Handbook of Research on Technology Integration in the Global World

Efosa C. Idemudia
Arkansas Tech University, USA

A volume in the Advances in Human and Social
Aspects of Technology (AHSAT) Book Series

Published in the United States of America by
IGI Global
Information Science Reference (an imprint of IGI Global)
701 E. Chocolate Avenue
Hershey PA, USA 17033
Tel: 717-533-8845
Fax: 717-533-8661
E-mail: cust@igi-global.com
Web site: http://www.igi-global.com

Library of Congress Cataloging-in-Publication Data

Names: Idemudia, Efosa C. (Efosa Carroll), 1970- editor.
Title: Handbook of research on technology integration in the global world /
    Efosa C. Idemudia, editor.
Description: Hershey, PA : Information Science Reference, an imprint of IGI
    Global, [2019] | Includes bibliographical references and index.
Identifiers: LCCN 2018008114| ISBN 9781522563679 (hardcover) | ISBN
    9781522563686 (ebook)
Subjects: LCSH: Communication in organizations--Data processing. | Virtual
    work teams. | Globalization. | Shared virtual environments. |
    Communication, International. | Online social networks.
Classification: LCC HD30.2 .H364298 2019 | DDC 658.4/0220285--dc23 LC record available at https://lccn.loc.
gov/2018008114

This book is published in the IGI Global book series Advances in Human and Social Aspects of Technology (AHSAT) (ISSN: 2328-1316; eISSN: 2328-1324)

British Cataloguing in Publication Data
A Cataloguing in Publication record for this book is available from the British Library.

For electronic access to this publication, please contact: eresources@igi-global.com.

Advances in Human and Social Aspects of Technology (AHSAT) Book Series

Ashish Dwivedi
The University of Hull, UK

ISSN:2328-1316
EISSN:2328-1324

MISSION

In recent years, the societal impact of technology has been noted as we become increasingly more connected and are presented with more digital tools and devices. With the popularity of digital devices such as cell phones and tablets, it is crucial to consider the implications of our digital dependence and the presence of technology in our everyday lives.

The **Advances in Human and Social Aspects of Technology (AHSAT) Book Series** seeks to explore the ways in which society and human beings have been affected by technology and how the technological revolution has changed the way we conduct our lives as well as our behavior. The AHSAT book series aims to publish the most cutting-edge research on human behavior and interaction with technology and the ways in which the digital age is changing society.

COVERAGE

- Gender and Technology
- Technology Dependence
- Cyber Behavior
- Information ethics
- Philosophy of technology
- Technoself
- Digital Identity
- Human Rights and Digitization
- Cultural Influence of ICTs
- Activism and ICTs

IGI Global is currently accepting manuscripts for publication within this series. To submit a proposal for a volume in this series, please contact our Acquisition Editors at Acquisitions@igi-global.com or visit: http://www.igi-global.com/publish/.

Titles in this Series

For a list of additional titles in this series, please visit: www.igi-global.com/book-series

Handbook of Research on Multicultural Perspectives on Gender and Aging
Rekha Pande (University of Hyderabad, India) and Theo van der Weide (Radboud University Nijmegen, The Netherlands)
Information Science Reference • copyright 2018 • 340pp • H/C (ISBN: 9781522547723) • US $225.00 (our price)

Narratives and the Role of Philosophy in Cross-Disciplinary Studies Emerging Research and Opportunities
Ana-Maria Pascal (Regent's University London, UK)
Information Science Reference • copyright 2018 • 198pp • H/C (ISBN: 9781522555728) • US $135.00 (our price)

Information Visualization Techniques in the Social Sciences and Humanities
Veslava Osinska (Nicolaus Copernicus University, Poland) and Grzegorz Osinski (College of Social and Media Culture, Poland)
Information Science Reference • copyright 2018 • 356pp • H/C (ISBN: 9781522549901) • US $195.00 (our price)

Handbook of Research on Civic Engagement and Social Change in Contemporary Society
Susheel Chhabra (Periyar Management and Computer College, India)
Information Science Reference • copyright 2018 • 445pp • H/C (ISBN: 9781522541974) • US $245.00 (our price)

Corporate and Global Standardization Initiatives in Contemporary Society
Kai Jakobs (RWTH Aachen University, Germany)
Information Science Reference • copyright 2018 • 394pp • H/C (ISBN: 9781522553205) • US $205.00 (our price)

Computational Psychoanalysis and Formal Bi-Logic Frameworks
Giuseppe Iurato (Independent Researcher, Italy)
Information Science Reference • copyright 2018 • 332pp • H/C (ISBN: 9781522541288) • US $215.00 (our price)

Psychological, Social, and Cultural Aspects of Internet Addiction
Bahadir Bozoglan (IF Weinheim Institute, Germany)
Information Science Reference • copyright 2018 • 390pp • H/C (ISBN: 9781522534778) • US $200.00 (our price)

Experience-Based Human-Computer Interactions Emerging Research and Opportunities
Petr Sosnin (Ulyanovsk State Technical University, Russia)
Information Science Reference • copyright 2018 • 294pp • H/C (ISBN: 9781522529873) • US $165.00 (our price)

701 East Chocolate Avenue, Hershey, PA 17033, USA
Tel: 717-533-8845 x100 • Fax: 717-533-8661
E-Mail: cust@igi-global.com • www.igi-global.com

This textbook is dedicated to the following family members because of their excellent and brilliant passion in my education:
My grandfather, Pa Idemudia Ogunbor
My parents, Mr. J. O. Idemudia and Mrs. E. M. Idemudia
My two great uncles, Dr. Taiwo Idemudia and Mr. Kehinde Idemudia
My late brother, Mr. Ikponmwosa Kizito Idemudia

List of Contributors

Abdelghaffar, Hany / *German University in Cairo, Egypt*.. 152

Abu-Taieh, Evon / *The University of Jordan – Aqaba, Jordan* 233

Acharya, Bhanu Bhakta / *University of Ottawa, Canada* 436

Akhter, Shameem / *Western Oregon University, USA* 166,189

Alfaries, Auhood / *King Saud University, Saudi Arabia & Princess Noura Bint Abdulrahman University, Saudi Arabia* 233

Al-Jenaibi, Badreya / *UAE University, UAE*.. 64

Al-Otaibi, Shaha / *Princess Nourah Bint Abdulrahman University, Saudi Arabi*........................ 233

Arpaci, Ibrahim / *Gaziosmanpasa University, Turkey*.. 114

Casillas, Luis / *University of Guadalajara, Mexico*.. 1

Chaudhary, Pankaj / *Indiana University of Pennsylvania, USA* 331

Daniel, Harold / *University of Maine, USA* 422

Demetriadis, Stavros / *Aristotle University of Thessaloniki, Greece*................................ 208

Djatej, Arsen / *Eastern Washington University, USA* 407

Doore, Brian / *University of Maine, USA*.. 422

Graham, Christian / *University of Maine, USA*.. 422

Gutierrez, Alfredo / *University of Guadalajara, Mexico*... 1

Gyftodimos, Georgios / *National and Kapodistrian University of Athens, Greece* 130

Hassan, Lobna / *German University in Cairo, Egypt*... 152

Hyde, Micki / *Indiana University of Pennsylvania, USA* 331

Lawrence, Japhet E. / *Deakin University, Australia*... 261

Magnisalis, Ioannis / *Aristotle University of Thessaloniki, Greece* 208

Makoza, Frank / *Cape Peninsula University of Technology, South Africa* 389

Papadimitriou, Alexandros / *School of Pedagogical and Technological Education, Greece* 130

Peña, Adriana / *University of Guadalajara, Mexico* 1

Rahman, Mohammad Nirjhar / *University of Rajshahi, Bangladesh* 189

Rahman, Nayem / *Portland State University, USA* 166,189

Rodger, James A. / *Indiana University of Pennsylvania, USA* 331

Samoilenko, Sergey / *Averett University, USA* 40

Saprikis, Vaggelis / *Western Macedonia University of Applied Sciences, Greece* 24

Sarikas, Robert / *Eastern Washington University, USA* 407

Senteney, David / *California State University – San Bernardino, USA & Ohio University, USA*.... 407

Sohn, Changsoo / *St. Cloud State University, USA* 290

Ullah, Mahmud / *University of Dhaka, Bangladesh* 166,189

Vejlgaard, Henrik / *Copenhagen Business Academy, Denmark* 373
Yaokumah, Winfred / *Pentecost University College, Ghana* 304
Yeo, Younsook / *St. Cloud State University, USA* 290
Zemmouchi-Ghomari, Leila / *Ecole Nationale Supérieure de Technologie (ENST), Algeria* 87
Zhou, Duanning / *Eastern Washington University, USA* 407

Table of Contents

Preface xix

Chapter 1
Automatic Approach to Evaluate Collaborative Interaction in Virtual Environments 1
    Luis Casillas, University of Guadalajara, Mexico
    Adriana Peña, University of Guadalajara, Mexico
    Alfredo Gutierrez, University of Guadalajara, Mexico

Chapter 2
Domestic vs. International E-Shopping: An Empirical Perceptions Analysis 24
    Vaggelis Saprikis, Western Macedonia University of Applied Sciences, Greece

Chapter 3
Do Investments in ICT Help Economies Grow? A Case of Transition Economies 40
    Sergey Samoilenko, Averett University, USA

Chapter 4
Reputation Management Techniques and E-Collaboration: UAE Public Relations Communication
Strategies During Crises Management 64
    Badreya Al-Jenaibi, UAE University, UAE

Chapter 5
Linked Data: A Manner to Realize the Web of Data 87
    Leila Zemmouchi-Ghomari, Ecole Nationale Supérieure de Technologie (ENST), Algeria

Chapter 6
A Theoretical Framework for IT Consumerization: Factors Influencing the Adoption of BYOD 114
    Ibrahim Arpaci, Gaziosmanpasa University, Turkey

Chapter 7
An Overview on Adaptive Group Formation Technique and the Case of the AEHS MATHEMA ... 130
    Alexandros Papadimitriou, School of Pedagogical and Technological Education, Greece
    Georgios Gyftodimos, National and Kapodistrian University of Athens, Greece

Chapter 8
Citizen-Government Collaborative Environment Using Social Networks: The Case of Egypt 152
Hany Abdelghaffar, German University in Cairo, Egypt
Lobna Hassan, German University in Cairo, Egypt

Chapter 9
Development of a Customer Information Database System 166
Shameem Akhter, Western Oregon University, USA
Nayem Rahman, Portland State University, USA
Mahmud Ullah, University of Dhaka, Bangladesh

Chapter 10
Shaping Competitive Strategies for the Computer Industry 189
Shameem Akhter, Western Oregon University, USA
Nayem Rahman, Portland State University, USA
Mahmud Ullah, University of Dhaka, Bangladesh
Mohammad Nirjhar Rahman, University of Rajshahi, Bangladesh

Chapter 11
Flexible Orchestration of Tools in E-Collaboration: Case Studies Analyzing the Developer, the
Teacher, and the Student Perspectives 208
Ioannis Magnisalis, Aristotle University of Thessaloniki, Greece
Stavros Demetriadis, Aristotle University of Thessaloniki, Greece

Chapter 12
Challenges Facing E-Publishing Over Cloud Computing on Scientists' Social Network Service: A
Comparative Study 233
Evon Abu-Taieh, The University of Jordan – Aqaba, Jordan
Auhood Alfaries, King Saud University, Saudi Arabia & Princess Noura Bint Abdulrahman
*   University, Saudi Arabia*
Shaha Al-Otaibi, Princess Nourah Bint Abdulrahman University, Saudi Arabi

Chapter 13
An Empirical Study of the Factors Influencing ICT Adoption in SMEs 261
Japhet E. Lawrence, Deakin University, Australia

Chapter 14
Web-Based PHR (Personal Health Records) Systems Adoption: Patients' Perspectives 290
Changsoo Sohn, St. Cloud State University, USA
Younsook Yeo, St. Cloud State University, USA

Chapter 15
Conceptualizing the Domain and an Empirical Analysis of Operations Security Management 304
Winfred Yaokumah, Pentecost University College, Ghana

Chapter 16
Executing a Real-Time Response in an Agile Information System 331
    Pankaj Chaudhary, Indiana University of Pennsylvania, USA
    James A. Rodger, Indiana University of Pennsylvania, USA
    Micki Hyde, Indiana University of Pennsylvania, USA

Chapter 17
The Rate of Adoption in Households and Organizations: A Comparative Study 373
    Henrik Vejlgaard, Copenhagen Business Academy, Denmark

Chapter 18
Learning From Abroad on SIM Card Registration Policy: The Case of Malawi 389
    Frank Makoza, Cape Peninsula University of Technology, South Africa

Chapter 19
Framework and Guidelines to Industry Web Portal Business.. 407
    Duanning Zhou, Eastern Washington University, USA
    Arsen Djatej, Eastern Washington University, USA
    Robert Sarikas, Eastern Washington University, USA
    David Senteney, California State University – San Bernardino, USA & Ohio University, USA

Chapter 20
Virtual Leadership: How Millennials Perceive Leadership Attribution and Its Impact on Database
System Development 422
    Christian Graham, University of Maine, USA
    Harold Daniel, University of Maine, USA
    Brian Doore, University of Maine, USA

Chapter 21
What Motivates Immigrants for ICT Adoption and Use? A Systematic Review of the 21st Century
Literature (2001-2017)... 436
    Bhanu Bhakta Acharya, University of Ottawa, Canada

Compilation of References 461

About the Contributors 524

Index... 533

Detailed Table of Contents

Preface xix

Chapter 1

Automatic Approach to Evaluate Collaborative Interaction in Virtual Environments 1

    Luis Casillas, University of Guadalajara, Mexico
    Adriana Peña, University of Guadalajara, Mexico
    Alfredo Gutierrez, University of Guadalajara, Mexico

Virtual environments for multi-users, collaborative virtual environments (CVE), support geographical distant people to experience collaborative learning and team training. In this context, monitoring collaboration provides valuable, and in time, information regarding individual and group indicators, helpful for human instructors or intelligent tutor systems. CVE enable people to share a virtual space, interacting with an avatar, generating nonverbal behavior such as gaze-direction or deictic gestures, a potential means to understand collaboration. This chapter presents an automated model and its inference mechanisms to evaluate collaboration in CVE based on expert human rules of nonverbal participants' activity. The model is a multi-layer analysis that includes data filtering, fuzzy classification, and rule-based inference producing a high-level assessment of group collaboration. This approach was applied to a task-oriented session, where two participants assembled cubes in a CVE to create a figure.

Chapter 2

Domestic vs. International E-Shopping: An Empirical Perceptions Analysis 24

    Vaggelis Saprikis, Western Macedonia University of Applied Sciences, Greece

Contemporary commerce is completely different as regards features some years ago. Nowadays, a considerable number of individuals and firms take advantage of the information and communication technologies and conduct transactions online. In particular, the mobile industry along with the broad use of social networks and improvements in the internet bandwidth worldwide has created a completely different business environment. Consequently, the technology incited many consumers to cross-border e-shopping, allowing access to a wider variety of products and services, and in numerous circumstances, access to cheaper goods. The purpose of this chapter is to investigate the perceptions internet users have towards e-shops focusing on Greece. More precisely, it aims to find out whether there are contingent differences on customers' perceptions regarding domestic vs. international e-shops, since a gradually augmented number of people have been expressing their preference on non-domestic e-stores for their purchases. Additionally, the chapter intends to shed light on the difficulty in understanding vital aspects of e-consumer behaviour.

Chapter 3

Do Investments in ICT Help Economies Grow? A Case of Transition Economies............................ 40
Sergey Samoilenko, Averett University, USA

A common assumption behind investments in information and communication technologies (ICT) is that of the resultant improvements in productivity. To substantiate this assumption with empirical evidence in the context of transition economies (TE), the authors use time series data sets spanning the period from 1993 to 2008 to inquire into the impact of investments in telecoms on total factor productivity (TFP). Results indicate that the improvements in productivity of the most of TEs in the sample was inconsistent and not based on the increase in the levels of investments and labor. Additionally, the results of the data analysis suggest that the dominant source of growth in productivity is not static, but changes over time. While in an earlier period (1993-2002) of transition, TEs grew based on technological change, it is efficient utilization of the already available technology that became a dominant source of growth in the later (2003-2008) period of transition.

Chapter 4

Reputation Management Techniques and E-Collaboration: UAE Public Relations Communication
Strategies During Crises Management 64
Badreya Al-Jenaibi, UAE University, UAE

Public relation is one of the significant communication methods in any organization. It leads the internal and external communication strategies, especially during crises. Some of the main goals of public relations are to create, maintain, and protect the organization's reputation, and—ever-increasingly—e-collaboration plays a vital role in accomplishing this goal. The aim of this study is to explore the approaches that help an organization rejuvenate its reputation after damage caused by various crises. It is important to know which PR approaches best engage stakeholders because companies must maintain healthy relationships with all stake-holding entities in order to survive. Qualitative case study was conducted to explore what circumstances can compromise a company's image and what role a PR department would optimally play in rejuvenating it.

Chapter 5

Linked Data: A Manner to Realize the Web of Data 87
Leila Zemmouchi-Ghomari, Ecole Nationale Supérieure de Technologie (ENST), Algeria

The data on the web is heterogeneous and distributed, which makes its integration a sine qua non-condition for its effective exploitation within the context of the semantic web or the so-called web of data. A promising solution for web data integration is the linked data initiative, which is based on four principles that aim to standardize the publication of structured data on the web. The objective of this chapter is to provide an overview of the essential aspects of this fairly recent and exciting field, including the model of linked data: resource description framework (RDF), its query language: simple protocol, and the RDF query language (SPARQL), the available means of publication and consumption of linked data, and the existing applications and the issues not yet addressed in research.

Chapter 6

A Theoretical Framework for IT Consumerization: Factors Influencing the Adoption of BYOD 114
Ibrahim Arpaci, Gaziosmanpasa University, Turkey

The chapter provided a comprehensive review of previous studies on the adoption of information and communication technology (ICT). The study further conducted a qualitative study on the adoption of "bring your own device" (BYOD). The study systematically reviewed technology acceptance theories and models such as TAM, TPB, and UTAUT at the individual level and technology adoption theories such as "innovation diffusion theory," "technology-organization-environment framework," and "institutional theory" at the organizational level. Thereby, key factors predicting the ICT adoption at the individual, organizational, institutional, and environmental level were identified. A theoretical framework that explains the ICT adoption and the consumerization process was proposed based on the theories. The qualitative data collected by semi-structured interviews with senior-level managers was analyzed using the content analysis. The findings suggested that perceived financial cost, compatibility, privacy, and security concerns were significant factors in predicting the enterprise's adoption of BYOD.

Chapter 7

An Overview on Adaptive Group Formation Technique and the Case of the AEHS MATHEMA ... 130
Alexandros Papadimitriou, School of Pedagogical and Technological Education, Greece
Georgios Gyftodimos, National and Kapodistrian University of Athens, Greece

This chapter presents the adaptive group formation and/or peer help technique implemented by various systems so far, and particularly, by web-based adaptive educational hypermedia systems (AEHSs). At first, some concepts about group formation and peer help are described, and a general description of the MATHEMA is made. Subsequently, the overview of the adaptive group formation considers extensively how several systems have implemented this technique so far. A comparative study of the presented systems with the MATHEMA is performed and conclusions are drawn. The systems that implement the adaptive group formation and/or peer help technique are the (M)CSCL, AELS, and AEHSs. In presentation of the adaptive grouping algorithm of the MATHEMA, the following are described: (1) how the priority list is created; (2) how the learners are supported in selecting their most suitable partner; (3) how the negotiation protocol works; and (4) how the peer groups are automatically linked up for a collaboration agreement using a peer-to-peer communication tool.

Chapter 8

Citizen-Government Collaborative Environment Using Social Networks: The Case of Egypt 152
Hany Abdelghaffar, German University in Cairo, Egypt
Lobna Hassan, German University in Cairo, Egypt

Electronic democracy is a concept which is used in some countries around the world with mixed success. Social networks helped in facilitating democracy and democratic change in several countries suggesting that they could be utilized as an e-democracy tool. This research proposed a new model of how the decision-making process for local governments could be improved via social networks. Quantitative approach was used to investigate how the use of a social network amongst people living in the same suburb could improve decision making on the local level. Findings showed that awareness building, deliberation, and consultation factors could be used to affect the decision making for their local governments.

Chapter 9
Development of a Customer Information Database System 166

Shameem Akhter, Western Oregon University, USA

Nayem Rahman, Portland State University, USA

Mahmud Ullah, University of Dhaka, Bangladesh

Organizations need to keep customer data safe and secure to run their everyday activities more credibly, promptly, and effectively. They need to use, and hence invest in customer database software to achieve these basic goals. Using well-designed software also allows them to increase operational efficiency of business. In this chapter, the authors discuss development of a customer inquiry database system for use by small businesses. The proposed database system is to help them store customer information, inquiries, and company product information too. The authors have used state-of-the-art software development technology to design and develop user interfaces (UI) for building business intelligence (BI) capability using this system. This chapter provides a holistic view of building a customer inquiry database system. The approach of an integrated view of customer inquiry system is different and offers more than the partial view of the existing literature or database system books on this issue.

Chapter 10
Shaping Competitive Strategies for the Computer Industry 189

Shameem Akhter, Western Oregon University, USA

Nayem Rahman, Portland State University, USA

Mahmud Ullah, University of Dhaka, Bangladesh

Mohammad Nirjhar Rahman, University of Rajshahi, Bangladesh

Accelerated response to competition with appropriate actions is one of the major determinants for a firm's sustenance and survival. Both operational and financial performances in terms of gaining and/or keeping competitive advantage always remain under the watchful eyes of the relevant stakeholders in an industry. A firm has to be very vigilant to cope with the internal and external changes it faces over the different phases of its growth. Just like any other industry, this is equally true, in fact more true for the computer industry as well. Continuous innovation in the computer industry has made it a very fast growing and fiercely competitive industry in the field of modern technologies. Firms in this industry always have to be on their toes to tackle the fierce competition created due to many obvious reasons. This study examines the computer industry in the light of Michael Porter's framework for analyzing the profitability. Threats of new entrants and substitute products, bargaining power of both suppliers and buyers, and regular rivalry among the competitors have been analyzed critically. This study may have significant implications in evaluating the competitive strategies developed and applied by the incumbent firms in and the new entrants into the computer manufacturing industry.

Chapter 11
Flexible Orchestration of Tools in E-Collaboration: Case Studies Analyzing the Developer, the
Teacher, and the Student Perspectives 208

Ioannis Magnisalis, Aristotle University of Thessaloniki, Greece

Stavros Demetriadis, Aristotle University of Thessaloniki, Greece

Relevant literature has emphasized the lack of a "tool orchestration" framework in e-collaboration environments (either for work or learning purposes). In this chapter, the MAPIS3 software architecture is suggested as a flexible solution to manage the key problem in tool orchestration, which is the efficient data transfer among various tools used in e-collaboration activities. The proposal is assessed by two case studies of flexible e-collaboration scenarios that cannot be implemented automatically with any known architectures or tools. These scenarios entail transfer and transformation of students' collaboration data through an IMS-LD compatible "player." The data emerge originally to a specific tool and are transferred to another tool. The overall implementations were evaluated from the developers', the instructors', and the students' perspectives. Results indicate that MAPIS3 supports seamless data flow among tools efficiently and flexibly. In particular, teachers are supported in monitoring the e-collaboration process by flexible visualizations of peer/student interactions.

Chapter 12

Challenges Facing E-Publishing Over Cloud Computing on Scientists' Social Network Service: A Comparative Study 233

Evon Abu-Taieh, The University of Jordan – Aqaba, Jordan
Auhood Alfaries, King Saud University, Saudi Arabia & Princess Noura Bint Abdulrahman University, Saudi Arabia
Shaha Al-Otaibi, Princess Nourah Bint Abdulrahman University, Saudi Arabi

This chapter illustrates the difficulties facing e-publishing over cloud computing pertaining to scientifically-oriented social network services from three axioms: the life cycle of the research document, an explanation of what a researcher juggles to conduct proper research, and the researcher knowledge pertaining to both scholarly search engines and citation indices. The chapter discusses the essential role of the researcher in teaching, being a beacon of hope, and explains the steps towards research conducting, when an original idea is deduced, as well as the step of writing research addressing the financial support for researchers: from submitting proposals, follow up proposals, grant management if funding is secured, whilst conducting the research, and publishing the results in accredited journals approved by the researcher's institute and financing partner, while publishing the research in accordance with the laws and regulations of the institute.

Chapter 13

An Empirical Study of the Factors Influencing ICT Adoption in SMEs 261

Japhet E. Lawrence, Deakin University, Australia

ICT has the potential to radically change the way business is conducted, offering a competitive edge and a gateway to the global marketplace. The explosive growth of ICT has opened a vast arena providing opportunities for businesses, particularly SMEs to sell their products and service to a global audience than they would have been able to afford to reach using the traditional methods. This chapter reports on the empirical study of ICT adoption in small to medium-sized enterprises. The intention of the study is to present evidence on the factors that influence SMEs' decision to adopt ICT in business. The study is chosen because of the strategic importance of SMEs to the economy and their contribution in creating jobs cannot be over emphasized. The study uses in-depth case studies, conceptualized within the grounded theory method to generate thick description to explain the phenomenon. The study uses diffusion theory and the technology acceptance model as a basis for the theoretical framework.

Chapter 14
Web-Based PHR (Personal Health Records) Systems Adoption: Patients' Perspectives 290
Changsoo Sohn, St. Cloud State University, USA
Younsook Yeo, St. Cloud State University, USA

The purpose of this study is to find factors which explain patients' intention to use web-based personal health records (PHR). It is hypothesized that patients' perceived value of information, perceived worthwhileness of searching, concerns about privacy issues, trust in information, and perceived security on web-based PHR systems are related to patients' intention to use PHRs. Using data from health information national trends survey (HINTS), direct and indirect effects of these factors on patients' intention to use PHRs were analyzed. The results show that perceived value of information, privacy, information trust, and security have significant and direct associations to intention to use PHRs. Meanwhile, perceived value of information is a strong antecedent of perceived worthwhileness of searching; however, it has no direct association to intention to use PHRs. The findings suggest that the efforts should be targeted to increase perceived value of the information and trust in privacy and security as well as the information to increase patients' intention to use PHRs.

Chapter 15
Conceptualizing the Domain and an Empirical Analysis of Operations Security Management 304
Winfred Yaokumah, Pentecost University College, Ghana

Operations security management integrates the activities of all the information systems security controls. It ensures that the entire computing environment is adequately secured. This chapter conducts an in-depth review of scholarly and practitioner works to conceptualize the domain of operations security management. Drawing upon the existing information systems security literature, the chapter classifies operations security management into 10 domains. Following, the chapter performs an empirical analysis to investigate the state-of-practice of operations security management in organizations. The findings show that the maturity level of operations security management is at the Level 3 (well-defined). The maturity levels range from Level 0 (not performed) to Level 5 (continuously improving). The results indicate that operations security processes are documented, approved, and implemented organization-wide. Backup and malware management are the most applied operations security controls, while logging, auditing, monitoring, and reviewing are the least implemented controls.

Chapter 16
Executing a Real-Time Response in an Agile Information System 331
Pankaj Chaudhary, Indiana University of Pennsylvania, USA
James A. Rodger, Indiana University of Pennsylvania, USA
Micki Hyde, Indiana University of Pennsylvania, USA

Agile information systems (AIS) is a current topic of interest in the IS industry. An AIS is defined as one that has ability to sense a change in real time, diagnose it in real time, and select and execute an action in real time. This study focuses on the properties or attributes of an AIS to execute an action in real time. The properties outlined in this research enable an AIS to select a response in real time and then execute a response in real time. The attributes are derived using industry literature, refined using interviews with industry practitioners and then verified for importance using a survey. From the exercise it is concluded that most properties or attributes are important for real-time execution in an AIS. Dimensions underlying these attributes are identified using EFA. Some recent frameworks and paradigms related to

IS configurations that can respond to changes in real time are discussed. These frameworks incorporate many of the properties that were arrived for executing a change in real time in an agile IS and hence provide additional validation for the research.

Chapter 17

The Rate of Adoption in Households and Organizations: A Comparative Study..............................373
    Henrik Vejlgaard, Copenhagen Business Academy, Denmark

The aim of this study is to investigate if households or organizations are faster in their adoption of an innovation. There does not appear to be existing research on this area of diffusion of innovations research. In this comparative study, the study object is digital terrestrial television (DTT), specifically the implementation of DTT in Denmark. By taking a service theory approach, DTT can be categorized as a service innovation. The rate of adoption is a concept in diffusion of innovations theory, which is used as the study's theoretical framework. For both units of analysis, three surveys were carried out. Based on the data, the rate of adoption for households and for organizations was established. It is clear that organizations adopt an innovation faster than households during the entire adoption process. Based on this research, a predictive model is constructed conceptually.

Chapter 18

Learning From Abroad on SIM Card Registration Policy: The Case of Malawi 389
    Frank Makoza, Cape Peninsula University of Technology, South Africa

This chapter presents an analysis of policy transfer in the context of a developing country. The case of Malawi was analyzed as an African country attempting to implement a mandatory subscriber identity module (SIM) card registration policy. The study used a qualitative research approach and secondary data including government reports and media reports. The findings showed that the SIM card registration policy was transferred through coercive transfer to meet security standards and international conventions, and voluntary transfer to address local social challenges related to the use of mobile technologies. Despite initiating the SIM card registration process on several occasions, the implementation process was met with constraints related to social, economic, and political factors that affected the policy transfer process.

Chapter 19

Framework and Guidelines to Industry Web Portal Business..407
    Duanning Zhou, Eastern Washington University, USA
    Arsen Djatej, Eastern Washington University, USA
    Robert Sarikas, Eastern Washington University, USA
    David Senteney, California State University – San Bernardino, USA & Ohio University, USA

This chapter discusses a growth framework for industry web portals which present a new opportunity in the internet business. The framework contains five stages: business plan stage, website development stage, attraction stage, entrenchment stage, and defense stage. The actions to be taken and strategies to be applied in each stage are set out. Two industry web portals are investigated in detail. The two examples illustrate the applicability of the proposed growth framework to the real world. The combination of a conceptual growth framework and the application of this conceptual framework to two real-world examples yields a set of guidelines based in large part on lessons learned from the two examples. Thus, this chapter provides a concept-based growth framework and a set of real-world-based guidelines that will very possibly provide a practical benefit to industry web portal business practitioners.

Chapter 20
Virtual Leadership: How Millennials Perceive Leadership Attribution and Its Impact on Database
System Development 422
Christian Graham, University of Maine, USA
Harold Daniel, University of Maine, USA
Brian Doore, University of Maine, USA

This chapter is an updated review of the results of a study completed in 2015 on leadership's impact on virtual team effectiveness and the quality of the completed virtual team project. Findings in 2015 suggested that leadership style and virtual team effectiveness did predict project quality, and specific leadership styles had a negative relationship with virtual team effectiveness. After summarizing the results of the studies purpose, methodology, and findings, the chapter concludes with a literature review of virtual team's leadership research between 2015 and present. It provides a discussion on the relationship between the previous studies' findings and what has been found since with recommendations on future research on shared leadership and relationship building in virtual teams.

Chapter 21
What Motivates Immigrants for ICT Adoption and Use? A Systematic Review of the 21st Century
Literature (2001-2017).. 436
Bhanu Bhakta Acharya, University of Ottawa, Canada

Several studies demonstrate that most immigrants feel positively about technology adoption and use, and they use information and communication technologies (ICTs) more than non-immigrants or earlier immigrants. What motivates immigrants to use ICTs? Is their motivation to use ICTs for back home connection with their families and friends, or to adjust to their new environment? What are the factors that influence immigrants' ICT behaviors most often? For this study, the author chose 24 peer-reviewed journal articles published in English between 2001-2017 to assess immigrants' motivations for ICT adoption and use. The chapter, based on the systematic review of the existing literature for a longitudinal assessment, will discuss primary motives for immigrants' ICT adoption and use, as well as identify factors that influence immigrants' behavior with respect to ICT adoption and use. Based on these influencing factors, the chapter proposes a framework of technology adoption and use by immigrants.

Compilation of References 461

About the Contributors 524

Index 533

Preface

INTRODUCTION

The chapters in this textbook claim that teaching technology integration in the global world is extremely important because today all disciplines, companies, organizations, and countries are using technology and data analytics to make better decisions and gain competitive advantages. Because all disciplines in different parts of the world are directly or indirectly using technology to survive and compete, the concepts, methodologies, tools, and skills in this textbook come from all the continents in the world (i.e., Asia, Africa, North America, South America, Antarctica, Europe, and Australia). Hence, the textbook is unique because it exposes students, professors, and employees to different cultures, norms, and traditions related to the adoption of a wide range of information systems platforms and usage. The textbook includes cases that expose students, professors, employees, practitioners, and government officials to appropriate methodologies, tools, and skills to create better decision making and competitive advantages. Lastly, this textbook exposes students to diverse industries, such as computer, education, health care, information, telecommunication, mass media, hospitality, financial services, technology, etc.

Every year for the past decade, I have taught my students that all companies and organizations are using data and technology to exceed customer expectations and to improve sales, revenues, profits, etc. Many studies have shown that the daily advances in technology bring significant and innovative improvements in applications, software, and hardware that help businesses, organizations, and governments increase productivity and accomplish their goals and objectives. Recently, rapid changes in technology have posed major challenges to corporations, academicians, practitioners, governments, and individual, particularly in the areas of cyber security, privacy, and adaptation to the market. This textbook helps to address these challenges by equipping professors, academicians, and practitioners with updated concepts and models on a wide range of information technology platforms in the global world.

In this textbook, readers will find concepts and cases from different continents to effectively and adequately address the demand from sophisticated users. The goal of this book is to expand the ability of individuals, organizations, and governments to adapt to changes in the market environment and emerging technologies to make better decisions, gain competitive advantages, and achieve objectives and goals. To that end, each chapter has discussion questions that empower students with communication, analytics, decision making, and critical thinking exercises to help them apply their problem-solving skills to real world situations.

WHY THIS TEXTBOOK FOR ACADEMICIANS, PRACTITIONERS, RESEARCHERS, AND STUDENTS?

This is a very interesting and fun textbook because students and professors will discover global information technology concepts that dominate headline news in television, social medial, and print journalism. Students will be exposed to concepts and practices from global cultures regarding a wide range of information systems platforms, updated frameworks and guidelines to industry web portal businesses, and case studies from different parts of the world. The textbook also includes a glossary of technical terms and useful programming codes.

The textbook equips academicians, practitioners, researchers, and students to use technology in the global world to make better decisions, improve competitive advantages, and create values in the work environments. For example, social media is valuable because students, professors, employees, and businesses are using social media for communication, research collaboration, marketing, contacting families/friends, sharing videos and files etc. Hence, this textbook exposes academicians, practitioners, researchers, and students with the skills and tools to see and appreciate the beauty in all technology for creating value, improving decision making, and creating competitive advantages. Some of the richest people in the world are using information systems and technology to create and add value for their global customers; for example:

- The CEO of Amazon, Jeff Bezos, is responsible for the growth of online shopping and e-commerce.
- The previous CEO of Microsoft, Bill Gates, is responsible for the proliferation of Microsoft products.
- The Berkshire Hathaway CEO, Warren Buffett, is responsible for the growth of e-investment.
- The chairman and CEO of Facebook, Mark Zuckerberg, is responsible for the growth of social media.
- The founder, chairman, and former CEO of software company Oracle, Larry Ellison, is responsible for the innovative growth of Oracle.

The above CEOs have made billions of US dollars revolutionizing global information technology and information systems through innovations and adding value to individual lives, companies, organizations, and governments.

This textbook provides the tools for academicians, practitioners, researchers, and students to use technology to do great and fantastic works in the global world. It also illustrates how academicians, practitioners, researchers, and students can use technology to advance their careers, secure dream jobs, increase earning potential, and be indispensable employees. Companies, organizations, and governments are increasingly depending on technology to make better decisions and improve competitive advantages. Companies and governments are looking for employees who can use technology to solve complex and difficult problems in the global world.

Technology is creating new jobs every day because technology is changing every day. For example, business data analytics, digital marketing, social media analysts, big data scientist, mobile developer, apps developer, data engineer, business intelligence developer, and business intelligence analyst are jobs that did not exist ten years ago, thus creating opportunities for individuals who are able to adapt to this swiftly changing environment. This textbook gives academicians, practitioners, researchers, and students the fantastic and great opportunity to use information technology and information systems to advance their careers by equipping them with the unique skills and tools to be able to predict technological innovations in the global world. Finally, this textbook provides a real world understanding of how technology and information systems are rapidly changing and transforming businesses, and informs readers how they can successfully participate in these transformations in the global world.

TEXTBOOK COMPONENTS

Data Mining and Linked Data

This textbook is important and unique because it presents the latest concepts in technology. For example, this textbook includes latest concepts, techniques, and research methods in data mining and linked data. The textbook explains how linked data can be used to explore web data from cookies and log files for better decision making and online advertisements and how link analysis can be implemented by companies and organizations to analyze the datasets collected from social media for marketing and advertising purposes to exceed customer, web user, and online visitor expectations. Readers will learn about linked data, semantic web, web of data, resources description framework, and Simple Protocol and the RDF Query Language (SPARQL). The linked data chapter exposes academicians, practitioners, researchers, and students to techniques and tools to successfully address issues and problems related to incompatibility datasets and formats to improve communication and data sharing. Readers will also discover the latest concepts and techniques to implement to make sure that machines understand semantic webs. The chapter effectively and efficiently discuss the similarities and differences between web of documents and web of data for decision making and competitive advantages.

European Union and E-Shopping

In Chapter 2, the textbook presents a holistic approach in the European Union by using a case study of Greece and empirically investigating how culture, norms, and political environments influence e-shopping. However, the textbook also provides a comprehensive case study comparing the e-shopping in Greece with other countries. These concepts provide insights and understanding to academicians, practitioners, researchers, and students on important factors to consider when designing e-shopping platforms that adapt to web user and online visitor expectations helping readers to make better decisions and experience competitive advantages. The textbook presents some of the problems and challenges associated with e-shopping features and functions and provides strategies and tools to implements to successfully address and overcome these challenges and problems. This textbook is unique because it exposes academicians, practitioners, researchers, and students to cross-country e-shopping.

Information and Communication Technologies (ICTs)

Another concern addressed in this textbook is immigrant use of Information and Communication Technologies (ICTs). Chapter 3 presents do Investments in ICT Help Economies Grow? A Case of Transition Economies; and chapter 21 discusses a holistic and systematic review of the 21st century literature relating to what motivates immigrants for ICT adoption and use. What are the critical factors that motivate immigrants to use ICTs? To answer this question, the textbook provides insights and understanding on how families, friends, and new environment influence ICT adoption and usage. It includes valuable concepts on how investments in ICTs help economies grow and gives insights and understanding to readers on how to improve decision makings for competitive advantages. Included is a case study using transition economies on the relationship between ICT and total factor productivity. The concept to academicians, practitioners, researchers, and students is that total factor productivity is not constant, and it changes with time, changes in the environments, and stakeholders' expectations. Also, the textbook present how investments in technologies is helping emerging, transitional, and developing economies to grow relating to big data and gaining knowledge and insights from big data for better decision making. The textbook includes key and significant factors that influence ICT adoption in Small to Medium-sized Enterprises (SMEs).

Reputation Management Techniques and E-Collaboration

Chapter 4 presents important concepts relating to reputation management techniques, and e-collaboration that are extremely very helpful to organizations, firms, and companies. Public relations is a significant communication method in most organization, and public relations have a significant influence on internal and external communication strategies during crisis. The textbook discusses important goals in public relations and how e-collaborations can be used to achieve such goals as creating, maintaining, and protecting organization integrity and reputation. In addition, the textbook provides insights and understanding to organizations, companies, and firms on important strategies for rejuvenating reputations after damage has been caused by various crises. Public relations approaches involve engaging effectively and efficiently managing all stakeholders because companies and firms must have excellent and healthy relationships with all stakeholders to survive. The textbook presents in detail how organizations can use qualitative case study and interviews to explore circumstances that compromise companies' images and the important roles the public relations department should play using e-collaboration that optimally rejuvenate the companies' reputation. It should be noted that the public relations department should always use e-collaboration to act quickly, efficiently, and competently to minimize the negative perceptions and impacts that crises have on the public.

Collaboration Information Systems

The textbook also presents important concepts that are extremely very valuable to companies, organizations, firms, and government agencies related to Collaboration Information Systems. It provides important concepts and strategies on how virtual environments for multi-users and Collaborative Virtual Environments (CVE) may be use by top officials to support geographically distant people to experience excellent meetings, learning sessions, and trainings that enhance decision making and competitive advantages. In the future, companies, organizations, and government agencies will use Collaboration Information Systems more often to provide valuable and real-time information related to individual and group performance that are helpful to human instructors or intelligence tutor systems. In addition, companies and organizations are using Collaborative Virtual Environments that enable employees to share virtual spaces for meetings and interact with avatars to improve decision makings, increase profits and sales, and save costs. The textbook provides insights and understanding to leading firms and organizations on how to successfully incorporate data filtering, fuzzy classification, and rule-based inference to effectively and efficiently produce a high-level assessment of group collaboration. The textbook provides updated models for future collaborative analysis, quality indicators/possible values, influence models, etc.

Adoption of Information and Communication Technologies/BYOD

Chapter 6 presents important theoretical factors that influence the adoption and usage of BYOD in organizations, companies, and governments by presenting a comprehensive and holistic review of prior studies related to the adoption and usage of Information & Communication Technologies/BYOD (ICT) in decision making. Important technology acceptance theories and models are discussed and presented, such as the technology acceptance model, theory of planned behavior, the unified theory of acceptance and use of technology, innovation diffusion theory, technology-innovation-environment-framework, institutional theory etc. Hence, students, organizations, firms, and governments are exposed to important and key factors that predict and influence ICT and BYOD adoption at the individual, organizational, institutional, and environmental levels. In addition, an updated conceptual model and framework are included that provide insights, understanding, and explanations on ICT/BYOD adoption, usage, and consumerization process. The chapter exposes organizations, firms, and companies to important concepts of content analysis and explains that perceived financial costs, compatibility, privacy, and security concerns are significant factors in predicting an enterprise's adoption of BYOD.

Adaptive Group Formation and Web-Based Adaptive Educational Hypermedia Systems (AEHSs)

In Chapter 7, the textbook presents techniques to top management and government officials on strategies to implement using different techniques to successfully form effective and efficient groups. The textbook discusses important factors that both positively and negatively influence adaptive group formation and web-based adaptive educational hypermedia systems (AEHSs). In addition, important concepts about group formation and peer help are discussed, described, and a general description of the MATHEMA is presented. The textbook describes the following in the presentation of the adaptive grouping algorithm of the MATHEMA: (a) how to create priority list, (b) how to support learners when selecting their most suitable group partners, (c) how negotiation protocol works relating to group formation, and (d) how using peer-to-peer communication tools has helped the peer groups to automatically link up during collaboration agreement.

Citizen-Government Collaborative Environment and Social Networking

Chapter 8 exposes academicians, practitioners, researchers, and students to African cultures by presenting a case study of a citizen-government collaborative environment using social networking. Electronic democracy is a concept that is used by most countries. E-democracy tools use social networks to facilitate democracy and democratic changes in both developed and developing countries. This textbook presents an updated model that helps to improve the decision-making processes for organizations, companies, and government agencies via social networks. Also, the textbook presents how governments can implement a quantitative approach to successfully and effectively investigate the use of social network among people living in villages, cities, states, countries to improve decision-making. The concepts discussed in this textbook provide insight and understanding to companies, firms, organizations, and government agencies on how awareness building, deliberation, and consultation factors influence decision making for governments.

Customer Inquiry Database System

Important concepts related to the development of a customer information database systems is presented in Chapter 9. To maintain and improve reputation, integrity, and credibility, organizations of all types are implementing strategies to ensure that customer and citizen data are safe, secure, protected, and private. This textbook presents updated techniques that readers can implement for investing in customer database software to improve operational efficiency and achieve the goals and objectives of businesses. This textbook provides insights and understanding on how to develop a customer inquiry database system that effectively and efficiently stores customer information, inquiries, and companies products. The textbook presents state of the art software development tools and techniques that can be used to design and develop user interfaces for building business intelligence related to better decision making and competitive advantages. The beauty of this concept is that it presents a holistic view of existing literature for database system development.

Computer Industry and Competitive Strategies

In Chapter 10, the textbook provides important insights and understanding for how the computer industry can use technology and information systems to share competitive strategies. Companies and organizations are using information systems to accelerate responses to competition with appropriate actions in order to compete and make better decisions. This chapter presents strategies for using information systems to improve operational and financial performances and to successfully adapt to both internal and external environments/changes. Technology is changing every day and organizations must make continuous improvements to adapt to the fast growing and fiercely competitive industry. The textbook examines the computer industry using Michael Porter's framework for analyzing the profitability. The framework includes discussions of the following topics: (a) threats of new entrants and substitute products, (b) bargaining power of both suppliers and buyers, and (c) regular rivalry among the competitors. These concepts have significant implications related to evaluating the competitive strategies developed and applied by firms and organization in the computer manufacturing industry.

Flexible Orchestration of Tools in E-Collaboration

Chapter 11 provides a detailed discussion of case studies analyzing the developer, teacher, and student perspectives using flexible orchestration of tools in e-collaboration. This textbook makes some recommendations to academia and government agencies on how to successfully improve both online and classroom education. Because of its reliability, efficiency, and robustness in transferring data among various tools used in e-collaboration tasks and activities, the MAPIS3 software architecture is a very good and flexible software that can be used to manage the key problem in tool orchestration. The textbook also presents two case studies that provide insights and understanding on e-collaboration architectures and tools, including scenarios that require the transfer and transformation of student e-collaboration data through an

IMS-LD compatible "player." The uniqueness of this approach is that the overall implementation was evaluated from the developer, instructor, and student's perspectives. The results from the case studies indicate that MAPIS3 strongly supports seamless data flow among e-collaboration tools effectively and efficiently with flexible visualizations.

E-Publishing and Cloud Computing

Chapter 12 presents recommendations and suggestions for how to address challenges facing e-publishing over cloud computing on a scientist social network service by implementing a comparative study. The challenges of e-publishing were addressed using three axioms: (1) life cycle of the research manuscript and documents, (2) explanation on what researchers do to conduct proper research, and (3) knowledge of the researchers relating to both scholarly search engines and citation indices. In addition, the chapter presents detailed information relating to the life circle for publishing in reputable journals and securing grants for research. Some techniques for assessing the reputation of journals such as Journal Citation Rank, Scientific Journal Ranking, ERA, Scopus, and ISI are presented. The processes involved in paper publishing are discussed, including terms of cost and time efficiency coupled with the copyright rules and regulations. Some current challenges in e-publishing are language barriers, level of knowledge of current technology, lack of skills and tools, savvy of the scholars etc. Strategies to address these challenges are discussed and presented in this textbook.

Adoption of Web-Based Personal Health Records (PHR)

In Chapter 14, the textbook presents and discusses the factors that significantly influence the adoption of web-based personal health records (PHR). Some of the factors that influences patients' intentions to use PHRs are perceived value of the information, trust in the information, perceived worthwhileness of searching for the information, perceived security on web-based PHR systems, and concerns about privacy issues. Using data from the Health Information National Trends Survey (HINTS), this chapter provides insights, explanations, and understanding on how to analyze and interpret data from the health care industry. The findings have a lot of managerial and research implications related to perceived value of the information in the PHRs; users' trust in privacy and security have a significant and positive influence on patients' intention to use PHRs.

Real-Time Responses and Agile Information Systems

Chapter 16 presents innovative and updated techniques that top managements and governments officials can implement in the execution of a real-time responses using agile information systems. This chapter provides a comprehensive and holistic literature review of agile information systems. In addition, it provides a holistic comparative study within the European Union of the rate of adoption of innovations in households and organizations that are helpful to organizations, firms, and companies for decision making and comparative advantages.

Other benefits of this textbook from Chapters 1, 5, 13, 15, 17, 18, 19, and 20 include that the textbook exposes students to African cultures, policies, and norms related to learning from abroad on SIM card registration using Malawi as a case study. Also, the textbook provides updated framework and guidelines to industry web portal businesses to increase profits and sales, increase competitive advantages, and improve decision making. Finally, the textbook provides many insights, understanding, and implications relating to millennials perceptions of virtual leadership.

ORGANIZATION OF THE BOOK

The book is organized into 21 chapters. A brief description of each of the chapters follows:

Chapter 1 presents updated techniques and approaches that firms and organization should implement to evaluate collaborative interaction in the virtual environments. Also, the authors present the future trends, benefits, challenges, processes, and opportunities relating to the different types of virtual environments that exist.

Chapter 2 discusses an empirical perception analysis of domestic versus International e-Shopping; and the author uses Greece as a case study by investigation the perception web users and online visitors have toward e-shopping. In addition, the author provides insights on the difficulty in understanding the challenges, vital aspects, and opportunity of e-consumer behaviors.

Chapter 3 presents a case study of transition economies by empirically investigating the effect of ICT on Economies. The author argues that the dominant source of growth in productivity is not constant but depends on time. Also, the chapter provides insights to government officials and top managements on strategies to implement so that investment in ICT positively and significantly influence economic development of emerging, transition, and developing economies.

Chapter 4 discusses a case study of UAE public relation communication strategies during crises management. The author argues that reputation management techniques and e-collaboration can be used to create, maintain, and protect the reputation of firms, organizations, and countries.

Chapter 5 provides an overview, challenges, opportunities, and the four principles of linked data. The author discusses on how linked data initiative can be a promising solution for web data and cookie integrations.

Chapter 6 reviews a theoretical framework for IT consumerization and factors influencing the adoption of BYOD. The author presents a detailed literature review and models relating to individual level of IT adoption and organization level of IT adoption. In addition, the author presents a theoretical framework for ICT adoption.

Chapter 7 reviews a holistic overview on adaptive group formation techniques and the case of the AEHS MATHEMA. Also, the authors present some of the most appropriate strategies to implement relating to the different types of group formation techniques. In addition, the authors present updated model relating to group formation techniques.

Chapter 8 presents a case study from Africa (i.e. Egypt) and a conceptual model on using social networks for citizen-government collaborative environments. The authors argue on strategies government officials and top managements should implement to make sure that social networks positively and significantly influence democracy and democratic changes.

Chapter 9 discusses a comprehensive review relating to the development of customer information database systems that are secure, protected, and private. The authors argue on strategies that top management should implement to make sure that customers' expectations are exceeded relating to protecting and making sure that customers data and information are protected and private.

Chapter 10 addresses how to shape competitive strategies for the computer industry by examining and investigating the computer industry in the light of Michael Porter's framework. The authors argue that Michael Porter's framework is an appropriate methodology that can be used to investigate the profitability of computer industry.

Chapter 11 presents a case study that analyses the developer, the teacher, and the student perspective relating to flexible orchestration of tools in e-collaboration. The authors discuss some of the challenges, problems, updated models, and proposed solutions relating to tool orchestration in e-collaboration.

Chapter 12 addresses the challenges and problems facing e-publishing over cloud computing on scientists social network service using a comparative study. In addition, the authors present strategies and updated models to implement to overcome the challenges and problems facing e-publishing over cloud computing.

Chapter 13 investigates and presents an empirical study of the factors that positively and significantly influence the adoption of ICT adoption in SMEs. The author develops a theoretical framework by using the diffusion theory and the technology acceptance model to investigate factors that influences ICT adoption in SMEs. The study has significant research and managerial implications.

Chapter 14 discusses web-based personal health records (PHR) systems adoption using patients' perspectives. The authors investigate and determine factors that positively and significantly influence patients' intention to use web-based personal health records. This study has significant research and managerial implications relating to the health industry.

Chapter 15 reviews the domain and an empirically analysis of operations security management; and the author presents strategies and IT models that can be used to improve operations security management relating to third-party systems, malware protection, backup restoration, etc.

Chapter 16 discusses on how to successfully execute a real-time response in an Agile Information Systems; and the authors discuss the attributes, functions, and design principles relating to Agile Information Systems for better decision making and competitive advantages.

Chapter 17 analyses and compares the rate of adoption of an innovation in households and organizations in Northern Europe (i.e. Denmark). The author presents an updated predictive model that provide insights and understanding on important factors that positively and significantly influence innovations in households and organizations.

Chapter 18 presents a case study from Africa (i.e. Malawi) relating to learning from broad on SIM card registration policy; and the author discusses the challenges, benefits, and opportunities of SIM card registration relating to better decision making and competitive advantages.

Chapter 19 presents an updated framework and a set of real world-based guidelines to industry web portal business; and the framework consists of five stages for better decision making and competitive advantages.

Chapter 20 discusses and analyses how millennials perceived leadership attribution and its impact on database system's development; and the authors discusses challenges, benefits, opportunities, research models, characteristics and design principles relating to virtual leadership.

Chapter 21 concludes and presents a comprehensive and holistic review (2001 – 2017) on what motivates immigrants for ICT adoption and use. The author presents insights and understanding on factors that positively and significant influence the adoption of ICT by immigrants. This study contributes significantly to the ICT literature.

Chapter 1
Automatic Approach to Evaluate Collaborative Interaction in Virtual Environments

Luis Casillas
University of Guadalajara, Mexico

Adriana Peña
University of Guadalajara, Mexico

Alfredo Gutierrez
University of Guadalajara, Mexico

ABSTRACT

Virtual environments for multi-users, collaborative virtual environments (CVE), support geographical distant people to experience collaborative learning and team training. In this context, monitoring collaboration provides valuable, and in time, information regarding individual and group indicators, helpful for human instructors or intelligent tutor systems. CVE enable people to share a virtual space, interacting with an avatar, generating nonverbal behavior such as gaze-direction or deictic gestures, a potential means to understand collaboration. This chapter presents an automated model and its inference mechanisms to evaluate collaboration in CVE based on expert human rules of nonverbal participants' activity. The model is a multi-layer analysis that includes data filtering, fuzzy classification, and rule-based inference producing a high-level assessment of group collaboration. This approach was applied to a task-oriented session, where two participants assembled cubes in a CVE to create a figure.

INTRODUCTION

Nowadays Collective Virtual Environments (CVE) are an intense setting for cooperative learning (Bratitsis & Demetriadis, 2013) and training (Peña & Jiménez, 2012), in which adherents can experience exploratory and self-coordinated learning. CVE enable sharing virtual places and objects, by allowing the integration of numerous participants to team up as groups; an environment with a visually-profuse

DOI: 10.4018/978-1-5225-6367-9.ch001

and intuitive interface in which information is managed in newfangled ways, bringing remote individuals and objects together into a spatial and social vicinity, and encouraging correspondence mindfulness (Wolff et al., 2008). In there, individuals cooperate within a virtual world and the players get a graphical representation as an avatar.

At the point when individuals team up, cooperation is performed through various correspondence channels other than words, that is our nonverbal conduct that involves the greater part of what we do, aside from the importance of the words (Patterson, 1983). Such that the symbol, as an embodied representation of the user in the CVE, aids conversation and understanding in the virtual space (Imai et al., 2000), adding nonverbal communication such as gaze-direction or by representing the pointing to a virtual object, deictic gestures.

Within this context, the automatic monitoring of collaboration in computer-supported learning or team training, represents a resource for human or intelligent tutor systems in different ways such as creating the student or apprentice profile to adapt or personalize activities, to track the students' involvement, understanding the individual factors that influence the group and vice versa, measuring the participation equality or to understand the dynamics of the group (Foutsitzis & Demetriadis, 2013; Graham & Doore, 2015; Papanikolaou & Gouli, 2013; Reinig & Mejias, 2014).

In CVE, as computer systems, each performed activity can be bound to indicators through the users' log files, allowing collecting the whole phenomena data, including the avatars' performance and the situation of the virtual objects in it. Such logs collect dense data assemblies, enabling to infer high semantic indicators. In our proposed model, the raw data collected from the log files of the CVE is gathered and classified, throughout a multilevel mechanism capable to automate the production of high-level indicators, with the aim to automatically evaluate collaboration, based on the nonverbal behavior displayed by the participants through their avatars in CVE. This is either an alternative or a complement to the analysis of dialogue, just as if a human expertise had made such judgment.

This chapter is organized as follows: "related work" section includes a review of previous efforts regarding the collaboration analysis, as well as the case for CVE; the "technological support" section focuses on featuring the technology-assets involved in this study; "modeling collaboration analysis" section is aimed at defining the analysis model throughout fuzzy logic and knowledge-based systems; "applying the model" section is devoted to providing evidence regarding model's operation. Finally, sections "conclusion" and "questions for discussion" close the present proposal including some remarks about the operation of the model and its possibilities to operate in some other contexts.

This work is an enhancement of a previous study developed at (Casillas, Peña & Gutierrez, 2016).

RELATED WORK

Nonverbal behavior has been broadly studied in the real world and for the creation of artificial behavior in robots or animation (Breazeal, Kidd, Thomaz, Hoffman, & Berlin, 2005). However, there are few studies of the nonverbal cues people display in CVE through their avatars. In some cases, the developed CVE are focused on the automatic generation and scripting of nonverbal behaviors for autonomous agents; and in others on a real-time interaction of human users with the primary goal to offer a tool that allows sending basic emotional nonverbal messages.

Guye-Vuillème et al. (1998) established the importance of non-verbal communication in face-to-face interaction and its conversion to an equivalent in virtual worlds, studying the advantages and disadvantages of complex embodiments. Using their Virtual Life Network (VLNET) they presented a solution that takes into account the practical limitations of input devices and social science aspects. Back then, their work exposed virtual environments as cold, dehumanized places, and with static avatars lacking emotions; while they stand out nonverbal communication as the most efficient way to communicate emotional content. Guye-Vuillème et al., (1998) recognized the importance of the avatars as the means for the interaction in virtual worlds and sensing various attributes of it. Also, the avatar becomes more important in CVE because of its crucial functions as perception, localization, identification, visualization of others' interest focus, visualization of others' actions, and a social representation of self through the customization of the avatar.

According to Fabri, Moore and Hobbs (2004) emotionally, expressive faces in avatars are beneficial for communication in CVE; and emotions can effectively be visualized with a limited number of facial features (they presented a set of exemplary facial expressions). Fabri, Moore and Hobbs (2004) argued about the insufficiency of existing distance communication media in terms of emotional context and means for emotional expression and suggested overcoming this problem by enabling people to meet virtually in a CVE, engaging in a fashion of face-to-face communication via their avatars. All of which reinforces the importance of nonverbal communication between humans, which transcends the spoken or written word.

In Breazal et al. (2005) conducted an experiment where humans guided robots in order to explore the positive impact of non-verbal social cues and behavior and to illustrate how non-verbal communication helps to coordinate teammates' actions in collaborative activities. The robots' communication was verbal (explicit) and non-verbal (implicit). Their results showed that implicit non-verbal communication positively impacted the task performance with respect to team understanding and task efficiency.

Particularly for object-focused interactions, Hindmarsh et al. (2002) published a work where a desktop CVE was developed and evaluated, to study how the system provided participants with the ability to refer and discuss features of the virtual environment, as well as their interaction around objects. They conclude with a number of proposals for the design of CVE to facilitate this type of interactions, in which stands out the semi-distorted views to support peripheral awareness that difficulties interaction in objects-based tasks.

Regarding collaboration, Manoharan et al. (2002) developed the Collaborative Urban Planner (CUP), a CVE system to aid shared analysis of urban planning proposals. It allows visualization and interaction with spatial data, sharing virtual experience and improving the collaboration among planning officers and other remote stakeholders, exploring alternative designs. The system has embedded spatial analysis tools to accelerate the acceptability of individual proposals, improving productivity, increasing public participation, and transparency in the planning process.

The automatic study of collaboration has been hardly relied on Social Network Analysis (SNA) to understand social structures such as connections, distribution or segmentation in a visual way by mapping the nodes. This approach was used, for example, by Lorenzo, Sicilia and Sánchez (2012) to evaluate interaction between tutors and learners in a Massively Multiuser Online Learning (MMOL), finding that interactions were dense, and the students' participation was broad-based, which indicates that the use of MMOL enhances tutor interactions and the group relationship.

In their study, Lehmann-Willenbrock et al. (2017) qualify groups, the core of organizational functioning, as an intriguing social phenomenon. They affirmed that group members share the need to interact with each other in order to fulfill their group goals, which can be identified, measured, and evaluated. That need creates and sustains relationships between group members who work together in common goals, interacting in verbal and nonverbal ways, resulting in an unpredictable group dynamic process.

Using a 3D meeting environment, Anderson et al. (2017), concentrates his attention in the role of avatars in group-work, and how the avatars' appearance affects the intergroup interaction and collaboration as well in the virtual world as in the physical world, giving more importance to the way the avatars can be used for nonverbal communication. The use of avatars resulted in conflicts reducing and cultural misunderstandings, and the use of collaborative tools in virtual worlds decreases the learning curve allowing teams to focus more on work tasks rather than the technology itself.

Regarding simulations and games in virtual educational environments, new studies are pointing to the highly difficult to capture and measure knowledge, skills, and abilities in participants using traditional tools. To solve this kind of issues, a real-time observation of students' affective and cognitive state, and how these are related whit their learning performance is required. So, the process and analysis of the data that the computerized environments collect can be used to study learning performance, at personal as well as at group level, including the understanding of human behaviors (Khan, 2017).

In our model, nonverbal interaction is then, the reference baseline to understand collaboration, individual features such as involvement or influence, and group features such as cohesion, during the accomplishment of a task, with the characteristic of being a spatial task that involves the use of objects, proper for a CVE.

A recent research made by Casillas and Jara (2018) refers to the use of a polyhedral model to capture and predict behavioral profiles involving avatars in 3D environments. Such model could be used to supervise additional features regarding collaboration analysis in CVE. The referred polyhedral model is enabled to collect mobility events along the virtual spaces. Those accumulated indicators enable an analysis involving the review of the virtual space. Collaborative interaction and task development are clearly fed by this kind of data. Future efforts from this research group will include that polyhedral structure to enhance monitoring capabilities and enrich feedback elements for users.

TECHNOLOGICAL SUPPORT

Data collected from collaboration scenarios consist of elements with complex and diverse constructions, the efforts involving assessment or judgment assignment over collaborative scenarios, require analyses on diverse sources with a mixture of formats and essences. Even though there is an automatic support to store, retrieve and process the different elements analyzed, computers cannot generalize from ensembles inputs of diverse nature. Data needs to be prepared, filtered and reorganized to discover patterns, consistent at certain levels and supported by each activity registration.

Our proposed model for the analysis of collaboration is based on human expertise, generating automated judgments regarding collaboration through the non-verbal interaction in a CVE, this approach requires considering the following assumptions. Although CVE facilitates the collaborative process, in contrast, the display of nonverbal cues is constrained in specific ways by the technology (Peña, Rangel, & Lara, 2015). The type of collaborative-task to be carried out implicates that people will focus attention on the space and the objects in it, that is, spatial tasks. Therefore, unlike in real life, the focus will be narrowed on a few objects and it will be expected that the participants will be engaged in the ongoing task (Schroeder, 2011). According to Patterson (1982), the involvement needed in task-oriented interaction seems to be barely variable and more likely to be impersonal, almost not engaged with personality or emotions. A better predictable type of nonverbal interaction delimited to the task regulations and related to the goals and outcomes of an interaction.

The proposed automated model is a fusion of two well-known technologies: knowledge-based systems and fuzzy logic, aiming to discover knowledge underlying in heaps of data. On one hand, the fuzzy logic provides a dynamic capacity to capture continuous and vast signaling from the scope by producing the corresponding representation inside the system (Kosko, 1993). And on the other hand, the knowledge-based systems technology (Hayes-Roth, 1983) enables to include machine-learning capabilities. The fusion of knowledge-based systems and fuzzy logic is justified because as Zadeh (1983) established "… management of uncertainty is an intrinsically important issue in the design of expert systems because much of the information in the knowledge base of a typical expert system is imprecise, incomplete or not totally reliable …"

Data is then treated in different stages. The fuzzy-logic stage focuses on dealing with the vastness of data in log-files produced by the users' interaction in the CVE; to get a discrete and nominal representation for this highly detailed numerical data. The nominal representation has inherent in the semantics of the terms. Following this strategy, the CVE log-files, reach a structured condition that enables a simplified treatment.

The knowledge-based systems stage deals with the organic inference mechanism, which mimics the assessment and judgment capabilities of the human experts, one of the most challenging duties for computers. Throughout the use of rules, nominal representations are linked, to discover behavioral patterns.

These first stages allow discovering primal interaction acts, the nominal and discrete representations from fuzzy modules are inserted into working memories, in a second and third stage, which have an overcharged behavior, storing and passing concepts between modules.

The combined effect of these technologies and the approach selected for this model allows the automated treatment for a task with high dependence on human capabilities. Due to the fast pace in the production from the CVE, as well as the need of assessment and supervision over collaboration, it becomes a priority to have an automated and robust infrastructure to collect, deal and assess primitive acts performed by participants in the observed CVE.

MODELING COLLABORATION ANALYSIS

A filtering tool was developed to gather raw data for specific indicators of the log files from the CVE, those that represent nonverbal cues, storing it in independent files. These separated indicators represent a set of magnitudes and real numbers such as *user_name, object_name, time_stamp, axes_position* or *activity_type,* among others; which requires a normalization effect over diverse nature indicators. Figure 1 illustrates this process.

From the log files, nonverbal interaction cues are obtained considering the nonverbal communication areas of:

- Paralanguage, described by Juslin & Scherer (2005) as the physical mechanisms for producing nonverbal vocal qualities and sounds.

Figure 1. Process to filter indicators from log files

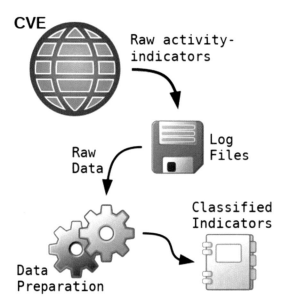

- Proxemics, the study of the use and perception of social and personal space, area (Hall et al., 1968).
- Kinesics, the body movements, and body positions.
- And those movements related to the task at hand (Peña, Rangel, & Lara, 2015).

In order to somehow measure the nonverbal interaction cues, a fuzzification process is performed. The volume of data will vary based on the sampling frequency performed in the CVE. A relaxed sampling might not produce enough or significant data for the analysis, but an intensive sampling involves huge volumes of data. A fuzzy mechanism is used to attenuate the exuberance of these indicators. Apparently, a paradox, a high rate frequency achieves precision, although the fuzzifying process implies a loss of precision. However, data precision is kept by using data averages, dispersion, and thresholds.

An *ad hoc* developed tool performs the fuzzifying process. This tool collects data from a specific indicator (indicator file) and calculates its mean (μ) and standard deviation (σ) to create the structure for the fuzzy sets. Throughout parameters, the tool receives the name of the indicator and the best names for the fuzzy sets.

Then, the quantity and width of the sets are calculated, as well as their position in a manifested range of the current indicator. These produce the segments sizes: the *meanSegment* with the Formula 1, and the *stdDevSegment* with the Formula 2; these formulas use the Pareto's principle for which data requires a normal distribution. The variable *numSets* in Formulas 1 and 2 corresponds to the number of segments or sets.

meanSegment $\leftarrow$ *[(μ*2)*0.8] / numSets*   (1)

stdDevSegment $\leftarrow$ *(σ*0.8) / numSets*   (2)

An iterative process gets the center (*center*) and the limits (*leftLimit* and *rightLimit*) for every fuzzy set, to classify the specific indicators measurements, see formulas 3, 4, and 5, where *i* corresponds to the number of fuzzy sets created. When one of the limits has the left or right assignment *value -1*, it is at the extreme in the fuzzy set, which requires being opened. Formulas 4 and 5 model this last case, when *i=0* or *i+1=numSets*.

$$\textbf{\textit{center}} \leftarrow meanSegment * (i + 1) \tag{3}$$

$$\textbf{\textit{leftLimit}} \leftarrow \textbf{\textit{if}}(i = 0): -1, \textbf{\textit{else}}: center - stdDevSegment * 2 \tag{4}$$

$$\textbf{\textit{rightLimit}} \leftarrow \textbf{\textit{if}}(i+1 = numSets): -1, \textbf{\textit{else}}: center + stdDevSegment * 2 \tag{5}$$

Another parameter specifies the sets nature: synthetic or organic. The synthetic approach analyzes the indicators with linear behavior; and the organic approach uses sigmoid shapes to match data from nature, economic or social sources. Figure 2 shows these two different cases of sets production.

This process turns quantitative raw data into qualitative descriptions. Collaboration goals are usually consistent when scrutinized by collaboration specialists in different scopes: real and virtual environments.

Figure 2. The first group {A, B, C}, are organic sets and the second group {D, E, F} are synthetic sets

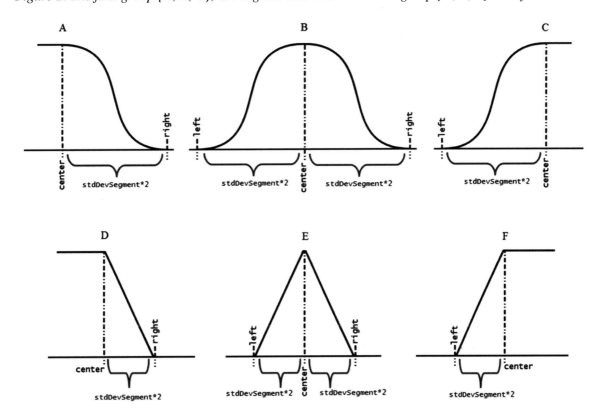

Table 1 contains the list of qualitative-indicators used in our model, the first column refers to indicator's name coming from the activity log-files and the second column is the linguistic values assigned to analyzed measurements. The linguistic values are the qualitative assessment corresponding to quantitative representations measuring activity in the studied CVE.

The qualitative indicators (QI) are then stored in a working memory see Figure 3, allowing a simplified rule-based analysis, implemented throughout a knowledge-based system that performs inference mechanisms. The inference mechanism is based on logical models that provide semantics by adding layers of meaning by using *modus ponens* transitions.

When fuzzification is finished, the Working Memory I contains qualitative indicators based on humans' expertise. From qualitative indicator in working memory, an inference procedure would produce low-level indicators to assess the collaboration acts. Figure 4 sketches the quantitative to qualitative relationships, as well as their transition to low-level indicators; where the round rectangles refer to the qualitative indicator as the inputs for rules to produce the low-level indicators, modeled as rhombuses.

Table 1. Qualitative Indicators and their possible values

Qualitative Indicator (QI)	Possible Values
Nodding Rate in Discussion Periods	Low Medium High
Head Shake Rate in Discussion Periods	Low Medium High
Pointing in Implementation	Low Medium High
Pointing in Discussion Periods	Low Medium High
Navigation Without Objects	Small distance Regular distance Long distance
Navigation Carrying Objects	Small distance Regular distance Long distance
Vocalization Rate	Low Medium High
Utterances Rate	Low Medium High
Discussion Initialization Rate	Low Medium High
Distance Among Group Members	Close to specific member Faraway from specific member Faraway from group formation
Manipulation of Task Objects	Low Medium High

Figure 3. Process from the indicators' files to a first working memory

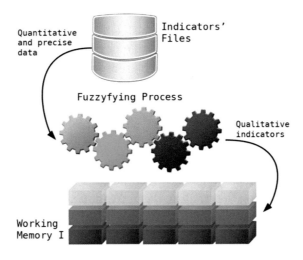

Figure 4. Influence models for rules in the first level inference

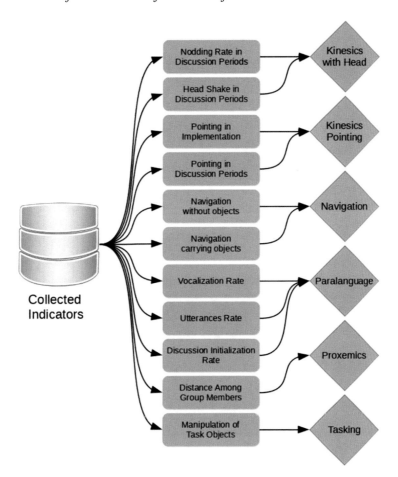

A knowledge-based system performs an inference through two-stages analysis. The first stage performs an inference process from fuzzified values in Working Memory I to produce low-level indicators for collaboration activity, as explained in the previous paragraph. This inference is shown in Figure 5. Such preliminary deduction produces a semantically improved version of collaboration that describes some interesting behaviors regarding participants' interaction.

The second inference process is now enabled. It is based on the ranges obtained from the first inference process. Nonverbal cues (low-level indicators) would be grouped in the same area, due to their relation as incomes to infer meaningful conclusions; for example, with two low-level values in nodding and head shaking in discussion periods will infer a high-level value for involvement in strategy. Table 2 contains, in the first column, a list of low-level indicators for collaborative interaction based on human experts in CVE, and in the second column shows their possible inferred values.

Hence when low-level indicators are ready and set in Working Memory II, the high-level inference is enabled to produce high-level indicators. Again, human experts in collaboration analysis defined these deep semantics indicators regarding CVE. Figure 6 sketches the influencing relationships among these low and high levered indicators, where the rhombuses refer to the low-level indicators as the inputs for rules that imply high-level indicators in hexagons. The produced high-level indicators are listed in Table 3. The first column in this table contains the indicators names and in the second one their possible inferred values.

Figure 5. First level inference fed with qualitative indicators (QI) produces semantic improved data as low-level indicators (LLI)

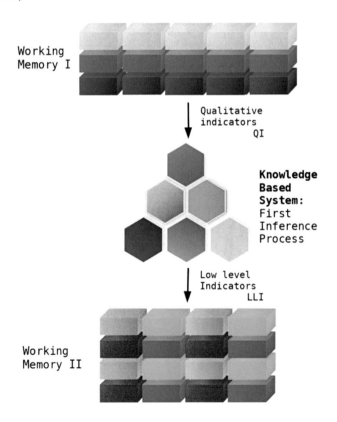

Table 2. List of Low Level Indicators, as well as their possible inferred alternatives

Low Level Indicator (LLI)	Possible Inferred Values
Kinesics with Head	Not Involved in Strategy Low Involvement in Strategy Involvement in Strategy High Involvement in Strategy
Kinesics Pointing	Low Influence in Strategy and Task Influence in Task Influence in Strategy Influence in Strategy and Task
Navigation	Low Involvement in Strategy and Task Involvement in Task Involvement in Strategy Involvement in Strategy and Task High Involvement in Task High Involvement in Strategy High Involvement in Strategy and Task
Paralanguage	Participation in Strategy Talkative Influence in Strategy High Influence in Strategy Leadership in Strategy
Proxemics	Close to Specific Member Involved in a Group and Subgroup Involved in Main Group Faraway from Specific Member Not Involved in a Group
Tasking	Not Involved in Task Accomplishment Involved in Task Accomplishment Taking Care of Task Accomplishment

This last process to create high-level indicators from Working Memory II is represented in Figure 7. High-level indicators are intended to be, somehow, an equivalent assessment for collaboration that would provide a human-expert. It is worth to mention that low-level and high-level indicators shown in this chapter have a specific implementation the rules in knowledge bases, which include all the alternatives for qualitative indicators, for low-level as well as high-level indicators.

Throughout the use of this model, it is possible to follow up the collaborative performance of participants in a CVE during the task accomplishment. Assessing every collaboration instant or action, due to model's dynamic nature. Thus, the collaboration-analysis can be performed during the session (online analysis), although the collaboration-analysis can be always performed at any moment after the session has finished (a posteriori analysis).

APPLYING THE MODEL

In order to verify model's feasibility, a CVE was developed, in which participants had to solve a puzzle in which 3D figures were reorganized in the space. The CVE collected data of all the activity performed by participants.

Figure 6. This model sketches the influence of low-level indicators over high-level indicators

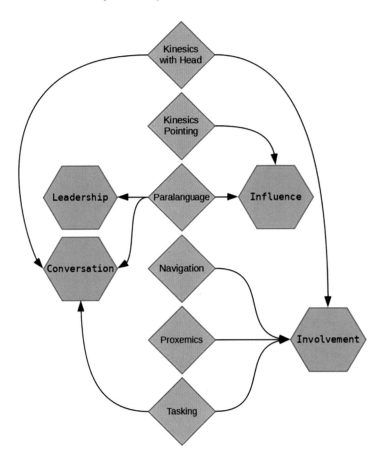

Table 3. List of high level indicators, as well as their possible inferred alternatives

High Level Indicator	Possible Inferred Values
Influence	Brief, Support, Significant
Leadership	Uncommitted, Engaged, Remarkable
Conversation	Silent, Reactive, Talkative
Involvement	Absent, Participative, Mingled

Regarding the testing method:

- **Participants:** Fourteen undergraduate students of a Computer Science School voluntarily participated in an exchange of desktop objects; five female students and nine male participants in the range of 18 to 25 years old randomly formed seven dyads.
- **Materials and Devices:** The sessions took place in a room with two desks facing to opposite directions, each with an Internet-connected computer Dell™ computer model Alienware X51 with a mouse, keyboard microphones, and earphones.

Figure 7. Low-level indicator (LLI) as input produce high-level indicators (HLI) to get the evaluation of collaborative activity in CVE

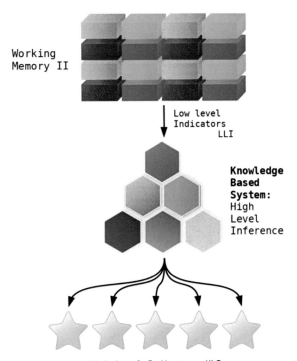

- **Procedure:** A CVE was developed in the OpenSim™ platform; it consisted in an island with 14 pieces placed in a circle, as seen in Figure 8. Participants had a humanoid avatar that matched their gender. The application saved in a text file a time stamp, the users' name, the avatar and the objects positions at each program cycle.

Dyads were asked to assemble three cuboid geometric figures: a cuboid of 4x3x2, a cube 3x3x3, and a cuboid 4x2x3; each one on a different session.

The sessions were taped with the aTube Catcher™ application. Sessions lasted on average 6.8 minutes, the fastest one was of two minutes and the one that lasts longer was 16 minutes. There was a difference of around two minutes between sessions for the dyads.

Data. Data was treated to get the average time that the participants:

- **Navigated Without Holding an Object:** Navigation without objects
- **Navigated Carrying an Object:** Navigation carrying object
- **Manipulated an Object:** Manipulation task object
- **Nodded:** Nodding rate in discussion period
- **Head Shacked:** Headshake rate in discussion period

The tapes were transcribed to get a rate of:

Figure 8. Top view of the CVE

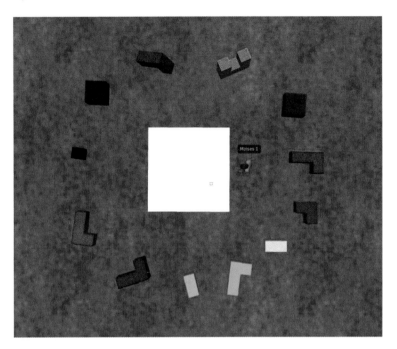

- **The Number of Words Pronounced:** Speech rate
- **The Number of Utterances:** Utterances rate
- **The Number That One of the Participants Initiated the Conversation Period:** Initiator rate

See Table 4, it shows the results of the fourteen participants at each session.

Each indicator listed in Table 4 goes through the fuzzy process. Table 5 contains the results of the produced fuzzy sets where the values for each set can be observed.

As an example, using the classified data in the fuzzy sets of the transactions 6 and 15, their results are:

The fuzzy classification for transaction **6**
Nodding_Rate_In_Discussion_Periods=6.4 | *NRD: Low*
Head_Shake_In_Discussion_Periods=20.2 | *HSD: High*
Navigation_Without_Objects=44.9 | *NWO: RegularDistance*
Navigation_Carrying_Objects=33.2 | *NCO: LongDistance*
Vocalization_Rate=0.46 | *VR: Medium*
Utterances_Rate=0.48 | *UR: Medium*
Discussion_Initialization_Rate=0.38 | *DIR: Low*
Manipulation_Of_Task_Objects=58.3 | **MTO: High**
The fuzzy classification for transaction **15**
Nodding_Rate_In_Discussion_Periods=14 | *NRD: High*
Head_Shake_In_Discussion_Periods=9.3 | *HSD: Medium*
Navigation_Without_Objects=18.2 | *NWO: SmallDistance*

Table 4. Data collected from CVEs' log files:The last two rows show the mean and the standard deviation

Indicator	Collected data	μ	σ
Navigation_Without_Objects (NWO)	26.2 30.8 24.7 21.1 30.5 44.9 25 34.9 19.9 44.4 22.7 22.5 14 21.8 18.2 18.5 28.9 14.7 66.8 66.8 66.8 19.7 23.4 18 27.5 64.7 23.1 33.2 34 39.8 20.7 20.7 20.7 36.6 23.8 81.7 38.6 19.8 103.4 46.6 22.3 82 ...	34.866666	20.95478
Navigation_Carrying_Objects (NCO)	13.5 17.5 9.2 19.1 2.4 33.2 4.8 25.4 32.7 25.5 26.9 26.3 21.7 24.1 16.5 19.4 23.9 11.3 16.3 16.7 10 12.1 6.8 4.5 17.5 12.1 10.8 17.2 15.4 18.7 11.6 14.2 23.6 11 17 7.1 21.4 7.6 25.3 ...	16.674358	7.649758
Nodding_Rate_In_Discussion_Periods (NRD)	10.5 8.4 6.5 11 6.5 6.4 6 8 5.5 4.5 11.5 12 11.5 15.5 14 6.5 8 5 7.5 7.5 7.5 6.9 9 8 8 6 5.5 4.5 11 7 13.1 12.5 14 7 10.5 6 8 8 6 6.5 10.5 6.5	8.47317	2.83857
Head_Shake_in_Discussion_Periods (HSD)	9.3 14.5 2 1.7 18.6 20.2 32.8 9.3 8.9 12.4 8.1 9.3 14.8 10.1 6.4 0.7 8 4 20.2 16.4 7.2 7.2 3.9 3.1 ...	10.508	7.2959
Manipulation_Of_Task_Objects (MTO)	5 56.6 21.3 38 25.3 4.5 58.3 12.7 43.5 43.6 30.4 45.4 43.3 41.3 27.2 55.3 50.2 39 19.2 44 33.1 15.7 53.3 40.1 29.6 64.2 35.3 15.1 31.8 43.5 61.9 32.1 30.8 22.3 41 30 24.116.1 40.2 4.2 35.8 ...	34.251219	15.46058
Vocalization_Rate (VR)	0.86 0.69 0.61 0.14 0.31 0.39 0.46 0.63 0.43 0.54 0.37 0.57 0.38 0.26 0.31 0.62 0.74 0.69 0.48 0.55 0.42 0.52 0.45 0.58 0.33 0.88 0.39 0.67 0.13 0.61 0.50 0.49 0.50 0.50 0.51 0.50 0.95 0.79 0.89 0.05 0.21 0.11 ...	0.500238	0.214026
Utterances_Rate (UR)	0.50 0.48 0.52 0.50 0.52 0.48 0.43 0.58 0.45 0.57 0.42 0.55 0.50 0.28 0.34 0.50 0.72 0.66 0.60 0.48 0.49 0.40 0.53 0.51 0.31 0.75 0.45 0.69 0.25 0.55 0.52 0.51 0.49 0.48 0.49 0.51 0.85 0.73 0.79 0.15 0.27 0.21 ...	0.500238	0.149885
Discussion_Initialization_Rate (DIR)	0.67 0.33 0.63 0.33 0.67 0.38 0.33 0.67 0.38 0.40 0.67 0.60 0.40 0.33 0.22 0.60 0.67 0.78 0.25 0.42 0.44 0.75 0.58 0.56 0.17 1.00 0.25 0.83 0.75 0.49 0.49 0.45 0.51 0.51 0.55 0.92 0.70 0.91 0.08 0.30 0.09 ...	0.513658	0.224006

Navigation_Carrying_Objects=24.1 | *NCO: LongDistance*
Vocalization_Rate=0.31 | *VR: Low*
Utterances_Rate=0.34 | *UR: Low*
Discussion_Initialization_Rate=0.22 | *DIR: Low*
Manipulation_Of_Task_Objects=27.2 | *MTO: Low*

Based on these results, the following stage of analysis implies expert inference process. As shown in Figures 6 and 7, different ensembles of indicators entail specific responses. Table 6 shows the first level inference for transactions 6 and 15, based on the qualitative classification produced by fuzzifying machinery.

The first inference process has already produced enough information to define some feedback for participants. Nevertheless, our model has an additional inference stage aimed to produce high-level indicators. Table 7 shows the results achieved by this second inference process for transactions 6 and 15.

Table 5. Results from the fuzzifying process over the collected data. Within the sections "Testing on collected data" in this table, a mark (*) has been set at those selected classified-entries for further analysis in the following stages.

Table 5. Continued

```
* Working variable: Navigation_Without_Objects (NWO)
- Mean received: 34.8666666666667
- Std Dev Received: 20.954779030752
* They were created 3 sets with the following dimensions:
+ meanSegment: 18.595555555555574
+ stdDevSegment: 5.5879410748672
- It was created the set: NWO: SmallDistance |
Z-Curve [ C: 18.595555555555574 RL: 29.771437705289976 ]
- It was created the set: NWO: RegularDistance |
Pi-Curve [ LL: 26.01522896137675 C: 37.19111111111115 RL:
48.36699326084555 ]
- It was created the set: NWO: LongDistance |
S-Curve [ LL: 44.61078451693232 C: 55.78666666666672 ]
* Testing on collected data:
- Value 26.2 => NWO: SmallDistance
- Value 30.8 => NWO: RegularDistance
- Value 24.7 => NWO: SmallDistance
- Value 21.1 => NWO: SmallDistance
- Value 30.5 => NWO: RegularDistance
* - Value 44.9 => NWO: RegularDistance
- Value 25.0 => NWO: SmallDistance
- Value 34.9 => NWO: RegularDistance
- Value 19.9 => NWO: SmallDistance
- Value 44.4 => NWO: RegularDistance
- Value 22.7 => NWO: SmallDistance
- Value 22.5 => NWO: SmallDistance
- Value 14.0 => NWO: SmallDistance
- Value 21.8 => NWO: SmallDistance
* - Value 18.2 => NWO: SmallDistance
- Value 18.5 => NWO: SmallDistance
...
```

```
* Working variable: Navigation_Carrying_Objects (NCO)
- Mean received: 16.674358974359
- Std Dev Received: 7.64975809554641
* They were created 3 sets with the following dimensions:
+ meanSegment: 8.892991452991467
+ stdDevSegment: 2.0399354921457094
- It was created the set: NCO: SmallDistance |
Z-Curve [ C: 8.892991452991467 RL: 12.972862437282885 ]
- It was created the set: NCO: RegularDistance |
Pi-Curve [ LL: 13.706111921691516 C: 17.785982905982934 RL:
21.86585389027435 ]
- It was created the set: NCO: LongDistance |
S-Curve [ LL: 22.599103374682983 C: 26.6789743589744 ]
* Testing on collected data:
- Value 13.5 => NCO: SmallDistance
- Value 17.5 => NCO: RegularDistance
- Value 9.2 => NCO: SmallDistance
- Value 19.1 => NCO: RegularDistance
- Value 2.4 => NCO: SmallDistance
* - Value 33.2 => NCO: LongDistance
- Value 4.8 => NCO: SmallDistance
- Value 25.4 => NCO: LongDistance
- Value 32.7 => NCO: LongDistance
- Value 25.5 => NCO: LongDistance
- Value 26.9 => NCO: LongDistance
- Value 26.3 => NCO: LongDistance
- Value 21.7 => NCO: RegularDistance
- Value 16.5 => NCO: RegularDistance
* - Value 24.1 => NCO: LongDistance
- Value 19.4 => NCO: RegularDistance
...
```

continued in next column

```
* Working variable: Nodding_Rate_In_Discussion_Periods (NRD)
- Mean received: 8.47317073170732
- Std Dev Received: 2.83857573355406
* They were created 3 sets with the following dimensions:
+ meanSegment: 4.519024390243904
+ stdDevSegment: 0.7569535289477494
- It was created the set: NRD: Low |
Z-Curve [ C: 4.519024390243904 RL: 6.0329314481394025 ]
- It was created the set: NRD: Medium |
Pi-Curve [ LL: 7.524141722592309 C: 9.038048780487808 RL:
10.551955838383307 ]
- It was created the set: NRD: High |
S-Curve [ LL: 12.043166112836214 C: 13.557073170731712 ]
* Testing on collected data:
- Value 10.5 => NRD: Medium
- Value 8.4 => NRD: Medium
- Value 6.5 => NRD: Low
- Value 11.0 => NRD: Medium
- Value 6.5 => NRD: Low
* - Value 6.4 => NRD: Low
- Value 6.0 => NRD: Low
- Value 8.0 => NRD: Medium
- Value 5.5 => NRD: Low
- Value 4.5 => NRD: Low
- Value 11.5 => NRD: Medium
- Value 12.0 => NRD: Medium
- Value 11.5 => NRD: Medium
- Value 15.5 => NRD: High
* - Value 14.0 => NRD: High
- Value 6.5 => NRD: Low
...
```

```
* Working variable: Head_Shake_in_Discussion_Periods (HSD)
- Mean received: 10.508
- Std Dev Received: 7.29594179435847
* They were created 3 sets with the following dimensions:
+ meanSegment: 5.604266666666667
+ stdDevSegment: 1.945584478495592
- It was created the set: HSD: Low |
Z-Curve [ C: 5.604266666666667 RL: 9.495435623657851 ]
- It was created the set: HSD: Medium |
Pi-Curve [ LL: 7.31736437634215 C: 11.208533333333333 RL:
15.099702290324517 ]
- It was created the set: HSD: High |
S-Curve [ LL: 12.921631043008816 C: 16.8128 ]
* Testing on collected data:
- Value 9.3 => HSD: Medium
- Value 14.5 => HSD: High
- Value 2.0 => HSD: Low
- Value 1.7 => HSD: Low
- Value 18.6 => HSD: High
* - Value 20.2 => HSD: High
- Value 32.8 => HSD: High
- Value 9.3 => HSD: Medium
- Value 8.9 => HSD: Medium
- Value 12.4 => HSD: Medium
- Value 8.1 => HSD: Low
- Value 14.8 => HSD: High
- Value 10.1 => HSD: Medium
- Value 6.4 => HSD: Low
* - Value 9.3 => HSD: Medium
- Value 0.7 => HSD: Low
...
```

continued on following page

Table 5. Continued

* Working variable: **Manipulation_Of_Task_Objects (MTO)**
- Mean received: 34.2512195121951
- Std Dev Received: 15.4605808744565
* They were created 3 sets with the following dimensions:
+ meanSegment: 18.26731707317072
+ stdDevSegment: 4.122821566521734
- It was created the set: **MTO: Low** |
Z-Curve [C: 18.26731707317072 RL: 26.51296020621419]
- It was created the set: **MTO: Medium** |
Pi-Curve [LL: 28.288991013297974 C: 36.53463414634144 RL: 44.780277279384904]
- It was created the set: **MTO: High** |
S-Curve [LL: 46.5563080864687 C: 54.80195121951216]
* Testing on collected data:
- Value 5.0 => MTO: Low
- Value 56.6 => MTO: High
- Value 21.3 => MTO: Low
- Value 38.0 => MTO: Medium
- Value 25.3 => MTO: Low
* - *Value 58.3 => MTO: High*
- Value 4.5 => MTO: Low
- Value 12.7 => MTO: Low
- Value 43.5 => MTO: Medium
- Value 43.6 => MTO: Medium
- Value 30.4 => MTO: Medium
- Value 45.4 => MTO: Low
- Value 43.3 => MTO: Medium
- Value 41.3 => MTO: Medium
* - *Value 27.2 => MTO: Low*
- Value 55.3 => MTO: High
...

* Working variable: **Vocalization_Rate (VR)**
- Mean received: 0.500238
- Std Dev Received: 0.214026
* They were created 3 sets with the following dimensions:
+ meanSegment: 0.2667936
+ stdDevSegment: 0.0570736
- It was created the set: **VR: Low** |
Z-Curve [C: 0.2667936 RL: 0.3809408]
- It was created the set: **VR: Medium** |
Pi-Curve [LL: 0.41944000000000004 C: 0.5335872 RL: 0.6477344]
- It was created the set: **VR: High** |
S-Curve [LL: 0.6862336000000001 C: 0.8003808000000001]
* Testing on collected data:
- Value 0.86 => VR: High
- Value 0.69 => VR: High
- Value 0.61 => VR: Medium
- Value 0.14 => VR: Low
- Value 0.31 => VR: Low
* - *Value 0.46 => VR: Medium*
- Value 0.39 => VR: Low
- Value 0.63 => VR: Medium
- Value 0.43 => VR: Medium
- Value 0.54 => VR: Medium
- Value 0.37 => VR: Low
- Value 0.57 => VR: Medium
- Value 0.38 => VR: Low
- Value 0.26 => VR: Low
* - *Value 0.31 => VR: Low*
- Value 0.62 => VR: Medium
...

Table 5. Continued

* Working variable: **Utterances_Rate (UR)**
- Mean received: 0.500238
- Std Dev Received: 0.149885
* They were created 3 sets with the following dimensions:
+ meanSegment: 0.2667936
+ stdDevSegment: 0.039969333333333336
- It was created the set: **UR: Low** |
Z-Curve [C: 0.2667936 RL: 0.3467322666666667]
- It was created the set: **UR: Medium** |
Pi-Curve [LL: 0.4536485333333334 C: 0.5335872 RL: 0.6135258666666668]
- It was created the set: **UR: High** |
S-Curve [LL: 0.7204421333333334 C: 0.8003808000000001]
* Testing on collected data:
- Value 0.5 => UR: Medium
- Value 0.48 => UR: Medium
- Value 0.52 => UR: Medium
- Value 0.5 => UR: Medium
- Value 0.52 => UR: Medium
* - *Value 0.48 => UR: Medium*
- Value 0.43 => UR: Low
- Value 0.58 => UR: Medium
- Value 0.45 => UR: Low
- Value 0.57 => UR: Medium
- Value 0.42 => UR: Low
- Value 0.55 => UR: Medium
- Value 0.5 => UR: Medium
- Value 0.28 => UR: Low
* - *Value 0.34 => UR: Low*
- Value 0.5 => UR: Medium
- Value 0.72 => UR: Low
...

* Working variable: **Discussion_Initialization_Rate (DIR)**
- Mean received: 0.513658
- Std Dev Received: 0.224006
* They were created 3 sets with the following dimensions:
+ meanSegment: 0.2739509333333333
+ stdDevSegment: 0.059734933333333344
- It was created the set: **DIR: Low** |
Z-Curve [C: 0.2739509333333333 RL: 0.3934208]
- It was created the set: **DIR: Medium** |
Pi-Curve [LL: 0.4284319999999999 C: 0.5479018666666666 RL: 0.6673717333333333]
- It was created the set: **DIR: High** |
S-Curve [LL: 0.7023829333333332 C: 0.8218527999999999]
* Testing on collected data:
- Value 0.67 => DIR: Low
- Value 0.33 => DIR: Low
- Value 0.63 => DIR: Medium
- Value 0.33 => DIR: Low
- Value 0.67 => DIR: Low
* - *Value 0.38 => DIR: Low*
- Value 0.33 => DIR: Low
- Value 0.67 => DIR: Low
- Value 0.38 => DIR: Low
- Value 0.4 => DIR: Low
- Value 0.67 => DIR: Low
- Value 0.6 => DIR: Medium
- Value 0.4 => DIR: Low
- Value 0.33 => DIR: Low
* - *Value 0.22 => DIR: Low*
- Value 0.6 => DIR: Medium
...

continued in next column

Table 6. First inference from the fuzzy classification results

Transaction 6	First Level Inference Results			
Input values	**Kinesics with Head**	**Navigation**	**Paralanguage**	**Tasking**
Nodding_Rate_In_Discussion_Periods *NRD: Low* Head_Shake_In_Discussion_Periods **HSD: High**	Involved in Strategy			
Navigation_Without_Objects **NWO: RegularDistance** Navigation_Carrying_Objects **NCO: LongDistance**		Involvement in task and strategy		
Vocalization_Rate **VR: Medium** Utterances_Rate **UR: Medium** Discussion_Initialization_Rate **DIR: Low**			Participation in strategy	
Manipulation_Of_Task_Objects **MTO: High**				Taking Care of Task Accomplishment
Transaction 15	**First Level Inference Results**			
Input values	**Kinesics with Head**	**Navigation**	**Paralanguage**	**Tasking**
Nodding_Rate_In_Discussion_Periods **NRD: High** Head_Shake_In_Discussion_Periods **HSD: Medium**	Involvement in Strategy			
Navigation_Without_Objects **NWO: SmallDistance** Navigation_Carrying_Objects **NCO: LongDistance**		Involvement in task		
Vocalization_Rate **VR: Low** Utterances_Rate **UR: Low** Discussion_Initialization_Rate **DIR: Low**			Low participation in strategy	
Manipulation_Of_Task_Objects **MTO: Low**				Involved in Task Accomplishment

The second inference process discovered high semantics assessment. In the case of transaction 6, this event collected from CVE implies a Reactive behavior regarding the HLI for Conversation and Mingled response regarding the HLI for Involvement. On the other hand, transaction 15 referring to another participant in the experiment implies a Silent behavior regarding the HLI for Conversation and Participative response regarding the HLI for Involvement. At this point, it is possible to assume that one participant was active and leading the task development meanwhile the other was less involved in the strategy or the task, although cooperative with the leader.

Table 7. Second inference process to produce high-level indicators

Transaction 6	
Kinesics_With_Head: **Involved in Strategy**	
Navigation: **Involvement in task and strategy**	Conversation: **Reactive**
Paralanguage: **Participation in strategy**	Involvement: **Mingled**
Tasking: **Taking Care of Task Accomplishment**	
Proxemics: *Does not apply in groups with two participants*	
Transaction 15	
Kinesics_With_Head: **Involvement in Strategy**	
Navigation: **Involvement in task**	Conversation: **Silent**
Paralanguage: **Low participation in strategy**	Involvement: **Participative**
Tasking: **Involved in Task Accomplishment**	
Proxemics: *Does not apply in groups with two participants*	

The enabled transactional analysis allows an instant response to every set of data collected from the system, providing a faster assessment of collaboration acts. This quick response could be used to produce an automated feedback to participants during collaboration. Such feedback can be aimed at producing better practices to achieve goals.

DISCUSSION QUESTIONS IN CLASSROOMS

The act of analyzing interactive collaboration implies challenging tasks to perform. Humans' intentions are not always manifested or even clear to be aware. The collaboration happens in diverse contexts at different commitment degrees from the parts. Hence collaborative analysis is clearly a difficult task for humans, although humans have complex intellect.

If collaboration analysis is transferred to computers, the task becomes even harder due to the absence of common sense in machines. Thus, knowledge engineers must define the features and treatment for collaboration analysis.

Regarding the philosophical approach for the automated analysis over the collaboration performed by humans, some questions can be made:

1. Can computers perform a reliable supervision of humans' collaboration?
2. Are computers enabled to discover the collaboration issues from humans' activity?
3. Could computers provide reliable recommendations regarding the collaboration issues?

Besides, there is a set of questions that could be considered to achieve a robust collaboration analysis. These questions are inspired by the strategy proposed at (Casillas & Daradoumis, 2012):
1. What are the features (direct and indirect) detected?
2. How can these features be discretized?

3.   What states can these indicators produce when merge using the cross product?

4.   Can states-list be optimized under the applicable constraints?

5.   Which actions can be applied to produce state changes?

6.   What is the collaborative achievement bound to the actions?

7.   What are the collaborative gains when following certain acting-sequences?

In fact, these questions were the research matter underlying the experimental development for present work.

CONCLUSION

The analysis of collaboration is an intricate task. The number of involved elements and the interaction dynamics from participants imply vibrant and complex scenarios that demand diverse efforts to understand collaboration. When a tutor or a teacher supervises collaboration, a number of human-senses are involved including intuition. And when collaboration is based on artificially supported scenarios, as CVE, complexity increases mainly due to the absence of primal communication elements. Even though machines can perform diverse processes over huge amounts of data, most of the produced information during collaboration is lost because of the machines limitation when gathering humans' manifestations.

It is a fact that significant amounts of data could be collected in the activity logs produced by CVE, but it is also a fact that the format and structure of this data are incompatible for humans' understanding. Log files are usually lines containing different sets of data separated by special characters, not easy to understand. The presented model faces this inconvenience using semantic layers between the data stored in CVE activity logs and high-level results for collaboration judgment or assessment.

The model presented in this work is provided with mechanisms to recover, filter, manage, translate, analysis and infer from data collected in log files to providing semantics for unbound pieces of data; by filtering, fuzzifying and two inferring stages, this model supplies the semantics for the activity performed in a CVE related to collaboration.

A performed test produced a series of responses, which are consistent with the expected results in isolated and controlled data. Because logs files are currently noisy and, in some cases, incomplete, various data-cleansing tasks must be undertaken over them, in order to have the needed infrastructure to run massive testing over results. Also, the current operating solution in the model is composed of isolated modules with a communication among them by passing files.

This is an adaptable model that can use customized rules accordingly to different experts' points of view regarding the field of knowledge or even increase the two rule stages if necessary to add semantic layers to the outcomes. Also, it can be used with partial data to get "snapshots" of the session.

The current research for this project involves an integrated-system feed with clean log-files directly coming from the CVE, operating as a black box that produces high-level indicators. The data-cleansing endeavor on log files for this project has thrown light on the opportunity to produce an additional layer in the middle of the process. This layer performs a preliminary analysis of data. With enough and clean data, a decision tree can produce a classification. Knowledge bases are segmented into specific bases, each of them aimed to discover a specific profile under the already defined classification.

Besides, the project by Casillas and Jara (2018) has enabled an additional analysis layer involving a detailed and microscopic supervision of avatars' mobility in CVE. That polyhedral learning-structure will allow the inclusion of new supervision layers involving navigation, strategy and task development.

REFERENCES

Anderson, A., Dossick, C. S., Iorio, J., & Taylor, J. E. (2017). The impact of avatars, social norms and copresence on the collaboration effectiveness of AEC virtual teams. *Journal of Information Technology in Construction*, *22*(15), 287–304.

Bratitsis, T., & Demetriadis, S. (2013). Research approaches in computer-supported collaborative learning. *International Journal of e-Collaboration*, *9*(1), 1–8. doi:10.4018/jec.2013010101

Breazeal, C., Kidd, C. D., Thomaz, A. L., Hoffman, G., & Berlin, M. (2005). Effects of nonverbal communication on efficiency and robustness in human-robot teamwork. *IEEE/RSJ International Conference on Intelligent Robots and Systems*, 383-388. 10.1109/IROS.2005.1545011

Casillas, L., & Daradoumis, T. (2012). An Ontological Structure for Gathering and Sharing Knowledge among Scientists through Experiment Modeling. *Collaborative and Distributed E-Research: Innovations in Technologies, Strategies and Applications: Innovations in Technologies, Strategies and Applications*, 165.

Casillas, L., & Jara, I. (2018). Learning Avatar's Locomotion Patterns Through Spatial Analysis in FPS Video Games. *International Journal of Organizational and Collective Intelligence*, *8*(1), 28–45. doi:10.4018/IJOCI.2018010103

Casillas, L., Peña, A., & Gutierrez, A. (2016). Towards an Automated Model to Evaluate Collaboration through Non-Verbal Interaction in Collaborative Virtual Environments. *International Journal of e-Collaboration*, *12*(4), 7–23. doi:10.4018/IJeC.2016100102

Fabri, M., Moore, D. J., & Hobbs, D. J. (2004). Mediating the expression of emotion in educational collaborative virtual environments: An experimental study. *International Journal of Virtual Reality*, *7*(2), 66–81. doi:10.100710055-003-0116-7

Foutsitzis, C. G., & Demetriadis, S. (2013). Scripted collaboration to leverage the impact of algorithm visualization tools in online learning: Results from two small scale studies. *International Journal of e-Collaboration*, *9*(1), 42–56. doi:10.4018/jec.2013010104

Graham, C. M., & Doore, B. (2015). Millennial leadership: The oppositional relationship between leadership type and the quality of database system's development in virtual environments. *International Journal of e-Collaboration*, *11*(3), 29–48. doi:10.4018/ijec.2015070103

Guye-Vuillème, A., Capin, T. K., Pandzic, I. S., Thalmann, N. M., & Thalmann, D. (1998). *Nonverbal communication interface for collaborative virtual environments. Collaborative Virtual Environments*. University of Manchester.

Hall, E. T., Birdwhistell, R. L., Bock, B., Bohannan, P., Diebold, A. R. Jr, Durbin, M., ... La Barre, W. (1968). Proxemics. *Current Anthropology*, *9*(2/3), 83–108. doi:10.1086/200975

Hayes-Roth, F. (1983). *Building knowledge based systems* (1st ed.). Addison-Wesley.

Hindmarsh, J., Fraser, M., Heath, C., & Benford, S. (2002). Virtually missing the point: Configuring CVEs for objectfocused interaction. In E. F. Churchill, D. Snowdon, & A. Munro (Eds.), *Collaborative virtual environments: Digital places and spaces for interaction* (pp. 115–139). London: Springer.

Imai, T., Qui, Z., Behara, S., Tachi, S., Aoyama, T., & Johnson, A. (2000). *Overcoming time-zone differences and time management problem with tele-immersion. 10th Annual Internet Society Conference (INET)*, Yokohama, Japan.

Juslin, P. N., & Scherer, K. R. (2005). Vocal expression of affect. The new handbook of methods in nonverbal behavior research, 65-135.

Khan, S. M. (2017). Multimodal Behavioral Analytics in Intelligent Learning and Assessment Systems. In *Innovative Assessment of Collaboration* (pp. 173–184). Cham: Springer. doi:10.1007/978-3-319-33261-1_11

Kosko, B., & Toms, M. (1993). *Fuzzy thinking: the new science of fuzzy logic.* New York: Hyperion.

Lehmann-Willenbrock, N., Hung, H., & Keyton, J. (2017). New frontiers in analyzing dynamic group interactions: Bridging social and computer science. *Small Group Research*, *48*(5), 519–531. doi:10.1177/1046496417718941 PMID:29249891

Lorenzo, C. M., Sicilia, M. A., & Sánchez, S. (2012). Studying the effectiveness of multi-user immersive environments for collaborative evaluation tasks. *Computers & Education*, *59*(4), 1361–1376. doi:10.1016/j.compedu.2012.06.002

Manoharan, T., Taylor, H., & Gardiner, P. (2002). *A collaborative analysis tool for visualisation and interaction with spatial data.* 7th International Conference on 3D Web Technology, New York, NY.

Papanikolaou, K., & Gouli, E. (2013). Investigating influences among individuals and groups in a collaborative learning setting. *International Journal of e-Collaboration*, *9*(1), 9–25. doi:10.4018/jec.2013010102

Patterson, M. L. (1982). A sequential functional model of nonverbal exchange. *Psychological Review*, *89*(3), 231–249. doi:10.1037/0033-295X.89.3.231

Patterson, M. L. (1983). *Nonverbal behavior. A functional perspective.* New York: Springer-Verlang. doi:10.1007/978-1-4612-5564-2

Peña, A., & Jiménez, E. (2012). Virtual environments for effective training. *Revista Colombiana De Computación, 13*(1).

Peña, A., Rangel, N., & Lara, G. (2015). Nonverbal interaction contextualized in collaborative virtual environments. *Journal on Multimodal User Interfaces*, *9*(3), 253–260. doi:10.100712193-015-0193-4

Reinig, B. A., & Mejias, R. J. (2014). On the measurement of participation equality. *International Journal of e-Collaboration*, *10*(4), 32–48. doi:10.4018/ijec.2014100103

Schroeder, R. (2011). *Being there together: Social interaction in shared virtual environments* (A. Kirlik, Ed.). New York: Oxford University Press.

Wolff, R., Roberts, D., Murgia, A., Murray, N., Rae, J., & Steptoe, W. (2008). *Communicating eye gaze across a distance without rooting participants to the spot.* Distributed Simulation and Real-Time Applications, 2008. DS-RT 2008. 12th IEEE International Symposium, Vancouver, British Columbia, Canada. 10.1109/DS-RT.2008.28

Zadeh, L. A. (1983). The role of fuzzy logic in the management of uncertainty in knowledge based systems. *Fuzzy Sets and Systems*, *11*(1), 197–198.

Chapter 2
Domestic vs. International E-Shopping:
An Empirical Perceptions Analysis

Vaggelis Saprikis
Western Macedonia University of Applied Sciences, Greece

ABSTRACT

Contemporary commerce is completely different as regards features some years ago. Nowadays, a considerable number of individuals and firms take advantage of the information and communication technologies and conduct transactions online. In particular, the mobile industry along with the broad use of social networks and improvements in the internet bandwidth worldwide has created a completely different business environment. Consequently, the technology incited many consumers to cross-border e-shopping, allowing access to a wider variety of products and services, and in numerous circumstances, access to cheaper goods. The purpose of this chapter is to investigate the perceptions internet users have towards e-shops focusing on Greece. More precisely, it aims to find out whether there are contingent differences on customers' perceptions regarding domestic vs. international e-shops, since a gradually augmented number of people have been expressing their preference on non-domestic e-stores for their purchases. Additionally, the chapter intends to shed light on the difficulty in understanding vital aspects of e-consumer behaviour.

INTRODUCTION

Online shopping is a fact. In reality, a large number of consumers do prefer to shop online than visiting a traditional brick-and-mortal store[1]. This 'phenomenon' is greatly based on Internet's wide utilization and bandwidth improvements, along with the continuous advancement of Information and Communication Technology (ICT). Furthermore, the mobile technology industry and social networking have also played a vital role, enticing even more individuals to e-purchases. The digital buyer penetration percentage is expected to reach 65.2% at the end of 2021 compared to 60.2% in 2017 (Statista, 2017). Thus, Internet users are will be purchasing online. Additionally, not only does the number of adopters grow, but also the

DOI: 10.4018/978-1-5225-6367-9.ch002

volume of their purchases is proportionally increased (Monsuwe et al., 2004). According to E-Commerce Europe (2015) and E-Commerce Foundation (2017), European e-commerce sales were expected to reach €477 billion in 2015, €530 billion in 2016 and €602 billion in 2017.

In Greece, business-to-customer (B2C) online shopping has been emerged quite late compared to developed countries worldwide. Based on the latest national survey, 31% of Greek Internet users have conducted online transactions and spent 4.5 – 5 billion euros annually, however, about 20% of them made their first purchase in 2017 (Eltrun, 2017)! These results are also confirmed by Eurostat, which mentioned that 32% of Greek internet users shop online (Eurostat, 2017). Thus, despite the continuous and noteworthy annual growth -25% in 2015, 29% in 2016 and 32% in 2017-, Greek B2C e-commerce is far away from the 57% of the European-28 average (E-Commerce Europe, 2015; Eltrun, 2017; Eurostat, 2017).

Online shopping can significantly help both customers and enterprises involved. Extended literature review has revealed a considerable number of benefits to both entities. For example, consumers state that convenience, lower prices, time saving, improved customer service and ease of shopping comparison are some vital reasons that positively impact them to purchase online (Ahmad et al., 2010; E-Commerce Europe, 2015; Eltrun, 2015, 2017). On the other hand, firms mention that e-purchases help them reduce administrative costs and extend their business activities well beyond their brick-and-mortal stores.

One key characteristic of online shopping is its limitless feature. Every potential customer can hypothetically buy from any enterprise worldwide and every enterprise can attract customers beyond its geographic boundaries; from any location in the world. Therefore, online shopping gives access to a global market that expands well beyond the geographically limited borders of brick-and-mortal stores (Ahmad et al., 2010) and has greatly stimulated the process of cross-border e-shopping. The purpose of this chapter is to investigate Internet users' e-shops perceptions focused on Greek reality. Specifically, it aims to examine potential differences on their perceptions regarding domestic versus international e-shops, as a growing number of individuals choose non-domestic online stores to buy from. Characteristically, recent studies revealed that Greek e-shoppers prefer to purchase abroad (Eltrun, 2014, 2015); 60% and 65% of them bought from Greek e-stores in 2013 and 2014 in correspondence, whereas the 80%-90% of European adopters prefer to purchase from national e-stores (Eltrun, 2014, 2015). Hence, this study intends to shed light on shed light vital aspects of e-shopping behaviour and interpret this situation.

The rest of the chapter is organized as follows. The literature review in consumers' online buying behavior and the factors that encourage or hinder online shopping are presented in the next section, which is then followed by study's the methodology and results. The last section concludes the chapter by reflecting on the implications of the study, its limitations and future research directions.

LITERATURE REVIEW

Online shopping catholic acceptance has forced many researchers to investigate e-consumer behavior. Hence, numerous studies have been taken place in e-commerce area from diverse perspectives trying to gain an improved insight of e-consumer behavior (Dennis et al., 2004). According to Dennis et al. (2009), there are two basic research streams that approach it. The first investigates technical specifications of an e-store; including interface, design and navigation (e.g. Hasan, 2016; Zhang & Von Dran, 2002), payment (e.g. Liao & Cheung, 2002; Yang et al., 2015), information (e.g. Mallagrada et al., 2016; McKinney et al., 2002), intention to use (e.g. Chakraborty et al., 2016; Chen & Hitt, 2002) and ease of use (e.g. Cho & Sagynov, 2015; Stern & Stafford, 2006). On the other hand, the second stream deals with the consumer-oriented approach of e-behavior. Demographics (e.g. Chahal, 2015; Hashim et al., 2009; Teo, 2006), shopping motivation (e.g. Al-Debei et al., 2015; Johnson et al., 2007), shopping orientation (e.g. Chang & Cheng, 2015; Jayawardhena et al., 2007), perceptions of benefits and risks -advantages and problems- (e.g. Saprikis et al., 2010; Teo, 2006; Thakur & Srivastava, 2015), and issues of psychological characteristics (e.g. Bilgihan, 2016; Wolfinbarger & Gilly, 2002) are examined.

Regarding the factors that positively or negatively impact on e-shopping and are investigated on this chapter, several researches have been conducted. For example, Antoniadis et al. (2014) proved that lower prices in e-stores compared to brick-and-mortal stores, wider variety of product options, convenience and less time spent are the most crucial factors that positively influence e-shopping adoption. Clemes et al. (2014) also confirmed the importance of product variety and convenience to online shopping adoption. Ernst & Young (2000) pointed out that Internet users buy online because of good product selection, competitive prices, and ease of use; but are concerned about lack of opportunity to prior examining the products, shipping costs, as well as the confidentiality of credit card and personal information. Similarly, Poon (2008) investigated consumers' concerns about payment security issues and their impact on customers' online shopping attitude. Furthermore, trust has been widely investigated and many researchers revealed its vital role in online shopping (Al-Debei et al., 2015; Antoniadis et al., 2014; Teo, 2006). The more experienced the e-shopper is, the more trustful the e-purchases tend to be (Oxford Internet Institute, 2005). A collection of the literature review regarding the factors that drive consumers to online shopping is provided by Monsuwe et al. (2004).

With reference to demographics and the perceived problems, numerous studies have already investigated e-shopping behavior. For example, Mahmood et al. (2004) pointed out that demographic and lifestyle characteristics do play a vital role in e-consumer behavior. Hashim et al. (2009) concluded that demographic variables, such as gender, age, salary, job description and marital status impact on e-shopping behavior. On the other hand, Clemes et al. (2014) confirmed that perceived risk negatively influence e-shopping adoption and Teo (2006) mentioned that non-adopters perceive e-shopping risk to a greater extent than e-consumers. Saprikis et al. (2010) proved that after-sales problems are perceived higher to traditional consumers than adopters of e-shopping. Antoniadis et al. (2014) claimed that the combination of the online and physical presence provides more opportunities to capture business than the pure online ones. Finally, Eurostat (2017) and Saprikis (2013) confirmed that perceptions related to security and privacy issues, as well as their desire to physically examine the product prevent many customers from buying online.

As a step forward, this chapter takes advantage of the relevant literature review and investigates Greek Internet users' e-shop perceptions. In Greece, about the 30% of Internet users buy online compared to the 57% in Europe-28 (Eltrun, 2017; Eurostat, 2017; Seybert, 2011). Despite the steady annual growth in Greece the last years the country still lags behind compared to the European average (Eltrun, 2014, 2017). Characteristically, a typical Greek e-adopter spends about 1500€ annually and buys online mostly travel and hotel e-booking services, computer equipment and clothes. On the contrary, in developed European countries, such as Austria, Norway and UK; this annual amount ranges between 2140€ and 2466€ (E-Commerce Europe, 2013; Eltrun, 2014, 2017). Thus, this chapter targets on revealing potential discrepancies on individuals' perceptions concerning domestic versus international e-shops because Greek e-adopters prefer to purchase abroad, whereas the vast majority of European e-shoppers prefer national e-business ventures (Eltrun, 2014, 2015). The analysis applied categorizes them in two groups; adopters and non-adopters of online shopping. As far as it is concerned there is a significant gap on this side of e-consumer behavior research, therefore, this study is expected to help in filling this gap and provide tangible results to both academicians and practitioners. Regarding the managerial standpoint, the industry is about to get vital information that helps various firms pursue strategies aimed to take full advantage of the consumers' online buying habits and intentions. Thus, the study is expected to draw lessons for professionals and assist their e-business venture to a great extent.

METHODOLOGY AND RESULTS

To examine Greek Internet users' perceptions regarding domestic versus international e-shops, an electronic questionnaire was developed aimed at gathering the required data. Data was collected from October to December 2012 via e-mailing lists. The sample selected was a representative subgroup of the population as has been in accordance with data from the 'Observatory for Digital Greece' and the 'Hellenic Statistical Authority'. However, it is to be emphasized the unusual situation of many unemployed respondents; despite they have been highly educated, because of the serious economic crisis of the country.

Concerning survey's data analysis, this empirical research is descriptive in nature. Therefore, apart from descriptive statistics, only simple statistics, namely chi-square[2] and t-tests[3], were applied to analyse respondents' perceptions. With the exception of demographic-related questions, five-point Likert scale was applied to the measurement items. All of them were designed on the basis of a comprehensive literature review and prior surveys approved for their validity and reliability. Therefore, prior to e-questionnaire's distribution, they were pretested from two academicians and two practitioners to ascertain the precision of the instructions and the content validity. Furthermore, a pilot test using a sample of twenty university students helped to identify possible problems in terms of clarity and accuracy; and a number of amendments took place to improve their presentation, based on comments and feedback. Table 1 provides the literature review in which the aforementioned issues were based on and Figure 1 presents the flow of the survey design.

Demographic Characteristics

Table 2 depicts the demographic characteristics of the sample. In this survey, a total of 624 respondents comprised its sample. Following previous surveys (e.g., Haque et al., 2007), adopters are mainly males and use e-shopping to a greater extent than female adopters. Furthermore, the vast majority of e-consumers

Table 1. Literature review of the study

Basic Categories of the Research	Source
Reasons for using online shopping (adopters only)	Ahmad et al., 2010; Chen, 2009; Ernst & Young, 2000; Kim et al., 2009; Osman et al., 2010
Reasons for not using online shopping (non-adopters only)	Ahmad et al., 2010; Chen, 2009; Ernst & Young, 2000; Osman et al., 2010; Poon, 2008
Consumers' perceptions of online stores	Ahmad et al., 2010; Poon 2008
Problems in online stores	Ahmad et al., 2010; Chen, 2009; Osman et al., 2010; Poon, 2008

Figure 1. Survey design

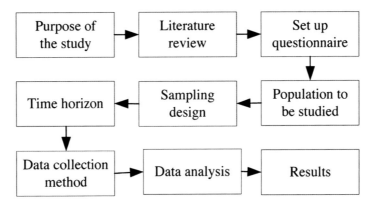

respondents have strong educational skills as the 86.3% of them have at least/ or attend a University degree/ program. Regarding their Internet activity, adopters are more experienced than non-adopters and they spend much more time on the Internet. These results can explain in a way that their greater familiarity with the new technologies make them more receptive to alternative methods of non-traditional shopping. However, they conduct quite a few online purchases (~8 every year). This may happen because of the serious economic situation in Greece. However, they are willing to buy online more in the near future. On the contrary, non-adopters are still sceptical about e-shopping and only the 16.5% referred that they will attempt to purchase online in the next year. Regarding chi-square statistics, a significant association is observed in all examined tests between adopters/ non-adopters and demographic characteristics.

Reasons for Buying (Adopters) or Not Buying Online (Non-Adopters)

Types of Purchased/ Interested Products and Services

Adopters mentioned that the main reasons for using the online stores are the lower prices compared to brick-and-mortal stores, the easiness of online buying procedures (convenience), the less time spent and the wider variety of available products (Table 3). Respondents' outcome is in full accordance with previous studies conducted from other researchers (e.g., Ahmad et al., 2010; Antoniadis et al., 2014; Clemes et al., 2014). Concerning their e-preferences, travel tickets/ e-booking services, computer hardware & software and consumer electronics top the list (Table 4) (Eltrun, 2014, 2017). However, it should be highlighted that e-banking services, along with clothing & accessories and e-tickets for shows, such as cinema and theatre, also scored quite high (Eltrun 2014, 2017).

On the contrary, non-adopters' expressed that the main reasons not to purchase online are their need to physically examine the product, their preference to purchase from traditional stores and security and privacy concerns (Table 4). The results are in full accordance with a contemporary study conducted in Greece (Eurostat, 2017). The non-use of credit card is a situation that takes place in the country. Thus, the vast majority of Greek e-stores do accept the cash on delivery option to overcome it (Eltrun, 2104). Finally, just like Eltrun (2017), a considerable number of non-adopters stated that they visit or search e-

Table 2. Demographic characteristics of the sample

Demographic profile	Adopters		Non adopters		Chi - Square
	No	%	No	%	
Gender					
Male	234	53.5%	73	39%	df = 1
Female	203	46.5%	114	61%	chi-sq = 11.031 p $\approx$ 0.001
Occupation					
Private employee	91	20.8%	31	16.6%	df = 4
Public Servant	67	15.3%	18	9.6%	chi-sq = 28.253 p $\approx$ 0.000
Freelancer	67	15.3%	9	4.8%	
Unemployed	180	41.3%	116	62%	
Other	32	7.3%	13	7%	
Education					
Elementary school	2	0.5%	1	0.5%	df = 3
High school	58	13.2%	32	17.1%	chi-sq = 10.805 p $\approx$ 0.000
University/ Technological College	262	60%	127	67.9%	
Master/ PhD	115	26.3%	27	14.5%	
Salary (in Euros/ month)					
<900€	188	43%	61	32.6%	df = 4
900€-1500€		19.5%	26	13.9%	chi-sq = 26.291 p $\approx$ 0.000
1501€-2400€	85	8%	8	4.3%	
>2400€	35	3.7%	5	2.7%	
I don't answer	16113	25.8%	87	46.5%	
Daily usage of the Internet					
1 hour and below	22	5%	21	11.2%	df = 4
1-3 hours	131	30%	69	36.9%	chi-sq = 26.491 p $\approx$ 0.000
3.1-5 hours	109	24.9%	58	31%	
5.1-7 hours	100	22.9%	27	14.5%	
7 hours and above	75	17.2%	12	6.4%	
Frequency of online purchases					
1-3 purchases annually	202	46.2%			
4-8 purchases annually	136	31.1%			
9-20 purchases annually	68	15.6%			
21 purchases and above annually	31	7.1%			
Intend to buy online in the next 12 months					
Absolutely No	2	0.5%	22	11.8%	df = 4
Probably No	12	2.7%	45	24.1%	chi-sq = 242.977 p $\approx$ 0.000
I do not know yet	80	18.3%	89	47.6%	
Probably Yes	160	36.6%	29	15.5%	
Absolutely Yes	183	41.9%	2	1%	

Table 3. Reasons for buying (adopters) or not buying online (non-adopters)

Reasons for Buying Online	Adopters		Reasons for Not Buying Online	Non-Adopters	
Lower prices	376	86%	Need to physically examine the product	105	56.1%
Easiness of online buying procedures (convenience)	218	49.9%	Do not use a credit card	61	32.6%
Wider variety of products	176	40.3%	Prefer to buy from brick-and-mortal stores	59	31.6%
Less time spent	176	40.3%	Security and privacy reasons	56	29.9%
High quality of products	57	13%	I don't trust online purchases	34	18.2%
Various payment options	57	13%	Are unaware of the buying procedure through the Internet	23	12.3%
Other reasons	15	3.4%	Unaffordable transportation fees	12	6.4%
			Shipping delays	9	4.8%
			Other reasons	3	1.6%

Table 4. Types of products/ services: adopters

Types of products/ services	Adopters				Non-Adopters			
	Intend to buy:		Bought in the future:		Searched information for:		Intend to buy in the future:	
Computer hardware & software	227	51.9%	153	35%	77	41.2%	52	27.8%
Travel	278	63.6%	199	45.5%	76	40.6%	73	39%
Consumer electronics	194	44.4%	166	38%	78	41.7%	43	23%
CDs & DVDs	54	12.4%	61	14%	75	40.1%	32	17.1%
Books	130	29.7%	135	30.9%	98	52.4%	49	26.2%
Clothing & accessories	168	38.4%	148	33.9%	78	41.7%	74	39.6%
Health & beauty	85	19.5%	81	18.5%	52	27.8%	30	16%
Jewellery & watches	62	14.2%	79	18.1%	57	30.5%	26	13.9%
Hotel e-booking	225	51.5%	162	37.1%	76	40.6%	61	32.6%
e-tickets (cinema, theatre and other events)	162	37.1%	147	33.6%	65	34.8%	48	25.7%
e-Banking	184	42.1%	121	27.7%	46	24.6%	29	15.5%
e-Gambling	59	13.5%	39	8.9%	30	16%	14	7.5%
Food & drink	23	5.3%	41	9.4%	38	20.3%	17	9.1%
Others	88	20.1%	62	14.2%	31	16.6%	14	7.5%

stores only to get information about a product/ service (e.g., characteristics, pricing, etc.); and expressed their positive intention to e-purchases in the near future (Table 5), which is a promising sign for sure. The results are of great interest and positive responses were recorded in the majority of the provided categories of products.

Table 5. Adopters' perceptions regarding online stores

General Perceptions	Greek e-shops Mean (SD[4])	International e-shops Mean (SD)	t-test value
Online stores provide sufficient information about available products	3.34 (0.92)	3.98 (0.79)	-11.38[a]
Online stores provide adequate payment options	3.56 (1.02)	3.71 (0.99)	-2.44[d]
Online stores provide simple and user-friendly procedures to cancel or return an order	3.13 (1.00)	3.52 (0.97)	-6.47[a]
Online stores offer sufficient number of value added e-services	3.42 (0.86)	4.00 (0.77)	-10.75[a]
Online stores provide contact options, like phone numbers and form to their customers	3.92 (0.89)	3.86 (0.92)	1.09
Online stores have a good reputation	3.44 (0.83)	3.83 (0.75)	-7.43[a]
Perceptions on privacy policy			
Online stores use sufficient security mechanisms to ensure the privacy of consumers' data	3.23 (0.86)	3.53 (0.83)	-5.81[a]
Online stores use consumers' data for statistic issues without consent	3.29 (0.98)	3.18 (0.96)	2.13[d]
Online stores ask for consumers' permission in order to send advertisements to their e-mail accounts	3.53 (1.21)	3.64 (1.05)	-1.86
Online stores forward consumers' information to marketing companies	3.35 (0.99)	3.18 (0.92)	3.53[a]
Online stores use sufficient mechanisms to ensure the security of consumers' transactions	3.34 (0.87)	3.66 (0.84)	-6.72[a]

[a]p<0.001 [b] p<0.005 [c] p<0.01 [d] p<0.05

Users' Perceptions Regarding Online Shopping

In order to investigate respondents' perceptions, two groups of them are revealed; a) general perceptions on e-shopping and b) perceptions on e-privacy policy (Tables 5 and 6). As it was expected, in the majority of them adopters scored higher compared to non-adopters. The former have already transacted online and have an empirical point of view of these types of shopping; therefore, they can easily understand the pros and cons of e-purchases. On the contrary, the latter are much more doubtful and clearly expressed their concerns. Therefore, the high mean scores of e-risks perceptions are not a surprise; followed similar results of previous researchers (e.g., Clemes et al., 2014; Poon, 2008; Teo, 2006).

To be more specific, regarding respondents' general perceptions on domestic versus international e-shops, the survey results do reveal significant differences. Specifically, respondents expressed that international e-business ventures provide much more than domestic e-ventures in the vast majority of the examined inquires. Thus, these discrepancies are so great that almost all t-test values reveal statistically significant differences to both respondents' groups (Tables 5 and 6). Thus, based on these dissimilarities, it comes as no surprise that numerous Greek e-shoppers prefer cross-border shopping. As a result, domestic e-stores should definitely try to improve their business models. For example, they should follow international trends and try to imitate the best practices. The Internet is a great power to customers and can help them being informed about any piece of information. Thus, it can make them much more demanding. E-ventures that are not able to follow the international trend will have serious problems to obtain a market share. Globalization along with the wide spread of the Internet may lead to catastrophic results; not only for their income, but also for their e-existence.

Table 6. Non-adopters' perceptions regarding online stores

General Perceptions	Greek e-shops Mean (SD)	International e-shops Mean (SD)	t-test value
Online stores provide sufficient information about available products	3.09 (0.97)	3.61 (0.89)	-6.25[a]
Online stores provide adequate payment options	3.17 (0.95)	3.46 (0.92)	-3.58[a]
Online stores provide simple and user-friendly procedures to cancel or return an order	2.94 (0.94)	3.31 (0.89)	-4.94[a]
Online stores offer sufficient number of value added e-services	3.20 (0.81)	3.60 (0.81)	-5.45[a]
Online stores provide contact options, like phone numbers and form to their customers	3.68 (0.99)	3.59 (0.94)	1.11
Online stores have a good reputation	3.04 (0.82)	3.40 (0.85)	-3.88[a]
Perceptions on Privacy Policy			
Online stores use sufficient security mechanisms to ensure the privacy of consumers' data	2.88 (0.84)	3.22 (0.88)	-4.73[a]
Online stores use consumers' data for statistic issues without consent	3.16 (0.97)	3.07 (0.95)	1.06
Online stores ask for consumers' permission in order to send advertisements to their e-mail accounts	2.99 (1.30)	3.16 (1.10)	-1.91
Online stores forward consumers' information to marketing companies	3.20 (0.98)	3.20 (0.90)	0.00
Online stores use sufficient mechanisms to ensure the security of consumers' transactions	2.90 (0.82)	3.38 (0.86)	-6.36[a]

[a]p<0.001 [b] p<0.005 [c] p<0.01 [d] p<0.05

Regarding the privacy and security issues, it goes without saying that both are at the top of the most important factors in all types of e-purchases (e.g., Monsuwe et al., 2004; Poon, 2008). Customers should feel safe and secure, thus, domestic e-shops should have as a first priority the privacy and security policies; no matter how much they need to invest on. Firms that lose their reputation are forced to fight for their future e-survival, especially on this impersonal way of contemporary e-shopping.

Perceived Problems in Online Shopping

In order to investigate respondents' perceived problems in online shopping, two groups of them are revealed; a) general problems and b) after-sales problems. As it was expected, statistically significant discrepancies between examined samples were revealed (Tables 7 and 8). To be more specific, adopters personal experience in e-purchases makes them realize that the anticipated problems are not such a deterrent for them compared to non-adopters.

Concerning their perceptions, both groups of respondents expressed their concerns about e-shops, especially the domestic ones. Their opinion is also clearly depicted in the vast majority of the examined questions; and the statistically significant differences revealed are high in both adopters and non-adopters answers. With reference to no statistically significant different questions, all of them came as no surprise; as the term 'distance' has been the common issue. 'Distance' is a vital characteristic of business transactions and more or less can affect everyone; even if he/ she currently purchases online or not. Therefore, the fact that there is no significant difference to these questions between examined groups is fairly normal.

Table 7. Adopters' perceived problems in online shopping

Problems Relating to Online Stores in General	Greek e-shops Mean (SD)	International e-shops Mean (SD)	t-test value
Online stores promise more than they can practically offer	3.14 (0.94)	2.77 (0.83)	6.77[a]
Consumers can not completely trust them	3.23 (0.98)	3.03 (0.96)	3.57[a]
Online stores are not always official representatives of their offered products	3.28 (0.90)	2.99 (0.85)	5.48[a]
Consumers find it difficult to confirm the reliability of the provided products	3.36 (0.94)	3.17 (1.02)	3.29[b]
It is possible to have your credit card data intercepted	3.10 (0.98)	2.99 (1.01)	2.26[d]
It is possible to buy a product that it would not value as much as you pay for it	3.54 (0.95)	3.31 (0.99)	4.41[a]
After-sales Problems			
It is difficult to return a product and get your money back	3.14 (1.07)	2.77 (1.11)	2.74[c]
Online stores can keep customers' money and do not send the agreed product	3.23 (0.97)	3.03 (1.07)	-2.02[d]
It is difficult to change a defective product with a new one	3.28 (1.04)	2.99 (1.06)	1.44
It s difficult to have after-sales services	3.36 (1.00)	3.17 (1.02)	3.25[b]
Product's guarantee is not assured	3.10 (1.06)	2.99 (1.04)	0.96
The delivery of the purchased product is time-consuming	3.54 (1.10)	3.31 (1.14)	-5.89[a]

p<0.001 [b] p<0.005 [c] p<0.01 [d] p<0.05

CONCLUSION

The aim of this chapter is to examine an unconventional case that takes place in Greek e-shopping reality; adopters prefer buying from an online store abroad to a national one. The survey conducted helps the main reasons of this situation be revealed providing a thorough analysis of adopters and non-adopters perceptions towards e-shopping features and problems, the reasons why the former buy and the latter do not purchase online, as well as the types of products and services that they buy, search or intent to e-purchase in the near future. Thus, this study intends to provide tangible results in an underexplored area of online shopping and shed light on the difficulty of understanding vital aspects of online commerce behavior. The findings are believed to provide interesting insights into Greek Internet users' perceptions towards online shopping. Adopters prefer to purchase online because of lower prices, wider variety of products and convenience compared to brick-and-mortal stores. The results are in accordance with those of previous researchers (e.g. Ahmad et al., 2010; Antoniadis et al., 2014; Clemes et al., 2014). E-tickets, computer hardware/ software and consumer electronics top the list of their preferences (e.g. Eltrun, 2017). On the other hand, non-adopters tend to physically examine the products and express serious concerns about security and privacy issues; however, they visit online stores to get informed about products and compare prices. Eurostat (2017) and Eltrun (2017) concluded to the same results as well. Furthermore,

Table 8. Non-adopters' perceived problems in online shopping

Problems Relating to Online Stores in General	Greek e-shops Mean (SD)	International e-shops Mean (SD)	t-test value
Online stores promise more than they can practically offer	3.38 (0.87)	3.16 (0.85)	2.94[b]
Consumers can not completely trust them	3.65 (0.91)	3.42 (0.94)	2.99[b]
Online stores are not always official representatives of their offered products	3.40 (0.83)	3.13 (0.91)	3.62[a]
Consumers find it difficult to confirm the reliability of the provided products	3.65 (0.92)	3.56 (0.93)	1.27
It is possible to have your credit card data intercepted	3.48 (0.93)	3.32 (0.93)	2.69[c]
It is possible to buy a product that it would not value as much as you pay for it	3.87 (0.91)	3.67 (0.91)	3.07[b]
After-Sales Problems			
It is difficult to return a product and get your money back	3.65 (0.98)	3.35 (0.97)	3.53[b]
Online stores can keep customers' money and do not send the agreed product	2.91 (1.09)	3.00 (1.03)	-1.10
It is difficult to change a defective product with a new one	3.40 (0.98)	3.21 (1.03)	2.32[d]
It s difficult to have after-sales services	3.43 (0.89)	3.20 (0.98)	2.96[b]
Product's guarantee is not assured	3.37 (0.99)	3.27 (0.96)	1.32
The delivery of the purchased product is time-consuming	3.21 (0.99)	3.36 (1.03)	-1.99[d]

[a]$p<0.001$ [b]$p<0.005$ [c]$p<0.01$ [d]$p<0.05$

the survey reveals significant differences between national and international e-shops. Characteristically, respondents expressed their concerns about reliability and trustworthiness of national e-stores. They mentioned that Greek e-ventures have more privacy and security problems compared to international e-stores. Greek e-stores provide fewer value added e-services, which are not as user friendly as the international ones. Additionally, they offer a lower variety and availability of products.

Based on the aforementioned, it is believed that this research can give important implications to both academia and practicing managers. The theoretical and managerial implications, as well as survey's limitations and future research directions are described below.

THEORETICAL AND MANAGERIAL IMPLICATIONS

Numerous researches have been conducted in e-commerce scientific field from different perspectives with the aim to understand better e-consumer behavior (e.g. Antoniadis et al., 2014; Clemes et al., 2014; Dennis et al., 2004). As a step forward, this chapter presents a significant number of recent studies examining the consumer-oriented approach of e-shopping behaviour and brings them into the academic community. Moreover, it provides a thorough empirical study in Greece where users' perceptions on domestic versus international e-shopping ventures are investigated. The importance of the results is also high if we take into consideration that a lot of differences have been revealed among the two examined categories of e-shops. Therefore, it is believed that the survey has set the groundwork for further scientific research and improvement, providing new inferences and insights on Internet users' perceptions towards cross-country e-shopping. It is expected that an analogous situation takes place in other countries worldwide as well.

On the other hand, practitioners are believed to be benefited from the results presented in this chapter as well. More specifically, the study's outcome can be of great assistance to them by making them evaluate their e-commerce ventures and follow specific strategies in order to adjust their e-shop structures with the aim to satisfy not only the existing customer base, but potential buyers as well. Especially in Greek reality where e-stores are considered lagged behind compared to similar international e-ventures. Alternatively, Greek practicing managers who are willing to invest in an e-shop business model could use the survey's results as a valuable guide to build an attractive e-store. For example, issues such as provided value added e-services, user friendly procedures, information about products and security concerns must be definitely taken into consideration.

Hence, online companies could use them as a consulting tool while organizing their work and implementing their e-business ideas. Additionally, the findings of this study could help e-ventures better understand Internet users' particular needs; and as a consequence, analogous marketing policies could be applied. To sum up, this chapter is believed to add value to both academia and the industry, as it provides meaningful information and a holistic approach concerning online consumers' behavior towards domestic and international e-stores.

LIMITATIONS AND FUTURE WORK

The survey has two basic limitations that need to be recognized. First, only simple statistics, namely t-tests and chi-square, have been applied. Therefore, the utilization of more advanced statistical methodologies helping to the development of a proposed model or framework would certainly offer a more holistic view and may provide additional important insights into academia and managers. Secondly, causal analysis that could study which factors are more important for e-commerce decisions has not been applied. Regarding further research, similar studies could be conducted in other countries, taking into consideration though the different cultural notions in order to get comparative data for a cross-cultural study or a meta-analysis of existing studies. Such a comparison could be beneficial for the better understanding of cross-country e-shopping perceptions and attitude.

DISCUSION QUESTIONS

1. Taking into consideration the cross-border e-commerce situation that takes place in Greece, can you mention some actions domestic e-stores should follow in order to attract these customers?
2. Supposing you are a manager in a Greek brick-and-mortal bookstore, what would you do in order to start business online?
3. How could Greek public authorities help domestic e-shops attract cross-border e-shoppers?

REFERENCES

Ahmad, N., Omar, A., & Ramayah, T. (2010). Consumer Lifestyles and Online shopping continuance intention. *Business Strategy Series*, *11*(4), 227–243. doi:10.1108/17515631011063767

Al-Debei, M. M., Mamoun, N., Akroush, N. M., & Ashouri, I. M. (2015). Consumer attitudes towards online shopping: The effects of trust, perceived benefits, and perceived web quality. *Internet Research*, *25*(5), 707–733. doi:10.1108/IntR-05-2014-0146

Antoniadis, I., Saprikis, V., & Politis, K. (2014). Investigating internet users' perceptions towards online shoping: An empirical study on Greek university students. *2nd International Conference on Contemporary Marketing Issues*, 66-71.

Bilgihan, A. (2016). Gen Y customer loyalty in online shopping: An integrated model of trust, user experience and branding. *Computers in Human Behavior*, *61*, 103–113. doi:10.1016/j.chb.2016.03.014

Chahal, P. (2015). A study on the role of consumers gender and age on online shopping. *International Journal in Comerce, IT &. Social Sciences*, *2*(7), 33–41.

Chakraborty, R., Lee, J., Bagchi-Sen, S., Upadhyaya, S., & Rao, R. (2016). Online shopping intention in the context of data breach in online retail stores: An examination of older and younger adults. *Decision Support Systems*, *83*, 47–56. doi:10.1016/j.dss.2015.12.007

Chang, C.-T., & Cheng, Z.-H. (2015). Tugging on heartstrings: Shopping orientation, mindset, and consumer responses to cause-related marketing. *Journal of Business Ethics*, *127*(2), 337–350. doi:10.100710551-014-2048-4

Chen, C. A. (2009). Information-oriented Online Shopping Behavior in Electronic Commerce Environment. *Journal of Software*, *4*(4), 307–314. doi:10.4304/jsw.4.4.307-314

Chen, P., & Hitt, L. (2002). Measuring switching costs and the determinants of customer retention in internet enabled businesses: A study of online brokerage industry. *Information Systems Research*, *13*(3), 255–274. doi:10.1287/isre.13.3.255.78

Cho, Y. C., & Sagynov, E. (2015). Exploring factors that affect usefulness, ease of use, trust, and purchase intention in the online environment. *International Journal of Management & Information Systems*, *19*(1), 21–36.

Clemes, D.-M., Gan, C., & Zhang, J. (2014). An empirical analysis of online shopping adoption in Beijing, China. *Journal of Retailing and Consumer Services*, *21*(3), 364–375. doi:10.1016/j.jretconser.2013.08.003

Dennis, C., Fenech, T., & Merrilees, B. (2004). *E-retailing*. Abingdon, UK: Routledge.

Dennis, C., Merrilees, B., Jayawardhena, C., & Wright, L. T. (2009). E-consumer behaviour. *European Journal of Marketing*, *43*(9), 1121–1139. doi:10.1108/03090560910976393

E-Commerce Europe. (2013). *Europe B2C E-Commerce Report 2013*. Retrieved February 1, 2014, from http://www.paymentscardsandmobile.com/wp-content/uploads/2013/08/Europe-B2C-Ecommerce-Report-2013.pdf

E-Commerce Europe. (2015). *Europe B2C E-Commerce Report 2015.* Retrieved January 15, 2016, from http://www.ecommerce-europe.eu/press/2015/european-e-commerce-turnover-grew-by-14.3-to-reach-423.8bn-in-2014

E-Commerce Foundation. (2017). *European E-Commerce Report.* Retrieved January 18, 2018, from https://ecommercenews.eu/ecommerce-europe-e602-billion-2017/

Eltrun. (2014). *Anuual e-Commerce survey in Greece.* Retrieved February 1, 2014, from http://www.eltrun.gr/wp-content/uploads/2013/12/ELTRUN_ecommerce_survey_20131.pdf (in Greek).

Eltrun. (2015). *Anuual e-Commerce survey in Greece.* Retrieved January 15, 2016, from http://www.eltrun.gr/wp-content/uploads/2015/12/%CE%97%CE%BB%CE%95%CE%BC%CF%80%CE%BF%CF%81%CE%B9%CE%BF2015-1.pdf (in Greek).

Eltrun. (2017). *Anuual e-Commerce survey in Greece.* Retrieved January 15, 2018, from http://www.greekecommerce.gr/gr/resources/ereynes-gia-ellada/etisia-ereuna-ecommerce-b2c-2017-2018/

Ernst and Young. (2000). *Global Online Retailing.* Retrieved January 27, 2003, from http://www.ey.com

Eurostat. (2017). *E-commerce statistics for individuals.* Retrieved January 20, 2018, from http://ec.europa.eu/eurostat/statistics-explained/index.php/E-commerce_statistics_for_individuals

Haque, H., Tarofder, A. K., Mahmud, S. A., & Ismail, A. Z. (2007). Internet advertisement in Malaysia: A study on attitudinal differences. *The Electronic Journal on Information Systems in Developing Countries*, *31*(9), 1–15. doi:10.1002/j.1681-4835.2007.tb00218.x

Hasan, B. (2016). Perceived irritation in online shopping: The impact of website designcharacteristics. *Computers in Human Behavior*, *54*, 224–230. doi:10.1016/j.chb.2015.07.056

Hashim, A., Ghani, E. K., & Said, J. (2009). Does consumers' demographic profile influence online shopping? *Canadian Social Science*, *5*(5), 19–31.

Jayawardhena, C., Wright, L. T., & Dennis, C. (2007). Consumers online: Intentions, orientations and segmentation. *International Journal of Retail & Distribution Management*, *35*(6), 515–526. doi:10.1108/09590550710750377

Johnson, E. J., Moe, W. W., Fader, P. S., Bellman, S., & Lohse, G. L. (2007). On the depth and dynamics of online search behaviour. *Management Science*, *50*(3), 299–309. doi:10.1287/mnsc.1040.0194

Kim, J. H., Kim, M., & Kandampully, J. (2009). Buying environment characteristics in the context of e-service. *European Journal of Marketing*, *43*(9/10), 1188–1204. doi:10.1108/03090560910976438

Liao, Z., & Cheung, M. T. (2002). Internet-based e-banking and consumer attitudes: An empirical study. *Information & Management*, *39*(4), 287–301. doi:10.1016/S0378-7206(01)00097-0

Mahmood, M. A., Bagchi, K., & Ford, T. C. (2004). On-line shopping behavior: Cross-country empirical research. *International Journal of Electronic Commerce*, *9*(1), 9–30.

Mallapragada, G., Chandukala, R. S., & Liu, G. (2016). Exploring the Effects of "What" (Product) and "Where" (Website) Characteristics on Online Shopping Behavior. *Journal of Marketing*, *80*(2), 21–38. doi:10.1509/jm.15.0138

McKinney, V., Yoon, K., & Zahedi, F. (2002). The measurement of web-customer satisfaction: An expectation and disconfirmation approach. *Information Systems Research, 13*(3), 296–315. doi:10.1287/isre.13.3.296.76

Monsuwe, T. P., Dellaert, B., & Ruyter, K. (2004). What drives consumers to shop online A literature review. *International Journal of Service Industry Management, 15*(1), 102–121. doi:10.1108/09564230410523358

Osman, S., Yin-Fah, B. C., & Hooi-Choo, B. (2010). Undergraduates and Online Purchasing Behavior. *Asian Social Science, 6*(10), 133–146. doi:10.5539/ass.v6n10p133

Oxford Internet Institute. (2005). *Oxford Internet Survey: Results of a Nationwide Survey of Britons aged 14 and Older.* Oxford, UK: Oxford Internet Institute.

Poon, W. C. (2008). Users' adoption of e-banking services: The Malaysian perspective. *Journal of Business and Industrial Marketing, 23*(1), 59–69. doi:10.1108/08858620810841498

Saprikis, V. (2013). Consumers' perceptions towards e-shopping advertisements and promotional actions in social networking sites. *International Journal of Electronic Adoption, 5*(4), 36–47. doi:10.4018/ijea.2013100103

Saprikis, V., Chouliara, A., & Vlachopoulou, M. (2010). Perceptions Towards Online Shopping: Analyzing the Greek University Students' Attitude. Communications of the IBIMA, Article ID 854516.

Seybert, H. (2011). *Internet use in the households and by individuals in 2011.* Eurostat - Statistics in focus 66/2011. Retrieved 24 July 24, 2012, http://epp.eurostat.ec.europa.eu/cache/ITY_OFFPUB/KS-SF-11-066/EN/KS-SF-11-066-EN.PDF

Statista. (2017). *Digital buyer penetration worldwide from 2016 to 2021.* Retrieved January 15, 2018, from https://www.statista.com/statistics/261676/digital-buyer-penetration-worldwide/

Stern, B. B., & Stafford, M. R. (2006). Individual and social determinants of winning bids in online auctions. *Journal of Consumer Behaviour, 5*(1), 43–55. doi:10.1002/cb.47

Teo, T. (2006). To buy or not to buy online: Adopters and non-adopters of online shopping in Singapore. *Behaviour & Information Technology, 25*(6), 497–509. doi:10.1080/01449290500256155

Thakur, R., & Srivastava, M. (2015). A study on the impact of consumer risk perception and innovativeness on online shopping in India. *International Journal of Retail & Distribution Management, 43*(2), 148–166. doi:10.1108/IJRDM-06-2013-0128

Wolfinbarger, M., & Gilly, M. C. (2002). *Q.com: dimensionalizing, measuring and predicting quality of the e-tail experience.* Working Paper No. 02-100, Marketing Science Institute, Cambridge, MA.

Yang, Q., Pang, C., Liu, L., Yen, C. D., & Tarn, M. (2015). Exploring consumer perceived risk and trust for online payments: An empirical study in China's younger generation. *Computers in Human Behavior, 50*, 9–24. doi:10.1016/j.chb.2015.03.058

Zhang, P., & Von Dran, G. M. (2002). User expectations and rankings of quality factors in different web site domains. *International Journal of Electronic Commerce, 6*(2), 9–33.

ENDNOTES

[1]   Brick-and-mortal store: company that has a physical presence and offer face-to-face customer experiences.

[2]   Chi-square is used to determine whether there is a significant difference between the expected frequencies and the observed frequencies in one or more categories examined.

[3]   T-test can be used to determine if two sets of data are significantly different from each other, and is most commonly applied when the test statistic would follow a normal distribution if the value of a scaling term in the test statistic were known.

[4]   SD: Standard Deviation is a measure that is used to quantify the amount of variation or dispersion of a set of data values. A standard deviation close to 0 indicates that the data points tend to be very close to the mean (also called the expected value) of the set, while a high standard deviation indicates that the data points are spread out over a wider range of values.

Chapter 3
Do Investments in ICT Help Economies Grow?
A Case of Transition Economies

Sergey Samoilenko
Averett University, USA

ABSTRACT

A common assumption behind investments in information and communication technologies (ICT) is that of the resultant improvements in productivity. To substantiate this assumption with empirical evidence in the context of transition economies (TE), the authors use time series data sets spanning the period from 1993 to 2008 to inquire into the impact of investments in telecoms on total factor productivity (TFP). Results indicate that the improvements in productivity of the most of TEs in the sample was inconsistent and not based on the increase in the levels of investments and labor. Additionally, the results of the data analysis suggest that the dominant source of growth in productivity is not static, but changes over time. While in an earlier period (1993-2002) of transition, TEs grew based on technological change, it is efficient utilization of the already available technology that became a dominant source of growth in the later (2003-2008) period of transition.

INTRODUCTION

The overall tendency associated with the outcome of investments in Information and Communication Technologies (ICT) is to expect an increasingly greater "bang for a buck." No longer ICT is viewed as a tool of an automation, but rather it is expected to be an agent of transformative change (Balcı, Medeni & Nohutçu, 2013; Abu Tair & Abu-Shanab, 2014). This expectation holds true regardless of the scale of implementation of ICT- be it a case of a bank (Haider & Tang, 2016) or a single economy (Eilu & Auma, 2017), or a group of economies (Samoilenko, 2016). Such expectations are well substantiated by the examples of the impact of investments in ICT on the macroeconomic bottom line in the United States (Oliner & Sichel, 2000; Van Ark *et al.*, 2002; Jorgenson, 2003) and in some of the OECD countries (Colecchia & Schreyer, 2002; Van Ark *et al.*, 2002).

DOI: 10.4018/978-1-5225-6367-9.ch003

But in the context of transition economies (TE) the outcomes of investments in ICT are mixed (Dewan & Kraemer, 2000), and more evidence is needed that such investments can be effectively and efficiently transformed into significant macroeconomic outcomes (Heeks, 2009). The case of TEs is not unique, for while some European economies increased their level of adoption of ICT in the period around 1998-2002, their levels of productivity actually started to decline, thus demonstrating the disparities in the outcomes of investments in ICT among economies (Daveri, 2002). Such a reduction in growth, even among well-heeled developed countries, clearly requires TEs to demonstrate that their limited technical, financial and human resources are not wasted (Indjikian & Siegel, 2005). The term *transition economy* refers to a country in the process of transitioning from a centrally planned economy to a market-oriented economy. It does not mean, however, that all TEs constitute a homogenous group in terms of the level of economic development. The World Bank, for example, groups some of them with the developed, and some with the developing countries, depending on the level of industrialization

In order to explore whether investments in ICT can impact the macroeconomic outcomes in the context of TEs, in this study we utilize the research framework of neoclassical growth accounting that is widely used in Information Systems (IS) research (McGuckin & Stiroh, 2002; Brynjolfsson & Hitt, 1996). Within the context of this framework, an increase in the macroeconomic bottom line (e.g., GDP) can come from two sources. The first source is represented by the "white-box" components, such as the available levels of capital (e.g., investments in ICT) and labor (e.g., ICT workforce). The origins of the "white-box" component are clear-cut and transparent. The second source is reflected by Total Factor Productivity (TFP), a "black-box" component origin and composition of which is less clear.

Resultantly, if we are to conceptualize the growth in GDP as a function of capital investments, labor, and "something else", then within the framework of neoclassical growth accounting the term "something else" is represented by TFP, where it serves as the residual (often referred to as *Solow's residual*) term capturing that contribution to GDP that is left unexplained by the inputs of capital and labor.

Of the three inputs used by the growth accounting model, only capital and labor are empirically observable, while the values for TFP must be derived computationally. Based on the idea of the productivity index, originally suggested by Malmquist (1953), Caves et al. (1982) defined the Malmquist index of TFP growth. Later, Färe et al. (1994) demonstrated that the Malmquist index could be constructed based on the results of Data Envelopment Analysis (DEA). Let us recall that DEA calculates the scores of the relative efficiency of Decision Making Units (DMU) (e.g., Transition Economies in the case of our study) relative to the efficient frontier which "envelops" the data set. Since DEA relative efficiency scores are calculated for each point in time t (e.g., year 1993), for a given DMU it is possible to calculate the change that took place between any pair of consecutive points in time t and $t+1$ (e.g., year 1993 and year 1994). The value of the Malmquist index captures the change in efficiency and reflects TFP.

Undoubtedly, TEs can grow via investing more and more money in ICT, and by hiring more and more ICT workers. But this is not the most efficient way to grow, and it is not clear, at this point, if TEs could grow efficiently - via increasing their productivity.

The overall purpose of this research, therefore, is to identify whether the ICT sector of TES exhibited growth in TFP (heretofore we use *TFP* and *productivity* interchangeably) associated with investments in ICT; specifically, we investigate two periods: a period of early transition (1993-2002) and a period of a later transition (2003-2008). In this investigation we use *telecoms* as a surrogate for general ICT. Not only it is a subset of ICT, but investments in telecoms are also common to almost all economies of the world.

Background

There are multiple ways in which ICT can produce an impact on an economy and society, and there are many levels where the impact can be detected. Not surprisingly, there are many different targets that researchers have investigated using a wide variety of methods in various contexts to assess the impact of ICT. Bankole, Osei-Bryson, and Brown (2013) used multivariate adaptive regression splines to investigate the impact of investments in ICT on human development. Beil, Ford, and Jackson (2005) and Wolde-Rafael (2007) used different versions of the Granger causality test to study the impact of investments in telecoms on economic activity in the United States. Cieślika and Kaniewska (2004) developed and tested a theoretical model linking telecoms and local levels of income in Poland. Piatkowski (2004) followed up an investigation of the impact of ICT capital on productivity in Poland (Piatkowski, 2003) with a similar study in the context of Bulgaria, Czech Republic, Hungary, Poland, Russia, Slovakia and Slovenia. Ziemba and Zelazny (2013) measured information society in Poland via assessment of the ICT Development Index and an evaluation of the impact of ICT on GDP. Datta and Agarwal (2004) identified the presence of the relationship between telecoms and economic growth in the context of 22 OECD countries. Lee, Levendis, and Gutierrez (2012) searched for the impact of telecoms on economic growth in Sub-Saharan Africa, Levendis and Lee (2013) studied the impact of ICT in the context of Asia, and Shiu and Lam (2008) studied the link between telecoms and economic growth in China. Chavula (2013) performed a cross-country analysis of 49 economies to assess the impact of telecoms on economic development in Africa, while Laguerre (2013) concentrated on the link between IT and development in Haiti. Swierczek, Shrestha, and Bechter (2005) investigated the impact of IT on productivity in Asia-Pacific. Kim, Kang, Sanders, and Lee (2008) studied the impact of investments in IT on GDP, while Samoilenko and Ngwenyama (2011) investigated the impact of IT on productivity in transition economies. Harindranath (2008) researched the impact of production and use of ICT in Hungary as the country becoming a market-driven economy.

Taking into consideration the existent body of knowledge, what differentiates our research from previous studies? The first differentiating factor is the context. While there have been investigations that have focused on groups of TEs (e.g., Samoilenko & Ngwenyama (2011), Piatkowski (2004)), or individual TEs (e.g, Harindranath (2008), Swierczek, Shrestha, and Bechter (2005), Piatkowski (2003)), this investigation focuses on a large group of TEs taken as a whole. The process of transition is intended to take less developed centrally-planned economies and, eventually, transform them into market-based developed economies. However, there is no uniform path of transition for TEs; there are *leaders* that perform better along the way, and there are *followers* that don't seem to do so well (Samoilenko, 2013).

The second differentiating factor is the time frame of the investigation; by analysing a period from 1993 to 2008, we have an opportunity to develop a clearer picture of the underlying process of transition than a study of a shorter period (or, a point-in-time case study) would allow. Another differentiating factor is the focus on the productivity component of macroeconomic growth. The process of globalization takes away any lasting opportunity of market economies to compete on the basis of low costs of resources or high prices of outputs; what is left is an opportunity to compete on the basis of efficient and effective transformation of inputs into outputs. The level of productivity directly impacts the level of transformative capacity of an economy, where economies that grow via increasing their productivity grow more efficiently (Samoilenko, 2013). If members of TEs aim to join the group of developed economies, then this is the path they will have to follow. Did they do so far? And if yes, what was the source of the growth? Could the source of growth be sustained and improved? And if yes, then how? Those are some of the questions that our study helps answering.

DO INVESTMENTS IN ICT IMPACT PRODUCTIVITY?

Research Questions

Overall, we pose two general questions: 1) Do the TEs in the sample exhibit continuous growth in TFP? and 2) What are some of the factors impacting growth in TFP? The potential for investments in ICT to generate high levels of productivity growth in the context of TEs has been noted (Indjikian & Siegel, 2005); however, it is not clear whether that potential has been realized. Previous investigations established that in order for investments in ICT to impact the economic bottom line, the level of investments must be above a certain threshold, and such investments must be complemented by other factors, notably, investments in human resources (Bresnahan *et al.*, 2002; Brynjolfsson *et al.*, 2000; OECD, 2004). We present the research questions of this study in Table 1.

To answer the research questions, we employ data envelopment analysis (DEA), multivariate regression (MR), and ordinary least squares regression (OLS) as our main data analytic tools. DEA is a widely used method for evaluating productivity and performance and is commonly combined with other techniques, such as cluster analysis (e.g. Shin & Sohn, 2004, Hirshberg & Lye, 2001; Lemos *et al.* 2005), neural networks (e.g. Samoilenko & Osei-Bryson, 2008a; Celebi & Bayraktar, 2008), decision trees (e.g. Samoilenko & Osei-Bryson, 2007; Wu, 2009), and regression analysis (e.g. Cooper & Tone, 1997).

We explore our research questions within the context of two periods, 1993-2002 and 2003-2008. This permits us to assess whether there are any significant differences between the period of early transition (1993-2002) and the period of late transition (2003-2008).

Table 1. Research questions of the investigation

RQ#	Formulation of the Research Question
1	Does a given TE exhibit annual growth in TFP?
2	Does the given TE exhibit continuous growth in TFP?
3	Is there a relationship between changes in the level of investments in telecoms and changes in TFP?
4	Is there a relationship between changes in the level of full-time telecom staff and changes in TFP?
5	Do changes in the level of investments in telecoms and changes in the level of full-time telecom staff produce a complementary effect on changes in TFP?
6	Is there a relationship between the level of investments in telecoms and TFP?
7	Is there a relationship between the level of full-time telecom staff and TFP?
8	Are the level of investments in telecoms and the level of full-time telecom staff complementary in terms of their effect on TFP?
9	Do changes in the ratio of revenues to investments impact TFP?
10	Does the ratio of revenues to investments have an impact on TFP?
11	What is the dominant source of growth in TFP?
12	Whether the dominant source of changes in TFP in the Later Period is different from that of the Earlier Period?

DATA AND METHODS OF THE STUDY

Data for this study were obtained from the *World Development Indicators* database (web.worldbank. org) and the *Yearbook of Statistics* of International Telecommunication Union (www.itu.int*)*. Looking at the twenty-five countries classified as transition economies in Europe and the former Soviet Union by IMF (2000), we selected the following 17 countries (data on the remaining was incomplete): Albania, Armenia, Azerbaijan, Belarus, Bulgaria, Czech Republic, Estonia, Hungary, Kazakhstan, Latvia, Lithuania, Moldova, Poland, Romania, Slovakia, Slovenia, and Ukraine. For the selected TEs we were able to construct two data sets: a data set covering the period of early transition from 1993 to 2002, and a data set spanning the period of later transition, from 2003 to 2008.

Now we offer a brief overview of Data Envelopment Analysis (DEA)- for a more complete coverage of the topic we refer our reader to Samoilenko and Osei-Bryson (2017). The DEA is a non-parametric technique that uses methods of linear programming to determine relative efficiencies of the Decision-Making Units (DMU, where a DMU could be an enterprise, an industry sector, a region, or a national economy). In the domain of DEA, a DMU receives inputs and produces outputs. A DEA model ensures functional similarities of all DMUs in the sample by specifying the common set of inputs and outputs for each DMU in the sample. In general, the specific definition of the DEA model is left to the decision maker and is rarely supported by a theory.

In order to calculate the score of the relative efficiency for each DMU in the sample, DEA collapses inputs and outputs into an abstract "meta input" and "meta output" and creates the ratio of the two for each DMU. The resultant score is then compared to the scores of other DMUs in the sample. The relatively efficient DMUs receive a score of "1" and constitute the efficiency frontier that envelops the DMUs in the sample. Depending on the orientation of the DEA model, the relatively inefficient DMUs receive the scores of less than "1" (in the case of the input-oriented model concerned with the minimization of inputs for achieving a given level of output), or greater than "1" (in the case of the output-oriented model concerned with the maximization of outputs for a given level of inputs). In the case of our study, we use an output-oriented DEA model.

In addition to the orientation of a DEA model, a researcher is given a choice regarding the return-to-scale, where an investigator can choose among constant return-to-scale (CRS), variable return-to-scale (VRS), and decreasing or non-increasing return-to-scale (NIRS) models. For the purposes of our study, we need to isolate yearly changes in TFP, as values of investments and revenues change from year-to-year. This is accomplished by means of Malmquist index.

The framework of the neoclassical growth accounting posits that an economic growth is determined by two factors. The first factor, resource accumulation, could lead to high rates of growth, albeit, due to the law of diminishing return, only for a limited period of time. Thus, it is the growth in productivity that is assumed to allow for attaining of the sustained economic growth. The productivity is commonly referred to as Total Factor Productivity (TFP) and its growth can be measured by Malmquist index. Based on the idea of productivity index, originally suggested by Malmquist (1953), Caves, Christensen and Diewert (1982) defined the Malmquist index of TFP growth. Later, Färe, Grosskopf, Norris, and Zhang (1994) demonstrated that the Malmquist index could be constructed based on the results of DEA.

Essentially, the approach is based on performing DEA analysis in two points in time; let us say t1 and t2. Then, for a given DMU, the period of time (t2-t1) could be represented as the distance between the data point at the time t1 and the data point at the time t2. For each DMU in the sample, the distance between these data points would be reflective of the change in this DMU's TFP, which is represented by the Malmquist index. In the case of economic growth, we expect that the efficiency frontier for a given set of DMUs would change its position over time. Let us suppose that a DMU A have changed its position over the period of time (t2 –t1). Such change is reflected by not only the new position of the DMU A, but also by the new position of the efficiency frontier itself. As a result, change in the position of each DMU in the sample could be perceived as consisting of the two components. The first component is the change in distance between a given DMU and the efficient frontier, which reflects the changes in efficiency (EC), and the second is the change in position of the efficient frontier itself, reflective of the technological change (TC) that took place over the period (t2-t1).

Now we offer our readers a brief overview of Multivariate Regression analysis. The overview that follows is not intended to reflect the true complexity of this topic; instead, our intent is to cover the subject sufficiently enough to explain our analysis. The reader who is interested in the subject of interpreting the interactions in MR, could refer to such sources as Jaccard et al. (1990), Aiken and West (1991), and Braumoeller (2004). For the purposes of this research, we are interested only in testing the null hypothesis of no interaction between the independent variables. Consequently, issues such as the presence of thresholds, level-dependent dynamic of the interacting variables, and so on are beyond the scope of this paper.

For our analysis it is necessary to state the general model of MR takes form of:

$$Y = a + b1*X1 + b2*X2 + b3*X1\ X2+...+ bn*Xn + bk*Xk + bm*Xn*Xk +e$$

The test for interaction then can be seen as testing the null hypothesis

$$H0: b3 = 0;$$

If from our empirical analysis we find that $b3 \neq 0$ we are able to reject the null hypothesis and state that there is no interaction between X1 and X2. The interpretation of the interaction term in MR, however, is not as straightforward as the interpretation of the slope coefficient of an independent variable. For example, b3 in the equation above reflects the relationship between Y and X1 and X2 when X1 and X2 increase jointly. Furthermore, b3 in the equation above reflects conditional relationship between Y and X1 and X2, for the impact of X1 on Y would depend on the level of X2 and vice versa. We will return to these issues in our analysis.

RESEARCH METHODOLOGY

In order to answer the eleven research questions of this study, we employ a four-phase methodology supported by three data analytic tools; a summary is provided in Table 2.

To approach our research problem, we rely on the neoclassical framework of growth accounting (Solow, 1957). A lack of theoretical support has been noted to be one of the serious limitations for conducting investigations assessing the impact of information and communication technologies (Gomez & Pather, 2012; Heeks, 2010); by employing a widely used theoretical framework we place this inquiry on a solid footing. The objective of growth accounting is to decompose, using a neoclassical production function, the rate of growth of an economy into the contributions from the different inputs. A neoclassical production function relates output and inputs in the following way:

Table 2. The four-phase methodology of the study

Phase	Research Question	Method
1	1. Does the given TE exhibit annual growth in TFP? 2. Does the given TE exhibit continuous growth in TFP?	DEA MI
2	3. Is there a relationship between changes in the level of investments in telecoms and changes in TFP? 4. Is there a relationship between changes in the level of full-time telecom staff and changes in TFP? 5. Do changes in the level of investments in telecoms & changes in the level of full-time telecom staff produce a complementary effect on changes in TFP? 6. Is there a relationship between the level of investments in telecoms and TFP? 7. Is there a relationship existed between the level of full-time telecom staff and TFP? 8. Are the level of Investments in telecoms & the level of full-time telecom staff complementary in terms of their effect on TFP?	MR
3	9. Do changes in the ratio of revenues to investments impact TFP? 10. Does the level of the ratio of revenues to investments have an impact on TFP?	OLS
4	11. What is the dominant source of changes in TFP?	DEA MI
5	12. Whether the dominant source of changes in TFP in the Later Period is different from that of the Earlier Period?	Statistical hypothesis testing

$Y = f(A, K, L),$

where Y = output (most often in the form of GDP),

A = the level of technology/total factor productivity (TFP),
K = capital stock (or, investments in telecoms, in our case), and
L = quantity of labor/size of labor force (e.g., quantity of full-time telecom employees).

From the three inputs used by growth accounting, only capital K and labor L could be observed in our data, while TFP serves as a residual (often referred to as *Solow's residual*) term capturing that contribution to Y (GDP or revenues from telecoms), which is left unexplained by the changes in the levels of capital K and labor L. The value of TFP could be obtained by calculating the value of Malmquist Index (MI) of TFP growth (Malmquist, 1953; Caves, Christensen & Diewert, 1982), which can be constructed based on the results of Data Envelopment Analysis (DEA) (Färe *et al.*,1994). Essentially, the approach is based on performing DEA in two points of time: let us say *Year1995* and *Year1996*. Then, for a given decision making unit (DMU), the period of time (*Year1996- Year1995*) can be represented as the distance between the data point at time *Year1995* and the data point at time *Year1996*. For each DMU in the sample the distance between these data points is reflective of the change in this DMU's TFP, which is represented by the Malmquist index. If the obtained value of MI is greater than 1, then the change is positive; conversely, if MI is less than 1, the change is negative.

In the case of our investigation we obtain nine values of MI for the first period (1993-2002) and five values of MI for the second period (2003-2008), where each value of MI serving as a measure of TFP for a given year. For the DEA part of the methodology we have identified a model consisting of the six input and four output variables, presented below in Table 3. The main goal that we pursue in performing DEA is to find out how efficient our set of TEs is in converting investment inputs into revenue outputs. Therefore, we did not include any other inputs or outputs such as those related to infrastructure, capa-

Table 3. Input and output variables of the DEA model

Input Variables of the DEA Model	Output Variables of the DEA Model
GDP per capita (in current US$) Full-time telecom staff (% of total labor force) Annual telecom investment per telecom worker (in current US $) Annual telecom investment (% of GDP in current US $) Annual telecom investment per capita (in current US $) Annual telecom investment per worker (in current US $)	Total telecom services revenue per telecom worker (in current US $) Total telecom services revenue (% of GDP in current US $) Total telecom services revenue per worker (in current US $) Total telecom services revenue per capita (in current US $)

bilities, utilization, etc. Instead of presenting the levels of investments and revenues in absolute dollar terms, we chose to represent them in relative units.

The second phase is dedicated to determining the presence of statistically significant relationships between the values of TFP, investments in telecoms, and a full-time telecom workforce. While Samoilenko and Osei-Bryson (2008b) presented evidence of the relationships between investments in ICT and full-time ICT labor and GDP in the context of TEs, it has not been shown that such a link exists in regard to TFP. Furthermore, we aim to determine whether these two variables (investments and labor) are complementary in their effect on TFP. The second and third phases of our investigation employ regression analysis. In this investigation we are interested in the presence of a statistically significant effect of the independent variables on the dependent variable. In this case, the general model of MR takes the form:

$$Y = a + b_{1*}X_1 + b_{2*}X_2 + b_{3*}X_1 X_2 + e,$$

and the test for presence of a statistically significant effect amounts to testing the null hypothesis

$$H_0: b_1, b_2, b_3 = 0$$

In the case of $b_1, b_2, b_3 \neq 0$ we are able to reject the null hypothesis of the study. However, because TFP represents change in productivity, we can also express the variable *annual telecom investment (in current US $)* in the form of the change in the level of investment that took place over the year; similarly, we can express the variable *full-time telecommunication staff* in the form of the change in the level of full-time telecom labor that took place over the same year. As a result, in the first MR model we use variables listed in Table 4.

Consequently, the first MR model takes the following form:

TFP = a + b$_{1*}$annual change in investments in telecoms + b$_{2*}$annual change in full-time telecoms staff+ b$_{3*}$ annual change in investments in telecoms$_*$annual change in full-time telecoms staff + e

Table 4. Variables in the first MR model

Term in the First MR Model	Variable
Y1	TFP
X1	Annual change in the level of telecom investment (in current US $)
X2	Annual change in the level of full-time telecommunication staff
X1*X2	Interaction term

We also aim to determine whether the values of TFP are affected by the levels of *annual telecom investment (in current US\$)* and *full-time telecommunication staff.* In the second MR model we use variables listed in Table 5.

As a result, the second MR model takes the following form:

TFP = a + b_{4*} annual telecom investment + b_{5*} full-time telecom staff + b_{6*} annual telecom investment $_*$full-time telecom staff + e

Now we can proceed with Phase 3 of the analysis. There appears to be an agreement on the importance of the effectiveness and efficiency of the workforce on productivity (Samoilenko & Osei-Bryson, 2008a). It is not clear, however, whether there is a relationship between the capacity of the workforce to convert investments into revenues and TFP in the context of TEs. In order to investigate this issue further, we employ a proxy variable *conversion efficiency*, which is represented by the ratio of the variable *total telecom services revenue in current US \$)* to the variable *annual telecom investment (in current US \$)*, per full-time telecom worker. The use of generalized indexes (e.g., *e-readiness, Network readiness, IT diffusion*) and proxy variables (e.g., *IT intensity, Access, Connectivity*) is common in studies of economic impact of IT (Indjikian & Siegel, 2005). Proxy variable *conversion efficiency* serves as a good intuitive representation of the state of a given economy in terms of investments in and revenues from telecoms, as well as the quality of its full-time telecom labor force. For example, given two hypothetical TEs with the values of 2 and 3 of the proxy *conversion efficiency*, one can immediately assess that a TE, *ceteris paribus*, can generate higher levels of revenues from the same level of investments while using the same level of workforce, than another TE. Once the values of *conversion efficiency* were calculated for TEs in our sample, we then calculated the values of *change in conversion efficiency*, representing the annual changes in the values of *conversion efficiency* for all of the economies in our sample. This allows us to construct two OLS models consisting of the variables listed in Table 6.

Table 5. Variables in the second MR model

Term in the Second MR Model	Variable
Y1	TFP
X3	Annual telecom investment (in current US \$)
X4	Full-time telecommunication staff
X3*X4	Interaction Term

Table 6. Variables in the OLS models

OLS Model	Term	Variable
First Model	Y1	TFP
	X1	*Change in conversion efficiency (*annual change in ratios of *Total telecom services revenue (in current US \$)* to *Annual telecom investment (in current US \$)*, per full-time Telecom worker.
Second Model	Y2	TFP
	X2	*Conversion efficiency (*ratio of *Total telecom services revenue (in current US \$)* to *Annual telecom investment (in current US \$)*, per full-time Telecom worker.

The first OLS model allows for determining the presence of statistically significant relationships between the values of TFP, and the values of *change in conversion efficiency,* and utilizes the formulation of the following OLS model:

$$TFP = a + b_{7*} \text{ Change in conversion efficiency} + e$$

Using the second OLS model allows for determining the presence of statistically significant relationships between the values of TFP, and the values of *conversion efficiency,* and utilizes the formulation of the following OLS model:

$$TFP = a + b_{8*} \text{ conversion efficiency} + e.$$

In Phase 4, again, we utilize DEA and MI. DEA allows an investigator not only to obtain the scores of the relative efficiency for each DMU in the sample and to calculate MI to evaluate the overall growth in productivity, but also to decompose the values of MI into two components. The first component is represented by the *change in technology* (TC), and the second component is represented by the *change in efficiency* (EC) that took place during a period of time. Consequently, taking into consideration that TFP is represented by MI, MI = (TC + EC), we can express the possible contribution of investments in telecoms to macroeconomic bottom line as a combination of two components:

1. *Investments in Telecoms - > Revenues from Telecoms -> GDP*, and
2. *Investments in Telecoms - > (TC + EC) -> GDP.*

By knowing relative values of TC and EC we can determine whether the growth in productivity was primarily due to the technology (in the case of TC > EC), or to the efficiency (in the case of EC > TC). This will allow us to gain insights into the nature of the weak link of the overall chain of the macroeconomic impact of the investments.

The last phase of our investigation aims is to determine whether the changes in productivity was primarily driven by a better technology (TC), or whether it was driven by the improvements in efficiency (EC). We will use the pair of difference measures in our statistical hypothesis testing provided in Table 7.

For our statistical analysis of differences in the two periods (e.g. $H_{o(Ld,*)}$; $H_{o(Fl,*)}$) we will used the a Mann-Whitney non-parametric test.

Table 7. Difference measures used in statistical hypothesis testing

Measure	Expression	Purpose
δ(EC,TC)	(EC – TC)	Used to measure the average difference between EC and TC in a given period. In the statistical analysis, we will: o Indirectly test for each period, whether EC dominates TC or vice versa. o Indirectly test whether different components of TFP dominate in the two periods.
Φ(EC,TC)	if (EC – TC) > 0 then **1** if (EC – TC) ≤ 0 then **0**	Used to measure the proportion of times that EC dominates TC in a given period. In the statistical analysis, we will directly test whether the proportion of times that EC dominates TC in the *Late Transition* period is significantly different than the proportion of times that EC dominates TC in the *Early Transition* period.

Our rationale for choosing a non-parametric test such as Mann-Whitney stems from the fact that such a test makes no assumptions (e.g. normality) about the data on which they can be used. It is used for testing differences between means when there are two conditions and different subjects have been used in each condition.

Null Hypotheses of the Study

For the first phase of our inquiry we formulate the following two hypotheses. Given the value of MI, representing the annual change in TFP, and the value of AMI, representing averaged value of TFP from 1993 to 2002:

$H_1 0$: For each of the 18 TEs in the sample for each year in the 1993-2002 period, MI < 1
$H_2 0$: For each of the 18 TEs in the sample for the period from 1993 to 2002, AMI <1

Similar hypotheses were formulated for the period from 2003 to 2008. Testing of $H_1 0$ allows us to identify TEs that exhibited annual growth in TFP, while testing $H_2 0$ allows us to identify TEs that exhibited continuous growth in TFP over the given period.

In Phase 2, given the first MR model

TFP = a + b$_{1*}$annual change in investments in telecoms + b$_{2*}$annual change in full-time telecom staff+ b$_{3*}$ annual change in investments in telecoms$_*$annual change in full-time telecom staff + e,

we formulate the following three hypotheses:

$H_3 0$: b_1 = 0 at α = 0.05 level of significance
$H_4 0$: b_2 = 0 at α = 0.05 level of significance
$H_5 0$: b_3 = 0 at α = 0.05 level of significance

Testing $H_3 0$ allows us to determine whether a given TE exhibited a statistically significant relationship between changes in the level of investments in telecoms and changes in TFP, while testing $H_4 0$ allows us to determine whether a given TE exhibited a statistically significant relationship between changes in the level of full-time Telecom staff and changes in TFP. Finally, testing $H_5 0$ allows us to determine whether for a given TE the changes in the level of investments in telecoms and changes in the level of full-time telecom staff produce a complementary effect on changes in TFP.

Similarly, given the second MR model

TFP = a + b$_{4*}$ Annual telecom investment + b$_{5*}$ Full-time telecom staff + b$_{6*}$ Annual telecom investment $_*$ Full-time telecom staff + ξ,

we formulate the following three hypotheses:

$H_6 0$: b_4 = 0 at α = 0.05 level of significance
$H_7 0$: b_5 = 0 at α = 0.05 level of significance
$H_8 0$: b_6 = 0 at α = 0.05 level of significance

Testing H_60 allows us to determine whether a given TE exhibited a statistically significant relationship between the level of investments in telecoms and TFP, while testing H_70 allows us to determine whether such relationship existed between the level of full-time telecom staff and TFP. Finally, Testing H_80 allows us to determine whether level of investments in telecoms and the level of full-time telecom staff are complementary in impacting TFP.

In Phase 3 the first OLS model utilizes the following formulation:

$$TFP = a + b_{7*} \text{ Change in conversion efficiency} + \xi,$$

and is concerned with the testing of the following null hypothesis:

H_90: *b_7 = 0 at* $\alpha = 0.05$ level of significance.

Testing H_90 allows us to determine whether for a given TE changes in *conversion efficiency* impact TFP. The second model takes the form of

$$TFP = a + b_{8*} \text{ conversion efficiency} + \xi,$$

and is concerned with the testing of the following null hypothesis:

$H_{10}0$: *b_8 =0 at* $\alpha = 0.05$ level of significance

Testing $H_{10}0$ allows us to determine whether for a given TE *conversion efficiency* has an impact on TFP. The fourth phase of our investigation relies on the following equation:

$$MI = TC + EC$$

And is concerned with testing the following hull hypothesis:

$H_{11}0$: TC > EC.

Testing $H_{11}0$ allows us to determine whether the growth in productivity was primarily driven by a better technology (e.g., via acquisition of a new technology), or whether it was driven by the improvements in efficiency (e.g., via more effective utilization of the available technology).

In the last phase of our inquiry we answer RQ12- to do so we generate and test two hypotheses. First, for the measure $\delta(EC, TC)$ we test

$H_{12}0$: There is no statistically significant difference between $\delta(EC, TC)_{\text{Late Period}}$ and $\delta(EC, TC)_{\text{Early Period}}$.

And for the measure $\Phi(EC, TC)$ we test

$H_{13}0$: There is no statistically significant difference between $\Phi(EC, TC)_{\text{Late Period}}$ and $\Phi(EC, TC)_{\text{Early Period}}$

RESULTS OF THE DATA ANALYSIS

In order to perform the DEA part of the data analysis we used the software application "OnFront," version 2.02, and *SAS Enterprise Miner* (EM) to conduct MR and OLS analysis. The data subjected to MR and OLS were standardized prior to analysis.

The results from Phase 1 that are displayed Table 8 suggested that most TEs exhibited continuous growth both in the period of the early transition (i.e. 1993-2002) and the period of late transition (2003-2008). Further with regard to the two research questions (i.e. RQ1, RQ2) of this phase, the performance of most of the TEs in the late transition period was similar to what it was in the early transition period.

The results of Phase 2 that are displayed in Table 9 suggest that the *level of investments in telecom*s and the *level of the full-time telecom staff* are not viable predictors of productivity growth.

This simply means that no TE in our sample, other than Belarus, can claim that the level of investment in telecoms serves as a determinant of the growth in productivity. It would appear that 17 TEs in our sample have already achieved a threshold level of investments sufficient enough to produce a stream of revenue, but insufficient in the absence of complementary investments to produce any significant changes in productivity.

Table 8. Results of phase 1: RQ1 and RQ2

Country	RQ1: Annual Growth in Productivity? (Y/N)		RQ2: Continuous Growth in Productivity? (Y/N)	
	1993-2002	2003-2008	1993-2002	2003-2008
Albania	N	N	Y	N
Armenia	N	N	Y	Y
Azerbaijan	N	N	Y	Y
Belarus	N	N	Y	Y
Bulgaria	N	N	Y	N
Czech Republic	N	Y	Y	Y
Estonia	N	N	Y	Y
Hungary	Y	N	Y	Y
Kazakhstan	N	N	Y	N
Latvia	N	N	Y	Y
Lithuania	N	N	Y	Y
Moldova	N	N	Y	Y
Poland	N	N	Y	N
Romania	N	N	Y	Y
Slovak Republic	N	N	Y	N
Slovenia	N	N	Y	Y
Ukraine	N	N	Y	Y
YES: Proportion	0.06	0.06	1.00	0.71
Similarity	0.88		0.71	

Table 9. Results of phase 2. RQ3, RQ4, & RQ5

Country	RQ3: Relationship Between Changes in the Level of Investments in Telecoms and Changes in Productivity		RQ4: Relationship Between Changes in the Level of Full-time Telecom Staff and Changes in Productivity		RQ5: Complementarity of Changes in the Levels of Investments in Telecoms and Full-time Telecom Staff on Changes in Productivity	
	1993-2002	2003-2008	1993-2002	2003-2008	1993-2002	2003-2008
Albania	N	N	N	N	N	N
Armenia	N	N	N	N	N	N
Azerbaijan	N	N	N	N	N	N
Belarus	Y	N	Y	N	Y	N
Bulgaria	N	N	N	N	N	N
Czech Republic	N	N	N	N	N	N
Estonia	N	N	N	N	N	N
Hungary	N	N	N	N	N	N
Kazakhstan	N	N	N	Y	N	N
Latvia	N	N	N	N	N	N
Lithuania	N	Y	N	Y	N	N
Moldova	N	Y	N	Y	N	N
Poland	N	N	N	N	N	N
Romania	N	N	Y	N	N	N
Slovak Republic	N	N	N	N	N	N
Slovenia	N	N	N	N	N	N
Ukraine	N	N	N	N	N	N
YES: Proportion	0.06	0.12	0.12	0.18	0.06	0.00
Similarity	0.82		0.71		0.94	

Also, no TE, other than Belarus or Romania, can demonstrate that the growth in productivity is determined by the level of the full-time telecom staff. This might mean that the rest of 16 TEs must concentrate not on increasing the quantity of full-time workers, but rather on increasing the efficiency and effectiveness of the utilization of investments, including increasing the quality of the existing level of their full-time workforce.

The results of Phase 2 displayed in Table 10 identified only Kazakhstan as having an economy in which the level of investments in telecoms and the level of full-time telecom staff have a statistically significant impact on changes in productivity (H_60 and H_70 were rejected).

These results also suggest a presence of the complementary effect of the levels of labor and capital on productivity (H_80 was rejected). The other 17 TEs exhibited no statistically significant relationship between the levels of capital investment and full-time labor, and productivity (H_60, H_70, and H_80 were accepted).

The results of Phase 3 displayed in Table 11 allow us to conclude that in the context of our set of TEs a higher *ratio of revenues* to *investments per full-time telecom worker* does not indicate a growth in productivity and the presence of a spillover effect.

Table 10. Results of phase 2: RQ6, RQ7, & RQ8

Country	RQ6: Rel. Between the Level of Investments in Telecoms & TFP		RQ7: Rel. Between the Level of Full-time Telecom Staff & TFP		RQ8: Complementarity of Investments in Telecoms & Telecom Staff in on TFP?	
	1993-2002	2003-2008	1993-2002	2003-2008	1993-2002	2003-2008
Albania	N	N	N	N	N	N
Armenia	N	N	N	N	N	N
Azerbaijan	N	N	N	N	N	N
Belarus	N	N	N	N	N	N
Bulgaria	N	N	N	N	N	N
Czech Republic	N	N	N	N	N	N
Estonia	N	N	N	N	N	N
Hungary	N	N	N	N	N	N
Kazakhstan	Y	Y	Y	Y	Y	Y
Latvia	Y	Y	N	N	N	N
Lithuania	N	N	N	N	N	N
Moldova	N	N	N	N	N	N
Poland	N	N	N	N	N	N
Romania	N	N	N	N	N	N
Slovak Republic	N	N	N	N	N	N
Slovenia	N	N	N	N	N	N
Ukraine	N	N	N	N	N	N
YES: Proportion	0.18	0.18	0.12	0.12	0.12	0.12
Similarity between Periods	1.00		1.00		1.00	

This is an interesting finding, for, intuitively, it would appear that the more productive workers should have a higher value of the ratio. However, this seems to be not the case in the context of TEs.

However, we can observe some dissimilarity between the two periods in regard to the RQ10 and RQ11 (see Table 12).

Based on the results of OLS it is reasonable to conclude that at least for some of the TEs economic growth associated with investments in telecoms is determined by the presence of the skilled full-time telecom workforce capable of efficiently and effectively converting investments into revenues.

The results of Phase 4 demonstrate a major difference between the two periods in regard to the sources of the growth in productivity (see Table 13). While during the period from 1993 to 2002 most of the TEs in our sample exhibited growth in productivity fueled by technological changes (e.g., TC component of MI), in the 2003-2008 period growth in productivity was based on improvements in efficiency (e.g., EC component of MI).

Finally, the results of Phase 5 are provided in Table 14, below. Results of Phase 5 demonstrate that the period of *Early Transition* was associated with the growth via TC component.

Table 11. Results of the phase 3: RQ9 & RQ10

Country	RQ9: Impact of Changes in the Ratio of Revenues to Investments un TFP		RQ10: Impact of Level of the Ratio of Revenues to Investments on TFP	
	1993-2002	2003-2008	1993-2002	2003-2008
Albania	Y	N	N	N
Armenia	N	N	N	N
Azerbaijan	Y	N	N	Y
Belarus	N	Y	N	N
Bulgaria	N	N	N	N
Czech Republic	N	N	N	N
Estonia	N	N	N	N
Hungary	N	Y	N	N
Kazakhstan	N	Y	N	N
Latvia	N	N	N	N
Lithuania	N	Y	N	N
Moldova	N	Y	N	Y
Poland	Y	N	N	N
Romania	Y	Y	N	N
Slovak Republic	Y	Y	N	N
Slovenia	Y	N	N	N
Ukraine	Y	N	N	N
YES: Proportion	0.41	0.41	0.00	0.12
Similarity	0.44		0.88	

Meaning, TEs of our sample were engaged in technological catch-up, spending money to purchase better technology. The situation changed during *Late Transition period*, where TEs exhibited a balanced growth in productivity with none of the components of MI dominating.

SOLUTIONS AND RECOMMENDATIONS

The results of the data analysis support the current perspective that ICT could, indeed, drive economic development of emerging, transition, and developing economies by impacting rates of growth (Samoilenko & Weistroffer, 2010a; Ngwenyama & Morawczynski, 2009). However, specific insights offered by the study are worth discussing further.

First, it would appear reasonable to expect, taking into consideration a limited economic power of TEs, that the period of late transition would be different from the period of early transition in regard to the annual growth in productivity. This is because the period of early transition could be characterized as a period of catching up in terms of the quality of technology, know-how of the workforce, and the amount of accumulated ICT-related capital. Thus, it is somewhat reasonable to expect that the growth

Table 12. Results of the phase 4: RQ 11

Country	RQ11: Do Changes in Technology Serve as a Primary Engine of growth of TFP?	
	1993-2002	**2003-2008**
Albania	Y	N
Armenia	Y	N
Azerbaijan	Y	N
Belarus	Y	N
Bulgaria	Y	N
Czech Republic	Y	N
Estonia	Y	N
Hungary	Y	Y
Kazakhstan	Y	Y
Latvia	Y	Y
Lithuania	Y	N
Moldova	N	N
Poland	Y	N
Romania	Y	N
Slovak Republic	Y	N
Slovenia	Y	Y
Ukraine	Y	N
YES: Proportion	0.94	0.18
Similarity between Periods	0.29	

in productivity would be inconsistent simply due to changes that TEs have gone through. After the first ten-year period we would expect to see TEs exhibiting a more stable, consistent annual growth in productivity, for the foundation laid by the period of early transition should serve as a solid platform for an economic take off. However, this turned out not be the case- while most of TEs indeed grew over the two periods, almost none of them grew consistently on the annual basis. Furthermore, approximately one third of TEs did not exhibit a continuous growth in productivity over the period of late transition. This is troubling, because it was noted that TEs increased their levels of investments in telecoms in the period of late transition compared to early years (Samoilenko, 2013), and yet, the increased investments did not translate into growth in productivity.

Moreover, the obtained evidence suggests that a level of investments in telecoms, as well as changes in the level of investments, do not serve as predictors of growth in productivity. While previous investigations determined that economies could obtain macroeconomic benefits by investing in telecoms (Samoilenko & Weistroffer, 2010b) via stream of revenues, our study provides evidence that the macroeconomic benefits of investments do not come in the form of growth in productivity. This is an important insight that suggests that TEs cannot pave the road to continuing growth in productivity with investment money. Additionally, when taking into consideration the absence of the impact of the level, as well as changes

Table 13. Comparison of sources of growth in productivity: 1993-2002 vs. 2003-2008

Country	Leader (L) or Follower (F)	1993-2002	2003-2008
Albania	F	TC	EC
Armenia	F	TC	EC
Azerbaijan	F	TC	EC
Belarus	F	TC	EC
Bulgaria	F	TC	EC
Czech Republic	L	TC	EC
Estonia	L	TC	EC
Hungary	L	TC	TC
Kazakhstan	F	TC	TC
Latvia	L	TC	TC
Lithuania	L	TC	EC
Moldova	F	EC	EC
Poland	L	TC	EC
Romania	F	TC	EC
Slovak Republic	L	TC	EC
Slovenia	L	TC	TC
Ukraine	F	TC	EC
EC: Proportion	**Overall**	0.06	0.76
	Leaders	0.00	0.63
	Followers	0.11	0.89
Similarity between Periods		0.29	

Table 14. Comparison of sources of growth in TFP

Period	Null Hypothesis	Results	Significant at p ≤ 0.01?	Inference
Early Transition	$H_{12}0$: $\delta(EC, TC) = 0$	The Z-Score is -2.7436.	The p-value is 0.00307. Significant.	EC < TC
Late Transition	$H_{13}0$: $\delta(EC, TC) = 0$	The Z-Score is 0.611.	The p-value is 0.27093. Not significant.	EC = TC

in the level of the telecom workforce on growth in productivity, we can conclude that TEs are not in the position when they can grow by simply spending more on technology or by hiring more workers. The absence of the complementarity of labor and investments indicate that TEs could not grow even if they invest more in telecoms while hiring more workers. What then, could serve as an indicator of growth?

According to the results of the data analysis our proxy *conversion efficiency* does not serve as a predictor of growth in productivity. The implication is simple, if counterintuitive - if one TE has a superior ratio of revenues to investments per telecom worker than another TE, then that does not imply that the economy with a higher ratio exhibited a stronger growth in productivity. While it was reasonable to expect that if an economy has a high revenue-to-investments ratio, then the higher ratio is due to a high level of productivity, this expectation turned out false. It is possible that while the impact of investments on revenues is straightforward, the impact of investments on the productivity component of the macroeconomic bottom line is indirect, being mediated by intermediate precursors and targets (Samoilenko, 2014).

However, it appears that the *change in conversion efficiency* does serve as a predictor of growth in productivity for some economies. This is an important finding, because this means that some TEs could manipulate their growth in productivity by monitoring revenues-to-investments ratio. Simply put, it is possible to grow by continuously "doing more with less", by employing a smaller number of highly skilled workers who are more efficient in utilization of investments in telecoms.

The results provided by the fourth phase of our inquiry are in line with "doing more with less" interpretation- we have determined that the sources of growth in productivity have shifted over time. If in the early stage of transition, the growth was primarily driven by investments in technology, the later period of transition has growth in productivity that is driven by the increases in efficiency of utilization of the available technology. However, keeping in mind that growth in productivity is comprised of two components- change in technology and change in efficiency, the best route to continuous growth in productivity is via balanced approach (Samoilenko, 2013), where both components contribute to growth. In the last phase of our inquiry we demonstrated that TEs grew via TC component during *Early Transition*, when economies allocated significant investments to establish the baseline for growth- to get the technological frontier up. However, by comparing periods of *Early Transition* and *Late Transition* we demonstrated that the growth in productivity was balanced during the period of *Late Transition*, with no components dominating the growth and TEs efficiently utilizing the available technology and not relying, solely, on technological advances for their growth.

FUTURE RESEARCH DIRECTIONS

The results raise questions that could serve as directions for future inquiries. First, what are some of the complementary factors that allow investments in telecoms to impact productivity growth? Second, what are some of the ways of improving the efficiency of conversion of investments in telecoms into revenues? Third, what is the optimal revenue-to-investment ratio per telecom worker that indicate the need for the expansion of the full-time workforce?

DISCUSSION QUESTIONS

1. The research described in this chapter utilizes the Framework of Neoclassical Growth Accounting as its theoretical foundation. What are some of the benefits of the framework? What are some of the shortcomings?
2. Investments in Information and Communication Technologies do not bring the results right away. Instead, there is a necessary delay between the point at which investments have been allocated, and the point at which the outcomes of investments start manifesting at the macroeconomic level. What is, in your opinion, a reasonable time lag between the two points?
3. It is commonly accepted that investments in ICT are capable of positively impacting the macroeconomic bottom line (e.g., GDP). However, such measure as GDP is an aggregate of a variety of

microeconomic outcomes. What are some of the routes by which investments in ICT impact the macroeconomic bottom line? What are some of the microeconomic targets of investments in ICT?

4. Investments in ICT are not made in isolation. Instead, such investments must be complemented by the investments in the qualified labor force that will serve as a "caretaker" of investments in ICT. What are some positive consequences of having an ICT-related labor force comprised of a small number of full-time ICT employees and a large number of part-time employees? What are the negative consequences of such composition?

5. Multifactor productivity, also commonly referred to as Total Factor Productivity (TFP), is not a term uniquely reserved for macroeconomic analysis. Quite contrary, the spillover effect (reflected by TFP) could manifest itself at any level. Give example of some of the personal purchases that resulted in the spillover effect and made you, or your household, more productive.

6. Discuss the issue of complementarity of investments- what are some of the areas of economics that require complementary investments? Give three examples of complementary investments (e.g., purchases) from your personal experience.

ACKNOWLEDGMENT

I express my gratitude to Professor Kweku-Muata Osei-Bryson for his contribution to the first research work published in the International Journal of Technology Diffusion with the title "Investigation of Determinants of Total Factor Productivity: An Analysis of the Impact of Investments in Telecoms on Economic Growth in Productivity in the Context of Transition Economies", which has been improved and presented in this chapter of the book.

REFERENCES

Abu Tair, H. Y., & Abu-Shanab, E. A. (2014). Mobile Government Services: Challenges and Opportunities. *International Journal of Technology Diffusion*, *5*(1), 17–25. doi:10.4018/ijtd.2014010102

Aiken, L., & West, S. (1991). *Multiple regression: Testing and Interpreting Interactions*. Newbury Park, CA: Sage Publications.

Balcı, A., Medeni, T. D., & Nohutçu, A. (2013). Turkish Case of E-Government Strategy Development and Policy-Formulation Process: Recent Developments on Evaluations of E-Government Rankings. *International Journal of Technology Diffusion*, *4*(4), 27–44. doi:10.4018/ijtd.2013100102

Bankole, F., Osei-Bryson, K.-M., & Brown, I. (2013). The Impact of ICT Investments on Human Development: A Regression Splines Analysis. *Journal of Global Information Technology Management*, *16*(2), 59–85. doi:10.1080/1097198X.2013.10845636

Beil, R., Ford, G., & Jackson, J. (2005). On the relationship between telecommunications investment and economic growth in the United States. *International Economic Journal*, *19*(1), 3–9. doi:10.1080/13511161042000320399

Braumoeller, B. (2004). Hypothesis Testing and Multiplicative Interaction Terms. *International Organization*, *58*(4), 807–820. doi:10.1017/S0020818304040251

Bresnahan, T. F., Brynjolfsson, E., & Hitt, L. M. (2002). Information technology, workplace organization, and the demand for skilled labor: Firm level evidence. *The Quarterly Journal of Economics*, *117*(1), 339–376. doi:10.1162/003355302753399526

Brynjolfsson, E., & Hitt, L. M. (1996). Paradox lost: Firm level evidence on returns to information systems spending. *Management Science*, *42*(4), 541–558. doi:10.1287/mnsc.42.4.541

Caves, D., Christensen, L., & Diewert, W. (1982). Multilateral comparisons of output, input and productivity using superlative index numbers. *Economic Journal (London)*, *92*(365), 73–86. doi:10.2307/2232257

Chavula, H. (2013). Telecommunications development and economic growth in Africa. *Information Technology for Development*, *19*(1), 5–23. doi:10.1080/02681102.2012.694794

Cieślika, A., & Kaniewska, M. (2004). Telecommunications Infrastructure and Regional Economic Development: The Case of Poland. *Regional Studies*, *38*(6), 713–725. doi:10.1080/0034340042000240996

Colecchia, A., & Schreyer, P. (2002). ICT Investment and Economic Growth in the 1990s: Is the United States a Unique Case? A Comparative Study of Nine OECD Countries. *Review of Economic Dynamics*, *5*(2), 408–442. doi:10.1006/redy.2002.0170

Cooper, W. W., & Tone, K. (1997). Measures of inefficiency in data envelopment analysis and frontier estimation. *European Journal of Operational Research*, *99*(1), 72–88. doi:10.1016/S0377-2217(96)00384-0

Datta, A., & Agarwal, S. (2004). Telecommunications and economic growth: A panel data approach. *Applied Economics*, *36*(15), 1649–1654. doi:10.1080/0003684042000218552

Daveri, F. (2002). The New Economy in Europe, 1992-2001. *Oxford Review of Economic Policy*, *18*(3), 345–362. doi:10.1093/oxrep/18.3.345

Dewan, S., & Kraemer, K. (2000). Information Technology and Productivity: Evidence from Country Level Data. *Management Science*, *46*(4), 548–562. doi:10.1287/mnsc.46.4.548.12057

Eilu, E., & Auma, T. O. (2017). Mobile Money Services as a Panacea to Financial Inclusion in Sub-Saharan Africa: The Case of Uganda. *International Journal of Technology Diffusion*, *8*(4), 77–88. doi:10.4018/IJTD.2017100106

Fare, R., Grosskopf, S., Norris, M., & Zhang, Z. (1994). Productivity growth, technical progress, and efficiency change in industrialized countries. *The American Economic Review*, *84*(1), 66–83.

Gomez, R., & Pather, S. (2012). ICT Evaluation: Are we asking the right questions? *The Electronic Journal on Information Systems in Developing Countries*, *50*(1), 1–14. doi:10.1002/j.1681-4835.2012.tb00355.x

Haider, A., & Tang, S. S. (2016). Maximising Value Through IT and Business Alignment: A Case of IT Governance Institutionalisation at a Thai Bank. *International Journal of Technology Diffusion*, *7*(3), 33–58. doi:10.4018/IJTD.2016070104

Harindranath, G. (2008). ICT in a Transition Economy: The Case of Hungary. *Journal of Global Information Technology Management, 11*(4), 33–55. doi:10.1080/1097198X.2008.10856478

Heeks, R. (2010). Do information and communication technologies (ICTs) contribute to development? *Journal of International Development, 22*(5), 625–640. doi:10.1002/jid.1716

Heeks, R., & Molla, A. (2009). *Impact Assessment of ICT-for-Development Projects: A Compendium of Approaches*. IDPM Development Informatics Working Paper no. 36. Retrieved from http://www.sed. manchester.ac.uk/idpm/research/publications/wp/di/index.htm

Hoskisson, R., Eden, L., Lau, C., & Wright, M. (2000). Strategy in Emerging Economies. *Academy of Management Journal, 43*(3), 249–267. doi:10.2307/1556394

IMF. (2000). *Transition Economies: An IMF Perspective on Progress and Prospects*. Retrieved May 20, 2009 from http://www.imf.org/external/np/exr/ib/2000/110300.htm#I

Indjikian, R., & Siegel, D. (2005). The Impact of Investments in IT on Economic Performance: Implications for Developing Countries. *World Development, 33*(5), 681–700. doi:10.1016/j.worlddev.2005.01.004

Jaccard, J., Turrisi, R., & Wan, C. (1990), Interaction effects in multiple regression. Thousand Oaks, CA: Sage Publications. Series: Quantitative Applications in the Social Sciences, No.72.

Jorgenson, D. W. (2003). *Information Technology and the G7 Economies*. Conference on Digital Transformations: ICT's Impact on Productivity, London Business School, London, UK.

Kim, Y. J., Kang, H. G., Sanders, L., & Lee, S.-Y. T. (2008). Differential effects of IT investments: Complementarity and effect of GDP level. *International Journal of Information Management, 28*(6), 508–516. doi:10.1016/j.ijinfomgt.2008.01.003

Lee, S., Levendis, J., & Gutierrez, L. (2012). Telecommunications and economic growth: An empirical analysis of sub-Saharan Africa. *Applied Economics, 44*(4), 461–469. doi:10.1080/00036846.2010.508730

Levendis, J., & Lee, S. (2013). On the endogeneity of telecommunications and economic growth: Evidence from Asia. *Information Technology for Development, 19*(1), 62–85. doi:10.1080/02681102.2012.694793

Malmquist, S. (1953). Index numbers and indifference curves. *Trabajos de Estatistica, 4*(1), 209–242. doi:10.1007/BF03006863

McGuckin, R. H., Streitwieser, M. L., & Doms, M. (1998). The effect of technology use on productivity growth. *Economics of Innovation and New Technology, 7*(1), 1–27. doi:10.1080/10438599800000026

Ngwenyama, O., & Morawczynski, O. (2009). Factors affecting ICT expansion in emerging economies: An analysis of ICT infrastructure expansion in five Latin American countries. *Information Technology for Development, 15*(4), 237–258. doi:10.1002/itdj.20128

OECD. (2002). OECD Information technology outlook: ICTs and the information economy. Paris: OECD.

OECD. (2005c). The Contribution of ICTs to Pro-Poor Growth: No. 379. *OECD Papers, 5*(1), 59–72.

Oliner, S. D., & Sichel, D. E. (2000). The Resurgence of Growth in the Late 1990's: Is Information Technology the Story? *The Journal of Economic Perspectives, 4*(14), 3–22. doi:10.1257/jep.14.4.3

Piatkowski, M. (2003). *The Contribution of ICT Investment to Economic Growth and Labor Productivity in Poland 1995-2000*. TIGER Working Paper Series, No. 43.

Piatkowski, M. (2004). *Does ICT Investment Matter for Growth and Labor Productivity in Transition Economies?* Development and Comp Systems 0402008, EconWPA.

Samoilenko, S. (2013). Investigating factors associated with the spillover effect of investments in telecoms: Do some transition economies pay too much for too little? *Information Technology for Development*, *19*(1), 40–61. doi:10.1080/02681102.2012.677710

Samoilenko, S. (2014). Investigating the impact of investments in telecoms on microeconomic outcomes: Conceptual framework and empirical investigation in the context of transition economies. *Information Technology for Development*, *20*(3), 251–273. doi:10.1080/02681102.2012.751572

Samoilenko, S. (2016). Where do Investments in Telecoms Come From? Developing and Testing a Framework of Sustained Economic Impact of Investments in ICT. *Journal of Information Technology for Development*, *22*(4), 584–605. doi:10.1080/02681102.2014.927348

Samoilenko, S., & Ngwenyama, O. (2011). Understanding the human capital dimension of ICT and economic growth in transition economies. *Journal of Global Information Technology Management*, *14*(1), 59–69. doi:10.1080/1097198X.2011.10856531

Samoilenko, S., & Osei-Bryson, K. M. (2008a). Strategies for Telecoms to Improve Efficiency in the Production of Revenues: An Empirical Investigation in the Context of Transition Economies. *Journal of Global Information Technology Management*, *11*(4), 59–79. doi:10.1080/1097198X.2008.10856479

Samoilenko, S., & Osei-Bryson, K. M. (2008b). An Exploration of the Effects of the Interaction between ICT and Labor Force on Economic Growth in Transitional Economies. *International Journal of Production Economics*, *115*(2), 471–481. doi:10.1016/j.ijpe.2008.07.002

Samoilenko, S., & Osei-Bryson, K.-M. (2017). Creating Theoretical Research Frameworks using Multiple Methods. *Insight (American Society of Ophthalmic Registered Nurses)*, ICT4D.

Samoilenko, S., & Weistroffer, H. R. (2010a). Improving the relative efficiency of revenue generation from ICT in transition economies: A product life cycle approach. *Information Technology for Development*, *16*(4), 279–303. doi:10.1080/02681102.2010.510461

Samoilenko, S., & Weistroffer, H. R. (2010b). Spillover Effect of Telecom Investments on Technological Advancement and Efficiency Improvement in Transition Economies. *Proceedings of the SIG GlobDev 3rd Annual Workshop ICT in Global Development*.

Shiu, A., & Lam, P.-L. (2008). Causal Relationship between Telecommunications and Economic Growth in China and its Regions. *Regional Studies*, *42*(5), 705–718. doi:10.1080/00343400701543314

Swierczek, F., Shrestha, P., & Bechter, C. (2005). Information Technology, Productivity and Profitability in Asia-Pacific Banks. *Journal of Global Information Technology Management*, *8*(1), 6–26. doi:10.1080/1097198X.2005.10856388

Van Ark, B., Inklaar, R., & McGuckin, R. (2002*). 'Changing Gear' - Productivity, ICT and Services Industries: Europe and the United States* (No. 02-02). Economics Program Working Papers, The Conference Board, Economics Program. Retrieved from http://econpapers.repec.org/RePEc:cnf:wpaper:0202

Wolde-Rufael, Y. (2007). Another look at the Relationship between Telecommunications Investment and Economic Activity in the United States. *International Economic Journal, 21*(2), 199–205. doi:10.1080/10168730701345372

Ziemba, E., & Zelazny, R. (2013). Measuring the information society in Poland - dilemmas and a quantified image. FedCSIS, 1173-1180.

Chapter 4
Reputation Management Techniques and E–Collaboration:
UAE Public Relations Communication Strategies During Crises Management

Badreya Al-Jenaibi
UAE University, UAE

ABSTRACT

Public relation is one of the significant communication methods in any organization. It leads the internal and external communication strategies, especially during crises. Some of the main goals of public relations are to create, maintain, and protect the organization's reputation, and—ever-increasingly—e-collaboration plays a vital role in accomplishing this goal. The aim of this study is to explore the approaches that help an organization rejuvenate its reputation after damage caused by various crises. It is important to know which PR approaches best engage stakeholders because companies must maintain healthy relationships with all stake-holding entities in order to survive. Qualitative case study was conducted to explore what circumstances can compromise a company's image and what role a PR department would optimally play in rejuvenating it.

INTRODUCTION

Current public relations incline to be obvious as performing within the management of the organization. "As public relations has shifted from an emphasis on the technical role of the communicator to the strategic communication role of the manager. Management theory has defined organizational effectiveness in a number of ways" (Okafor & Malizu, 2015).

Public relations play a vital role during crises and is critical to their effective management. Turney (2008) posits that PR practitioners typically have daily responsibilities identical to those during crises, such as "maintaining and improving their organization's relationships by effectively communicating

DOI: 10.4018/978-1-5225-6367-9.ch004

with its target audiences. Public relations practitioners are not normally responsible for resolving the underlying problem(s) that created a crisis situation" (p. 1). Therefore, PR practitioners cannot (and should not) exercise their roles independently or direct the organization's actions without considering and adhering to the organization's overarching goals.

Out of necessity, an intense amount of internal scrutiny is directed towards reputation during times of crisis. Rather than seeing this as a negative, Turney (2008) points out that times of crisis can be turned into opportunity for strengthening and growing a company if they are managed well, saying that "Effective crisis communication can actually enhance an organization's reputation" (p.1). Jennex (2004) defines crises and disasters as unexpected circumstances or situations that demand a swift and effective response that is "different from their normal operating procedures" (p. 86).

Even though in any crisis, PR is always looking to manage the immediate reactions, maintaining a longer-term perspective that focuses on increasing ongoing communications with targeted populations is good practice, and contributes to a better overall outcome. Latonero and Shklovski (2011) discussed the importance of quick responses during crises, and they agreed that "the general goal of risk and crisis communication...is to inform the public of potential or current events and to persuade the public to adapt their behavior in ways that would improve health and safety" (p. 5).

Occasionally, situations require immediate damage control, in which case an appropriate set of actions must be quickly devised in order to manage the situation. In the concise and memorable words of Brigulio (2004), during times of crisis, organizations must "tell the truth, tell it all, and tell it fast." According to Shaw (2006), crisis management is:

...the coordination of efforts to control a crisis event consistent with strategic goals of an organization. Although generally associated with response, recovery and resumption of operations during and following a crisis event, crisis management responsibilities extend to prevent awareness, prevention and preparedness and post event restoration and transition (p. 66).

A longtime public relations scholar and professional leader, the late Farlow (1976), compiled almost 500 definitions for the term "public relations." From these, he then identified the major common elements in an attempt to arrive at a cohesive definition of "public relations." His resulting definition encompasses both conceptual and operational elements (Farlow, 1976). In essence, public relations can be defined as a professional field concerned with maintaining public image for high-profile people, organizations, or programs.

Public relations practitioners help others establish and maintain effective relationships with third parties. This work is usually performed through a public relations firm or an agency, independent consultants, or as a part of the communication staffs of corporations, not-for-profit organizations, or government agencies (Latimore, Baskin, Heiman, Toth & Van, 2004). To establish a holistic understanding of the public relations function, the following definition serves well (Seitel, 2004):

Public relations is a leadership and management function that helps achieve organizational objectives, define philosophy, and facilitate organizational change. Public relations practitioners communicate with all relevant internal and external public to develop positive relationships and to create consistency between organizational goals and societal expectations. Public relations practitioners develop, execute, and evaluate organizational programs that promote the exchange of influence and understanding among an organization's constituent parts and public. (p. 5)

Fearn-Banks (2007) describes a crisis as "a major occurrence with a potentially negative outcome affecting the organization, company, or industry, as well as its public, products, services, or good name. A crisis interrupts normal business transactions and can sometimes threaten the existence of the organization" (p.2). Barton (1993) defines a crisis as "a major unpredictable event that has potentially negative results" (p.2). Fink (1986) further adds that a crisis is an event that increases in intensity and is given much scrutiny by the media. Crisis management most often falls under the responsibility of an organization's public relations practitioner(s). One of the key components to handling a crisis successfully is controlling the flow of information by developing and disseminating a set of key messages to the media and the organization's public. "Staying on message" is a common term among public relations practitioners when engaging with the public or members of the media during a crisis, and it refers to the importance of maintaining control of the situation by sticking by the key messages that were established by PR before communication with the media/public regarding the crisis began (Howard & Mathews, 2000; Shin & Cameron, 2005).

RESEARCH PROBLEM

Coombs (2007) stated that crisis management is a serious organizational function. Failure can result in grave harm to stakeholders, losses for an organization, or end its very existence. Crises generally figure as negative events in an organization's developmental trajectory, ushering in many types of competition, both healthy and unhealthy. Crises have the potential to destroy livelihoods and property, and they have the capability to ruin the images of organizations and countries, as investors become skeptical and hesitant to invest. Effective public relations is crucial to overcoming crises. If an organization or country wishes to prosper during or after a crisis, it must focus on public relations during this critical time. In an age of multinational corporations where the internet reigns supreme, e-collaboration has become the standard mode for quickly dealing with major problems.

Research Goals

There are limited studies have examined PR, and particularly its role in managing crises in the UAE, because the individuals and communities there consider crises to be a sensitive issue. As a result, the involved parties are often reticent about discussing crises earnestly in their aftermath. Also, because of the difficulty in collecting the data from PR employees, researchers don't frequently attempt to investigate it. Difficulties concerning this type of research can involve police needing to withhold information for legal reasons, or the necessity of obtaining official approval to access sensitive information. This study is intended to help government officials, countries, and public and private organizations determine best practices for maintaining their images in the wake of crisis situations. It identifies the nature of crises, elucidates the significance of PR to various stakeholders during crisis management, examines how companies have handled those situations, and explores frameworks and activities to overcome crises through effective PR. In the literature review, causes of crises in the UAE are highlighted, including various methods used to overcome them. Successful and unsuccessful methods are explored, followed by proposals for the most effective PR solutions to cope with future crises.

Qualitative methods used in this study include case studies and interviews, chosen because they offered unique, qualitative perspectives from PR professionals' own opinions about challenges they have encountered in their work. Overall, respondents were cooperative and supplied answers to the questions posed, but there were still several limitations while gathering data, which are outlined below. Crossman (2017) argued that 'Qualitative research is a type of social science research that collects and works with non-numerical data and that seeks to interpret meaning from these data that help us understand social life through the study of targeted populations or places" (p.1)

A qualitative research technique—in-depth interviews—was chosen to investigate the perceptions of a limited number of respondents because significant crisis is (luckily) not a routine issue. "In-depth interviewing involves conducting intensive individual interviews to explore their perspectives on a particular idea, program, or situation"(Boyce & Neale, 2006, p. 3). Structured interviews were conducted, and respondents answered the questions both in-person and through emails. The latter option was preferred by two people, who considered the topic particularly sensitive. All the interviewees were coded and given numbers (e.g. Interviewees #5 or #6). The in-depth interviews were helpful in exploring the subjects' views, actions and behaviors and to explore more specific issues in-depth (Patton, 2002).

Most significantly, participants were quite reluctant to discuss crisis management strategies in interviews due to the fierce competitive markets in which they operate. Interviewees discussed their roles as PR practitioners, their communication tools and action plans during and after the crises appeared. Six UAE companies that have faced critical situations between 2000- 2013 were selected for case studies, and 35 PR professionals were selected from among them for face-to-face interviews. The affirmative response rate, however, was very low: 28 of the selected individuals either declined or did not respond at all. These people were between 32 and 45 years old, and held either BS or BA degrees. The companies were equally represented in the selection of 3 PR representatives each from 9 different organizations. The research questions and hypotheses addressed in this study were:

Q1: How well do PR practitioners cope with crises and their effects in UAE firms?
H1: PR practitioners in the UAE employ a specific set of management techniques to effectively manage crises that arise within organizations, and keep collateral damage to a minimum.
Q2: What strategies and approaches are most effective for restoring trust?
H2: PR firms have developed several key communication and e-collaboration strategies such as emails and text messages to deal with crises in UAE firms effectively.

This paper explores the practice of crisis management from the unique perspective of PR practitioners in the UAE. It highlights the approaches media entities undertake in times of crisis, the role PR departments play in crisis management, and the strategies PR professionals used to rebuild a company's image. The rewards companies can reap by rebuilding a positive image after facing a crisis are also discussed.

LITERATURE REVIEW

Meaning of Crises and Crisis Management?

Betts (2017) defined the what the crises is as "The critical thing is to quickly ascertain all the facts to fully understand exactly what the crisis is and what its potential impact might be. Identify the key people who might be affected and what the longer-term ramifications will be. Without this information, it is impossible to determine the best solution" (p.2).

According to Nwosu (1996), a crisis is an event of extreme difficulty or danger. This definition is equally applicable to the individual and organization, and most of us, both individually and as part of a larger organization, are likely to face a time of crisis—if not many—over the course of our lives. Black (1989) defines crisis management as a process an organization adopts to handle unexpected events that are harmful to the image, reputation, or survival of an organization. Often, a company has no specific plan prepared in advance in order to tackle such events. If an organization's history is examined carefully, it is often revealed that crises and responses to crises prompted the organization to evolve or further develop its communication plans. Few UAE universities teach crisis management; in fact, of twenty-four UAE universities, only two offer crisis management courses (Ey-Ling, 2011).

Due to advancing technology, contemporary UAE companies are handling news, information, and communication differently during crisis management. Agnes (2017) and Britton(2017) agreed that one of the best crises techniques is gain access to valuable data from individuals, businesses, and even government agencies. According to Kirat (2005), major crisis management techniques in the UAE focus on effective management of news, managing media and people, and dealing with information technologies, with the bottom line emphasis being that all media be used effectively and efficiently during crises. But PR is meant to do more than just devise strategies (Ashcroft, 1997); it is a critical organizational tool during a crisis. Effective crisis planning is important to all firms since a crisis can destroy an organization, affecting many different stakeholders negatively. Past crises suggest that PR practitioners are important during planning and restructuring of an organization's image. Crisis management consists of three phases: 1.) planning before a crisis, 2.) response to a crisis, and 3.) *separative* measures taken after a crisis.

Crisis Communication Plan

Bernstein (2016) stated that crises is "any situation that is threatening or could threaten to harm people or property, seriously interrupt business, significantly damage reputation and/or negatively impact the bottom line" (p.1) So, many plans must be done before the crises. According to Barton (2011), the best practice an organization can adapt to reduce the threat of crises is to have a plan based on the experiences of other organizations in the industry that is updated regularly. Second, a team should exist that is devoted to handling crises. Third, the team should occasionally practice theoretical crisis management so it knows what to do when a crisis occurs, much like an organization that practices evacuating a building in case of a fire. Finally, PR should have redrafted messages to deliver during a crisis, and the company's legal department should review those messages in advance in order to reduce financial losses (Banks, 2001).

The Effect of Financial Crises on UAE Companies' Reputations

Seter (2017) wrote about "How PR Crises Impact Brand Reputation", she believed that "brand reputation is incredibly important for a company's ability to succeed. To build long-term brand reputation, short-term PR strategies must be ready to be implemented at all times." (p.1). According to Thafer (2013), much like other oil-rich states in the UAE, Dubai is not only an oil-rich entity; its growth depends on tourism and other industries. It is important that Dubai maintain its image to attract new businesses after suffering from a financial crisis in 2008. If Dubai is unable to maintain its image and reputation as a hub that attracts investors worldwide, it could suffer great losses. The 2008 crisis caused a collapse in Dubai's real estate industry, and investors still remain hesitant to invest in its infrastructure, especially regarding hotel construction. Two of the negative effects of the crisis included: a) projects from

India that were delayed or abandoned, and b) the resultant surge in unemployment from those delayed/ abandoned projects, (Jain, 2012). According to Bitar (2013), areas most affected by the economic crisis are the financial, real estate, and construction sectors. Both public and private sectors took preventative measures to reestablish their reputations and manage the crisis. Some private companies reduced activities or merged with other companies to remain solvent, and for some public companies, authorities passed laws to prevent excision of investor rights. Following the crisis, companies are striving to resurrect their reputations. With the increased transparency and good corporate governance following the crisis, investors are enjoying more opportunities from the relaxing of laws that allow entrance into new markets, and diversifying risk.

Best Performs for Media Training during a Crisis

Garcia (2017) discussed the avoidance of Social Media Turbulence and PR Disasters, she wrote "during a crisis, in today's social media-driven news cycle, "you've got 15 minutes or fewer to say sorry.. **Executives** should be prepared to respond immediately when the unexpected happens." (p.2). Lerbinger (1997) argues that when an organization faces a crisis, it should never respond with the phrase "no comment" because it makes stakeholders think the organization is hiding something that, if discovered, would implicate the company or its managers. Whatever statement a PR department offers, it should be clear; statements given without clarity and containing too many technical terms result in a confused and mistrustful public (Coombs, 2007). Also, it is important that a spokesperson representing an organization during a crisis should not appear nervous; he/she should have controlled expressions and avoid nervous habits such as pacing. Statements should lack linguistic fillers such as "uhm" that reflect unpreparedness (EU Crisis Management, 2002). Finally, the PR team and its spokesperson should have access to all points and information they need in order to convey a coherent and accurate message to the public.

How to Communicate Effetely During a Crisis

Barnes & Indie Bound (2017) wrote about the effective communication tools during crises they agreed that "If the crisis is a result of a natural disaster, state of emergency or other unforeseen catastrophic event, your initial response statement should include a clear explanation of what your company is doing to manage operations, keep customers safe (both physically and digitally in terms of data) and the expected path to recovery." (p.2). Regarding a company's virtual presence, a web page should be made that is dedicated to handling the crisis (Downing, 2003). It is best to use intranets to target internal stakeholders, but the Internet should target external stakeholders. It is also a best practice to use mass notification, since it notifies all public actors simultaneously (Kent, 2007).

The Role of PR in Crisis Management

Hazarika (2016) agreed that "Public relations (PR) concerns professions working in public message shaping for the functions of communication, community relations, crisis management, customer relations, employee relations, government affairs, industry relations, investor relations, media relations, mediation, publicity, speech-writing, and visitor relations." (p. 3). According to Coombs (2007), PR's role is important during crisis management because news travels faster than anything else, and if a crisis is handled inefficiently, much is at stake. A company should defend itself as quickly as possible. The first hour following a crisis is usually the most critical, during which PR practitioners must provide an explanation for the crisis. The future of a company depends wholly on PR professionals in these moments; their choices and actions can literally make or break the company. Ideally, PR practitioners should use three steps to prevent damage from crises: a) attempt to prevent crises from happening in the first place, b) address crises before they escalate, and c) find creative ways to turn adverse situations to the company's favor. Conducting PR requires a good deal of planning; PR without planning is like running a business without a growth plan. Contemporary businesses are different from businesses of the past; they are highly exposed to the public, media, and other threats and they constantly need to maintain their images. Consequently, they must involve PR in every business decision (Ebersole, 2013).

Reputation Building After a Crisis

Shadbolt (2016) argued that reputation rebuilding related to time "It's about being quick and being confident and taking responsibility," he wrote. "Companies should not be in denial. Those that have tried to hide these things in the past have paid a much higher price in terms of loss of consumer trust." (p. 4) A crisis can threaten a company's reputation or public safety and harm both internal and external stakeholders. Commonly, the entire public suffers from crises organizations face (Kirat, 2005). Crises usually conclude with negative consequences, and PR practitioners charged with the task of improving the image or reputation of the company. Common threats crises cause include loss of reputation, capital, and safety of associated public actors. Sometimes a crisis is so extreme that it costs lives (e.g., the Tylenol contamination incident). Product harm and accidents are examples that take lives, and a company faces a shrinking market share and major lawsuits as a result (Dilenschneider, 2000). To repair a reputation after initial crisis management, public safety is the first threat a company needs to address. If public safety addressed properly, the crisis intensifies (Coombs, 2004). Financial losses and reputation-building/repairing addressed in a later stage. The role of PR during crisis management is to protect the organization and its stakeholders, and to perceive and minimize potential threats caused by crisis management (Coombs, 2007).

Response to Initial Crisis

Jorden (1993) suggests that the most effective news travels quickly and accurately, so the first hour after crisis is a crucial opportunity for PR to reach stakeholders. Care should be taken that all facts conveyed are accurate and consistent (Cohen, 1999). When there are threats of both financial loss and to public safety, public safety should be the primary concern. All available communication channels should be employed to notify stakeholders. A spokesperson should appear sympathetic toward the situation, but without appearing nervous (Dean, 2004). Internal stakeholders and external stakeholders should be kept equally informed of the situation. Employees and their families often experience post-traumatic stress after crises, so free consultation and training should be offered to help avoid further negative outcomes (Hearit, 2006).

Approaches to Repair Reputations

According to Shadbolt (2016), admitting responsibility was a vital part of the process, and the company took full responsibility on the day of the accident. If there is no evidence of a crisis and someone is accusing the organization for no apparent reason, the best repair strategy is to confront the accuser with evidence (Kellerman, 2006). During less critical situations, a spokesperson denies the allegation by stating that the media has not portrayed any such situation. A scapegoat strategy is also possible, in which PR blames someone internal or external to the organization. Crisis managers and PR practitioners sometimes use excuses, and simply apologize for events that triggered a crisis (Lerbinger, 1997). Provocation used as a repair strategy, suggesting that a crisis was inevitable and the organization had to take corrective measures in response to an unwanted event. Events also sometimes called accidents or unexpected happenings—a situation that gets out of control no matter how well the crisis was planned and managed. To save an organization's reputation, managers occasionally invent justifications for a crisis, sometimes giving the impression that losses were smaller than the actual losses realized (Tyler, 1997). A sandwich strategy occurs when a manager tells stakeholders about the good the organization has done for them, and then discusses recent negative events before closing with optimism and a promise of a better future. To minimize the effect of a crisis, victims are compensated for losses, and sometimes after admitting culpability, a PR spokesperson asks for forgiveness from the public, thereby suggesting the public and corporation are united (Ulmer, 2006).

E-Collaboration, PR and Crises Management

According to Kock and D'Arcy (2002), there are several definitions of e-collaboration one of them is collaboration using electronic technologies among different individuals to accomplish a common task. Kock (2005) defined the e-collaboration as "collaboration among individuals engaged in a common task using electronic technologies" (p. 37). Arinze (2012) believes that e-collaboration has come of age in the last decade. Communication and collaboration is no longer limited to simple electronic communication through networks and programs such as Microsoft Word (Kock, 2004). The use of electronic collaboration between institutions and individuals requires effort and continuity to achieve the goals of the enterprise through permanent contact (Nosek, 2006). According to Kock and Nosek (2005), after the telephone emerged as a communication tool in 1870, later followed by the computer, that crossover is very high cost, with the technological development and the emergence of e-mail, collaboration tools and networking computers increased use of e-mail that serve institutions in times of crisis or time shaking the institution's reputation. Therefore, Kock and Nosek (2005) find that development of new technologies and communication is very important for any institution or organizations.

Between the early 1970s and 1980s with the emergence of corporate development and public relations offices in institutions, communications increased, especially as e-mail gained thousands of users (Kock, 2005). The internet and e-mail serve not only as a tool for communication, but they are the fastest tool for strengthening communication and restoring the reputations of institutions during times of crisis. According to Kock (2008a), with the increase in the scope of coverage and the growing number of public institutions, each institution have evolved means of electronic communication

Kock and DeLuca (2007). In their article *improving business processes electronically: An action research study in New Zealand and the US*, the authors discussed a study and analyzed a case study done by Munkvold, who published an article titled "Experiences from global e-collaboration: Contextual influences on technology adoption and use. "In the article, he wrote about the experiences of several organizational communication methods and the importance of e-collaboration. Munkvold studied the use of technology in the electronic collaboration of two large, globally-recognized companies. It was found that the correlation between implementation of the organizational success depended on the successful implementation of global e-collaboration, especially in alignment with existing collaborative work practices.. In other research conducted by Gallivan and Benbunan-Fich (2005) entitled "A framework for the analysis of the analysis of issues in studies of electronic collaboration levels," the researchers analyzed a range of issues using a multilevel approach and 63 experimental studies on e-collaborations. They found that most empirical studies have focused on the importance of electronic communication in organizations and cooperative groups to achieve the objectives of each institution, such as a joint collaboration between groups and individuals with communication and collaborative technology.

Arinze (2012) argued that researchers need to be aware of the importance of electronic collaboration. He believes that many of the issues related to e-collaboration are vague and need to discuss interpretations and analysis of institutional challenges such as conflicts, crisis managements, recruitment of staff and means of communication in resolving crises. Many of the phenomena related to electronic collaborations are still vague and need to be clarified through experimental, theoretical, and academic research studies.

Kock (2008b) mentioned that the research inevitably and active researches make a means of communication, and has a scientific value and benefits that outweigh the costs. In many cases, companies in times of crisis are using e-collaborations to promote, resort, and diversify the means of communication, ensuring that they reach the target audience, whereupon using collaborative communication to support group communication inside institutions such as e-mail and instant messages to bulletin boards on the Internet, and other means such as teleconferencing, and systems management the supply chain.

It can be said one of the most widely used computer today's applications, is the cooperation of electronic technology, which aims to support forms a quick and relatively simple communications. Certain electronic collaboration techniques more oriented support complex communication and decision-making, such as a group decision support system. Other electronic collaboration technologies between the various departments involved in the production and delivery of goods and services (Kock, 2008, p.1).

Kock (2005) and Arinze (2012) debated the importance of cooperative communication PR crisis management such as practitioners of public relations and their need for electronic communication facilities of different cooperative types like dealing with publics. In this study, for example, there is no center or institution without the unity of public relations, such as cases in this study like IKEA or the global village and Damas in the United Arab Emirates, which used means of communication and electronic communication. Kock (2005) believes that the research, the use of questionnaires, survey research and the study of the behavior of the public towards a particular commodity in times of crisis complements the use of means of communication in order to reach the public in a timely manner, as happened with IKEA in the UAE. Especially when the company used the posters and advertisements published in on-line networks to solve the crises that they face and announced not to be used for horses meat where the non-Muslim communities don't eat this kind of meat. Overall, public relations does not dispense with the electronic means of communication in any organization, especially profitability by it seeks to raise its image and reputation through the promotion of e-mails and text. This can only be done by means of collaborative communication. In summary, e- collaboration theory associated with practitioners of public relations who strive to save the image of the institution in times of crisis find e-collaboration to be an ideal way to reach the most segments of society.

METHOD

This paper uses a case study approach, an appropriate method for examining in-depth how UAE companies rebuild their reputations after crises (Feagin, Orum, & Sjoberg, 1991). When multiple cases are examined, such as in this study, it is called a collective case study approach (Yin, 1993). A case study is usually based on an example, a holistic understanding of context, analysis of a problem, and sometimes proposed solutions. Case study analysis is qualitative because the focus is on achieving thick descriptions (Stake, 2006). The cases in this study were selected not only to describe places and people, but also to analyze interpretations subjects hold concerning a complex context. Relativity was constructed between practitioners and cases, especially to answer "why" and "how" questions in a complex context (Yin, 2005). Six cases were considered, chosen especially since they contained issues (e.g., crises) that aid in building explanatory theories and methodologies. All cases dealt with crises and an organization forced to cope with not only the crisis, but also rebuilding its reputation in the wake of it.

When all research in a field suggests the same findings, it is usually referred to as a case study, not a type of sampling research like a survey study. In this scenario, the researcher used six UAE companies to formulate hypotheses and discover what each company did to rebuild its reputation after facing a crisis. Benefits of case studies are that they are selective and focus on only one or two issues, which in this case is rebuilding image and reputation, and outlining the varying systems used for crisis management. Analysis of published news in some local newspapers in the UAE were cited and analyzed such as the National, CBC, Gulf News, and Emirates newspapers.

Interviews with PR professionals from within the organizations that faced the crises were collected in the research process for this paper. The case study method was used because it helps organizations learn directly from the experiences of other organizations—i.e. it helps in devising crisis management plans before a crisis actually occurs. In-depth interview analysis was used to explore how organizations deal with crises.

Instrument

A structured interview guide was developed and followed. All questions were open-ended, and prompting was used to gain additional responses and insights from the subjects, who were all crisis-management managers and PR spokespersons. All content included in the guide was related to the role PR plays during crisis management. Various methods were used to conduct the interviews, including telephone interviews, face-to-face interviews, and e-mail exchanges. The highest response rate and most valuable insights were gathered from e-mail conversations. Data were collected from seventeen organizations, including hospitals, municipalities, and banks as well as companies. The first interviews were with people employed in the analyzed local case studies, such as IKEA and Freij Entertainment. Because of the sensitive nature of the topic, respondents were not entirely cooperative and open, but the researcher used many published articles in the local newspaper to analyze the case studies. The comments of these respondents were included in the case studies analysis sections. The second set of interviews were with PR people in local hospitals, banks, and municipalities including AlFardan exchange, Dubai Islamic Bank, Saderat Iran Bank, National Bank of Abudhabi, AlAin, AlNoor and Tawam hospitals, Al Ain and Abu Dhabi municipality. Twenty-six subjects were interviewed face-to-face, but others preferred to reply through email due to the sensitive nature of the topic. Sixteen females and twelve males between

30 and 55 years of age were interviewed. Of those subjects, twenty interviewees held bachelor's degrees and 8 other people had a diploma.

Validity and Reliability of the Instrument

The interview guide was pilot tested on sample respondents to ensure the appropriateness of the questions and the secondary probing questions were designed around yes/no answers to ensure instrument reliability. The interview guide was prepared by considering oral interviews since they offer in-depth insights. All statements were neutral so they would not lead respondents to answer a certain way. The instrument was tested and retested on various samples until all respondents understood its content similarly.

IKEA

Ikea is a Swedish company founded by Ingvar Kamprad in 1926. It is known for producing high-quality products at low prices, and it operates in forty countries globally. The IKEA horse meat scandal nearly ruined the company's reputation, but PR tactics saved the company. The Swedish meatball scandal began in February 2013. Horse DNA was found in packets marked as pork and beef. The scandal originated in Sweden, and the meat was supplied to thirteen countries. As soon as the controversy began, the company pulled its stock from twenty-one countries to ensure public safety and company reputation (Masudi, 2013). IKEA believed meat supplied to the UAE was *halal*, coming from Arabic origin instead of Sweden, so there was no threat of horse meat contamination in that country. To satisfy its customers, IKEA sent the meat to laboratories in Abu Dhabi for further testing, proving the meat supplied to the UAE was free from the controversy that had arisen in Sweden (DuBois, 2013).

After the controversy, the company's popularity decreased, and the company now monitors popularity figures daily. IKEA isolated the scandal to one area and mitigated its effects in other areas by sending products to local labs for testing, helping the company reduce the scope of the crisis (Kavoussi, 2013). Also, IKEA PR practitioners capitalized on e-collaboration methods like sending messages to publics through media and newspapers. IKEA markets itself as an economy seller, and some people believed it was trying to reduce costs by selling horse meat. The company stated that the problem stemmed from lack of supervision at the supplier's end, and immediately cancelled orders of meatballs and sausages from the same supplier to demonstrate the company's integrity to its customers. Stock suspected of being infected was pulled from stores worldwide, and although the action resulted in short-term losses, it ultimately restored customer loyalty so consumers felt safe returning to IKEA for food. A senior manager in the UAE indicated, "We took this matter very seriously when the issue happened. The meatballs recalled in other IKEA stores came from another supplier. The meatballs we serve here [the UAE] in IKEA are specially made for us. They all came from Saudi which is a different supplier [than the one] who had the issue. To avoid (sic., appease) loyal customers, we requested certification from our supplier for the meat origin. Thus, it's ensured that it's beef of origin as expected" (Personal Communication, January, 2014).

Public safety and sympathy for customers figured more importantly than profit for IKEA during the crisis, proved by its strict measures (News, 2013). Public perception is important, and it was important that the company take responsibility and remedy the crisis. The scapegoat strategy (blaming the supplier for the initial problem) places culpability where it belongs. It consoles the public, and shifts negative perceptions to other entities more directly responsible for the breach in trust, while effectively dodging the issue of Ikea's ultimate responsibility for quality assurance from its suppliers. Public safety should be given prime importance because breaches of it are capable of inflicting the most severe and lasting type of damage to a company's reputation. News and television are the most important media to manage during crisis, and companies must be sure to hear and address public and consumer concerns before communicating sympathy.

FREIJ ENTERTAINMENT

Another example comes with Freij, the world's largest outdoor entertainment provider, which originated in Europe in 1987. It's a part of the Global Village, which is the region's leading family outdoor cultural and entertainment destination and one of Dubai's most unique tourism and cultural destinations. The theme park offers a variety of multicultural entertainment and retail options. It specializes in amusement rides, outdoor events, circuses, travel, and other forms of entertainment. The company diversified its operations worldwide, and one of its hubs in the Middle East is located in Dubai. It was the first entertainment company to provide mobile rides in the UAE, and its rides are renowned for reliability since the company upgrades and maintains them constantly.

Despite a good reputation for safety, Freij suffered a crisis in January 2013 when an iron rod fell from the Ferris wheel in Dubai Global Village. The event would not have been an issue, but unfortunately the rod fell on the head of a visitor, causing instant death. This was a critical situation because it is the primary duty of every organization to ensure public safety in the environment in which they operate. As an immediate response, all rides owned by Freij entertainment were closed. Two men testified that they told the operator about the fault, but he did nothing to prevent the accident. The wheel continued to operate for thirty minutes after the incident, and it took approximately two hours to unload all of the riders (Subaihi, 2013). To manage the crisis, the people responsible for the event were arrested immediately, and all rides were closed. The company admitted its fault, apologized to the public, and participated in the investigation; it did not place blame elsewhere. New work-process and ride-maintenance policies were passed, and in the future, rides would be evaluated more frequently and complaints about rides from customers would be handled more efficiently (Emirates247, 2013). Freij communicated openly with the media so that they knew the facts, helping to align media with the company, and thereby the public. The marketing mentioned that "the crises supporters are Bur Dubai Police Station at Global Village and the Dubai Municipality underwent thorough investigation and handled the situation, as they are hand-in-hand with The Global Village" (Personal Communication, March, 2014). After calling the marketing manager of The Global Village, he assured that the crisis had not affected the number of visitors they have per season because the theme park has a variety of facilities as the incident only happened at the games' area, and occurred due to the "will of god." The Global Village tried to enhance information and launched new promotion by using e-collaboration. The website of the village has listed new services for the year 2013-2014, for example:

- Bigger and exciting entertainment acts for families
- Dancing fountain (including fire, sound, light)
- Customized décor and lighting
- New information booths

- New food court
- New gates with new exciting themes
- Enhancement on public toilets

"After seeing these enhancements on the website, it occurred that these are the actions that were taken after the incident had occurred to entice future and existing audiences" (Personal Communication, March, 2014). The company apologized and asked for forgiveness because if it had not, people would have boycotted the product. The Freij case study offers several insights into effective crisis management. Since public safety is the primary concern, financial losses should not be projected or discussed when interfacing with the public. The victim's family should be compensated to earn respect from stakeholders. Companies should avoid media pollution and fill communication gaps where needed. Therefore, companies must use different types of e-collaboration tools to solve crises, such as texting and emailing customers and stakeholders.

DAMAS

Damas is a leading jewelry brand in the Middle East (Damas, 2013). The company operates in more than six countries, with approximately 240 retail outlets. The company also deals in valuable watches. The group originated in Syria, and has been in business since 1900. The company bases its target audience according to demographics. Damas operated only in the UAE until it decided to go global with its brand name in 2000. Practices and systems within the organization were both opaque and corrupt: officials took money from the organization's accounts for personal use, promising to return the borrowed money, but never following through. This sparked questions regarding the integrity of the company, and stakeholders began losing faith. Due to fraud, the share price of Damas decreased 13.5% in the UAE. The organization shifted from private to public ownership, after which it was discovered that there was confusion or accusation about the disclosure of the theft of money to stakeholders. To demonstrate good faith to stakeholders and to show that the business could operate normally after facing a financial crisis, the brothers who held the company were fined and banned by the government from exercising executive roles (Complinet, 2010).

An external audit was conducted to remedy all financial flaws as soon as the theft was discovered. Officials who were indicted were replaced in order to restore the faith of stakeholders. Business was backed by heavy investments, and funds were returned to help normal operations and work, such as repairing the company image and improving the e-collaboration methods and communication. The company cooperated with officials to unveil the facts, and later communicated those facts to the public once they were confirmed by authorities. People still trust the company and continue to buy Damas' products. The brothers were punished—a lesson for the entire business community—and they suffered this fate because they were unable to communicate at multiple levels effectively (Hope, 2009). Instead of communicating at one level, PR practitioners should communicate to all levels so everyone receives the same message. Building a positive image is advantageous, but PR must not confuse image and reality in the minds of consumers. A company should give consumers what it promises because false commitments can be more damaging than none at all, thereby tarnishing an organization's reputation. Proactive approaches and planning are paramount, but they cannot prevent or save a company from crisis. The

Damas case study suggests that PR professionals would be well-served to plan for the worst, cater to the genuine concerns of customers, not wait until the crises increase, and demonstrate an organization's humane side to consumers.

INTERVIEW ANALYSIS

Significance of Organization Reputation

In a world where information represents knowledge and power, reputation is everything to an organization. In the words of one respondent, "A good reputation earns loyal customers and ushers huge investment opportunities for stakeholders, and a bad reputation can ruin an organization" (Interviewee #3, 2014). A company's goodwill depends on reputation, which is paramount to being awarded contracts and negotiating mergers and acquisitions; a bad reputation means total loss. "Public actors, stakeholders, employees, and investors benefit from the stability of a company" (Interviewee #5, 2014). If a company is unstable, or if PR does not communicate stability, growth and profit are impossible. PR communicates products to customers and creates a path to government and legislation. It enhances the image of a company and thus increases production by attracting opportunities, customers, and reducing the effects of recession. Ten interviewees agreed that a company's positive reputation stems from honesty and trust. For instance, "Sending true information is the first step to build the company reputation" (Interviewee #13, 2014). Interviewee #18 added that "answering the people during crises and providing them with accurate information is another step." In summary, most interviewees agreed that communication and trust are the foundation of a company's reputation, and that e-collaboration is the most efficient means of coordinating efforts across a company to create and execute a plan to preserve a company's reputation during times of crisis.

Public Relations Practitioners Rolls During a Crisis

During a crisis, PR practitioners must enhance corporate image and turn adverse situations into opportunities. They must also increase awareness of products and services, communicate flaws and achievements, and introduce gatekeepers to control the flow of information. One interviewee expressed, "The approach of every PR practitioner must be transparent and professional because PR is superior to marketing regarding branding an organization and its products" (Interviewee #11, 2014). Organizations invest in a good PR team because they need to communicate internal happenings to stakeholders and develop two-way communication between managers and the public; PR bridges the gap between suppliers and buyers. The e-collaboration is one of the main priorities of the PR practitioners such as using website and social media to inform and communicate with public. As one interviewee stated, "news and information are communicated to external actors through a reliable PR team" (Interviewee #1, 2014). Eight interviewees agreed that PR practitioners are responsible for problem solving and securing customer satisfaction. Interviewee #6 provided the example of refunding the customer for bad services as being a helpful step in resolving a crisis.

Rewards for Developing a Positive Organizational Image

When the PR practitioners were asked about the rewards they receive when they achieve their goals, most reported that they are rewarded with leaves, and in extreme cases, the promise of promotions with fringe benefits. Both intrinsic and extrinsic reward systems are common in organizations. "Some organizations compensate better monetarily, and others focus on recognition and appreciation," one interviewee stated (Interviewee #27, 2014). High-level PR practitioners may gain more access to top managers and are sometimes offered shares in the company. On the other hand, most of the interviewees mentioned that they believe there is discrimination between them and Western professionals in the same field, since local professionals are rarely promoted. Interviewee #23 said "I was working all the time during events and emergencies and I did not get even an overtime." Overall, PR practitioners seem unsatisfied with the rewards and there is no encouragement for employees during crises. But still they report that they enjoy their work despite the unfair treatment inside the companies.

Principles to Measure Firm Reputation

Standards developed by PR practitioners to measure reputation (good or bad) of their organizations include whether stakeholders and the organization have low interactivity and feel distant, suggesting firm reputation is at-risk. For instance, "If a firm's e-collaboration, communication strategy is transparent, honest, and clear, and people enjoy socializing, the company can assume a good reputation both in and out of the firm" (Interviewee#24, 2014). Some respondents believed market share and awareness of a firm are indicators. Cumulative indicators are used sometimes to measure awareness, customer satisfaction, and brand image. One respondent reported that "if the majority—say eighty percent—of customers are satisfied, a company has a good reputation" (Interviewee #15, 2014). 11 interviewees mentioned that surveying people and filling online responses are types of measurement but that the public is generally uninterested in participating. Respondents felt that "the solution is coming through face-to-face communication and using e-collaboration techniques"(Interviewee #14, 2014), increment of subscribers" (Interviewee #8, 2014), and demand of services which increase the companies' income (Interviewee #15, 2014).

Crisis Examples Relevant to Company Image

Two respondents believed they had not faced full-blown crises due to their rigid and regularly updated crisis management programs. One respondent from a municipality reported that "sometimes a customer must visit a new building because the old building is having technological issues" (Interviewee #19, 2014). Companies usually try to overcome small problems to enhance their image by addressing customer complaints and maintaining infrastructures. Also, crises spread when the customers create scandals such as "other customers get benefits and we are not" (Interviewee #3, 2014). Five interviewees agreed that there is no company or organization free of struggles and crises and that these challenges may create opportunities for success for companies.

Tactical Planning During a Crisis

Some processes defined by respondents regarding strategic planning during a crisis include handling complaints effectively and efficiently, without delays. Standard pre-made communication messages must be drafted and approved by legal departments, systems must be kept honest and transparent, and errors must be admitted and rectified as soon as possible. For instance, one respondent stated that "avoiding rumors and improving interactions among departments are some good strategies" (Interviewee #22, 2014). In contrast, other interviewees were unaware of whether their organizations had a crisis management program. Two respondents mentioned that planning and taking action as soon as possible will eliminate the problem. However another interviewee said that "planning needs time and taking the action and refunding the people be the fastest way." He added that the international financial crises affected Dubai and that many managers left the country. When customers asked for refunds, no action was taken and people went to the courts without seeing any other solution.

IMPLICATION TO THEORY

Karl Marx's structural conflict theory provides some useful insights into crisis management. The theory suggests that the structure and organization of society leads to conflicts and crises, arising when organizations compete for scarce resources (Ademola, 2007). Sources of crises include poverty, oppression, injustices, shirking responsibilities, exploitation, and exclusion, and crises occur in society due to class oppression and unjust behaviors from other entities. The theory implies that competing benefits and interests of multiple groups influence economic and social settings (Oyekola, 1995). The theory also proposes that economic and social-setting disruptions cause crises in both societies and organizations. Every organization competes for resources, and resources appear at the core of crises. While obtaining resources, crises are inevitable, but the fittest have learned and developed crisis-management strategies to survive adverse conditions. When equilibrium in society is not maintained, critical situations arise, especially when there is power and abundance on one end and adversity on the other end (Kothari, 1979). To develop crisis-management strategies, companies must understand both the nature of conflict and factors that contribute to crises. The structural theory of conflict defines and explains both a framework for crisis management and how PR practitioners can address conflicts and crises. The theory suggests that during a crisis, how stakeholders perceive a company's reputation and how PR manages the crisis determine whether a company will be able to salvage its reputation.

RESULTS

To answer the research questions, the researcher find that the theory of E-collaboration which discusses in Kock (2008a) and Kock (2005) is closely related to the subject of research and crises in public relations. Kock, Davison, Ocker, and Wazlawick (2001) argued that there is a need of e-collaboration in the business and research fields. Therefore, all the staff of public relations who interviewed in this study resort to the use of means of communication and focus on them in times of crisis and in particular e-collaboration and communication cooperative such as the use of web pages and to respond to what is published in newspapers, as has happened in IKEA when it was published the news of the sale shop for horse meat. The shop staff were informing the public credibly news as soon as possible, they also diversify the means of communication such as telephone answering and interviews in the newspapers. And the credibility of practitioners of public relations researcher finds that a lot of companies dims some of the facts in times of crisis and in particular the bad news that harm the institution, as happened in the global village and Damas, where they did not respond to the researcher permanently and refused to give their opinion about the crisis, such as "the researcher must contact the police station and get approval to investigate the crises " while many local newspaper published their crises such as *The National.* The researcher finds that credibility is the foundation of the institution and the institutions of freedom to express an opinion and not to intimidate the public relations practitioners to show that the statements being kept from the institution and spread rumors. When the disappearance of the facts, for example, the global village or Damas spread misinformation and bad news will be traded, creating another crisis. Kock and Antunes (2007), in their article *Government Funding of E-Collaboration Research in the European Union: A Comparison with the United States Model,* discussed that true and strong e-collaboration is supporting and increasing the success of organizations like what happen in European Union when some companies and government area about the e-collaboration, it increased its funding.

When examining the hypotheses, the researcher finds that the first hypothesis, a

- **H1:** PR practitioners in the UAE employ a specific set of management techniques to effectively manage crises that arise within organizations, and keep collateral damage to a minimum.

Hypothesis is positive, the public relations staff have the control and management of public relations by using different types of communication strategies like posters, announcements and advertisements but does not circulate on all in IKEA and found solutions to positive and positive. Therefore, the administration in companies that dims the information problems are exacerbated by not publishing or announcing transparency and accuracy full information about crises.

For the second hypothesis:

- **H2:** PR firms have developed several key communication and e-collaboration strategies to deal with crises in UAE firms effectively.

The researcher finds that it is a positive hypothesis: search results emphasize the use of several tools and methods and means of communication. As suggested in several of the case studies and interviews with PR practitioners, PR should immediately engage television, social media, and other news media in order to communicate transparently and begin to re-build an organization's image. In connecting the literature review with the results, according to Bitar (2013), finance, real estate, and construction industries have been heavily impacted by economic crises. However, it is evident from the case studies and interview analysis that PR firms are dealing effectively with crises in UAE firms. In addition, PR firms have developed effective strategies to deal with crises similar to those faced by firms such as IKEA, Freij, and Damas and these best practices will continue to shape corporate success in the future. Knock (2008) mentioned that "this will, in turn, lead to technological improvements that will eventually make e-collaboration through virtual worlds attractive as the benefits of e-collaboration outweigh the costs "(P. 7). Also, Knock, 2008 argued that strength communication tools is one of the main issues that led to increase the power of entertainment and business purposes "and a corresponding growing interest from researchers in the impact of virtual worlds on e-collaboration behavior and outcomes" (Kock, p. 1, 2008).

As mentioned by the interviewees, e-collaboration is a necessary tool for PR practitioners, also (Kock, 2006) agreed that tasks and community engagement will create success. Because of the main role of PR people be to connect their workplaces with the community, they have specific plans and tasks like dealing with crises and following administrative orders in order to solve crises by using different technologies and communication tools.

DISCUSSION

PR plays a critical role during crisis management. With skill, advance planning, and proper execution, PR teams have the potential to turn adverse situations to their favor and build a company's reputation that would otherwise be irrevocably tarnished. As suggested by Karl Marx's structural conflict theory, if a crisis is handled improperly, a company's reputation can be gravely compromised. The loss of a company's reputation, e-collaboration may be followed by loss of public opinion, sales, and investment opportunities. Common sources of crises include natural disasters, ineffective complaint handling, low-quality products, non-sympathetic behaviors toward stakeholders, lack of interaction, lack of resources, and increasing competition.

The case studies in this article strongly support that PR practitioners may play a key role in resolving crises, but to do so they must be involved in e-collaboration, communicating effective messages to the media and public. PR practitioners should not delay assignation of blame. Rather, they should confront crises head-on, convey clear messages, and be cooperative with any authorities investigating the matter. As Mausdi (2013) explains regarding the IKEA case, as soon as the controversy arose, the company pulled stock from twenty-one countries in order to ensure public safety and protect the company's reputation. This earned generally favorable views from the public that benefitted the firm in the long-run.

As suggested in several of the case studies, PR should immediately engage e-collaboration, television, social media, and other news media in order to communicate transparently and begin to re-build an organization's image. According to Bitar (2013), finance, real estate, and construction industries have been heavily impacted by economic crises. However, it is evident from the case studies and interview analysis that PR firms are dealing effectively with crises in UAE firms. On the whole, PR firms have developed effective strategies to deal with crises similar to those faced by firms such as IKEA, Freij, and Damas and these best practices will continue to shape corporate success in the future.

LIMITATIONS OF THE STUDY

This study qualitatively determines the significance of PR during crisis management regarding various stakeholders, identification of the nature of a crisis, how companies handled crises in the past, and what PR strategies are most effective in overcoming crises in the age of e-collaboration and new media. In the literature review, previous causes of crises in the UAE are highlighted, including methods employed by PR departments during a crisis. Analysis of successful and unsuccessful methods used to handle crises are highlighted, followed by a proposal of PR best practices regarding crisis management. The study is covering managing crises, e-collaboration and public relation in the UAE which considered a sensitive topic. Information regarding the topic is hardly collected after assuring the employees that their names are anonymous. Few studies were published about PR in general but there is no study published in the UAE about crises managements, e-collaboration and PR roles. However, the cases covered international companies in the UAE such as IKEA, Damas and one local company which is the Global village. Future researches can focus on crises in the private or public sectors in the local places in the UAE and effectiveness of e-collaboration in the PR departments. Researchers are advised to get formal approval to interview employees to collect this sensitive topic.

QUESTIONS FOR SCHOLARS AND STUDENTS

1. What are the main causes of crises in organizations?
2. What is the main role of PR practitioners cope with crises and their effects in firms?
3. Write about the main management techniques of PR practitioners in that arise within organizations, and keep collateral damage to a minimum?
4. What strategies and approaches are most effective for restoring trust?
5. Discuss the PR key communication and e-collaboration strategies to deal with crises in effectively?

REFERENCES

Ademola, F. S. (2007). Theories of social conflict in best, 5.An Edited Introduction to Peace and Conflict Studies in. Ibadan: Spectrum Books limited.

Agnes, M. (2017). *3 Important Crisis Management Trend Projections For 2017*. Retrieved on January, 2018, from https://www.forbes.com/sites/melissaagnes/2017/01/11/3-important-crisis-management-trend-projections-for-2017/#39d5a22663e0

Arinze, B. (2012). E-Research Collaboration in Academia and Industry. *International Journal of e-Collaboration*, *8*(2), 1–13. doi:10.4018/jec.2012040101

Ashcroft, L. S. (1997). Crisis Management - Public Relations. *Journal of Managerial Psychology*, *12*(5), 325–332. doi:10.1108/02683949710183522

Banks, K. F. (2001). *Crisis Communications: A case Book Approach 2nd Edi*. Mahwah, NJ: Lawrence Erlbaum.

Barnes, A., & Indie Bound, N. (2017). *How to Communicate Effectively During a Crisis*. Retrieved on January, 2018, from https://www.entrepreneur.com/article/290446

Barton, L. (2011). *Crisis in Organizations II* (2nd ed.). Cincinnati, OH: College Divisions South-Western.

Bernstein, J. (2016). *The 10 Steps of Crisis Communications*. Retrieved on January 31, 2018, from https://www.bernsteincrisismanagement.com/the-10-steps-of-crisis-communications/

Betts, K. (2017). *Crisis management for entrepreneurs: how to deal with PR disasters*. Retrieved on January, 2018, from https://www.theguardian.com

Black, S. (1989). *Introduction to Public Relations*. West African Book Publishers Ltd.

Boyce, C., & Neale, B. (2006). *Conducting In-depth Interviews: A Guide for Designing and Conducting In-Depth Interviews for Evaluation Input*. Pathfinder International.

Briguglio, P. (2004). *Crisis Management: A White Paper*. Retrieved on August, 2013, from MMI Public Relations: http://www.mmipublicrelations.com/white/paper/crisis-management-a-white-paper/

Britton, C. (2017). *Crisis Management Planning in 2017: 3 Emerging Threats*. Retrieved on January 31, 2018, from https://www.rockdovesolutions.com/blog/crisis-management-planning-in-2017-3-emerging-threats

Cohen, J. R. (1999). Advising Clients to Apologize. California Law Review, 129-131.

Complinet. (2010). *DFSA Takes Action Over Damas Failures*. Thomson Reuters.

Coombs, W. T. (2004). Structuring Crisis Discourse Knowledge: The West Pharmaceutics Case. *Public Relations Review*, 467–474. doi:10.1016/j.pubrev.2004.08.007

Coombs, W. T. (2007). *Crisis Management and Communications*. Institute of PR.

Coombs, W. T. (2007). Ongoing Crisis Communication: Planning, Managing, and Responding. Academic Press.

Coombs, W. T. (2007). Protecting Organization Reputations During a Crisis: The Development and Application of Situational Crisis Communication Theory. *Corporate Reputation Review*, 1–14.

Crossman, A. (2017). *An Overview of Qualitative Research Methods*. Retrieved on January 31, 2018 from https://www.thoughtco.com/qualitative-research-methods-3026555

Damas. (2013). *About Damas*. Retrieved on August 31, 2013, from Damas: http://www.damasjewel.com/articledisplay.aspx?mid=33&id=25

Dean, D. H. (2004). Consumer Reaction to Negative Publicity: Effects of Corporate Reputation, Response, And Responsibility For a Crisis Event. *Journal of Business Communication*, *41*(2), 192–211. doi:10.1177/0021943603261748

Dilenschneider, R. L. (2000). *The Corporate Communications Bible: Everything you Need to Know to Become a Public Relations Expert*. Beverly Hills, CA: New Millennium.

Downing, J. R. (2003). American Airlines' Use of Mediated Employee Channels After the 9/11 Attacks. *Public Relations Review*, 37–48.

DuBois, S. (2013). *How IKEA Can Get Back On The Horse After a Meat Scandal*. Retrieved on September 01, 2013, from CNN Money: http://management.fortune.cnn.com/2013/02/26/ikea-horsemeat/

Ebersole, G. (2013). *The Importance of Public Relations and Crisis Management Planning To Your Business*. Retrieved on September 1, 2013, from Crisis Management: http://www.crisistraining.net/crisis-media-training_workshops_The-Importance-of-Public-Relations-and-Crisis-Management-Planning-To-Your-Business.htm

Emirates247. (2013). *Global-village Rides Closed After Visitors Death Arrested*. Retrieved on September 1, 2013, from Emirates 247: http://www.emirates247.com/news/emirates/global-village-rides-closed-after-visitor-s-death-3-arrested-2013-01-26-1.492484

EU Crisis Management and Conflict Prevention. (2002). *Guidelines on Fact-Finding Missions Col 15461/02*. Author.

Ey-Ling, S. (2011). Practice Analysis: Professional Competencies and Work Categories in Public Relations Today. *Public Relations Review*, 187–196.

Feagin, J., Orum, A., & Sjoberg, G. (1991). *A Case for Case Study*. Chapel Hill, NC: University of North Carolina Press.

Fearn-Banks, K. (2007). *Crisis Communications: A Casebook Approach* (3rd ed.). Mahwah, NJ: Lawrence Erlbaum.

Fink, S. (1986). *Crisis Management: Planning For The Inevitable*. New York: AMACOM.

Gallivan, M. J., & Benbunan-Fich, R. (2005). A Framework for Analyzing Levels of Analysis Issues in Studies of E-Collaboration. *IEEE Transactions on Professional Communication*, *48*, 87–104.

Garcia, M. (2017). *Avoiding Social Media Turbulence and PR Disasters: Airline CEOs Speak Out on Crisis Communications*. Retrieved January 30, 2018, from https://apex.aero/2017/06/09/avoiding-social-media-turbulence-pr-disasters-airline-ceos-crisis-communications

Hazarika, B. (2016). *The Role of PR in Crisis Management*. Retrieved February 1st, 2018, from http://www.dsc.edu.in/the-role-of-pr-in-crisis-management/

Hearit, K. M. (2006). *Crisis Management By Apology: Corporate Response to Allegations of Wrongdoing*. Lawrence Erlbaum Associates.

Hope, T. G. (2009). *Damas Says It Must Restructure, Delay Debt Payments to Survive*. Retrieved August 30, 2013, from The National: http://www.thenational.ae/business/banking/damas-says-it-must-restructure-delay-debt-payments-to-survive

Howard, C., & Mathews, W. K. (2000). *On Deadline: Managing Media Relations* (3rd ed.). Lone Grove, IL: Waveland Press.

Jennex, M. E. (2004). Emergency Response Systems: The Utility Y2K Experience. *Journal of Information Technology Theory and Application*, *6*(3), 85–102.

Jorden, C. (1993). Prepare for Business-Related Crises. *The Public Relations Journal*, 34–35.

Kavoussi, B. (2013). *Ikea Horse Meat Controversy Hurts Company's Reputation: Analysis*. The Huffington Post.

Kellerman, B. (2006). When Should a Leader Apologize and When Not? *Harvard Business Review*, 73–81. PMID:16579415

Kent, M. T. (2007). Taxonomy of mediated crisis responses. *Public Relations Review*, 140–146.

Kirat, M. (2005). Public relations practice in the Arab World: A critical assessment. *Public Relations Review*, *31*(3), 323–332. doi:10.1016/j.pubrev.2005.05.016

Kirat, M. (2006). Public relations in the United Arab Emirates. *Public Relations Review*, *32*(3), 254–260. doi:10.1016/j.pubrev.2006.05.006

Kock, N. (2004). The Psychobiological Model: Toward a New Theory of Computer-Mediated Communication Based on Darwinian Evolution. *Organization Science*, *15*(3), 327–348. doi:10.1287/orsc.1040.0071

Kock, N. (2005). What is E-collaboration? *International Journal of e-Collaboration*, *1*(1), i–vii.

Kock, N. (2006). Car Racing and Instant Messaging: Task Constraints as Determinants of E-Collaboration Technology Usefulness. *International Journal of e-Collaboration*, *2*(2), i–v.

Kock, N. (2008). E-Collaboration and E-Commerce in Virtual Worlds: The Potential of Second Life and World of Warcraft. *International Journal of e-Collaboration*, *4*(3), 1–13. doi:10.4018/jec.2008070101

Kock, N., & Antunes, P. (2007). Government Funding of E-Collaboration Research in the European Union: A Comparison with the United States Model. *International Journal of e-Collaboration*, *3*(2), 36–47. doi:10.4018/jec.2007040103

Kock, N., & D'Arcy, J. (2002). Resolving the E-collaboration Paradox: The Competing Influences of Media Naturalness and Compensatory Adaptation. *Inform. Manage. Consulting*, *17*(4), 72–78.

Kock, N., Davison, R., Ocker, R., & Wazlawick, R. (2001). E-collaboration: A look at Past Research and Future Challenges. *Journal of Systems and Information Technology*, *5*(1), 1–9. doi:10.1108/13287260180001059

Kock, N., & DeLuca, D. (2007). Improving Business Processes Electronically: An action Research Study in New Zealand and the US. *Journal of Global Information Technology Management*, *10*(3), 6–27. doi:10.1080/1097198X.2007.10856447

Kock, N., & Nosek, J. (2005). Expanding the Boundaries of E-Collaboration, IEEE *Transactions on Professional Communication. Special Issue on Expanding the Boundaries of E-Collaboration*, *48*(1), 1–9.

Kothari, R. (1979). *The North-South Issue*. Mazingria, No 10.

Latimore, D., Baskin, O., Heiman, S., Toth, E., & Van, J. (2004). *Public Relations: The Profession and the Practice*. New York: McGraw-Hill.

Latonero, M., & Shklovski, I. (2011). Emergency Management, Twitter, and Social Media Evangelism. *International Journal of Information Systems for Crisis Response and Management*, *3*(4), 1–16. doi:10.4018/jiscrm.2011100101

Lerbinger, O. (1997). *The Crisis Manager: Facing Risk and Responsibility*. Lawrence Erlbaum.

Masudi, F. (2013). *Meatballs on Menu Are Halal*. Retrieved on September 01, 2013, from Gulf News: http://gulfnews.com/news/gulf/uae/general/meatballs-on-menu-are-halal-ikea-says-1.1152651

News, C. (2013). *Horsemeat Found in Ikea Meatballs in Europe*. Retrieved on September 1, 2013, from CBC NEWS World: http://www.cbc.ca/news/world/story/2013/02/25/horse-meat-ikea-meat-balls.html

Nwosu, I. E. (1996). Mass Media and African War. Star Printing and Publishing Corporation Limited.

Okafor, G., & Malizu, C. (2015). Effective Public Relations and Organizational Management: The Bond. *Journal of Social Sciences & Humanities Research, 1*(1), 1–7.

Oyekola, O. (1995). *Foundations of Public Relations*. Ibadan Bombshell Publication.

Patton, M. Q. (2002). *Qualitative Research & Evaluation Methods*. Thousand Oaks, CA: Sage Publications.

Rex, F. F. (1976). Building a Public Relations Definition. *Public Relations Review, 2*, 4.

Seitel, F. P. (2004). *The Practice of Public Relations*. Prentice Hall.

Seter, J. (2017). *How PR Crises Impact Brand Reputation*. Retrieved on January 31, 2018, from http://www.instituteforpr.org/pr-crises-impact-brand-reputation/

Shadbolt, P. (2016). *How can a company repair a damaged reputation?* Retrieved on February 1st, 2018, from http://www.bbc.com/news/business-37630983

Shaw, G. L., & Harrald, J. (2006). The Core Competencies Required of Executive Level Business Crisis and Continuity Managers. Disaster Resource Guide. 11th Annual 2006/2007.

Stake, R. E. (2006). *Multiple Case Study Analysis*. New York: Guilford Press.

Subaihi, T. A. (2013). *Operator Warned Before Global Village Ferris Wheel Death*. Retrieved on September 01, 2013, from *The National*: http://www.thenational.ae/news/uae-news/operator-warned-before-global-village-ferris-wheel-death-says-family

Turney, M. (2008). *Performing public relations during a crisis*. Retrieved on September 12, 2014, from The www.nku.edu/~turney/prclass/tips/crisis_response.pdf

Tyler, L. (1997). Liability Means Never Being Able to Say You're Sorry: Corporate Guilt, Legal Constraints, and Defensiveness in Corporate Communication. *Management Communication Quarterly, 11*(1), 51–73. doi:10.1177/0893318997111003

Ulmer, R. R. T. L. (2006). Effective Crisis Communication: Moving from Crisis to Opportunity. Thousand Oaks, CA: Sage.

Yin, R. K. (1993). *Applications of Case study Research*. Newbury Park, CA: Sage Publishing.

Yin, R. K. (2005). *Case Study Research: Design & Methods* (3rd ed.). Beverly Hills, CA: Sage.

Chapter 5
Linked Data:
A Manner to Realize the Web of Data

Leila Zemmouchi-Ghomari
Ecole Nationale Supérieure de Technologie (ENST), Algeria

ABSTRACT

The data on the web is heterogeneous and distributed, which makes its integration a sine qua non-condition for its effective exploitation within the context of the semantic web or the so-called web of data. A promising solution for web data integration is the linked data initiative, which is based on four principles that aim to standardize the publication of structured data on the web. The objective of this chapter is to provide an overview of the essential aspects of this fairly recent and exciting field, including the model of linked data: resource description framework (RDF), its query language: simple protocol, and the RDF query language (SPARQL), the available means of publication and consumption of linked data, and the existing applications and the issues not yet addressed in research.

INTRODUCTION

Web data is often stored in isolated silos; these isolated silos are unable to exchange their content with other web systems. Incompatibility between data formats leads to low level of communication and data sharing (Herman, 2010). The contextual interpretation of data sets can be expensive, difficult, and time-consuming; in addition, it requires the intervention of developers. Furthermore, data is integrated into web pages and is only available for human consumption; thus, it is essential to adopt a framework based on coherent (homogeneous) principles that allow automatic processing, information sharing, cooperation, and collaboration, in lieu of the current framework. The primary objective of the Semantic Web is to enable machines to understand and process data contained in web pages and documents; it aims to create a structured Web of Data to complement the existing Web of Documents.

According to many researchers, including Bizer and Heath (2009), Wood et al. (2014) and Hogan (2014), The Linked Data Initiative1 is a promising approach, which includes a set of standards and tools that enable publishing and interlinking structured data on the web. The Linked Data technologies render the conceptual models on which these data are based to be explicit and transparent. In particular, these

DOI: 10.4018/978-1-5225-6367-9.ch005

Linked Data technologies support data integration in dynamic and distributed environments, such as large enterprises, intergovernmental organizations, and the World Wide Web (Mendez & Greenberg, 2012).

In fact, if the Resource Description Framework (RDF) is adopted and shared by data providers and consumers, automated data exchange would be considerably easy with common tools for accessing data, such as the Simple Protocol and the RDF Query Language (SPARQL). Linked Data enables development of new web pages using data extracted from multiple other web pages, i.e., Linked Data allows for uncoordinated cooperation (Wood et al., 2014).

However, the publication of Linked Data does not guarantee their publication, because publication requires the provenance, quality, credit, attribution, and implementation of methods to ensure reproducibility for the validation of results (Bechhofer et al., 2013; Schmachtenberg et al., 2014); thus, several challenges still need to be addressed by researchers in this field.

Exploration, description, and explanation are the main purposes of survey research (Pinsonneault & Kraemer, 1993). This work involves exploration, which is a method that aims to make readers more familiar with a topic and explain the related basic concepts; thus, the aim of this chapter is to highlight the efforts of the Semantic Web community towards the realization of the Web of Data using Linked Data principles for publishing and consuming data on the web. The best practices and recommendations of the World Wide Web Consortium (W3C) are explored; in particular, web data modeling and querying, interlinking techniques, dataset reuse, and challenges for future research, are discussed.

The remainder of this chapter is organized as follows. Section 2 describes the features of the Web of Data and compares them with those of the Web of Documents; in addition, several approaches for Web of Data are presented. Section 3 defines the Linked Data principles. Section 4 describes the Linked Data model: RDF. Section 5 presents SPARQL, the Linked Data query language, and its capabilities. The method of consumption of Linked Data datasets is explained in Sections 6. Then, Section 7 discusses the existing approaches and tools for the publication of Linked Data. Section 8 presents some of the most common applications of Linked Data technologies. The issues with Linked Data along with their probable causes and possible solutions are summarized in Section 9. Finally, Section 10 concludes the chapter by highlighting the role of Linked Data in realizing the full potential of the web.

WEB OF DATA DESCRIPTION AND APPROACHES

Bizer and Heath (2011) define the Web of Data as another layer that is linked with the classic document Web, and it has the following features:

- **Generic:** Can contain any type of data.
- **Interlinked:** Entities are connected by links that enable the visualization and the exploration of a unique giant global graph.
- **Open:** Data sources are dynamic and can be exploited in the framework of applications, in addition, anyone can publish data to the Web.

A comparison between the Web of Data and the Web of Documents is presented in Table 1 (Zemmouchi-Ghomari, 2015).

Table 1. Comparison between web of documents and web of data

Web of Documents	Web of Data
Primary objects: documents	Primary objects: things or concepts (or description of things)
Links between documents (or parts of them)	Links between things
Degree of structure in data: fairly low	Degree of structure: high (based on RDF data model)
Implicit semantics of contents	Explicit semantics of contents and links
Designed for human consumption	Designed for both machines and humans

The origins of the Web of Data lie in the activities of theW3C Linking Open Data (LOD) project[2] founded in January 2007.

Data can be considered as open if anyone is free to use, reuse, and redistribute it; indeed, a sustainable and consequent strategy of publishing and linking data on the web requires the data to be open. Most websites are developed using HTML language, which structures textual documents rather than data. As data is embedded into the text, applications cannot extract structured data from these HTML pages.

Several means have been proposed to enable extraction of data from web pages: microformats, web APIs and Linked Data.

Microformats are simple conventions for embedding semantics in HTML to enable decentralized development. Microformats are a set of simple, open data formats built upon existing and widely adopted standards, and thus, applications can extract data from web pages. However, microformats are restricted to represent data about a small set of different types of entities; they only provide a small set of attributes describing these entities. In addition, it is often not possible to express relationships between entities. Therefore, microformats are not suitable for extracting random data on the web.

Web APIs allow the availability of structured data on the web. They provide interrogation facilities for structured data via the HTTP protocol. APIs consist of two related elements. The first is a specification that describes how information is exchanged between programs, done in the form of a request for processing and a return of the necessary data. The second is a software interface written to that specification and published to be used. Therefore, these small applications associate data from different sources, each of which is read through an API specific to the data provider.

It is clear that these two approaches are not generic and do not allow extracting and linking arbitrary data on the web. In fact, linking data across the web requires a way for specifying the existence and the semantics of connections between things described in such data. This mechanism is provided by RDF[3]. Compared with HTML documents and web APIs, RDF provides more semantics and more generality for the following reasons:

- RDF links things or concepts extracted from web documents
- RDF links are typed: the relationships are explicitly specified

The use of HTTP as a standardized data access mechanism and RDF as a standardized data model simplify data access and linking. As an example, Python can be used with RDF lib and HTML5 to extract RDF data from datasets and display it as HTML.

LINKED DATA DEFINITION AND PRINCIPLES

Linked Data is described as follows: The term Linked Data refers to a set of best practices for publishing and connecting structured data on the Web (Bizer & Heath, 2009). Data on the web that is in RDF and is linked to other RDF data is Linked Data, which forms a giant global database that can be queried using SPARQL[4].

Linked Data allows discovery and consumption (standards-based data sharing) and reduces redundancy. It also provides the following:

1. A unifying data model. Linked Data relies on RDF as a data model
2. A standardized data access mechanism (the HTTP protocol)
3. Hyperlink data discovery. Because URIs are worldwide identifiers for entities, Linked Data are able to connect entities in different data sources via hyperlinks
4. Self-descriptive data. Linked Data eases the integration of data from different sources from shared vocabularies; this makes it easier for data consumers to discover, access, and integrate data

Thus, Linked Data depends on two technologies that are fundamental to the web: Uniform Resource Identifiers (URIs) and the Hypertext Transfer Protocol (HTTP).

The RDF model (Section 4) encodes data in the form of subject, predicate, and object triples expressed by means of URIs. The predicate specifies how the subject and object are related.

The Linked Data life cycle (Figure 1) unfolds in several phases according to Auer et al. (2012):

Figure 1. Linked data life cycle (Auer et al., 2012)

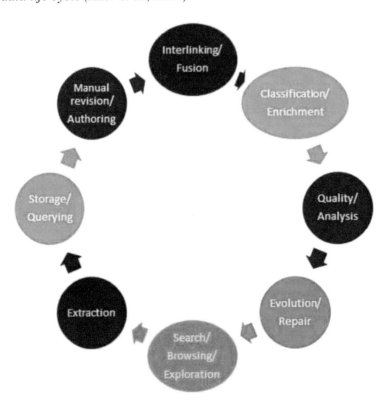

- Storage/querying that involves RDF data management
- Authoring of knowledge bases
- Interlinking between datasets to facilitate data integration
- Classification and integration with upper-level ontologies
- Quality analysis according to several dimensions: provenance, context, coverage, and structure
- Evolution/repair in a dynamic environment
- Search/browsing/exploration of explicit web data for end users

As mentioned previously, the term Linked Data denotes a set of best practices for publishing and connecting structured data on the web. These best practices were presented as the Linked Data principles by Tim Berners-Lee (2009) in his web architecture notes. These principles are as follows:

1. Use URIs as designations for things: URI references to detect Web documents, concrete objects (e.g. person, book) and abstract concepts (e.g. emotions)
2. Use HTTP URIs so that they can be dereferenced over the HTTP protocol into a description of the identified entity. In this context, there are two different means to make URIs that identify entities dereferenceable, namely, 303 URIs and hash URIs.
   a. **303 URIS:** The server does not send the entity over the network; in fact, it answers to the client with the HTTP response code 303 or redirection. In this case, there is a content negotiation with the server: Does the client ask for the HTML or the RDF+XML document?
   b. The hash URI strategy builds on the characteristic that URIs may contain a special part that is separated from the base part of the URI by a hash symbol (#). This fragment is called the fragment identifier. Thus, a URI that comprises a hash does not automatically identify a Web document.
3. A URI has to provide beneficial information, using a data model for publishing structured data on the Web, i.e. RDF. RDF data on the web can be serialized in different formats. The two RDF serialization formats most commonly used to publish Linked Data on the Web are RDF/XML (Beckett, 2004) and RDFa (Adiba & Birbeck, 2008). RDFa allows RDF to be embedded into HTML code; consequently, the content negotiation mentioned above is unnecessary.
4. Include links to other URIs, so that they can discover more things: Hyperlinks that connect things in a Linked Data context have types that describe the relationship between the things. These links enable applications to access the data.

Concretely, these links can be created using several means, such as OWL: Same As, RDFS: See Also or SKOS object properties to refer to external equivalent resources (see Figure 2).

However, these powerful properties may introduce errors because Linked Data includes entailments in addition to the implicit import of properties (Halpin et al., 2010) because *OWL: Same As* is symmetric and transitive.

The example presented in (Wood et al., 2014) is very illustrative. The New York Times used *OWL: Same As* to show the equivalence between three URIs describing the population of Rhode Island. Unfortunately, the numbers reported in these resources were different because of the difference in terms of the census year. This situation leads to three answers to the query '*what is the population of Rhode Island*?' when a single answer is expected.

Figure 2. Means to include links pointing to external datasets

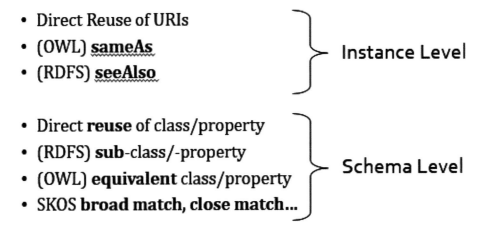

The Web of Data is open to arbitrary vocabularies being used in parallel. Despite this general openness, it is considered a good practice to reuse terms from well-known RDF vocabularies, such as Friend Of A Friend (FOAF)[5], Simple Knowledge Organization System (SKOS)[6], Dublin Core[7], and Semantically-Interlinked Online Communities (SIOC)[8], wherever possible in order to make it easier for client applications to process Linked Data. Descriptions of some common vocabularies are provided in Table 3. Some of these vocabularies can be found on these URLs:

- https://www.w3.org/wiki/TaskForces/CommunityProjects/LinkingOpenData/CommonVocabularies,
- http://lov.okfn.org/dataset/lov/.

Most of these vocabularies are specific to a particular domain, except schema.org, which supports a wide range of entities belonging to several domains, such as article, blog, recipe, photography, review, movie, and map.

The LODstats project[9] generates statistics for the most commonly used vocabularies.

LINKED DATA MODEL: RDF

The Semantic Web aims to represent web data with a model that yields a dynamic web of information in a systematic way (Allemang & Hendler, 2011). Linked Data is structured data based on the RDF data model. RDF is a simple and highly flexible data model for semantically describing resources on the web (Domingue et al., 2011), recommended by the W3C. RDF addresses the issue of managing distributed data; it relies on the infrastructure of the web and some of its most common features (Allemang & Hendler, 2011), i.e. URIs.

An RDF triple is of the form subject-property-object. RDF annotates web resources in terms of named properties. The values of the named properties can be URIrefs of web resources or literals, representations of data values such as integers and strings. RDF subjects must be URIs. A set of RDF statements is called an RDF graph (Staab & Studer, 2010). An example of an RDF graph is illustrated by Figure 3.

Figure 3. Example of RDF triples provided by the RDF 1.1 W3C Primer

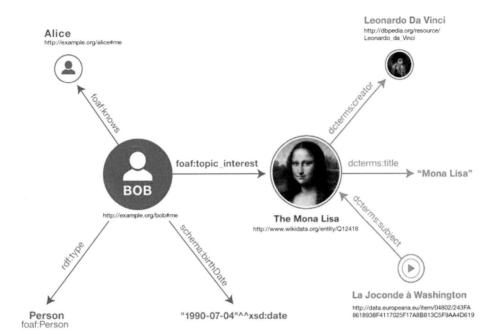

RDF formats (RDF/XML, Turtle, RDFa, JSON-LD) used in Linked Data are compatible because they share a common data model. Every RDF format can be selected for a user's preferences without negatively influencing data interoperability (See Table 2). RDF/XML was the first RDF format, and it is still used widely in enterprises. Turtle is the simplest and most human-readable format. RDFa is the preferred way to embed RDF data into web pages. JSON-LD is a relatively new format intended for web developers having structured data in JSON. Using RDFa in the development of web pages means that every item related to a vocabulary in such a page is associated with its semantics, as shown in Figure 4. Some of the most common RDFa attributes are presented in Table 4.

Thus, RDFa enables search engines to retrieve more relevant results and helps to publish the content as Linked Data on the web. Search engines prefer using RDFa Lite because they care about scalability; however, RDFa Lite has limited expressivity because it consists of only five attributes, namely, vocab, typeOf, property, resource, and prefix. The RDFa elements are used in conjunction with HTML tags. An example of Tim Berners-Lee's information (image, name, job title, and homepage) is shown in Figure 5.

Table 2. Some RDF serializations examples

RDF/XML: Standard serialization in XML <Description about="subject"> <property> value </property> </Description>
NTriples: Simple (verbose) reference serialization (for specifications only) <http:// ....subject> <http:// ...predicate> "value".
N3 and Turtle: Developer-friendly serializations :subject:property "value"

Table 3. Some common vocabularies

Vocabulary	Description
Bibo	Describes citations and bibliographic references
DC (Dublin Core)	Describes web pages and all types of publications
DOAP (Description Of A Project)	Describes software projects
FOAF (Friend Of A Friend)	Allows description of people and their interests, activities, and relationships with other people
Geonames	Specifies geographic location
GoodRelations	Describes e-commerce domains
MO (Music Ontology)	Describes musical domain
Schema.org	Provides common schema for structured data markup on web pages
SIOC (Semantically-Interlinked Online Communities)	Describes online communities
SKOS (Simple Knowledge Organization System)	Describes taxonomies, labels, and links between concepts
VoID (Vocabulary of Interlinked Data)	Describes datasets and sitemaps that describe websites

Table 4. RDFa attributes

Attribute Role	Attribute	Description
Syntax	Prefix	List of prefix-name IRIs pairs
	Vocab	IRI that specifies the vocabulary where the concept is defined
Subject	About	Specifies the subject of the relationship
Predicate	property	Express the relationship between the subject and the value
	Rel	Defines a relation between the subject and a URL
	Rev	Express reverse relationships between two resources
Resource	href	Specifies an object URI for the rel and rev attributes
	resource	Same as href (used when href is not present)
	src	Specifies the subject of a relationship
Literal	Datatype	Express the datatype of the object of the property attribute
	Content	Supply machine-readable content for a literal
	xml:lang, lang	Specifies the language of the literal
Macro	Typeof	Indicate the RDF type(s) to associate with a subject
	Inlist	An object is added to the list of a predicate.

LINKED DATA QUERY LANGUAGE: SPARQL

SPARQL aims to be the language for querying data published on the web, but actually, it is a query language for RDF either stored natively as RDF or viewed as RDF via middleware (Domingue et al., 2011). It has been a recommendation of the W3C since 2008.

The SPARQL recommendation not only defines a query language for RDF but also a protocol for sending queries to and receiving results from remote endpoints (Ngomo et al., 2014).

SPARQL is to RDF as SQL is to relational databases. The use of triple patterns in the WHERE clause is one of the syntactic differences between SQL and SPARQL; another is the use of prefixes in SPARQL (used to abbreviate long URIs). RDF data can be queried locally (using tools such as TWINKLE) or online (using SPARQL endpoints such as Virtuoso SPARQL editor).

SPARQL endpoints are web query services that return results in different formats such as text, HTML, XML, and JSON. They are not intended to be used only by humans; they accept SPARQL queries in the parameters of HTTP GET or POST requests.

A SPARQL query consists of five parts (Domingue et al., 2011): zero or more prefix declarations (introduce shortcuts for long URIs), a query result clause, zero or more FROM or FROM NAMED clauses, a WHERE clause, and zero or more query modifiers. A SPARQL query can take four forms: SELECT, ASK, CONSTRUCT, and DESCRIBE.

- SELECT queries provide answers in a tabular form, such as for an SQL query executed against a relational database
- ASK form checks whether the SPARQL endpoint can provide at least one result; the answer to the query is YES or NO
- CONSTRUCT form provides the answer to the query as an RDF graph
- DESCRIBE form is used to retrieve information without knowing the vocabulary in use, producing an RDF graph as the result

The optional set of FROM or FROM NAMED clauses defines the dataset against which the query is executed. The WHERE clause is the core of a SPARQL query. It is specified in terms of a set of triple patterns. SPARQL also provides a set of optional query modifiers such as ORDER BY, which orders the results set, and LIMIT and OFFSET, which allow results to be obtained in a specified number. An example of a SPARQL query[10] is: '*To find landlocked countries with a population greater than 15 million, with the highest population country first*'; see Figure 6.

SPARQL defines other core features that can be used to create complex query patterns (Hogan, 2013):

- **UNION:** Defines a disjunction of query patterns that the query should match.
- **OPTIONAL:** Specifies optional query patterns that the query should try to match.
- **FILTER:** Specifies further conditions that a query solution should match.

Figure 4. RDFa added value in a web page (Wood et al., 2014)

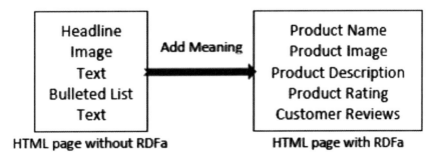

Figure 5. HTML+RDFa Code Example

```
<div vocab="http://schema.org/" typeof="Person">
 <a property="image" http://www.w3.org/
        Press/Stock/Berners-Lee/2001-europaeum-eighth.jpg ">
  <span property="name">Tim Berners Lee</span></a>,
  <span property="jobTitle">Web Inventor</span>
 <div>
  Links: <a property="url" href=" http://www.w3.org/
        People/Berners-Lee/">Tim Berners Lee's Homepage</a>
 </div>
</div>
```

Figure 6. SPARQL Query Example

```
PREFIX type: <http://dbpedia.org/class/yago/>
PREFIX prop: <http://dbpedia.org/property/>
SELECT ?country_name ?population
WHERE {
    ?country a type:LandlockedCountries ;
         rdfs:label ?country_name ;
         prop:populationEstimate ?population .
    FILTER (?population > 15000000 &&
    langMatches(lang(?country_name), "EN")) .
} ORDER BY DESC(?population)
```

Solution modifiers are available for use in SPARQL:

- **ORDER BY [ASC j DESC]:** Assigns a list of variables by which to sort results
- **LIMIT:** The LIMIT clause allows for specifying a non-negative integer that represents the maximum number of results to return.
- **OFFSET:** The OFFSET clause takes a non-negative integer n to skip over the first n results that would be returned.

SPARQL 1.1 (http://www.w3.org/TR/sparql11-query/) extends SPARQL with new features. Some of the main novelties are.

- **Property Paths:** Allow for specifying chains of non-fixed paths in a query clause using a limited form of regular expressions over RDF predicates.
- **Aggregates:** Allow for grouping results in such a manner that functions like max, min, sum, avg, count, etc., can be applied over solutions grouped by common terms bound to a given set of variables.
- **Binding Variables:** Enables initializing new variables to hold the result from the execution of a function, or a set of constant terms.
- **Subqueries:** Allow for nesting sub-SELECT queries, where nested queries are executed first and the results projected to the outer query.
- **Entailment**: SPARQL does not leverage RDF(S) or OWL Semantics when running queries. The SPARQL 1.1 Entailment Regimes proposal offers optional support for such semantics when running SPARQL queries, allowing to find additional answers through formal entailment mechanisms.
- **Update:** Allows for modifying the content of the index, based on the results of a nested query clause.
- **Federation:** SPARQL federation involves executing a single query over a selection of SPARQL endpoints. SPARQL 1.1 Federated Query centers on the SERVICE clause, which can be nested in a SPARQL query clause and allows for invoking a sub-query against a remote endpoint at a given URL.
- **Service Descriptions:** To allow for automated discovery of SPARQL endpoints on the Web, the SPARQL 1.1 Service Descriptions proposal provides a vocabulary to describe the features supported by that endpoint. This is possible by performing an HTTP lookup against the endpoint URL requesting content in an RDF format.
- **CSV, TSV, and JSON Output:** New formats for outputting results to SPARQL SELECT and ASK queries have been formalized, allowing for easier integration of SPARQL engines into software applications.

HOW TO PUBLISH LINKED DATA

Linked Data publishers should preferably follow some best practices in order to fully exploit the potential of Linked Data. Therefore, it is possible to optimize the discovery of the datasets in Semantic Web search results by:

- Publishing DOAP files related to projects (using DOAP A MATIC, for example)
- Publishing VoID files for describing datasets (using Ve2 editor, for example)
- Publishing semantic sitemaps for websites (using Semantic Web crawling, for example)
- Providing metadata (labels and comments) to enhance the retrieval of datasets

Techniques for web Linked Data publication[11] depend on the possible forms of data available on the web (Bizer & Heath, 2011). More explicitly:

- Datasets stored in relational databases can be published as Linked Data by using relational database-to-RDF wrappers. These tools allow mappings to be defined between relational databases and RDF graphs

- Structured data related to a custom API (such as the Flickr or Amazon web APIs). In this case, a wrapper has to be developed according to the API
- Text documents are transformed into Linked Data by using Linked Data entity extractors such as Calais[12], Ontos[13], or DBpedia Spotlight[14], which annotate documents with the Linked Data URIs of entities referenced in the documents

Figure 7 summarizes all possible transformation scenarios from heterogeneous web data sources to web Linked Data.

Alignment of multiple data sources using Linked Data principles (Wood et al., 2014) is possible because of:

- The use of URIs as unique identifiers
- The use of common vocabularies
- The use of *OWL:SameAs* or *RDFS:SeeAlso* properties to highlight equivalences between primitives

We want to place particular emphasis on a specific data source shown in Figure 7, i.e. RDF databases, because of its status with regard to Linked Data. RDF databases fall into the category of NoSQL (Not only SQL) databases as opposed to traditional relational databases.

Figure 7. Linked data publication scenarios (Bizer & Heath, 2011)

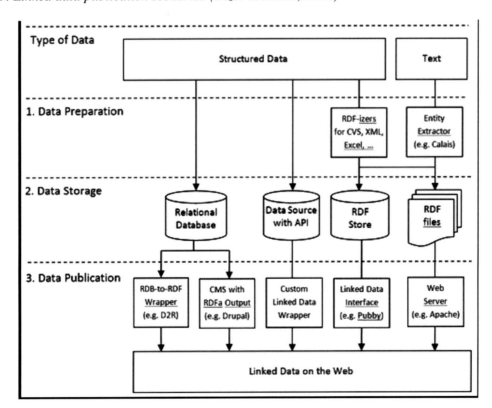

The distributed and changing nature of the web makes NoSQL databases more suitable than relational databases for storing web data. RDF databases are triple stores that allow the running of SPARQL queries on such data, e.g. AllegroGraph, Virtuoso, and Big Data.

More generally, Tim Berners-Lee has described Linked Datasets in terms of a five-star rating scheme (Berners-Lee, 2009); in other words, he proposes that stars should be awarded to published datasets according to the following criteria:

- **1 Star:** Data is available on the web (whatever format), but with an open license
- **2 Stars:** Data is available as machine-readable structured data (e.g., Microsoft Excel instead of a scanned image of a table)
- **3 Stars:** Data is available as machine-readable structured data but in a non-proprietary format (e.g., CSV instead of Excel)
- **4 Stars:** In addition to the above principles, the use of standards from the W3C (RDF and SPARQL) to identify entities
- **5 Stars:** Data is available according to all of the above, plus outgoing links to other people's data to provide context

Figures 8 and 9 show how the number of datasets published on the web as Linked Data has increased since the foundation of the Linking Open Data project.

In the most recent LOD cloud, datasets are categorized into the following domains: geographic, government, media, libraries, life science, commerce, user-generated content, and cross-domain datasets.

A dataset can be published in this diagram if it complies with the following conditions:

Figure 8. Linked open data cloud May 2007

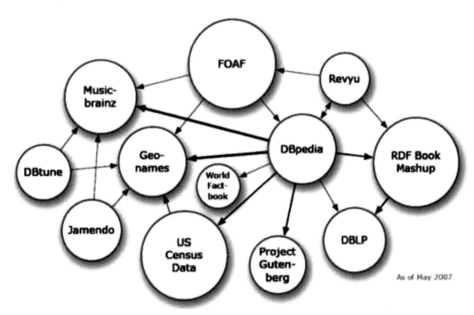

Figure 9. Linked open data cloud August 2017

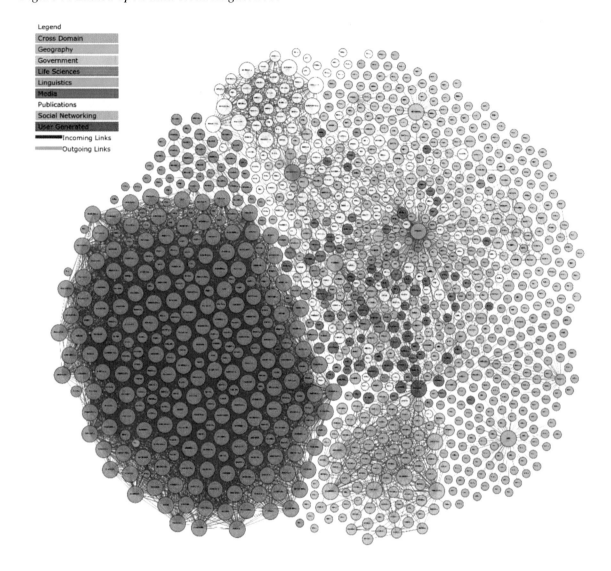

- Data is published according to the Linked Data principles
- Data must resolve (with or without content negotiation) to RDF data in one of the popular RDF formats (see Section 4)
- The dataset must contain at least 1000 triples
- The dataset must be connected via RDF links to a dataset that is already in the diagram.

This means that each dataset must use URIs from the other. At least 50 links are required

- Access to the dataset must be possible via RDF crawling, an RDF dump, or a SPARQL endpoint

The LOD cloud consists of more than 300 datasets from various domains, over 31 billion data items, and 500 million links between them. More information about each of these datasets can be obtained by exploring the LOD Cloud Data Catalog[15], which is maintained by the LOD community in the Comprehensive Knowledge Archive Network (CKAN)[16]. Some of the best-known publication tools are Virtuoso Universal Server[17], Pubby[18], CKAN registry, and Sitemap4rdf[19].

Additional tools dedicated to web Linked Data manipulation are shown in Figure 10.

HOW TO CONSUME LINKED DATA

Once the data is published, it has to be described efficiently in order to enable its discovery via search engines by means of two primary mechanisms available for publishing descriptions of a dataset:

- **Semantic Sitemaps (Cyganiak et al., 2008):** This is an extension of the well-established Sitemaps protocol[20], which provides search engines with hints about pages in a website that are available for crawling. This extension allows data publishers to state where documents containing RDF data are located and web clients to choose the most efficient means of access for the task at hand.
- **VoID (Alexander et al., 2009):** Vocabulary of Interlinked Datasets (VoID) is the standard vocabulary for describing Linked Datasets descriptions (metadata). It is intended as a bridge between the publishers and users of RDF data, with applications ranging from data discovery to cataloging and archiving of datasets.

There are several ways to consume published Linked Data on the web:

1. **Linked Data Browsers:** These enable users to navigate between different data sources by following RDF links. An RDF link means that one piece of data has some type of relationship to another piece of data. These relationships can have different types, for example, two persons who have

Figure 10. Linked data tools (Deirdre, 2012)

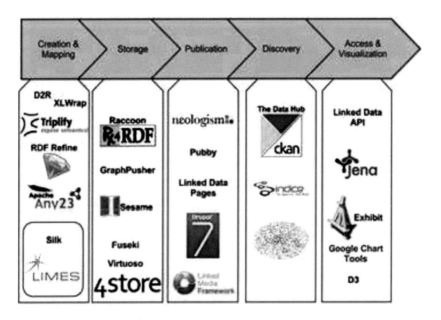

FOAF profiles may be linked by the relation 'know'. Some of these Linked Data browsers are the Disco hyperdata browser[21], Tabulator Browser[22], Marbles[23], and OpenLink RDF Browser[24].

2. **Linked Data Mashups:** Multiple sources can be queried and combined on the fly using Linked Data mashups, which are domain-specific applications. These mashups conduct the following phases (Bizer & Heath, 2011):

   ◦ Discover data sources that provide data about a specific entity by following RDF links from an initial seed URI into other data sources
   ◦ Download data from the discovered data sources and store the data together with provenance Meta information in a local RDF store
   ◦ Retrieve information to be displayed using SPARQL

Some of the Linked Data mashups are Revyu[25] (website for rating everything), DBtune Slashfacet[26] (visualizes music-related Linked Data), and DBpedia mobile[27] (geospatial entry point into the Web of Data)

3. **Search Engines:** Traditional search engines such as Google and Yahoo have also started to use structured data from the web within their applications. Google crawls RDFa and microformat data describing people, products, businesses, organizations, reviews, recipes, and events. It uses the crawled data to provide richer and more structured search results to its users in the form of Rich Snippets. Whereas SWSE[28] and Falcons[29] provide search functions for human needs, other search engines have been developed to serve the needs of applications built on top of distributed Linked Data, such as Swoogle[30] (Ding et al., 2005), Sindice[31] (Oren et al., 2008), and Watson[32] (d'Aquin et al., 2009); these provide APIs through which Linked Data applications can discover RDF documents on the web that reference a certain URI or contain certain keywords (Bizer & Heath, 2009).

LINKED DATA APPLICATIONS

Linked Data is being used beyond the LOD cloud and is becoming the basis for data sharing in many contexts. As stated by Wood, '*Linked Data successes are difficult to see because they are under the hood*' (Wood et al., 2014).

Linked Data allows concretization of the following purposes (Mendez & Greenberg, 2012):

- Making the meaning of data and information more explicit, visible, and linkable
- Integration of data from different sources in dynamic environments such as the web (Jaffri, 2010)
- Generating search functionalities and reports on top of integrated data in a cost-efficient way
- Using the web and web technologies to publish data and/or metadata to leverage the value of assets

A linked data application is a web application that consumes, manipulates and produces linked data. This type of application should include three main components: a data integrator from several sources, such as the LOD cloud or a semantic indexer, an RDF store and a data re publisher according to LD principles, as illustrated by Figure 11.

Some concrete applications of Linked Data are reported in the case studies of the W3C consortium[33]. These case studies are descriptions of systems that have been deployed within an organization and are now being used within a production environment, such as Google's Rich Snippets, which provide richer

Figure 11. A linked data-driven web application (Hausenblas, 2009)

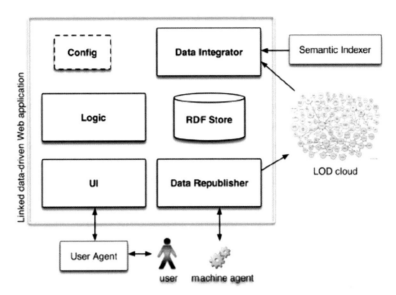

and more structured search results to users. Google embedded RDFa in its web pages, which resulted in an increase of 15%–30% in the click-through rate for its global results (Wood et al., 2014).

Some other success stories are presented below:

- The case of the British Broadcasting Corporation (BBC) is the most widely reported success story of linked data technology usage in the literature (Zemmouchi-Ghomari et al., 2018). This success stems from the use of linked data in the BBC web portal, which enables the site to present rich content that is automatically updated from linked data cloud. The BBC is the largest broadcasting corporation in the world. The BBC's team of developers builds the BBC website by integration of the available Linked Data. For example, BBC Nature aggregates data from different sources, including Wikipedia, WWF WildFinder, the IUCN Red List of Threatened Species, the EDGE of Existence program of the Zoological Society of London, and the Animal Diversity Web. BBC Wildlife Finder repurposes that data and puts it in a BBC context, linking out to program clips extracted from the BBC's Natural History Unit archive.
- In April 2010, Facebook launched the Open Graph protocol to manage users' interests and their preferences using vocabularies from the Linked Data cloud, such as FOAF and Semantically-Interlinked Online Communities (SIOC) (Bojars et al., 2008). The point is that if a person's friends recommend something, he or she will be more inclined to like it. Less than a month after the rollout of Open Graph, more than 100,000 sites had integrated the technology (Heitmann et al., 2010). In fact, every time someone clicks on a like button, two RDFa triples are generated; one of them is stored in Facebook's database and the other one is sent to the supplier of the product that is liked (Wood et al., 2014).
- In 2010, Facebook launched the Open Graph protocol to manage users' interests and their preferences using vocabularies from the Linked Data cloud, such as FOAF and Semantically-Interlinked Online Communities (SIOC) (Bojars et al., 2008). The point is that if a person's friends recom-

mend something, he or she will be more inclined to like it. Less than a month after the rollout of Open Graph, more than 100,000 sites had integrated the technology (Heitmann et al., 2010). In fact, every time someone clicks on a like button, two RDFa triples are generated; one of them is stored in Facebook's database and the other one is sent to the supplier of the product that is liked.

- The Open Government Data (OGD) is an international collaboration between the governments of the US, the UK, France, and Singapore for sharing machine-readable datasets covering government activities. "The Linked Open Government Data project investigates the role of Semantic Web technologies, especially Linked Data, in producing, enhancing and utilizing government data published on Data.gov and other websites" (Ding et al., 2011). Datasets are produced by governments or government-controlled entities. One significant benefit of the OGD initiative is greater governmental transparency, i.e. the creation of services that deliver social and commercial value and encourage participatory governance. Another example of OGD initiatives is: The Tetherless World Constellation (TWC) Data-gov corpus (Maali et al., 2012), yielded by the Data-gov project at RPI (Rensselaer Polytechnic Institute) which published over than 5 billion RDF triples converted from hundreds of Data.gov datasets covering a wide range of topics (e.g. US government spending, energy usage and public healthcare).
- The Google Knowledge Graph enables the search engine to collect and to deliver information about objects in the real world (Pelikánová, 2014) efficiently. This graph is rooted in public sources such as Freebase, Wikipedia, and the CIA World Factbook. The Knowledge Graph enhances Google Search using several means, such as: (1) disambiguate the semantics of words by proposing all possible matches with categories to which belong searched terms, for example users can search for Taj Mahal the monument, or Taj Mahal the musician, (2) Propose summaries of relevant content around the topic of searched items. For example, if a user is looking for Marie Curie, relevant content about her is suggested such as its date of birth and death, her education and scientific discoveries, by using the relationships with related items. The relevance of the proposed content is obtained by combining information that other users found useful, (3) Explore new facts: the knowledge graph as a linked data structure enables to discover new facts about the same topic, so new connections are revealed.

Linked Data technologies certainly allow large organizations to set up data integration with relatively little effort as compared to traditional data warehousing solutions that require the design of a global schema (Bizer & Heath, 2011). Gradually, these organizations can invest in Linked Data by reusing shared vocabularies or schema mappings between datasets.

DISCUSSION

In this section, we discuss open challenges related to Linked Data, their origins, and possible approaches for solving them (see Table 5).

If we have to arrange these challenges in terms of priority, we approve Needleman's (Needleman, 2011) summary of the most significant Linked Data issues, which are:

- **Quality and Relevance:** Data quality is a problem in every data management system. Ensuring that data most relevant or appropriate to the user's needs are identified and made available is an

Table 5. Linked data issues : causes and potential solutions

Issue Category	Cause: Lack of	Effect: Difficulty of	Potential Solution(s): Development of
Description and Provenance	Metadata: Provenance, ownership, versioning (Bechhofer et al., 2013) (Dividino, 2017)	Reuse, reproducibility	Research objects (container infrastructure of data resources, relationships, experiments conducted on Linked Datasets) (Bechhofer et al., 2013)
	Mechanisms to track the provenance of the published data on the web	Determining the provenance of Linked Data For the users, difficulty to have answers concerning data provenance: Where is this data from? Who provided the data? When was this data provided? Was the provider certain about the truth of this data? Was the data believed by others?	(Hartig & Zhao, 2009) proposed an approach consisting of 3 steps: collecting elements of provenance information, deciding on its influence, and applying a function to calculate the quality Tools that explore provenance information when ranking and updating caches of Web data (Dividino, 2017).
	Formal description of LOD Cloud datasets(Jain et al., 2010) Reference dataset per domain (Zemmouchi-Ghomari & Ghomari, 2009)	Knowledge discovery (especially systematically)	Formal descriptions of datasets LOD sets Description rules Domain Reference Ontologies
Domain Knowledge Coverage	Detailed knowledge of the dataset structures Adequate number of LOD datasets to answer complex and frequent queries (Polleres et al., 2010)	Querying of the LOD cloud (Hartig et al., 2009; Naumann, 2002)	Available detailed and formal descriptions of queried datasets at the endpoints. Reuse of query results by means of query subsumption (based on analyzing graph patterns of cached SPARQL queries)
	Different datasets cover the same knowledge domain	Selection from a set of different results of a given query	(Toupikov et al., 2009) mechanisms for classification of datasets according to their popularity among end users
	Subjective and individual design of real-world objects Differences in contexts of represented knowledge	Contradictory facts reported about common entities from different knowledge bases	Mechanisms for entity disambiguation
Interlinking, Reasoning and Maintenance	Interlinking or mappings between datasets (schema and instance level) (Biessmann & Harth, 2010) Link maintenance is expensive Publishers continue to use locally defined URIs (Polleres et al., 2010)	Link discovery (Jain et al., 2010; Bechhofer et al., 2013) in terms of recall (all links) and precision (correctness)	Development of more efficient link discovery platforms than LIMES or SILK (Jain et al., 2010) use of an upper-level ontology such as SUMO to formalize relationships and descriptions of the datasets, (Reed & Lenat, 2002) use of CYC, (Bergman & Giasson, 2008) use of UMBEL Propose ontology based framework for formally specifying Linked Data Mashup views (Vidal et al., 2015)
	Language Expressivity used to design datasets	Knowledge reasoning, inferring new facts	Use of more expressive languages such as OWL 2 instead of RDFa, RDF Lite, or OWL Lite
	Human design errors Soundness and completeness (in terms of formal semantics) by means of existing reasoning systems (Hitzler et al., 2010)	Incoherencies and inconsistencies in the LOD sets, examples: use of the foaf: image property to relate an arbitrary resource with an image, missing the fact that foaf:person is the domain of this property (Polleres et al., 2010)	The web community can resolve inconsistencies by working with data providers (pointing out mistakes and helping to fix them) such as the pedantic web group Semi-automatic repair algorithms, such as explanation of OWL entailments[35], a protégé plugin, or model-based revision operators that remove axioms causing inconsistencies (Qi & Du, 2009)

continued on following page

Table 5. Continued

Issue Category	Cause: Lack of	Effect: Difficulty of	Potential Solution(s): Development of
	Services to exploit datasets	Disinterest/underuse of available LOD datasets (Jain et al., 2010) Understanding dataset semantics	Efficient Tools to achieve data parsing, data transformation, data standardization, and data fusion (Alba et al., 2017).
Exploitation & Scalability	Mechanism to identify dataset domain performance: still, substantial penalties compared to relational datasets (Auer & Lehmann, 2010) Large-scale processing (usually cannot be loaded in standard OWL reasoners) (Bizer & Schultz, 2009) Data fusion mechanisms Missing end-user tools	Data consumption Data Usability	The Semantic Web community should conduct more applied research to demonstrate Linked Data cloud possibilities (Polleres et al., 2010) Large community-driven effort, such as efforts in and around SIOC and FOAF Adaptive automatic data indexing technologies (Auer & Lehmann, 2010) Existing machine learning algorithms have to be extended (from DL) and they have to be optimized for processing large-scale knowledge bases (Auer & Lehmann, 2010) Open licenses or at least clear information about licensing (Neumaier et al., 2017) Very large RDF data management platforms Adaptive UI interfaces
Quality & Relevance	No common and standardized evaluation metrics Data providers do not receive feedback on its use No consensual and formalized quality metrics are explicitly defined to assess LD datasets. No fully automated tools with little user involvement are implemented and inability to produce interpretable results.	Evaluation of the quality of the dataset (Harting & Zhao, 2009) LD datasets are often affected by errors, inconsistencies, missing values and other quality issues that may lower their usage (Kontokostas et al., 2014),(Cappiello et al., 2016), (Radulovic et al., 2017), (Heinrich et al., 2018). If quality metrics are not well defined, this can lead to wrong decisions and economic losses (Heinrich et al., 2018) Assessment tools Configuration is difficult and time-consuming. Technology and domain knowledge Expertise of users is required.	Use of upper-level ontologies (e.g. SUMO) to do reasoning and propagation of the queries from concepts of upper-level ontologies to LOD set instances User feedback mechanism Evaluation approach of the data quality integrated as part of the publication process (Hartig & Zhao, 2009) such as: -(Motro & Rakov, 1998): automatic assessment for evaluating soundness and completeness -(Bobrowski et al., 1999): use of questionnaire based on user input -(Yang et al., 2002): measurement of information quality from soundness, dependability, usefulness User input (instance and schema mappings) for machine learning techniques (inductive reasoning) and results can be assessed again by end users (iterative refinement) Services to execute constant evaluation of links between knowledge bases Precision and recall measures as more realistic evaluation metrics (Hitzler et al., 2010) Framework for LD quality assessment. Quality metrics must be explicitly defined or consist of precise statistical measures (Zaveri et al., 2016). Quality assessments approaches must be accompanied by implemented tools to enhance their usability. Develop extensions of the W3C Data Quality Vocabulary using it to capture quality information specific to Linked Data (Radulovic et al., 2017)

enduring issue. Recent studies have shown that the majority of Linked Data datasets suffer from data quality problems (Zaveri et al.,2016; Capello et al., 2016; Debattista et al., 2017). Several models and approaches have been proposed to assess the quality of data (Radulovic, 2017), however, these methods focus on some dimensions and are adequate for some use cases, consequently, LD quality assessment is still an open issue.

- **Maintenance and Interlinking:** Keeping links valid is quite difficult, especially with the evolution of Linked Data clouds. Robust mechanisms that can automatically check and update links will be needed for this purpose. It is crucial to think about a strategy for the incremental maintenance of linked data mashup views (Vidal et al., 2015)
- **User Interfaces Design and Licensing (Exploitation):** A Linked Data browser has to dynamically integrate access to data from distributed and heterogeneous data sources. This may involve the integration of data from sources not explicitly selected by the user. In addition, some data will have licensing restrictions. Not all Open Data is completely open and most data on the Web is attached to different licenses, terms, and conditions, so how and whether these licenses can be interpreted by machines (Neumaier et al., 2017). How online user interfaces, such as web browsers, will tackle this type of data remains an open question.

CONCLUSION

The Linked Data project has been initiated to enable computers to understand online content in order to help users easily find, share, and combine information, i.e. to fulfill the purposes of the Semantic Web. One of the most evident benefits of Linked Data is that it presents the web as a giant global database that can be queried using tools such as SPARQL endpoints.

Linked Data is a viable means of concretizing the idea of the Web of Data, in addition to the existing Web of Documents, if all stakeholders (web data publishers) agree to publish data according to the principles articulated by Tim Berners-Lee. These principles aim to realize standardization in terms of creation, mapping, storage, publication, discovery, access, and visualization of web Linked Data.

In spite of these restrictions, data publishers in this framework have some flexibility in their actions because they are not constrained in their choice of vocabulary to represent data, and they can freely represent disagreement and contradictory information about an entity.

Annotated data with RDF vocabularies using RDFa Lite is found more easily by search engine crawlers, contributing significantly to the publication of Linked Data. Furthermore, the Web of Data is sufficiently generic for anyone to publish any type of data. Standardization will accelerate the progress of the Linked Data community.

There are several unresolved issues concerning Linked Data in spite of its promise. These include quality, maintenance, licensing, and end-user consumption. Nevertheless, we are convinced that Linked Data will constitute a significant evolutionary step in realizing the full potential of the web.

Our future efforts will be dedicated to developing approaches to assess, monitor, maintain and improve Linked Data quality based on a combination of ontology evaluation approaches.

DISCUSSION QUESTIONS

1.   What is the difference between the web of documents and the web of data?
2.   What is the web of data approaches?
3.   What are the four principles of linked data?
4.   What are the linked data purposes?
5.   What are linked data technologies?
6.   What is the linked data model?
7.   What is the linked data query language?
8.   What are the means to publish linked data?
9.   How to consume linked data?
10. What are the most prominent linked data applications?
11. What are the linked data challenges and possible solutions?

REFERENCES

Adida, B., & Birbeck, M. (2008). RDFa primer - bridging the human and data webs. *W3C Recommendation*. Retrieved from http://www.w3.org/TR/xhtml-rdfa-primer/

Alba, A., Coden, A., Gentile, A. L., Gruhl, D., Ristoski, P., & Welch, S. (2017, December). Multi-lingual Concept Extraction with Linked Data and Human-in-the-Loop. In *Proceedings of the Knowledge Capture Conference*. ACM. 10.1145/3148011.3148021

Alexander, K., Cyganiak, R., Hausenblas, M., & Zhao, J. (2009). Describing linked datasets. *Proceedings of the WWW Workshop on Linked Data on the Web*.

Allemang, D., & Hendler, J. (2011). *Semantic Web for the Working Ontologist, Effective Modeling in RDFS and OWL* (2nd ed.). Morgan Kaufmann publishers.

Auer, S., Buhmann, L., & Dirschl, C. (2012). Managing the life-cycle of linked data with the lod2 stack. *Proceedings of the International Semantic Web Conference, ISWC*. 10.1007/978-3-642-35173-0_1

Auer, S., & Lehmann, J. (2010). Creating knowledge out of interlinked data. *Semantic Web Journal*, *1*(1), 97–104.

Bechhofer, S., Buchan, I., de Roure, D., Missier, P., Ainsworth, J., Bhagat, J., & Goble, C. (2013). Why linked data is not enough for scientists. *Future Generation Computer Systems*, *29*(2), 599–611. doi:10.1016/j.future.2011.08.004

Beckett, D. (2004). Rdf/XML syntax specification (revised). *W3C Recommendation*. Retrieved from HTTP:// www.w3.org/TR/rdf-syntax-grammar/

Bergman, M. K., & Giasson, F. (2008). *Umbel ontology*. Technical report, Structured Dynamics LLC. Retrieved from https://github.com/structureddynamics/UMBEL/blob/master/Doc/UMBEL_TR-11-2-10.pdf

Berners Lee, T. (2009). *Linked data design issues*. Retrieved from http://www.w3.org/DesignIssues/LinkedData.htmls

Biessmann, F., & Harth, A. (2010). Analysing dependency dynamics in Web data. *Proceedings of the Linked AI: AAAI Spring Symposium.*

Bizer, C., & Heath, T. (2011). *Evolving the Web into a Global Data Space.* Morgan and Claypool Publishers. doi:10.1007/978-3-642-24577-0_1

Bizer, C., Heath, T., & Berners Lee, T. (2009). Linked data – the story so far. *International Journal on Semantic Web and Information Systems, 5*(3), 1–22. doi:10.4018/jswis.2009081901

Bizer, C., & Schultz, A. (2009). The Berlin SPARQL benchmark. *International Journal on Semantic Web and Information Systems, 5*(2), 1–24. doi:10.4018/jswis.2009040101

Bobrowski, M., Marrie, M., & Yankelevich, D. (1999). A homogeneous framework to measure data quality. *Proceeding of Information Quality workshop.*

Bojars, U., Passant, A., Breslin, J., & Decker, S. (2008). Social Network and Data Portability using Semantic Web Technologies. *Proceedings of the Workshop on Social Aspects of the Web.*

Cappiello, C., Di Noia, T., Marcu, B. A., & Matera, M. (2016, June). A quality model for linked data exploration. In *International Conference on Web Engineering* (pp. 397-404). Springer. 10.1007/978-3-319-38791-8_25

Cyganiak, R., Stenzhorn, H., Delbru, R., Decker, S., & Tummarello, G. (2008). Semantic sitemaps: Efficient and flexible access to datasets on the semantic web. *Proceedings of the 5th European Semantic Web Conference.* 10.1007/978-3-540-68234-9_50

D'Aquin, M., Motta, E., Sabou, M., Angeletou, S., Gridinoc, L., Lopez, V., & Guidi, D. (2008). Toward a new generation of semantic web applications. *IEEE Intelligent Systems, 23*(3), 20–28. doi:10.1109/MIS.2008.54

Debattista, J., Lange, C., Auer, S., & Cortis, D. (2017). Evaluating the Quality of the LOD Cloud: An Empirical Investigation. *Semantic Web Journal.*

Deirdre, L. (2012). *Linked open data.* Retrieved from http://fr.slideshare.net/deirdrelee/linked-opendata-15303345

Ding, L., Lebo, T., Erickson, J. S., DiFranzo, D., Williams, G. T., Li, X., & Hendler, J. A. (2011). Twc logd: A portal for linked open government data ecosystems. *Journal of Web Semantics, 9*(3), 325–333. doi:10.1016/j.websem.2011.06.002

Ding, L., Pan, R., Finin, T., Joshi, A., Peng, Y., & Kolari, P. (2005). Finding and ranking knowledge on the semantic web. *Proceedings of the 4th International Semantic Web Conference.* 10.1007/11574620_14

Dividino, R. Q. (2017). *Managing and using provenance in the semantic web* (Doctoral dissertation). Universität Koblenz-Landau.

Domingue, J., Fensel, D., & Hendler, J. (2011). *Handbook of semantic web technologies.* Springer. doi:10.1007/978-3-540-92913-0

Halpin, H., Hayes, P., & Mccusker, J. (2010). When owl: same as is not the same: An analysis of identity in linked data. In *Proceedings of the International Semantic Web Conference, ISWC* (pp. 305-320). Springer Berlin Heidelberg.

Hartig, O., Bizer, C., & Freytag, J.-C. (2009). Executing SPARQL queries over the Web of Linked Data. *Proceedings of the International Semantic Web Conference.* 10.1007/978-3-642-04930-9_19

Hartig, O., & Zhao, J. (2009). Using web data provenance for quality assessment. *CEUR Workshop Proceedings.*

Hausenblas, M. (2009). *Linked data applications. First Community Draft.* DERI.

Heinrich, B., Hristova, D., Klier, M., Schiller, A., & Szubartowicz, M. (2018). Requirements for Data Quality Metrics. *Journal of Data and Information Quality, 9*(2), 12. doi:10.1145/3148238

Heitmann, B., Kim, J. G., Passant, A., Hayes, C., & Kim, H. G. (2010). An architecture for privacy-enabled user profile portability on the Web of Data. In *Proceedings of the 1st International Workshop on Information Heterogeneity and Fusion in Recommender Systems* (pp. 16-23). ACM Publishers. 10.1145/1869446.1869449

Herman, I. (2010). Introduction to semantic web technologies. *Proceedings of the Semantic Web Activity Lead World Wide Web Consortium. Semantic Technology Conference.*

Hogan, A. (2014). Linked Data and the Semantic Web Standards. In *Linked Data Management* (pp. 3–48). CRC Press. doi:10.1201/b16859-3

Jaffri, A. (2010). *Linked data for the enterprise - an easy route to the semantic web.* Retrieved from HTTP://www.capgemini.com/blog/capping-it-off/2010/03/linked-data-for-the-enterprise-an-easy-route-to-thesemantic-web

Jain, P., Hitzler, P., Yeh, P. Z., Verma, K., & Sheth, A. P. (2010). Linked Data Is Merely More Data. *Proceedings of the AAI Spring Symposium: linked data meets artificial intelligence.*

Kontokostas, D., Westphal, P., Auer, S., Hellmann, S., Lehmann, J., Cornelissen, R., & Zaveri, A. (2014, April). Test-driven evaluation of linked data quality. In *Proceedings of the 23rd international conference on World Wide Web* (pp. 747-758). ACM.

Lee, Y. W., Strong, D. M., Kahn, B. K., & Wang, R. Y. (2002). AIMQ: A methodology for information quality assessment. *Information & Management, 40*(2), 133–146. doi:10.1016/S0378-7206(02)00043-5

Maali, F., Cyganiak, R., & Peristeras, V. (2012). A publishing pipeline for linked government data. *The semantic web: Research and applications*, 778-792.

Mendez, E., & Greenberg, J. (2012). Linked data for open vocabularies and hive's global framework. *El Profesional de la Información, 21*(3), 236–244. doi:10.3145/epi.2012.may.03

Motro, A., & Rakov, I. (1998). Estimating the quality of databases. In *Flexible query answering systems* (pp. 298–307). Springer Berlin Heidelberg. doi:10.1007/BFb0056011

Naumann, F. (2002). *Quality-driven query answering for integrated information systems.* Springer Verlag. doi:10.1007/3-540-45921-9

Needleman, M. (2011). Linked data: What is it and what can it do? *Serials Review*, *37*(3), 234. doi:10. 1080/00987913.2011.10765392

Neumaier, S., Polleres, A., Steyskal, S., & Umbrich, J. (2017, July). Data Integration for Open Data on the Web. In Reasoning Web International Summer School. Springer.

Ngomo, A. C. N., Auer, S., Lehmann, J., & Zaveri, A. (2014). Introduction to linked data and its life-cycle on the web. In *Reasoning Web. Reasoning on the Web in the Big Data Era* (pp. 1–99). Springer International Publishing. doi:10.1007/978-3-319-10587-1_1

Oren, E., Delbru, R., Catasta, M., Cyganiak, R., Stenzhorn, H., & Tummarello, G. (2008). Sindice.com: A document-oriented lookup index for open linked data. *Journal of Metadata. Semantics and Ontologies*, *3*(1), 37–52. doi:10.1504/IJMSO.2008.021204

Pelikánová, Z. (2014). *Google Knowledge Graph*. Academic Press.

Pinsonneault, A., & Kraemer, K. L. (1993). Survey research methodology in management information systems: An assessment. *Journal of Management Information Systems*, *10*(2), 75–105. doi:10.1080/07 421222.1993.11518001

Polleres, A., Hogan, A., Harth, A., & Decker, S. (2010). Can we ever catch up with the Web? *Semantic Web Journal*, *1*(1), 45–52.

Qi, G., & Du, J. (2009). Model-based revision operators for terminologies in description logics. *Proceedings of the 21st International Joint Conference on Artificial Intelligence*.

Radulovic, F., Mihindukulasooriya, N., García-Castro, R., & Gómez-Pérez, A. (2017). A comprehensive quality model for linked data. *Semantic Web*, 1-22.

Reed, S., & Lenat, D. (2002). *Mapping ontologies into Cyc* (Technical report). Cycorp, Inc. Retrieved from http://www.cyc.com/doc/white papers/

Schmachtenberg, M., Bizer, C., & Paulheim, H. (2014). Adoption of the linked data best practices in different topical domains. In *International Semantic Web Conference* (pp. 245-260). Springer. 10.1007/978-3-319-11964-9_16

Staab, S., & Studer, R. (2010). *Handbook on ontologies*. Springer.

Toupikov, N., Umbrich, J., Delbru, R., Hausenblas, M., & Tummarello, G. (2009). DING! Dataset ranking using formal descriptions. *Proceedings of the WWW2009 Workshop on Linked Data on the Web*.

Vidal, V. M., Casanova, M. A., Arruda, N., Roberval, M., Leme, L. P., Lopes, G. R., & Renso, C. (2015, June). Specification and incremental maintenance of linked data mashup views. In *International Conference on Advanced Information Systems Engineering* (pp. 214-229). Springer. 10.1007/978-3-319-19069-3_14

Wood, D., Zaidman, M., Ruth, L., & Hausenblas, M. (2014). *Linked Data, Structured Data on the Web*. Manning Publishers.

Zaveri, A., Rula, A., Maurino, A., Pietrobon, R., Lehmann, J., & Auer, S. (2016). Quality assessment for linked data: A survey. *Semantic Web*, *7*(1), 63–93. doi:10.3233/SW-150175

Zemmouchi-Ghomari, L. (2015). Linked Data, Towards Realizing the Web of Data: An Overview. *International Journal of Technology Diffusion*, 6(4), 20–39. doi:10.4018/IJTD.2015100102

Zemmouchi-Ghomari, L., & Ghomari, A. R. (2009). Reference Ontology. *Proceedings of the International IEEE Conference on Signal-Image Technologies and Internet-Based System*.

Zemmouchi-Ghomari, L., Sefsaf, R., & Azni, K. (2018). Using linked data resources to generate web pages based on a BBC case study. *Proceedings of the IEEE Computing Conference*.

ENDNOTES

[1] http://linkeddata.org
[2] http://esw.w3.org/topic/SweoIG/TaskForces/CommunityProjects/ LinkingOpenData
[3] http://www.w3.org/RDF/
[4] http://www.w3.org/TR/rdf-sparql-query/
[5] http://rdfweb.org/foaf/
[6] http://www.w3.org/2004/02/skos/
[7] http://dublincore.org/
[8] http://sioc-project.org/
[9] http://stats.lod2.eu/
[10] http://www.w3.org/2009/Talks/0615-qbe/
[11] http://www.w3.org/TR/swbp-vocab-pub/
[12] http://viewer.opencalais.com/
[13] http://www.ontos.com/20-10-2010-ontos-links-lod/
[14] https://github.com/dbpedia-spotlight/dbpedia-spotlight
[15] http://datahub.io/group/lodcloud
[16] http://ckan.org/
[17] http://virtuoso.openlinksw.com/
[18] http://wifo5-03.informatik.uni-mannheim.de/pubby/
[19] http://lab.linkeddata.deri.ie/2010/sitemap4rdf/
[20] http://www.sitemaps.org/fr/protocol.html
[21] http://wifo5-03.informatik.uni-mannheim.de/bizer/ng4j/disco/
[22] http://www.w3.org/2005/ajar/tab
[23] http://mes.github.io/marbles/
[24] semanticweb.org/wiki/OpenLink_RDF_Browser
[25] http://revyu.com/
[26] http://dbtune.org/
[27] http://dbpedia.org/DBpediaMobile
[28] http://swse.deri.org/
[29] http://ws.nju.edu.cn/falcons/objectsearch/index.jsp
[30] http://swoogle.umbc.edu/
[31] http://sindice.com/

[32]   http://watson.kmi.open.ac.uk/WatsonWUI/
[33]   http://www.w3.org/2001/sw/sweo/public/UseCases/
[34]   http://www4.wiwiss.fu-berlin.de/lodcloud/state/#license
[35]   http://owl.cs.manchester.ac.uk/explanation/

Chapter 6

A Theoretical Framework for IT Consumerization:
Factors Influencing the Adoption of BYOD

Ibrahim Arpaci
Gaziosmanpasa University, Turkey

ABSTRACT

The chapter provided a comprehensive review of previous studies on the adoption of information and communication technology (ICT). The study further conducted a qualitative study on the adoption of "bring your own device" (BYOD). The study systematically reviewed technology acceptance theories and models such as TAM, TPB, and UTAUT at the individual level and technology adoption theories such as "innovation diffusion theory," "technology-organization-environment framework," and "institutional theory" at the organizational level. Thereby, key factors predicting the ICT adoption at the individual, organizational, institutional, and environmental level were identified. A theoretical framework that explains the ICT adoption and the consumerization process was proposed based on the theories. The qualitative data collected by semi-structured interviews with senior-level managers was analyzed using the content analysis. The findings suggested that perceived financial cost, compatibility, privacy, and security concerns were significant factors in predicting the enterprise's adoption of BYOD.

INTRODUCTION

This study conducted a systematic review that provides a bibliography of the relevant literature, both qualitative and quantitative. During the review process, the study first formulated the research problem, and then performed a literature search, and finally, analyzed and interpreted the findings. The keyword combinations including "technology adoption" and "organizational adoption" were searched in the Scopus and ISI Web of Science databases that were selected to ensure quality and comprehensive data collection. Thereby, the articles indexed in Scopus or SSCI/SCI/ESCI and published in peer-reviewed journals between 2004 and 2017 were included in the study. This study conducted a content analysis to analyze the bibliographic data. Thereby, the articles were coded based on the research purpose, research

DOI: 10.4018/978-1-5225-6367-9.ch006

method, research design, data collection/analysis method and findings. Thereby, this study identified theoretical underpinnings of the theoretical framework for the ICT adoption. The theoretical framework suggested the consumerization of ICT as a solution for organizations, specifically, for small-and-medium sized enterprises. Accordingly, this study conducted a qualitative study on the adoption of BYOD based on data collected from senior level managers. The findings suggested the key factors predicting enterprise's adoption decisions on BYOD.

LITERATURE REVIEW

Individual Level Adoption

The literature classifies technology acceptance or adoption theories and models based on the applicability to individuals or organizations. Well-known theories that explain ICT adoption by individuals are "Technology Acceptance Model" (TAM) (Davis, Bagozzi, & Warshaw, 1989; Davis, 1989), "Theory of Planned Behavior" (TPB) (Ajzen, 1985, 1988, 1991), and "Unified Theory of Acceptance and Use of Technology" (UTAUT) (Venkatesh, Morris, Davis, & Davis, 2003).

Technology Acceptance Model

TAM focused on two main theoretical constructs, including "perceived usefulness" and "perceived ease of use," which were argued to be key determinants of the ICT adoption. Davis (1989) developed and validated a psychometric scale to measure "perceived usefulness" and "perceived ease of use" through a longitudinal study and found that both constructs were significantly correlated with the ICT adoption. Moreover, Davis (1989) suggested that "perceived ease of use" and "perceived usefulness" can predict the attitudes toward using a technology or system. Attitudes can also predict individuals' behavioral intentions to use a technology or system. Further, use or acceptance of the technology or system is predicted by the behavioral intentions (See Appendix A for the definitions of terms).

TAM has been adapted to understand individuals' acceptance or use of a new technology or system. For example, Arpaci (2016) used the TAM as a theoretical framework and reported that subjective norm, perceived usefulness, and trust were significant factors in predicting the cloud services adoption. In another study, Arpaci, Yardimci Cetin, and Turetken (2015) argued the impact of perceived security on the smartphone adoption and suggested that security, perceived usefulness, and perceived ease of use significantly affect the adoption. In a recent study, Arpaci (2017) found that knowledge management functions have a significant effect on perceived usefulness and innovativeness. Further, training and education have a significant effect on the perceived ease of use of cloud computing services.

Theory of Planned Behavior

Ajzen (1991) developed the TPB by extending "Theory of Reasoned Action" (TRA; Fishbein & Ajzen, 1975; Ajzen & Fishbein, 1980). The TPB theorized that a behavior could be determined by behavior intentions, which are predicted by three external factors, including "subjective norms," "perceived behavioral control," and "attitudes." These were also related to a set of normative, control, and behavioral beliefs toward that behavior.

Unified Theory of Acceptance and Use of Technology

Venkatesh et al. (2003) investigated main technology acceptance theories and formulated a unified theory that integrates significant constructs of the previous models. Accordingly, empirical and conceptual similarities of eight models were utilized to design the UTAUT, which proposes that "effort expectancy," "performance expectancy," and "social influence" are significant determinants of behavioral intentions and behavioral intentions and facilitating conditions significant determinants of the actual use. Further, significant moderating effects of gender, experience, age, and voluntariness were also confirmed. Arpaci (2015) used UTAUT as a theoretical framework in order to explain mobile learning adoption by university students and found that experience, "performance expectancy," and "effort expectancy" were significantly associated with the adoption.

It is important to note that theories may inspire each other, and naturally, they may have empirical and conceptual similarities. For instance, "perceived ease of use" of the TAM is similar to the notion of "effort expectancy" in the UTAUT and "complexity" in the IDT. Further, Fishbein and Ajzen (1975) developed the TRA, which suggests that an individual's behavior can be predicted by the behavioral intention, which can be explained by "subjective norms" and attitudes. Ajzen (1991) extended the TRA and proposed the TPB suggesting that behavioral intention can be explained by the subjective norm, attitude, and perceived behavioral control. Davis (1989) proposed the TAM based on the TRA, and finally, the UTAUT integrated significant constructs of the eight theories, including the TAM, TRA, and TPB.

Organizational Level Adoption

Innovation Diffusion Theory

"Innovation Diffusion Theory" (IDT), formulated by Rogers (2003), argues the adoption of an innovation can be predicted by innovation characteristics such as "relative advantage," "complexity," "compatibility," "observability," and "trialability." These characteristics operate at both organizational and individual level. Several studies have employed this theory to explain the ICT adoption at the organizational level. For example, Ax and Greve (2017) investigated adoption of management accounting systems at the organizational level based on data collected form 165 Swedish manufacturing firms. Their results suggested that compatibility is positively associated with the adoption. Yang, Sun, Zhang, and Wang (2015) investigated cloud-computing adoption by 173 organizations. They reported that top management support as an organizational factor; relative advantage, simplicity, compatibility, and experience as technological factors; competitor pressure and partner pressure as environmental factors were significant in predicting the adoption.

Arpaci et al. (2015) focused on the adoption of smartphones based on data obtained from senior level managers at 141 and 213 organizations in Canada and Turkey, respectively. They found that complexity, compatibility, trialability, and security as technological factors; top management support, innovativeness, and expertise as organizational factors; competitive pressure, partner and customer expectations as environmental factors were significant in predicting the adoption. Grublješič and Jaklič (2015) investigated organizational adoption of business intelligence systems based on data obtained from interviews with managers and practitioners. They reported that result demonstrability, facilitating conditions, and social influence were significant determining factors in the adoption.

Technology-Organization-Environment Framework

Tornatzky and Fleischer (1990) developed "Technology-Organization-Environment" (TOE) framework, which suggests three dimensions affecting organizations' decisions on ICT adoption: Technological context (i.e. external or internal technologies), organizational context (i.e. size, scope, and structure) and environmental context (i.e. competitors, industry, legislation). Several studies have used this framework to explain ICT adoption by organizations. For example, Sucahyo, Utari, Budi, Hidayanto, and Chahyati (2016) investigated knowledge management adoption based on data collected from 51 Indonesian large-scale companies. The results suggested that ease of use and usefulness perceptions as personal factors; structure, management support, organization culture as organizational factors; IT infrastructure as a technological factor; mimetic pressure as an environmental factor were significant determinants of the adoption. Dedrick, Venkatesh, Stanton, Zheng, and Ramnarine-Rieks (2015) identified key factors affecting organizational adoption of smart grid technologies based on the data from interviews with managers at 12 U.S. companies. They found that perceived benefits as a technological factor; structure, top management leadership, technology champions expertise, and innovation culture as organizational factors; competition, consumer pressure, and external knowledge resources as environmental factors were significant determinants of the adoption. Ainin, Naqshbandi, and Dezdar (2016) investigated the adoption of green IT practices based on data collected from 277 managers in Tehran. They reported that manager' considerations for future consequences and openness as personal factors; institutional pressure and economic performance as organizational factors; environmental performance and customer satisfaction as environmental factors were significant determinants of the adoption. Kim, Jang, and Yang (2017) investigated Software as a Service (SaaS) adoption in small businesses and found that technological risks (i.e. performance, security) and benefits (i.e. quality, cost, business process improvement) as technological factors; top management support as an organizational factor; vendor support as an environmental factor were significant determinants of the adoption. Martins, Oliveira, and Thomas (2015) investigated antecedents of the information systems outsourcing based on data obtained from 261 firms. The results suggested that top management support, relative advantage, competitive pressure, and firm size were significant determinants of the adoption.

Institutional Theory

DiMaggio and Powell (1983) suggested three types of environmental pressures, which significantly affect an organization's institutional isomorphism. These environmental pressures were coercive (i.e. legitimacy issues, political pressure), mimetic (i.e. competitor pressure) and normative (i.e. customer and partner expectations). Several studies have used this theory to explain an organization's ICT adoption decision. For example, Kharuddin, Foong, and Senik (2015) investigated ERP adoption by organizations and found that expected economic benefits, mimetic pressures, and organizational performance were significant factors. Karoui, Dudezert, and Leidner (2015) investigated the adoption of a SAP based social-networking system based on data obtained from 38 interviews across the two organizations. Their results suggested that symbolic notions attached to SNS and social capital were important institutional factors affecting the adoption. Oguz (2016) focused on the adoption of digital libraries by organizations and found that management style, organizational structure, focus & direction of the program, and external relationships were significant in the adoption. Table 1 summarizes the organizational, technological, and environmental factors that affect the organizations' ICT adoption.

Table 1. ICT adoption at the organizational level

Reference	Domain	Technological Factors	Organizational Factors	Environmental Factors	Controls
Kim, Jang, & Yang (2017)	Software as a Service	**Technological Risks, Benefits**	IT Capacity, Slack Resource, **Top Management Support***	Competition, **Vendor Support***, Government Support	
Sucahyo, Utari, Budi, Hidayanto, & Chahyati (2016)	Knowledge Management Systems	**IT infrastructure** (perceived usefulness** and ease of use** as personal factors)	Structure, **Management Support**, Organization Culture**,** Strategic Planning	**Mimetic Pressure**,** Industry and Market	
Dedrick, Venkatesh, Stanton, Zheng, & Ramnarine-Rieks (2015)	Smart Grid Technologies	**Perceived Benefits**	**Structure, Top Management Leadership, Technology Champions Expertise, Innovation Culture**	**Competition, Consumer Pressure, External Knowledge Resources**	
Arpaci, Yardimci Cetin, & Turetken (2015)	Smartphone	**Compatibility***, Complexity***, Trialability**, Security***	**Innovativeness***, Top Management Support***, Expertise***	**Competitive Pressure***, Partner Expectations***, Customer Expectations***	
Yang, Sun, Zhang, & Wang (2015)	Cloud-computing	**Relative Advantage*, Simplicity*, Compatibility*, Experience***	IT infrastructure, **Top Management Support**	**Competitor Pressure*, Partner Pressure***	
Lian, Yen, & Wang (2014)	Cloud computing	**Cost*, Complexity*, Data security*,** Compatibility	**Top manager's support*, Perceived technical competence*,** Relative advantage, Adequate resource, Benefits, CIO innovativeness,	Government policy, Perceived industry pressure	
Ciganek, Haseman, & Ramamurthy (2014)	Service-oriented architecture	Compatibility, Complexity, Relative Advantage	**Culture**,** Management Support	**Coercive Isomorphism*, Normative Isomorphism*,** Mimetic Isomorphism	Industry Type, Firm Size, IT Department Size
Ajjan, Kumar, & Subramaniam (2013)	IT Project Portfolio Management	**Cost**,** Expected benefits, Compatibility	**Data quality***, Stakeholder support**, Business stakeholder resistance**, Number of projects***	**External pressure***	organization size
Bernroider & Schmöllerl (2013)	DSS	**IT support*, Method support**,** Framework support	**Management support***	**Legislative regulation***	
Sila (2013)	B2B e-commerce	**Cost**, Data security*, Network reliability**, Scalability**,** Complexity	**Top management support**,** Trust	**Pressure from trading partner**, Pressure from competition***	
Yoon & George (2013)	Virtual Worlds	Relative Advantage, Security Concern, Compatibility	**Organization Readiness***, Top Management Support, Organization Size, Firm Scope	**Competitors Pressure**, Normative Pressure*,** Customers Pressure, Intensity of Competition	Social Desirability, Firm Age, Industry
Saldanha & Krishnan (2012)	Web 2.0	**Importance to Open Standards***	**Organization Size***	**Industry Knowledge Intensity*,** Industry Competitive Intensity	
Ifinedo (2011)	Internet/E-Business		**Management Commitment & Support*,** Organizational IT Competence	**External Pressure**,** Financial Resources Availability, IS Vendor Support & Pressure	Size, Industry
Low, Chen, & Wu (2011)	Cloud Computing	**Relative Advantage*,** Complexity, Compatibility	**Top Management Support*, Firm Size*,** Technology Readiness	**Competitive Pressure*, Trading Partner Pressure***	
Wang, Wang, & Yang (2010)	RFID	**Complexity***, Compatibility*,** Relative Advantage	**Firm Size**,** Top Management Support, Technology Competence	**Competitive Pressure*, Trading Partner Pressure*, Information Intensity**.**	
Chong, Ooi, Lin, & Raman (2009)	Collaborative Commerce	**Information Distribution**, Information Interpretation**, Trust**,** Relative Advantage, Compatibility, Complexity	**Feasibility*, Top Management Support*, Project Champion Characteristics***	**Competitive Pressure*, Expectations of Market Trends***	
Teo & Ranganathan (2009)	E-procurement	**Perceived Costs*,** Perceived Direct Benefits, Indirect Benefits	**Firm Size*, Information Sharing Culture*,** Top Management Support	Business Partner Influence	
Ramdani, Kawalek, & Lorenzo (2009)	Enterprise Systems	**Relative Advantage**, Trialability **,** Compatibility, Complexity, Observability	**Organizational Readiness*, Top Management Support***	Competitive Pressure, External IS Support	**Size **,** Industry
Lin & Lin (2008)	E-Business	**IS Infrastructure**, IS Expertise***	Organizational Compatibility, **Expected Benefit of E-Business***	**Competitive Pressure*,** Trading Partner Readiness	

continued on following page

Table 1. Continued

Reference	Domain	Technological Factors	Organizational Factors	Environmental Factors	Controls
Li (2008)	E-procurement	**Relative Advantage***, Complexity, Compatibility	Financial Slacks, **Top Management Support***.	**External Pressure***, External **Support***, Government Promotion	
Soares-Aguiar & Palma-Dos-Reis (2008)	E-procurement	**IT Infrastructure***, IT Expertise, B2B Know How	**Firm Size***	**Trading Partner Readiness***, **Perceived Extent of Adoption among Competitors****	Industry, **Sector****
Liu (2008)	E-commerce	**Support from Technology and Human Capital****	**Management Level for Information***, Firm Size	**User Satisfaction****, E-Commerce **Security***	Firm Property
Pan & Jang (2008)	ERP	IT Infrastructure, **Technology Readiness***	**Size***, **Perceived Barriers***	**Production and Operations Improvements****, Competitive Pressure, Regulatory Policy, Enhancement of Products and Services	
Chang, Hwang, Hung, Lin, & Yen (2007)	E-signature	System Complexity, Security Protection	User Involvement, **Adequate Resources***, **Hospital Size***, Internal Need	**Vendor Support***, **Government Policy***	
Hong & Zhu (2006)	E-commerce	**Technology Integration****, Web Functionalities****, EDI Use	**Web Spending****, Perceived Obstacles	**Partner Usage***	**Size****, Industry
Teo, Ranganathan, & Dhaliwal (2006)	B2B E-commerce	Lack of Interoperability, **Unresolved Technical Issues***, Lack of IT Expertise and Infrastructure	Difficulties in Organizational Change, **Lack of Top Management Support***, Problems in Project Management, **Difficulties in Cost-Benefit Assessment***, Lack of E-Commerce Strategy***	Unresolved Legal Issues, Fear and Uncertainty	
Zhu, Dong, Xu, & Kraemer (2006)	E-business	**Relative Advantage****, Compatibility****, Costs***, Security Concern**** Technology Competence****	**Organization Size***	**Competitive Pressure***, Partner Readiness****	
Raymond, Bergeron, & Blili (2005)	E-business	**Manufacturing Technology***	Strategic Orientation, **Managerial Context***, Manufacturing Context***	**Networking Intensity***	
Zhu & Kraemer (2005)	E-business	**Technology Competence****	**Size***, International Scope, **Financial Commitment***	**Competitive Pressure***, Regulatory Support****	
Xu, Zhu, & Gibbs (2004)	Internet	**Technology Competence****	Firm Size, Global Scope; **Enterprise Integration***	**Competition Intensity***, Regulatory Environment****	

*$p < .05$; **$p < .01$; ***$p < .001$ (Significant factors are shown in **bold**). **A Theoretical Framework for ICT Adoption**

TAM (Davis, 1989) posits that "perceived ease of use" and "perceived usefulness" can significantly predict an individual's behavioral intention to use a new technology. Whereas, the studies on the organizational adoption suggested that organizational characteristics such as organizational readiness, financial resources, innovativeness, information intensity, and top management support have significant effects on the ICT adoption at the organizational level. Finally, "Institutional Theory" suggests that environmental pressures exerted on organizations such as partner expectations, customer expectations, and competitive pressure have significant effects on the ICT adoption at the industry level.

Figure 1 illustrates the aforementioned theoretical arguments and implies that ICT adoption proceeds at three phases. At the personal or individual level, individuals adopt an ICT. At this level, perceived usefulness and ease of use of the ICT have a strongly significant effect on the adoption decision. At the organizational level, ICT is adopted by organizations and organizational characteristics of top management support, organization readiness, financial resources, innovativeness, information intensity, and security have a significant effect on the adoption. At the final phase, ICT adoption diffuses within the industry. Environmental characteristics such as customer and partner expectations and competitive pressure have a significant effect on the adoption at the industry level.

Figure 1. The theoretical framework

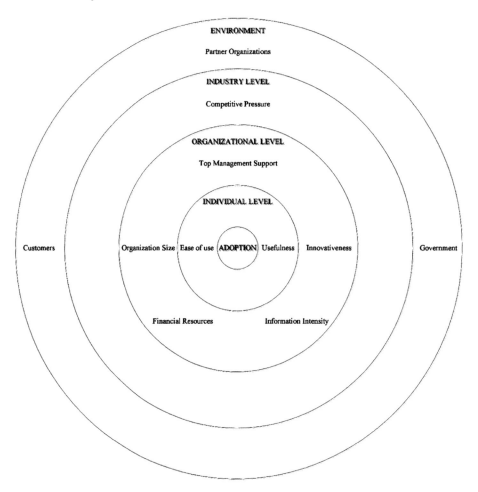

Despite the fact that key determining factors of the ICT adoption at the organizational level were different from that of at the individual level, organizational level adoption is positively correlated with individual level adoption. For example, employees' level of expertise or prior knowledge in an ICT may significantly affect the organizations' adoption decision. IT consumerization is another example that support this argument. For example, BYOD practice that supports adoption of employee or consumer devices in the workplace has been rapidly adopted by organizations.

METHODOLOGY

Data Collection

A qualitative research design, which has a unique potential in identifying grounded concepts, is considered as the most suitable research design for the present study. Since senior level managers has a responsibility in deciding to allow employees to bring their own mobile devices such as smartphones, tablets, and digital cameras in order to use them in the workplace, opinions from senior level management are elicited for the study.

Qualitative data was collected from senior level managers at 14 private sector organizations in Turkey. Table 2 shows a detailed information about the interview informants. Participants were randomly selected and contacted by a telephone call to schedule a place and time for the interviews. The semi-structured interviews were approximately 20 minutes in length. Interviewees were requested to read a short description of research and signed a consent form. All recorded interviews were transcribed into text files. The participants were requested to answer a series of open-ended questions from the following interview guide:

1.   "Do you allow employees to bring their own portable devices and use them in the organization?"
2.   "What are the main factors affecting your decisions about the BYOD practice?"
3.   "Why do you think that the factors affecting your decision are important?"

Data Analysis

A content analysis using the constant-comparative-method was employed to identify concepts from data obtained from the transcription of the interviews. Data analysis involved three levels including "open coding, axial coding, and selective coding" (Corbin, Strauss, & Strauss, 2014). First, different categories are identified within data, then the connections between categories are identified, and finally, the core categories are identified (Corbin, Strauss, & Strauss, 2014).

Table 2. Interviewee profiles

Organization	Title	Sector	Industry	Adopter	Size
1	CIO	Service	IT	Yes	250
2	CEO	R&D	Machinery	No	15
3	CFO	Service	IT	Yes	11
4	Owner	Manufacturing	Electronics	No	25
5	Owner	R&D	IT	No	15
6	CIO	Service	Machinery	No	15
7	Owner	R&D	IT	No	16
8	CEO	R&D	IT	Yes	15
9	Owner	Service	IT	Yes	25
10	Owner	Manufacturing	IT	Yes	40
11	CEO	Commerce	Furniture	Yes	140
12	CEO	Commerce	Construction	No	10
13	Owner	Manufacturing	Consulting	Yes	16
14	Owner	Service	Machinery	Yes	38

Note: CEO: Chief Executive Officer, CIO: Chief Information Officer, CFO: Chief Financial Officer

Matrices were constructed to extract information in a systematic manner by following the coding procedure: 1) read text from logs, 2) encode text in information segments, 3) code the segments, 4) refine the codes, and 5) collapse the codes into the themes. Table 3 shows the codes, categories, and statements.

Table 3. Codes, categories and statements

Codes	Categories	Statements
"The amount of money to purchase these technologies for each employee was very high…"	Perceived financial cost	Organization 1: "Each employee who works with us has a mobile technology such as tablets or smartphones. Since we are a large-sized company, the amount of money to purchase these technologies for each employee was very high. Therefore, we have adopted these technologies, which increase employee morale and satisfaction."
"There is a risk that the organization's sensitive documents could end up in the hands of unauthorized parties…"	Security	Organization 2: "Our organization experienced a leakage of confidential documents. There is a risk that the organization's sensitive documents could end up in the hands of unauthorized parties, and therefore, we do not allow our employees to connect corporate network and access corporate database from their own device."
"Compatible with other technologies available in the firm… compatible with the firm's values and beliefs…"	Compatibility	Organization 3: "Our firm is an entrepreneur; we have an open support policy for BYOD practice, which are compatible with other technologies available in the firm. Moreover, implementing the changes caused by a BYOD policy is compatible with the firm's values and beliefs."
"Mobile devices present a significant security risk, guarded with the type of information shared online…"	Security, privacy	Organization 4: "Documents accessed by the mobile devices present a significant security risk. Therefore, we do not allow our employees to use their own devices for work related activities. We are also guarded with the type of information shared online. "
"No security policy to protect sensitive corporate information…"	Security	Organization 5: "Our company has no security policy to protect sensitive corporate information. Thus, we never allow our employees to use their own devices to access corporate databases."
"Loss of confidential documents, confidential documents are not fully protected…"	Security	Organization 6: "As we experienced a loss of confidential documents, I believe that our organization's confidential documents are not fully protected. We therefore do not support organizational adoption of BYOD practice."
"Information technology use policy…"	Security	Organization 7: "Since we have no information technology use policy integrated with a BYOD plan, our firm do not allow employees to use their own devices in the workplace.
"Substantial modification in our existing IT infrastructure…"	Compatibility	Organization 8: "Installation and use of mobile devices do not require substantial modification in our existing IT infrastructure. Therefore, we adopted BYOD practice."
"They do not disrupt other technologies…"	Compatibility	Organization 9: "We therefore allow our employees to bring their own devices to work as they do not disrupt other technologies available in the organization."
"Strong security policy, safe access to corporate data, compatible with existing technologies…"	Security, compatibility	Organization 10: "There is always a risk that organizations' sensitive documents could be accessed by third parties. However, our company has a strong security policy to protect corporate data. Security ensuring safe access to corporate data, lead us to adopt BYOD practice, which are compatible with existing technologies."
"Sufficient budget to purchase the mobile devices, cost of monthly payments of these devices for each employee is very high…"	Perceived financial cost	Organization 11: "Our firm has no sufficient budget to purchase the mobile devices for each employee. Moreover, costs of monthly payments of these devices for each employee are very high. Therefore, employees are allowed to use their own devices for work emails, phone calls, etc. Our firm operates 7/24 with no break times; therefore, key managers need to be accessible at all times. These technologies allow for managers to be accessible out of their office."
"Security policy determining which user has access to what application…"	Security	Organization 12: "We have a security policy determining which user has access to what application. Based on this, we allow only a limited number of managers to access specific applications using their own devices."
"Security issues that it creates…	Security	Organization 13: "Consumer adoption of mobile devices such as tablets and smartphones is pushing us to adopt them more rapidly. Even it creates some security issues, we allow our employees to use their own devices for work purposes."
Audit logging and log analysis to access, employees' privacy…"	Security, privacy	Organization 14: "Our firm employs audit logging and log analysis to access sensitive information. We also care about our employees' privacy. We support BYOD practice with a plan that describes how to use mobile devices."

Findings

The results suggested privacy and security concerns, perceived financial cost, and compatibility were key factors that affect managers' decision concerning the adoption of BYOD. Adopter organizations that allow employees to bring and use their own mobile devices for work-related purposes reported that compatibility and perceived financial cost affect their adoption decision. Two relatively large scale organizations having more than a hundred employees reported that perceived financial cost was one of the main factors affecting their adoption decision. Finally, two adopter organizations reported that compatibility was a significant factor affecting their decision.

Whereas, the non-adopter organizations argued that privacy and security concerns were significant factors affecting their adoption decision. This suggests that organizations dealing with sensitive and confidential documents do not allow their employees to bring and use their own portable devices in the workplace. It is important to note that security and privacy concerns are two key determining factors for the non-adopter organizations.

CONCLUSION

TOE framework, proposed by Tornatzky and Fleischer (1990), has been successfully used by a number of studies on ICT adoption at the organizational level. However, some of the studies enhanced this framework by including the IDT to better explain ICT adoption (Chong et al., 2009; Ciganek et al., 2014; Hsu et al., 2006; Low et al., 2011; Li, 2008; Wang et al., 2010; Zhu et al., 2006). The results suggested that technological characteristics of compatibility, relative advantage, and complexity have significant effects on the ICT adoption.

The TOE framework has also been enhanced by "Institutional Theory" to explain organizational behavior within different domains as in (Gibbs & Kraemer, 2004; Iacovou, Benbasat, & Dexter, 1995; Soares-Aguiar & Palma-Dos-Reis, 2008; Yoon & George, 2013). Their findings suggested that environmental characteristics of competitive pressure, trading partner pressure, and regulatory environment have significant effects on the ICT adoption.

Previous studies suggested that organizational factors such as top management support, organizational readiness, financial resources, and organization size were consistently significant determining factors in the adoption. Particularly, organizational readiness was one of the significant factors in predicting the organizational adoption decision.

Previous studies along with the current findings suggested that privacy and security issues were important determining factors for the organizations. Sila (2013) argued that information security has a significant impact on the B2B e-commerce adoption. In the same vein, Park and Kim (2014) argued that user acceptance of mobile services is significantly affected by perceived security. Further, main challenges of cloud services were security, privacy, and standardization (Lin & Chen, 2012). One of the key aspects that can impede BYOD adoption is the security of wireless data transfer and mobile devices (Arpaci, 2015). The results implied that the organizations with a low tolerance in security risks might defer their BYOD adoption. Likewise, there is a risk of monitoring private data when employees or customers connect their own mobile devices to the company's networks. This suggests that organizations should have a strong policy to protect privacy of both customers and employees. The organizations should also fortify both device and network level security to protect intellectual properties of the organization.

The findings indicated that compatibility of portable devices has a positive impact on the organizations' adoption decision. This construct has been identified as a significant factor in prior studies as well. For instance, Bellaaj, Bernard, Pecquet, and Plaisent (2008) reported compatibility as a significant factor in predicting web site adoption. In similar study, Zhu et al. (2006) suggested that compatibility has a significant impact on the e-business adoption.

Several limitations of the study should be addressed by a future research. Quantitative data should be included to test and confirm the proposed theoretical framework and qualitative findings. Further, corporate culture can significantly affect organizations' adoption behavior. For example, organizations with a low uncertainty avoidance can adopt the BYOD easier and quicker than that of organizations with a high uncertainty avoidance. Thus, this investigation of the effects of corporate culture on the organizational adoption is a potential avenue of the future research.

DISCUSSION QUESTIONS

1. What are the differences between individual and organizational level ICT adoption?
2. What are the similarities between technology acceptance or integration theories?
3. What connection is there between individual, organizational and industry level ICT adoption?
4. How would you explain ICT adoption by individuals?
5. What is the importance of organizational factors affecting enterprises' ICT adoption?
6. What is the meaning of BYOD?
7. How BYOD provides a solution for small-and-medium sized enterprises?
8. Which factors reported in the book chapter have positively affect BYOD adoption?
9. Which factors reported in the book chapter have a negative impact on the BYOD adoption?
10. What original and unique was in this book chapter?
11. What did you already know about the subject before you read this book chapter?
12. How well do you think the author built the theoretical framework in the book chapter?

REFERENCES

Ainin, S., Naqshbandi, M. M., & Dezdar, S. (2016). Impact of adoption of Green IT practices on organizational performance. *Quality & Quantity*, *50*(5), 1929–1948. doi:10.100711135-015-0244-7

Ajjan, H., Kumar, R. L., & Subramaniam, C. (2013). Understanding differences between adopters and non-adopters of information technology. Project portfolio management. *International Journal of Information Technology & Decision Making*, *12*(6), 1151–1174. doi:10.1142/S0219622013400129

Ajzen, I. (1985). From intentions to actions: A theory of planned behavior. In J. Kuhl & J. Beckman (Eds.), *Action-control: From cognition to behavior* (pp. 11–39). Heidelberg, Germany: Springer. doi:10.1007/978-3-642-69746-3_2

Ajzen, I. (1988). *Attitudes, personality and behaviour.* Milton Keynes, UK: Open University Press.

Ajzen, I. (1991). The theory of planned behavior. *Organizational Behavior and Human Decision Processes, 50*(2), 179–211. doi:10.1016/0749-5978(91)90020-T

Ajzen, I., & Fishbein, M. (1980). *Understanding attitudes and predicting social behavior.* Englewood Cliffs, NJ: Prentice-Hall.

Arpaci, I. (2013). *Organizational adoption of mobile communication technologies* (Doctoral dissertation). Department of Information Systems, Middle East Technical University.

Arpaci, I. (2015). A qualitative study on the adoption of bring your own device (BYOD) Practice. *International Journal of E-Adoption, 7*(2), 1–14. doi:10.4018/IJEA.2015070101

Arpaci, I. (2016). Understanding and predicting students' intention to use mobile cloud storage services. *Computers in Human Behavior, 58*, 150–157. doi:10.1016/j.chb.2015.12.067

Arpaci, I. (2017). Antecedents and consequences of cloud computing adoption in education to achieve knowledge management. *Computers in Human Behavior, 70*, 382–390. doi:10.1016/j.chb.2017.01.024

Arpaci, I., Yardimci Cetin, Y., & Turetken, O. (2015). A cross-cultural analysis of smartphone adoption by Canadian and Turkish organizations. *Journal of Global Information Technology Management, 18*(3), 214–238. doi:10.1080/1097198X.2015.1080052

Arpaci, I., Yardimci Cetin, Y., & Turetken, O. (2015). Impact of Perceived Security on Organizational Adoption of Smartphones. *Cyberpsychology, Behavior, and Social Networking, 18*(10), 602–608. doi:10.1089/cyber.2015.0243 PMID:26383763

Ax, C., & Greve, J. (2017). Adoption of management accounting innovations: Organizational culture compatibility and perceived outcomes. *Management Accounting Research, 34*, 59–74. doi:10.1016/j.mar.2016.07.007

Bellaaj, M., Bernard, P., Pecquet, P., & Plaisent, M. (2008). Organizational, environmental, and technological factors relating to benefits of web site adoption. *International Journal of Global Business, 1*(1), 44–64.

Bernroider, E. W. N., & Schmöllerl, P. (2013). A technological, organisational, and environmental analysis of decision making methodologies and satisfaction in the context of IT induced business transformations. *European Journal of Operational Research, 224*(1), 141–153. doi:10.1016/j.ejor.2012.07.025

Chang, I. C., Hwang, H. G., Hung, M. C., Lin, M. H., & Yen, D. C. (2007). Factors affecting the adoption of electronic signature: Executives' perspective of hospital information department. *Decision Support Systems, 44*(1), 350–359. doi:10.1016/j.dss.2007.04.006

Chong, A. Y. L., Ooi, K. B., Lin, B. S., & Raman, M. (2009). Factors affecting the adoption level of c-commerce. An empirical study. *Journal of Computer Information Systems, 50*(2), 13–22.

Ciganek, A. P., Haseman, W. D., & Ramamurthy, K. (2014). Time to decision: The drivers of innovation adoption decisions. *Enterprise Information Systems*, *8*(2), 279–308. doi:10.1080/17517575.2012.690453

Corbin, J., Strauss, A., & Strauss, A. L. (2014). *Basics of qualitative research*. Newbury Park, CA: Sage.

Davis, F. D. (1989). Perceived usefulness, perceived ease of use, and user acceptance of information technology. *Management Information Systems Quarterly*, *13*(3), 319–339. doi:10.2307/249008

Davis, F. D. (1993). User acceptance of information technology: System characteristics, user perceptions and behavioral impacts. *International Journal of Man-Machine Studies*, *38*(3), 475–487. doi:10.1006/imms.1993.1022

Davis, F. D., Bagozzi, R. P., & Warshaw, P. R. (1989). User acceptance of computer technology: A comparison of two theoretical models. *Management Science*, *35*(8), 982–1003. doi:10.1287/mnsc.35.8.982

Dedrick, J., Venkatesh, M., Stanton, J. M., Zheng, Y., & Ramnarine-Rieks, A. (2015). Adoption of smart grid technologies by electric utilities: Factors influencing organizational innovation in a regulated environment. *Electronic Markets*, *25*(1), 17–29. doi:10.100712525-014-0166-6

DiMaggio, P. J., & Powell, W. (1983). The iron cage revisited: Institutional isomorphism and collective rationalizing in organizational fields. *American Sociological Review*, *48*(2), 147–160. doi:10.2307/2095101

Fishbein, M., & Ajzen, I. (1975). *Belief, attitude, intention and behavior: An introduction to theory and research*. Reading, MA: Addison-Wesley.

Gibbs, J. L., & Kraemer, K. L. (2004). A cross-country investigation of the determinants of scope of e-commerce use: An institutional approach. *Electronic Markets*, *14*(2), 124–137. doi:10.1080/10196780410001675077

Grublješič, T., & Jaklič, J. (2015). Business intelligence acceptance: The prominence of organizational factors. *Information Systems Management*, *32*(4), 299–315. doi:10.1080/10580530.2015.1080000

Hong, W., & Zhu, K. (2006). Migrating to Internet-based e-commerce: Factors affecting e-commerce adoption and migration at the firm Level. *Information & Management*, *43*(2), 204–221. doi:10.1016/j.im.2005.06.003

Iacovou, C., Benbasat, I., & Dexter, A. (1995). Electronic data interchange and small organisations: Adoption and impact of technology. *Management Information Systems Quarterly*, *19*(4), 465–485. doi:10.2307/249629

Ifinedo, P. (2011). Internet/E-Business technologies acceptance in Canada's SMEs: An exploratory investigation. *Internet Research*, *21*(3), 255–281. doi:10.1108/10662241111139309

Karoui, M., Dudezert, A., & Leidner, D. E. (2015). Strategies and symbolism in the adoption of organizational social networking systems. *The Journal of Strategic Information Systems*, *24*(1), 15–32. doi:10.1016/j.jsis.2014.11.003

Kharuddin, S., Foong, S. Y., & Senik, R. (2015). Effects of decision rationality on ERP adoption extensiveness and organizational performance. *Journal of Enterprise Information Management*, *28*(5), 658–679. doi:10.1108/JEIM-02-2014-0018

Kim, S. H., Jang, S. Y., & Yang, K. H. (2017). Analysis of the determinants of Software-as-a-Service adoption in small businesses: Risks, benefits, and organizational and environmental factors. *Journal of Small Business Management*, *55*(2), 303–325. doi:10.1111/jsbm.12304

Li, Y. H. (2008). An empirical investigation on the determinants of e-procurement adoption in Chinese manufacturing enterprises. *15th International Conference on Management Science & Engineering*, 32-37. 10.1109/ICMSE.2008.4668890

Lian, J. W., Yen, D. C., & Wang, Y. T. (2014). An exploratory study to understand the critical factors affecting the decision to adopt cloud computing in Taiwan hospital. *International Journal of Information Management*, *34*(1), 28–36. doi:10.1016/j.ijinfomgt.2013.09.004

Lin, A., & Chen, N. C. (2012). Cloud computing as an innovation: Perception, attitude and adoption. *International Journal of Information Management*, *32*(6), 533–540. doi:10.1016/j.ijinfomgt.2012.04.001

Lin, H. F., & Lin, S. M. (2008). Determinants of e-business diffusion: A test of the technology diffusion perspective. *Technovation*, *28*(3), 135–145. doi:10.1016/j.technovation.2007.10.003

Liu, M. (2008). Determinants of e-commerce development: An empirical study by firms in Shaanxi, China. *4th International Conference on Wireless Communications, Networking and Mobile Computing*, 9177-9180. 10.1109/WiCom.2008.2143

Low, C., Chen, Y., & Wu, M. (2011). Understanding the determinants of cloud computing adoption. *Industrial Management & Data Systems*, *111*(7), 1006–1023. doi:10.1108/02635571111161262

Martins, R., Oliveira, T., & Thomas, M. A. (2015). Assessing organizational adoption of information systems outsourcing. *Journal of Organizational Computing and Electronic Commerce*, *25*(4), 360–378. doi:10.1080/10919392.2015.1087702

Moore, G. C., & Benbasat, I. (1991). Development of an instrument to measure the perceptions of adopting an information technology innovation. *Information Systems Research*, *2*(3), 192–222. doi:10.1287/isre.2.3.192

Morgan, G. (1986). *Images of organization*. London: Sage.

Oguz, F. (2016). Organizational influences in technology adoption decisions: A case study of digital libraries. *College & Research Libraries*, *77*(3), 314–334. doi:10.5860/crl.77.3.314

Pan, M. J., & Jang, W. Y. (2008). Determinants of the adoption of enterprise resource planning within the technology-organization-environment framework: Taiwan's communications. *Journal of Computer Information Systems, 48*(3), 94–102.

Park, E., & Kim, K. J. (2014). An integrated adoption model of mobile cloud services: Exploration of key determinants and extension of technology acceptance model. *Telematics and Informatics*, *31*(3), 376–385. doi:10.1016/j.tele.2013.11.008

Ramdani, B., Kawalek, P., & Lorenzo, O. (2009). Predicting SMEs' adoption of enterprise systems. *Journal of Enterprise Information Management*, *22*(1/2), 10–24. doi:10.1108/17410390910922796

Raymond, L., Bergeron, F. O., & Blili, S. (2005). The assimilation of e-business in manufacturing SMEs: Determinants and effects on growth and internationalization. *Electronic Markets*, *15*(2), 106–118. doi:10.1080/10196780500083761

Rogers, E. M. (1986). *Communication technology: The new media in society*. New York: The Free Press.

Rogers, E. M. (2003). *Diffusion of innovations* (4th ed.). New York, NY: The Free Press.

Saldanha, T. J. V., & Krishnan, M. S. (2012). Organizational adoption of Web 2.0 technologies: An empirical analysis. *Journal of Organizational Computing and Electronic Commerce*, *22*(4), 301–333. doi:10.1080/10919392.2012.723585

Sila, I. (2013). Factors affecting the adoption of B2B e-commerce technologies. *Electronic Commerce Research*, *13*(2), 199–236. doi:10.100710660-013-9110-7

Soares-Aguiar, A., & Palma-Dos-Reis, A. (2008). Why do firms adopt e-procurement systems? Using logistic regression to empirically test a conceptual model. *IEEE Transactions on Engineering Management*, *55*(1), 120–133. doi:10.1109/TEM.2007.912806

Sucahyo, Y. G., Utari, D., Budi, N. F. A., Hidayanto, A. N., & Chahyati, D. (2016). Knowledge management adoption and its impact on organizational learning and non-financial performance. *Knowledge Management & E-Learning*, *8*(2), 387–413.

Teo, T. S. H., & Ranganathan, C. (2009). Adopters and non-adopters of E-Procurement in Singapore. *Omega*, *37*(5), 972–987. doi:10.1016/j.omega.2008.11.001

Teo, T. S. H., Ranganathan, C., & Dhaliwal, J. (2006). Key dimensions of inhibitors for the deployment of web-based business-to-business electronic commerce. *IEEE Transactions on Engineering Management*, *53*(3), 395–411. doi:10.1109/TEM.2006.878106

Venkatesh, V., & Davis, F. D. (2000). A theoretical extension of the technology acceptance model: Four longitudinal field studies. *Management Science*, *46*(2), 186–204. doi:10.1287/mnsc.46.2.186.11926

Venkatesh, V., Morris, M. G., Davis, G. B., & Davis, F. D. (2003). User acceptance of information technology: Toward a unified view. *Management Information Systems Quarterly*, *27*(3), 425–478. doi:10.2307/30036540

Wang, Y. M., Wang, Y. S., & Yang, Y. F. (2010). Understanding the determinants of RFID adoption in the manufacturing industry. *Technological Forecasting and Social Change*, *77*(5), 803–815. doi:10.1016/j.techfore.2010.03.006

Xu, S., Zhu, K., & Gibbs, J. L. (2004). Global technology, local adoption: A cross-country investigation of Internet adoption by companies in the United States and China. *Electronic Markets*, *14*(1), 13–24. doi:10.1080/1019678042000175261

Yang, Z., Sun, J., Zhang, Y., & Wang, Y. (2015). Understanding SaaS adoption from the perspective of organizational users: A tripod readiness model. *Computers in Human Behavior*, *45*, 254–264. doi:10.1016/j.chb.2014.12.022

Yoon, T. E., & George, J. F. (2013). Why aren't organizations adopting virtual worlds? *Computers in Human Behavior*, *29*(3), 772–790. doi:10.1016/j.chb.2012.12.003

Zhu, K., Dong, S., Xu, S., & Kraemer, K. L. (2006). Innovation diffusion in global contexts: Determinants of post-adoption digital transformation of European companies. *European Journal of Information Systems*, *15*(6), 601–616. doi:10.1057/palgrave.ejis.3000650

Zhu, K., & Kraemer, K. L. (2005). Post-adoption variations in usage and value of e-business by organizations: Cross-country evidence from the retail industry. *Information Systems Research*, *16*(1), 61–84. doi:10.1287/isre.1050.0045

Chapter 7

An Overview on Adaptive Group Formation Technique and the Case of the AEHS MATHEMA

Alexandros Papadimitriou
School of Pedagogical and Technological Education, Greece

Georgios Gyftodimos
National and Kapodistrian University of Athens, Greece

ABSTRACT

This chapter presents the adaptive group formation and/or peer help technique implemented by various systems so far, and particularly, by web-based adaptive educational hypermedia systems (AEHSs). At first, some concepts about group formation and peer help are described, and a general description of the MATHEMA is made. Subsequently, the overview of the adaptive group formation considers extensively how several systems have implemented this technique so far. A comparative study of the presented systems with the MATHEMA is performed and conclusions are drawn. The systems that implement the adaptive group formation and/or peer help technique are the (M)CSCL, AELS, and AEHSs. In presentation of the adaptive grouping algorithm of the MATHEMA, the following are described: (1) how the priority list is created; (2) how the learners are supported in selecting their most suitable partner; (3) how the negotiation protocol works; and (4) how the peer groups are automatically linked up for a collaboration agreement using a peer-to-peer communication tool.

INTRODUCTION

Adaptive Educational Hypermedia Systems (AEHSs) combine ideas about hypermedia and intelligent tutoring systems (ITS) to produce applications whose content is adapted to each student's learning goal, knowledge level, performance, background, interests, preferences, stereotypes, cognitive preferences, and learning style, and they are stored in the learner's model. A number of research groups have independently realized that a hypermedia system coupled with an ITS can offer more functionality than a traditional static educational hypermedia (Brusilovsky & Peylo, 2003). AEHSs can be considered as a

DOI: 10.4018/978-1-5225-6367-9.ch007

solution to the problems of traditional online educational hypermedia systems. These problems are due to the static content, the "lost in hypermedia" syndrome and the "one-size-fits-all" approach. In Web-based AEHSs, several adaptive and intelligent techniques have been applied to introduce adaptation, such as curriculum sequence, adaptive presentation, adaptive navigation support, interactive problem solving support, intelligent analysis of student solutions, example-based problem solving support, and adaptive collaboration support or adaptive group formation and/or peer help (Brusilovsky & Peylo, 2003). According to Brusilovsky and Peylo (2003), a real AEHS should carry out all the above-mentioned techniques. Some examples of AEHSs are the AHA! (De Bra & Calvi, 1998), TANGOW (Carro, Ortigosa, Martin, & Schlichter, 2003), CA-OLE (Santamaria, 2006), and MOT 2.0 (Cristea & Ghali, 2011).

According to Brusilovsky and Peylo (2003), the technologies for adaptive group formation and/or peer help attempt to use knowledge about collaborating peers (most often represented in their student models) to form a matching group of kinds of collaborative tasks.

One major goal of learner-centeredness is to give active and collaborative learning environments (Lambert & McCombs, 1998). The learner-centered characteristic refers to students' independent learning by doing, combining personalized and collaborative learning, encouraging student interest in problem-solving and critical thinking, monitoring the development of students' knowledge and skills by the teacher, and the adaptability to each student (Jamal & Tilchin, 2016; Doyle & Tagg,2008). Dillenbourg (2002) defined collaborative learning as a situation in which two or more people learn or try to learn something together. Also, he supports that the decision on forming homogeneous or heterogeneous groups will primarily depend on the aim of collaborative learning activity (Dillenbourg, 2002). Heterogeneous groups that keep the differences between group members high, but not extreme will allow students to learn from each other. Collaborative learning can also enhance motivation when students care about the group they become more engaged with the task and achieve better learning outcomes (Slavin, 2010).

Recently, the nature of collaborative learning and the dynamics of group interactions in learning environments have gained much interest. The *group productivity* (the ability of a group to solve a problem) is determined by how well the group members work together. The *group effectiveness* is defined as both high performances of group members and their quality of work life (Cohen, Ledford, & Spreitzer, 1996). One way to enhance the effectiveness of collaborative learning is to structure interactions by engaging students in well-defined scripts. A collaboration script is a set of instructions prescribing how students should form groups, how they should interact and collaborate and how they should solve the problem (Dillenbourg, 2002). The group effectiveness is influenced by the task, traits, and skills (Vosniadou, 2008), as well as by the *willingness* and the *ability* of the group members to work efficiently together (Hersey & Blanchard, 1988).

Several studies have been conducted to find out how learning is improved by collaborating in learner dyads. Various studies have shown that problem solving which requires some kind of transfer can be improved after knowledge acquisition in pairs (Olivera & Straus, 2004). Hausmann, et al., (2008) suggest that the dyads solve more problems and request fewer hints during physics problem-solving than individuals. Research of Chester (2009) showed that the physics achievement of cooperative learning dyads was significant. Tao (1999) suggests that the rich collaborative talk of the dyads shows that peer collaboration provided students with experiences of co-construction and a conflict that is conducive to successful physics problem-solving. In addition, students' success in physics problem-solving depended not so much on their ability but on how they interacted and whether and how they invoked the relevant physics principles and strategies.

Group formation as a starting point of computer-supported collaborative learning (CSCL) plays a key role in achieving pedagogical goals. Various approaches have been reported on the literature to address this problem but none has offered an ideal solution (Sadeghi, 2016). Group learning outcomes may depend on many factors, including characteristics of each member, group composition, task context, behavior of each group, skills, and inclinations (Mujkanovic & Bollin, 2016). Parameters of learner profile such as personal details (marks, level of education, country of origin), individual learning style, experiences and interests (skills) are used as group formation policies (Spoelstra, van Rosmalen, Houtmans, & Sloep, 2015; Sun & Shen, 2014).

Peer help is the informal sharing of what we have learned from our experiences with other peers. A kind of peer help is an informal conversation with peers via the internet.

Forming suitable learning groups is one of the factors that figure ure the efficiency of collaborative learning activities. Moreover, the group effectiveness should be one of the goals of a system supporting collaboration. These goals are adopted by the AEHS MATHEMA. It combines both the constructivist and socio-constructivist didactic models, and it also supports both personalized and collaborative learning. The general aim of the AEHS MATHEMA is to support senior high school students or novices of higher education, through an interactive and constructivist educational material, in learning science, individually and/or collaboratively, and overcoming their possible misconceptions and learning difficulties. So far, the AEHS MATHEMA has supported curriculum sequencing, adaptive presentation, adaptive and meta-adaptive navigation, interactive problem solving, and adaptive group formation and peer help techniques. This chapter focuses on the adaptive group formation techniques implemented by various systems to date, mainly from the AEHSs, it also compares them with that of AEHS MATHEMA and then follows the full description of the adaptive group formation and peer help technique implemented by the AEHS MATHEMA.

The innovation of the adaptive group formation and peer help technique of the MATHEMA that makes it distinguishing from other systems, and particularly from AEHSs, is that the learner is given the full control for the choice of his or her collaborators, including the negotiation of a collaboration agreement with them, through a list of matching candidate peers, generated by the implemented algorithm, which takes into account their learning styles and their knowledge level on the current learning goal.

Unlike, the CSCL, MCSCL, AELS, and AEHSs, which have been developed so far and presented in this chapter, are based on a system-controlled and/or upon an educator-controlled design, that is, the group formation is decided by the system and/or by the educator while the learners are not allowed to change their group and/or negotiate a collaboration agreement with their possible candidate collaborators.

The rest of this chapter is structured as follows. Section 2 presents an overview of the systems that support group formation and/or peer help. Section 3 describes the learner-controlled adaptive group formation and peer help technique offered by the AEHS MATHEMA, and Section 4 summarizes the most significant points of the work and refers to future research directions.

AN OVERVIEW ON ADAPTIVE GROUP FORMATION AND/OR PEER HELP

Until recently, the primary goal of collaborative learning was the investigation whether and under what circumstances, collaborative learning was more effective than individual learning (Dillenbourg, Baker, Blaye, & O'Malley, 1996). Under the premise that the collaborative learning process depends on contextual, physical, and temporal factors (Vosniadou, 2008), several conditions have been studied such as the composition of the group, the individual prerequisites, the features of the task, the context of collaboration, and the medium available for communication.

Group formation may be used for a variety of purposes such as for grouping students, that could potentially benefit from cooperation, based upon their individual characteristics or needs, for mediating *peer help* by matching peer learners, and for facilitating instructors proposing an initial grouping approach (Christodoulopoulos & Papanikolaou, 2007). In this sense, group formation is a key issue to offer a successful collaborative experience. Peer helping can be considered as a subcategory of group formation for dyads since the system is trying to find the most suitable group member to carry out a task with a specific partner (Greer, McCalla, Collins, Kumar, Meagher, & Vassileva, 1998). The *adaptive group formation* research concerns two main questions: what are the group formation techniques and where exactly are the group formation results used? According to the group formation techniques, groups are formed either by combining the members' individual models or by observing, analyzing and finally measuring the quality and/or the quantity of the workgroup and use these results to form groups (Demetriadis & Karakostas, 2009). The aim of adaptive group formation might be to design a group of students all at a similar cognitive level and of similar interests or one where the participants bring different but complementary knowledge and skills (Muehlenbrock, 2006). The effective formation of learning groups is considered as one of the important keys to succeeding the collaborative learning activities (Dillenbourg, 2002).

The formation of student groups is taken into account by several researchers for personal characteristics and each difference between learners in teaching and learning. As students show development and each difference in teaching and learning, it is particularly important to take these differences into account in the group formation process (Vosniadou, 2008).

Spoelstra et al. (2015) presented a group formation model to decide a fitness value for a group of learners for a particular project. The model determined three types of variables that manage the group formation process: knowledge, personality, and preferences. According to Spoelstra et al. (2015) the knowledge is the most important feature to be used in the group formation process, over preferences and finally personality.

Hórreo and Carro (2007) studied the impact of personality and group formation on learner performance. The information obtained by this study can be incorporated into collaborative systems as criteria for group formation, with the aim of favoring Computer Supported Collaborative Learning (CSCL) situations where students are prone to get better results.

Computer technology can be applied to support the adaptive group formation and/or peer help. In the domain of educational technology, the CSCL has been developed, and it is based on the socio-cultural theory of Vygotsky (1978). The socio-cultural approach focuses on the causal relationship between social interaction and personal cognitive change. Until recently, most support for group formation in CSCL systems was based on learner profile information such as gender, class and other features of the learner (e.g., Cavanaugh, Ellis, Layton, & Ardis, 2004). In traditional classrooms, the teachers form group students in work groups, but in CSCL systems, group formation can be performed either by the educator (in the classroom or using the information stored in the system) or automatically by the system (Carro et al., 2003; Bratitsis & Demetriadis, 2012, 2013).

If the group formation is performed by the system, it can be done randomly or by taking into account personal features included in the user and group models. Cavanaugh et al. (2004) designed the *Team-Maker*, a web-based system that aims at reducing instructors' time in allocating students to groups. The system takes some learner characteristics such as gender, skills, and students' schedules, and the instructor's criteria for the creation of homogeneous or heterogeneous groups. Read et al., (2006) designed and implemented the *COPPER* system, where personalized and collaborative learning is combined within a constructivist approach to help second language learning. The adaptive group formation algorithm dynamically generates communicative groups based on the linguistic capabilities of available students and a collection of collaborative activity templates. The results of a student's activity within a group are evaluated by a student's monitor that empowers students and further consolidates what have been previously learned. Students, therefore, initially work individually in this framework of certain linguistic concepts and after taking part in authentic collaborative communicative activities.

Some researchers forming groups of students, according to the learning style of learners. Cristodoulopoulos and Papanikolaou (2007) presented a web-based group formation tool that supports the instructor to manually create both homogeneous and heterogeneous student groups based upon specific criteria, as well as, the learners are informed about the formed groups, as well as they are allowed to negotiate their group assignment. The criteria used by the authors are the knowledge level for the current lesson, the learning style according to the Felder-Silverman model, the Reflective/Active and the Pragmatist/Theorist dimensions of the Honey and Mumford's model.

Kyprianidou, Demetriadis, Pombortsis, and Karatasios (2009) implemented a Web-based system named *PEGASUS*. PEGASUS is expected to help students and teachers towards two distinct goals: enhancing metacognition (students and teachers are supported to identify their learning and teaching preferences, which in turn is used as a framework for reflection), and group formation (the system suggests homogeneous or heterogeneous workgroups based upon the student's learning style, supporting also teacher-students negotiations of the last group participation.) In similar research, a multi-agent intelligent system was introduced called *I-MINDS* (Soh, Khandaker, & Jiang, 2008) where the instructor, each student, and each group is represented by an intelligent agent. The student agent profiles the student and finds compatible students to form the student's "body group." The agents communicate and form coalitions dynamically. Since the group formation, each student agent bid to join its favorite group based upon their earlier performance in group activities.

A newer system is the *PopCorm* (Popular Collaborative Platform) presented by Srba and Bieliková (2015), which supports kinds of collaboration scenarios in formal or informal learning settings. In formal learning settings, students can collaborate on short-term tasks which supplementary learning materials provided by the particular course. These tasks can be prepared by a teacher who plays the role of the instructor. A teacher can check students' collaboration with the provided statistics and even by observing the current created content in real-time. In informal learning, members of different communities (e.g. workplace teams, communities of practice) can collaborate on tasks which support their involvement in their organizations.

There have been many approaches of the field of AI and Education for providing adaptive group formation and/or peer help for the learner. Examples of adaptive group formation and/or peer help include forming a group for collaborative problem solving (Ikeda & Mizoguchi, 1997), for finding peers who are ready, willing and able to help with tasks (Greer et al., 1998) or peer helper suggestion based upon contextual parameters (Muehlenbrock, 2006), and for self-, peer-, and collaborative-assessment process (Gouli, Gogoulou, & Grigoriadou, 2006).

Ikeda and Mizoguchi (1997) suggest the *"Opportunistic Group Formation"* to form a collaborative learning group dynamically and context dependently. The term "Opportunistic" implies that the model can prescribe the right situation to form the collaborative learning group. When the system detects the situation for a learner to shift from individual learning mode to collaborative learning mode, it forms a learning group of which each member is assigned a reasonable learning goal and a social role which are consistent with the goal for the group. When the negotiation mechanism finds a learner who asks collaboration, it initiates a negotiation with other tutoring systems to dynamically form a learning group proper to the learner's goal. The goal of negotiation is the learner to get the largest social utility from collaborative learning.

Greer et al. (1998) presented a system called *PHelpS* which supports the workers as they do their tasks, offers help in finding peer helpers when required, and mediates communication with task-related topics. When a worker runs into difficulty in carrying out a task, PHelpS provides a list of other workers who are ready, willing and able to help him or her. The worker then selects a particular helper with PHelpS supporting the subsequent help interaction. The PHelpS system acts as a facilitator to stimulate learning and collaboration, and not as a directive agent imposing its perspectives on the workers. In this way, PHelpS facilitates the creation of extensive informal peer help networks, where workers help one another with tasks.

Muehlenbrock (2006) combines information from learner profiles and information on the learner context. It allows for the ad-hoc creation of learning groups, which is especially useful either for peer help for immediate problems or for reducing the risk of disruptions. The building of learning groups could also be enriched by information available on the experience of previous collaborations, which could be provided by peers but also from a teacher if available. Furthermore, the group formation could include information on the type of support needed, among others. Using a networked infrastructure of easily available sensors and context-processing components, an application has been developed for peer helper suggestion and opportunistic group formation based upon contextual parameters such as location, activity, and availability.

Gouli et al. (2006) developed the *PECASSE* system which implements self-assessment, peer-assessment, and collaborative-assessment in a Web-based educational environment. It offers facilities for group formation, collaboration, activity submission, a review process, revision of the activity, assignment and evaluation of assessors. Peer assessment refers to those activities of learners in which they judge and test the work and/or the performance of their peers.

MATEO (Arias-Báez, Pavlich-Mariscal, & Ramos, 2013) is a generic system for adaptive group formation taking into account group candidates' characteristics, context (both individual and collective), and team-forming criteria. The candidates' characteristics are gender, age, culture, knowledge, competencies, and personality. MATEO can yield three types of output: empty groups (no group could be formed to satisfy the required criteria); unique group (only one group could be formed to satisfy the required criteria); or, multiple groups (several groups could be formed to satisfy the required criteria).

In recent years, an attempt has been made to form groups in Adaptive E-Learning Systems (AELS) and in Mobile Computer Supported Collaborative Learning (MCSCL). In the *COFALE* (Chieu, 2007), which is based on cognitive flexibility theory, through Learner Model Manager, stereotyped learner (or user) models can be defined according to the different groups of learners like novices or experts. Different communication tools are also available like discussion forums, chat room, inbox for sending & receiving messages and immediate messaging facility to online learners, and learners' hyperspace area for group solving situations. COFALE may suggest some "experts" students to a "novice", so that he or she can ask them some questions about problems, or may suggest an "expert" student to another "expert" student so that they can exchange ideas.

Topolor (Shi, Qudah, Qaffas, & Cristea, 2013) is a social personalized adaptive e-learning system based on the connectivist learning theory that combines adaptive group formation and project management recommendations with social learning domain adaptation. Topolor approaches for providing adaptive recommendations to support students' decisions on project choice based on students' knowledge and skills; group membership, based on student's profile characteristics; project tasks, based on students' personality; and communication tools. The aim of these recommendations is to offer performance monitoring and dynamic support to the user, to increase the acceptance of the virtual team project.

Walker, Rummel, and Koedinger (2014) implemented in the *APTA* system an adaptive group formation based on learning styles, which are determined systematically based on the students' profile. The APTA system provides adaptive support to enhance the tutoring ability of peer tutors and uses multiple sources of information to assess collaborative state: a combination of problem-solving information, student self-classifications of their own chat, and machine classifications of student chat. APTA focuses on peer tutoring actions and models, both correct and incorrect behaviors.

Kompan and Bieliková (2016) in the *ALEF* system bridge the gap between an active collaborative learning and the usage of students' Felder and Silverman learning styles in the e-learning. They designed a group recommendation module which demonstrates the usage of the method for enhancing e-learning systems with students' learning styles, and the collaborative group learning by the construction of study groups based on the similar members' learning styles and construction of group recommendations.

In the *ELARS* (Knez, Dlab, & Hoic-Bozic, 2017) the grouping algorithms enable the automatic creation of groups that meet the pedagogic criterion set by the teacher as well as the students' preferences. The criterion for automatic group formation includes the following characteristics: the program of study, gender, learning styles, knowledge level, Web 2.0 tools preferences, and activity level. The automatic group formation supports the teacher in dividing the students enrolled in the e-tivity into groups according to the specific criterion. This is accomplished by implementing group formation algorithms and recommending grouping of the students to the teacher.

In the Mobile Computer Supported Collaborative Learning (MCSCL), Amara, Macedo, Bendella, and Santos (2015) proposed a group formation mechanism that is based upon the combination of three types of grouping criteria: learner's Felder and Silverman's learning styles, learner's behaviors, and context information. The instructors can freely select the type, the number, and the weight of grouping criteria with other settings such as the number, the size, and the type of learning groups (homogeneous or heterogeneous).

Examples of adaptive group formation in AEHSs are the following: In the *TANGOW* system (Carro et al., 2003) the adaptation techniques dynamically generate adaptive collaborative Web-based courses. These courses are generated at runtime by selecting the most suitable tasks for each student and at every step, the time in which the tasks are presented, the specific problems to be solved, the most suitable partners to cooperate with, and the collaborative tools to support the group cooperation. This choice is based on the users' personal features, preferences, knowledge, and behavior while interacting with the course. In the *TANGOW-WOTAN* system (Martin & Paredes, 2004) the default criteria for group formation consist of combining active students with reflective ones of Felder-Soloman model in similar percentages. They studied the impact on learning styles and group homogeneity/heterogeneity based on the results obtained by students in collaborative tasks. Thus, they concluded that some dimensions of the learning style model seem to affect the quality of the resulting work.

In the *CA-OLE* system (Santamaria, 2006) the adaptive group formation is done by placing students with a similar level of knowledge in the same group. By allowing collaboration between students within the group, teamwork and group effort are developed and the learning experience is improved. Students collaborate with peers assigned to the same group. CA-OLE analyses score and time for each of the tests and for each of the sections included in the lesson. A new group may be assigned based on this analysis and this new group is the team the student will be interacting with for the next learning lesson.

In the *MOT 2.0* system (Cristea & Ghali, 2011) the grouping mechanism is based upon the given course. MOT 2.0 as a social-AEHS supports both social interactions between students (via a chat tool) and interaction between students and system (via adaptive content recommendations). MOT 2.0 can create multiple groups and assign different privileges to different users based upon their knowledge, social and grouping features (such as tagging, rating, feedback, subscriptions) as well as it offers help to learners in finding peer helpers.

ADAPTIVE GROUP FORMATION AND PEER HELP IN THE AEHS MATHEMA

The Table 1 lists the main features of all the above mentioned CSCL, MCSCL, AELS, and AEH systems supporting the adaptive group formation and/or peer help technique.

Most of the systems presented in Table 1 are based upon several learners' characteristics to support the adaptive group formation and/or peer help, and they also carry out it based upon a system-controlled and/or upon an educator-controlled design. That is, the system or the educator decides the group formation and the learners are informed without having the ability changing it or negotiating a *collaboration agreement* with their candidate collaborators.

Exceptions are the CSCL tools of Christodoulopoulos and Papanikolaou (2007) and Kyprianidou et al. (2009) mentioned above, where the system categorizes the learners into groups and then it allows them to communicate with the educator to negotiate their final group participation. However, these CSCL systems do not offer the learners the control and appropriate help to choose their collaborators and negotiate with them a collaboration agreement.

In addition, two of the CSCL systems of Table 1 (Muehlenbrock's system and PHelpS) offer help to the learners in finding peer helpers making use of the following learner characteristics: agenda information, availability of preferred communication channels, activity, location, willingness, ability, availability, and knowledge profile. However, these systems present the peer helpers in a list without taking into account the learning styles about their group effectiveness, as well as these systems do not use the student's learning style in combination with his or her knowledge level to form groups.

In Ikeda & Mizoguchi's system (1997) the negotiation is done with other tutoring systems to dynamically form a learning group proper to the learner's goal.

The AEHSs listed in Table 1 (CA-OLE, MOT 2.0, TANGOW, TANGOW/WOTAN) make use of the knowledge level, social and grouping features (tagging, rating, feedback subscriptions), users' personal features, preferences, behavior while interacting with the course, and learning styles as characteristics for the adaptive group formation. The group formation is decided by the system, and the learners are informed without having the ability to change it or to negotiate a collaboration agreement with their possible candidate collaborators. Moreover, none of these systems uses learning styles combined with the level of learner knowledge to support the adaptive group formation and/or peer help.

Table 1. Adaptive group formation and/or peer help implementations in (M)CSCL, AELS, and AEHSs

System	(M) CSCL or AEHS or AELS	Learner Characteristics for Group Formation and/or peer help	Method of Group Formation and/or Peer Help	Assistance to the Learners in Selecting Their Collaborator and Negotiating a Collaboration Agreement
ALEF (Kompan & Bieliková, 2016)	AELS	Felder and Silverman's learning styles.	Adaptive group formation.	-
Amara's et al. group formation mechanism (2015)	MCSCL	Felder and Silverman's learning styles, and learner's behaviors.	Adaptive group formation.	-
APTA (Walker et al., 2014)	AELS	Learning styles.	Adaptive group formation.	-
CA-OLE (Santamaria, 2006)	AEHS	Knowledge level.	Adaptive group formation.	-
Christodoulopoulos & Papanikolaou's system (2007)	CSCL	Knowledge level for the current lesson, learning styles.	Adaptive group formation.	Teacher-students negotiations of the final group participation.
COPPER (Read et al., 2006)	CSCL	Linguistic capabilities of available students, and a collection of collaborative activity templates.	Adaptive group formation.	-
COFALE (Chieu, 2007)	AELS	Experts and novices.	Adaptive group formation.	-
ELARS (Knez, et al., 2017)	AELS	Gender, learning styles, Web 2.0 tools preferences, knowledge level, and activity level.	Adaptive group formation.	-
Ikeda & Mizoguchi's system (1997)	CSCL	Learning goal and social role.	Adaptive group formation.	Negotiation with other tutoring systems to dynamically form a learning group proper to the learner's goal.
I-MINDS (Soh, et al., 2008)	CSCL	Previous performance in group activities.	Adaptive group formation.	-
MATEO (Arias-Báez, et al., 2013)	CSCL	Gender, age, knowledge, culture, competencies, personality.	Adaptive group formation.	-
MOT 2.0 (Cristea & Ghali, 2011)	AEHS	Knowledge level, social and grouping features (tagging, rating, feedback, subscriptions).	Adaptive group formation and peer help.	Assistance in finding peer helpers.
Muehlenbrock's system (2006)	CSCL	Agenda information, availability of preferred communication channels.	Adaptive group formation and peer help.	Assistance in finding peer helpers.
PECASSE (Gouli et al., 2006)	CSCL	Learners' proficiency and learners' ability as assessors.	Adaptive group formation for collaborative assessment.	-
PEGASUS (Kyprianidou et., 2009)	CSCL	Learning style.	Adaptive group formation and negotiations.	Teacher-students negotiations of the final group participation.
PHelpS (Greer et al., 1998)	CSCL	Willingness, ability, availability, and knowledge profile.	Peer helping.	Assistance in finding peer helpers.
PopCorm (Srba and Bieliková, 2015)	AELS	Interests, knowledge or any other personal characteristics (e.g. age, gender), and students' collaborative behavior.	Adaptive group formation.	-
Spoelstra et al. model (2015)	AELS	Knowledge, personality, and preferences.	Adaptive group formation.	-
TANGOW (Carro et al., 2003)	AEHS	Users' personal features, preferences, knowledge and behavior while interacting with the course.	Adaptive group formation.	-
TANGOW/WOTAN (Martin & Paredes, 2004)	AEHS	Active/reflective of Felder-Soloman model.	Adaptive group formation.	-
Team-Maker (Cavanaugh et al., 2004)	CSCL	Gender, skills, students' schedules, and the instructor's criteria for the creating groups.	Adaptive group formation.	-
Topolor (Shi, et al., 2013)	AELS	Students' knowledge, skills, profile, and personality.	Adaptive group formation.	-

Taking into consideration the:

- Importance of the learning style as one of the learners' characteristic influencing positively on the group productivity and effectiveness (Gardner & Korth, 1997);
- Learner-centeredness as the main goal of active and collaborative learning environments (Lambert & McCombs, 1998), as well as the collaboration willingness as a significant factor influencing the group effectiveness (Hersey & Blanchard, 1988);

A learner-controlled adaptive group formation and peer help technique were designed and implemented in the AEHS MATHEMA by using the abstract and concrete dimensions of learning styles and knowledge level on the current learning goal of learners as characteristics for adaptation.

In the current version, the MATHEMA offers physics lessons on electromagnetism. It is well-known that physics consists of difficult abstract concepts. Piaget (1983) has identified the concrete-abstract continuum as the main dimension along which human cognitive growth occurs and represents the major directions of cognitive development. Taking into consideration both of them, the selection of the abstract-concrete dimension of student learning styles to form student groups was decided. Some students may grasp abstract concepts readily while others need concrete imagery to learn (Wolfe & Kolb, 1979). Abstract dimension allows learners to visualize, conceiving ideas, to understand or believe in what they cannot actually see. Concrete dimension enables learners to register information directly through their five senses.

A learning style model, recognizing the abstract-concrete dimension of student learning style is Kolb's one which is based on his *Experiential Learning Theory* (ELT) (Kolb, 1984). Kolb argues that most people prefer to learn with one of the following four learning styles: *Diverging, Assimilating, Converging and Accommodating*. Diverging is characterized as concrete and reflective, Assimilating is characterized as abstract and reflective, Converging is characterized as abstract and active, and Accommodating is characterized as concrete and active. How students prefer to learn can have a significant impact on their performance in group work. The use of Kolb's experiential learning model in conjunction with the learning groups enhances the learning process, reinforces the link between theory and practice, and facilitates the transfer of learning to the workplace (Gardner & Korth, 1997). Kolb and Kolb (2005) have developed a revised questionnaire to recognize the learners' learning styles, the Kolb's LSI questionnaire.

In order to restrict the parameters making the design of adaptive group formation more complex, investigations into Kolb's learning style model were studied, and especially, investigations examining the influence of active-reflective dimensions on students' performance when they collaboratively solve problems. A relative research of Sandmire, Vroman, and Sanders (2000) studied the influence of students' individual learning style preference (active and reflective dimensions of Kolb's learning styles) on collaborative performance. For this research, they used 78 occupational and physical therapy students in a problem-solving activity. The students were randomly assigned in pairs to one of three subsets (active-active groups, active-reflective groups, and reflective-reflective groups) based on their Kolb's LSI scores (active vs. reflective). The students viewed a videotape of a quadriplegic patient's physical examination (neuroscience course) and completed a collaborative exercise that required performance skills at all levels of Bloom's taxonomy of learning. The results of this research indicated that *the active-active, reflective-reflective, and active-reflective student groups have no significant performance differences, when they collaborate in problem-solving activities.*

Taking all the above into consideration, an experimental study was conducted in order to investigate the influence of concrete and abstract dimensions of Kolb's learning style model on the group effectiveness (both high performance and quality of work life of students) in problem-solving activities (Papadimitriou & Gyftodimos, 2007). The conclusions of the experimental study are the following:

1. A Diverging (concrete) collaborates better with a Diverging (concrete) than with an Assimilating (abstract).
2. An Assimilating (abstract) collaborates better with an Assimilating (abstract) than with a Diverging (concrete).
3. A Converging (abstract) collaborates better with a Converging (abstract) than with an Accommodating (concrete).
4. An Accommodating (concrete) collaborates better with an Accommodating (concrete) than with a Converging (abstract).
5. In the same research, the collaboration willingness and the ability of the student group members were also confirmed that they are significant factors of the group effectiveness.

According to the above results, the learning style is considered that not only is a factor of decisive importance when designing modern educational systems, but also the chosen dimensions of student's learning style for group formation should fit with the scope. For example, if the scope consists of difficult abstract concepts (e.g., physics) then, it will be best to use the abstract and concrete dimensions of student's learning style for forming groups.

Of course, it should be taken into consideration that the results of the experiment performed concern only the specific context and scope, and they might be verified on a large scale of subject matter experiments, on different domains and levels of knowledge and students' age as well, in order to constitute a generalized rule on forming students' groups for any educational purpose. However, they indicate a path to follow as a method applicable to different contexts.

Taking all those mentioned above into consideration, the adaptive group formation and peer help technique were designed and implemented in the AEHS MATHEMA.

IMPLEMENTATION OF THE ADAPTIVE GROUP FORMATION AND PEER HELP

In order to design and carry out the adaptive group formation algorithm in the AEHS MATHEMA, the following conditions were taken into consideration:

1. The importance of learning style, as one of the learners' characteristics influencing positively on the group productivity and effectiveness (Gardner & Korth, 1997);
2. The learner-centeredness as the main goal of active and collaborative learning environments (Lambert & McCombs, 1998), as well as the collaboration willingness as a significant factor influencing the group effectiveness (Hersey & Blanchard, 1988);
3. The results of our experimental study in forming groups for problem-solving activities (abstract and/or concrete groups with the same active or reflective dimension of learning style) and the results of Sandmire et al. (2000) research.

As those mentioned above, the results of the experimental study of forming student groups are the following:

1. A Diverging (concrete) collaborates better with a Diverging (concrete) than with an Assimilating (abstract).
2. An Assimilating (abstract) collaborates better with an Assimilating (abstract) than with a Diverging (concrete).
3. A Converging (abstract) collaborates better with a Converging (abstract) than with an Accommodating (concrete).
4. An Accommodating (concrete) collaborates better with an Accommodating (concrete) than with a Converging (abstract).

It is important to point out that the participants of this research have had the same active or reflective dimension of learning style.

According to Sandmire's et al. (2000) research that mentioned above, the active-active, reflective-reflective and active-reflective student groups have no significant performance differences when they collaborate in problem-solving activities. Seeing that the active-reflective dimension of students' learning style has no significant performance differences when students collaborate in problem-solving activities, the results of our experimental study to abstract and concrete students that have different active or reflective dimension of learning style were extended, and the following results were obtained:

1. A Diverging (concrete) collaborates better with an Accommodating (concrete) than with a Converging (abstract).
2. An Assimilating (abstract) collaborates better with a Converging (abstract) than with an Accommodating (concrete).
3. A Converging (abstract) collaborates better with an Assimilating (abstract) than with a Diverging (concrete).
4. An Accommodating (concrete) collaborates better with a Diverging (concrete) than with an Assimilating (abstract).
5. An example explaining our argument is as follows: in (5) the conclusion that the Diverging (concrete) collaborates better with an Accommodating than with a Converging (concrete) arises from the conclusion of our experimental study, that is, the concrete-concrete students collaborate significantly better on problem-solving activities than the concrete-abstract students.

Furthermore, it was taken into consideration that the learner-centeredness should be the main goal of active and collaborative learning environments (Lambert & McCombs, 1998) and that the willingness and ability of the group members are significant factors influencing the group effectiveness (Hersey & Blanchard, 1988), the algorithm was decided to be designed in such a way that the system to give each learner a priority list of candidate collaborators taking into account the learner's concrete or abstract dimension of learning style and the concrete or abstract dimension of learning style and knowledge level on the current learning goal of his or her candidate collaborators, and the learner to have also the ability (full control) to select his or her candidate collaborator. The learners who choose a different learning goal do not appear on the priority list.

Table 2 demonstrates the way that the adaptive group formation algorithm sorts the matching candidate collaborators of a certain student in the priority list. For example, in the first row of Table 2, according to (1) the *"Diverging"* is placed in the first position and the *"Assimilating"* is placed in the second position, according to (5) the *"Accommodating"* is placed in the third position and the *"Converging"* is placed in the fourth position.

In case that more than one candidate collaborator belongs to the same learning style category, then the algorithm takes into account the knowledge level on the current learning goal of each candidate collaborator and it sorts them according to their knowledge level on the current learning goal. The knowledge level on the current learning goal of each candidate collaborator is the sum of all his or her grades in the assessment tests of main concepts derived from his or her study of the current learning goal (a chapter of physics) until that moment.

Table 3 shows how the algorithm selects and sorts the possible candidate collaborators for a student who has Diverging learning style, taking into account his or her collaborators learning style and knowledge level on the current learning goal.

Example explaining the sequence of collaborators according to each collaborator's knowledge level on the current learning goal, is the following: the Students 4, 3, and 10 have *"Assimilating"* learning style but the Student 4 is placed on the ordering list before the Student 3 because the knowledge level of the Student 4 on the current learning goal is greater than the knowledge level of the Student 3 on the same learning goal (45>28), as well as the Student 3 is placed on the ordering list before the Student 10 because the knowledge level of the Student 3 on the current learning goal is greater than the knowledge level of the Student 10 on the same learning goal (28>25). In this table, the characterizations Student 1, 2, 3 etc. were used in order to hold the students anonymous for ethic and personal data reasons.

The learner can select a peer or to declare his or her collaboration willingness through the adaptive group formation and peer help tool offered by the AEHS MATHEMA (see Figure ure 1).

Whenever learners wish to collaborate with peers, then they have two options on the group formation tool, as follows:

Table 2. Priority of a learner's candidate collaborators according to their learning style

Learning Style of a Student	Ordering of his or her Candidate Collaborators in the Priority List According to Their Learning Style			
	1st Position	**2nd Position**	**3d Position**	**4th Position**
Diverging (concrete) (reflective)	*Diverging* (concrete) (reflective)	*Assimilating* (abstract) (reflective)	*Accommodating* (concrete) (active)	*Converging* (abstract) (active)
Assimilating (abstract) (reflective)	*Assimilating* (abstract) (reflective)	*Diverging* (concrete) (reflective)	*Converging* (abstract) (active)	*Accommodating* (concrete) (active)
Converging (abstract) (active)	*Converging* (abstract) (active)	*Accommodating* (concrete) (active)	*Assimilating* (abstract) (reflective)	*Diverging* (concrete) (reflective)
Accommodating (concrete) (active)	*Accommodating* (concrete) (active)	*Converging* (abstract) (active)	*Diverging* (concrete) (reflective)	*Assimilating* (abstract) (reflective)

Table 3. Selection and sorting candidate peers of a student with a diverging learning style

Priority	Candidate Collaborators	Learning Style	Knowledge Level on the Current Learning Goal
1	Student 5	Diverging	40
2	Student 1	Diverging	30
3	Student 4	Assimilating	45
4	Student 3	Assimilating	28
5	Student 10	Assimilating	25
6	Student 11	Accommodating	50
7	Student 7	Accommodating	40
8	Student 9	Accommodating	32
9	Student 8	Converging	45
10	Student 6	Converging	32
11	Student 12	Converging	20

Figure 1. Adaptive group formation and peer help tool implemented in the AEHS MATHEMA

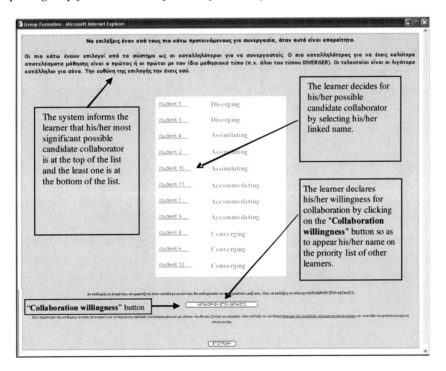

1. They can select a candidate collaborator, who declared willingness for collaboration, by clicking on his or her linked name. In this case, the system informs the learner that his or her most significant possible candidate collaborator is at the top of the list, and the least significant one is at the bottom of the list. The learner decides for his or her collaborator by selecting his or her linked name on the priority list and the chat tool automatically opens (see Figure . 2). Then, the learner

can negotiate a collaboration agreement with his or her candidate collaborator. Figure . 1 shows a snapshot containing the linked names of the possible candidate collaborators for a learner who has the "Diverging" learning style.

2. They can click on the "Collaboration willingness" button to declare their willingness for collaboration (see Figure 1) aiming at negotiating with other learners a collaboration agreement. In this case, the system informs the learner that his or her collaboration willingness (his or her linked name) will appear on the priority list of other learners. Then, the learner opens the chat tool and waits for a negotiation request from another learner.

The *negotiation protocol* via the chat tool (synchronous communication) of the AEHS MATHEMA is as follows:

1. The learner declares the willingness to collaborate either by selecting his or her partner from the priority list of candidate collaborators or by declaring a desire for collaboration so that others that would like to work with him or her to be able to choose his or her linked name, and then activates the synchronous communication tool.

2. The peers negotiate collaboration agreement and if they agree with each other, then both state it in the system by clicking on the "Collaboration agreement" button (see Figure 2) to drop their linked name from the priority list of other learners that would like to collaborate with them. Also, when a peer-to-peer connection is made through the synchronous communication tool, then no other learner is allowed to join. It happens because the chat tool allows for only two peers (a dyad) to collaborate synchronously.

3. After negotiating and updating the system that they agree with each other to collaborate, learners can start the collaboration, communicating with the chat tool synchronously, to exchange their experience, opinions, and findings. They also can interchange Web pages and files.

More information about the negotiation protocol and chat tool handling are given by the system through the "Help" option in the toolbar area of the AEHS MATHEMA.

Figure 2 shows the dialogue between two peers via the chat tool where they negotiate a collaboration agreement.

The dialogue between the two peers shown in the snapshots of Figure 2 is as follows:

Giannis: Hello Mary.

Mary: Hello Giannis.

Giannis: Do you want to collaborate with me?

Mary: Yes, of course!

Giannis: OK! Let us click on the "Collaboration agreement" button.

Mary: OK! Please, send me the page with last results to compare with my own and then to negotiate with them.

Figure 2. Snapshots of the dialogue between two peers via the chat tool

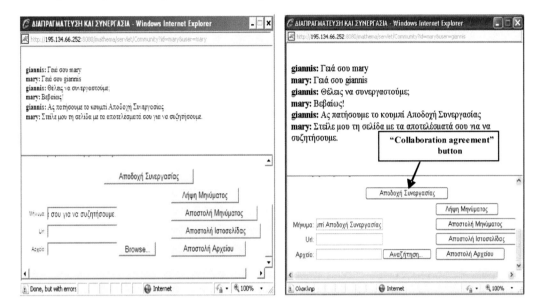

Chat tool interactions are considered informal. Thus, the chat tool supporting the learners' collaboration might be considered as an *informal peer help network*.

DISCUSSION AND FUTURE RESEARCH DIRECTIONS

This chapter is particularly focused on the adaptive group formation and/or peer help technique offered by various CSCL, MCSCL, AELS, and AEHS as well as by the AEHS MATHEMA.

From the systems shown in Table 1, only the PHelpS system uses the willingness and ability as characteristics for adaptive group formation and peer help. The AELS tools usually use students' knowledge and skills, collaborative behavior, profile, activity level, preferences, and personality as well experts and novices as learner characteristics for adaptive group formation. The recent AELS uses learning style as learners' characteristics for adaptive group formation. The CSCL tools usually use knowledge level, learning goal, social role, performance, gender, motivation, attitudes, interests, and learning styles as learners' characteristics for adaptive group formation. The AEHS tools usually use knowledge level, social and grouping features personal features, preferences, and learning styles as learners' characteristics for adaptive group formation.

In general, the tendency in recent years is the use of learners learning style as learner characteristic for adaptive group formation, as it supported by the systems ALEF, APTA, PEGASUS, ELARS, Amara's et al. group formation mechanism, etc. In the CSCL, MCSCL, and AELS tools, such as those mentioned above, are not offered to the learners the control and the assistance in selecting peers and negotiating a collaboration agreement with them. Two of the CSCL systems offer help to the learners in finding their peer helpers. However, these systems present the peer helpers on a list without taking into account their classmates' learning styles and group effectiveness, as well as those systems, do not use the peers learning style combined with their knowledge level to form groups.

The adaptive group formation and peer help technique of the AEHS MATHEMA is an innovative technique in the area of AEHSs because the AEHSs developed so far, such as those mentioned above, are based on a system-controlled and/or upon an educator-controlled design. That is, the system or the educator decides the group formation and the learners are informed without having the ability changing it or negotiating a *collaboration agreement* with their candidate collaborators. Moreover, none of those systems uses learning styles combined with the knowledge level of learners in supporting the adaptive group formation and/or peer help.

The way in which the adaptive group formation algorithm generates a priority list with the matching candidate collaborators for a certain student, the way in which the algorithm supports the learners in selecting the most suitable collaborator, and the way in which the algorithm automatically links the candidate collaborators (peers) up via a chat tool for the aim of negotiating a collaboration agreement, are described in this chapter.

In the design of the MATHEMA, has taken into account that a significant factor influencing the performance of students is their ability to collaborate effectively together as well as that the learner-centeredness, the group productivity, and group effectiveness should be the main goals of a system supporting collaboration.

At this time, the improvement in the adaptive group formation algorithm is in progress. Our effort has been focused on forming a more generalized algorithm to be able to engage with groups of learners that follow different curricula in different schools. The system will decide on the formation of groups taking into account the new parameters involved such as the level of the subject matter achieved in each student's class at the time of each experiment, the assessments of the teacher on the open-ended questions, and the time obligations of each learner.

DISCUSSION QUESTIONS IN CLASSROOM

1. What are Adaptive Educational Hypermedia Systems (AEHS) and what problems are they try to solve?
2. What is the major goal of learner-centeredness?
3. Why is collaborative learning effective?
4. What is group productivity and effectiveness?
5. What does peer help mean?
6. What is the positive contribution of students' dyads to collaboration?
7. What is the innovation of adaptive group formation and peer help technique of the MATHEMA?
8. What basic types of Web-based applications use the adaptive group formation and/or peer help technique?
9. What basic characteristics of the learner have been used by the main types of Web-based educational technology topics for the adaptive group formation and/or peer help technique?
10. What is the main characteristic of learners used in recent years for adaptive group formation and/or peer help technique?
11. What basic problem is trying to solve the adaptive group formation and/or peer help technique of the MATHEMA?
12. What basic issues do the design of the adaptive group formation and peer help technique of the MATHEMA take into account?

13. Homogeneous or heterogeneous groups are formed in the AEHS MATHEMA? Who are they?
14. According to the research carried out, what dimensions of Kolb's learning style do not improve the performance of problem-solving skills through peer collaboration?
15. What learner's characteristics are used for adaptive group formation and why by the AEHS MATHEMA?
16. How is the AEHS MATHEMA informal peer helping achieved?
17. What is the tendency towards recent years for adaptive group formation with regard to the use learner characteristics?
18. Describe the operation of the negotiation protocol in the AEHS MATHEMA.
19. How is the automatic connection between two peers in adaptive group formation technique of the AEHS MATHEMA done?
20. What is the primary and what is the secondary learner characteristic used in the adaptive group formation technique of the AEHS MATHEMA?

ACKNOWLEDGMENT

We express our gratitude to Professor Emeritus Grigoriadou Maria for her contribution to first research work published in the International Journal of e-Collaboration with the title "A Web-based Learner-Controlled Adaptive Group Formation Technique", which has been improved and presented in this chapter of the book.

REFERENCES

Amara, S., Macedo, J., Bendella, F., & Santos, A. (2016). Group Formation in Mobile Computer Supported Collaborative Learning Contexts: A Systematic Literature Review. *Journal of Educational Technology & Society*, *19*(2), 258–273.

Anderson, T. (2008). *The Theory and Practice of Online Learning*. Athabasca University Press.

Arias-Báez, M. P., Pavlich-Mariscal, J. A., & Ramos, A. C. (2013). Forming adapted teams oriented to collaboration: Detailed design and case study. *journal. Dyna (Bilbao)*, *10*(1), 87–94.

Bratitsis, T., & Demetriadis, S. (2012). Perspectives on Tools for Computer-Supported Collaborative Learning. *International Journal of e-Collaboration*, *8*(4), 1–7. doi:10.4018/jec.2012100101

Bratitsis, T., & Demetriadis, S. (2013). Research Approaches in Computer-Supported Collaborative Learning. *International Journal of e-Collaboration*, *9*(1), 1–8. doi:10.4018/jec.2013010101

Brusilovsky, P., & Peylo, C. (2003). Adaptive and Intelligent Web-Based Educational Systems. *International Journal of Artificial Intelligence in Education*, *13*, 156–169.

Carro, R. M., Ortigosa, A., Martin, E., & Schlichter, J. (2003). Dynamic Generation of Adaptive Web-based Collaborative Courses. *Journal of Lecture Notes on Computer Science*, *2806*, 191–198. doi:10.1007/978-3-540-39850-9_17

Cavanaugh, R., Ellis, M., Layton, R., & Ardis, M. (2004). *Automating the Process of Assigning Students to Cooperative-Learning Teams.* Paper presented at the American Society for Engineering Education Annual Conference and Exposition, Salt Lake City, UT.

Chester, V. (2009). *The relationship between cooperative learning and physics achievement in minority students (Doctoral dissertation).* Walden University.

Chieu, V. M. (2007). COFALE: An Authoring System for Creating Web-based Adaptive Learning Environments Supporting Cognitive Flexibility. *Journal of Computers, 2*(5), 27–37. doi:10.4304/jcp.2.5.27-37

Christodoulopoulos, C. E., & Papanikolaou, K. A. (2007). *A Group Formation Tool in an E-Learning Context.* Paper presented at the 19th IEEE International Conference on Tools with Artificial Intelligence (ICTAI 2007), Patras, Greece. 10.1109/ICTAI.2007.155

Cohen, S. G., Ledford, G. E. Jr, & Spreitzer, G. M. (1996). A predictive model of self-managing work team effectiveness. *Journal of Human Relations, 49*(5), 643–676. doi:10.1177/001872679604900506

Cristea, A. I., & Ghali, F. (2011). Towards adaptation in e-learning 2.0. *Journal of New Review of Hypermedia and Multimedia, 17*(2), 199–238. doi:10.1080/13614568.2010.541289

De Bra, P., & Calvi, L. (1998). AHA! An open adaptive hypermedia architecture. *Journal of New Review of Hypermedia and Multimedia, 4,* 15–139.

Demetriadis, S., & Karakostas, A. (2009). Introduction to Adaptive Collaboration Scripting: Pedagogical and Technical Issues. *Journal of Intelligent Collaborative e-Learning Systems and Applications Studies in Computational Intelligence, 246,* 1-18.

Dillenbourg, P. (2002). Over-scripting CSCL: The risks of blending collaborative learning with instructional design. In Three worlds of CSCL. Can we support CSCL? Heerlen, Open Universiteit Nederland.

Dillenbourg, P., Baker, M., Blaye, A., & O'Malley, C. (1996). The evolution of research on collaborative learning. In E. Spada & P. Reiman (Eds.), *Learning in Humans and Machine: Towards an interdisciplinary learning science* (pp. 189–211). Oxford, UK: Elsevier.

Dlab, M. H., Boticki, I., Hoic-Bozic, N., & Looi, C.-K. (2017). Adaptivity in Synchronous Mobile Collaborative Learning. *Proceedings 9th International Conference on Education and New Learning Technologies.* 10.21125/edulearn.2017.1097

Doyle, T., & Tagg, J. (2008). *Helping Students Learn in a Learner-Centered Environment: A Guide to Facilitating Learning in Higher Education.* Stylus Publishing.

Gardner, B. S., & Korth, S. J. (1997). Classroom strategies that facilitate transfer of learning to the workplace. *Journal of Innovative Higher Education, 22*(1), 45–60. doi:10.1023/A:1025151609364

Gouli, E., Gogoulou, A., & Grigoriadou, M. (2006). Supporting Self- Peer- and Collaborative-Assessment through a Web-based Environment. In E. Pearson, & P. Bohman (Eds.), *Proceedings of World Conference on Educational Multimedia, Hypermedia and Telecommunications* (pp. 2192-2199). Chesapeake, VA: AACE.

Graf, S., & Bekele, R. (2006). Forming heterogeneous groups for intelligent collaborative learning systems with ant colony optimization. LNCS, 4053, 217–226. doi:10.1007/11774303_22

Greer, J., McCalla, G., Collins, J., Kumar, V., Meagher, P., & Vassileva, J. (1998). Supporting Peer Help and Collaboration in Distributed Workplace Environments. *International Journal of Artificial Intelligence in Education*, 9, 159–177.

Hausmann, R. G. M., van de Sande, B., & VanLehn, K. (2008). Are Self-explaining and Coached Problem Solving More Effective When Done by Pairs of Students Than Alone? *Proceedings of the 30th Annual Cognitive Science Society* (p. 744). Washington, DC: Cognitive Science Society

Hersey, P., & Blanchard, K. H. (1988). *Management of organizational behavior: utilizing human resources*. Prentice-Hall.

Hórreo, V. S., & Carro, R. M. (2007). Studying the Impact of Personality and Group Formation on Learner Performance. *Journal of Lecture Notes in Computer Science*, *4715*, 287–294. doi:10.1007/978-3-540-74812-0_22

Ikeda, M., Go, S., & Mizoguchi, R. (1997). *Opportunistic group formation*. Paper presented at the 8th World Conference on Artificial Intelligence in Education, Amsterdam, The Netherlands.

Jamal, A.-H., & Tilchin, O. (2016). Teachers' Accountability for Adaptive Project-Based Learning. *American Journal of Educational Research*, *4*(5), 420–426.

Kolb, A. Y., & Kolb, D. A. (2005). *The Kolb Learning Style Inventory, version 3.1: 2005 technical specifications*. Boston: Hay Resources Direct.

Kolb, D. A. (1984). *Experiential Learning: Experience as the Source of Learning and Development*. Englewood Cliffs, NJ: Prentice-Hall Inc.

Kompan, M., & Bieliková, M. (2016). Enhancing existing e-learning systems by single and group recommendations. *Int. J. Cont. Engineering Education and Life-Long Learning*, *26*(4), 386–404. doi:10.1504/IJCEELL.2016.080980

Kyprianidou, M., Demetriadis, S., Pombortsis, A., & Karatasios, G. (2009). PEGASUS: Designing a system for supporting group activity. *Journal of Multicultural Education and Technology*, *3*(1), 47–60. doi:10.1108/17504970910951147

Lambert, N. M., & McCombs, B. L. (1998). *How students learn: Reforming schools through learner-centered education*. Washington, DC: American Psychological Association. doi:10.1037/10258-000

Martin, E., & Paredes, P. (2004). *Using learning styles for dynamic group formation in adaptive collaborative hypermedia systems*. Paper presented at the First International Workshop on Adaptive Hypermedia and Collaborative Web-based Systems (AHCW 2004). Retrieved from http://citeseerx.ist.psu.edu/viewdoc/download?doi=10.1.1.106.9315&rep=rep1&type=pdf

Muehlenbrock, M. (2006). Learning Group Formation based on Learner Profile and Context. *International Journal on E-Learning*, *5*(1), 19–24.

Mujkanovic, A., & Bollin, A. (2016). Improving learning outcomes through systematic group reformation: the role of skills and personality in software engineering education. *Proceedings of the 9th International Workshop on Cooperative and Human Aspects of Software Engineering*, 97-103. 10.1145/2897586.2897615

Olivera, F., & Straus, S. G. (2004). Group-to-individual transfer of learning: Cognitive and social factors. *Small Group Research*, *35*(4), 440–465. doi:10.1177/1046496404263765

Papadimitriou, A., & Gyftodimos, G. (2007). Use of Kolb's learning cycle through an adaptive educational hypermedia system for a constructivist approach of electromagnetism. *Proceedings of 4th WSEAS/ IASME International Conference on Engineering Education*, 226-231.

Piaget, J. (1983). Piaget's theory. In P. Mussen (Ed.), Handbook of Child Psychology (pp. 703–732). New York, NY: Wiley.

Read, T., Barros, B., Barcna, E., & Pancorbo, J. (2006). Coalescing Individual and Collaborative Learning to Model User Linguistic Competences. *Journal of User Modeling and User-Adapted Interaction*, *16*(3-4), 349–376. doi:10.100711257-006-9014-5

Rubens, V., & Okamoto. (2009). Automatic group formation for informal collaborative learning. *Proceedings of the 2009 IEEE/WIC/ACM International Joint Conference on Web Intelligence and Intelligent Agent Technology*, *3*, 231-234 10.1109/WI-IAT.2009.270

Sandmire, D. A., Vroman, K. G., & Sanders, R. (2000). The Influence of Learning Styles on Collaborative Performances of Allied Health Students in a Clinical Exercise. *Journal of Allied Health*, *29*(3), 143–149. PMID:11026115

Santamaria, P. G. (2006). *CA-OLE: a collaborative and adaptive online learning environment* (Master's thesis). Retrieved from: http://dspace.uta.edu/bitstream/handle/10106/229/umi-uta-1528.pdf?sequence=1

Shi, L., Qudah, D., Qaffas, A., & Cristea, A. I. (2013). Topolor: A social personalized adaptive e-learning system. In User Modeling, Adaptation, and Personalization (pp. 338-340). Springer Berlin Heidelberg. doi:10.1007/978-3-642-38844-6_32

Slavin, R. E. (2010). Co-operative learning: what makes group-work? In D. Hanna, I. David, & B. Francisco (Eds.), *The nature of learning: Using research to inspire practice* (pp. 161–178). Chicago: OECD Publishing. doi:10.1787/9789264086487-9-en

Soh, L. K., Khandaker, N., & Jiang, H. (2008). I-MINDS: A Multi-agent System for Intelligent Computer-Supported Collaborative Learning and Classroom Management. *International Journal of Artificial Intelligence in Education*, *18*(2), 119–151.

Spoelstra, H., van Rosmalen, P., Houtmans, T., & Sloep, P. (2015). Team formation instruments to enhance learner interactions in open learning environments. *Journal of Computers in Human Behavior*, *45*, 11–20. doi:10.1016/j.chb.2014.11.038

Srba, I., & Bieliková, M. (2015). Dynamic Group Formation as an Approach to Collaborative Learning Support. *IEEE Transactions on Learning Technologies*, *8*(2), 173–186. doi:10.1109/TLT.2014.2373374

Sun, G., & Shen, J. (2014). Facilitating social collaboration in mobile cloud-based learning: A teamwork as a service (TaaS) approach. *IEEE Transactions on Learning Technologies*, *7*(3), 207–220. doi:10.1109/TLT.2014.2340402

Tao, P.-K. (1999). Peer collaboration in solving qualitative physics problems: The role of collaborative talk. *Research in Science Education*, *29*(3), 365–383. doi:10.1007/BF02461599

Vosniadou, S. (2008). *International handbook of Research on Conceptual Change*. New York, NY: Taylor and Francis Group.

Vygotsky, L. S. (1978). *Mind in Society. The Development of Higher Psychological Processes*. Cambridge, MA: Harvard University Press.

Walker, E., Rummel, N., & Koedinger, K. R. (2014). Adaptive intelligent support to improve peer tutoring in algebra. *International Journal of Artificial Intelligence in Education*, *24*(1), 33–61. doi:10.100740593-013-0001-9

Wolfe, D. M., & Kolb, D. A. (1979). Career Development, Personal Growth, and Experiential Learning. In *Organizational Psychology: A Book of Readings*. Englewood Cliffs, NJ: Prentice-Hall Inc.

Zakrzewska, D. (2009). Cluster Analysis in Personalized E-Learning. *Intelligent Systems for Knowledge Management*, *252*, 229–250. doi:10.1007/978-3-642-04170-9_10

KEY TERMS AND DEFINITIONS

Ability: Is defined as the knowledge, experience, and skill that an individual or group brings to a particular task or activity.

Algorithm: Is a finite set of actions or rules, strictly defined and executable at a finite time that precisely defines a sequence of operations, aimed at solving a problem.

Dyad: Is a group of two people.

Heterogeneous Group: Consists of the learners with different characteristics.

Homogeneous Group: Consists of the learners with the same or similar characteristics.

Informal Peer Help Network: The learners choose their helpers without being absolutely explicit about what kind of help they need and without knowing much about the candidate helpers.

Learning Style: Refers to the particular way in which the student captures, processes, comprehends, and retains information.

Negotiation Protocol: Is the set of rules that govern the interactions between the negotiating parties.

Problem-Solving: Is the process of finding solutions to difficult or complex issues.

Technique: Is a particular method of doing an activity, usually a method that involves practical skills or special facilities.

Willingness: Refers to the extent to which an individual or group has the confidence, commitment, and motivation to accomplish a specific task.

Chapter 8
Citizen–Government Collaborative Environment Using Social Networks:
The Case of Egypt

Hany Abdelghaffar
German University in Cairo, Egypt

Lobna Hassan
German University in Cairo, Egypt

ABSTRACT

Electronic democracy is a concept which is used in some countries around the world with mixed success. Social networks helped in facilitating democracy and democratic change in several countries suggesting that they could be utilized as an e-democracy tool. This research proposed a new model of how the decision-making process for local governments could be improved via social networks. Quantitative approach was used to investigate how the use of a social network amongst people living in the same suburb could improve decision making on the local level. Findings showed that awareness building, deliberation, and consultation factors could be used to affect the decision making for their local governments.

INTRODUCING THE RESEARCH

Electronic democracy (e-democracy) is a way to engage citizens and politicians with their government through Information and Communication Technology (ICTs) (Tambini, 1999; Riley & Law, 2003). Its main objective is to change citizens from being passive to become active and to engage in the democratic processes in their governments (Lee & Berry, 2011). Web 2.0 is one of the technologies that could potentially have an impact on achieving e-democracy (Chadwick, 2008; Hull et al., 2010; Mahrer & Krimmer, 2005).

DOI: 10.4018/978-1-5225-6367-9.ch008

Different web 2.0 technologies such as social networks, wikis, and blogs are available for governments to interact with citizens for very cheap costs (Hull et al., 2010). Nevertheless; some governments lack the motivation to adopt new web 2.0 technologies. On the other hand, citizens are moving from using the traditional bureaucratic means of information sharing to use new web 2.0 technologies such as social networks. This movement towards the use of social networks is hard for governments to control (Murugesan, 2007). Social networks help people to group their opinions and improve the public policy decision making which will lead to improving the democratic process and to reshaping public services (Chadwick, 2003; Flak et al., 2005).

This paper is proposing a model of how governments can use social networks to listen to citizens' opinions so they could enhance their decision making. Accordingly, the paper is aiming to answer the following research question: How social networks support the local government decision making to enhance e-democracy? The paper structure starts by presenting the theoretical background for understanding e-democracy followed by proposing the suggested e-democracy model. This is followed by the methodology used in research and ended by the discussion section.

THEORETICAL BACKGROUND

There are several benefits which could be achieved from e-democracy. E-democracy helps to increase citizens' participation in the political life (Riley & Law, 2003; Thomas an&d Streib, 2005). Citizens are empowered to say their input to the decisions made by their governments which lead to having two ways of communications rather one way only (Stahl, 2005). Small governorates or states are more responsive to e-democracy than larger ones (Riley, 2003; 84) while young citizens are more responsive to e-democracy compared to elder citizens (Hull et al, 2001).

Williamson (2007) develops a new model that explains the lifecycle of e-democracy. The model combines two models to understand how e-democracy develops on the local level. The first is the trans-theoretical stages of change that explores how change and awareness occurs in a society and consists of five awareness stages that depend on the level of an individual motivation:

- **Pre-Contemplation:** A person doesn't recognize the need for any change
- **Contemplation:** The person considers the change but is still resisting it
- **Preparation:** The person accepts the need for change and considers how it is to be carried out
- **Action:** Implementing the change and adopting to it
- **Maintenance:** Maintain the change and ways thing are done after it

The second model is the social movement lifecycle model that talks about the actors in a social movements, and divides them into four categories. Each of these individuals has to exist in a society for a social movement to start and continue (Williamson, 2007):

- **Citizens:** The general public in a society
- **Reformers:** Are those who have the power to implement the change
- **Change Agents:** Individuals who would spread awareness of the issues rebels are challenging in a society and support the change they call for
- **Rebels:** Individuals ready to challenge established conditions

Figure 1. E-democracy life cycle (Williamson, 2007)

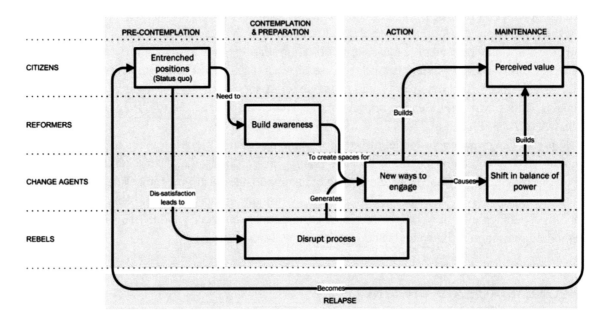

Areas of E-Democracy

There are different areas that need to exist to have e-democracy. The first area is information provision which aims to provide citizens with the correct information which is usually done by the government in a top-down approach. However it's important to focus on the down-top information provision from the citizens to the government and politicians (Riley, 2003). This help to reduce the information overload to citizens from different sources (Chadwick, 2003). The second area of e-democracy is deliberation. Deliberation represents the political discussions conducted on the web between citizens (Dahlberg, 2001; Riley, 2003). It helps into making citizens more involved in the community and its problems, as well as in forming the public opinion of the citizens (Dahlberg, 2001). Consultation is very similar to deliberation and conducted by governmental organizations (Päivärinta & Sæbø, 2006).

Community building helps to achieve collaborative work of citizens to form a unified community and to support a shared goal (Jimenez & Polasek, 2003; Päivärinta & Sæbø, 2006). This would help governments to get solid feedback from citizens regarding discussed issues rather than having different opinions for the same issue. Finally, organization of campaign to achieve a certain goal would help to reach the stage of citizens' opinion is considered for certain issue (Päivärinta & Sæbø, 2006).

The challenge for developing countries is that the digital divide for citizens is high (Abdelghaffar & Magdy, 2012; Pinkett, 2000). compared to developed countries. For example, the Internet reach in many developing countries ranges from 1% to 5% of a country's population (Riley, 2003). Consequently, when citizens do not have the same computer literacy skills or internet access, e-democracy becomes unrepresentative, and potentially undemocratic.

PROPOSED MODEL AND HYPOTHESES DEVELOPMENT

Reviewing the literature shows that there is almost no research conducted on the use of social networks on improving e-democracy in Arab Spring countries. To overcome this gap, this research answers the following question: How social networks support the local government decision making to enhance e-democracy? Accordingly, a conceptual model is introduced (figure 2) which is based on the e-democracy lifecycle model developed by Williamson (2007). List of constructs and definitions are listed in table (1).

Information Provision

The first area of e-democracy is information provision. Information provision is to provide citizens with important information (Coldow, 2004; Paivarinta & Sæbo, 2006). A citizen that is well informed is able to holistically understand problems that governments could face and effectively participate in the decision making process (Irvin & Stansbury, 2004; Davis & Metcalf, 2016). Social network, as a web 2.0 tool, is considered to be a powerful internet tool that allows users to access governments' information (Murugesan, 2007). Accordingly, governments could make use of information provision during both pre-contemplation and contemplation stages. Through this there are different techniques governments might use such as the look and layout of the social network pages to send information to citizens (Cormode & Kirshnamurthy, 2008).

The advantage of using social networks is that it allows governments to keep citizens updated with the new information without having to log into several governmental websites. Moreover, governments

Figure 2. Proposed conceptual model

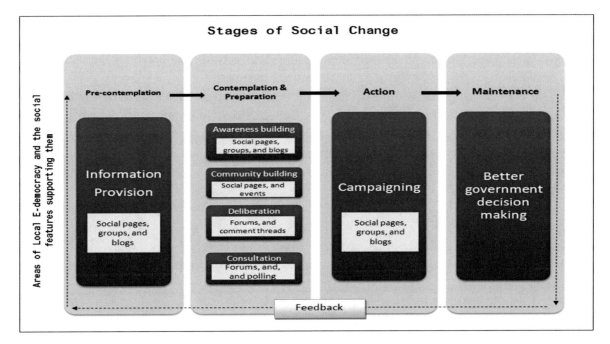

have the ability to tag and categorize the content of the pages, photos and videos. This would make it easy for citizens to find information relevant to the keywords they are searching for (Murugesan, 2007). Accordingly, social networks would be a good tool for information provision to citizens (Mergel & Bretschneider, 2013) since they are updated without efforts and reach large number of citizens at the same time. Based on this, we posit the following hypothesis:

- **H1:** Information provision via social networks significantly influences the local government decision making.

Deliberations and Consultations

Both of consultation and deliberations are important for e-democracy. Deliberation is defined as the use of ICT for political discussions among citizens to help them get involved in the community and its obstacles (Dahlberg, 2001; Elstub & McLaverty, 2014; Papadopoulos, 2012). Different actors in the society are involved in the deliberation. It is highly present through all the stages of changes explained by Williamson (2007) and it has a major rule in moving the society through the change stages (Hassan & Abdelghaffar, 2016). The features of social networks would allow deliberations as they provide social interaction and collaborative abilities (Murugesan, 2007). Citizens will be able to share their opinions by writing contents on the social network through leaving their comments (breindl & Franq, 2008; Murugesan, 2007). Such interactivity enable citizens to collectively create and discuss content with each other (Chadwick, 2008; Hull et al., 2001). Deliberations are not contradicting with the governments' provision of information, but rather information provision might lead the citizens into new deliberations.

Consultation has some similarity to deliberation; however the government or other organizations takes an official role in the discussion over the internet. Hendriks (2015) explained that citizens have problem to interact with discrete systems and websites offered by government organizations (Hull et al., 2011). This lead to inconsistency of achieving better deliberation with citizens regarding specific problem. Accordingly, Hendriks suggests to couple citizens with different types of governmental websites. By using both discussions boards and separate forums using social network, deliberations and consultations would be conducted successfully between social network members.

Citizens who are using social networks could get in touch with any other citizen, including public figures such as politicians (Mislove et al., 2007; Pena-Lopez, 2010). Government officials and politicians need to be get engaged with citizens to get closer to how citizens think of a certain issue or problem. However, this needs champions who are willing to do the changes through the use of social networks Hendriks (2015). Even more, these public figures could get in touch with citizens and consult them in matters of importance. It is thought that, if citizens are willing to participate in deliberations over a social network, they are more likely to take part in consultations sponsored by the government. Hence, we hypothesize that:

- **H2:** Deliberation via social networks significantly influences the local government decision making.
- **H3:** Consultations via social networks significantly influences the local government decision making.

Communities Building

Community building is essential before the action stage of social change towards e-democracy. This is due to the fact that citizens need to work collaboratively to be able to form unified community that has a common interest. This will help communities to get organized to start action movements (Paivarinta & Sæbo, 2006).

Communications between the community members are done using different form such as text, audio, and video (Birdsall, 2007). One of the best technologies to provide such type of interaction between citizens is social networks (Birdsall, 2007; Murugesan, 2007). Social networks help citizens to collaborate horizontally to eliminate any hierarchies that might inhibit the community creation process (Bertot, Paul, & Justin, 2012; Mergel & Bretschneider, 2013). Accordingly, governments will be able in a understand citizens' needs and enhance the way they take decisions by assessing the opinion of citizens (Bertot, Paul, & Justin, 2012; Irvin & Stansbury, 2004).

The social networks features make the researcher assumes that the use of a social network in e-democracy would lead to forming of community or interest groups that have common interests and opinion. Hence, we hypothesize that:

- **H4:** Community building via social networks significantly influences the local government decision making.

Campaigning and Awareness Building

Since social networks allow for two way communications between the campaign organizers and the public, and vice versa, it can be an effective campaigning tool in elections (Williams and Gulati, 2007). However, to achieve success of campaigning, there is a need to increase the awareness of top management in the government that the use of social networks would increase awareness between citizens. This needs to be spread across government organizations (Mergel & Bretschneider, 2013). This might draw the attention to the impact of the local culture inside governments' organizations which ban spreading information to citizens. This culture issue need to be addressed before using social networks to increase awareness of citizens regarding specific issue.

Social networks campaigns and awareness building activities have especially shown a transformational role of the society. This was clear through different examples happened in both developed and developing countries. In United States, Obama's presidential campaign in 2008 is a clear example of how he used the internet and specifically social networks in campaigning. Social networks such as MySpace. Facebook, and Youtube were utilized in connecting with the public, seeking volunteers and better organizing the activities of the campaign (Kes-Erkul & Erkul, 2009). On the other hand, social networks such as Facebook and Twitter played a significant role in the Arab spring revolutions in 2011. For example, Facebook and Twitter had a strong influence on grouping protesters during the Egyptian revolution in 2011 (Lotan et al., 2011; Timeline, 2011). This emphasizes the importance of campaigning and awareness (Abdelghaffar, 2009) building via social networks (Lotan et al., 2011). Based on this, we can conclude that campaigning and awareness building are essential during the contemplation and action stages of change.

Since social networks have already shown a great impact in organizing campaigns and change, this research proposes that the use of social networks would have massive impact in campaigning and awareness for the community. It is assumed that citizens would be willing to use social networks in organizing social campaigns related to local political matters. Hence, we hypothesize that:

- **H5:** Campaigning via social networks significantly influences the local government decision making.
- **H6:** Build awareness via social networks significantly influences the local government decision making.

Table 1 below presents each of the variables measure through the developed hypothesis and their definition.

METHODOLOGY

The proposed model was tested to answer the research question of how social networks support the local government decision making to enhance e-democracy. A survey method was employed to collect data from citizens. Egypt has been selected for investigation which is considered as a good example of how social networks such as Facebook and Twitter had great impact on the success of the Egyptian 25th January revolution in 2011 (Timeline, 2011). Moreover, citizens after the revolution have become more active in the political life and share their opinions online.

Table 1. Constructs summary

Constructs	Definition	References
Information Provision	- provision of laws, regulations, issues of interest etc online - takes a bottom down approach from government to citizens	Coleman & Norris, 2005; Riley an&d Law, 2003; Williamson, 2007; Davis & Metcalf, 2016
Awareness Building	- Political awareness in general. - Awareness of local issues.	Williamson, 2007
Deliberation	- Discussion of political matters amongst citizens	Chadwick, 2003; Riley & Law, 2003; Williamson, 2007; Papadopoulos, 2012; Elstub & McLaverty, 2014
Consultation	- government's discussions of matter of concern with the citizens - initiated by the government - aims at helping the government with taking a decision regarding the issue at discussion	Kersten, 2004; Caldow, 2004; Williamson, 2007
Campaigning	- citizens ability to organize themselves - citizen's ability to mobilize themselves in the service of a certain cause	Coleman & Norris, 2005; Päivärinta & Sæbø, 2006; Williamson, 2007; Mergel & Bretschneider, 2013.
Community Building	- The ability of citizens to build communities amongst themselves These communities share a common set of values, causes or ideologies	Paivarinta & Sæbo, 2006; Birdsall, 2007; Murugesan, 2007

Prototype

In order to make it easier for citizens to understand how social networks work, a prototype of social networks has been created to allow citizens to visualize the social network. The website that has been developed for the demonstration of the suggested social network was created using "wordpress" open source Content Management System (CMS) and necessary "plugins" were added to improve the functionality of the network.

Sample and Instruments Design

Since the research is investigating the impact of social networks on enhancing the e-democracy, therefore, participants should be able to use computers and the internet. Accordingly, the survey was distributed online to Egyptian internet users to ensure that the respondents have digital literacy. Only 24% of Egypt's population (19.2 million) during the time of the study had stable internet access, mostly through internet cafés, internet clubs, or mobile phones (Arthur, 2011). The sample consisted of citizens above eighteen years old as this is the minimum age for voting in Egypt. A total of 150 participants successfully completed the questionnaires which were used in the analysis. Questionnaires were divided into several sections. Each of these sections measured a different variable of the proposed model through Likert scales.

Demographic Data

Respondents' demographics profile included information about age, gender, income level and educational levels presented in table (1). 76% of the participants were from age 18-30. 44% of respondents were females while 56% were males. Regarding the internet usage, access, and familiarity with the Internet and social, 92.7% of respondent used the internet daily. 96.7% of the respondent answered that they see the internet an effective tool of communication with the government and with other citizens.

When it comes to the political awareness and political participation of the surveyed participants, it was found that 94% of the respondents agreed that they used the internet to follow political news and contributing with their opinions. Furthermore, 96% of respondents agreed on the impact of the social network as a tool of communication between citizens. 72% of the respondents have participated in both the referendum on the constitutional amendments in 2011 and the parliamentary elections in 2012.

ANALYSIS AND RESULTS

Validity and Reliability

The composite reliability of each construct was assessed using Cronbach's alpha. A reliability coefficient of 0.70 is marked as a lowest acceptable limit for Cronbach's alfa (Robinson et al., 1991). The calculated Cronbach's Alpha for this research is equal to 0.862.

Convergent validity has been used to check validity which shows that there is a significant correlation and relation among all dimension and sub factors. The correlation was high as shown in table (3), which is an evidence of a convergent validity. All the independent factors are significant at level 0.05. Discriminant validity is assessed to measure the extent to which constructs are different. To evaluate

Table 2. Demographic description of the sample

Characteristics		Percentage
Age	18-30	76%
	31-45	17.3%
	Above 45	6.7%
Gender	Male	44%
	Female	56%
Education	High school	40.7%
	Bachelor	44.7%
	Master	10%
	PhD	4.7%
Internet usage	Daily	92.7%
	Weekly	5.3%
	Rarely	2%
Social network effectiveness in communication	Yes	96.7%
	No	3.3%
Political usage of Internet	Yes	94%
	No	6%
Political participation on ground	Participated in both the referendum and elections	72%
	Participated in only one of them	11.3%
	Did not participate at all	16.7%

discriminant validity, the AVE is used. All constructs have an AVE of at least 0.5 (Fornell & Larcker, 1981) and all the square roots of each AVE value are higher than the off-diagonal correlation elements.

The table (3) presents the correlations between factors. All factors are at a positive direction meaning that the decision making is affected by each factor.

Since multicollinearity might exist in regression analysis and negatively affects the predictive ability, computing the variance inflation factor (VIF) of each variable might help to detect multicollinearity

Table 3. Correlation analysis

	Decision Making	Campaigning	Information Provision	Deliberation	Consultation	Awareness Building	Community Building
Decision Making	1						
Campaigning	0.580	1					
Information Provision	0.396	0.422	1				
Deliberation	0.245	0.343	0.526	1			
Consultation	0.612	0.524	0.461	0.318	1		
Awareness Building	0.657	0.649	0.547	0.463	0.706	1	
Community Building	0.569	0.589	0.440	0.302	0.482	0.601	1

(Myers, 1986). If the VIF of an explanatory variable exceeds 10, the variable is considered to be highly collinear and it can be treated as a candidate for exclusion from the regression model (Kleinbaum et al., 1988). Findings show that VIF range from 1.98 to 2.56 suggesting that multicollinearity is not an issue with this data set.

The multiple regression analysis has been used to test the hypotheses. The R calculated through the regression analysis is equal to 0.733 and R Square is equal to 0.537. Results from the regression test show that there is a positive strong relationship between the independent and the dependent variables. Any change in the independent variable would affect the dependent variable in the same direction and in a certain degree. The R value is above 0.5 meaning that there is a high probability that any changes in the independent variable would affect the dependent variable by 73% change.

DISCUSSION, RECOMMENDATIONS AND LIMITATIONS

Social networks such as Facebook and Twitter played a vital role in the Egyptian revolution and almost all of the Arab spring revolutions e.g. Tunisia. During the uprisings, protestors organized themselves mainly through the use of social networks (Arthur, 2011; Shenker, 2011). So, protestors were able to utilize social networking to enforce democratic change. This paper proposed a hypothetical model to investigate how governments could make use of social networks to enhance the e-democracy process and changing the way of interaction between governments and citizens. The research provided a theoretical contribution by validating the proposed model and identifying the significant variables governments' have to take them into consideration.

Findings confirmed that awareness building (β=0.657, p<0.05), which is in contemplation & preparation stage, is the highest independent factor that significantly affect the local government decision making (Williams & Gulati, 2007). Respondents considered that the use of social networks would help to spread awareness of political issues. Once citizens are aware of their local issues, they are able better to form a precise opinion and exercise political pressure on the decision maker. Moreover, respondents believed that consultation (β=0.612, p< 0.05) would improve the local decision-making as the government could ask citizens for their input on a certain issue and consequently would be used to form a decision.

Community building affects the government decision making (β=0.569, p< 0.05). When citizens form communities and unify their opinion in some major directions, it makes it easier for them to channel their opinions to the government. Accordingly, the government would be able to expect and analyze the opinions of each of the communities they govern and thus would be able to make better decisions. Once

Table 4. Regression analysis

Hypotheses	Variable	β	Significance
H1	Information provision	0.396	0.665
H2	Deliberation	0.245	0.791
H3	Consultation	0.612	<0.05
H4	Community building	0.569	<0.05
H5	Campaigning	0.580	<0.05
H6	Awareness	0.657	<0.05

community building achieved, the next step is to move to campaigning. While participants believed that social networks could facilitate the organization of campaigning (β=0.580, p< 0.05), they also believed that virtual campaigning would not have much effect on local decision making if it is not successfully transferred from the virtual world to real life (Arthur, 2011). This was the case for both of the Egyptian and Tunisian revolutions occurred in 2011.

Deliberation variable had non-significant impact on decision-making ($\beta = 0.245$, p=0.791). Respondents agreed that the use of a social network to debate on matters of interest with other citizens is of the least importance to decision-making. This is because deliberation allows discussion between members to argue regarding different viewpoints without a mechanism to facilitate reaching a final decision that could then be communicated to the government (Chadwick, 2008). Information provision ($\beta = 0.396$, p=0.665) from the government to the citizens has not influenced the decision making of the government. The reason is that the simple act of providing information could be faced by a passive reception by citizens and this would not affect decision making (Cormode & Kirshnamurthy, 2008). On the other hand, information provision is significantly correlated with awareness building as sharing information is essential to build awareness which is a factor that can significantly affect decision making.

Recommendations

The research suggests recommendations for politicians and practitioners for the effective use of social networks in enhancing e-democracy. Social networks could be used by governments to improve the e-democracy process on the local government level which would improve their decision making. Consequently, this would lead to reducing the gap between government decisions and citizens' expectations. Governments could use social networks to facilitate increase awareness of vital issues among citizens and support citizens in building their communities so they have more input in the governmental decision making. It is important to consider that social networks should be free of government surveillance so citizens can freely share their opinion even if they are opposing the government. However, governments need to think about what should be done about citizens who do not use social network and how they could be get involved in the decision making.

Research Limitation and Future Research Directions

In this research, the sample size is considered limited and focusing on Egypt only which could be expanded in future research. Also, the study is limited to the decision making on the local level and not covering central government decision making. However, there is a greater need to investigate the government's opinion regarding involving citizens in the decision making process.

CONCLUSION

More and more citizens are asking to be given the chance to participate in the decision making of their governments. The use of internet technology and social networks showed an excellent opportunity to enhance the democratic process of how citizens could participate in decisions in different countries. This research proposed a model that investigates how social networks could be used to support the decision making and to enhance e-democracy. Findings show that awareness building, deliberation and consultation could be used by citizens to affect the decision making for their local governments. Moreover, governments could use social networks to facilitate awareness of information among citizens and support citizens in building their communities.

QUESTIONS

Q1: What is the e-democracy lifecycle? And how actors are interacting in the e-democracy?

Q2: How social networks support the local government decision making to enhance e-democracy?

Q3: How governments make use of social networks to enhance citizens' deliberation?

Q4: How governments could protect citizens' privacy when they use public social networks such as Facebook?

Q5: How governments could move to the next level of e-democracy?

REFERENCES

Abdelghaffar, H. (2009). Citizens' Readiness for E-government in Developing Countries (CREG). In *Proceedings of the 8th European Conference on Information Warfare and Security, Military Academy, Lisbon and the University of Minho, Braga, Portugal, 6-7 July 2009* (p. 11). Academic Conferences Limited.

Abdelghaffar, H., & Magdy, Y. (2012). The Adoption Of Mobile Government Services In Developing Countries: The case of Egypt. *International Journal of Information*, 2(4), 333–341.

Arthur, C. (2011). Egypt blocks social media websites in attempted clampdown on unrest. *The Guardian*. Retrieved from http://www.guardian.co.uk/world/2011/jan/26/egypt-blocks-social-media-websites

Bertot, J., Paul, J., & Justin, G. (2012). Promoting Transparency and Accountability through ICTs, Social Media, and Collaborative E-Government. Transforming Government: People, Process, and Policy, 6(1), 78–91.

Birdsall, W. F. (2007). Web 2.0 as a Social Movement. *Webology*, 4(2), 5–11.

Breindl, Y., & Francq, P. (2008). Can Web2.0 Applications Save E-Democracy? A Study Of How New Internet Applications May Enhance Citizen Participation In Political Process Online. *International Journal of E-Democracy, 1*(1), 14-31.

Chadwick, A. (2003). Bringing E-Democracy Back. *Social Science Computer Review*, 21(4), 443–455. doi:10.1177/0894439303256372

Chadwick, A. (2008). Web 2.0: New challenges for the study of e-democracy in an era of informational exuberance. *ISJLP*, 5, 9.

Coldow, J. (2004). *E-Democracy: Putting Down Global Roots*. Institution of Electric Government.

Cormode, G., & Krishnamurthy, B. (2008). Key Differences between Web 1.0 and Web 2.0. *First Monday, 13*(6). Retrieved December, 2012, from http://www.uic.edu/htbin/cgiwrap/bin/ojs/index.php/

Dahlberg, L. (2001). The Internet and Democratic Discourse: Exploring the Prospects of Online Deliberative Forums Extending the Public Sphere. *Information Communication and Society*, *4*(4), 615–633. doi:10.1080/13691180110097030

Davis, L., & Metcalf, G. (2016). Does Better Information Lead to Better Choices? Evidence from Energy-Efficiency Labels. *Journal of the Association of Environmental and Resource Economists*, *3*(3), 589–625. doi:10.1086/686252

Elstub, S., & McLaverty, P. (2014). Conclusion: The future of deliberative democracy. In *Deliberative democracy: Issues and cases*. Edinburgh, UK: Edinburgh University Press.

Flak, L., Olsen, D., & Wolocott, P. (2005). Local E-Government in Norway: Local status and emerging issues. *Scandinavian Journal of Information Systems*, *17*(2), 41–84.

Fornell, C., & Larcker, D. F. (1981). Evaluating Structural Equation Models with Unobservable Variables and Measurement Error. *JMR, Journal of Marketing Research*, *18*(1), 39–50. doi:10.2307/3151312

Hassan, L., & Abdelghaffar, H. (2016). Social Development of Rules: Can Social Networking Sites Benefit E-Rulemaking? *Transforming Government: People, Process and Policy. Emerald, 10*(2).

Hendriks, C. (2015). Coupling citizens and elites in deliberative systems: The role of institutional design. *Europena Joural of Politicial Research, 55*, 43–60.

Hull, D., West, H. G., & Cecez-Kecmanovi, D. (2011). Two Models of E-Democracy: A Case Study of Government Online Engagement with the Community. University of New South Wales, Australia.

Irvin, R. A., & Stansbury, J. (2004). Citizen Participation In Decision Making: Is It Worth The Effort? *Public Administration Review*, *64*(1), 55–65. doi:10.1111/j.1540-6210.2004.00346.x

Jimenez, J. M., & Polasek, W. (2003). E-democracy and Knowledge. A multi criteria Framework for The New Democratic Area. *Journal of Multi-Criteria Decision Analysis*, *12*, 163-176.

Kersten, G. E. (2003). E-Democracy and Participatory Decision Processes: Lessons From-Negotiation Experiments. *Journal of Multi-Criteria Decision Analysis*, *12*(2-3), 127–143. doi:10.1002/mcda.352

Lee, C. P., Chang, K., & Berry, F. S. (2011). Testing the Development and Diffusion of E-Government and E-Democracy: A Global Perspective. *Public Administration Review*, *71*(3), 444–454. doi:10.1111/j.1540-6210.2011.02228.x

Lotan, G., Graff, E., Amanny, M., Gaffney, D., Pearce, I., & Boyd, D. (2011). The Revolutions Were Tweeted: Information Flows During The 2011 Tunisian And Egyptian Revolutions. *International Journal of Communication*, *5*, 1375–1405.

Mahrer, H., & Krimmer, R. (2005). Towards The Enhancement of E-Democracy: Identifying The Notion Of The 'Middleman Paradox'. *Information Systems Journal*, *15*(1), 27–42. doi:10.1111/j.1365-2575.2005.00184.x

Mergel, I., & Bretschneider, S. (2013). A Three-Stage Adoption Process for Social Media Use in Government. Public Administration Review, 73(3), 390-400.

Mislove, A., Marcon, M., Gummadi, K. P., Druschel, P., & Bhattacharjee, B. (2007). Measurement and analysis of online social networks. *Proceedings of the 7th ACM SIGCOMM conference on Internet measurement.* 10.1145/1298306.1298311

Murugesan, S. (2007). Understanding Web 2.0. *IT Professional, 9*(4), 34–41. doi:10.1109/MITP.2007.78

Paivarinta & Sæbo. (2006). Models Of E-Democracy. *Communications of the Association for Information Systems, 17*, 818–840.

Papadopoulos, Y. (2012). On the embeddedness of deliberative systems: Why elistist innovations matter more. In J. Parkinson & J. Mansbridge (Eds.), *Deliberative systems: Deliberative democracy at the large scale.* Cambridge, UK: Cambridge University Press. doi:10.1017/CBO9781139178914.007

Pinkett, R. (2000). Bridging The Digital Divide: Sociocultural Constructionism and an Asset-Based Approach to Community Technology and Community Building. *Proceeding of the 81st annual meeting of the American educational research association (AERA).*

Riley. C. G. (2003). The Changing Role of The Citizen In The E-Government And E-Democracy Equation. *Commonwealth Centre for E-Government.*

Riley, C. G., & Law, M. A. (2003). E-Governance & E-Democracy Equation. *Commonwealth Center for E-Governance*, 2-111.

Shenker, J. (2011). Fury over advert claiming Egypt revolution as Vodafone's. *The Guardian.* Retrieved from http://www.guardian.co.uk/world/2011/jun/03/vodafone-egypt-advert-claims-revolution

Stahl, B. C. (2005). The paradigm of e-commerce in e-government and e-democracy. *Electronic Government Strategies and Implementation, 9*(2) 1-19.

Tambini, D. (1999). New Media and Democracy: The Civic Networking Movement. *New Media & Society, 1*(1), 305–329. doi:10.1177/14614449922225609

Thomas, J. C., & Streib, G. (2005). E-Democracy, E-Commerce, and E-Research Examining the Electronic Ties between Citizens and Governments. *Administration & Society, 37*(3), 259–280. doi:10.1177/0095399704273212

Timeline: Egypt's revolution. (2011). *Aljazeera online.* Retrieved December, 2012, Accessed from http://www.aljazeera.com

Williams Whyte, C. B., & Gulati, G. J. (2007). Social Networks in Political Campaigns. *Annual Meeting of The American Political Science Association.*

Williamson, A. (2007). Empowering Communities to Action: Reclaiming Local Democracy Through ICT. *Community Informatics Research Conference.*

Chapter 9
Development of a Customer Information Database System

Shameem Akhter
Western Oregon University, USA

Nayem Rahman
Portland State University, USA

Mahmud Ullah
University of Dhaka, Bangladesh

ABSTRACT

Organizations need to keep customer data safe and secure to run their everyday activities more credibly, promptly, and effectively. They need to use, and hence invest in customer database software to achieve these basic goals. Using well-designed software also allows them to increase operational efficiency of business. In this chapter, the authors discuss development of a customer inquiry database system for use by small businesses. The proposed database system is to help them store customer information, inquiries, and company product information too. The authors have used state-of-the-art software development technology to design and develop user interfaces (UI) for building business intelligence (BI) capability using this system. This chapter provides a holistic view of building a customer inquiry database system. The approach of an integrated view of customer inquiry system is different and offers more than the partial view of the existing literature or database system books on this issue.

INTRODUCTION

The 18th century Industrial Revolution is considered to be a major turning point in the history of mankind. Newly invented machines and technology contributed to many-fold increase in material production capability. Consequently, human life-style based on a manual-labor-based economy gradually shifted to an economy centered on a machine-based manufacturing. Many players appeared in manufacturing business to produce bulk of goods, resulting into escalated competition among businesses to sell their products to an expanding global marketplace. As part of proactive customer orientation, providing prompt

DOI: 10.4018/978-1-5225-6367-9.ch009

customer services, and releasing quick resolutions to the customer inquiries are vital to do business in the 21st century (Akhter & Rahman, 2015). Skilled use of information technology (IT) by a business is obvious to become so proactive, and to augment its competitive capabilities to have an edge in the market.

Amazon CEO Jeff Bezos said, "In the offline world 30% of a company's resources are spent providing a good customer experience and 70% goes to marketing. But online 70% should be devoted to creating a great customer experience and 30% should be spent on "shouting" about it" (Zeithaml et al., 2002). This exemplifies the importance of speedy handling of and resolution to customer inquiries. These days, customers expect sellers to respond effectively to their expressed needs and be innovative enough to proactively address their latent and future needs. Farouk (1987) and Blocker et al. (2011) assert that proactive customer orientation is the most consistent driver of customer value in a business. They propose a proactive customer orientation construct in terms of "proactive customer orientation → value → satisfaction → loyalty chain" (Blocker et al., 2011). Szymanski and Henard (2001) observed that by sensing the importance of customer satisfaction many companies in the US have come up with slogans such as 'Our focus is customer satisfaction' –Gulfstream Aeronautics; 'Our customers will be totally satisfied with the products services and technology we supply' –Shell Chemical Company; and 'Satisfaction Guaranteed' –Wal-Mart Stores, Inc.

A few quotes from successful business entrepreneurs (Morris, 2012, 2013; Murphy Jr., 2018):

Your most unhappy customers are your greatest source of learning. – Bill Gates, Founder, Microsoft

If you work just for money, you'll never make it, but if you love what you're doing and you always put the customer first, success will be yours. – Ray Kroc, Founder, McDonalds

There is only one boss. The customer. And he can fire everybody in the company from the chairman on down, simply by spending his money somewhere else. – Sam Walton, Founder, Wal-Mart

You've got to start with the customer experience and work back toward the technology – not the other way around. – Steve Jobs, Founder, Apple

If you do build a great experience, customers tell each other about that. Word of mouth is very powerful. – Jeff Bezos, CEO, Amazon.com

Quality in a service or product is not what you put into it. It is what the client or customer gets out of it. – Peter Drucker

An entrepreneur is someone who jumps off a cliff and builds a plane on the way down. – Reid Hoffman

An organization's ability to continuously "generate intelligence about customers' expressed and latent needs, and about how to satisfy those needs, is essential for it to continuously create superior customer value" (Slater & Narver, 2000). With the advent of computer hardware, software (Sommerville, 2004), the internet and other emerging technologies (Rahman et al., 2014) business organizations have been taking advantage of computer application-based customer service systems (Umar, 2005). Internet technology has opened the flood-gate of both global opportunities and competition for business organizations. Ever-growing competition in the early 21st century has compelled business organizations to pay more attention to customer services. Organizations were forced to switch from mere product selling to customer relationship and service-oriented ones. Business organizations have embarked upon a paradigm shift from a transaction-based economy to a relationship-based economy (Romano, Jr. & Fjermestad, 2003). Business organizations have started taking advantage of information technology to match with this transformation. Some companies have adopted e-business initiatives to better manage their internal business processes and their interfaces with the external environment (Wu et al., 2003). Strategic use of IT has significant impacts on business performance (Huang, 2013).

This chapter describes the build of a customer inquiry database system for small businesses to automate the customer service and inquiry system. Typically, most of the small businesses do not have any or much computer information system at the start. This has motivated us to come up with a simple to implement customer inquiry database system. Assuming that a small business does not have a customer support data collection system to collect and track the volume and type of customer inquiries received, it is very likely for that business to fail in resolving their customer queries, and losing the customers eventually. The business owner then will certainly start feeling the need of having some sort of system due to the failure to handle an expected increase in business and customer service requirements. To handle the continuously increasing data volume related to customer inquiries and services, small businesses need an effective tool to assist in providing timely resolution to customer issues and a way to report on what has been done. We create an inquiry database system that will retain and centralize customer inquiry information from receipt to resolution. The database is to include query and reporting capabilities to help determine the volume and types of inquiries that are being received (Akhter & Rahman, 2015; Inmon, 2002).

To build a customer inquiry database system for a company, the nature of business, customer inquiry and user inputs (Keil & Carmel, 1995) are important and need to be taken into consideration. Under this initiative, we would like to work on a few user specifications and requirements, and reflect them in this application system. Our customer inquiry system should be able to create, change and remove records via a UI. We propose using Microsoft® Visual Studio .NET as front-end and Microsoft® Access as the backend database. The customer inquiry database system should also be able to track and trace all customer service issues; report writer and BI capabilities; generate historical and current data; and query capabilities (e.g., Inquiry Type, Inquiry Status). A typical customer inquiry database system is designed to answer several important queries (Akhter & Rahman, 2015):

1. Inquiry Status (e.g. Open/ Closed Inquiries)
2. Customer Information (e.g. Name and way to contact)
3. Product Information (e.g. ID, description)
4. Investigator's name (who is working the request)
5. Type of Customer Inquiry (e.g. question, complaint)
6. Add Product and Customer Information into database (tables)
7. Search Capabilities (e.g., Customer Inquiry Number, Customer ID, and Product ID)
8. Auto-fill capabilities for certain fields (e.g., Customer Inquiry Number)
9. Look up capabilities in form (e.g., Customer ID, Product ID, Date fields)
10. Reporting Capabilities consisting of information from multiple tables

This chapter is organized as follows: Section 2 briefly discusses the use of IT by business organizations in general and related work in this area. Section 3 provides an overview of software development life cycle (Sommerville, 2004) for this application. Section 4 provides an entity-relationship diagram for the underlying database system. Section 5 provides actual work done. Section 6 summarizes and concludes the chapter.

LITERATURE REVIEW

Companies need to run their business based on IT infrastructure for strategic agility (Rahman, 2016; Weill et al., 2002). "Companies must employ information technology with a sophisticated understanding of the requirements for competitive advantage (Porter & Miller, 1985)." In this case, small businesses are not exceptions. They must take advantage of information technology to stay competitive and reduce operating costs and increase bottom line. Research suggests that firms, especially large ones, have been continuing to develop new, valuable IT-enabled business process innovations (Tambe & Hitt, 2012; Smith et al., 2015). "In more competitive industries, firms tend to deploy IT more intensively and use it more efficiently (Chang & Gurbaxani, 2013)." Bardhan et al. (2013) propose that IT investments create additional business value through interactions with other business processes. Given that IT delivers productivity and efficiency in business, Li et al. (2013) suggest managers to "motivate employees to leverage implemented (information) systems to extract their value potential more effectively." Im et al. (2013) observed that there is an interaction between IT and firm size: as a firm grows in size, its coordination activities increase; the firm then uses more IT; this increased use of IT, in turn, decreases coordination costs.

Chakravarty et al. (2013) research suggests that IT has two distinct roles: an enabling role and a facilitating role. In its enabling role, IT helps to enhance entrepreneurial and organizational agility. In its facilitating role, IT competencies enhance firm performance in terms of implementation of entrepreneurial and adaptive actions (Rahman, 2017a). Drnevich and Croson (2013) argue that IT activities remain integral to the functional-level strategies of the firm as well as significant roles in business strategy, with substantial performance implications. Organizational agility is vital to the innovation and competitive performance of firms. There is a relationship between IT capabilities and organizational agility (Lu & Ramamurthy, 2011). Firms are increasingly relying on information technologies, including process, knowledge, and communication technologies, to enhance their agility (Sambamurthy et al., 2003). Research findings indicate that the influence of IT investment on the firm is statistically significant on firm value beyond that exclusively on the accounting performance measures (Kohli et al., 2012).

In the customer support sphere, prominent software and hardware firms including SAP®, Apple®, and Oracle® complement their traditional models of customer support (help desks, product documentation, troubleshooting, etc.) by enabling user-generated support in the form of online technical forums which helps to support users at a relatively low cost (Jabr et al., 2014). The findings of Mithas et al. (2011) suggest that information management capability plays an important role in developing other firm capabilities such as customer management, process management, and performance management. These capabilities, in turn, positively influence customer, financial, human resources, and organizational effectiveness measures of firm performance (Mithas et al., 2011). Roberts and Grover (2012) investigate as to how information technology (IT) facilitates a firm's customer agility and, in turn, competitive activity. Customer agility captures the extent to which a firm is able to sense and respond quickly to customer-based opportunities for innovation and competitive action (Smith et al., 2015). So IT has a prominent role to play in present day business organizations by increasing agility, adding business value, improving business performance and providing strategic directions. Adopting an automated customer inquiry system will positively bring efficiency in small businesses (Akhter & Rahman, 2015).

THE SOFTWARE DEVELOPMENT LIFE CYCLE (SDLC)

Typically, a software development project goes through a set of distinct phases called a software development life cycle (SDLC). Phases include requirements analysis and specifications; design and development; testing (unit testing, system testing, and user acceptance testing); and deployment to production. Here we briefly discuss these phases of SDLC.

Requirements Analysis and Specification

In a software development project, typically the systems analysts will do requirement analysis with users, data analysts and other stakeholders on a rolling basis for each of the iterations of development throughout the project life. Figure 1 provides possible field requirements of customer inquiry system of a Returned Material Authorization (RMA) department.

Figure 1. Typical field requirements of an inquiry system

Field Requirements:	
Open Date (required- possible to have it automatically fill with "today's" date)	
Close Date (upon completion)	
Field to assign in Customer Inquiry (CI) Number automatically once	
Customer information fields (required)	
a. Company Name	
b. Address	
Contact Name (required)	
Contact's phone number (optional)	
Contact's email address (optional)	
Investigator's name (who is working the request-required)	
Drop-down list for:	
a. Retrun Material Authorization (RMA) number	
b. Investigation Issue number	
c. Customer Inquiry Number	
Large history field to enter notes (optional):	
a. Incluse capability to insert attachments or cut and paste from other source	
Drop-down list for status to include (required):	
a. New/Open	
b. Pending	
c. Closed	
Drop-down list for type of CI numebr to include (required):	
a. Disposition	
b. Return to customer	
c. Miss-shipment (wrong warehouse)	
d. Invalid return	
e. Reprot request	
f. Process question	
g. Other	
Product return group (PRG) contact (optional)	
PRG contact's phone number (optional)	
Capability to send email with pertinent information from this application	
Section to enter or add product information	

For this proposed application, we did a thorough analysis of business requirements and listed the items/ tasks that need to be done to make this customer inquiry system a real-world application (Rahman, 2018). From the requirements it is clear the application needs a database system. Given the target customer is a small company, acquiring an expensive database system such as Microsoft® SQL or Oracle® won't be a viable option. We have decided to use Microsoft Access® which is less expensive and affordable by small businesses. Some open source database system could also be a possibility. For a robust inquiry system of a large and medium business organization other scalable database systems such as Oracle® or Microsoft® SQL server could be considered.

For this application, we would also need a user interface. Some database systems (Hernandez, 2013) offer UI for underlying database tables. But in this case that is not a viable option due to high cost involvement. We decided to use MS Visual Studio-based .NET software development architecture.

Designing Solutions

In the design phase, we invested time to perform technical analysis of the business requirements and define deliverables. Deliverables include mapping documents for database tables and VB .NET application development, VB .NET-based UI and report mockups, success criteria, and basic test cases.

From a modeling standpoint, we came up with table names along with primary key (PK) and foreign key (FK) column(s) for individual tables. We brain-stormed to list pertinent columns for each table to make sure we are storing necessary information. Regarding the user interface design we discussed making certain fields automated so users do not have to type-in values manually (Akhter & Rahman, 2015).

Building Solutions/Implementation

In the development phase, the Application Developers write code and prepare utility scripts to load database tables via UI and/or utility scripts. Forms and reports are created for users and business intelligence (BI) team to retrieve data from the underlying database tables. Software development is laborious, complex and takes significant amounts of time.

We have come up with meaningful data for each table. We made sure data integrity (Evermann, 2008) is maintained while preparing data set for each table. In the forms development we made sure that the forms are intuitive, friendly and users can see a row including the one being inserted real-time.

Testing

The testing phase needs to ensure that not only the code works correctly (Khramov, 2006), but also that UI, Reports, and data quality (Garvin, 1987; Idris & Ahmad, 2011) are not compromised. Without successful testing by developers, testers and end users (Melnik et al., 2006) software projects should not be released to production (Rahman, 2017b).

Before releasing an application to end-users we made sure that all objects were tested thoroughly (Rahman, 2018). First we performed unit tests of each individual component and then end-to-end testing of the whole application. After both development and testing is completed any software application is made available to business users to perform user acceptance testing (Ghanam & Maurer, 2011). The data validation in terms of rows and individual column values is a huge task. The more complex an application is the more complex the scenarios are. Each of the scenarios must be tested thoroughly.

As part of testing, we inserted data via each form and checked if certain fields populated automatically as expected. Example: CustInqNbr, CustomerID, ProductID, and date fields. We ran the reports to validate correct data was displayed as expected.

THE ENTITY-RELATIONSHIP (E-R) DIAGRAM

The entity-relationship diagram is crucial to any database schema (Rahman et al., 2012; Kroenke & Auer, 2013). This is needed to make sure data quality is not compromised due to bad relations (Evermann, 2008) or referential integrity issues (Ordonez & Garcia-Garcia, 2008) among the tables in a database schema. In this project, we have come up with three tables required at a minimum. The customer table holds all customer information. The product table holds data values for each of the products sold by the company. The customer inquiry table holds information relating to customer inquiry, complaints, status, and resolutions (Akhter & Rahman, 2015).

Figure 2 shows the Customer Inquiry Database System consists of these three core tables. At any point a customer might have one-to-many inquiries and/or a product might belong to one-to-many inquiries. These tables have relationships with one another in terms of primary key (PK) and foreign key (FK). We did analyze and design these tables in terms of normal forms (NF).

- **Customer:** CustomerID (PK); Highest Normal Form: 4NF; Domain: Text.
- **Product:** ProductID (PK); Highest Normal Form: 4NF; Domain: Text, Currency, Number, Date/Time.

Figure 2. Customer inquiry system E-R diagram

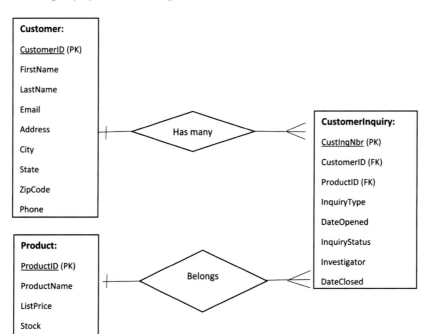

- **CustomerInquiry:** CustInqNbr (PK); CustomerID (FK), ProductID (FK); Highest Normal Form: 4NF; Domain: AutoNumber, Text, Date/Time.

THE CUSTOMER INQUIRY SYSTEM UI DEVELOPMENT

In this section, we show the design and development of database schema, forms (UI) and reports. We used Microsoft® Visual Studio 2013 – Visual Basic (VB) .NET to build the required user interface (UI). .NET is a powerful and scalable industry standard object-oriented architecture. It gives the flexibility to design a custom-made UI versus that of database-table specific forms native to Microsoft® Access. .NET also will integrate well and compliment the backend database system. We have decided to use Microsoft® Access 2010. Both VB .NET and Microsoft® Access are viable options in terms of cost and availability of knowledgeable resources by making them wise and affordable choices for our target small business organizations (Akhter & Rahman, 2015).

Designing the Database Schema

Database design is often described as an intuitive, even artistic, process (Storey & Goldstein, 1993; Coronel & Morris, 2014) and for this application we have come up with a database design for the customer inquiry system to satisfy both database professional and user experience.

We showed the design (Figure 2) of the customer inquiry database tables. The table definitions are called data definition language (DDL) and were created using the Microsoft® Access table-design tool.

Our proposed database inquiry system is capable respond to queries that can be performed on the Customer Inquiry Database System to demonstrate the data structure and relationships. These queries consist of single or multi-table query. Example: (1) List all inquiries showing customer names and their inquiry status (use multi-table query). (2) List all inquiries showing product names and customer inquiry types (multi-table query). (3) List all customer inquiries that have status Open. (4) Show all products being sold by this company. (5) Lastly, we provide a Business Intelligence (Rahman and Sutton, 2016) query to get the TOP 10 customers in terms of purchase amount:

1. List ALL inquiries showing customer names and their inquiry status (use multi-table query).

```
SELECT CI.CustInqNbr, CI.CustomerID, C.FirstName, C.LastName, CI.Status
FROM CustomerInquiry AS CI, Customer AS C
WHERE CI.CustomerID = C.CustomerID
ORDER BY CI.CustomerID;
```

2. List ALL inquiries showing product names and customer inquiry types (multi-table query).

```
SELECT CI.CustInqNbr, CI.CustomerID, CI.ProductID, P.ProductName,
CI.InquiryType
FROM CustomerInquiry AS CI, Product AS P
WHERE CI.ProductID = P.ProductID
ORDER BY CI.ProductID;
```

3.   List ALL customer inquiries that have status Open.

```
SELECT *
FROM CustomerInquiry AS CI
WHERE CI.Status = 'Open';
```

4.   Show ALL products being sold by this company.

```
SELECT P.ProductID, P.ProductName
FROM Product AS P;
```

5.   Get the TOP 10 customers in terms of purchase amount.

```
SELECT DRV.*
FROM (
SELECT CI.CustomerID AS CustomerID, C.FirstName AS FirstName
, C.LastName AS LastName, SUM(P.ListPrice) AS TotalPurchAmount
FROM CustomerInquiry AS CI, Customer AS C, Product AS P
WHERE CI.CustomerID = C.CustomerID
AND CI.ProductID = P.ProductID
GROUP BY CI.CustomerID, C.FirstName, C.LastName
) AS DRV
INNER JOIN
(SELECT TOP 10 CI2.CustomerID AS CustomerID
FROM CustomerInquiry AS CI2, Customer AS C2, Product AS P2
WHERE CI2.CustomerID = C2.CustomerID
AND CI2.ProductID = P2.ProductID
GROUP BY CI2.CustomerID
ORDER BY SUM(P2.ListPrice) DESC
) AS DRV2
ON DRV.CustomerID = DRV2.CustomerID
ORDER BY TotalPurchAmount DESC;
```

Design and Development of the User Interface

When building an IT infrastructure an organization needs to take into consideration the performance, reliability and security requirements. Budget can only be set after taking into account these deliverables and if those requirements are important to business. Martin (2006) asserts that the organizations that shelter in the trailing edge of technology might be at risk from scalability, performance (Rahman & Sutton, 2016) and security standpoint. Research suggests that tough "non-functional requirements including performance, reliability, and security can result in high performance to time/budget" (Martin, 2006).

In our case, we have decided to use Visual Studio® .NET 2013 as the development environment. .NET is the latest software development technology from Microsoft. VB.NET offers many controls to help organize forms more effectively, ease the data entry process, and improve functionality for user interfaces including calendar control, checked list-box and main menu controls. The UI's are destined to sit on top of the tables of the database schema.

Figure 3 shows the main form of our Customer Inquiry Database System. Figure 4 shows the code to launch this form. The first two rows in the form provide the text boxes to show a customer inquiry record. Only one row shows at a time to reduce clutter and ensure accurate data entry. This form has a search button to pull up a known customer inquiry number. Figure 5 shows the syntax executed by a "Search a Cust Inq Nbr" button 'click' that searches for a particular customer inquiry number. The next and previous buttons are used to scroll forward and backward through the existing records. With each scroll forward or back the database system is querying the database to retrieve data for the records to

Figure 3. Customer inquiry database system main form

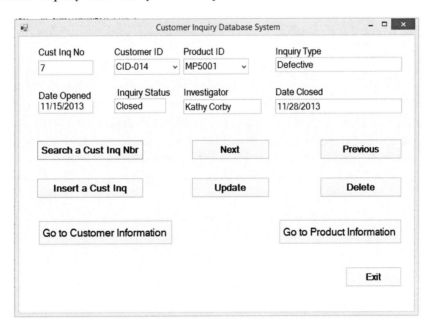

Figure 4. Code to launch customer inquiry main form

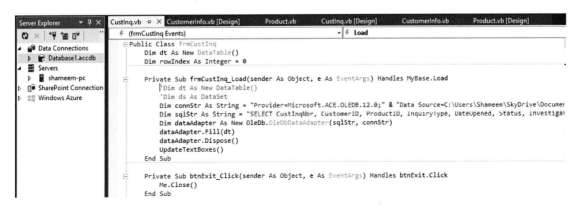

Figure 5. Code-block to find an existing customer inquiry number

```
Private Sub btnFind_Click(sender As Object, e As EventArgs) Handles btnFind.Click

    Dim sCustInqNbr As Integer
    Dim sCustInqNbrFound As Boolean = False

    sCustInqNbr = intCustInqNbr.Text    'this also works: InputBox("Enter a CustInqNbr:")
    For i As Integer = 0 To (dt.Rows.Count - 1)
        If CStr(dt.Rows(i)("CustInqNbr")) = sCustInqNbr Then
            sCustInqNbrFound = True
            rowIndex = i
            UpdateTextBoxes()
        End If
    Next
    If (Not sCustInqNbrFound) Then
        MessageBox.Show("Cannot find the requested CustInqNbr: " & sCustInqNbr)
    End If
End Sub
```

be viewed by the user. The main form has functionality to create (insert), change (update) and remove (delete) records. The main form shows two other buttons named 'Go to Customer Information' and 'Go to Product Information'. These buttons are used to jump to customer (Figure 9) and product information (Figure 10) forms. Each of those forms has functionalities to manipulate data relating to customer and product. The 'Exit' button lets to leave the Customer Inquiry Database System.

Figure 6 shows code-block that enables scrolling records to the next or previous customer inquiry numbers.

In .NET for Windows Forms to bind data to form controls, it is necessary to create a DataSet. We add the components to the form to enable the form to use the data in the Dataset. Figure 4 shows that on the Form's Load event, dataset is filled using DataAdapter.Fill(Dataset). The variable, connStr creates a unique session to database and the variable sqlStr points to a prepared query to retrieve the required records. The variable dataAdapter retrieves (SELECT) and commits (UPDATE) data from and to the

Figure 6. Code to scroll to the next/previous customer inquiry number

```
, btnNext                                              ▼ | ⚡ Click

    Private Sub btnNext_Click(sender As Object, e As EventArgs) Handles btnNext.Click
        If (rowIndex < dt.Rows.Count - 1) Then
            rowIndex += 1
            UpdateTextBoxes()
        End If
    End Sub


    Private Sub btnPrev_Click(sender As Object, e As EventArgs) Handles btnPrev.Click
        If (rowIndex > 0) Then
            rowIndex = rowIndex - 1
            UpdateTextBoxes()
        End If
    End Sub
```

database. In .NET, forms are disconnected from the database. To bind controls to the database, projects are created that contain classes and objects to specifically handle database operations. Also in .NET, it is necessary to explicitly specify when connections are opened and closed on the database for the queries run to populate the form and commit data back to the database. This helps to optimize network traffic.

Figure 7 shows creation of the Data Access Components (Cogan & Valabjee, 2004). Four types of objects are used in this process: SqlConnection, SqlDataAdapter, DataSet and DataRelation. These objects are created for each table used in the solution. SqlDataAdapters from the DataAccess project is instantiated and then used to fill the corresponding DataSets. DataSet stores an in-memory copy of the data for use in the application. DataRelation maintains a relationship between two tables in a dataset, much like relationships in a relational database.

Figure 8 shows the act of an Insert/Add of a new record. All text fields in the form are populated first and then the user clicks-on 'Insert a Cust Inq Nbr' button to add the new record. Note that a message window is used as visual feedback to the user to confirm that one new record was created. 'Cust Inq No' is the record identifier (aka, PK). The PK value is auto-generated incremental record number and is accomplished by setting the column in the table to auto-generate sequence number.

The code-block in Figure 9 sits under 'Insert a Cust Inq' button (Figure 8). By clicking on 'Insert a Cust Inq' button user will be able to insert a new record in CustomerInquiry table. In Figure 9, simple error handling is evident in the Try/Catch block.

In .NET, because forms are bound to a local in-memory copy of the data and not the actual database, Update (or Save/Add) button is used in the form which, when clicked, will perform the database update.

In the Update button's Click event (Figure 10), the syntax dataAdapter.Update(dt) is used to tell the data adapter to commit changes made to the in-memory dataset back to the database. In Figure 10,

Figure 7. Data access project components

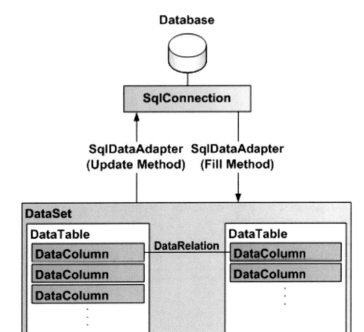

Figure 8. Inserting a new customer inquiry

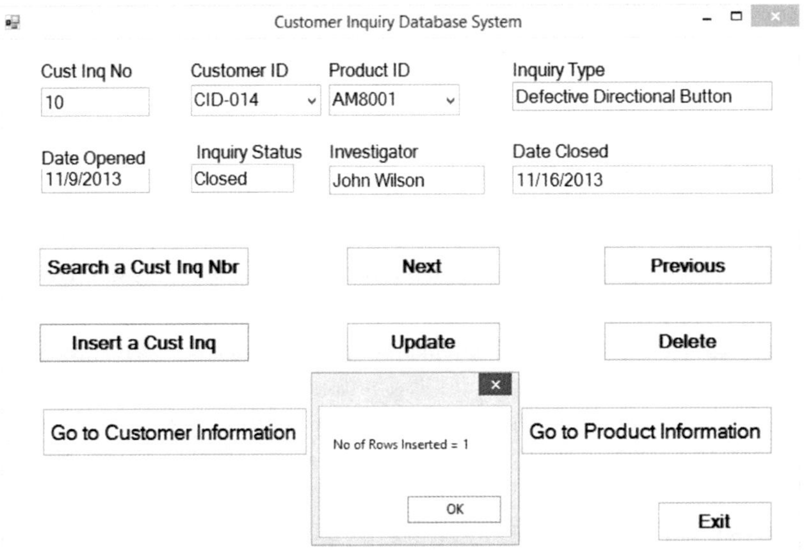

Figure 9. Code-block that inserts a new customer inquiry

```
Private Sub btnInsert_Click(sender As Object, e As EventArgs) Handles btnInsert.Click
    Dim i As Integer
    Dim sCustomerID, sProductID, sInquiryType, sStatus, sInvestigator, v_DateOpend, v_DateClosed As Strin
    Dim rw As DataRow
    Dim connStr As String = "Provider=Microsoft.ACE.OLEDB.12.0;" & "Data Source=C:\Users\Shameem\SkyDrive
    Dim sqlStr As String = "SELECT * FROM CustomerInquiry"
    Dim dataAdapter As New OleDb.OleDbDataAdapter(sqlStr, connStr)
    Dim CommandBuilder As New OleDb.OleDbCommandBuilder(dataAdapter)
    dataAdapter.Fill(dt)
    rw = dt.NewRow
    sCustomerID = cmbCustomerID.Text   'txtCustomerID.Text
    sProductID = cmbProductID.Text     'txtProductID.Text
    sInquiryType = txtInquiryType.Text
    sStatus = txtStatus.Text
    sInvestigator = txtInvestigator.Text
    v_DateOpend = txtDateOpened.Text
    v_DateClosed = txtDateClosed.Text
    rw.Item("CustomerID") = sCustomerID
    rw.Item("ProductID") = sProductID
    rw.Item("InquiryType") = sInquiryType
    rw.Item("Status") = sStatus
    rw.Item("Investigator") = sInvestigator
    If String.IsNullOrEmpty(v_DateOpend.ToString().Trim) = True Then
        rw.Item("DateOpened") = Today    'This works in INSERT but not in UPDATE: DBNull.Value
    Else : rw.Item("DateOpened") = v_DateOpend
    End If
    If String.IsNullOrEmpty(v_DateClosed.ToString().Trim) = True Then
        rw.Item("DateClosed") = "12/31/9999"    'This works in INSERT but not in UPDATE: DBNull.Value
    Else : rw.Item("DateClosed") = v_DateClosed
    End If
    Try
        dt.Rows.Add(rw)
        i = dataAdapter.Update(dt)
    Catch ex As Exception
        MessageBox.Show(ex.Message)
```

Figure 10. Code-block that updates/changes an existing customer inquiry

```
btnUpdate                                                    Click
    Private Sub btnUpdate_Click(sender As Object, e As EventArgs) Handles btnUpdate.Click
        Dim sCustInqNbr As Integer
        Dim sCustomerID, sProductID, sInquiryType, sDateOpened, sStatus, sInvestigator, sDateClosed As String
        Dim ObjectConnection As System.Data.OleDb.OleDbConnection
        Dim ObjectCommand As System.Data.OleDb.OleDbCommand
        sCustInqNbr = CInt(intCustInqNbr.Text)
        sCustomerID = CStr(cmbCustomerID.Text)
        sProductID = CStr(cmbProductID.Text)
        sInquiryType = CStr(txtInquiryType.Text)
        If String.IsNullOrEmpty(txtDateOpened.Text.ToString().Trim) = True Then
            sDateOpened = Today 'This works in INSERT but not in UPDATE: DBNull.Value
        Else : sDateOpened = txtDateOpened.Text
        End If
        sStatus = CStr(txtStatus.Text)
        sInvestigator = CStr(txtInvestigator.Text)
        If String.IsNullOrEmpty(txtDateClosed.Text.ToString().Trim) = True Then
            sDateClosed = "12/31/9999"  'This works in INSERT but not in UPDATE: DBNull.Value
        Else : sDateClosed = txtDateClosed.Text
        End If
        ObjectConnection = New System.Data.OleDb.OleDbConnection("Provider=Microsoft.ACE.OLEDB.12.0;" & "Data
        ObjectConnection.Open()
        ObjectCommand = New System.Data.OleDb.OleDbCommand
        ObjectCommand.Connection = ObjectConnection
        Try
            ObjectCommand.CommandText = "UPDATE CustomerInquiry SET CustomerID = '" & sCustomerID & "' ,Produ
            ObjectCommand.CommandType = CommandType.Text
            ObjectCommand.ExecuteNonQuery()
            ObjectConnection.Close()
            MessageBox.Show("Row Updated with CustInqNbr = " & sCustInqNbr)

        Catch ex As Exception
            MsgBox(ex.ToString)
        End Try
    End Sub
```

simple error handling is also shown. Any changes that are made to the DataSet need to be committed back to the database. In Figure 3, once the user clicks on 'Update' button a message window appears to confirm the update/change of the record.

Any changes that are made to the DataSet need to be committed back to the database. In Figure 11, once the user clicks on 'Update' button a message window appears to confirm the update/change of the record.

- **Switching to Sub Forms**: In the main form (Figure 3), that is, Customer Inquiry Form, there are two buttons: *'Go to Customer Information'* and *'Go to Product Information'*. These two buttons lets user to go to Customer and Production forms to insert, update, and search records operations.
- **Sub Form-1: Customer Information:** Connect to Customer Information Form via the main form - Customer Inquiry Form.

The 'Customer Information' form (Figure 12) lets the user view, insert, and change customer information. The 'Scroll to Next Customer' and 'Scroll to Previous Customer' buttons enables users to scroll through the records in the customer table. By clicking on 'Go Back to Cust Inq System' the user is able to go back to the main Customer Inquiry Form.

Figure 11. Message to confirm an existing customer inquiry updated

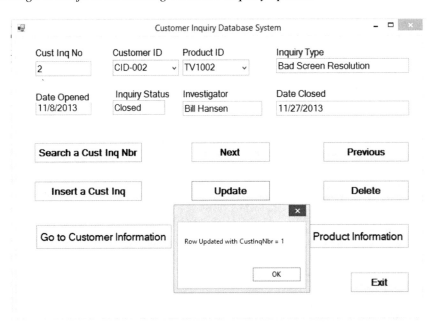

Figure 12. Customer Form to add a new customer

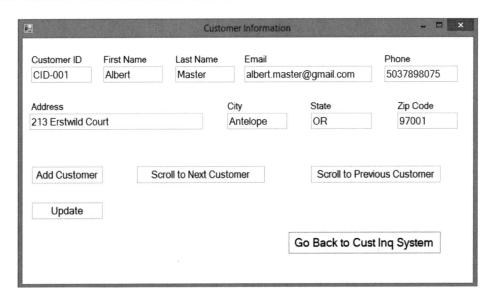

- **Sub Form-2: Product Information**: Connect to Product Information Form via the main form - Customer Inquiry Form.

The Product Information form in Figure 13 facilitates updating product information in the Product table in the database. The user is able to create/add a new record and change/update an existing record. When the user changes the product and clicks "Update Product", the database table is updated instantly.

Figure 13. Product information form to add or update a new product

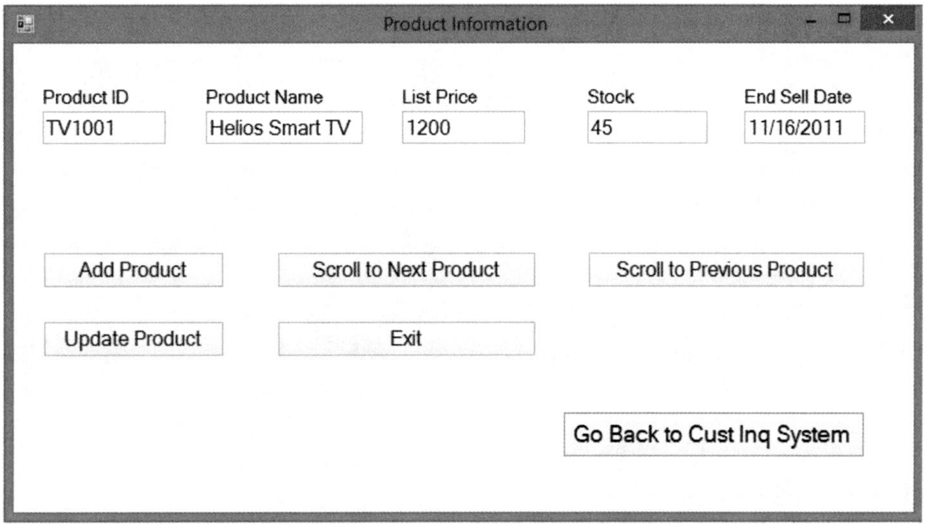

The 'Scroll to Next Product' and 'Scroll to Previous Product' buttons provide back and forth record navigation capability. Finally, the 'Go Back to Cust Inq System' lets the user to return to the main Customer Inquiry Form.

Design and Development of the Reports

This section discusses the design process (Figure 14) and results to generate reports based on customer inquiry database system tables. Reporting, online analytical processing (OLAP) or other business intelligence (Chaudhuri et al., 2011; Heer & Shneiderman, 2012) tools built upon database systems reflect an asset for every organization in the decision making process (Brohman, et al., 2000; Lehner et al., 2002; Rutz et al., 2012).

- **Customer Inquiry Report-1**: Generate a Customer Inquiry report showing Customer Name and Product Name along with other important information from the Customer-Inquiry Table (multi-table report).

Using the native report builder within Microsoft® Access (Figure 14) the format and desired data fields were laid out to produce a Customer Inquiry Report (Figure 15) showing Customer Name and Product Name along with other important information from Customer-Inquiry table (use multi-table report) based on Below SQL:

```
SELECT CI.CustInqNbr, CI.CustomerID, C.FirstName & " " & C.LastName AS Customer-
erName, CI.Status, CI.ProductID, P.ProductName, CI.InquiryType
FROM CustomerInquiry AS CI, Customer AS C, Product AS P
WHERE CI.CustomerID = C.CustomerID
```

Figure 14. Design view of customer inquiry report

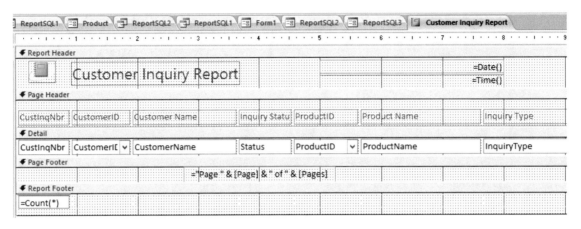

Figure 15. Customer inquiry report generated

Customer Inquiry Report

CustInqNbr	CustomerID	Customer Name	Inquiry Statu	ProductID	Product Name	Inquiry Type
7	CID-014	Margaret Lawson	Closed	MP5001	Eos Mobile Phone	Defective
8	CID-015	Lana Beatty	Closed	CA6108	Uranus Compact System Camera	Defective Pixels Map
9	CID-014	Margaret Lawson	Closed	CA6108	Uranus Compact System Camera	Defective Pixels Map
10	CID-014	Margaret Lawson	Open	AM8001	Persephone MP3 Player	Defective Directional Button
11	CID-038	James Henry	Open	AM8001	Persephone MP3 Player	Defective Directional Button
12	CID-009	Ben Miller	Open	CG0002	Rhea GPS Nevigation	Gives Inaccurate Information
13	CID-012	Roy Jaeger	Open	CG0003	Rhea GPS Nevigation	Gives Inaccurate Information
14	CID-034	Andy Mitchel	Closed	MP5001	Eos Mobile Phone	Defect in Manufacturing
15	CID-010	Donald Quinn	Open	MP5003	Eos Mobile Phone	Defect in Manufacturing
16	CID-011	Jane Miller	Open	MP5004	Eos Mobile Phone	Defect in Manufacturing
17	CID-011	Jane Miller	Closed	TV2001	Selene Smart TV	Defective - Channels won't change
18	CID-014	Margaret Lawson	Open	TV1001	Helios Smart TV	Defective - A black box blocking the picture

```
AND CI.ProductID = P.ProductID
ORDER BY CI.CustInqNbr;
```

- **Customer Inquiry Report-2**: Generate a Report showing product names and customer inquiry types (multi-table report). The report provides product names and customer inquiry types (multi-table report) are based on SQL below:

```
SELECT CI.CustInqNbr, CI.ProductID, P.ProductName, CI.InquiryType
FROM CustomerInquiry AS CI, Product AS P
WHERE CI.ProductID = P.ProductID
ORDER BY CI.CustInqNbr;
```

- **Customer Inquiry Report-3:** Generate a Report showing customer inquiries that have status Open (single-table report). The report provides customer inquiries that have status Open is based on below SQL:

```
SELECT CI.CustInqNbr, CI.CustomerID, CI.ProductID, CI.InquiryType,
CI.DateOpened, CI.Status
FROM CustomerInquiry AS CI
WHERE CI.Status = 'Open'
ORDER BY CI.CustInqNbr;
```

DISCUSSION AND CONCLUSION

IT has a prominent role to play in present day business organizations in terms of increasing agility, adding business value, improving business performance and providing strategic directions. Adopting an automated customer inquiry system will positively bring efficiency in small businesses.

In this chapter, we provided the detailed steps of software development life cycle (SDLC) to implement a Customer Inquiry Database System. We have designed and developed a database schema with required columns for each table and have shown the referential integrity (RI) among the tables in terms of primary and foreign keys.

We walked through the steps to build the required UI for the Inquiry System using Microsoft Visual Studio®, VB. NET to design and develop the forms. We have provided examples of VB .NET code to insert, update, and delete rows and perform other operations. We have discussed other useful functionality in the forms enabling users to scroll through records and switch from one form to another.

We have designed and developed basic, necessary reporting environment to provide decision support system (DSS) utility. Traditional isolated, stand-alone DSS has been recently facing new challenges. In order to improve the performance of DSS to meet the challenges, research has been actively carried out to develop integrated decision support systems (Liu & Duffy, 2010). We make contributions in reporting and BI space. We hope that IT professionals and small business will find this customer inquiry database system beneficial.

REVIEW QUESTIONS

1. What is the purpose of a customer information database?
2. Describe why a small database is not necessarily simpler than a large one.
3. What is Structured Query Language (SQL), and why is it important?
4. What are the downsides of a poorly designed database?
5. What are the steps of a software development life cycle?
6. Why are requirement analyses important in implementing a database application project?
7. What is entity-relationship and why is it important in database design?
8. What factors need to be considered in developing a customer support system?
9. What testing is so important for a user interface development?
10. What is the Visual Basic .NET syntax to setup connection with the underlying database system?

ACKNOWLEDGMENT

An earlier version of this book chapter entitled, Building a Customer Inquiry Database system appeared in the International Journal of Technology Diffusion (Akther & Rahman, 2015). This chapter has been revised and enhanced, based on book chapter publishing guidelines from IGI Global. They include change of title of the original article, modifications of the abstract to reflect the enhanced content, changes in references and literature review sections to incorporate the most current research findings, and adding and changing of graphs and tables to ensure that they are up-to-date. The authors would like to thank the anonymous reviewers and editor of this book for their constructive comments provided on earlier version of this book chapter.

REFERENCES

Akhter, S., & Rahman, N. (2015). Building a customer inquiry database system. *International Journal of Technology Diffusion*, *6*(2), 59–76. doi:10.4018/IJTD.2015040104

Bardhan, I., Krishnan, V., & Lin, S. (2013). Research note—business value of information technology: Testing the interaction effect of IT and R&D on Tobin's Q. *Information Systems Research*, *24*(4), 1147–1161. doi:10.1287/isre.2013.0481

Blocker, C. P., Flint, D. J., Myers, M. B., & Slater, S. F. (2011). Proactive customer orientation and its role for creating customer value in global markets. *Journal of the Academy of Marketing Science*, *39*(2), 216–233. doi:10.100711747-010-0202-9

Brohman, M. K., Parent, M., Pearce, M. R., & Wade, M. (2000). The business intelligence value chain: Data-driven decision support in a data warehouse environment: An exploratory study. In *Proceedings of the 33rd Hawaii International Conference on System Sciences (HICSS-33)*. IEEE. 10.1109/HICSS.2000.926905

Chakravarty, A., Grewal, R., & Sambamurthy, V. (2013). Information technology competencies, organizational agility, and firm performance: Enabling and facilitating roles. *Information Systems Research*, *24*(4), 976–997. doi:10.1287/isre.2013.0500

Chang, Y. B., & Gurbaxani, V. (2013). An empirical analysis of technical efficiency: The role of IT intensity and competition. *Information Systems Research*, *24*(3), 561–578. doi:10.1287/isre.1120.0438

Chaudhuri, S., Dayal, U., & Narasayya, V. (2011). An overview of business intelligence technology. *Communications of the ACM*, *54*(8), 88–98. doi:10.1145/1978542.1978562

Cogan, A., & Valabjee, J. (2004). *How to migrate access forms to. NET windows forms*. Retrieved on 02/15/2018 from: http://www.ssw.com.au/ssw/Standards/DeveloperDotNet/MSUS_02_How_To_Migrate_Access_Forms_To_Dot_Net_Whitepaper_ver15.doc

Coronel, C., & Morris, S. (2014). Database systems: Design, implementation, & management (11th ed.). Cengage Learning.

Drnevich, P. L., & Croson, D. C. (2013, June). Information technology and business-level strategy: Toward an integrated theoretical perspective. *Management Information Systems Quarterly, 37*(2), 483–509. doi:10.25300/MISQ/2013/37.2.08

Evermann, J. (2008). An exploratory study of database integration processes. *IEEE Transactions on Knowledge and Data Engineering, 20*(1), 99–115. doi:10.1109/TKDE.2007.190675

Farouk, A. (1987). *Retail marketing in Dhaka city, Research Report.* Dhaka, Bangladesh: Bureau of Business Research, University of Dhaka.

Garvin, D. A. (1987, November). Competing on the eight dimensions of quality. *Harvard Business Review*, 101–109.

Ghanam, Y., & Maurer, F. (2011). Using acceptance tests for incremental elicitation of variability in requirements: An observational study. *Proceedings of AGILE 2011 Conference (AGILE'11), IEEE 2011.* 10.1109/AGILE.2011.21

Heer, J., & Shneiderman, B. (2012). Interactive dynamics for visual analysis. *Communications of the ACM, 55*(4), 45–54. doi:10.1145/2133806.2133821

Hernandez, M. J. (2013). Database design for mere mortals: A hands-on guide to relational database design (3rd ed.). Addison-Wesley Professional.

Huang, H. L. (2013). Performance effects of aligning service innovation and the strategic use of information technology. *Service Business.* doi:10.100711628-013-0192-z

Idris, N., & Ahmad, K. (2011). Managing data source quality for data warehouse in manufacturing services. *Proceedings of the 2011 IEEE International Conference on Electrical Engineering and Informatics.* 10.1109/ICEEI.2011.6021598

Im, K. S., Grover, V., & Teng, J. T. C. (2013). Research note - Do large firms become smaller by using information technology? *Information Systems Research, 24*(2), 470–491. doi:10.1287/isre.1120.0439

Inmon, W. H. (2002). *Building the data warehouse* (3rd ed.). John Wiley.

Jabr, W., Mookerjee, R., Tan, Y., & Mookerjee, V.S. (2014). Leveraging philanthropic behavior for customer support: The case of user support firms. *MIS Quarterly, 38*(1), 187-208.

Keil, M., & Carmel, E. (1995). Customer-developer links in software development. *Communications of the ACM, 38*(5), 33–44. doi:10.1145/203356.203363

Khramov, Y. (2006). The cost of code quality. In *Proceedings of the Agile 2006 Conference (AGILE'06).* IEEE. 10.1109/AGILE.2006.52

Kohli, R., Devaraj, S., & Ow, T. T. (2012). Does information technology investment influence a firm's market value? A case of non-publicly traded healthcare firms. *Management Information Systems Quarterly, 36*(4), 1145–1163.

Kroenke, D. M., & Auer, D. J. (2013). Database processing: fundamentals, design, and implementation (13th ed.). Prentice Hall.

Lehner, W., Hummer, W., & Schlesinger, L. (2002). In processing reporting function views in a data warehouse environment. In *Proceedings of the 18th International Conference on Data Engineering (ICDE'02)*. IEEE. 10.1109/ICDE.2002.994707

Li, X., Hsieh, J. J. P., & Rai, A. (2013). Motivational differences across post-acceptance information system usage behaviors: An investigation in the business intelligence systems context. *Information Systems Research*, *24*(3), 659–682. doi:10.1287/isre.1120.0456

Liu, S., Duffy, A. H. B., Whitfield, R. I., & Boyle, I. M. (2010). Integration of decision support systems to improve decision support performance. *Knowledge and Information Systems*, *22*(3), 261–286. doi:10.100710115-009-0192-4

Lu, Y., & Ramamurthy, K. (2011). Understanding the link between information technology capability and organizational agility: An empirical examination. *Management Information Systems Quarterly*, *35*(4), 931–954. doi:10.2307/41409967

Martin, A. (2006). Successful IT application architecture design: An empirical study. *Information Systems and e-Business Management*, *4*(2), 107–135. doi:10.100710257-005-0029-y

Melnik, G., Maurer, F., & Chiasson, M. (2006). Executable acceptance tests for communicating business requirements: Customer perspective. *Proceedings of AGILE 2006 Conference (AGILE'06), IEEE 2006*. 10.1109/AGILE.2006.26

Mithas, S., Ramasubbu, N., & Sambamurthy, V. (2011). How information management capability influences firm performance. *Management Information Systems Quarterly*, *35*(1), 237–256. doi:10.2307/23043496

Morris, T. (2012). *12 customer service quotes to inspire you this year*. Retrieved on 03/23/2014 from: http://www.parature.com/12-customer-service-quotes-to-inspire-you-this-year/

Morris, T. (2013). *12 customer service quotes to inspire you in 2013*. Retrieved on 02/15/2018 from: http://www.parature.com/12-customer-service-quotes-inspire-2013/

Murphy, B., Jr. (2018). *Here Are the Best Inspirational Quotes for 2018*. Retrieved on 2/15/2018 from: https://www.inc.com/bill-murphy-jr/here-are-best-inspirational-quotes-for-2018.html

Ordonez, C., & Garcia-Garcia, J. (2008). Referential integrity quality metrics. *Decision Support Systems*, *44*(2), 495–508. doi:10.1016/j.dss.2007.06.004

Porter, M. E., & Millar, V. E. (1985, July). How information gives you competitive advantage. *Harvard Business Review*, 101–109.

Rahman, N. (2016). Enterprise data warehouse governance best practices. *International Journal of Knowledge-Based Organizations*, *6*(2), 21–37. doi:10.4018/IJKBO.2016040102

Rahman, N. (2017a). An empirical study of data warehouse implementation effectiveness. *International Journal of Management Science and Engineering Management*, *12*(1), 55–63. doi:10.1080/17509653.2015.1113394

Rahman, N. (2017b, October-December). Lessons from a successful data warehousing project management. *International Journal of Information Technology Project Management, 8*(4), 30–45. doi:10.4018/IJITPM.2017100103

Rahman, N. (2018). A simulation model for application development in data warehouses. *International Journal of Operations Research and Information Systems, 9*(1), 66–80. doi:10.4018/IJORIS.2018010104

Rahman, N., Marz, J., & Akhter, S. (2012). An ETL metadata model for data warehousing. *CIT. Journal of Computing and Information Technology, 20*(2), 95–111. doi:10.2498/cit.1002046

Rahman, N., Rutz, D., Akhter, S., & Aldhaban, F. (2014, November). Emerging technologies in business intelligence and advanced analytics. *ULAB Journal of Science and Engineering, 5*(1), 7–17.

Rahman, N., & Sutton, L. (2016). Optimizing SQL performance in a parallel processing DBMS architecture. *ULAB Journal of Science and Engineering, 7*(1), 33–44.

Roberts, N., & Grover, V. (2012). Leveraging information technology infrastructure to facilitate a firm's customer agility and competitive activity: An empirical investigation. *Journal of Management Information Systems, 28*(4), 231–269. doi:10.2753/MIS0742-1222280409

Romano, N. C. Jr, & Fjermestad, J. (2003). Electronic commerce customer relationship management: A research agenda. *Information Technology Management, 4*(2/3), 233–258. doi:10.1023/A:1022906513502

Rutz, D., Nelakanti, T. K., & Rahman, N. (2012). Practical implications of real time business intelligence. *CIT. Journal of Computing and Information Technology, 20*(4), 257–264. doi:10.2498/cit.1002081

Sambamurthy, V., Bharadwaj, A., & Grover, V. (2003). Shaping agility through digital options: Reconceptualizing the role of information technology in contemporary firms. *Management Information Systems Quarterly, 27*(2), 237–263. doi:10.2307/30036530

Slater, S. F., & Narver, J. C. (2000). Intelligence generation and superior customer value. *Journal of the Academy of Marketing Science, 28*(1), 120–127. doi:10.1177/0092070300281011

Smith, A. W., Rahman, N., & Ullah, M. (2015). Intrapreneurship: Is more than just innovation. In *Proceedings of the 1st Biennial Conference of Bangladesh Academy of Business Administration (BABA'15)*, 19-20.

Sommerville, I. (2004). *Software engineering*. Pearson Education Limited.

Storey, V. C., & Goldstein, R. C. (1993). Knowledge-based approaches to database design. *Management Information Systems Quarterly, 17*(1), 25–46. doi:10.2307/249508

Szymanski, D. M., & Henard, D. H. (2001). Customer satisfaction: A meta-analysis of the empirical evidence. *Journal of the Academy of Marketing Science, 29*(1), 16–35. doi:10.1177/0092070301291002

Tambe, P., & Hitt, L. M. (2012). The productivity of information technology investments: New evidence from IT labor data. *Information Systems Research, 23*(3), 599–617. doi:10.1287/isre.1110.0398

Umar, A. (2005). IT infrastructure to enable next generation enterprises. *Information Systems Frontiers, 7*(3), 217–256. doi:10.100710796-005-2768-1

Weill, W., Subramani, M., & Broadbent, M. (2002). Building IT infrastructure for strategic agility. *MIT Sloan Management Review*, (Fall): 57–65.

Wu, F., Mahajan, V., & Balasubramanian, S. (2003). An analysis of e-business adoption and its impact on business performance. *Journal of the Academy of Marketing Science, 31*(4), 425-447. DOI: 10.1177/0092070303255379

Zeithaml, V. A., Parasuraman, A., & Malhotra, A. (2002). Service quality delivery through web sites: A critical review of extant knowledge. *Journal of the Academy of Marketing Science, 30*(4), 362–375. doi:10.1177/009207002236911

Chapter 10
Shaping Competitive Strategies for the Computer Industry

Shameem Akhter
Western Oregon University, USA

Nayem Rahman
Portland State University, USA

Mahmud Ullah
University of Dhaka, Bangladesh

Mohammad Nirjhar Rahman
University of Rajshahi, Bangladesh

ABSTRACT

Accelerated response to competition with appropriate actions is one of the major determinants for a firm's sustenance and survival. Both operational and financial performances in terms of gaining and/ or keeping competitive advantage always remain under the watchful eyes of the relevant stakeholders in an industry. A firm has to be very vigilant to cope with the internal and external changes it faces over the different phases of its growth. Just like any other industry, this is equally true, in fact more true for the computer industry as well. Continuous innovation in the computer industry has made it a very fast growing and fiercely competitive industry in the field of modern technologies. Firms in this industry always have to be on their toes to tackle the fierce competition created due to many obvious reasons. This study examines the computer industry in the light of Michael Porter's framework for analyzing the profitability. Threats of new entrants and substitute products, bargaining power of both suppliers and buyers, and regular rivalry among the competitors have been analyzed critically. This study may have significant implications in evaluating the competitive strategies developed and applied by the incumbent firms in and the new entrants into the computer manufacturing industry.

DOI: 10.4018/978-1-5225-6367-9.ch010

INTRODUCTION

Computer usage has been pervasive for pretty long time now, and there is no sign of slowing down, rather it is becoming increasingly pervasive every day. Computer is needed for family, for business, for low income people, for high income people, for developed nations, for developing nations, for underdeveloped nations, for whom not in fact. And everybody in every sector is embracing this need enthusiastically, because it is not possible to stay away but doing so.

Auspicious availability of all the most user friendly application software, worldwide diffusion of internet with ever increasing high speed but decreasing low cost, emergence of number of companies with innovative appliances and specialized internet sites etc. have made computer usage one of the easiest possible behavior even for a laymen, and one of the most essential aspects at every facets of our daily life. Consequently, computers in different innovative forms have become the most inevitable devices for mankind. The emergence of popular sites such as Google and Yahoo as search engines and email communication vehicles; social networking tools such as Face-book, Linked-in, Twitter and many online shopping sites including Amazon.com have made computer use part of life for most people in developed nations and in increasing numbers in developing nations as well (Akhter et al., 2014).

The International Business Machines (IBM) Corporation played major role in making computer familiar initially, and popular gradually throughout the whole world. IBM® was the pioneer in introducing the personal computer (PC) to household and business users. Being a renowned high tech company for decades; IBM®'s entrance in computer industry nearly fifty years ago has legitimized the industry and expanded its growth (Moy & Terregrossa, 2009). However, IBM followed their strategic business models to operate in personal computer industry too. They did not make all the components and parts required to manufacture PCs on their own. The two major components of a PC - microprocessors and operation systems (OS), were outsourced from Intel® and Microsoft® respectively. Outsourcing some services to the specialized companies has been used as effective strategies by IBM®. Both Intel and Microsoft offered to join IBM in successful lunching of PCs to household and business users, seeing it mutually beneficial for them to join a company like IBM®, which has been established for decades with enormous goodwill as a renowned business machine company. Although IBM was the leading firm for high technology and computers for decades, it is no longer the leading manufacturer of personal computers. IBM's one-time dominance of the computer industry has been diminishing in part to a software manufacturer, Microsoft, and in part to a microprocessor manufacturer, Intel (Waldman, 2008). Microsoft's decision to align itself with IBM's microcomputer project is one of the great business decisions of all time (Akhter et al., 2014; Moy & Terregrossa, 2009).

Since IBM's pioneering of the PC, a good number of computer manufactures have emerged over the years, including HP, Lenovo, Dell, Acer, ASUS, Toshiba, Sony, Samsung, Gateway, Apple, etc. During the last decade Taiwan, Singapore, Mexico, and China (Kraemer & Dedrick, 2002) also began to emerge as key players in the PC industry. The computer industry is now one of the fastest growing industries. "Gartner, the research company, predicts the global devices market will grow by 2 per cent in 2018 to 2.35bn units. That would represent the fastest rate of growth since 2015" (Fildes, 2017).

This chapter is organized as follows: Section 2 briefly discusses the related work done in this area. Section 3 discusses the present state of the computer industry. Section 4 provides a critical analysis of the computer industry profitability in terms of five competitive forces proposed by Porter. Section 5 summarizes and concludes the chapter.

LITERATURE REVIEW

Competitive strategy of a firm is thought to be of major importance in its success in the industry (Gatignon & Robertson, 1989; Goolsbee, 2001; Kumar et al., 2011; Lawless & Fisher, 1990; Mathews, 2002; Porter, 2008; Prahalad & Hamel, 1990; Tambe & Hitt, 2012). These studies reinforce the importance of understanding different forces of competition. This is true for both incumbent and the new entrants. Bush (2012) asserts that developing an organization's competitive strategies is instrumental in staying ahead of the competition. Research has shown that competitive strategies need to be assessed from the standpoint of the threat of new entrants (which matters to incumbents), the bargaining power of suppliers (true for both incumbents and new comers), the bargaining powers of buyers, the threat of substitute products (matter of concern for incumbents), and rivalry among competitors (Porter, 2008).

A number of empirical studies have examined certain aspects of the internal and external factors affecting competition in the computer industry (Akhter et al., 2014). Goolsbee (2001) provides an insight in terms of online versus retail competition in the competitive industry. Kumar et al. (2011) studied the influence of market orientation on performance. Their analysis suggests that market orientation has a positive impact on business performance both in the short and long term. Their study also suggests that the earlier firms adopt market orientation, the better they can exploit the market opportunities to fetch more sales, and consequently more profit. Firms that are late in understanding and adopting market orientation are very likely to stay behind, and may not be able to catch up their competitors ever on sales making and profit earning rate. Prahalad and Hamel (1990) suggest that a firm's growth depends on top executives' ability to identify, cultivate, and exploit the core competencies.

Zhou et al. (2005) study suggests that the market orientation of a firm helps in innovations that use advanced technology. This in turn offers greater benefits to mainstream customers (Ives & Learmonth, 1984). Firms in the computer industry must come up with innovations (Swanson & Ramiller, 2004) by taking market orientation into consideration. This should definitely be an essential practice in the highly competitive computer industry, because customers are continuously looking for more and more innovative and user friendly features in every newer generation and form of computers (Rahman, 2018). Heil and Walters (1993) present a conceptual model to analyze the strength of competitive reactions to new product introductions. This model could be used to generate insights before introducing computer products to the market. Life cycles of maximum products in the computer industry are very short, lasting three to five years at most. Hence, computer firms frequently introduce a new version of the product or create a completely new product to stay competitive. In this study we make an attempt to analyze the computer industry based on existing literature about firms' competitive strategies.

THE COMPUTER INDUSTRY IN THE EARLY 21ST CENTURY

The computer industry includes: designing computer components, devices, and peripherals; manufacturing computer components; and assembling personal computers (PCs), laptops, handheld computers and servers (IBIS World, 2011). The U.S. Census Bureau (2007) gives a comprehensive definition of computer industry:

Computer and Peripheral Equipment Manufacturing (CPEM) industry comprises establishments primarily engaged in manufacturing and/or assembling electronic computers, such as mainframes, personal computers, workstations, laptops, and computer servers; and computer peripheral equipment, such as storage devices, printers, monitors, input/output devices and terminals.

Emerging Technologies and Products in Computer Industry

In this section we provide an overview of emerging technologies and products in computer industry. We also discuss relative advantages of substitute products from competitive strategy perspective (Akhter et al., 2014).

A *Server* consists of a physical computer, which provides services to all terminals or computers connected to it, such as granting permissions or allocating resources. The advantages of computer servers include increased reliability and performance, scalability, security, reduced administration and lower total cost of ownership. Business and other organizations are buyers of computer servers. Dell, Lenovo, Apple, Asus, and HP supply top rated servers. Banerjee (2017) provides a list of best -selling computer servers and accessories as of 2017 which include 2017 Newest Dell PowerEdge, High-End Virtualization Server (by TechMikeNY), Microsoft Server 2016 Essentials, Enterprise Dell PowerEdge, POWEREDGE T30 (Dell), New Dell PowerEdge T30 Mini Tower Server, HP ProLiant DL360, and iStarUSA D-260HN Bay (by iStarUSA).

A *Desktop* Computer is a personal computer designed to be used at a desk. A desktop computer is relatively cheaper than a laptop computer of similar specifications. It is easy to upgrade; and defective accessories and components on a desktop are easy to replace. A desktop computing system has bigger monitor and more comfortable keyboard. However, consumers have a tendency to switch from desktop to laptops because of its portability. Is desktop a substitute for laptop? The main difference between a desktop and laptop is portability (Akhter et al., 2014).

Desk top is not portable but laptop is; hence, desktop cannot be a substitute of laptop. Domingo and Brant (2017) provide ten best desktop computers for 2018. Their assessment is based on power and flexibility, and stylish designs: Corsair One Pro, Dell Precision 5720 All-in-One, Origin Neuron, Apple

Figure 1. Computer industry products

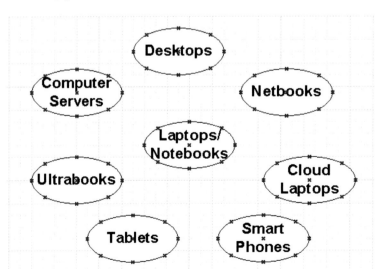

iMac 21.5-Inch With 4K Retina Display, Dell XPS Tower Special Edition (8930), Dell XPS 27 (Kaby Lake, 2017), HP Z2 Mini G3, Microsoft Surface Studio, Polywell B250G-i7, and Velocity Micro Raptor Z95 (2017). According to IDC, shipment of desktop PCs worldwide had gradually declined each year from 157 million in 2010 to 103 million in 2016.

A *Laptop* computer is a personal computer for mobile use. One great advantage of laptop is its portability. Dell Corporation takes pride in being the first company to introduce the notebook computer system (Akhter et al., 2014). Laptop computers are categorized according to size. Is a Laptop a substitute for a Desktop? Yes, from a user's point of view, it is. Laptop has all features and functionalities that a desktop might have. The additional benefit of the laptop is its portability. Manufacturers might be able to switch their production. A manufacturer needs all components and technologies to make both desktop and laptop. From manufacturer's point of view, switching its production requires huge financial involvement, technological undertaking, marketing strategy; and it is not that easy compared to switching by a user from desktop to laptop. Today, a laptop has similar functionalities and processing power to those of a desktop. New players have entered into computer market with laptop computer. Who are these new entrants? There are many. Table 1 shows the top ten computer brands world-wide. Samsung has entered the computer industry lately. In the future many more might come.

We also provide a list of computers which are ordered in terms of price (lowest to highest) ranging from $258 to $1450 as of February 2018. These laptops are selected by taking several factors into considerations: budget, productivity, gaming and many other factors.

A *Tablet* is relatively small in size and weight. It is sleeker, and does not have a keyboard (to save space) which is available on most notebooks. The main input device of tablets is the touch screen which differentiates it from desktops and laptops. Due to its uniqueness, user-friendliness and popularity, tablets cost more compared to notebooks. Is the Tablet a substitute for a Laptop/Notebook? No. A laptop has certain functionalities that a Tablet does not have. The Laptop is portable like a Tablet. It has a keyboard which makes it easier to type larger documents. Some consumers have a tendency to switch from Laptop to Netbook depending on the purpose of their computer use (Akhter et al., 2014).

The tablet market got momentum in 2010 and subsequent years. But lately the tablet market is on the decline. IDC (2017) reports that smartphone size increase is the reason for gradual decrease of tablet

Table 1. World's best computer brands

Rank	Brands	Country of Origin
1.	Dell	Texas, USA
2.	Apple Computer	California, USA
3.	Hewlett-Packard	Palo Alto, California, USA
4.	ASUS	Taipei, Taiwan
5.	Acer	New Taipei City, Taiwan
6.	Lenovo	Beijing, China
7.	Alienware	Subsidiary of Dell, USA
8.	Sony	Tokyo, Japan
9.	Toshiba	Tokyo, Japan
10.	Samsung	Seoul, South Korea

(TheTopTen, 2018)

Table 2. Top 10 Laptops, 2018; PC Magazine

Order by Price	Laptops
1.	Acer Swift 1
2.	Dell XPS 13 (9360)
3.	HP Spectre x360 13
4.	Lenovo ThinkPad T470
5.	Acer Aspire E 15 (E5-575-33BM)
6.	Alienware 17 R4
7.	Apple MacBook Pro 13-Inch
8.	Lenovo IdeaPad Miix 520
9.	Microsoft Surface Book 2
10.	Razer Blade Stealth (13.3" QHD+)

(Domingo, 2018).

market. Tablet market's overall growth declined 5.4% in Q3 2017 for the twelve quarters in a row (IDC, 2017). The top five tablet companies as of third quarter of 2017 include (in order of ranking) Apple (Apple-iPad), Samsung (Galaxy Tab A-7.0), Amazon (Fire HD 10), Huawei (Huawei MediaPad), and Lenovo (Tab 7 Essential) (IDC, 2017).

A *Netbook* is another variety of laptop computer system which falls into a super small notebook category. Netbooks are small, inexpensive, less powerful laptop computers. For example, netbook might use older processor versions such as Pentium processors and many users might find it okay given the tasks they want to do using Netbook. It is like a Dollar Tree commodity as opposed to a Shopping Mall commodity. Is a Netbook a substitute for a Laptop? Yes, Netbooks have all features that a Laptop might have. Some users might switch from Laptop to Netbook, but others might not, from a user's point of view. From a manufacturer's point of view it does not use powerful processors and latest or premium versions of PC components in a Netbook. A Netbook has all kinds of functionality that a desktop has but, not necessarily it needs to have the latest technology and latest processing powers. *Ultra-book* computers are a bit larger, thinner, much more expensive and more powerful than Netbooks. The Ultra Notebook is like a Shopping Mall commodity as opposed to Dollar Tree commodity. Is an Ultrabook a substitute for a Laptop/Notebook? Yes. An Ultrabook has most functionality that a Laptop/Notebook does not have. Ultrabooks use advanced technology, extended battery life and a new line of powerful processors. Some consumers, those who can afford, might want to switch from a Laptop to the Ultrabook laptop (Akhter et al., 2014).

As of 2017 top ten best netbooks include: 1. Lenovo 110s Premium Built High Performance Netbook, 2. HP Stream Laptop PC 11-y010nr, 3. ASUS E200HA Portable Lightweight Netbook, 4. Dell i3168-0027, 5. HP Pavilion x2 Detachable Premium 2-in-1 Laptop Tablet, 6. HP X360 11-AB011DX, 7. Acer AO1-132-C129 N306, 8. Lenovo ThinkPad Yoga 11E, 9. ASUS Transformer Mini T102HA-D4-GR, 10. Dell Inspiron i3000-101SLV.

The Google *Chromebook* is a light, simple laptop which comes along with Google products such as Search, Gmail and YouTube, etc. It relies on cloud computing, so it is only useful if one is online. Google's Chromebook is entirely dedicated to cloud computing. Top five Chromebooks as of February

2018 include Chromebook 14 (Acer), Chromebook 14 Intel Celeron (HP), 14" IdeaPad Chromebook (Lenovo), Chromebook Pro (Samsung), and Chromebook C202 (ASUS).

A *Smartphone* is a mobile phone that contains certain advanced features which are not available on a standard cell phone. Smartphones are based on an operating system just like any personal computer. Apple iOS and Android OS are the two fast developing mobile operating systems which share similarities and differences on the basis of their hardware and software. These operating systems are devised for smart phones. Apple iOS is restricted and kind of proprietary. On the other hand Google's Android is open source. Any phone manufacture can use it at no charge and they can customize the OS as needed. The latest models of smartphones are Apple's iPhone 8 and 8 Plus and Samsung's Galaxy S9. Mobile phone ownership has increased significantly since 2000. Ninety five percent of Americans own cellphone. The share of smartphones ownership has increased from about 35% in 2011 to 77% in 2018 (Pew Research Center, 2018). Gartner (2018) predicts that in 2018, smartphone sales will grow by 6.2 percent, to represent 87 percent of mobile phone sales.

In this chapter, we focus our analysis on the main devices such as personal computer (PC) that includes Laptop computers/ Notebooks. There is a handful of vendors/ manufacturers of laptops. This market is very competitive. The laptops have a large number and a wide variety of customers. Gradually, more and more users are switching to Laptops for many purposes and from Laptops to smartphone for many reasons as well.

Computer Products Market Segments

Pervasive use of computers may entice computer manufacturing firms to focus on all segments of the market to increase market share. The U.S. computer manufacturers' major buyers include consumers, small and medium businesses, large enterprises, export and government agencies. The buyers like to buy from the manufactures that have good reputation of being quality producers. They prefer reliable, technically sound, and latest technology based computer products. They expect prompt post-purchase services such as warranty, return policy, etc. Computer manufacturers, who emphasize the inclusion of maximum features and functionalities in a computer system to serve numerous purposes of different kinds of users spreading over different market segments, may expect to gain wider market share (Akhter et al., 2014).

Laptop Industry Supply Chain

Laptop companies get their laptops built by contract manufacturers (CM), original design manufactures (ODM), or Electronic manufacturing services (EMS). The top six ODM companies include Compal, Quanta, Wistron, Inventec, Pegatron, Asus, and Foxconn. 2017 list of the Manufacturing Market Insider (MMI) Top 10 EMS providers includes 1. Hon Hai Precision Industry (Foxconn), New Taipei, Taiwan. 2. Pegatron, Taipei, Taiwan. 3. Flex, Singapore. 4. Jabil, St. Petersburg, FL. 5. Sanmina, San Jose, CA. 6. Celestica, Toronto, Canada. 7. Wistron, Taoyuan, Taiwan. 8. New Kinpo Group, New Taipei, Taiwan. 9. Plexus, Neenah, WI. 10. Benchmark Electronics, Angleton, TX. (Evertiq, 2017). All these ODM and EMS companies are located mostly in china, the rest in other Asian countries including Taiwan. They take contract orders from Laptop vendors and/or Assemblers from all over the world including the U.S. Figure 2 provides typical laptop industry supply chain.

World's leading laptop vendors include HP, Lenovo, Dell, Acer Group, ASUS, and Toshiba. The ODM and EMS companies collect all kinds of computer components, design and manufacture laptops as per

Figure 2. Laptop industry supply chain (manufactures to consumers)

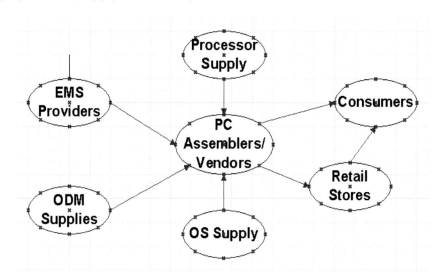

specifications form the laptop vendors. Top ODM company Quanta, ships 98% of its orders within two days (Dean & Tam, 2005; Akhter et al., 2014) after taking orders. The shipments to the US vendors are made via global logistics companies such as FedEx, UPS, etc. The laptop companies (HP, Dell, Toshiba, and Apple) then send the laptops to consumers directly or via distribution channels and retailers. Laptop companies distribute through various channels (Akhter et al., 2014; Dedrick & Kraemer, 2002) including wholesalers (Ingram Micro, Tech Data), corporate resellers, department stores, electronics super-stores (Best Buy, Target, Fry's, CostCo, CompUSA), and specialty retailers. Besides selling laptops via wholesalers and retailers, Dell and Gateway sell their products directly to consumers (Magretta, 1998).

COMPUTER INDUSTRY AND PORTER'S FIVE COMPETITIVCE STRATEGIES

The five competitive forces model is a framework for understanding the structure of an industry developed by Michael Porter (2009). The framework consists of the forces that determine industry profitability. Well-managed companies try to avoid or diminish these forces in an attempt to beat the average rate of return for the industry (Kaiser, 2009). We will evaluate competitive forces in laptop industry in terms of Porter's five strategic market forces. Figure 3 provides an overview of competitive forces in terms of threat of new entrants, bargaining power of suppliers, bargaining power of buyers, rivalry among competitors, and threat of substitute products or services in computer industry.

Threat of New Entrants Into the Industry Segment

"New entrants to an industry put pressure on prices, costs, and the rate of investment necessary to compete" (Porter, 2008). The incumbents try their best to prevent new entrants from joining the industry. Usually, economies of scale, product differentiation and capital requirements, cost advantages, access to distribution channels are the barriers to entry in an industry (Kaiser, 2009).

Figure 3. Five forces in computer industry

	THREAT OF NEW ENTRANTS: Economies of scale - no barrier to entry; no high requirements on technologies - no technological barrier; from supply side no existing manufacturer has adavntage over other - no cost disadvantage for new entrant; new entrant can enter with breakthrough technology - no barrier to entry from demand side benefits of scale; no cost of switching from one computer brand to another - no barrier to entry.	
BARGAINING POWER OF SUPPLIERS: OS provider Microsoft has bargaining power; Microprocessor provider Intel has bargaining power; No visible threat of forward integration.	RIVALRY AMONG COMPETITORS: PC industry is highly concentrated; Only four largest companies control 80% of industry revenue; High rivalry exist among PC vendors; Price competition is intense in the industry; Severe competition has caused declining profit margin.	BARGAINING POWER OF BUYERS: PC products are standardized (OS, processor, etc) - buyers can switch to another brand; Zero switching cost in changing vendors; Competion is fierce - buyers have power to ask for better price, reliability, quality, and warranty; no threat of backward integration.
	THREAT OF SUBSTITUTE PRODUCTS OR SERVICES: PC products' function or capability almost similar - threat of substitute is high; Switching from laptop to tablet involves no switching cost; availability of substitutes makes PC industry competitive; and decreases profitability of the firms.	

Manufacturing or producing up to the optimum level by utilizing the optimum capacity of a production or manufacturing concern brings the unit cost of production to the lowest, as the fixed cost is shared over maximum possible units. This continuity in cost reduction with the increase in each unit of production / manufacturing up to a certain level, leads to economies of scale that may be used to reduce the per unit production or manufacturing cost to the minimum. This phenomenon leads to the idea of economies of scale, which can be considered from both internal and external point of view (Akhter et al., 2014).

In the laptop industry, leading laptop makers (Brand owners, such as HP, Dell) make laptops through contract manufacturers (Dean & Tam, 2005) such as ODM (Original Design Manufacturers) companies. These laptop makers do not need to make huge investment in capital machinery, technological innovation, etc. So, no lowering of per unit cost is involved as such, and hence no internal economies of scale exist. This indicates that, new entrants do not face much of a barrier to enter into laptop industry. As a side note, an incumbent might have a strong distribution channel or might allocate huge advertising budget or might have brand recognition (Prahalad & Hamel, 2012). Here, we assume that a new entrant can do the same too. Thore (1996) asserts that large established companies fall behind in the technology race while startups grow rapidly by possessing emergent new technology (Kohli et al., 2012), leadership (Beyer & Browning, 1999), and management. "A new kind of innovator can wipe out incumbents in a flash" (Downes & Nunes, 2013).

Now, let us shift our focus to external economies of scale. Overall, in the laptop industry, there is a lot of standardization happening over the years as the laptop industry is maturing (Biddle et al., 2010). Some major reasons like expanded laptop user base, standardization of various components of laptops and other related technologies etc. make external economies of scale happen in this industry. The main components of a laptop, including motherboards, HDD, chipsets, OS, and LCD, are manufactured by a handful of suppliers. According to Moore's Law (Schaller, 1997) chip density doubles every 18 months, higher chip densities and smaller components result in less raw material, and increase in computer speed and memory (Venkataraman & Haftka, 2004). Combined with the maturing and standardizing of laptop components result in much lower unit prices. So, from external economies of scale standpoint also, there is no barrier to entry to the laptop industry by a new entrant. Both incumbents and new entrants are supposed to use the same standardized components of laptops and most likely will use the same OMD companies as contract manufacturer (leading manufacture, Quanta Computer Inc.).

Due to external economies of scale and tremendous growth of laptop market, new companies emerge in the laptop industry with innovative ideas (Zhou et al., 2005) and new business strategies (Bush, 2012) that eventually bring computer prices down, increase sales volume and thereby allows for greater profits. Example, Samsung is historically a TV manufacturer but, recently it joined the computer industry. On the other hand, Taiwanese company, Asustek, in 2007 introduced the first netbook identifying consumer demand that was not recognized by any of the top industry players (Shah & Dalal, 2009).

Although there is not much, still any sort of entry barriers into the industry may work as advantages for the incumbents compared to the new entrants. Sometimes the supply-side of economies of scale cause entry barrier. These economies arise when firms that produce at larger volumes enjoy lower costs per unit, employ more efficient technology (Ernst, 2000), or command better terms from suppliers (Porter, 2008). Laptop production technology is easy to learn for the new entrants. The start-up cost of laptop production is not very high (Cui, 2009). Most of the components such as chips, OS, graphics cards, HDD come from specialized companies. Laptop makers get the laptops manufacturers by ODM companies. Laptop makers' main tasks involve assembling (some cases) and marketing. Technological requirements are not too high to manufacture a laptop. Hence, there are no technological barriers either for new entrants of laptop industry (Akhter et al., 2014).

Mostly ODM and OEM companies assemble or build laptops for all the vendors in the laptop market. Two other major players in the laptop industry supply chain are Intel (supplies processors) and Microsoft (supplies OS and application software). Both of these global suppliers of laptop components have standardized products which they offer the same way to any laptop manufacturer. Laptop manufacturers build their products according to a set industry standards which allows a wide degree of compatibility (IBIS World, 2011; Akhter et al., 2014). So, supply side does not allow any manufacture to have an extra advantage over other manufacture. This uniformity in supply of the required components sets uniform price as well which help the new entrants get protected from manufacturing cost disadvantage against the incumbents. Consequently, the new entrants do not have to go for a large scale operations to compete with existing big fishes in the industry.

However, sometimes the demand side may impose some entry barriers to the new entrants. This is because buyers have a tendency to trust larger companies more due to their established brand image. Buyers probably feel more comfortable to be assured of product reliability, quality, and warranty, which matter to them most, if they buy their laptops from the larger companies. "Demand side benefits of scale discourage entry by limiting the willingness of customers to buy from a newcomer and by reducing the price the newcomer can command until it builds up a large base of customers" (Porter, 2008). In the tablet market, Apple's iPad is extremely popular and it adopts a product differentiation strategy. In this case, a new entrant will find it very difficult to compete (Heil & Walters, 1993). In the laptop industry, a new entrant can balance the demand side benefits of scale of the incumbent by virtue of innovation (Mathews, 2002). A new entrant is able to secure advantages by entering the industry utilizing the most advanced technologies (Gatignon & Robertson, 1989). Entering the laptop industry with a breakthrough technology and production differentiation (an example could be Apple's iPad) should be the two key factors a new entrant can use to be able to overcome the demand side benefits of scale of the incumbents (Akhter et al., 2014).

Buyers may have to incur switching cost when they choose to buy a new brand than the one they have or had been using. This is a disadvantage to the new entrants, as they find it hard to get the customers switch to their brands departing from the ones they i.e. the customers have or had already been loyal to. "The larger the switching costs, the harder it will be for an entrant to gain customers" (Porter, 2008). It does not matter much for the household users switching from one laptop brand to another. Because, the basic technology of different brands of laptops are pretty much the same, and the extent and level of household use need not a big difference either. Two main components, microprocessor (Intel) and operating systems (MS) are from the same companies in any laptop (except Apple). So, not much switching cost is involved as no additional training is required to use a new brand leaving the existing one. Switching cost might incur when an individual or a large enterprise wants to switch from Windows-based laptop to Apple OS-based laptop. Most of the application software used in Windows laptop could no longer be compatible with Mac Laptop. The laptop user will need to purchase applications software compatible with Apple MacBook.

The new entrants might suffer from the cost or quality advantage that incumbents might enjoy. "These advantages can stem from such sources as proprietary technology, established brand identities, or cumulative experience that has allowed incumbents to learn how to produce more efficiently" (Porter, 2008). For incumbent, Lawless and fisher (1990) propose a framework consisting of several components affecting strategic non-imitability. These include product form, product function, product tangibles, pricing, promotion, distribution, and firm characteristics. In laptop industry, there are several top rated brands including HP, Dell, Lenovo, ASUS, and Acer. They have an established distribution channel as well. These reputed brands will have incumbency advantage over new entrants. Technological innovation by laptop makers is minimal (IBIS World, 2011) as all components are manufactured by different manufacturers. So there is no proprietary technology advantage for laptop makers, at least, for Windows-based laptop makers. Samsung is a new entrant in laptop industry. Although Samsung has reputation of being good TV maker, still it is yet to see how they do with laptop. A new entrant is supposed to do well as long as it has an innovative organization and strong leadership (Hagel & Brown, 2017). Apple laptops consist of proprietary technology and Apple certainly has incumbency advantage in terms of proprietary technology and product differentiation over new entrants.

A new entrant must have great plan for smooth distribution of its products and services. "Sometimes access to distribution is so high a barrier that new entrants must bypass distribution channels altogether or create their own" (Porter, 2008). In laptop industry, an incumbent might already have established distribution channel. A new entrant might find it difficult to manage space to place its laptop brands in retail stores. However, if the new entrant is a reputed company for other related products, it might not find it difficult to manage distribution channels. Samsung being a reputed TV maker, or Intel as top chip maker, may not find it difficult to manage distribution channel or manage space in retail stores as a new entrant in laptop industry. In the age of Internet, a new entrant may find it easy to sell laptops through a unique distribution strategy namely the Internet and UPS and FedEx services. For individual consumers, online purchases might be preferable if discounts are offered. Given a consumer's intent of buying a computer, the elasticity of buying remotely with respect to retail store prices is about 1.5 (Goolsbee, 2001).

Bargaining Power of Suppliers

Suppliers can charge higher prices if they have higher bargaining power. "Powerful suppliers gain more of the value for themselves by charging higher prices, limiting quality or services, or shifting costs to industry participants" (Porter, 2008). In the laptop industry, suppliers are quite limited in terms of bargaining power by virtue of increased commoditization of hardware components (Shah & Dalal, 2009). Intel and AMD, the two major microprocessor suppliers, compete for increased market share. Intel competes to retain its market share. On the other hand AMD competes with Intel to take market share from Intel. The ODM companies compete with one another fiercely. In order to control the ODMs, laptop makers such as HP, Dell do periodic negotiations and have contracts with half a dozen ODMs (Dean & Tam, 2005) at any point in time. For hardware such as external hard drives suppliers' bargaining powers are gradually declining as there are several brands on the market (Top brands: LaCie, Lenovo, Samsung, Western Digital, Seagate). In case of motherboards, many a brands are available on the market (Top brands: Intel, MSI, Gigabyte, ASUS, ASRock) even though Intel has advantage because of its reputation as the world's top semiconductor company.

Unlike the microcomputer industry, the microprocessor industry consists of two prominent companies: Intel and AMD. The PC makers (buyers) had little bargaining power over the microprocessor industry, which consisted of Intel with significantly large market share (Dolkart & Pronina, 2007). "Entrance into the industry was difficult because of the patents and the amount of R&D and capital investment that was necessary to produce a chip. The operating system industry, which Microsoft controlled, had similar favorable fundamentals" (Moy & Terregrossa, 2009).

Is the supplier industry more concentrated than the industry it sells to? Are there a few substitutes for suppliers' input? In laptop manufacturing there is a high concentration of ODMs. The top five ODMs are Quanta Computer Inc., Compal Electronics Inc., Wistron Corp., Inventec Corp. and Pegatron Corp. In laptop making, one of the main suppliers is Microsoft (for OS). And for processors the suppliers are Intel and AMD. Do the suppliers pose credible threat of forward integration into the product market? Suppliers' evaluation of their profitability in their current lines of business, and their capability to invest in different lines will determine this forward integration. If they assume low profitability in their existing business, the suppliers might enter into new business to improve their profits. Intel might pose a threat to manufacture laptops itself. But, this might be a departure from Intel's core business. By concentrating on non-core business Intel might distract itself from its core business. However, (hypothetically) if Intel finds that its processor business is declining, it might actively consider another line of business such as Laptop or Smartphone business. So, Intel might pose a threat to laptop makers, but the laptop industry would definitely want to evaluate the seriousness of such threats. However, there is no visible forward integration threat at this point of time.

Bargaining Power of Buyers

"Powerful customers - the flip side of powerful suppliers - can capture more value by forcing down prices, demanding better quality or more service (thereby driving up costs), and generally playing industry participants off against one another, all at the expense of industry profitability" (Porter, 2008). The Laptop industry's products are standardized or undifferentiated. If buyers believe they can always find an equivalent product, they tend to play one vendor against another. For Windows laptops buyers (consumers) there should be zero switching costs in changing vendors. In the laptop industry, users/

consumers have such advantage over laptop makers. All laptops have processors from Intel or AMD and OS from MS. Nevertheless, buyers may switch from brands to brands incurring some switching cost. Because, besides processor and OS, laptop buyers look for better price (George & Venkatesan, 2012), guarantee of reliability and quality (Garvin, 1987; Xiaolam & Jun, 2010) of the laptop, latest features, warranty, better post-purchase services (Nasir et al., 2006), and user-friendliness and ergonomically correct devices (Suomalainen et al., 2010). However, as already mentioned before, if an individual consumer or large enterprise wants to switch from Windows-based laptop maker to Apple OS-based laptops and vice versa, there might be higher switching cost, as application software used in these two OS based laptops might not be compatible.

Threat of Substitute Products or Services

A substitute product is something which can provide the same or similar functions, values, and utilities as the other products in the industry. "When the threat of substitutes is high, industry profitability suffers. Substitute products or services limit an industry's profit potential by placing a ceiling on prices" (Porter, 2008). The laptop industry faces a significant threat. Advances in computing power and communication technologies such as 5G mobile networks and WiFi technology (to exchange data or to connect to the Internet wirelessly) have enabled devices such as smart-phones (iPhone, iPad, etc.) to compete with laptops by providing similar capabilities and more user-friendliness (Shah & Dalal, 2009). So with the development of the technologies, many other products begin to have the functions of laptops and become the potential substitutes for laptop. Availability of substitutes makes an industry competitive and decreases the profitability of firms in the industry. On the other hand, lack of close substitutes makes an industry less competitive and increases the profit potentials for firms in the industry. The buyer's cost of switching to the substitute is low (Porter, 2008). Switching from a laptop to tablet involves no switching costs.

Given that there is a fierce competition among the top five laptop makers, there are constant threats of close substitutes from other computer products. Nevertheless an existing competitor or a new entrant may survive through unique business strategies (DuBois et al., 1993) such as, direct service, customer service, advanced technology, and improved usability (Ozok et al., 2008). There is an availability of substitutes from outside industry as well. Is a Tablet/iPad a close substitute for laptop? The answer is yes. Both laptop and tablet are portable. Using tablet, a user can perform most tasks a laptop can do. Recent industry data shows that laptop industry is facing annual decline of laptop shipment due to tablet and smartphone products. However, individual consumers use laptop or tablet based on the purposes of their use. Some consumers might find a Tablet/iPad a close substitute for a laptop, but some others might not. For heavy typing, Tablet might not be a close substitute.

Rivalry Among Existing Competitors

The laptop industry is highly concentrated. Only four largest companies control about 80% of computer industry revenue. "Rivalry among existing competitors takes many familiar forms, including price discounting, new product introductions, advertising campaigns, and service improvements. High rivalry limits the profitability of an industry" (Porter, 2008). Severe competition among competitors and competition from abroad has tightened the profit margins and laptop prices have reduced significantly over the last decade. Manufactures have been making only 1.0% profit for consumer-oriented computers (IBIS World, 2011) and currently (2018) there is no possibility of profit margin increase as users are switching to smartphones. Because of gradual standardization of laptop components among Windows laptops, switching costs are low and therefore competition is driven by pricing instead of product differentiation. On the other hand, Apple products are proprietary. Apple competes on product differentiation by promoting premium products instead of low prices (Shah & Dalal, 2009).

What is the degree of seller concentration in laptop industry? Laptop seller concentration is limited within a few manufacturers/sellers. A few sellers are dominating the market – Lenovo, Dell, Asus, HP, and Apple. So, there is high rivalry among these sellers. Price competition is intense in the industry now. This has led to declining computer prices during the last decade. What is the rate of laptop industry growth? According to IBIS World (2011), laptop manufacturing industry has gradually been experiencing declining revenue. Rivalry has brought laptop price down significantly. In 90's laptop price was more than 2K and now it is below 1K.

CONCLUSION

In order to gain a competitive advantage (Kumar et al., 2011; Brentani & Droge, 1988), laptop companies must keep up with the rapid technological change (Rahman et al., 2013) occurring in this field and take strategic business decisions accordingly. Laptop manufacturing companies need to capitalize on the market by focusing on the development of new products that are offered and sold to the consumer. Laptop companies need to fully analyze the threats, opportunities, and profitability of the industry.

In this study we examined the laptop industry with Michael Porter's competitive forces. In our analysis we have shown that barriers to entry into the laptop industry are low and steady. This poses a high threat to the incumbents. The Laptop industry is facing a threat of substitutes as well. Recently introduced tablets in the market have gained significant attention. Apple introduced iPad in 2010. Competing tablet manufactures (Samsung) started lunching tablets on Windows and Android operating systems. Laptop industry has started facing annual decline in revenue due to tablet and smartphone products. This means that profitability in laptop industry will be razor-thin.

Does the laptop industry face threat from suppliers? Laptop manufacturers get their laptops built by ODM companies. In order to control the ODM companies and decrease their supplying power, laptop manufacturers work with multiple ODMs to retain their bargaining power. So, from a supplier point of view, the laptop industry faces a weak threat. Profitability is also not impacted from this point of view. However due to increased standardization of laptop components and advances in semiconductor industry, product cost is decreasing. This impacts profitability in the industry.

Given that computer components of laptops are rapidly getting standardized, all Windows laptop makers use the same components to build laptops resulting virtually into no product differentiation. So, individual consumers might switch from one brand to the other quite easily and without any switching costs. Hence, individual companies might face threats from buyers' point of view. This could be a low threat given a laptop manufacturer can resort to innovative business strategies to increase customer loyalty.

Laptop seller concentration is limited within a few manufacturers/sellers. A few sellers are dominating the market – Lenovo, Dell, Asus, HP, and Apple. So, there is high rivalry among these sellers. A high threat exists due to rivalry among the competitors. Price competition is intense in the industry now. This impacts profitability of the industry.

Finally, should one enter laptop industry as a new entrant? Despite the increased consumer base of laptop products, profit margins on laptop industry remain at or below 1% (Akhter et al., 2014; IBIS

World, 2011). This is happening due to several factors including low barriers to entry, standardized computer components, and price competition. Laptop industry is highly concentrated. Four top laptop companies hold about 80% of the revenue in the US. So, one might not want to enter this industry as a new entrant. One might venture to enter tablet products market which is gaining consumer interest. For incumbents, they might want to develop a sustainability metrics (Rahman & Akhter, 2010) to monitor individual firm's performance. They also might want to measure the performance periodically using a balanced scorecard (BSC) approach (Rahman, 2013).

REVIEW QUESTIONS

1. Is tablet a substitute for a laptop/notebook?
2. Is laptop a substitute for a desktop computer?
3. Is smartphone a substitute for a tablet?
4. Briefly describe ODM and EMS companies.
5. Describe supply chain of smartphone industry.
6. Describe Porter's five competitive forces model.
7. What are the challenges for a new entrant to enter a mature market with strong competition in it? How do you overcome the challenges?
8. In smartphone industry what are the possible threats of substitute products or services?
9. Explain the rivalry among laptop companies.
10. What kind of rivalry exists between Apple and Samsung in smartphone market?

ACKNOWLEDGMENT

An earlier version of this book chapter entitled, Competitive Strategies in the Computer Industry appeared in the International Journal of Technology Diffusion (Akther et al., 2014). This chapter has been revised and enhanced, based on book chapter publishing guidelines from IGI Global. They include change of title of the original article, modifications of the abstract to reflect the enhanced content, changes in references and literature review sections to incorporate the most current research findings, and adding and changing of graphs and tables to ensure that they are up-to-date. The authors would like to thank the anonymous reviewers and editor of this book for their constructive comments provided on earlier version of this book chapter.

REFERENCES

Akhter, S., Rahman, N., & Rahman, M. N. (2014). Competitive strategies in the computer industry. *International Journal of Technology Diffusion*, 5(1), 73–88. doi:10.4018/ijtd.2014010106

Banerjee, S. (2017). *Top 10 Best Selling Computer Servers & Accessories. RS-WebSols.* Retrieved on 2/19/2018 from: https://www.rswebsols.com/reviews/product-reviews/top-10-best-selling-computer-servers-accessories

Best Reviews. (2018). Best Chromebooks - Updated February 2018. *Best Reviews*. Retrieved on 2/19/2018 from: http://bestreviews.com/best-chromebooks

Beyer, L. M., & Browning, L. D. (1999). Transforming an industry in crisis: Charisma, routinization, and supportive cultural leadership. *The Leadership Quarterly*, *10*(3), 483–520. doi:10.1016/S1048-9843(99)00026-0

Biddle, B., White, A., & Woods, S. (2010). How many standards in a laptop? (And other empirical questions). *Proceedings of the ITU-T, Beyond the Internet? – Innovations for Future Networks and Services, Kaleidoscope Conference*. Available at SSRN: http://ssrn.com/abstract=1619440

Brentani, U. D., & Droge, C. (1988). Determinants of the new product screening decision: A structural model analysis. *International Journal of Research in Marketing*, *5*(2), 91–106. doi:10.1016/0167-8116(88)90062-6

Bush, T. (2012). Developing an organization's competitive strategies: Staying ahead of the competition. In *Proceedings of the 2nd International Conference on Management and Artificial Intelligence (IPEDR)* (*Vol. 35*, pp. 88-92). Academic Press.

Cui, X. (2009). In-depth analysis of PC industry in China. *International Journal of Business and Management*, *4*(11), 150–157. doi:10.5539/ijbm.v4n11p150

Dean, J., & Tam, P. (2005, June 9). The laptop trail - The modern PC is a model of hyper-efficient production and geopolitical sensitivities. *The Wall Street Journal*.

Dedrick, J., & Kraemer, K. L. (2002). *Globalization of the personal computer industry: Trends and implications. Globalization of I.T. CA*. Center for Research on Information Technology and Organizations, UC Irvine.

Dolkart, V. M., & Pronina, L. V. (2007). Change in computer hardware and software paradigms. *Russian Electrical Engineering*, *78*(10), 548–553. doi:10.3103/S1068371207100082

Domingo, J. S. (2018). The Best Laptops of 2018. *PC Magazine*. Retrieved on 2/18/2018 from: https://www.pcmag.com/article2/0,2817,2369981,00.asp

Domingo, J. S., & Brant, T. (2017). The Best Desktop Computers of 2018. *PC Magazine*. Retrieved on 2/19/2018 from: https://www.pcmag.com/article2/0,2817,2372609,00.asp

Downes, L., & Nunes, P. F. (2013). The big idea: Big-bang disruption. *Harvard Business Review*, 1–12.

DuBois, F. L., Toyne, B., & Oliff, M. D. (1993). International manufacturing strategies of U.S. multinationals: A conceptual framework based on a four-industry study. *Journal of International Business Studies*, *24*(2), 307–333. doi:10.1057/palgrave.jibs.8490234

Ernst, D. (2000). Inter-organizational knowledge outsourcing: What permits small Taiwanese firms to compete in the computer industry? *Asia Pacific Journal of Management*, *17*(2), 223–255. doi:10.1023/A:1015809609118

Evertiq. (2017). *List: Top10 EMS-providers of 2016*. Manufacturing Market Insider (MMI). Retrieved on 2/19/2018 from: http://evertiq.com/news/41361

Fildes, N. (2017). PC market set to return to growth in 2018. *Financial Times*. Retrieved on February 19, 2018, from https://www.ft.com/content/1d525464-b282-11e7-aa26-bb002965bce8

Gartner, Inc. (2018). *Gartner Says Worldwide Device Shipments Will Increase 2.1 Percent in 2018*. Gartner, Inc. Retrieved on February 19, 2018 from https://www.gartner.com/newsroom/id/3849063

Garvin, D. A. (1987). Competing on the eight dimensions of quality. *Harvard Business Review*, 100–109.

Gatignon, H., & Robertson, T. S. (1989). Technology diffusion: An empirical test of competitive effects. *Journal of Marketing*, *53*(1), 35–49. doi:10.2307/1251523

George, S., & Venkatesan, N. (2012). Marketing strategies for laptop using conjoint analysis. *International Academic Research Journal of Business and Management*, *1*(1), 39–48.

Goolsbee, A. (2001). Competition in the computer industry: Online versus retail. *The Journal of Industrial Economics*, *XLIX*(4).

Hagel, J., & Brown, J. S. (2017). Shaping Strategies for the IoT. *Computer*, *50*(8), 64–68. doi:10.1109/MC.2017.3001254

Heil, O. P., & Walters, R. G. (1993). Explaining competitive reactions to new products: An empirical signaling study. *Journal of Product Innovation Management*, *10*(1), 53–65. doi:10.1016/0737-6782(93)90053-S

IBIS World. (2011). *IBIS world industry report 33411a: Computer manufacturing in the US*. Retrieved October 1, 2013 from www.ibisworld.com

IDC. (2017). *IDC: Worldwide Tablet Market Declines 5.4% in Q3 2017*. XDA Developers. Retrieved on 2/19/2018 from: https://www.xda-developers.com/idc-q3-2017-tablet-market-decline/

Ives, B., & Learmonth, G. P. (1984). The information system as a competitive weapon. *Communications of the ACM*, *27*(12), 1193–1201. doi:10.1145/2135.2137

Kaiser, U. (2009). *A primer in entrepreneurship*. Retrieved February 19, 2018, from http://www.business.uzh.ch/professorships/entrepreneurship/teaching/past/hs08/primer/Kap1primerentrepreneuruka.pdf

Kohli, R., Devaraj, S., & Ow, T. T. (2012). Does information technology investment influence a firm's market value? A case of non-publicly traded healthcare firms. *Management Information Systems Quarterly*, *36*(4), 1145–1163.

Kraemer, K. L., & Dedrick, J. (2002). Enter the dragon: China's computer industry. *Computer*, *35*(2), 28–36. doi:10.1109/2.982913

Kumar, V., Jones, E., Venkatesan, R., & Leone, R. P. (2011). Is market orientation a source of sustainable competitive advantage or simply the cost of competing? *Journal of Marketing*, *75*, 1–31. doi:10.1509/jmkg.75.2.1

Lawless, M. W., & Fisher, R. J. (1990). Sources of durable competitive advantage in new products. *Journal of Product Innovation Management*, *7*(1), 35–44. doi:10.1016/0737-6782(90)90030-I

Magretta, J. (1998). The power of virtual integration: An interview with Dell computer's Michael Dell. *Harvard Business Review*, 73–84. PMID:10177868

Mathews, J. A. (2002). Competitive advantages of the latecomer firm: A resource-based account of industrial catch-up strategies. *Asia Pacific Journal of Management, 19*(4), 467–488. doi:10.1023/A:1020586223665

Moy, R. L., & Terregrossa, R. (2009). Nerds: A case study of the PC industry. *Journal of Business Case Studies, 5*(6), 23–34. doi:10.19030/jbcs.v5i6.4729

Nasir, V. A., Yoruker, S., Gunes, F., & Ozdemir, Y. (2006). Factor influencing consumers' laptop purchases. *Proceedings of the 6th Global Conference on Business & Economics*, 1-9.

Ozok, A. A., Benson, D., Chakraborty, J., & Norcio, A. F. (2008). A comparative study between tablet and laptop PCs: User satisfaction and preferences. *International Journal of Human-Computer Interaction, 24*(3), 329–352. doi:10.1080/10447310801920524

Pew Research Center. (2018). *Mobile Fact Sheet*. Retrieved on February 19, 2018 from: http://www.pewinternet.org/fact-sheet/mobile/

Porter, M. E. (2008). The five competitive forces that shape strategy. *Harvard Business Review*, 1–18. PMID:18271320

Prahalad, C. K., & Hamel, G. (1990). The core competence of the corporation. *Harvard Business Review*, 1–15.

Preetam. (2017). 10 Best Netbooks – 2017. *Best World*. Retrieved on 2/19/2018 from: http://bestlaptopsworld.com/best-netbooks/

Rahman, N. (2013). Measuring performance for data warehouses - A balanced scorecard approach. *International Journal of Computer and Information Technology, 4*(1), 1–7.

Rahman, N. (2018). Environmental Sustainability in the Computer Industry for Competitive Advantage. In Green Computing Strategies for Competitive Advantage and Business Sustainability (pp. 110-130). IGI Global. doi:10.4018/978-1-5225-5017-4.ch006

Rahman, N., & Akhter, S. (2010). Incorporating sustainability into information technology management. *International Journal of Technology Management & Sustainable Development, 9*(2), 95–111. doi:10.1386/tmsd.9.2.95_1

Rahman, N., Aldhaban, F., & Akhter, S. (2013). Emerging technologies in business intelligence. In *Proceedings of the IEEE Portland International Center for Management of Engineering and Technology (PICMET 2013) Conference*. San Jose, CA: IEEE.

Schaller, R. J. (1997). Moore's Law: Past, present and future. *IEEE Spectrum*, 53–59.

Shah, A., & Dalal, A. (2009). *The global laptop industry*. Retrieved October 1, 2013, from http://srl.gatech.edu/Members/ashah/laptop_industry_analysis_aditya_abhinav.pdf

Suomalainen, P. (2010). A comparison of the usability of a laptop, communicator, and handheld computer. *Journal of Usability Studies, 5*(3), 111–123.

Swanson, E., & Ramiller, N. C. (2004). Innovating mindfully with information technology. *Management Information Systems Quarterly, 28*(4), 553–583. doi:10.2307/25148655

Tambe, P., & Hitt, L. M. (2012). The productivity of information technology investments: New evidence from IT labor data. *Information Systems Research, 23*(3), 599–617. doi:10.1287/isre.1110.0398

TheTopTen. (2018). Best Computer Brands. *The Top Ten.* Retrieved on 2/18/2018 from: https://www.thetoptens.com/best-computer-brands/

Thore, S. (1996). Economies of scale in the US computer industry: An empirical investigation using data envelopment analysis. *Journal of Evolutionary Economics, 6*(2), 199–216. doi:10.1007/BF01202594

U.S. Census Bureau. (2007). *NAICS 334: Computer and electronic product manufacturing.* Retrieved from http://www.census.gov/econ/industry/def/d334.htm

Venkataraman, S., & Haftka, R. T. (2004). Structural optimization complexity: What has Moore's law done for us? *Structural and Multidisciplinary Optimization, 28*(6), 375–387. doi:10.100700158-004-0415-y

Xiaolan, Z., & Jun, J. (2010). A research on the selection and evaluation of supplier for laptop. *IEEE Xplore*, 674-676.

Zhou, K. Z., Yim, C. K., & Tse, D. K. (2005). The effects of strategic orientations on technology- and market-based breakthrough innovations. *Journal of Marketing, 69*(2), 42–60. doi:10.1509/jmkg.69.2.42.60756

Chapter 11
Flexible Orchestration of Tools in E-Collaboration:
Case Studies Analyzing the Developer, the Teacher, and the Student Perspectives

Ioannis Magnisalis
Aristotle University of Thessaloniki, Greece

Stavros Demetriadis
Aristotle University of Thessaloniki, Greece

ABSTRACT

Relevant literature has emphasized the lack of a "tool orchestration" framework in e-collaboration environments (either for work or learning purposes). In this chapter, the MAPIS3 software architecture is suggested as a flexible solution to manage the key problem in tool orchestration, which is the efficient data transfer among various tools used in e-collaboration activities. The proposal is assessed by two case studies of flexible e-collaboration scenarios that cannot be implemented automatically with any known architectures or tools. These scenarios entail transfer and transformation of students' collaboration data through an IMS-LD compatible "player." The data emerge originally to a specific tool and are transferred to another tool. The overall implementations were evaluated from the developers', the instructors', and the students' perspectives. Results indicate that MAPIS3 supports seamless data flow among tools efficiently and flexibly. In particular, teachers are supported in monitoring the e-collaboration process by flexible visualizations of peer/student interactions.

INTRODUCTION

Previous research work (Dillenbourg et al., 2011) has identified the multifaceted benefits emerging from collaboration either at work or educational settings. E-collaboration (or technology-supported collaboration) is usually considered as an advantage to the toolbox of a company or educational organization (Prinz et al., 2010). However, it has been also highlighted that integrating advanced e-collaboration

DOI: 10.4018/978-1-5225-6367-9.ch011

technologies into a traditional workplace or classroom is a complex procedure (Dillenbourg et al., 2011). Among others, one technological factor that reasons such difficulty is what we call the "tool orchestration" problem. This problem denotes the requirement of supporting a seamless communication and data flow pattern among the various tools that may be included in a specific e-collaboration scenario.

In this work, we start by analyzing the tool orchestration problem and we present the MAPIS3 architecture to address this problem. We limit this work's scope and avoid tackling other technical issues such as security concerns (Bracher & Padmanabhan, 2012). Then, we challenge our proposal with other similar solutions presented in the literature, emphasizing the expected benefits and possible limitations. Moreover, we provide architecture evaluation data based on two case studies, exploring the developer's, the instructor's and user's perspective. This is an enhanced work of an already published study (Magnisalis & Demetriadis, 2015) which was based on case study 2 of the current manuscript. Case study 2 is also included here, yet enhanced with the viewpoint of the instructor, including requirements for visualizing peer interaction data that occur during e-collaboration. Focusing on case study 1, we present the development of a technological system that deploys visualized peer interaction data from a Moodle forum and supports mobility (i.e. a widget application in mobile devices). We discuss: a) the information model used to represent the peer interaction data, and b) the visualization implementation in order to support end users (focusing on teachers) in monitoring some key online discussion parameters. We also highlight future application of such a system which connects e-collaboration tools in order to both support monitoring of the discussion stream and beneficially affect collaboration outcomes.

BACKGROUND

The Tool Orchestration Problem and Proposed Solutions

E-Collaboration activities, either in the work environment (Kristensen & Kijl, 2010) or for learning purposes (Hayne & Smith, 2005), are usually guided by an e-collaboration scenario defined at an abstract, technologically independent level (Kock, 2008). In the area of computer-supported collaborative work (Bouras et al., 2009), this is typically referred to as "scenario" (Dillenbourg et al., 2011), while in the computer-supported collaborative learning (CSCL) field it is known as "learning design", "collaboration script" or simply "script" (Dillenbourg et al., 2011). For reasons of simplicity and generalization, in the current work, we call this abstract design as e-collaboration scenario or simply scenario or script.

By integrating scenario techniques, e-collaboration has gradually evolved to a setting of considerable complexity because of multiple human-human and human-technology interactions. In the context of such e-collaboration scenarios with many component activities and consequently tools, there are several technical challenges that have to be addressed (Munkvold & Zirus, 2005). Designers have to decide which e-collaboration tools to use and, most importantly, how these tools will interoperate with each other. Moreover, proposals for reference architectures (Peristeras et al., 2010) towards integration of collaborative work environments mainly focus on the support of the individual during collaboration, possibly underestimating group dynamics and learning or work effects.

A common example illustrating the needs and limitations in e-collaboration scenarios is when "flexibility" (i.e. adaptation) is needed for learner-tailored activities (Dillenbourg et al., 2011). A learning environment can adapt in order to scaffold interactions or to provide individual support. In doing so, the environment has to model parameters and modify them in real time. Such parameters maybe the content, the level of support, etc. (Dimitrakopoulou et al., 2006). The motivation of this study is to address open issues related to flexibility, interaction analysis, and representation in CSCL. Furthermore, the added value of this study is the use of e-collaboration tools to compare feedback modes utilizing simple, though comprehensive models of collaboration (Soller et al., 2005). One topic, we specifically address is the issue of providing standards-based systems capable of flexibly changing representation of peer interactions, upon learner/teacher demand. Consequently, we describe as "e-collaboration tool orchestration" a situation where e-collaboration activity data need to be forwarded to and processed by various tools in a transparent and unobtrusive manner for the participants.

Research works close to the "tool orchestration" concept so far emerge from computer supported collaborative learning (CSCL) research field and utilize IMS-LD specification (IMS-LD, 2003). IMS-LD allows for flexible design of an e-collaboration scenario, linking various activities with tools. Using an IMS-LD compliant authoring tool, one can formally express an e-collaboration scenario, which is a complete, self-contained unit of education or training, such as a course, a module, a lesson, etc. All relevant background has been deeply analyzed in already published work (Magnisalis & Demetriadis, 2015). Here, we focus on extending specific aspects of that study, by including aspects of flexible peer interaction visualization in e-collaboration environments with CSCL features. Furthermore, we analyze the perspective of the instructor/teacher who wishes to connect e-collaboration tools in CSCL contexts and visualize relevant peer interaction data in order to monitor and control the e-collaboration process.

There have been some major efforts to tackle the problem of e-collaboration tool orchestration, which stem from the CSCL context and are related to IMS-LD standard specification (IMS-LD, 2003), including:

1. A generic architecture for extending IMS-LD through specific application interfaces (APIs) (De-la-Fuente-Vanentin et al., 2011). This approach introduces the use of APIs in order to link tools with an IMS-LD representation.
2. Architectures that try to integrate every possible external component with bidirectional communication through a service adapter acting as a middle layer (Alario-Hoyos et al., 2013) and (Prieto et al., 2014).
3. LeadFlow4LD, a learning design and workflow-based method aiming to achieve a computational representation of data with tools in e-collaboration processes in an interoperable and standard way (Palomino-Ramirez et al., 2013).
4. Recently, community has developed the Learning Tools Interoperability (LTI) specification (IMS-LTI, 2014), to allow remote tools and content to be integrated into a Learning Management System (LMS).
5. Several technological tools (e.g. Recourse, Reload, Collage, LDShake etc. (The Learning Design Grid, 2017) have been developed and are currently available to instructors/teachers to help them implement/author e-collaboration scripts of varying degrees of flexibility.
6. There are some efforts to support teachers encode in their e-collaboration settings flexibility. For instance, in Moodle (Moodle, 2017), an instructor can encode rules that adapt the scenario according to certain parameters.

Unfortunately, one or more of the abovementioned limitations are still present in each of these solutions, as will be detailed in Section "Comparison with existing solutions". One common shortcoming of the above approaches is that they do not focus on flexible usage of data retrieved from tools required in e-collaboration scenarios, but mainly provide solutions for reusing existing tools and establishing links between them and IMS-LD. For instance, they showcase how an IMS-LD modeled activity can link to tools used by businesses in e-collaboration activities (like an online discussion forum (ODF) and a chat tool (Lam W. et al., 2008)), without, however, establishing any data-transfer connection between them, or among the tools and the IMS-LD based rules of the scenario.

These tools have not evolved from prototype to production level so as to support actual delivery of courses. A flexible CSCL scenario may require the interoperable linking of several learning enactment tools. CSCL is not simply implying the use of technology for communication purposes. Successful e-collaboration applications aim to capture and model information and knowledge of group activity and use it to achieve a more effective group monitoring and support, thus leading to the development of more adaptive and intelligent CSCL systems (Caballé et al., 2007). We argue that, in order to be successful from teachers and learners viewpoint, a mobile CSCL system has to cater for: a) collaboration skills and learning enhancement by fostering peer interaction (PI), and b) mobility in the deployment of components supporting CSCL activities. Many e-collaboration tools, especially in the CSCL context, attempt to deal with the former by monitoring PI through interaction analysis and learning analytics methods and providing visualized PI representations to learners and teachers (Suthers et al., 2010).

The MAPIS3 Architecture

In our previous work, we have proposed that the tool orchestration problem can be successfully managed by an architecture that combines the IMS-LD specification with web services (Magnisalis & Demetriadis, 2015). We named this architecture "MAPIS3" (Mediating Adaptation Patterns &Intelligent Services) and the core idea is to implement a mediator component (MC) which acts as "glue" between any two different e-collaboration tools that need to be orchestrated. A fine-grained analysis of MAPIS3 architecture is presented in Figure 1, highlighting the 3 included layers: data flow, orchestration and user layer.

- **Data Flow Layer:** this layer is responsible for storing data, such as user characteristics, interaction data or learner's prior knowledge. In this layer, the Mediator Component (MC) handles data from/to web services and tools.
- **Orchestration Layer:** The Mediator Component (MC) along with the IMS-LD compatible e-collaboration scenario constitutes the orchestration layer. MC plays the role of an intermediate component which: 1) fetches or sets data from tools into MC own "data hub/bus", 2) "understands" and controls IMS-LD properties, 3) communicates with appropriate web services. All the above actions are performed by MC in an attempt to orchestrate the tools used in the scenario activities.
- **User Layer:** From the user layer viewpoint, a designer (e.g. a teacher) authors a specific scenario for e-collaboration using an IMS-LD compatible design tool. He/she cooperates closely with the developer (or programmer) responsible for implementing the MC in order to enable the data flow between the coupled tools that are used in the abovementioned scenario. Finally, the end-user (worker/learner/student) is the one who participates in the implementation of the e-collaboration scenario. It is worth mentioning that a user may also have access to the data handled by the MC. For example, a teacher could have the privilege to control through the MC: a) what kind of data is sent from tool A to tool B, b) the setting of IMS-LD properties, or even c) the selection and use of web services, thus affecting the amount and type of data that MC retrieves, stores and transforms.

Figure 1. The three layers of MAPIS3 architecture

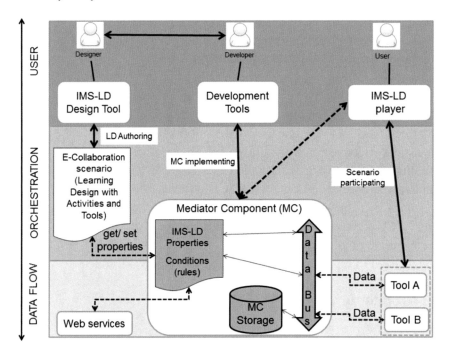

Comparison With Existing Solutions

We believe that efforts for building an efficient 'tool orchestration' framework should be based on already existing tools for collaborative activity modeling. Thus, MAPIS3 relies heavily on IMS-LD, the currently existing modeling standard in the area. It also employs Web services (Peltz, 2003), which is the de facto standard way for facilitating management of data flow among heterogeneous systems.

The differences of MAPIS3 with other proposed solutions for "tool orchestration" that have already been mentioned (Magnisalis & Demetriadis, 2015) are very briefly cited here. Other differences, not mentioned in the past are pointed out. All these differences are summarized as follows:

1. MAPIS3 is based solely on current widely accepted standards, i.e. IMS-LD and Web services for the interconnectivity part. This is in contrast to (De-la-Fuente-Vanentin et al., 2011; Alario-Hoyos et al., 2013; Prieto et al., 2014) works.
2. The MAPIS3 approach maintains full compatibility with IMS-LD, as it does not introduce any new element in IMS-LD to model and perform any adaptive operations in e-collaboration scenarios. This is in contrast to (De-la-Fuente-Vanentin et al., 2011; Palomino-Ramirez et al., 2013) works.
3. MAPIS3 achieves seamless data transfer among tools in e-collaboration activities, contrary to other approaches (Alario-Hoyos et al., 2013; Prieto et al., 2014).
4. In MAPIS3 terms, tool interoperability is the seamless data flow among tools controlled by a pedagogical objective expressed in IMS-LD rules. Our approach surpasses the basic use case of the IMS-LTI specification, which is mainly focused on facilitating the seamless connection (login functionality) of web-based, externally hosted tools.

5. MAPIS3 may provide an efficient solution in e-collaboration scenarios that require flexible peda-
    gogy and coordination of complex situations like the following: a) User grouping (shown in case
    study 2) and regrouping (not shown in this work but could be an extension of case study 2), b)
    User - or device-adjusted - interface adaptation (as presented in case study 1) c) Dynamic (on-
    the-fly) modification of learning flow and d) peer interaction visualization (see case study 2). An
    example that we showcase in this work is τηε flexible provision of peer interaction visualization
    to instructors and learners. Our approach reuses standards (IMS-LD, web services) and leverages
    functionality offered by technological tools like Recourse. Thus, we develop means to support
    instructors/teachers implement/author e-collaboration scripts of varying degrees of flexibility.
6. Instructors take pedagogic design decisions that can be syntactically supported by IMS-LD Level-B
    properties and rules, task that -although not trivial- is semantically necessary for teachers demanding
    flexible scripting. MAPIS3 specifically caters for this issue. While Moodle and other approaches
    focus on flexibility offered towards the individual, not taking into account collaborative parameters.

MAPIS3 supports loose coupling and high cohesion among tools used, thus there are no requirements
for the IMS-LD editors (and run-time players). Moreover, the practitioners (teachers and developers) do
not have to make changes to these applications in order to get a MAPIS3-based system to run. Depending
on the case, tool data transfer is based on a learning flow controlled either totally by IMS-LD rules and/or
by rules shared between MC and IMS-LD. In technological terms this orchestration layer is implemented
by IMS-LD Level-B constructs and MC programmed control logic. In fact MC acts as facilitator of the
adaptive behavior of the whole CSCL script, which is controlled –otherwise orchestrated by IMS-LD
rules. Thus, the MC acts as the connector between IMS-LD and external tools/services, implements
the complex parts of synchronizing services and facilitates adaptive behavior controlled by IMS-LD.

Reviewing the area of CSCL interaction analysis, we have concluded that there is abundance and
diversity of works trying to model and study the interactions in a CSCL process. Many tools are available
for capturing the progress of a collaborative activity (Martínez-Monés et al., 2011). However, despite the
great interest and some proposals (Martínez-Monés et al., 2011) in the area of peer interaction support,
no standard way has been agreed by the community in order to study the essence of collaboration in a
consistent manner and be capable of comparing results.

The concept of supporting (as opposed to enabling) peer-to-peer interaction in CSCL systems is still
in its infancy (Jermann, Soller, & Lesgold, 2004). There is a great diversity of approaches for providing
interaction feedback to peers. Such diversity might be explained by the fact that each system draws upon
a different theoretical perspective (Soller et al., 2005). Based upon work by Magnisalis et al., (2011)
we have not seen a system that can behave flexibly enough to enable easy mobile deployment of PI
visualizations. Our motivation is to provide a real world (i.e. as mobile as possible) implementation and
a visual presentation of PIs within a known CSCL tool (e.g. Moodle forum). The current study focuses
on this aspect and how this is supported by MAPIS3 approach. Research motivation was to recommend
specific instructor-led design strategies and guidelines that orchestrate e-collaboration tools in CSCL
contexts hopefully fostering pedagogical objectives.

Framework for Architecture Evaluation

Evaluating a proposed software architecture can be a complex endeavor that integrates and triangulates
data emerging from various resources, including experts in different fields and users in various settings

and scenarios (Martinez et al., 2011). We suggest that a helpful first step for researchers is to draft a general evaluation framework analyzing the major evaluation dimensions of interest for the evaluated architecture. For MAPIS3, we highlight these evaluation dimensions (EDs) as follows:

- **ED1:** Tool orchestration support: Can MAPIS3 successfully support e-collaboration scenarios incorporating a wide range of tools (e.g. open source) orchestrated in various contexts?
- **ED2:** Transparent data flow support: Can MAPIS3 support seamless data transfer for users of orchestrated tools? This dimension highlights the importance of achieving seamless data interchange among tools for users (learners/teachers).
- **ED3:** Support for flexible scenario adjustments during runtime: Can MAPIS3 manage efficiently and flexibly any necessary adjustments in complex adaptive e-collaboration scenarios? The emphasis, of this work is on case study 1 to follow, when compared with the already previously work that focused on case study 2. Thus, focus is on supporting on the fly interventions that may have an impact on collaboration and consequently on project/learning results. In this work, we challenge the flexibility of our e-collaboration environments by adding various layers of required flexibility. That is, we require that our approach supports peer interaction visualizations that: a) are flexibly adapted to individuals, groups and teachers, b) are offered through various delivery modus operandi (e.g. within or outside an orchestrated tool) and c) are accessible through different devices (e.g. mobile).

CASE STUDIES

To provide data relevant to the above MAPIS3 evaluation perspectives, we showcase the implementations of MAPIS3 in the context of two e-collaboration scenarios entailing data flow among tools to support their orchestration. In the following, we describe the developer's, the teachers' and learners' experience of the integrated system. The case studies that are described are: a) Case study1: Supporting flexible visualization of peer interaction data, and b) Case study2: Supporting data flow among tools in the CSCL context. Case study 2 has already been published (Magnisalis & Demetridis, 2015) and discussed analytically. For completion reasons of the current work, we replicate specific information from that work.

For both case studies, a developer with advanced programming skills in PHP and MySQL open source tools was introduced into MAPIS3 architecture. He was asked to apply MAPIS3 guidelines to implement the specific e-collaboration scenario. He was not knowledgeable of IMS-LD or Web services technologies, therefore he followed simple guidelines to implement a system orchestrating tools and handling data flow among them for the purposes of the given scenario.

Case Study 1: Method

We administered an e-collaboration scenario as a case study in a university learning context, where students were able to collaborate remotely using one discussion tool (i.e. forum). Qualitative and quantitative data were recorded from three perspectives: a) the developer, who was responsible for developing (programming and integrating in the architecture) the required Mediator Component and all necessary MC APIs, according to a specific e-collaboration scenario; b) the learners, who participated in the e-collaboration scenario and provided feedback for the various aspects of the e-collaboration setting, and c) the teachers/instructors who wish to flexibly design and monitor the e-collaboration process.

Case Study 1: Participants

The study was conducted in a Second Chance school in Thessaloniki, Greece. The participants were 176 students (ages 18-50, M=42, SD=3.7), with most of them having low familiarization level with online communication tools; only 13 had used forum/chat tools before -but none of them for educational purposes- with an average computers and in-formation literacy level of 3.8 out of 10 (based on 35 questions, similar to (Simonson et al., 1987), and designed according to the B-Tile (Beile, 2005). The students were randomly distributed into 44 groups of 4 peers.

Case Study 1: Design of the E-Collaboration Scenario

Here we depict the whole procedure for case study 1. This is similar, although using different tools, to procedure of case study 2, already presented (Magnisalis & Demetriadis, 2015). At pedagogical level the e-collaboration scenario involved interconnection of the following tools within a system allowing for flexible peer interaction visualizations (fPIv system):

- **Forum:** students formed new groups and were engaged in a Moodle forum-based asynchronous online discussion. Each group member provided anonymous feedback to peers within the same group. Each student had been attributed to a pseudo name in the system and rated posts of peers anonymously. All ratings were calculated, summarized and visualized as feedback to collaborating peers (see Figure 2, PR at both group and individual levels are depicted). Thus, Moodle was enhanced with an anonymous peer rating tool (PRT) based on a rubric-based qualitative model.

Figure 2. Data representation of peer interaction data of e-collaboration in a Moodle-forum

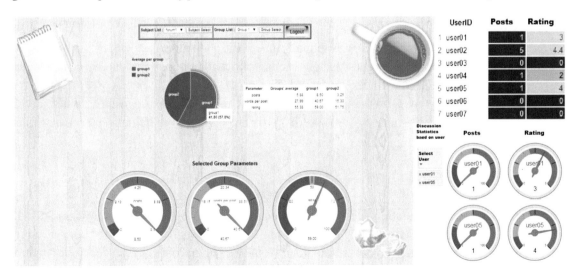

- **Peer Interaction Data Management with MC:** Peer interaction data management by the teacher included two interventions: a) activation/deactivation of individual and group data concerning peer interaction in a forum-based collaboration; b) selecting the type of peer interaction visualization. Type of visualization, means that the teacher could select various types (e.g. mirroring, meta-cognitive, guiding) of peer interaction visualization offered to him/her and learners. However, this detail is out of the scope of the current work.

- **A Shared Visualization Tool (SVT):** students used SVT as a feedback tool for peer posts, replies and ratings (PRR). It was based on Google's Visualization API, an intuitive interactive interface supporting both individual and group awareness. PRT allowed the group members to rate peer cognitive contribution chunked into posts, and shared this information anonymously with all group members. Rating in fPIv was based on the same models applied in Dehler et al. (2011).

The procedure of the study is illustrated in Table 1:

1. **Pre-Test:** Students were asked to individually answer a pre-test with 20 questions related to the subject of the domain knowledge the case study aimed to cover.
2. **Group Formation:** The system randomly formed groups of 4.
3. **Forum Discussion with Mode of Support:** The Moodle forum tool was used as the discussion activity that lasted for 4 weeks. During this study phase the students had to study 10 most important sightseeing of the city within a presentation deliverable. Collaborative work and deliverable could only be produced within the Moodle forum. The system locked each group to a feedback mode/ type of visualization and messages, according to teacher's selection. Anonymous peer rating was obligatory and a grade penalty was introduced for the students that did not rate their peers' posts. The system provided a specific representation to teachers to monitor the collaboration process in each group at-real time (Figure 3). Thus, the teacher could identify if a group deliverable was the product of a continuous collaborative work among peers.
4. **Presentation-Discussion:** Each group presented its work in front of the whole class. A discussion followed and monetary prizes to the three best assessed groups were attributed.
5. **Post-test:** Students answered individually an on-line post-test including 20 multiple choice questions similar to the ones of the pre-test.
6. **Questionnaire:** Students answered individually an on-line questionnaire focusing on the collaboration process and containing closed-type questions, followed by open-type ones in which students could further elaborate on their responses.
7. **Interviews:** We spent one week analyzing log files, tests and questionnaire results. In the individual interviews that followed, students were asked to provide details about their experience in the activity and the fPIv system.

Case Study 2: Method

We administered an e-collaboration scenario as a case study in a university learning context, where students were able to collaborate remotely using two tools successively; first a chat and later on a forum tool. Qualitative and quantitative data were recorded from two perspectives: a) the developer, who was responsible for developing (programming and integrating in the architecture) the required Mediator

Table 1. Activities of implemented case study

Activity	Day (Time)	Social Plane	Mode
1) Pre-test	Day 1	Individual	Asynchronous
2) Group formation	Day 2		
3)Supported forum discussion	Days 3-30 (4 weeks)	Groups of 4	Asynchronous
5) Presentation-Discussion	Day 31	Whole class	Synchronous
6) Individual Post-test	Day 32	Individual	Asynchronous
7) Questionnaire	Day 33	Individual	Asynchronous
8) Interviews	Day 40-47	Individual	Synchronous

Component and all necessary MC APIs, according to a specific e-collaboration scenario; b) the learners, who participated in the e-collaboration scenario and provided feedback for the various aspects of the e-collaboration setting.

Case Study 2: Participants

As learners, we recruited 39 undergraduate computer science students (16 females). The majority of the students were familiar with synchronous and asynchronous communication technologies such as forums and dialogue-based systems. In particular, 33 of them had already used a forum tool before and all of the students were also familiar with chat tools.

Case Study 2: Design of the E-Collaboration Scenario

At pedagogical level the e-collaboration scenario included the following three tools:

- **Chat:** students were engaged in chat-based synchronous online discussion using a specific chat environment. Students working in pairs were asked to discuss and collaboratively provide an answer to a learning issue. In each student team one peer was assigned the 'author' role, who was responsible for initiating the discussion and submitting the final answer of the pair.
- **Group Management with MC:** Group management by the teacher included two interventions: a) group formation for the upcoming forum-based asynchronous collaboration, based on students' interaction data recorded at the previous chat-based phase; b) assigning group moderators in each forum group based on students' performance data recorded also at the chat-based collaboration phase.
- **Forum:** students formed new groups and were engaged in forum-based asynchronous online discussion. Moodle installment forum was chosen for this study.

DATA COLLECTION AND ANALYSIS

In order to record and analyze the developer's experience in both case studies, he kept an activity diary with all his major actions during the implementation of the case study. Based on this diary, we later transcribed the details of his work. For the learners/students, case study data were collected and analyzed as follows:

- **Log files of the Activity and e-Mail Communication Among Students and Teacher:** Students' activity within each tool was logged. The following data were logged for each participant: posts sent, posts read, the moment posts were read and duration of their display, access time of resources like forum or visualization tool, time and duration the visualizations were viewed, individual pre and post-tests, evaluation of group deliverables.
- **Questionnaire:** Participants were asked to fill in an appropriate attitude questionnaire. These questionnaires included both closed-type questions (Likert scale from 1-Totally Disagree to 5-Totally Agree), and open-ended ones, where participants freely expressed their opinions. For closed-type questions the mean (M) and standard deviation (SD) statistical measures were calculated (Table 1), while open-ended ones were content analyzed and classified. This classification was provided as an input to the interviews that followed.
- **Interviews:** After the analysis of questionnaires and extraction of major conclusions, we performed individual interviews with each student. Each interview lasted 15 minutes on average and focused on deeper understanding of the students' comments and suggestions that were already extracted from their answers in the open-ended questions. The interviews were transcribed and the classification of conclusions extracted both from the interviews and the replies to the open-type questions were the results of interviews analysis.

For the teachers' input data from both case studies were collected through a questionnaire and interviews, the same way as we performed for leaners.

Data analysis followed the principles of a mixed evaluation method (Creswell, 2013). By following these principles we reviewed quantitative data and checked whether answers to closed-type questions matched reasonably to the answers of open-ended questions. Comments concerning the architecture were content analyzed and classified to extract valuable conclusions for the system.

RESULTS

In this section we present the results of our case study from the developer's, the teacher's and students' perspectives. Thus, the following sections apply for both case studies 1 and 2. In fact, we observed that case study 1 confirmed results of case study 2, although participating students of case studies had different profile. Results are congregated for both case studies. The reader who wishes to compare results can refer to our previous work (Magnisalis & Demetriadis, 2015).

Developer Perspective

Each of the following sub-sections describes the developer's effort and experience to orchestrate e-collaboration tools that exchange data by applying our MAPIS3 proposal. We focus on case study 1 that followed chronologically case study 2. However, we have verified that the developer can implement flexible tool orchestration solutions for e-collaboration following MAPIS3 architecture.

Scenario Design and Model of Peer Interactions

The developer was not knowledgeable of IMS-LD authoring and player tools and had to follow a 2 hour tutorial about those tools. Afterwards he designed the given e-collaboration scenario in an IMS-LD authoring tool and tested it on an IMS-LD player tool. A small number of iterations/meetings took place between the developer and the teacher in each case study. Initially, the developer identified the data provided as input(s) and received as output(s) for the tools involved, which would enable the required tool orchestration and data transfer functionality for the specific scenario. As a result, he produced a table mapping activities, tools, inputs and outputs from each tool. The developer along with the teachers agreed on the forum-based activity data relevant to students' collaboration to be collected according to the following PRR data model. This data model refers to specific indicators/parameters modeling the peer interactivity within the chat-based activity. These indicators, which were visualized as in Figure3, are:

- **"P" (Posts):** The total number of chat messages (posts) that a student posted.
- **"R" (Replies Per Message):** The average replies per message for a user, calculated across all forum-messages that a student posted.
- **"R" (Rate of Participation):** The rating of messages exchanged, as the average of the rating that each post gathered from peers working within same discussion forum.

Mediator Component (MC)

After the scenario and system design, an iterative and rapid development process was followed, during which the developer and the instructor discussed face-to-face two times. This discussion led to decisions concerning technical issues such as "visualized information for individuals and groups should be provided throughout forum discussion activity, in well-known representations (e.g. gauges)". The developer implemented a MC to enable data flow from one tool to the other. MC acted as the data transfer mechanism between tools involved (i.e. Moodle forum and visualization tool) and IMS-LD run engine. MC facilitated: a) provision of peer interaction visualization data of in forum-based activity to both teachers and learners, upon relevant choice of the teacher (see Figure4) and b) provide peer interaction visualization data of in forum-based activity via various delivery channels (i.e. through mobile devices, as information integrated within forum tool, as information outside the forum tool, etc.). In Figure 3 we depict a mobile visualization of PRR indicators that was available to both learners and teachers of case study 1.

fPIv Development

After a quick review of the available technologies, the developer selected Google Visualization API as the programming means to realize the required visualization. Figure 4 illustrates our "visualization" (Bachour et al., 2010; Soller et al., 2005; Falakmasir et al., 2012) mechanism, which aims to reflect the information about individual interactions within the forum tool. The MC transformed available forum data to a visualization of three useful indicators, namely posts, replies and ratings of the posts. Additionally, as a measure of comparison, the deployed visualization presented the mean of the group and the mean of the classroom for these indicators. Thus, in fPIv system, PI representation covered three levels (Figure 4): a) Individual, b) Group, c) All groups working in parallel in the forum discussion. Notice

Figure 3. Mobile PI visualization to support Teacher identify learner performance based on PRR model

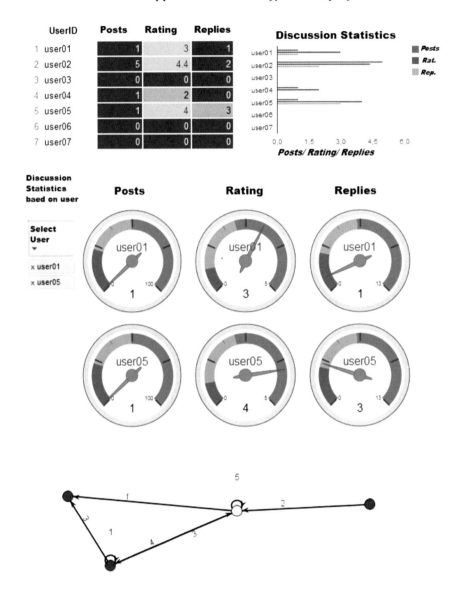

that the teacher (and even learner) can select (Figure4, step 2) the type of visualization and information depicted to him/her via SVT tool (Figure 4 step 3) in order to monitor e-collaboration within the forum tool (Figure 4, step 1). Notice that in Figure 4 some text appears in Greek.

Student Perspective

Case study 1 was organized during a classroom activity and lasted 4 weeks in total. Case study 2 was organized during a classroom activity and lasted 6 days in total. After the end of these activities, a student questionnaire was filled-in and interviews were conducted, lasting another week. This section presents the results collected from the log files, the questionnaires and the interviews.

Figure 4. Case study 1 (fPIv system): Flexible peer interaction visualization based on teacher's selection

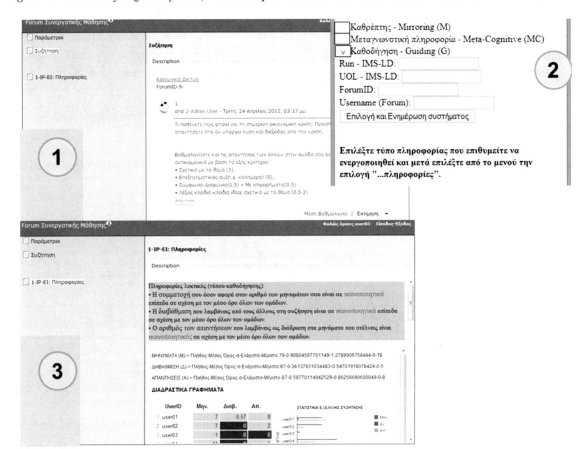

Log File Observations

Major observations from activity log files aggregated for both case studies are the same as presented in already published work (Magnisalis & Demetriadis, 2015).

- **L1:** From system integrity point of view, no login problems were identified.
- **L2:** No problems were met throughout the whole activity. Moreover, no complaints and problems were reported through the e-mail communication channel used between students and teacher.
- **L3:** The students did not spend much time to read the instructions (average: 5.9 minutes), neither needed to access help information frequently (average: 1.6 accesses).
- **L4:** The students spent a considerable amount of time watching the visualized feedback information about their collaboration (24% of their activity time).
- **L5:** There was no system down-time during the whole scenario. No problematic system operation was recorded that could affect students' collaboration.
- **L6:** The students did not mention any technical problem concerning system functional (e.g. system usability) and non-functional (e.g. system response time) parameters.

Questionnaire Results

The responses on a few questions of the students' questionnaire, which was not anonymous, are depicted in Table 2 and presented in accordance with Kock (2013). For comparison reasons, we mention that the analytic results of case study 2 alone are already published (Magnisalis & Demetriadis, 2015). Table 2 ascertains the validity of those results.

Interview Evidence

The major conclusions emerging from the student interviews that apply for both case studies of case study 1 include:

Table 2. Evaluation questionnaire (part)

ID	Question for Students from case studies 1 & 2 (N = 176 + 39)	Mean (Standard deviation)	Statistical Control (t-test)
Q1	Tool orchestration: System Integrity & Usability		
Q1.1	It was easy to use the system efficiently and understand what to do according to scenario	4.38 (0.92)	t=5.03 *p < .001
Q1.2	The system gave me the impression of a unified system/scenario	4.28 (0.83)	t=4.82 *p < .001
Q2	Transparent Data flow support		
Q2.1	There was data exchange among tools during e-collaboration scenario	4.58 (0.73)	t=6.11 *p < .001
Q2.2	Tools were easily identifiable during e-collaboration scenario	4.03 (0.82)	t=6.12 *p < .001
Q3	Support for flexible interventions: Effect on Collaboration & Learning		
Q3.1	Information on "collaborative Participation indicators (CPI)" during forum discussion was simple & understandable	4.20 (1.19)	t=4.08 *p < .001
Q3.2	CPI information instigated thoughts/feelings	3.39 (0.90)	t=1.43 p = .15
Q3.3	CPI information put me into thoughts about my participation in chat tool	4.37 (0.71)	t=5.41 *p < .001
Q3.4	CPI information affected my behavior in forum	3.24 (0.91)	t=.86 p = .39
Q3.5	Peer discussion must be balanced	4.03 (1.06)	t=3.74 *p < .001
Q3.6	CPI information could affect my behavior in chat tool	3.71 (1.16)	t=2.45 *p = .017
Q3.7	Moderator assignment is more significant than CPI information during forum discussions	3.53 (1.25)	t=1.76 *p = .078
Q3.8	CPI information helped individual and group reach better learning domain outcomes	4.31 (0.61)	t=5.44 *p < .001
Q3.9	Group formation helped individual and group reach better learning domain outcomes	4.89 (0.34)	t=8.13 *p < .001
Q3.10	Moderator assignment helped individual and group reach better learning domain outcomes	4.37 (0.53)	t=5.76 *p < .001

* Statistically significant at the 0.05 level

- **I1:** Most of the users (96%) agreed that the system's use was simple and straightforward. Many stated "…system was really a WYSIWYG system", while others said that "…system from the first till the end was simple to use".
- **I2:** The majority of the students (86%) declared that they were under the impression of a unified system and only 2.5% of the sample (5 students) declared that he/she perceived the system as many independent systems, while the other 12.8% (28 out of 215) did not form an opinion. Many indicated "…we thought of the tool as a new custom unified tool".
- **I3:** Most students (90%) easily understood the instructions and system use for the whole e-collaboration scenario. Most stated "…instructions were clear and no further explanations were needed".
- **I4:** Learners found that PRR model (case study 1) is comprehensive (88%) and representative (89%) of peer interactions within group (all groups).
- **I5:** Learners wanted to have some statistical data depicting the PRR model (case study 1) of the whole class (74%).

Instructor/Practitioner Perspective

Interview Evidence

The major conclusions emerging from the teacher interviews that apply for both case studies include:

- **I6:** the system is easy to deploy and control, provided that a developer supports for the implementation of the "glue" (i.e. mediator component) between tools (78% of teachers).
- **I7:** 76% of teachers believe that "IMS-LD based script is innovative but it seems difficult to be implemented in the context of K-12 Education". When discussed in depth, the teachers argued that "script is very motivating, but I (as a teacher) may encounter difficulties while creating the material and script with current IMS-LD tooling" but also "… MAPIS3 with its flexible features may allow for such implementations".
- **I8:** Regarding the complexity of the authoring phase and the use of questionnaire tools, external specialized tools, like a GoogleForm, are preferred over IMS-LD vocabulary and related standards (e.g. IMS-QTI) (89% of teachers).
- **I9:** A well-designed interface makes easy for the learners to interpret the data transferred among tools when using data visualization (64% of teachers).
- **I10:** Many teachers (63%) agreed that interconnecting systems may enable the setting up of useful educational services, such as viewing students' progress using graphical representations.
- **I11:** Teachers (86%) agreed that scenarios support a flexible course of action, while retaining clear the main/normal course flow. Many stated "…now I see the possibility of developing scripts where I can mix and match data and tools".
- **I12:** Teachers (87%) agreed that fPIv (case study 1) supports for interaction and sensemaking. Many stated "…system design should support direct pointing upon information and interactive feedback. For instance, we should be able to provide one click interactions and feedback to most of the information objects provided".
- **I13:** Teachers (83%) agreed that fPIv (case study 1) supports group and individual awareness. Many stated "… interface design should support hierarchical retrieval of information from class through group towards individual level for both learners and teachers".

- **I14:** Teachers (85%) agreed that fPIv (case study 1) supports provision of meta-cognitive type visualizations. Many stated "MAPIS3 should support us in peer interaction visualizations to maximize cognitive productivity (see figures 2 and 3 the gauges as meta-cognitive awareness tools with color scaling).

Questionnaire Results

The responses selected and relevant questions of the teachers' questionnaire, which was not anonymous, are depicted in Table 3 and presented in accordance with Kock (2013).

DISCUSSION

In this section we reflect on and discuss the developer's, the teachers' and students/learners' experiences as seen through the three dimensions of our evaluation framework. We conclude by investigating the implications for practitioners.

ED1: Tool Orchestration

- **Developer's Perspective:** To implement tool orchestration according to MAPIS3 guidelines, the developer has to be competent in certain high-level programming languages to build the MC. Knowledge of IMS-LD and Web service technologies is an advantage as he/she will need less time to develop the MC and the IMS-LD component in any given e-collaboration scenario.
- **Students/Learners' Perspective:** Students evaluated the simplicity, transparency and integrity of the showcased system. From the questionnaire results shown on Table 2, items Q1.1, Q1.2 and from the interview conclusions I1, I2, and I3 it is evident that using the system was simple, straightforward and transparent. The students worked in a system that: (a) managed to hide from its users the complexities or technicalities related to the e-collaboration tools involved, and b) revealed to them only the necessary information and interactions for their collaborative activi-

Table 3. Evaluation questionnaire (part)

ID	Question for Teachers from case study 1 & 2 (N = 9)	Mean (Standard deviation)	Statistical Control (t-test)
QT1	Peer interaction visualization to support monitor and control of e-collaboration		
QT1.1	The showcased script was realistic (providing peer interaction visualization to support monitor and control of e-collaboration)	4.56 (0.74)	t=5.03 *p < .001
QT1.2	The showcased system supports for interaction and sensemaking	4.06 (0.88)	t=5.01 *p < .001
QT1.3	The showcased system supports for group and individual awareness	4.73 (0.46)	t=5.01 *p < .001
QT1.4	The showcased script is rich (e.g. supports provision of meta-cognitive type visualizations)	4.53 (0.73)	t=5.02 *p < .001

* Statistically significant at the 0.05 level

ties (I1, I3). Regarding system integrity, no problems were identified and the scenario was easily followed as shown by log file observations L1, L2, L3 and interview conclusion I2. Overall, the students experienced the system as an integrated solution in an e-collaboration scenario connecting various tools, such as forum and visualization widgets.

- **Teacher Perspective:** Teachers are supported by MAPIS3 in order to monitor and control e-collaboration activities. In case study 1, we put special effort to provide peer interaction visual feedback to teachers (and learners), Teachers are supported to orchestrate tools like a forum and a visualization tool by derived guidelines for teachers when designing scenarios that require orchestrated data flow among these e-collaboration tools. Thus, we support for interaction and sensemaking (I12), support for group and individual awareness (I13) and provision of meta-cognitive type visualizations (I14). For instance, in figure 3, when a learner clicks on a group pie data, gauges appear below to reflect the PI parameters (i.e. PRR) of that group. fPIv has such an integrated model of navigation so that one can drill down to each individual contribution within the Moodle forum discussion. For instance, selecting a group moves hierarchically towards individual PI data and parameters (see figure 2). Also, many teachers stated "…learners and teachers are now supported to easily understand their group and individual collaboration status according to the PI information model used".

ED2: Data Flow Support

- **Developer's perspective:** The developer implemented MC with web services following MAPIS3. In both case studies, but in particular in case study 1, the developer has facilitated easy orchestration of data flow between a peer interaction visualization tool and a forum communication tool
- **Students/Learners' perspective:** Most students understood the data transfer taking place in the background during the activity (Table 2, item Q2.1) and the pedagogical objective that this transfer served (Table 2, item Q2.2 and I4, I5). Thus, while the successful integration between discrete technological tools gave its users the impression of a unified system (Q1.2), they could also understand and model data transfer between involved tools (Q2.2).
- **Teacher perspective:** Focusing on case study 1, the specific pedagogical design features were inspired by relevant literature suggesting that communication tools that provide data feedback to peers on their collaboration status may also trigger peer interactivity and sometimes improve learning conditions and outcomes (Graf et al., 2011; Vatrapu et al., 2011; Long & Aleven, 2011; Falakmasir et al., 2012). In our case, the instructor explored how the data transfer from an e-collaboration tool (forum) could have influenced students' behavior and strategy during a real-time visualization tool. This design was of value to the teachers (I6-I10), supports a flexible course of action, while retaining clear the main/normal course flow (I11), supports for interaction and sensemaking (I12), supports group and individual awareness (I13) and most importantly supports provision of meta-cognitive type visualizations (I14). These findings are supported by the questionnaire results (Table 3, set of items QT). The conclusion drawn is that data transfer can provide the basis for sound pedagogical design in an e-collaboration learning setting. More general, data flow accomplished flexibly by MAPIS3 architecture could support design decisions at a strategic level, exploiting user interaction data generated by any tool of the e-collaboration scenario. In contrast other approaches in the area (e.g. De-la-Fuente-Vanentin et al., 2011; Alario-Hoyos et al., 2013; Prieto et al., 2014) have not dealt with such issues.

ED3: Runtime Intervention

- **Developer's Viewpoint:** Once again, like in case study 2, the developer's implementation in case study 1 has proven that MAPIS3 flexibly allows for interventions like visualization of peer interactions: a) to address additional needs of any involved stakeholder (teachers, students), b) in various representational modes (e.g. visual etc.), c) through various delivery channels (e.g. mobile).

- **Students/Learners' Perspective:** During the forum activity, a visual graphical representation was provided to the students so that they could compare their personal participation level against their peers during chat activity. An initial observation is that students spent considerable time watching the visualized feedback information regarding their collaboration (L4). Moreover, no interruptions of the collaborative activity were mentioned for the forum activity and the whole scenario (L5). System was functional all the time and its operation did not cause any complaints from the students (L6).

- **Teacher Perspective:** Although answers suggest that the cases studied were realistic and could be useful in real situations and in situations where the participants experience in their working environments (see QT1.1 and I7, I8, I9, I10), we analyzed more the negative answers of questions during interviews. Teachers answering negatively, feel the applicability of such a type of learning material in a real situation is matter of research. Despite the positive view of the case studies' systems, they expressed their lack of confidence on their adoption and application in their working situations (I7). Data shown in Table 3 reinforces this view: Teachers considered the scenarios to provide support for interaction and sensemaking (QT1.2), for group and individual awareness (QT1.2) and being rich (QT1.4). However, teachers believe that the option of MAPIS3 to utilize a range of tools (especially Web 2.0) with various affordances is a key factor to overcome limitations of IMS-LD modeling capabilities of flexible CSCL scripts/scenarios (see I7).

Implications for Practitioners

The implication of our study for the practitioners is that the proposed architecture initially offers a technique to interconnect tools in an e-collaboration scenario based on the capability of MC to transfer data among these tools. However, to achieve this, practitioners must consider that an instructor (pedagogical expert) needs to work in close collaboration with a developer (technological expert).

Before concluding our study, we summarize the implications that MAPIS3 proposal has from a practitioners' viewpoint. Practitioners may include all interested stakeholders such as, developers implementing e-collaboration solutions, instructors designing e-collaboration activities, or a company using e-collaboration services and tools. Therefore, the following points, that challenge MAPIS3 from practitioners' perspective, should be taken under consideration:

- **Instructor's and Developer's Training:** From the instructor's viewpoint we believe that an instructor with a basic one-day training session, can design flexible e-collaboration scenarios entailing various tools and data flows among them and being coded in IMS-LD rules. The developer should know Web service technologies and a programming language to implement the MC.

- **Design and Development Costs:** As discussed before, the only cost requirement for the practitioners' and developers' team is to invest a small amount of time on standard technologies and open-source tools.

- **Standards and Open-Source Tools:** Unlike other relevant solutions, our approach follows well-established standards such as IMS-LD Level B rules and web services. As our proposal focuses on reusing tools, it works more efficiently when utilizing open-source and even on-line tools/services tools for the "tool orchestration" part. Thus, in case study 1 we have used an on-line tool-service to support peer interaction visualization.

- **Support for Peer Interaction Monitoring:** In case study 1, we introduced the teachers' requirement to monitor peer interaction in e-collaboration scenarios. In this work we have particularly discussed MAPIS3 based implementations that facilitate: a) data flow among tools, b) orchestration of tools/services conducted by IMS-LD, c) peer interaction visualizations that cover various needs (e.g. teacher and learner) and devices (e.g. desktop and mobile). Focusing on the last, we have presented technological solutions for the visualization in mobile context of peer interaction data emerging in e-collaboration settings. Thus, a mobile application, in a system called fPIV, was implemented to support monitoring of asynchronous collaboration within a Moodle forum. While similar systems are scarce (Ogata & Yano, 2004; Caballé et al., 2007), our approach comprises some advantageous features worth mentioning, as it: a) follows up a general architecture, b) models PI in a flexible way to support alternative models for both teachers and learners, c) supports easy deployment of mobile components (e.g. mobile widgets, desktop widgets etc.) for interactive visualized monitoring of CSCL PIs, d) implements clear design guidelines for mobile PI visualizations, e) follows IMS-LD standard (unlike other proposals of "Comparison with existing solutions" section).

Despite promising evidence, however, it is a fact that the systems that supports flexible orchestration of tools and data-flows in e-collaboration are at an early stage. An explanatory observation is that there exist an abundance of tools and services built for specific purposes and e-collaboration settings. In fact, most of the tools or services used in CSCL scripts were not initially designed taking into account collaborative usage. Moreover, many studies (Dimitracopoulou & Petrou, 2005) have pointed out the lack of a standardized approach to model CSCL activities and generated data. That is, CSCL community lacks ways to include in a CSCL script design these tools (Burgos et al. 2007), exploit the data these tools handle and generate and eventually visualize peer interactivity in fruitful ways for the cognitive process. One reason for this is the fact that the currently available interoperability standard IMS-LD is not capable of expressing the computationally complex and demanding constructs necessary for implementing adaptive techniques (Magnisalis et al., 2011). However, MAPIS3, alleviates for this deficit of IMS-LD by introducing MC.

CONCLUSION, LIMITATIONS AND FUTURE RESEARCH DIRECTIONS

The presented MAPIS3 architecture is a flexible solution that takes advantage of IMS-LD and web service technologies to support efficient tool orchestration in e-collaboration settings. In this work we implemented the architecture to interconnect various tools and facilitate transparent data transfer between them. The evaluation (from the developer, the teacher and the learner's perspective) revealed that MAPIS3 architecture can support: a) flexible tool orchestration for e-collaboration scenario execution, b) transparent data flow among tools, and c) runtime interventions and d) flexible peer interaction visualizations to assist in monitoring and control of the e-collaboration process.

The current study did not test the flexibility of receiving data from past runs of the system being an input in an e-collaboration scenario. We believe that data about peers and groups could be exploited to introduce well-informed higher level decisions and interventions during the scenario runtime. This may require complex strategies and tools to mediate control of important aspects, affecting the collaboration process itself (Kock, 2013). Moreover, we have already started working on supporting e-collaboration scenario design by studying efforts worldwide (Van Ostrand et al., 2016; Kock, 2016; Bratitsis & Demetriadis, 2012) utilizing various e-collaboration tools.

The 'tool-orchestration-involving-data-flow' problem is technically demanding. However, we believe that we have provided a well-defined solution for a team of practitioners (teachers in collaboration with a capable developer) to implement flexible e-collaboration scenarios. How to further automatize our solution for the end-user is a matter of future research. Thus, a possible future MAPIS3 development could be an IMS-LD editor/player using a semantic based repository to dynamically search, discover and select tools suitable for the flexible script/scenario interventions to be realized. Additionally, a mechanism for automatic (or at least semi-automatic) MC composition is currently being investigated to be deployed over MAPIS3 architecture.

We argue that adaptive functionalities can be available to IMS-LD designers either as software add-ons or web services that are invoked by a script editor (i.e. the software extends its functionalities depending on the available add-ons library or list of web services). Then, the designer/teacher could integrate the desired adaptations at the appropriate point of the computerized scenario representation and parameterize the properties and methods of the pattern as desired. In this way the "adaptive logic" can reside at a separate software component (outside IMS-LD manifest) and pedagogically effective CSCL scenarios are decoupled from the flexibility it is desired to have under certain circumstances. Also, this way we take advantage of modifying the adaptive strategy without touching the original pedagogy pattern expressed with IMS-LD. We have already started working towards the latter in an attempt to provide/integrate flexibility in e-collaboration scenarios. Thus, we aim to support teacher undertake the role of authoring a course and gradually need the developer less.

QUESTIONS FOR STUDENTS AND TEACHERS TO USE FOR DISCUSSIONS IN CLASSROOM

1. **For Students and Teachers:** Briefly outline two e-collaboration scenarios that include more than one communication tool (e.g. forum, chat, wiki). Do you imagine cases where data among these tools may be used? Please explain how and why?

2. **For Students and Teachers:** What might be the purpose of transferring data among tools used within an e-collaboration scenario? Do you identify any benefits and limitations (e.g. technological)?

3. **For Students and Teachers:** What might be a fruitful intervention of a teacher or a learner during e-collaboration within a tool in a classroom? Could this be easily supported from a conversational agent (or bot) in a MOOC (massive on-line open courses) setting?

4. **For Students and Teachers:** Is peer interaction visualization a valuable feedback to you? Do you foresee any advantages when this information is available when compared to cases where this information is not available? Imagine usage of this information in MOOCs.

5. **For Students and Teachers:** What kind of information could be useful for you when working in a set of e-collaboration systems. Imagine also systems that can be used for informal types of learning

(e.g. Facebook). For instance, is information about how many peers like or rate your posts highly providing any added value?

6. **For Teachers:** What kind of information could be useful for you when administering a set of e-collaboration systems. Imagine also systems that can be used for informal types of learning (e.g. Facebook). For instance, is information about how many peers like a post providing any added value when monitoring learners' collaboration?

7. **For Students:** Is information about collaboration within a collaborative setting useful for you and your institution? How is it compared to information about your achievements (e.g. passing a test)?

8. **For Students:** Is information about collaboration within a collaborative setting useful for you and your institution? How can this insight help you in monitoring and control of your courses, students etc.?

9. **For Students and Teachers:** Do you believe that solutions like MAPIS3 deal with the problem of data transfer among tools used in e-collaboration scenarios adequately? Do you identify any short comings (e.g. ethical, legal, security hindrances)?

10. **For students and teachers:** Does MAPIS3 proposal involve any overlapping and common areas of interest with web analytics data that might be used for learning purposes (i.e. learning analytics)?

11. **For Students and Teachers:** Do you believe that there are issues for future research when applying a proposal such as MAPIS3 (e.g. tools that support the teacher in designing the course that uses e-collaboration communication tools)?

12. **For Students and Teachers:** Do you believe that the way peer interaction feedback is visualized affects perception, self-awareness and usage of this feedback from the end-user (teacher/learner)? What kind of feedback might be more effective for him/her and efficient for his/her work when collaborating?

REFERENCES

Alario-Hoyos, C., Bote-Lorenzo, M. L., Gómez-Sánchez, E., Asensio-Pérez, J. I., Vega-Gorgojo, G., & Ruiz-Calleja, A. (2013). GLUE! An architecture for the integration of external tools in Virtual Learning Environments. *Computers & Education*, *60*(1), 122–137. doi:10.1016/j.compedu.2012.08.010

Bachour, K., Kaplan, F., & Dillenbourg, P. (2010). An interactive table for supporting participation balance in face-to-face collaborative learning. *IEEE Transactions on Learning Technologies*, *3*(3), 203–213. doi:10.1109/TLT.2010.18

Beile, P. M. (2005). *Development and Validation of the Beile Test of Information Literacy for Education (B-TILED)* (PhD thesis). College of Education, Central Florida Univ., Orlando, FL.

Bouras, C., Giannaka, E., & Tsiatsos, T. (2009). E-Collaboration Concepts, Systems, and Applications. In N. Kock (Ed.), *E-Collaboration: Concepts, Methodologies, Tools, and Applications* (pp. 8–16). Hershey, PA: Information Science Reference. doi:10.4018/978-1-60566-652-5.ch002

Bracher, S., & Krishnan, P. (2012). Supporting Secure Information Flow: An Engineering Approach. *International Journal of e-Collaboration*, *8*(1), 17–35. doi:10.4018/jec.2012010102

Bratitsis, T., & Demetriadis, S. (2012). Perspectives on Tools for Computer-Supported Collaborative Learning. *International Journal of e-Collaboration*, *8*(4), 1–7. doi:10.4018/jec.2012100101

Burgos, D., Tattersall, C., & Koper, R. (2007). Representing Adaptive and Adaptable Units of Learning. In B. Fernández Manjon, J. M. Sanchez Perez, J. A. Gómez Pulido, M. A. Vega Rodriguez, & J. Bravo (Eds.), *Computers and Education: E-learning – From Theory to Practice* (pp. 41–56). Springer. doi:10.1007/978-1-4020-4914-9_4

Caballé, S., Daradoumis, T., & Xhafa, F. (2007). Efficient embedding of information and knowledge into CSCL applications. In *International Conference on Technologies for E-Learning and Digital Entertainment* (pp. 548-559). Springer. 10.1007/978-3-540-73011-8_53

Creswell, J. W. (2013). *Research design: Qualitative, quantitative, and mixed methods approaches*. Thousand Oaks, CA: Sage Publications.

De-la-Fuente-Vanentin, L., Pardo, A., & Kloos, C. D. (2011). Generic service integration in adaptive learning experiences using IMS learning design. *Computers & Education*, *57*(1), 1160–1170. doi:10.1016/j.compedu.2010.12.007

Dehler, J., Bodemer, D., Buder, J., & Hesse, F. W. (2011). Guiding knowledge communication in CSCL via group knowledge awareness. *Computers in Human Behavior*, *27*(3), 1068–1078. doi:10.1016/j.chb.2010.05.018

Dillenbourg, P., Zufferey, G., Alavi, H., Jeremann, P., Do-Lenh, S., Bonnard, Q., & Kaplan, F. (2011). Classroom Orchestration: The third circle of usability. In *Proceedings of the 9th International Conference on Computer Supported Collaborative Learning* (pp. 510-517). Hong Kong: International Society of the Learning Sciences.

Dimitracopoulou, A., & Petrou, A. (2005). Advanced collaborative distance learning systems for young students: Design issues and current trends on new cognitive and metacognitive tools. *THEMES in Education, International Journal*.

Falakmasir, M. H., Hsiao, I. H., Mazzola, L., Grant, N., & Brusilovsky, P. (2012). The Impact of Social Performance Visualization on Students. In *Proceedings of the 12th International Conference on Advanced Learning Technologies,* (pp. 565-569). Washington, DC: IEEE Computer Society Press. 10.1109/ICALT.2012.218

Graf, S., Ives, C., Rahman, N., & Ferri, A. (2011). AAT: a tool for accessing and analysing students' behaviour data in learning systems. In *Proceedings of the 1st International Conference on Learning Analytics and Knowledge* (pp. 174-179). New York, NY: ACM. 10.1145/2090116.2090145

Hayne, S. C., & Smith, C. A. P. (2005). The relationship between e-collaboration and cognition. *International Journal of e-Collaboration*, *1*(3), 17–34. doi:10.4018/jec.2005070102

IMS-LD. (2003). *IMS Global Learning Consortium: Learning Design Specification*. Retrieved February 2, 2015, from http://www.imsglobal.org/learningdesign/

IMS-LTI. (2014). *IMS Global Learning Consortium: Learning Tools Interoperability*. Retrieved February 2, 2015, from http://www.imsglobal.org/lti/

Kock, N. (Ed.). (2008). *Encyclopedia of e-collaboration*. Hershey, PA: Information Science Reference. doi:10.4018/978-1-59904-000-4

Kock, N. (2013). Using WarpPLS in e-collaboration studies: What if I have only one group and one condition? *International Journal of e-Collaboration*, *9*(3), 1–12. doi:10.4018/jec.2013070101

Kock, N. (2016). Visualizing Moderating Effects in Path Models with Latent Variables. *International Journal of e-Collaboration*, *12*(1), 1–7. doi:10.4018/IJeC.2016010101

Kristensen, K., & Kijl, B. (2010). Collaborative Performance: Addressing the ROI of Collaboration. *International Journal of e-Collaboration*, *6*(1), 53–69. doi:10.4018/jec.2010091104

Lam, W., Kong, E., & Chua, A. (2008). Managing Online Discussion Forums for Collaborative Learning. In N. Kock (Ed.), *Encyclopedia of E-Collaboration* (pp. 437–443). Hershey, PA: Information Science Reference. doi:10.4018/978-1-59904-000-4.ch067

Long, Y., & Aleven, V. (2011). Students' Understanding of Their Student Model. *International Journal of Artificial Intelligence in Education*, *67*(38), 179–186.

Magnisalis, I., & Demetriadis, S. (2015). Tool Orchestration in e-Collaboration: A Case Study Analyzing the Developer and Student Perspectives. *International Journal of e-Collaboration*, *11*(4), 40–63. doi:10.4018/ijec.2015100103

Magnisalis, I., Demetriadis, S., & Karakostas, A. (2011). Adaptive and intelligent systems for collaborative learning support: A review of the field. *IEEE Transactions on Learning Technologies*, *4*(1), 5–20. doi:10.1109/TLT.2011.2

Martínez-Monés, A., Harrer, A., & Dimitriadis, Y. (2011). An interaction-aware design process for the integration of interaction analysis into mainstream CSCL practices. In *Analyzing interactions in CSCL* (pp. 269–291). Boston, MA: Springer. doi:10.1007/978-1-4419-7710-6_13

Moodle. (n.d.). Retrieved from https://moodle.org/

Munkvold, B. E., & Zigurs, I. (2005). Integration of e-collaboration technologies: Research opportunities and challenges. *International Journal of e-Collaboration*, *1*(2), 1–24. doi:10.4018/jec.2005040101

Ogata, H., & Yano, Y. (2004). Knowledge awareness map for computer-supported ubiquitous language-learning. In *Wireless and Mobile Technologies in Education, 2004. Proceedings. The 2nd IEEE International Workshop on* (pp. 19-26). IEEE.

Palomino-Ramirez, L., Bote-Lorenzo, M. L., Asensio-Pérez, J. I., Vignollet, L., & Dimitriadis, Y. A. (2013). LeadFlow4LD: A Method for the Computational Representation of the Learning Flow and Data Flow in Collaborative Learning. *Journal of Universal Computer Science*, *19*(6), 805–830.

Peltz, C. (2003). Web services orchestration and choreography. *Computer*, *36*(10), 46–52. doi:10.1109/MC.2003.1236471

Peristeras, V., Martínez-Carreras, M. A., Gómez-Skarmeta, A. F., Prinz, W., & Nasirifard, P. (2010). Towards a Reference Architecture for Collaborative Work Environments. *International Journal of e-Collaboration*, *6*(1), 14–32. doi:10.4018/jec.2010091102

Prieto, L. P., Asensio-Pérez, J. I., Muñoz-Cristóbal, J. A., Jorrín-Abellán, I. M., Dimitriadis, Y., & Gómez-Sánchez, E. (2014). Supporting orchestration of CSCL scenarios in web-based Distributed Learning Environments. *Computers & Education*, *73*, 9–25. doi:10.1016/j.compedu.2013.12.008

Prinz, W., Martínez-Carreras, M. A., & Pallot, M. (2010). From Collaborative Tools to Collaborative Working Environments. *International Journal of e-Collaboration*, *6*(1), 1–13. doi:10.4018/jec.2010091101

Simonson, M. R., Maurer, M., Montag-Torardi, M., & Whitaker, M. (1987). Development of a standardized test of computer literacy and a computer anxiety index. *Journal of Educational Computing Research*, *3*(2), 231–247. doi:10.2190/7CHY-5CM0-4D00-6JCG

Soller, A., Martínez, A., Jermann, P., & Muehlenbrock, M. (2005). From mirroring to guiding: A review of state of the art technology for supporting collaborative learning. *International Journal of Artificial Intelligence in Education*, *15*(4), 261–290.

Suthers, D. D., Dwyer, N., Medina, R., & Vatrapu, R. (2010). A framework for conceptualizing, representing, and analyzing distributed interaction. *International Journal of Computer-Supported Collaborative Learning*, *5*(1), 5–42. doi:10.100711412-009-9081-9

The Learning Design Grid. (2017). *Tools*. Retrieved from http://www.ld-grid.org/resources/tools

Van Ostrand, A., Wolfe, S., Arredondo, A., Skinner, A. M., Visaiz, R., Jones, M., & Jenkins, J. J. (2016). Creating Virtual Communities That Work: Best Practices for Users and Developers of E-Collaboration Software. *International Journal of e-Collaboration*, *12*(4), 41–60. doi:10.4018/IJeC.2016100104

Vatrapu, R., Teplovs, C., Fujita, N., & Bull, S. (2011). Toward visual analytics for teachers' dynamic diagnostic pedagogical decision-making. In *Proceedings of the 1st International Conference on Learning Analytics and Knowledge* (pp. 93-98). New York, NY: ACM. 10.1145/2090116.2090129

Chapter 12
Challenges Facing E-Publishing Over Cloud Computing on Scientists' Social Network Service:
A Comparative Study

Evon Abu-Taieh
The University of Jordan – Aqaba, Jordan

Auhood Alfaries
King Saud University, Saudi Arabia & Princess Noura Bint Abdulrahman University, Saudi Arabia

Shaha Al-Otaibi
Princess Nourah Bint Abdulrahman University, Saudi Arabi

ABSTRACT

This chapter illustrates the difficulties facing e-publishing over cloud computing pertaining to scientifically-oriented social network services from three axioms: the life cycle of the research document, an explanation of what a researcher juggles to conduct proper research, and the researcher knowledge pertaining to both scholarly search engines and citation indices. The chapter discusses the essential role of the researcher in teaching, being a beacon of hope, and explains the steps towards research conducting, when an original idea is deduced, as well as the step of writing research addressing the financial support for researchers: from submitting proposals, follow up proposals, grant management if funding is secured, whilst conducting the research, and publishing the results in accredited journals approved by the researcher's institute and financing partner, while publishing the research in accordance with the laws and regulations of the institute.

DOI: 10.4018/978-1-5225-6367-9.ch012

INTRODUCTION

This chapter will shed light on the difficulties facing e-publishing over cloud computing pertaining to scientifically-oriented social network service from three axioms: the life cycle of the research document, after which, the chapter will clarify what a researcher juggles throughout the production of the document related to research. As such, the first part of the chapter will show the life cycle of the research paper and illustrates how each segment of the cycle ripple affect the next segment, then the chapter will present the different force affecting a scholar and the many balls a scholar juggles. Subsequently the chapter will reflect how a scholar knows about scientifically-oriented social network service but does not know the important parts of the different indices that is affected by the citation. In fact, the least known citation indices SCI & SSCI are the most important indices used to rank universities.

Afterwards, the chapter discusses the essential role of the researcher in teaching, being a beacon of hope, as well as being a mentor when molding human minds of young students, then how the research is conducted, and how the ideas are construed in the researcher's mind by reading other research, conducting experiments, discussions, seminars, and from life. The chapter will explain the steps towards research conducting, when an original idea is either deduced or the researcher resort to going back to the drawing board. When an original idea is reckoned, the researcher embarks on the quest and conduct more researcher either by experimenting or working on other research and reading. Subsequently, the step of writing research would be the next topic to be discussed, then the chapter will address the financial support for researchers that entails submitting proposals, follow up proposals, grant management if funding is secured, whilst conducting the research, and publishing the results in accredited journals approved by the researcher's institute and financing partner. In addition, the chapter will discuss the importance of publishing the research in accordance with the laws and regulations of the institute. Consequently, the chapter sheds more light on the rate of the journal based on reputation of the journal and Journal Citation Rank (JCR) or scientific Journal Ranking (SJR), accordingly, the next section of this chapter discusses the three most important words in ranking journals: ERA, Scopus, and ISI.

In this context, the chapter discusses paper publishing process, in terms of the cost and time efficiency coupled with the copy rights rules and regulations. Then the chapter discussed the language barrier, in view that most of the web-based search engines and scientifically-oriented social network services are in English mainly, subsequently the chapter discusses that being knowledgeable of current technology is becoming more indispensable.

Subsequently, the chapter will unveil two discovering studies conducted at the University of Jordan – Aqaba and Princess Nourah Bint Abdulrahman University (PNU), to determine the level of being tech savvy of the scholars at both universities. The study aims to discover if the researchers know/don't know about the different Scientifically-oriented Social network service, citation indices, bibliographic software, scholar search engines etc. The questionnaire identified whether teaching staff know of "Scientifically-Oriented Social network service", bibliographic software, scholar search engines, and their knowledge of different citing indices, whereby, measuring the savviness of the faculty members of the university, indicated the level of alignment of the faculty members with the university strive to become a globally recognized university.

Accordingly, in subsequent sections, the chapter will investigate the web-metrics, university ranking, accreditation bodies, and address the cause of accreditation, before discussing the survey results then the chapter will conduct a comparison between the survey respondents from both universities.

BACKGROUND: THE LIFE CYCLE OF RESEARCH PAPER

Faculty members normally have two prominent tasks to successfully fulfill their job description; to teach and research. In this context, academics need to conduct research regularly, and stay up-to-date, in order to not only be the beacons of hope, but also be mentors when molding human minds of young students. An integral part to understand the Difficulties Facing E-Publishing over Cloud Computing pertaining to Social network service for scientists is to navigate the stages of today's life cycle of the research paper. The first stage would be an explicit tacit knowledge (idea) that has been proven by scientific methodology, then the paper is written, edited and sent out for publishing consideration at either a scientific conference or scientific journal. There are many conferences and journals where research papers are published, nevertheless choosing the proper journal/conference/book is not an easy job. Researcher investigates the rank of the journal/conference/book through ranking agencies like ERA, ISI, and Scopus. After appropriate review (peer & blind), paper is either published and indexed in digital library or simply rejected and returned to the researcher to improve the paper. While writing a research paper, researchers may look at results of fellow researchers to use in their own work. Researchers usually cite such usage of work of others in their own work, in view that cited papers are regarded highly since it proves useful to others.

For a paper to be cited digital libraries feed into search engine the paper metadata or the document itself. Hence, when a researcher looks for a paper, such paper would be available. When a paper is cited frequently in search engines i.e. Google scholar and Social network service for scientists i.e. Research-Gate index the paper hence increasing the citing index of the researcher and the journal/conference/book. Such indices like i10-index, h-index RG score, SCI (Scientific Citation Index), SSCI (Social Science Citation Index) are used in ranking the researcher university and enhancing the image and the rank of the university and enhance the citing score of the journal/conference /book. Figure 1 illustrates the life cycle of a research paper. There are many relations that can be shown in this cycle.

First, there is a positive relation between a researcher citing rate and the paper published by the researcher. The higher the citing rate of the paper the higher the citing index of the researcher and vice versa. The citation score of the paper reflects on the citation score of the journal/conference/book. Hence, such relation reflects positively or negatively on the publisher. The publisher in turn has a positive effect on the credibility of the paper: renowned publishers like ACM, IEEE, IGI and Springer may give the paper credibility and respect. Hence, the need for the ranking system used in ISI, ERA, and Scopus.

Universities that strive for positive stature and ranking are seeking the citation through their scholars; furthermore, universities require faculty members to publish in reputable, highly cited, highly ranked journals.

Social network sites are web-based services that allow individuals to construct a public or semi-public profile within a bounded system. This would be the first step to link with other users with whom they share common interests, in addition to viewing and navigating their list of connections and those made by others within the system" (Ellison, 2007), accordingly, such sites facilitate the development of online social networks by connecting a user's profile with those of other individuals and/or groups ((Buettner, 2016). In this context, social network can be categorized based on their orientation into the following: Social; such as *Facebook, Twitter, Instagram, Myspace*, or Professional; like *LinkedIn, Google+*, or Scientific, for example *ResearchGate, Academia.edu*, or socially intellectual such as *Goodreads for books*.

Figure 1. Research paper life cycle (Abu-Taieh, 2016)

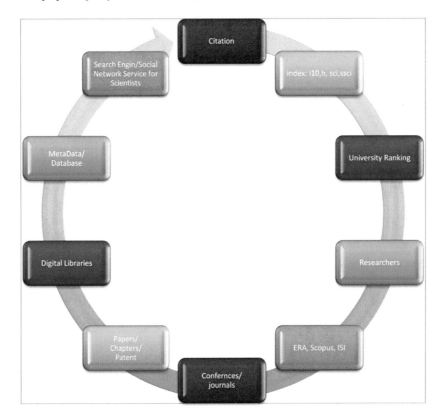

SCIENTISTS SOCIAL NETWORK SERVICE AND CITATION INDICES

In light of the aforementioned, the scientifically oriented social network service and how they interrelate with citation indices are discussed in this section. Unlike social networks, the scientifically oriented social network services only accommodate the needs of the scholars for instance: ResearchGate, Google scholar, and academia.edu, Zotero, Coins, and Figshare. CiteSeerX, getCITED, MyScienceWork, Mendeley. In addition, this section provides an overview of citation indices used in regards to scientifically oriented social network service for scientists and scholar search engines: i10-index, h- index, SCI, SSCI, and RG score.

ResearchGate was established in 2008 with 10,000 researchers, however, now has more than 9 million members from 193 countries, more than 81 million publications, and more than 19 million full-text documents (RG facts, 2016). ResearchGate claims 2.5 million new publications is added every month; With 24 different discipline (RG Trending, 2016).

Academia.edu was established in 2008, and claims to have 35,551,064 academics 11,364,859 papers and 1,846,788 research interests and attracts 36 million unique visitors a month (AcademiaEdu, 2016).

Mendelcy was bought by Elsevier in 2013, at the time it had 2.3 users. Mendeley was established in 2008. According to Lunden (2013), the competitors of Mendeley is EndNote which is owned by Thomson Reuters.

MyScienceWork was established in 2010 and has open access to a vast range of over 30 million scientific publications according to Bridges (2014). MyScienceWork is available in English, French, Chinese, Spanish, German, Italian, Portuguese, Russian.

CiteSeerX considers itself a search engine and digital library with focus on scientific literature pertains to computer science. Indexed more than 750,000 documents. CiteSeerX was established in 1997 in NEC Research Institute (Princeton, New Jersey), then in 2003 The service transitioned to the Pennsylvania State University's College of Information Sciences and Technology (CiteSeer, 2016).

Zotero a software first released in 2006 to help manage data of bibliographic nature, the software was developed in George Mason University. Zotero was associated with word processors and internet explorers. Hence, Zotero is not Social network service for scientists but it does influence the citation vicious cycle.

COinS is short for ContextObjects in Spans created in 1990s by Ghent University. Gives researchers an easier way to link OpenURLs into library subscription resources (Chudnov, 2006).

Figshare is an online digital repository *helps academic institutions store, share and manage all of their research outputs* (figshare, 2016). Figshare was developed by Mark Hahnel in 2011 and now belongs to Macmillan Publishers (Hane, 2013).

getCITED *was a website database that listed publication and citation information on academic articles whose information was entered by members. getCITED aimed to include publications, both peer-reviewed and non-reviewed* (Burden, 2010).

Google Scholar launched in 2004, is web search engine and index both full text and metadata of publications of journals in both Europe and America. (Orduña-Malea, Ayllón, Martín-Martín, & Delgado López-Cózar, 2014) claims that Google Scholar has 160 million documents. Some researchers had criticism for Google Scholar regarding: screening for quality (Beall, 2014), Vulnerability to spam (Labbe, 2010), Incorrect field detection (Jacsó, 2010).

Science Citation Index (SCI) was created in 1955 aiming to *eliminate the uncritical citation of fraudulent, incomplete, or obsolete data* (Garfield, 1955) as bibliographic system for science literature. SSCI is short for Social Sciences Citation Index used for interdisciplinary and was developed by ISI from SCI (Thomson Reuters., 2016).

h-index is Hirsch index or Hirsch number developed in 2005 by (Hirsch, 2005) is used by Google Scholar. The h-index was criticized by (Dorogovtsev & Mendes, 2015) as favoring "modestly performing researchers" in their paper titled Ranking scientists and was criticized by Yong (2014) for the same reason.

Google Scholar developed i10-index which indicates the number of publication with at least 10 citations (Google Scholar Blog, 2011).

ResearchGate index called RG Score *The RG Score is a metric that measures scientific reputation based on how all of your research is received by your peers* (RG facts, 2016). Claims ResearchGate on their website. RG score includes: publications, questions, answers and followers of the researchers to calculate the RG score.

THE RESEARCHER THE JUGGLER

The researcher is an integral factor in understanding the difficulties facing e-publishing over cloud computing pertaining to scientifically oriented social network service. There are many factors that influence the researcher, especially when juggling other correlated factors. On one hand the researcher must increase his/her citation indices, that manifest in affecting university ranking and web matrices while conducting research, writing the research document, conduct classes exams etc. Additionally, the researcher must raise funds for her/his research, tactfully deal with copyrights of the publisher, while at the same time deal with the different language barriers whilst being a tech savvy to deal with websites and computers. As such, the researcher must play many roles, as stipulated in Figure 2.

Students, Classes, Exams

An essential role of the researcher is teaching, being a beacon of hope, as well as being a mentor when molding human minds of young students. On average a researcher in the university must teach 12-15 credit hours per week in addition to at least 3 office hours allocated to receive and consult students. Such load carries with it lecturing, seminars, exams, quizzes, grading and following up on students' absences. In addition, each faculty member must carry managerial work such as weekly meetings with faculty, faculty strategy discussions and write up, quality assurance tasks. With simple calculations, the aforementioned requires 20-25 working hours per week which leaves only 20-15 hours for research per week. Such amount of time is not enough to conduct research, hence the researcher resort to work on his/her own time while eating up family and social time.

Figure 2. Researchers juggling 14 elements affecting their work (Abu-Taieh, 2016)

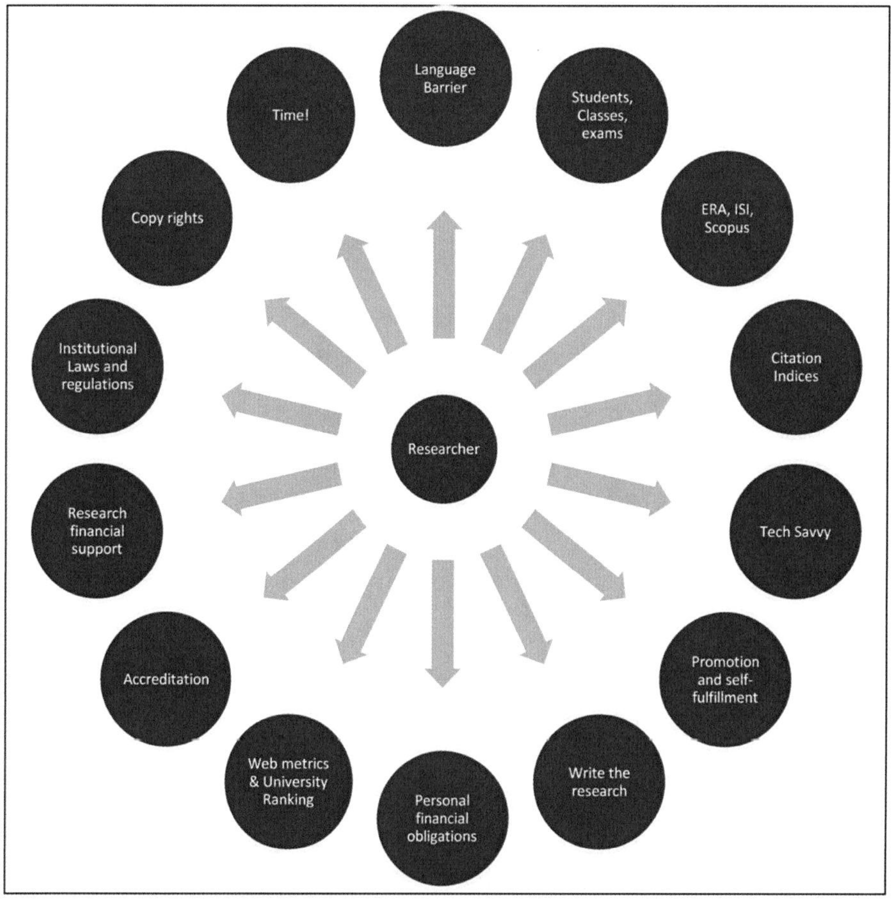

Researching

Ideas are construed in the researcher's mind by reading other research, conducting experiments, discussions, seminars, and from life. After conducting some research, an original idea is either deduced or the researcher resort to going back to the drawing board. When an original idea is reckoned, the researcher embarks on the quest and conduct more researcher either by experimenting or working on other research and reading. Subsequently, the step of writing research is the next topic to be discussed.

Writing Research

To write a research paper, a series of steps will be followed, starting with developing a research question, identifying an original idea, and conducting the research, which is an agonizing process that entails many hours on part of the researcher to present the tacit knowledge then convert to explicit written knowledge. The written paper must be clear, succinct, concise, formatted, strong, with original idea. The process of writing is an art that carries with it the writing style where some scholars over simplify and others over complicate the idea of the research.

Research Financial Support

Researchers are obligated to finance their research from a number of organizations. Such task entails submitting proposals, follow up proposals, grant management if funding is secured, whilst conducting the research, and publishing the results in accredited journals approved by his/her institute and financing partner. As such, the researcher will take up the roles and responsibilities of a manager, an accountant, a lawyer, and a scientist simultaneously. Research financial support is an essential element in conducting research. Many researchers and research centers flaunt how much research fund has a scholar raised for research projects.

In this context, indubitably, the funds from the scholar's academic institution or other funding agencies does not become available without conditions, as such, funds are secured to address a topic desired and aligned with the goals of the funding institutions. As such, funds that target for example cancer research; heart disease may not be geared to fund computer science research. In the same token, the scholar has to attain the skills, techniques and know how to capture and be eligible for research funding opportunities, which can be torturous, and lengthy process.

Funding agencies solicit their funding money to scholars, yet there are many legal issues that regulates the way a fund is spent. Furthermore, different funding agencies have different requirements and rules for grant applications, to which the scholar must abide, more notably, the scholar's academic institution has another set of rules and regulations governing the acceptance and spending of the funds.

Institutional Laws and Regulations

The researcher must publish their research in accordance with the laws and regulations of their institute and promote their institute through the different search engines and scientifically oriented social network service. Likewise, the academic institution normally encourages their scholars to publish in highly cited journals, whereby such citing would entice the ranking of the institution. In this context, the University of Jordan awards points to each published paper according to the journal ranking. Some journals are awarded 1 point, others 2 points, the highest is 3 points. The points awarded to the scholar through the published article is used later to promote the scholar from Assistant Professor to Associate Professor, or from associate professor to Full Professor. To be promoted to associate Professor, a scholar must accumulate more than 8 points; whereas to be promoted to Full professor an Associate Professor must accumulate more than 12 points. Some institutes encourage sole authored papers while other institutes encourage shared research papers. It is worth noting that papers published in first grade journal are not treated as papers published in second grade journals. A committee decides the rate of the journal based on reputation of the journal and Journal Citation Rank (JCR) or scientific Journal Ranking (SJR), accordingly, the next section of this paper will discuss the three most important words in ranking journals: ERA, Scopus, and ISI.

Institute for Scientific Information (ISI)

ISI is short for Institute for Scientific Information, which is a citation indexing service that is maintained by Clarivate Analytics, an intellectual property of Thomson Reuters. There are six main citation indices kept by ISI, namely: social science that has 3200 journals, Science citation that has 8850 journals, arts & humanities citation index which has 1700 journals, books citation which has 80,000 books where 10,000 books are added each year, conference proceedings citation index which has 180,000 conference proceedings, the sixth citation index is emerging source citation index (Clarivate, 2018). Clarivate Analytics publishes Journal Citation Rank (JCR) report which ranks the journals according to citation counts.

Scopus

Scopus is Elsevier's abstract and citation database launched in 2004, Scopus is owned by Elsevier's (Burnham, 2006). Scopus has four types of quality measure for each title; those are h-Index, CiteScore, SJR (SCImago Journal Rank) and SNIP (Source Normalized Impact per Paper) (Kulkarn, Aziz, Shams, & Busse, 2009). Scopus covers literature: scientific journals, books and conference proceedings. In the fields of science, technology, medicine, social sciences, and arts and humanities according to Scopus (2018).

In this regard, it is worth noting that the University of Jordan awards scholars publishing in Scopus Journals with two points towards promotion, while Princess Nourah Bint Abdulrahman University (PNU) encourages publishing in ISI and Scopus ranked journals alike and promote such actions with recognition across the university.

Excellence in Research for Australia (ERA)

ERA stands for *Excellence in Research for Australia* (ERA), ranking list for journals administered by Australian government Research Council (ARC). The ARC has four tiers of quality rating namely A*, A, B, and C. (ARC, 2018). The ARC has announced that Clarivate Analytics will provide citation information for the 2018 round of Excellence in Research for Australia (era-2018, 2018). According to same source, the Discipline groupings for administrative purposes (8 groups), as follows: MIC = Mathematical, Information and Computing Sciences, PCE = Physical, Chemical and Earth Sciences, EE = Engineering and Environmental Sciences, BB = Biological and Biotechnological Sciences, MHS

= Medical and Health Sciences, HCA = Humanities and Creative Arts, EHS = Education and Human Society, EC = Economics and Commerce.

In this context, the University of Jordan (JU) awards researcher who publish in quality rating journals A*, A, and B only, with three points towards promotion as stated on University web site (JU, 2018). Moreover, Princess Nourah Bint Abdulrahman University (PNU) encourages publishing in ISI and Scopus ranked journals and provides the Mechanism for checking journals categorized under ISI or Scopus databases (PNU, 2018)

Management of Time and Money

Peer review is very expensive and time-consuming task, towards this issue, Price (2012) claims in his article that review process takes up to $80 million, furthermore, review process takes six months to two years. Hence, the researcher must manage time and money pertaining to aspects of his document and his research. Some journals charge the scholar publishing and review fees while others do not. The fees range from few dollars to thousands of dollars, while others publish for free and compensate their loss with royalties. The review process time also varies according to the journal, some take weeks, months while others may take years.

Time management efficiently is an adamant concern, and "how to manage time" is the most frequent questions among scholars, on average a research paper takes months after the actual research is conducted, to undergo the cycle of writing, editing, validating a paper through colleagues, checking and double checking the results, referencing and using the proper referencing style, then submitting the paper to the proper journal. More notably, the submission process goes through much research and investigation for the proper journal with high indexing and citation rate.

Both the University of Jordan and Princess Nourah Bint Abdulrahman University (PNU) try to support and elevate such burdens on the scholar by offering some rewards like granting certain amount of money to support publishing.

Legal Issues and Copy Rights

To upload a copy of research paper on scientifically-oriented social network is hindered by the copy rights rules and regulations, in this context, many papers had to be taken down from scientifically-oriented Social network service due to objections from publishers. According to Howard (2013) Acadmia.edu received 2800 take-down notice from Elsevier, however, later, Elsevier, bought Mandely a social network for researchers (Lunden, 2013), thereby showing two points publishing houses resisted the idea of an author showing their papers on scientific social network yet could not resist forever, as such, Elsevier bought Mandely. Such instance not only shows the tug of war between publishing houses and social network, but also proves the intensity and magnitude of such conflict on researchers. Accordingly, scholars are advised to read legal documents and copyrights to stay on the safe side (El-Mahied, Alkhaldi, & Abu-Taieh, 2009). Indeed, scholars must be equipped with legal skills and to be wary, in view that such knowledge and efforts are needed to walk the maze. Nonetheless, another solution that was provided by the industry is Open Access Journals, which allow the researcher to publish on-line and such that others can refer and access the research for free.

Language Barrier

Even though determining which languages are spoken most in the world is a more difficult task, based on which web-based tools, services and applications can be devised. Nevertheless, most of the web-based search engines and scientifically-oriented social network services are in English mainly, yet, some like *MyScienceWork* is available in English, French, Chinese, Spanish, German, Italian, Portuguese, Russian. More notably none is available in Arabic, Urdu, Dutch, Korean, Japanese, Bengali, Malay/Indonesian, Persian and other less main-stream languages. Taking into consideration that there are more than 100 languages in the world, the eight languages used in *MyScienceWork* represent merely 34% of the world population languages. As such, scholars who do not master one of the predominant languages are not only discouraged from participating in the dissemination of knowledge among peers, but also, depriving none-English speakers from benefiting from the knowledge available, thereby, creating a language barrier among scholars (El-Mahied & Abu-Taieh, 2006). Furthermore, publishing in Arabic, for example, will hinder the work for lack of citation and index. In this context, the University of Jordan awards publishing in Arabic Journals with only one point towards promotion, while Princess Nourah Bint Abdulrahman University (PNU) encourages publish in Arabic and supports *Sharia Sciences and Arabic Language Journal*.

Tech Savvy

Being knowledgeable of current technology is becoming more indispensable, yet, unfortunately, not all researchers are tech savvy; many cannot understand nor comprehend the different interfaces with search engines and scientifically-oriented social network service, as such, a tailored training is required to help the researcher overcome this difficulty. In this regard, it is worth noting that the different types of indexing and indexing algorithms are an enigma to some researchers. Furthermore, the distinction between some search engines and scientifically-oriented social network services can be vague and confusing to none-tech savvy researchers. Some terms are not obvious such as; i10-index and h-index in Google scholar, RG Score in Research Gate. As such, this section will discuss a study about the level of knowledge the different types of scholars regarding citation indices, scientific social networks, scholarly search engines, etc. In two discovering studies conducted at the University of Jordan – Aqaba and Princess Nourah Bint Abdulrahman University (PNU), shown below, most people know about the scientific social networks but when it comes to citation indices some scholars were oblivious regarding such network services.

It is worth to note that the there are many aspects to further signify this hurdle, one of which is the needed skills of word processing using Microsoft word, Latex style, Overleaf, among others. Equally needed skill is the use of the different search engines like google, Bing, Dogpile, coupled with another needed skill, which is the knowledge of the use of websites of Scopus, ISI, ERA; as well as understanding the different meaning of all the numbers and acronyms related to each site. Accordingly, in subsequent sections, the chapter will investigate the web-metrics, university ranking, accreditation bodies, and address the cause of accreditation.

Web Metrics and University Ranking

Ranking universities is done by many agencies according to a number of variables, noting that all the different rankings have one thing in common, namely: the citation of papers published by researchers in the university. In this regard, there are more than 20 different rankings in the world thus far.

The following seven different ranking each holds the greater mark based on the citation of the paper published by the academic researchers: (1) Higher Education Evaluation and Accreditation Council of Taiwan (HEEACT) developed Performance Ranking of Scientific Papers for World Universities based on research productivity, impact and excellence data was drawn on Science Citation Index and Social Science Citation Index both are owned by Thomson Reuters, noting that back in 2012 HEEACT stopped. (2) QS World University Rankings by Quacquarelli Symonds (QS) based on Academic peer review, Faculty/Student ratio, Citations per faculty, Employer reputation, International student ratio, International staff ratio. (3) Times Higher Education World University Rankings by Times Higher Education (THE) magazine based on Industry Income – innovation, International diversity, Teaching – the learning environment, Research – volume, income and reputation, Citations – research influence (32%). (4) the Academic Ranking of World Universities (ARWU), by Shanghai Ranking Consultancy based in China based on Quality of education, Quality of faculty, Research output (40%), Per capita performance. (5) The CWTS Leiden Ranking by the Centre for Science and Technology Studies based on Citation impact and scientific collaboration. (6) Global University Ranking using the RatER, an autonomous, non-commercial, Russian rating agency. (7) G-Factor is based on Google search engine and measures the presence of the institute on the internet.

It is worth noting that aforesaid ranking systems include research in their ranking, nonetheless, only two of these ranking systems that weigh the research as 32% and 40% of university rank, to be based on research output and research influence. Subsequently, the discernable inquiry would be; why universities do care about web Metrics and University Ranking; because both are needed for accreditation and ranking the universities which in turn reflect positive or negative in accrediting universities internationally. Consequently, the next section would discuss accreditation bodies whereby addressing the question of why accredit?

Accreditation Bodies

The ultimate goal of accreditation bodies of higher education is to first, standardize education and maintain the quality of education in the different educational institutes. Second enhance the credit transferability among different educational institutes and furthermore different countries. In this regard, subsequently, below an illustrated of some international and national Quality assurance and accreditation organizations from: Germany, Spain, Hong Kong, Pakistan, Canada, Swiss, Austria, and USA. In addition to two important information technology-based organization i.e ABET which is IEEE based organization and ACM.

There are two international organizations, namely: The International Network for Quality Assurance Agencies in Higher Education (INQAAHE) which has 280 members (INQAAHE, 2017), the second, a US based organization; Council for Higher Education Accreditation that has 467 quality assurance bodies, accreditation bodies, and ministries of Education from 175 countries, and has 3000 member institutions (chea, 2017). CHEA is member in INQAAHE. CHEA replaced Council on Postsecondary Accreditation (COPA) and Federation of Regional Accrediting Commissions of Higher Education (FRACHE). In Europe there is European Association for Quality Assurance in Higher Education (ENQA) which has 51 organizations and 28 countries. ENQA (ENQA, 2017) established The European Quality Assurance Register for Higher Education (EQAR), the European Students' Union (ESI), the European University Association (EUA) and the European Association of Institutions in Higher Education (EURASHE) and

ENIC – NARIC (National Academic Recognition Information Centre) comprises all countries of Europe as well as Australia, Canada, Israel, the United States of America and New Zealand.

In Germany Kultusministerkonferenz (KMK) (KMK, 2017) was founded in 1948, then in 1957 German Council of Science and Humanities (Wissenschaftsrat) was founded. KMK established Accreditation Council (Akkreditierungsrat). Associated with the Accreditation Council 10 agencies which are: Swiss Agency for Accreditation and Quality Assurance(AAQ), Accreditation, Certification and Quality Assurance Institute (ACQUIN), Accreditation Agency for Study Programmes in Health and Social Sciences (AHPGS), Agency for Quality Assurance and Accreditation of Canonical Study Programmes (AKAST), Agency for Quality Assurance and Accreditation Austria(AQ Austria), Agency for Quality Assurance by Accreditation of Study Programmes (AQAS), Accreditation Agency for Degree Programmes in Engineering, Informatics/Computer Science, the Natural Sciences and Mathematics (ASIIN), evaluation agency Baden-Württemberg(evalag), Foundation for International Business Administration Accreditation (FIBAA), and Central Evaluation- and Accreditation Agency Hannover(ZEvA)

In Spain, the Agencia Nacional de la Evaluación de la Calidad y Acreditación (National Agency for Quality Assessment and Accreditation) which is dubbed (ANECA) founded in 2002 (ANECA, 2017). ANECA is full member of European Association for Quality Assurance in Higher Education (ENQA), International Network for Quality Assurance Agencies in Higher Education(INQAAHE), and. European Quality Assurance Register for Higher Education(EQAR).

In the United Kingdom there is Quality Assurance Agency (QAA) which is a member of INQAAHE and ENQA (PSRB, 2016). In Hong Kong, the Hong Kong Council for Accreditation of Academic and Vocational Qualifications (HKCAAVQ) replaced the Hong Kong Council for Academic Accreditation (HKCAAVQ, 2017).

In India there are 12 professional councils: All India Council for Technical Education (AICTE), Distance Education Council (DEC),Indian Council for Agriculture Research (ICAR), Bar Council of India (BCI), National Council for Teacher Education (NCTE),Rehabilitation Council of India (RCI),Medical Council of India (MCI), Pharmacy Council of India (PCI),Indian Nursing Council (INC), Dentist Council of India (DCI),Central Council of Homeopathy (CCH),Central Council of Indian Medicine (CCIM) (HE_India, 2017).

In Pakistan under Quality Assurance Agency of Higher Education Commission of Pakistan there are: National Accreditation Council for Teachers Education (NACTE), National Agricultural Education Accreditation Council (NAEAC), National Business Education Accreditation Council (NBEAC), National Computing Education Accreditation Council (NCEAC) (NACTE, 2017), (NAEAC, 2017), (NBEAC, 2017), and (NCEAC, 2017).

In Canada the Canada's Association of I.T. Professional (CIPS) is a Full Member of the Association of Accrediting Agencies of Canada (AAAC). CIPS has established the Computer Science Accreditation Council (CSAC), the Information Systems and Technology Accreditation Council (ISTAC) and the Business Technology Management Accreditation Council (BTMAC) as autonomous bodies. CIPS was established with this name in 1968. CIPS accredits the University, college/applied degree programs. The programs include: Computer Science Degree Programs, Software Engineering Degree Programs, Interdisciplinary Programs, Management Information Systems Degree Programs, Business Management Technology Programs, Computer Systems Technology type Diploma Programs, and Applied Information Technology Degree Programs.

In the USA the Higher education accreditation in the United States is categorized: regional, national, programmatic, and faith-based accreditors. There are 6 regional accreditors namely: Middle States Commission on Higher Education, New England Association of Schools and Colleges, Northwest Commission on Colleges and Universities (NWCCU), Higher Learning Commission (HLC) (formerly, North Central Association of Colleges and Schools (NCA)), Southern Association of Colleges and Schools (SACS) Commission on Colleges, and Western Association of Schools and Colleges (WASC-ACCJC). There are 6 national accreditors (nationwide not international): Accrediting Bureau of Health Education Schools (ABHES) (recognized by USDE), Accrediting Commission of Career Schools and Colleges (ACCSC) (recognized by USDE), Accrediting Council for Continuing Education and Training (ACCET) (recognized by USDE), Council on Occupational Education (COE) (recognized by USDE), Distance Education Accrediting Commission (DEAC) (recognized by USDE and CHEA), Accrediting Council for Independent Colleges and Schools (ACICS) (U.S. Department of Education, 2017). The specialized or programmatic accreditors are generally under CHEA or Department of Education US (USDE) there are 76 agencies.

ABET is programmatic Accreditation established in 1932 and has 3369 programs (chea, 2017). ABET accredited 3,852 programs at 776 colleges and universities in 31 countries according to (ABET, 2017).

ABET covers disciplines of applied and natural science, computing, engineering and engineering technology at the associate, bachelor and master degree levels. ABET has four accreditation commissions: Applied and Natural Science Accreditation Commission (ANSAC), Computing Accreditation Commission (CAC), Engineering Accreditation Commission (EAC), and Engineering Technology Accreditation Commission (ETAC). ABET is a federation of 35 societies and organizations (ABET, 2017) furthermore, ABET stemmed from 7 engineering societies. The first computer engineering program accredited by ABET was in 1971 at Case Western Reserve University (ACM& IEEE, 2016).

The Association for Computing Machinery (ACM) was established in 1947 has 100,000 members ACM is an organization for academic and scholarly interest in computer science. ACM has 171 local chapters, 37 special interest groups and more than 50 scholarly peer-reviewed journals (ACM, 2017).

Both Saudi Arabia and Jordan have their own accreditation bodies and quality assurance: In Saudi Arabia the accreditation body is Education Evaluation Commission (EEC) was established in 2016 formally. (EEC, n.d.), a center that pertains to accreditation is National Center for Academic Accreditation (ncaaa, 2018). In Jordan Accreditation and Quality Assurance Commission for Higher Education was established formally in 2007 (HEAC, 2018). Both commissions in both countries adhere to the highest level of accreditation and quality assurance. Their experience is best lined with international laws and standards.

Why Accredit

Accreditation is equally important and crucial for academic institutions ranking, because accreditation is the process and implementation phase of the body of knowledge. Accordingly, a body of knowledge "can be very useful to provide a comprehensive and integrative view of the discipline, for assessment of professionals and organizations, for self-assessment as well as for curriculum development for academic or professional development courses and degree programs" (Oren, 2005). Accreditation in accordance to body of knowledge affects students, institutions, public and professionals. The ultimate goal of both that the idea (Body of knowledge) and the process (accreditation) is to create a better-educated computer professional. Such computer professional shall practice with an ethical manner to the well-being of the ordinary user, organization, establishment, and the public. Such professional is needed in industry and government hence all parties need to cooperate to create the proper environment for such professional to spring to life. Industry standards must be met by the Institutions in the supply-demand manners. Furthermore, properly accredited institute can provide computer students with proper education that will prepare them to further advance their higher education. Also, institutes can self-evaluate, analyze, and bridge the gap between industry and education.

The accreditation process must be fair, unswerving, confidential with clear process, transparent and objective. The accreditation agency must be independent and autonomous from educational institute. The accreditation process must be carried out by qualified reviewers. Resources must be available to carry process effectively. Accreditation process, goals, steps and time must be clear and set. Such Guidelines are set by (CIPS, 2017).

DISCOVERING STUDY: UNIVERSITY OF JORDAN-AQABA

In light of the aforementioned, a study was conducted to determine the level of being tech savvy of the scholars at the university of this chapter's researcher. The study aimed to discover if the researchers know/don't know about the different Scientifically-oriented Social network service, citation indices, bibliographic software, scholar search engines etc. The questionnaire aimed to discover:

- Does teaching staff know of "Scientifically-Oriented Social network service", bibliographic software, scholar search engines?
- Does teaching staff know of the different citing indices?

Whereby, measuring the savviness of the faculty members of the university, will indicate the level of alignment of the faculty members with the university strive to become a globally recognized university.

Population of the Study

The University of Jordan –Aqaba Campus is composed of five faculties: Faculty of Information Technology and Systems, Faculty of Languages, Faculty of Management and Finance, Faculty of Marine sciences, Faculty of Tourism and Hospitality. In this regard, the Faculty of Information Technology and Systems has two programs Business Information Technology and Computer Information Systems. The Faculty of Languages has 4 programs: English Language and Literature, French language and literature, Applied English, and Arabic language and literature. The Faculty of Management and Finance has 3 programs: Business Management, Accounting, Risk Management and Insurance. The Faculty of Marine sciences has 3 programs: Marine Biology, Coastal environment, and a master program. The Faculty of Tourism and Hospitality has 3 programs: Hotel Management, Travel and Tourism Management, Food and Beverage Management. The teaching staff is comprised of a total of 75 PhD academics and master holders, where 26 are master holders and 49 are PhD holders.

A questionnaire was sent to all 75-teaching staff, yet only 47 (62.6%) responded to the questionnaire, of whom 32(68%) are PhD holder and 15 (31.9%) master holder. Also, among the responding scholars are 8 (17.0%) female scholars. The responding scholars represented the faculties as follows: Faculty of Management and Finance (13) which represents (27.7%) of the study population, Faculty of Information Technology and Systems (10) which represents (21.3%) of the study population, Faculty of Tourism and Hospitality (9) which represents (19.1%) of the study population, Faculty of Languages

(8) which represents (17.0%) of the study population, Faculty of Marine sciences (3) which represents (6.4%) of the study population. Taking into account that four respondents forgot to fill the faculty part of the questionnaire.

Results of the Questionnaire

Upon analyzing the received replies, it is worth to note that 96% knew Google Scholar and 91% knew ResearchGate, however, fewer scholars knew of citation indices h-index and i10-index related to Google scholar, in view that only (51%) knew of the h-index and (49%) knew of the i10-index, more notably, the least known citation index was the SSCI index, as only (28%) knew the SSCI index.

Accordingly, Figure 3 illustrates the questionnaire's results, which shows that ResearchGate, Google scholar, and academia.edu are most known, while least known are Zotero, Coins, and Figshare. Furthermore, CiteSeerX, getCITED, MyScienceWork, Mendeley are partially known (26%, 26%, 21%, 13%) respectively by the scholars.

Likewise, the results of this questionnaire further prove that citation indices like RG Score, h-index, i10-index, SCI, SSCI are not well known among the responded academic researchers. The RG score related to ResearchGate was known by only 20 (*43%*) respondents, while the h-index was known by only 24 (*51%*) of the respondents, whereas the i10-index related to Google Scholar was known by 23 (*49%*) of the respondents, and SCI index is known by 15 (*32%*) of the respondents, whilst SSCI is known by 13 (*28.2%*) of the respondents. Figure 4 reflects the knowledge of the scholars in general of the citation indices.

It is noteworthy, upon taking a closer look at the academic researchers' knowledge and how each faculty member knows of h citation index, Table 1 summarizes the results, whereby 23 (*48.9%*) faculty members do not know h- index, of whom 13 (56.5%) of masters' level and 10 (43.4%) of PhD level.

Figure 3. Academic researchers knowledge of different scientists social media in JU (Abu-Taieh, 2016)

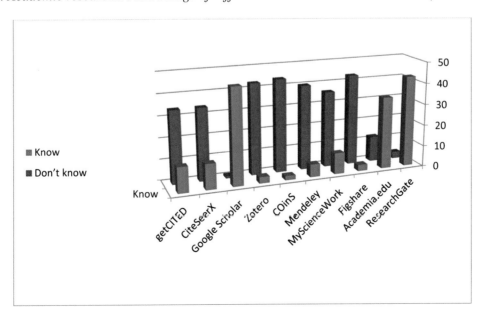

Figure 4. Scholars knowledge of citation indices in JU (Abu-Taieh, 2016)

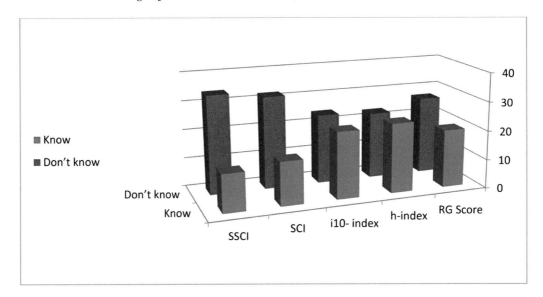

When concluding the result analysis of the questionnaire, and the Table 1, another pattern among the academic researchers was recognized; the following faculties had more knowledge of h-index: Information Technology and Systems, Tourism and Hospitality, Marine sciences, while; Management and Finance faculty and Languages faculty exerted less knowledge.

DISCOVERING STUDY: PRINCESS NOURAH BINT ABDULRAHMAN UNIVERSITY

In conjunction with the aforementioned study, a similar study was conducted at the Princess Nourah Bint Abdulrahman University (PNU). As such, this section presents a study that was conducted to discover the level of being tech savvy of the researchers in the Princess Nourah Bint Abdulrahman University. The

Table 1. The h citation Index level of knowledge among academic researchers in JU (Abu-Taieh, 2016)

Faculty	Know h-index	Don't Know h-Index	Grand Total
Information Technology and Systems	8	2	10
Tourism and Hospitality	5	4	9
Languages	2	6	8
Marine sciences	2	1	3
Management and Finance	5	8	13
NA	2	2	4
Grand Total	**24**	**23**	**47**

study aimed to discover if the researchers know/don't know about the different scientifically-oriented Social network service, citation indices, bibliographic software, scholar search engines etc. The questionnaire aimed to discover:

- Does teaching staff know of "Social network service for scientists", bibliographic software, scholar search engines?
- Does teaching staff know of the different citing indices?

Upon measuring the technological savviness of the faculty members of the university, whereby an indication of the alignment of the faculty members with the university strive to become a globally recognized university.

Population of the Study

Established in 2008, Princess Nourah Bint Abdulrahman University(PNU) is all female campus that is composed of six colleges; namely the College of Education for Liberal Arts Disciplines, the College of Education for Scientific Disciplines, the College of Education for the Development of Teachers, the College of Social Services, the College of Home Economics and the College of Fine Arts.

There are 3 main streams in PNU: Humanities, Sciences and Medicine. The College of Humanities has College of Education, College of Arts, College of Social Services, and College of Languages. The College of Science has College of Sciences, College of Computer and Information Sciences, College of Business Administration, and College of Arts and Design. The College of Medicine has College of Nursing, College of Pharmacy, College of Health and Rehabilitation Sciences, College of Dentistry, College of Medicine.

College of Education consists of Teaching Methods, Early childhood, Special Education, Psychology Departments. College of Social Services has one department Social Service which includes the following programs: Bachelor of Social Service, Master of Social Planning, PhD in Social Planning, Bachelor of Social Service, Master in Service of Individuals, PhD in Service of Individuals, Bachelor of Social Service, Master in Community Planning, PhD in Community Planning, Bachelor of Social Service, Master in Community Service, PhD in Community Service. College of Languages includes: English Department and French Department.

College of Science includes 4 departments: The Biology Department., The Chemistry Department, The Physics Department, and The Mathematical Sciences Department.

College of Computer and Information Sciences has 3 departments with 150 faculty members: Information Technology has (42 faculty members), Computer Sciences (29 faculty members) and Information Systems (35 faculty members).

College of Business Administration includes: Business Administration, International Finance, Marketing and Innovation & Technology, Economics, Law, Accounting. College of Arts and Design includes: Graphic Design and Digital Media, Interior Design, Visual Design and Printing, Fashion Design and Fabrics, Innovation & Product Design Department.

The College of Nursing encompasses the following departments: Surgical and Internal Medicine Nursing, Maternity, Obstetrics, and Gynecology Nursing, Pediatrics Nursing, Psychological nursing,

Community Service Nursing, Nursing Management. College of Health and Rehabilitation Sciences: Biomedical Technology, Communication Sciences, Rehabilitation Sciences, Health Sciences. College of Medicine: Clinical Sciences, Basic health sciences, Basic Science and Training.

A questionnaire was sent to all 41-teaching staff, and 41 responded (100%) responded to the questionnaire among them 26(63%) PhD holder and 15 (37%) master holder. Also, since PNU is all female campus the respondents are all (100%) female scholars. The responding scholars represented the faculties as follows: College of Arts (2) which represents (5%) of the study population, College of Education (2) which represents (5%) of the study population, College of Business Administration (1) which represents (2%) of the study population, College of Science (2) which represents (5%) of the study population, College of Health & Rehabilitation (1) which represents (2%) of the study population, College of Languages (2) which represents (5%) of the study population, College of Computer & information Science (30) which represents (73%) of the study population, College of Arts & Design (2) which represents (5%) of the study population.

Results of the Questionnaire

Upon analyzing the received replies, it is worth to note that 95% knew Google Scholar and 85% knew ResearchGate, however, fewer scholars knew of citation indices h-index and i10-index related to Google scholar, in view that only (51%) knew of the h-index and (34%) knew of the i10-index, whilst the least known citation index was the RG Score index, as only (34%) knew the RG Score index.

Accordingly, Figure 5 illustrates the questionnaire's results, which shows that ResearchGate, Google scholar are most known, while least known are Zotero, Coins, MyScienceWork, getCITED, and Figshare. Furthermore, CiteSeerX, Academia.edu and Mendeley are partially known (46%, 56%, and 59%) respectively by the scholars.

Figure 5. Academic researchers knowledge of different scientists social media in PNU

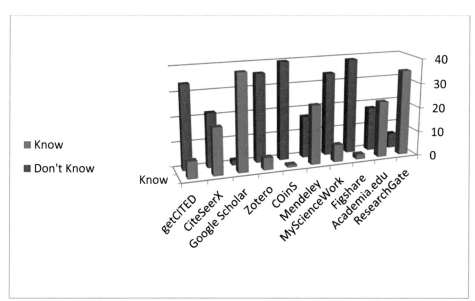

Likewise, the results of this questionnaire further prove that citation indices like RG Score, h-index, i10-index, SCI, SSCI are not well known among the examined academic researchers. The RG score related to ResearchGate was known by only 27 (*34%*) respondents, while the h-index was known by only 21 (*51%*) of the respondents, whereas, the i10-index related to Google Scholar was known by 21 (*34%*) of the respondents, whilst SCI and SSCI index is known by 15 (*37%*) of the respondents, in this regard Figure 6 reflects the knowledge of the scholars in general of the citation indices.

Figure 6. Scholars knowledge of citation indices in PNU

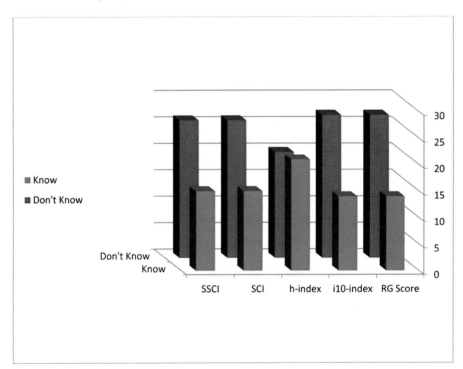

Table 2. The h citation Index level of knowledge among academic researchers in PNU

College	Know h-index	Don't Know h-Index	Grand Total
College of Arts	1	1	2
College of Education	0	2	2
College of Business Administration	0	1	1
College of Science	1	1	2
College of Health & Rehabilitation	1	0	1
College of Languages	0	2	2
College of Computer & information Science	17	13	30
College of Arts & Design	0	1	1
Total	**20**	**21**	**41**

It is noteworthy, upon taking a closer look at the academic researchers' knowledge and how each faculty member knows of h citation index, accordingly Table 2 summarizes the results, whereby there are 21 (*51%*) faculty members do not know h- index.

When concluding the result analysis of the questionnaire, and the Table 2, another pattern among the academic researchers was recognized; the following faculties had more knowledge of h-index: College of Computer & information Science, while; other faculty exerted less knowledge.

Comparison Between JU and PNU

Upon explicit comparison between the results of the surveyed respondents from the two universities, PNU and JU, the following is noted:

1. PNU and JU respondents knew Google Scholar with close proximity (95%, 96%) respectively.
2. Both PNU and JU participants knew ResearchGate with close proximity (85%, 91%) respectively.
3. PNU participants least known are Zotero, Coins, MyScienceWork, getCITED, and Figshare, whereas, CiteSeerX, Academia.edu and Mendeley are partially known (46%, 56%, and 59%) respectively by the scholars. On the other hand, JU participants least known are CiteSeerX, getCITED, MyScienceWork, Mendeley are partially known (26%, 26%, 21%, 13%) respectively by the scholars.
4. Both universities PNU and JU participants knew ResearchGate citation indices h-index and i10-index with close proximity (51%,34%; 51%, 49%) respectively.
5. PNU participants least known citation index was the RG Score index, as only (34%) knew the RG Score index, while JU participants least known citation index was the SSCI index, as only (28%) knew the SSCI index.
6. Looking closer at the h-index, in both PNU and JU respondents from the faculty of information technology know the h-index

FUTURE RESEARCH DIRECTIONS

This paper proved that the vicious cycle of knowledge shown above is the driving power for scholars, publishers, universities and technology towards perfection. There are many venues where scholars can present their work: video, sound, animation, simulation such elements are not taken into account in citation battle field, hence the future will bring technology that can accommodate such work.

CONCLUSION

This paper discussed the difficulties facing e-publishing over cloud computing pertaining to scientifically-oriented social network service from three axioms: the life cycle of the research document, after which, the paper gave a clarification of what a researcher juggles throughout the production of the document related to research. Then paper discussed discovering study of the researcher knowledge pertaining to both Social network service for scientists, scholarly search engines and citation indices.

The first part of the paper showed the life cycle of the paper and illustrated how each segment of the cycle ripple affect the next segment, then the paper illustrated the different force affecting a scholar and the many balls a scholar juggles. Subsequently the paper reflected how a scholar knows about scientifically-oriented social network service but does not know the important parts of the different indices that is affected by the citation. In fact, the least known citation indices SCI & SSCI are the most important indices used to rank universities. Then the paper discussed the scientifically oriented social network service and how they interrelate with citation indices.

Afterwards, the paper discussed the essential role of the researcher in teaching, being a beacon of hope, as well as being a mentor when molding human minds of young students, then how the research is conducted, and how the ideas are construed in the researcher's mind by reading other research, conducting experiments, discussions, seminars, and from life. After conducting some research, an original idea is either deduced or the researcher resort to going back to the drawing board. When an original idea is reckoned, the researcher embarks on the quest and conduct more researcher either by experimenting or working on other research and reading. Subsequently, the step of writing research was the next topic to be discussed, then the paper discussed the financial support for researchers that entails submitting proposals, follow up proposals, grant management if funding is secured, whilst conducting the research, and publishing the results in accredited journals approved by the researcher's institute and financing partner. In addition, the paper discussed the importance of publishing the research in accordance with the laws and regulations of the institute. Consequently, the paper discussed the rate of the journal based on reputation of the journal and Journal Citation Rank (JCR) or scientific Journal Ranking (SJR), accordingly, the next section of this paper discussed the three most important words in ranking journals: ERA, Scopus, and ISI.

In this regard, the paper discussed paper publishing process, in terms of the cost and time efficiency coupled with the copy rights rules and regulations. Then the paper discussed the language barrier, in view that most of the web-based search engines and scientifically-oriented social network services are in English mainly, subsequently the paper discussed that being knowledgeable of current technology is becoming more indispensable, yet, unfortunately, not all researchers are tech savvy; many cannot understand nor comprehend the different interfaces with search engines and scientifically-oriented social network service, as such, a tailored training is required to help the researcher overcome this difficulty.

Subsequently, the paper discussed two discovering studies conducted at the University of Jordan – Aqaba and Princess Nourah Bint Abdulrahman University (PNU), to determine the level of being tech savvy of the scholars at both universities. The study aimed to discover if the researchers know/don't know about the different Scientifically-oriented Social network service, citation indices, bibliographic software, scholar search engines etc. The questionnaire identified whether teaching staff know of "Scientifically-Oriented Social network service", bibliographic software, scholar search engines, and their knowledge of different citing indices, whereby, measuring the savviness of the faculty members of the university, indicated the level of alignment of the faculty members with the university strive to become a globally recognized university.

Accordingly, in subsequent sections, the paper investigated the web-metrics, university ranking, accreditation bodies, and address the cause of accreditation, before discussing the survey results then conducted a comparison between the survey respondents from both universities.

DISCUSSION QUESTIONS

1. What is an impact factor, and why is important in the Academic world?
2. Why publishers and university push for highly cited journals/books and conferences?
3. What is the dilemma behind this researcher chapter? And why e-publishing is important?
4. What is the difference between ERA, ISI, and Scopus?
5. Why would a researcher publish papers, and conduct research?

REFERENCES

ABET. (2017). Retrieved from ABOUT ABET.: Http://www.abet.org/about-abet/

Abu-Taieh, E. (2016). Social Network Service for Scientists Difficulties Facing E-Publishing over Cloud Computing. International Journal of Technology Diffusion, 7(3), 10-20. doi:10.4018/IJTD.2016070102

Abu-Taieh, E. (2017). *Cyber Security Body of Knowledge. SC2 IEEE Conference*. IEEE. Retrieved from https://grid.chu.edu.tw/sc2-2017/AcceptedPaperList.php

Academia.edu. (2016). About academia.edu. Retrieved from http://www.academia.edu

ACM. (2017). *About*. Retrieved from The ACM Orgnization: www.acm.org

ACM & IEEE. (2013). *Curriculum Guidelines for Undergraduate Degree Programs in Computer Science*. New York: ACM IEEE; doi:10.1145/2534860

ACM & IEEE. (2016). *Curriculum Guidelines for Undergraduate Degree Programs in Computer Engineering*. New York: ACM IEEE; doi:10.1145/3025098

ACM & IEEE. (2017). Information Technology Curricula 2017. ACM IEEE. doi:10.1145/3173161

Adcock, R., Hutchison, N., & Nielsen, C. (2016). Defining an architecture for the Systems Engineering Body of Knowledge. *2016 Annual IEEE Systems Conference (SysCon)* (pp. 1-7). Orlando, FL: IEEE. 10.1109/SYSCON.2016.7490640

Alberts, C., Allen, J., & Stoddard, R. (2010). *Integrated Measurement and Analysis Framework for Software Security(CMU/SEI-2010-TN-025)*. Carnegie Mellon University. Retrieved 9 5, 2017, from http://resources.sei.cmu.edu/library/asset-view.cfm?AssetID=9369

Alberts, C., & Dorofee, A. (2012). *Mission Risk Diagnostic (MRD) Method Description(CMU/SEI-2012-TN-005)*. Carnegie Mellon University. Retrieved 12 12, 2017, from https://resources.sei.cmu.edu/asset_files/TechnicalNote/2012_004_001_15431.pdf

Alberts, C., & Woody, C. (2017). *Prototype Software Assurance Framework (SAF):Introduction and Overview (CMU/SEI-2017-TN-001)*. Carnegie Mellon University. Retrieved 12 12, 2017, from https://resources.sei.cmu.edu/asset_files/TechnicalNote/2010_004_001_15191.pdf

ANECA. (2017). Retrieved from National Agency for Quality Assessment and Accreditation of Spain ANECA: www.aneca.es/

ARC. (2018, Feb 18). Retrieved from The Australian Research Council: http://www.arc.gov.au/news-media/media-releases/arc-seeks-sectors-views-journal-rankings-era-initiative

Beall, J. (2014). *Google Scholar is Filled with Junk Science.* Retrieved 3 30, 2016, from Scholarly Open Access: https://scholarlyoa.com/2014/11/04/google-scholar-is-filled-with-junk-science/

Benslimane, Y., Yang, Z., & Bahli, B. (2016). Information Security between Standards, Certifications and Technologies: An Empirical Study. *Information Science and Security (ICISS), 2016 International Conference on* (pp. 1-5). Pattaya, Thailand: IEEE. doi:10.1109/ICISSEC.2016.7885859

Bijwe, A., & Mead, N. (2010). *Adapting the SQUARE Process for Privacy Requirements Engineering (CMU/SEI-2010-TN-022). Carnegie Mellon University.* Retrieved from https://resources.sei.cmu.edu/library/asset-view.cfm?AssetID=9357

Bourque, P., & Fairley, R. (2014). Guide to the Software Engineering Body of Knowledge (Swebok(R)): Version 3.0 (3rd ed.). Los Alamitos, CA: IEEE Computer Society Press.

Bridges, T. (2014). Retrieved 3 30, 2016, from MyScienceWork raises $1.1 million to fuel its international growth and roll-out new services: http://www.rudebaguette.com/2014/04/10/mysciencework-raises-1-1-million-fuel-international-growth/

Buettner, R. (2016). Getting a Job via Career-oriented Social Networking Sites: The Weakness of Ties. In *49th Hawaii International Conference on System Sciences (HICSS-49).* Kauai, Hawaii: IEEE. 10.1109/HICSS.2016.272

Burden, P. (2010). *A subject guide to quality Web sites.* Scarecrow Press, Inc. Retrieved from https://dl.acm.org/citation.cfm?id=1942832

Burnham, J. F. (2006, March 8). Scopus database: A review. *Biomedical Digital Libraries, 3*(1), 1. doi:10.1186/1742-5581-3-1 PMID:16522216

Chabrow, E. (2016). *IST Unveils a Cybersecurity Self-Assessment Tool:Gauging the Effectiveness of Risk Management Initiatives.* Princeton, NJ: Information Security Media Group, Corp. Retrieved from https://www.bankinfosecurity.com/aligning-cyber-framework-organizations-strategy-goals-a-9401

CHEA. (2017). Retrieved from Council for Higher Education Accreditation: http://www.chea.org/

Chen, P., Dean, M., Ojoko-Adams, D., Osman, H., Lopez, L., & Xie, N. (2004). *Systems Quality Requirements Engineering (SQUARE) Methodology: Case Study on Asset Management System* (CMU/SEI-2004-SR-015). Carnegie Mellon University. Retrieved 07 12, 2017, from https://resources.sei.cmu.edu/library/asset-view.cfm?assetid=6841

Chudnov, D. (2006). 6). COinS for the Link Trail. *Library Journal, 131*(12), 8–10.

CIPS. (2017). *Accredited Programs.* Retrieved from Canada's Association of I.T. Professionals: http://www.cips.ca/

CiteSeer. (2016). *History.* Retrieved 11 11, 2016, from CiteSeer: http://csxstatic.ist.psu.edu/about/history

Clarivate. (2018). *Databases.* Retrieved from clarivate: https://clarivate.com/products/web-of-science/databases/

Craigen, D., Diakun-Thibault, N., & Purse, R. (2014). Defining Cybersecurity. *Technology Innovation Management Review, 4*(10), 13-21. Retrieved from http://timreview.ca/article/835

Davis, Z. (2017). Definition of computer security. *PCMag.* Retrieved 11 3, 2017, from http://www.pcmag.com/encyclopedia/term/40169/computer-security

Dorogovtsev, S., & Mendes, J. (2015). Ranking Scientists. *Nature Physics, 11*(11), 882–884. doi:10.1038/nphys3533

Duarte, A., Duarte, D., & Thiry, M. (2016). aceBoK: Toward a Software Requirements Traceability Body of Knowledge. In *2016 IEEE 24th International Requirements Engineering Conference (RE)* (pp. 236-245). Beijing: IEEEXPLORE. doi:10.1109/RE.2016.32

EEC. (2018). *About EEC.* Retrieved from Education Evaluation Commission (EEC): https://www.eec.gov.sa/

El-Mahied, M. T., & Abu-Taieh, E. (2006). Information Systems in Developing Countries: Reasons for Failure –Jordan, Case Study. In M. Khosrow-Pour (Ed.), *IRMA-2006. 1* (p. 868). Idea Group Inc. Retrieved from http://www.irma-international.org/viewtitle/32934/

El-Mahied, M. T., Alkhaldi, F., & Abu-Taieh, E. M. (2009). Discovering Knowledge Channels in Learning Organization: Case Study of Jordan. In E. Abu-Taieh, A. El-Sheikh, & J. Abu-Tayeh (Eds.), *Utilizing Information Technology Systems Across Disciplines: Advancements in the Application of Computer Science* (pp. 190–209). Hershey, PA: IGI Global; doi:10.4018/978-1-60566-616-7.ch013

Ellison, N. B. (2007). Social network sites: Definition, history, and scholarship. *Journal of Computer-Mediated Communication, 13*(1), 210–230. doi:10.1111/j.1083-6101.2007.00393.x

ENQA. (2017). Retrieved from ENQA:European Association for Quality Assurance in Higher Education: Enqa.eu

era-2018. (2018, Feb 21). Retrieved from Excellence in Research for Australia (ERA): http://www.arc.gov.au/era-2018

Federal Financial Institutions Examination Council. (2015). *FFIEC Cybersecurity Assessment Tool.* Federal Financial Institutions Examination Council. Retrieved 6 6, 2017, from https://www.ffiec.gov/pdf/cybersecurity/FFIEC_CAT_June_2015_PDF2.pdf

figshare. (2016). *About figshare.* Retrieved from figshare: figshare.com/

Garfield, E. (1955). Citation Indexes for Science: A New Dimension in Documentation through Association of Ideas. *Science, 122*(3159), 108–111. doi:10.1126cience.122.3159.108 PMID:14385826

Gasser, M. (1988). *Building a Secure Computer System* (1st ed.). Van Nostrand Reinhold. Retrieved from https://ece.uwaterloo.ca/~vganesh/TEACHING/S2014/ECE458/building-secure-systems.pdf

Google Scholar Blog. (2011). *Google Scholar Citations Open To All.* Retrieved 3 30, 2016, from Google Scholar Blog: googlescholar.blogspot.com/2011/11/google-scholar-citations-open-to-all.html

Hane, P. (2013). *Sharing Research Data—New figshare For Institutions.* Retrieved 3 3, 2016, from Against The Grain Designed: www.against-the-grain.com/2013/09/sharing-research-data-new-figshare-for-institutions-2/

HEAC. (2018). *about HEAC.* Retrieved from Accreditation and Quality Assurance Commission for Higher Education: http://heac.org.jo

HE_India. (2017). *HE_India.* Retrieved from Higher Education in India: www.education.nic.in/higedu.asp

Hirsch, J. E. (2005). An index to quantify an individual's scientific research output. *Proceedings of the National Academy of Sciences.* 102, pp. 16569–16572. 10.1073/pnas.0507655102

HKCAAVQ. (2017). Retrieved from Hong Kong Council For Accreditation Of Academic & Vocational Qualifications HKCAAVQ: https://www.hkcaavq.edu.hk/en/

Howard, J. (2013). *Posting Your Latest Article? You Might Have to Take It Down.* Retrieved 3 3, 2016, from The Chronicle of Higher Education: https://www.chronicle.com/blogs/wiredcampus/posting-your-latest-article-you-might-have-to-take-it-down/48865

INQAAHE. (2017). *INQAAHE.* Retrieved from The International Network for Quality Assurance Agencies in Higher Education: http://www.inqaahe.org/presentation

Jacsó, P. (2010). Metadata mega mess in Google Scholar. *Online Information Review, 31*(1), 175–191. doi:10.1108/14684521011024191

JU. (2018, Feb 20). *Deanship of Academic Research and Quality Assurance.* Retrieved from The University of Jordan: http://research.ju.edu.jo/ar/arabic/Pages/AccreditedJournals.aspx

Kajko-Mattsson, M., Sjögren, A., & Lindbäck, L. (2017). Everything Is Possible to Structure - Even the Software Engineering Body of Knowledge. In *2017 IEEE/ACM 1st International Workshop on Software Engineering Curricula for Millennials (SECM)* (pp. 61-67). Buenos Aires: IEEE. doi:10.1109/SECM.2017.5

Khabsa, M., & Giles, C. (2014). The Number of Scholarly Documents on the Public Web. *PLoS One, 9*(5), e93949. doi:10.1371/journal.pone.0093949 PMID:24817403

Kissel, R. (2013). *Glossary of Key Information Security Terms.* doi: 10.6028/NIST.IR.7298R2

Klein, D., & Chiang, E. (2004). 4 1). The Social Science Citation Index: A Black Box—with an Ideological Bias? *Econ Journal Watch, 1*(1), 134–165.

KMK. (2017). *KMK.* Retrieved from German Council of Science and Humanities: http://www.akkreditierungsrat.de/

Kulkarn, A., Aziz, B., Shams, I., & Busse, J. (2009, September 9). Comparisons of citations in Web of Science, Scopus, and Google Scholar for articles published in general medical journals. *Journal of the American Medical Association, 302*(10), 1092–1096. doi:10.1001/jama.2009.1307 PMID:19738094

Labbe, C. (2010). Ike Antkare one of the great stars in the scientific firmament. *ISSI Newsletter, 6*(2). Retrieved 6 6, 2016, from http://evaluation.hypotheses.org/files/2010/12/pdf_IkeAntkareISSI.pdf

Lipner, S. (2015). Security Assurance. *Communications of the ACM, 58*(11), 24–26. doi:10.1145/2822513

Lunden, I. (2013). Confirmed: Elsevier Has Bought Mendeley For $69M-$100M To Expand Its Open, Social Education Data Efforts. *Techcrunch*. Retrieved 4 4, 2016, from https://techcrunch.com/2013/04/08/confirmed-elsevier-has-bought-mendeley-for-69m-100m-to-expand-open-social-education-data-efforts/

McGettrick, A. (2013). *Toward Curricular Guidelines for Cybersecurity- Report of a Workshop on Cybersecurity Education and Training*. ACM. Retrieved 12 12, 2017, from https://www.acm.org/education/TowardCurricularGuidelinesCybersec.pdf

Mead, N., Allen, J., Ardis, M., Hilburn, T., Kornecki, A., Linger, R., & McDonald, J. (2010). *Software Assurance Curriculum Project Volume I: Master of Software Assurance Reference Curriculum* (CMU/SEI-2010-TR-005). Software Engineering Institute. Carnegie Mellon University. Retrieved from http://resources.sei.cmu.edu/library/asset-view.cfm?AssetID=9415

Mead, N., Hilburn, T., & Linger, R. (2010). *Software Assurance Curriculum Project Volume II: Undergraduate Course Outlines* (CMU/SEI-2010-TR-019). Carnegie Mellon University. Retrieved 10 2017, 10, from http://resources.sei.cmu.edu/library/asset-view.cfm?AssetID=9543

Mouratidis, H., & Giorgini, P. (2007). *Integrating Security and Software Engineering: Advances and Future Visions*. Hershey, PA: Idea Group Publishing. doi:10.4018/978-1-59904-147-6

NACTE. (2017). Retrieved from National Accreditation Council for Teacher Education (NACTE): http://www.nacte.org.pk

NAEAC. (2017). Retrieved from About NAEAC: http://www.naeac.org.pk/

NBEAC. (2017). Retrieved from National Business Education Accreditation Council (NBEAC): www.pbeac.org.pk/

Ncaaa. (2018, Feb 2). Retrieved from national center for acadmic accrediatation: https://www.ncaaa.org.sa/Pages/default.aspx

NCEAC. (2017). Retrieved from National Computing Education Accreditation Council: http://www.nceac.org

NICCS. (2017). Retrieved from National NSA/DHS Centers of Academic Excellence in Information Assurance/Cyber Defense Focus Areas: https://niccs.us-cert.gov/sites/default/files/documents/pdf/cae_ia-cd_focusareas.pdf?trackDocs=cae_ia-cd_focusareas.pdf

NICE. (2013). Retrieved from National Cybersecurity Workforce Framework: https://www.nist.gov/itl/applied-Cybersecurity/nice/resources/nice-Cybersecurity-workforce-framework

Orduña-Malea, E., Ayllón, J., Martín-Martín, A., & Delgado López-Cózar, E. (2014). About the size of Google Scholar: playing the numbers. *EC3 Working Papers*, 18. Retrieved from https://arxiv.org/abs/1407.6239

Oren, T. I. (2005). Toward the body of knowledge of modeling and simulation. In *Interservice/Industry Training, Simulation, and Education Conference (I/ITSEC) 2005*. Orlando, FL: Simulation Conference. Retrieved 7 13, 2017, from http://www.site.uottawa.ca/~oren/pubs-pres/2005/pub-0513-MSBOK-IITSEC.pdf

Penzenstadler, B., Fernandez, M., Richardson, D., Callele, D., & Wnuk, K. (2013). The requirements engineering body of knowledge (rebok). In *Requirements Engineering Conference (RE) 2013 21st IEEE International*, (pp. 377-379). Rio de Janeiro, Brazil: IEEE. 10.1109/RE.2013.6636758

PNU. (2018, Feb 20). *Mechanism for Checking Journals Categorized under ISI or SCOPUS Databases*. Retrieved from Deanship of Scientific Research: http://www.pnu.edu.sa/arr/Deanships/Research/Documents/%D8%A2%D9%84%D9%8A%D8%A9%20%D8%A7%D9%84%D9%83%D8%B4%D9%81%20%D8%B9%D9%84%D9%89%20ISI%20or%20Scopus.pdf

Price, R. (2012). The Future of Peer Review. *TechCrunch*. Retrieved 4 4, 2016, from https://techcrunch.com/2012/02/05/the-future-of-peer-review/

PSRB. (2016). *Retrieved from Professional, Statutory and Regulatory Bodies (PSRBs) and professional accreditation of undergraduate programmes*. Higher Education Statistics Agency: www.hesa.ac.uk

Quezada-Sarmiento, P. A., Enciso-Quispe, L. E., Garbajosa, J., & Washizaki, H. (2016). Curricular design based in bodies of knowledge: Engineering education for the innovation and the industry. In *SAI Computing Conference (SAI), 2016* (pp. 843-849). London: IEEE. 10.1109/SAI.2016.7556077

RG facts. (2016). *Fact Sheet – ResearchGate*. Retrieved from ResearchGate: www.researchgate.net/aboutus.AboutUsPress.downloadFile.html?

Scopus. (2018, Feb 10). *About Scopus*. Retrieved from ELSEVIER: https://www.elsevier.com/solutions/scopus

Thomson Reuters. (2016). *Fact Sheet*. Retrieved from Thomson Reuters.: thomsonreuters.com/content/dam/openweb/documents/pdf/scholarly-scientific-research/fact-sheet/wos-next-gen-brochure.pdf

Trending, R. G. (2016). *Discover the world's top research*. Retrieved from RG Trending: www.researchgate.net/trending/publications

U.S. Department of Education. (2017, 8 9). Retrieved from Regional and National Institutional Accrediting Agencies: https://www2.ed.gov/admins/finaid/accred/accreditation_pg6.html

Walrad, C. C. (2016). The IEEE Computer Society and ACM's Collaboration on Computing Education. *Computer*, *49*(3), 88–91. doi:10.1109/MC.2016.67

Yong, A. (2014). Article *Notices of the American Mathematical Society*, *61*(9), 1040–1050. doi:10.1090/noti1164

ADDITIONAL READING

Burnham, J. F. (2006, March 8). Scopus database: A review. *Biomedical Digital Libraries*, *3*(1), 1. doi:10.1186/1742-5581-3-1 PMID:16522216

Garfield, E. (1955). Citation Indexes for Science: A New Dimension in Documentation through Association of Ideas. *Science*, *122*(3159), 108–111. doi:10.1126cience.122.3159.108 PMID:14385826

Harhoff, D., Narin, F., Scherer, F. M., & Vopel, K. (1999). Citation frequency and the value of patented inventions. *The Review of Economics and Statistics*, *81*(3), 511–515. doi:10.1162/003465399558265

Hirsch, J. E. (2005, 11 15). An index to quantify an individual's scientific research output. *Proceedings of the National Academy of Sciences*. 102, pp. 16569–16572. PNAS. 10.1073/pnas.0507655102

Jacsó, P. (2010). Metadata mega mess in Google Scholar. *Online Information Review*, *31*(1), 175–191. doi:10.1108/14684521011024191

Khabsa, M., & Giles, C. (2014). The Number of Scholarly Documents on the Public Web. *PLoS One*, *9*(5), e93949. doi:10.1371/journal.pone.0093949 PMID:24817403

Kulkarn, A., Aziz, B., Shams, I., & Busse, J. (2009, September 9). Comparisons of citations in Web of Science, Scopus, and Google Scholar for articles published in general medical journals. *Journal of the American Medical Association*, *302*(10), 1092–1096. doi:10.1001/jama.2009.1307 PMID:19738094

Lunden, I. (2013). Confirmed: Elsevier Has Bought Mendeley For $69M-$100M To Expand Its Open, Social Education Data Efforts. *techcrunch*. Retrieved 4 4, 2016, from https://techcrunch.com/2013/04/08/confirmed-elsevier-has-bought-mendeley-for-69m-100m-to-expand-open-social-education-data-efforts/

Page, L., Brin, S., Motwani, R., & Winograd, T. (1999). *The PageRank citation ranking: Bringing order to the web*. Stanford InfoLab.

Price, R. (2012). The Future of Peer Review. *TechCrunch*. Retrieved 4 4, 2016, from https://techcrunch.com/2012/02/05/the-future-of-peer-review/

KEY TERMS AND DEFINITIONS

Citation Index: An indicator that represents the number of intellectual work cited by other than author.

Cloud Computing: The use of internet and storage devices on-line and processing.

E-Publishing: Electronic publishing is publishing on-line intellectual work.

Search Engines: A website that allows a computer user to search the internet.

Chapter 13
An Empirical Study of the Factors Influencing ICT Adoption in SMEs

Japhet E. Lawrence
Deakin University, Australia

ABSTRACT

ICT has the potential to radically change the way business is conducted, offering a competitive edge and a gateway to the global marketplace. The explosive growth of ICT has opened a vast arena providing opportunities for businesses, particularly SMEs to sell their products and service to a global audience than they would have been able to afford to reach using the traditional methods. This chapter reports on the empirical study of ICT adoption in small to medium-sized enterprises. The intention of the study is to present evidence on the factors that influence SMEs' decision to adopt ICT in business. The study is chosen because of the strategic importance of SMEs to the economy and their contribution in creating jobs cannot be over emphasized. The study uses in-depth case studies, conceptualized within the grounded theory method to generate thick description to explain the phenomenon. The study uses diffusion theory and the technology acceptance model as a basis for the theoretical framework.

INTRODUCTION

Small to Medium-sized Enterprises (SMEs) are extremely important to many countries, in some countries these group of organizations provide the foundation for the entire economy (Mason, 1997), their contribution to the economy cannot be over emphasised. These enterprises serve as drivers of economic growth and innovation. SMEs comprise firms that make up a sizeable proportion of UK industry (Oftel, 2000). They account for more than 50% of private sector employment in the UK and are currently contributing most of private sector employment growth (DTI, 1998). In most countries, SMEs constitute more than 98% of the total number of businesses (OECD, 2000). However, these categories of enterprises face multiple challenges. To minimise the challenges, several solutions have been suggested including the adoption of ICTs to boost efficiency and competitiveness.

DOI: 10.4018/978-1-5225-6367-9.ch013

Technologies are being adopted and incorporated into nearly all organizations, particularly Information communication technologies (ICTs) which have the potential to radically change the way businesses are conducted (Lawrence, 2002). ICTs refer to the wide range of computerised information and communication technologies. These covers all technologies used for the handling and communication of information and their use, specifically in organisation. For example, the Internet, wireless networks, email, mobile telephony, digital recording equipment, tablet, PCs, laptops and other communication mediums, computer networks as well as necessary enterprise software, middleware, storage, and audio-visual systems, which enable users to access, store, transmit, and manipulate information (Ashrafi & Murtaza, 2008). ICTs provide a great deal of opportunities, as well as challenges for SMEs. In an increasingly global world, both information and information technology are of great significance to organisations of all sizes. The adoption and use of ICT in business is widely seen as critical for the competitiveness of SMEs in the global marketplace (Lawrence, 2013).

The adoption of ICT presents a unique opportunity for SMEs to participate in electronic commerce and extend their capabilities and grow in a global market. The Internet provides more opportunities for businesses, particularly SMEs to sell their products and services to a global audience than they would have been able to afford to reach using the traditional methods. The effective use of ICT can add significant value to an organisation in terms of productivity increase and performance improvements (Lawrence, 2009). The establishment of an environment in which SMEs can grow and prosper in the global market is considered critical to the development and expansion of businesses in the economy.

The purpose of this study is to empirically investigate the factors that influence the adoption of ICT in SMEs business and to generate a grounded theory, not to test a theory that has been determined a priori. Previous studies (Orlikowski, 1993) show that theoretical grounding for understanding and developing clear process of ICT adoption, integration and implementation has been lacking. The present study aims to fill this gap by building on the work done so far by using grounded theory method to develop a model designed to explain and enhance the understanding of the factors that influence SMEs' decision to adopt ICT in business.

BACKGROUND

SME is chosen as the main context of this study because of the strategic importance of this sector to growth and job creation. Businesses in this sector include those which are flexible to new working patterns and who are innovators in the adoption of new business practice. There is no universal definition of SMEs that is widely accepted, the definition varies from country to country but is often based on employment, assets or a combination of the two. The term Small to Medium-sized Enterprises (SMEs) incorporates two primary classifications - small business and medium business. Hence, different definitions are used in different countries. For instance, OECD (2004) defines SMEs as enterprises that have less than 500 employees. while in Australia, SMEs are defined as enterprises that have between five and 199 employees (Kotey & Folker, 2007). In Britain, the Department of Trade and Industry (DTI) defines SMEs as a company employing between 1-249 employees. The current study is based on DTI SME definition of small business thus: independently owned and managed; being closely controlled by owners/managers who also contribute most, if not all, of the operating capital, having the principal decision-making functions resting with the owner/manager; with total number of employees less than 50. While Medium-sized enterprise is defined as business that is larger than small business and smaller than large business with total employees greater 50 and less than 250.

SME comprises firms that make up the sizeable proportion of UK industry (99.8%), and are therefore very important to the UK economy. SMEs account for more than 59% of private sector employment in the UK and currently are contributing most of the private sector employment growth (BERR, 2008). According to the Observatory of European SMEs (2007), the average SME across all European enterprises employ 6.8 people. At both the European Union and national level, SMEs lie at the heart of policy making with the emphasis on encouraging enterprise and promoting business growth. SMEs are an important link to boosting the levels of innovation in the national economy and fostering greater competition both domestically and increasingly, internationally. In Canada, where SMEs account for 45% of GDP, much of the economy's growth, 60% of all jobs in the economy, and 75% of net employment growth. SMEs are an integral part of the country's economic fabric and are important to the economy. "The success of SMEs affects the well-being of the Canadian society as engines of job creation, economic growth and innovation" (CFIB, 2000). Apart from the economic significance of SMEs, the sector's social significance is widely recognized. In many cases, SMEs reflect the more personal and unique characteristics of a community than larger firms do. SMEs often serve specific market niches, the very presence of which can be a manifestation of special social and cultural characteristics. The greater independence and entrepreneurial nature of SMEs are thought to embody desirable social values and their presence is regarded as an important source of social stability (Lawrence, 2015).

Barnes et al. (2008) argue that the advent of the digital economy has made the adoption and use of ICT a significant issue for most SMEs. Yet, many SMEs find themselves in a tricky situation. Research shows (Barnes et al., 2008) that SMEs may be too small to be able to employ a dedicated IT expert and lack the resources to buy consultancy advice. SMEs often have limited experience in selecting, implementing and evaluating suggested IT solutions. Barnes et al. (2008) note that SMEs find themselves caught in a trap, lack of resources means that while there may be an aggregate demand for IT service and advice, individually, the varying nature of that demand makes it uneconomical for other firms to provide a service meeting that demand.

MAIN FOCUS OF THE CHAPTER

The Nature and Characteristics of SMEs

Literature shows that SMEs posses' specific attributes that distinguish them from the large organisations most often studied regarding information systems usage (Auger & Gallaugher, 1997; Cragg & King, 1993). Other studies (Lawrence, 2008, 2013; MacGregor et al., 1998) have shown that SMEs' characteristics are different from larger organizations. SMEs differ from large companies in the way they develop their corporate strategies and their technology policies (Lawrence, 2008; MacGregor et al., 1998). Large companies typically have well-defined processes for developing and implementing strategies through a corporate planning process (Pool et al., 2006). While SMEs often use less structured approaches, strategies and policies that may not be formulated but may 'emerge' from a set of actions and experiments (Lawrence, 2008).

MacGregor et al. (1998) and Cragg and King (1993) show the differences in management style between large businesses and SMEs. These studies have shown that among other characteristics, SMEs tend to have a small management team (often one or two individuals), they are strongly influenced by the owner and the owner's personal habits. SMEs have little control over their environment (this is supported by the studies of Barnes et al., 2008; and Lawrence, 2008). SMEs have strong desire to remain independent. Other studies (Lawrence, 2002, 2013) show that small businesses tend to be riskier than their larger counterpart. Most SMEs lack technical expertise (Cragg & King, 1993; Blili & Raymond 1993), lack adequate capital to undertake technical improvements (Wymer & Regan, 2005; Auger & Gallaugher, 1997) and most suffer from inadequate organizational planning.

Majority of SMEs may be too small to employ a dedicated IT expert (Wymer & Regan, 2005; Auger & Gallaugher, 1997), lack resources and expertise both financial and intellectual and especially in terms of management of innovative technologies to buy consultancy advice (MacGregor et al., 1998). These authors agree that SMEs are more vulnerable because of their lack of financial and human resources, as well as information resources that are needed to sufficiently understand and master the organisation and its environment (Wymer & Regan, 2005). Many SMEs do not possess the technological background, which would enable them to use and evaluate ICT, or lack the time to explore it (Barnes et al., 2008). SMEs find themselves caught in a trap and lack of resources means that while there may be an aggregate demand for ICT service and advice, individually. The varying nature of that demand makes it uneconomical for other firms to provide a service meeting that demand. It is often the skill and enthusiasm of the owner-manager that typically drives the business forward and shapes the character of investment decisions (Barnes et al., 2008; Dixon et al., 2002). Yet the need to remain flexible and innovative is the criteria for survival and success for most SMEs.

On the other hand, Cameron and Clarke (1996) add that some of the features of SMEs' made ICT use ideal for their businesses. These include flexibility and their ability to change and adapt quickly to innovations compared to large organisations, which are very slow to respond to changes (Blili & Raymond, 1993). SMEs are generally less formal in their organisational and managerial practices and have less sophisticated IT capabilities and expertise than larger organisations. They are less likely to suffer 'lock-in' with respect to existing plants; technologies or organisational structure. SMEs tend to exhibit more informal communication and a less bureaucratic mode of operation and less rigid functional divisions (Lawrence, 2009).

Potential Use of ICTs in SMEs

The use of ICT in organisations has been the focus of many research studies because of its importance in improving organisation performance (Lawrence, 2002). Businesses both large and small have seized the opportunity to explore its use and how to become more productive and competitive. ICT is already being put to a myriad of different uses: educational, recreational, commercial etc. According to Lawrence (2002), the explosive growth and commercialisation of ICT has led to widespread usage of online services such as shopping, audio and video applications including telephony and videoconferencing. Research indicates that commercial activities now account for a substantial proportion of growth of the Internet (Lawrence, 2013). ICT offers an increasingly diverse platform for innovative ways of doing business and new opportunities through which SMEs can conduct ecommerce (Golden & Griffin, 2000). It offers opportunities to businesses that transcend those of the traditional media; for example, easy access to global markets (DTI, 1998).

There is tremendous potential for SMEs to harness the power of ICT to improve their productivity and sharpen their competitive edge in both local and international markets (Chatteqee & Sarnbamurthy, 1999). The adoption and use of ICT presents a unique opportunity for SMEs to participate in ecommerce, extend their capabilities and grow in a global market. Lawrence (2013) argues that ICT use is becoming increasingly important as a mechanism to increase productivity, reduce costs and facilitates flexibility in SMEs business. ICT provides global connectivity based on non-proprietary technology and allows SMEs to access global markets, foster relationships from a business to business (B2B) and business to customer (B2C) perspective. ICT is a relatively low-cost information technology infrastructure, which enables SMEs to be involved in ecommerce technologies most appropriate to their business requirements (Chatterjee & Sambamurthy, 1999).

The participation of SMEs in global market is possible due to the absence of barriers to entry, it is argued that ICT tears down boundaries of time and space, enabling smaller firms to create entirely new businesses and reach new markets they could never have reached before. The global reach of ICT and its range of services (e.g. information dissemination, interactive communication, and transactional support) makes it a potentially powerful business resource for SMEs (Chatterjee & Sambamurthy, 1999). ICT presents an arena in which small companies can create an ecommerce strategy that can enable them to compete effectively against large companies. Despite the unprecedented growth in the use of ICT in organisations, however, there are some unresolved issues that have accompanied the growth of ICT such as security of information and legal issues (Clarke, 1996). Added to these are technology problems such as the lack of standards and overloaded communication lines, resulting in inaccessibility of sites and sources of information and poor response times (Auger & Gallaugher, 1997).

LITERATURE REVIEW

This study interrogates two key theoretical issues on the adoption of ICT in SMEs: (a) the diffusion of innovation theory and (b) technology acceptance model. These theoretical perspectives offer differing, but overlapping, insight into the factors that influence SMEs decision to adopt ICT in business.

The use of these models widens the scope of inquiry and pools the lessons learned from research that spans disciplines and methodologies and provide insights that may help to extend the depth and breadth of understanding the adoption of ICT in SMEs.

Diffusion of Innovation Theory

Rogers (1995) diffusion of innovation theory is used to study a variety of innovations. Rogers defines diffusion as "the process by which an innovation is communicated through certain channels over time among the members of a society". Rogers' diffusion of innovation theory focuses on the adoption of innovation from a sociological perspective and has been successfully applied in the Information Systems context to explain the adoption of innovations (Tornatzky & Klein, 1982). Most past studies on adoption have used Rogers' (1995) diffusion of innovations theory to identify the attributes of innovation that influence technological adoption at individual or organisational level (Fichman, 1992). The theory is one of the most enduring and widely cited theories for studying adoption of information technologies, it offers useful insights into the reasons surrounding the widespread uptake of innovative ideas such as ICT in organisation (Galliers & Swan, 1999). Wolfe (1994) argues that most often, the adoption of innovation could not be understood without careful attention to the personal, organisational, technological and environmental contexts with which it takes place. Within the context of ICT adoption in SMEs, both organisational and individual level factors are undoubtedly important in understanding the factors that influence ICT adoption in SMEs. Rogers (1995) defines innovation as an idea, practice, or object (ICT) that is perceived as new by the adopter (SMEs). Thus, an innovation can be a new idea such as a new way of doing things, e.g. email or a new hardware technology. Technological innovation like ICT can create uncertainty in the minds of potential SMEs (e.g., about its expected consequences on the breach of security of information) as well as representing an opportunity for SMEs to reduce uncertainty in another sense (its ability to reach global audience). The latter type of potential uncertainty reduction represents the possible efficacy of ICT in solving SME's felt need or perceived problems.

Rogers (2003) states that characteristic of an innovation as perceived by members of a social system (SMEs) determines its rate of adoption. He identifies five innovation characteristics that may contribute to the rate of adoption of innovation as relative advantage, compatibility, complexity, observability, and trialability; explained as follows: i) Relative advantage: "the degree to which an innovation is perceived as better than the idea it supersedes". Rogers (1995) suggests that the greater the perceived relative advantage of an innovation, the more rapid its rate of adoption is going to be. ii) Compatibility: "the degree to which an innovation is perceived as being consistent with the existing values, past experiences, and needs of potential adopters". Tornatzky and Klein (1982) found that innovation is more likely to be adopted when it is found to be compatible with potential adopter's job responsibilities and the value system (Ndubisi & Sinti, 2006). iii) Complexity: "the degree to which an innovation is perceived as difficult to understand and use". Rogers suggests that novel ideas that are simpler to understand are adopted rapidly than the ones that require the adopter to develop new skills and understanding. Lawrence (2013) found that complexity could negatively influence the adoption of ICT. iv) Trialability: "the degree to which an innovation may be experimented with on a limited basis". It measures the extent to which potential adopters perceive an opportunity to experiment with the innovation prior to committing to its usage (Agarwal and Prasad, 1998). v) Observability: "the degree to which the results of an innovation are visible to the others".

The relationship between an innovation's characteristics and adoption has been examined in several past empirical works, most notably by Orlikowski (1993), Cragg and King (1993), Galliers and Swan (1999), Fichman (1992) and Wolfe (1994). These studies are particularly helpful in the effort to understand the factors that influence ICT adoption in SMEs. However, in each of these studies, one must use caution in applying concepts derived from the large organisational context to the SME context (Mason, 1997). Tornatzky and Klein (1982) assert that relative advantage, compatibility and complexity are the three most relevant constructs for the adoption of innovation. The five elements of Rogers' diffusion of innovation theory have considerable domination in the innovation diffusion studies and have been successfully adapted to study the diffusion of technological innovation (Patel & Connolly, 2007).

Technology Acceptance Model

To understand the factors influencing adoption and acceptance of technology, information systems research has taken a wider perspective to study the factors affecting adopter's behaviour to adopt technology. Davis (1989) proposes Technology Acceptance Model (TAM), which provides a firm theoretical foundation for the stream of information systems research with an objective to predict behaviour of individuals or organisation to adopt a technology. According to Davis, Bagozzi, and Warshaw (1989), "the goal of TAM is to provide an explanation of the determinants of computer acceptance that is general and capable of explaining user behaviour across broad range of end-user computing technologies and user populations, while at the same time being both parsimonious and theoretically justified". Davis (1989) technology acceptance model is an adaptation of theory of reasoned action (Ajzen & Fishbein, 1980) that is specifically meant to explain factors that influence users' acceptance and actual use of information technology in a work place. It represents an important theoretical contribution toward understanding Information Systems usage and Information Systems acceptance behaviours (Patel & Connolly, 2007). TAM offers promising theoretical base for examining the factors that influence ICT adoption in SMEs.

TAM posits that two distinct constructs, Perceived Usefulness and Perceived Ease of Use, directly affect the attitude toward target system use and indirectly affect actual system use (Davis, 1993). TAM posits that beliefs, attitudes, and intentions are crucial factors in the adoption of ICT in organisation. Davis (1989) defines perceived usefulness as "the prospective user's subjective probability that using a specific application system will increase his or her job performance within an organisational context". A system high in perceived usefulness, in turn, is one for which a user believes in the existence of a positive use-performance relationship. Perceived ease of use, in contrast, refers to "the degree to which a prospective user believes that using a particular system would be free of effort". All else being equal, Davis claims, an application perceived to be easier to use than another is more likely to be accepted by users (Davis, 1989). Several researchers have used TAM in their work to examine the factors influencing web technology adoption by consumers (Gefen, Karahanna & Straub 2003; Gefen & Straub 2000). Adams, Nelson, Todd (1992) report that there are a wide variety of ways in which perceived usefulness and perceived ease of use can be applied. The model may be used in organisations to make selections between contending software packages and it may also be used by researchers interested in understanding factors that influence the success of information systems or it may be used in studies within and across organisations by researchers who are interested in understanding the diffusion of information technology and the determinants of technology adoption (Patel & Connolly, 2007).

RESEARCH QUESTION

The study is cross-sectional in nature and the data for this study was collected over a six-month period. The objective of the study is to contribute toward a fuller understanding of ICT adoption in SME setting and hence contribute to the cumulative body of research in this area. To achieve this, the study proposes a more enriched model for conceptualising the technological, organisational, environmental and contextual issues around the adoption of ICT—issues that have been largely missing from contemporary discussions of ICT usage (Orlikowski, 1993). To realise this research objective, the study, especially the data-gathering process, is guided by the main research question. What are the factors that influence ICT adoption in SMEs? The research uses in-depth case studies, conceptualised within the grounded theory method to generate thick description to explain the phenomenon.

RESEARCH DESIGN

The study takes the form of exploratory and descriptive research, focusing on the factors that influence ICT adoption in SMEs. To achieve the study objectives, multi-case study of seven SMEs was conducted to provide answers to ICT adoption in SMEs. The study uses qualitative approach to provide an in-depth description, conceptualised within the grounded theory method to explain the factors that influence ICT adoption in SMEs business, the research approach used for this study is shown in figure 1.

Data Collection

Case Study Design

The study uses an emergent, exploratory, inductive qualitative case study approach. This is because the basis of such an approach is one that does not predetermine or delimit the directions the investigation might take. According to Lincoln and Guba (1985), the emergent design of a naturalistic inquiry does not allow for a detailed plan before the research began "the research design must therefore be 'played by ear'; it must unfold, cascade, roll and emerge". The design for the case study began as a broad outline of contingency plans open for modification and extension as necessary during the study. The design assumes a worldview in which there are multiple realities, that is the world is not an objective thing out there, but a function of interactions and perception (Merriam, 1988) and these realities are complex, dynamic and change overtime. This view is important to this research which is attempting to bring understanding and interpretations to processes or events as perceived by SMEs in their natural setting.

A multi-case study of seven SMEs was used to provide reasons why SMEs adopt ICT in their business. Case study method lends itself to getting out into the natural setting of the phenomenon under

Figure 1. Outline of research approach
Source: Adapted from Walsham, 1993

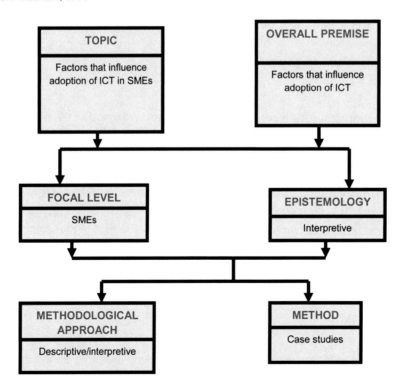

investigation. The benefits of multi-case study have been discussed by other information systems researchers (Yin, 1984). According to Yin, case study can involve single or multiple cases and numerous levels of analysis. Yin suggests that multiple case designs are desirable when the intent of the research is descriptive, theory building or theory testing. Benbasat et al. (1987) argue that multiple case studies enable the researcher to relate differences in context to constants in process and outcome, and multiple cases allow for cross case analysis and the extension of theory. Miles and Huberman (1984) add that multiple cases enable the researcher to verify that findings are not merely the result of idiosyncrasies of the research setting. The multi-case study was designed as a series of interviews and site visits. Most authors are vague when it comes to suggesting how many cases to study, Eisenhardt (1989) suggests that multiple case designs require the study of at least four, but not more than ten cases. The number of cases in this study was planned in advance and the study involved seven SME cases. These cases were purposefully selected from the SMEs that had previously completed the survey questionnaire in phase one of the studies. The case studies employed multiple data sources and have as their focus, the factors that influence ICT adoption in SMEs. The multiple data sources have been chosen to give as many insights into the phenomenon as is feasible and to assist in theory generation.

Case Participants

Twenty-six SMEs were approached to participate in the case study. The criteria for inclusion were based on a need for each participating SME to conform to the definition of SMEs and a willingness on the part of the SME owners/mangers to disclose details of their business. Several potential SMEs were rejected because they did not satisfy the criteria. A total of seven SMEs that satisfied the criteria were chosen to participate in the study. These SMEs were chosen across business sectors so that the study could investigate the existence of sector-independent issues. This was important to avoid observations specific to a sector. The first SME was selected at random from the seven SMEs that participated in this study, to provide the first body of data. Then subsequent data collection was guided by the theoretical sampling principle of grounded theory as defined by Strauss and Corbin (1990); i.e. sampling based on concepts that have proven theoretical relevance to the evolving theory. Letters were emailed to the owner/managers of each of the selected SMEs requesting a one-hour interview. An availability form indicating choices of available dates and time for interview was also sent. The purpose of the study and the nature of the research were clearly spelled out as were assurance of confidentiality. The participants were asked open-ended questions. The primary details of the SMEs that participated in the case study are shown in table 1 in no significant order.

Interview

Interviews are arguably the primary data sources where interpretive case study research is undertaken (Yin, 1994), as it is through interviews that researchers can best access case participant's views and interpretations of actions and events (Walsham, 1995). Kaplan and Maxwell (1994) indicate that the primary goal of interview is to elicit the respondent's views and experiences in his or her own words rather than to collect data that are simply a choice among pre-established response categories. Interviews are flexible enough to favour adaptation to each context, organisation and to pursue unexpected paths and cues suggested by the theoretical sensitivity (Glaser & Strauss, 1967) developed by the researcher throughout the research process. Interview was selected as one of the suitable forms to collect data in the

Table 1. Details of SMEs that participated in the case study

SMEs	Type of Business	Size (employees)
BIL	Peugeot cars franchise holder	20
BPC	Publishing	25
SAH	Health care	200
MGL	Manufacturer of contract carpets	9
AL	Manufacturer and seller of educational engineering equipment	40
FP	Specialist flooring manufacturer	110
CLR	Cigarette paper manufacturer	180

Source: (Case study data, 2017)

case study, because the technique provided face-to-face contact with the social actors also it provided the additional benefit of allowing the researcher to recognise and process non-verbal communications. The interviews were structured to gather data about the widest possible range of issues associated with the phenomenon under study. The research questions guided the data-gathering process. The structure and content of subsequent interviews were determined after the data analysis process had commenced. The interviews were used to gather new data about known concepts and categories that have been developed about the phenomenon and to involve the SMEs in a process of testing and verifying data and the emerging theory. The use of interview made it possible for the researcher to probe and explore responses and to develop insight into how the participants interpret and make meaning of the world. All data was treated in a way that it protected the confidentiality and anonymity of the SMEs involved in the study. Coding was used during the gathering and processing of interview notes, tapes and transcripts.

DATA ANALYSIS

The process of data analysis in qualitative research "involves working with data, organising it, breaking it down, synthesising it, searching for patterns, discovering what is important and what is to be learned, and deciding what you will tell others" (Bogdan & Biklen, 1982). Throughout data collection, data analysis took place through systematic procedures, regarding abstraction and comparison outlined in the grounded theory method (Glaser & Strauss, 1967). The grounded theory approach uses an iterative pathway moving from data collection to emergent theory and back again until theoretical saturation is reached.

Grounded Theory Method

The selection of grounded theory (Glaser & Strauss, 1967; Strauss & Corbin, 1990, 1998) amongst a myriad of other qualitative analysis methods is to generate a descriptive and explanatory theory of adoption of ICT rooted in the experiences of SMEs. The defining characteristic of grounded theory is that of a general methodology for discovering theory that is grounded in data systematically gathered and analysed. The objective of the study is the development of a conceptual model that explains the adoption of ICT in SMEs and it fits well with the philosophical nature of grounded theory, which is useful in understanding the contextual elements that constitutes the focus of this study. The theory evolves during actual research, and it does this through a continuous interplay between analysis and data collection; data analysis guides data collection. Strauss and Corbin (1990) identify three levels of analysis: (a) present the data without interpretation and abstraction, the participants tell their own story; (b) create a "rich and believable descriptive narrative" using field notes, interview transcripts and researcher interpretations and (c) build a theory using high levels of interpretation and abstraction. This study combines the second and third approaches, to present rich and detailed descriptions that allows the reader to make sufficient contextual judgements to transfer the study findings to alternative settings. The concern here is with the multiple constructions of reality as experienced by SMEs.

Data analysis in grounded theory involves specific procedures which, when applied appropriately and with vigilance will result in theory that is rigorous and well-grounded in the data. The grounded theory coding methods are: open coding, axial coding and selective coding with the understanding that a researcher may alternate between all three forms of analysis depending upon the changing circumstances of the study (Glaser & Strauss, 1967). Coding is "the crucial link between collecting data and developing an emergent theory to explain the data". Strauss and Corbin (1990) recommend line-by-line open coding that gets researcher off the empirical level by fracturing the data, then conceptually grouping it into codes that then become the theory, which explains what is happening in the data. Axial coding involves re-building the data (fractured through open coding) in new ways by establishing relationships between categories and their subcategories. Selective coding is to integrate and refine the categories into a theory, which accounts for the phenomenon being investigated and validates the statements of relationships among concepts, and fills in any categories in need of further refinement. Memo writing is occurring throughout the analytic process whereby memos elaborate processes, assumptions, and actions that are subsumed under codes.

CASE STUDY ANALYSIS

The aim of the case study is to produce an in-depth, holistic study (Yin, 1984), which is fully grounded in the data that gives the reader sufficient contextual and environmental descriptions to allow them to transfer the case studies based on conceptual applicability (Dey, 1993). The case studies are reported with sufficient detail and precision to allow judgements about transferability. The material here is drawn from seven separate field studies carried out within the broad tradition of interpretive case study (Orlikowski, 1991; Walsham, 1993), which involved extensive interviewing of key participants (e.g. company owner or manager in each of the SMEs), coupled with the use of documentary evidence such as company reports. Seven SMEs were studied and analysed in turn, a strategy adopted by Orlikowski (1993), the data analysis process involved identifying patterns in the case study data. These patterns included issues raised repeatedly across interviews, commonly found in ICT usage in business activities or opinions, which kept re-appearing. The data were analysed within each case as well as across the cases to detect similarities and compare differences. The initial concepts that emerged in one case context were then contrasted, elaborated, and qualified in the other. Within the first case, the iterative approach of data collection, coding, and analysis was more open-ended, and generative, focusing on the development of concepts, properties, and relations, and following the descriptions of how to generate grounded theory set out by Glaser and Strauss (1967) and Eisenhardt (1989).

The detailed write-up of the cases and all the data generated by interviews, and documentation were examined and coded by focusing on the factors that influence ICT adoption in business. The case data was read and categorised into concepts that were suggested by the data rather than imposed from outside. This is known as open coding (Strauss & Corbin, 1990, 1998) and it relies on an analytic technique of identifying possible categories and their properties and dimensions. Once all the data were examined, the concepts were organised by recurring theme. These themes became prime candidates for a set of stable and common categories, which linked several associated concepts. This is known as axial coding (Strauss & Corbin, 1990) and it relies on a synthetic technique of making connections between subcategories to construct a more comprehensive scheme. The case data were then re-examined and re-coded using this proposed scheme, the goal being to determine sets of categories and concepts that covered as much of the data as possible. This iterative examination yielded a set of broad categories and associated concepts that described the salient conditions, events and experiences associated with adoption of ICT in this first SME case. These initial concepts guided the remaining case study, allowing the process of data collection, coding, and analysis to be more targeted. Following the constant comparative analysis method (Glaser & Strauss, 1967), the initial SME case's experiences were systematically compared and contrasted with the second SME case. This analysis also used Miles and Huberman's (1984,1994) technique for across-site pattern comparison and clustering that involves matrix displays to compare key events, triggers, and outcomes, see table 2. The presence of these categories is indicated by a 'Yes' in the table.

Data from the second SME case was first sorted into the initial concepts generated by the first SME data. It soon became clear however, that the initial concepts generated by the first SME case did not accommodate some of the findings emerging from the second SME case. Accommodating the second SME case's experiences, led to some important elaborations and clarifications in the emerging theoretical framework, and forced a reconsideration of some of the first SME case's experiences. For example, the category environmental factor did not include a concept of external pressure from trading partners,

Table 2. Across case pattern comparison

Core Categories	Subcategories	Small to Medium-Sized Enterprises						
		AL	SAH	BIL	BPC	FP	MGL	CLR
SME Characteristic	Knowledge of ICT	Yes	Yes	Yes	Yes	Yes	Yes	Yes
	Attitude toward ICT	Yes	Yes	Yes	Yes	Yes	Yes	Yes
Technological	Compatibility	Yes	Yes	Yes	Yes	Yes	Yes	Yes
	Cost effectiveness	Yes	Yes	Yes	Yes	Yes	Yes	Yes
	Benefits of using ICT	Yes	Yes	Yes	Yes	Yes	Yes	Yes
	Perceived usefulness of ICT	Yes	Yes	Yes	Yes	Yes	Yes	Yes
	Perceived ease of use of ICT	Yes	Yes	Yes	Yes	Yes	Yes	Yes
Organizational	Management support	Yes	Yes	Yes	Yes	Yes	Yes	Yes
	Organizational resources	Yes	Yes	Yes	Yes	Yes		Yes
	Organizational size						Yes	
Environmental	Competitive pressure	Yes			Yes	Yes	Yes	Yes
	External pressure			Yes	Yes		Yes	

Source: (Case study data, 2017)

as this was not salient in the first SME case. The second SME case's experiences, however, indicated that they started using ICT because they were pressurised into doing so by their trading partners, which was indeed very relevant in shaping the interpretations and use of ICT, and substantially influenced their ICT adoption.

The process of comparing and contrasting the SME case data was repeated for the remaining SME cases. Redefining the initial concepts to incorporate considerations of the second SME case's experiences required returning to the first SME case data, and re-sorting and re-analysing them to take account of the richer concepts and more complex relations now constituting the framework. This ability to incorporate unique insights during the study is one of the benefits of a grounded theory approach, an example of what Eisenhardt (1989) labels "controlled opportunism," where "researchers take advantage of the uniqueness of a specific case and the emergence of new themes to improve resultant theory" (Eisenhardt, 1989). The iteration between data and concepts ended when enough categories and associated concepts had been defined to explain what had been observed at all the SME cases, and no additional data was found, to develop or add to the set of concepts and categories, a situation Glaser and Strauss (1967) refer to as "theoretical saturation". The resultant framework is empirically valid as it accounts for the unique data of each SME case, as well as generalise patterns across all the SME cases (Eisenhardt, 1989). The core categories and subcategories that emerged from the analysis are shown in table 3.

Table 3. Core categories and subcategories that emerged from the case data analysis

Core Categories	Subcategories
SME Characteristic factors	Knowledge of ICT
	Attitude toward ICT
Technological factors	Compatibility
	Complexity
	Cost effectiveness
	Benefits of using ICT: • *The ICT generates new business opportunities* • *Communication medium to improve organizational efficiency* • *Easy entry into new markets* • *Promotional and adverting* • *Global markets reach* • *Easy access to global information*
	Perceived usefulness of ICT
	Perceived Ease of use of ICT
Organizational factors	Management Support
	Organizational resources
	Organizational size
Environmental factors	Competitive pressure
	External pressure

Source: (Case study data, 2017)

DISCUSSION OF CASE STUDY RESULTS

This section presents the results of the SMEs' experiences with the adoption of ICT in business. The results from the case study were used to develop a theoretical model for conceptualising the organisational issues around the adoption of ICT--issues that have been largely missing from contemporary discussions of ICT usage (Orlikowski, 1993). The results of the multiple case studies are discussed in terms of the categories that emerged from the grounded theory analysis process. The intention is to identify and give substance to each of the categories. The adoption factors that emerged from the SMEs' experiences with ICT are depicted in figure 2.

Figure 2 shows the categories and concepts that emerged as salient from the case data analysis, as well as their relationships. This theoretical model is proposed as an initial formulation of the key factors that influenced SMEs decision to adopt ICT in business. It attempts to show a 'map of the territory' based on the analysis developed from the case study data. It is "the researcher's first cut at making some explicit theoretical statements" (Miles & Huberman, 1994). The researcher sees the theoretical model as simply the current version of the map of territory being investigated. No claim is made that the factors and categories presented here are exhaustive. Further organisational studies of the adoption of ICT should add to or modify the ideas presented here. The categories constituting the factors that influence SMEs' decision to adopt ICT in business are discussed below.

Figure 2. Proposed conceptual model of ICT adoption
Source: Case study data, 2017

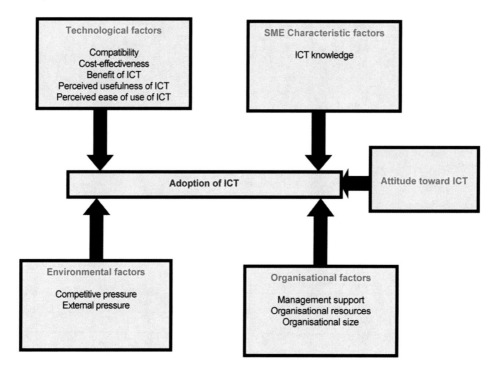

Adoption of ICT

Researchers have identified several indicators of IT acceptance. The most generally accepted measures of IT in organisations appear to be user satisfaction (Yap et al., 1992), system usage and frequency of use has been employed as measure of implementation success (Davis, et al., 1989). However, system usage has been the primary indicator of technology acceptance (Adams et al., 1992), system usage has a notable practical value for managers interested in evaluating the impact of IT. The focus of the case study is on the factors influencing ICT adoption in SMEs. Therefore, adoption of ICT is used as an indicator of ICT adoption in SMEs. It is important to note that ICT usage relates to the ICTs in its entirety rather than to a specific function (email, web or Internet) of ICT.

Attitude Toward ICT

Attitude toward ICT refers to SMEs' general feeling of favourable or unfavourable use of ICT in business process. The attitudes of SMEs toward ICT can influence adoption of ICT, if SMEs have negative attitudes toward technology, providing them with excellent ICT facilities may not influence them to use it in their business. The case study result shows that all the SMEs that participated in the study have positive attitude towards the use of ICT. The case results support others (Schiller, 2003) which found attitudes of SMEs toward technology greatly influence adoption of ICT in business. Lawrence (2008) concurs with Schiller that found attitude as a crucial factor in adoption of ICT in business. Lawrence argues that to successfully implement technology in business depends strongly on SMEs' support and attitudes. It is believed that if SMEs perceived technology as neither fulfilling their needs nor their customers' needs, it is likely that they will not adopt the technology into their Business. If SMEs' attitudes are positive toward the use of technology then they can easily provide useful insight about the adoption of ICT (Lawrence, 2008). SMEs' attitude is supported by Davies (1989) that found SMEs' attitudes towards technology influence their acceptance of the usefulness of technology and its adoption in business.

SME Characteristics Factors

The adoption of ICT is strongly governed by SMEs' characteristics such as ICT knowledge, resources, time and attitude towards ICT can influence adoption. SME that has ICT knowledge is in a better position to judge the usefulness of adopting and using ICT in business activities. The study evidence shows that SME's ICT knowledge is an important concept in understanding the adoption of ICT. According to Koehler and Mishra (2009), technology knowledge includes understanding ICT broadly enough to apply it productively and being able to recognize when ICT can assist or impede the achievement of a goal. SMEs adopt and use ICT into their business activities, if they have the skill or knowledge alongside their pre-existing content and knowledge to judge the effectiveness of the technology and not by its sheer existence. Literature shows that inadequate ICT knowledge and improper perceptions of SMEs towards technologies may hinder the adoption of ICT and their respective usage in business. According to Finger et al. (2013), the basic technical knowledge and skills related to technologies are necessary to adopt them into business effectively. SMEs tend to adopt and use more technology in their business if they have high levels of confidence in technologies being useful in their business (Karatas et al., 2017). The case result shows that all the SMEs in the case study use some form of technology in their business activities. The case study finding is supported by Schiller (2003) that found adopter characteristics such as experience with computer and attitude towards computers can influence the adoption of technology in business. SMEs' computer experience relates positively to their attitudes toward ICT usage. The more experience SMEs have with computers, the more likely that they will show positive attitudes towards computers (Lawrence, 2008).

Technological Factors

Technological factors represent the perceived characteristics of ICT. The adoption is strongly governed by how SMEs perceive ICT and its capability to leverage it for business use. If SMEs perceive that the use of ICT offers relative advantage over other technologies, for example reducing cost of communications, then it is likely to be adopted. The technological factor is described by five characteristics of ICT that emerged from the case study analysis, which are found to explain the adoption of ICT in SMEs. These characteristics are compatibility of ICT, cost effectiveness, benefits of using ICT, perceived usefulness of ICT as a business tool and perceived ease of use of ICT in carrying out tasks. Evidence from previous study suggests that technological characteristics as perceived by SMEs influence the rate of adoption (Rogers, 2003).

Compatibility

The compatibility of ICT refers to the degree to which the use of ICT is perceived as being consistent with the existing practices, values, past experiences, and the needs of SMEs. The objectives of most SMEs using any technology in business is to improve efficiency and reduce operational costs. The case results show that across all SMEs, there is evidence of compatibility of ICT to existing business practices. BPC reports: "The use of ICT enables us to co-ordinate and work more efficiently". While BIL reports: "The use of ICT levels the playing field, giving us the opportunity to advertise to a global market and compete with larger companies". The case result shows that compatibility is a significant factor contributing to the adoption of ICT, the emphasis lies in the fit between the characteristics of the technology and the characteristics of the task. The more an innovation is compatible with the current situation of a potential adopter and its needs, the lesser are the switching costs and uncertainties, the more probable the innovation will be adopted (Frambach, 1993). The case findings provide support for diffusion of innovation theory and it is consistent with prior research which has shown that successful innovations occur when the task and the technology are compatible (Tornatzky & Klein, 1982). Greater compatibility of technological innovation with the existing technical systems, hardware, software, operating practices, and the value and belief systems of the adopting unit has been cited to be favourable to its rate of adoption and diffusion (Rogers, 2003).

Cost-Effectiveness

The cost-effectiveness of ICT compares to the initial cost of introducing the technology in the organisation to the potential paybacks that can be generated. From the early days of its conception, IT has been used to save money (Kimbrough & Lee, 1997). The use of ICT enables SMEs to place brochure, catalogue, corporate information, and support material on-line for a fraction of the cost of print counterparts. The positive reaction toward the web's low cost of entry reinforces Rogers' (1995) claim that trialability is a significant factor in the adoption of an innovation. A favourably low cost-benefit ratio helps to convince and reinforce the advantages of ICT, and hence promotes its adoption. The low costs of Internet presence made it a low-risk strategy and very appealing to SMEs that lack the financial resources to use other methods of communicating to customers and marketing their products (Cragg & King, 1993). Most SMEs do not have the resources of big companies to advertise their products in the traditional way; however, ICT offers them the opportunity to mount aggressive advertisement just as the big companies. It provides SMEs with the cheapest form of advertisement relative to the number of people that it can reach. AL reports: "A small company with a suitable product or service to sell can create as much of an impact in its own domain as a large business". CLR reports: "We sell our merchandise through online and we regard it as a more cost-effective means of selling merchandise than the traditional route". The case result shows that cost benefit is the most important when deciding to use ICT. This is certainly not surprising, since business decisions must be financially viable and because of SMEs limited financial resources (Cragg & King, 1993). While SMEs commonly use ICT to reach more customers globally, the most immediate business case justification is cost reduction (Auger & Gallaugher, 1997). The cost effectiveness of ICT is found to be a crucial factor that influences adoption and use of ICT (Kimbrough & Lee, 1997). Kimbrough and Lee (1997) indicate that the most profound consequences of using ICT in business is the dramatic decrease in the transaction costs of conducting and maintaining inter-organisational relationships. ICT as an innovation is significant in that SMEs perceive the financial obstacles to their participation in ecommerce have been reduced to the point where they can experiment without an overly burdensome commitment (Auger & Gallaugher, 1997).

Benefit of ICT

Benefits of using ICT is similar to Rogers (1995)' relative advantage. ICT benefit deals with the degree of managerial valuation of the relative advantage that can be derived from the use of ICT in business. The degree of relative advantage is often expressed in economic profitability, savings in time and effort, cost reduction or status given (Cragg & King, 1993). A higher managerial recognition of ICT benefits (i.e., direct and indirect benefits) increases the likelihood of the allocation of the managerial, financial, and technological resources necessary to the adoption and use ICT (Lawrence, 2002). The case result shows the greater the perceived relative advantage of an innovation, the more rapid its rate of adoption is going to be. This is consistent with the findings of other diffusion scholars that have found relative advantage as the only variable that has been consistently identified as one of the most critical adoption factors (Rogers, 2003; Tornatzky & Klein, 1982) and as the most crucial factor for information technology growth in small firms (Cragg & King, 1993). Mason (1992) reports similar findings that most SMEs decide to adopt innovative technologies based on perceived benefits and costs savings. The case evidence shows some of the major benefits gained from the use of ICT as cost reduction, ability to generate new business opportunities, operational efficiency, increased ability to compete, promotional and image building, global market reach, easy access to global information and easy entry to new markets. The evidence of these perceived benefits is presented and discussed in turn.

ICT Generates New Business Opportunities

The case study result indicates that six of the SMEs (BPC, FP, MGL, AL, BIL and CLR) report generating businesses through using ICT. The others had either improved their competitiveness and business performance or access to international markets. Using ICT to conduct transactions remove all the geographic constraint found in the traditional method and it is considered the most cost-effective means to sell products to wider markets. Most of the SMEs believe that engaging in ecommerce, have allowed them to capture unexpected business opportunities. BPC reports: "Customers are more willing to communicate to us through email". FP reports: "We have received overseas investors' inquiries concerning special floor tile, we wouldn't have had it without being online". MGL reports: "... ICT is a very important source for getting and ordering products for our business". AL reports: "The sales we have generated from being online have all been outside our area and would not have occurred otherwise". BIL reports: "The online platform is another selling tool to provide information and advertise products to the global audience". CLR reports: "The use of ICT has enabled us to sell CLR wear to a wider audience".

Communication Medium to Improve Organizational Efficiency

The evidence reveals that SMEs most often use ICT as a communication medium to improve organisational efficiency and as a 'dynamic' and 'interactive way of communicating to customers. All the SMEs used ICT primarily in this way and they reported that its use had made communication easier, better and faster. The speed of communication and speed of access to information and the documentary record of action of email was regarded as beneficial. Email delivers flexibility and convenience to communications, particularly for many small businesses that rely on personal contact with their customers. AL reports: "With email, documents could be exchanged as email attachments and this greatly reduced the turnaround time and without added communication costs". BPC reports: "We use email to exchange design documents with our business partners". BIL reports: "Email is a quick and effortless way to communicate to customers on a global basis". AL reports: "Having an email was as necessary as the need for a fax number". FP reports: "The use of email for communication has been quite a breakthrough, because there is less paper about". MGL reports: "We can easily and quickly communicate to customers and potential customers at a very low cost". CLR reports: "The good thing about email is that you've got a written record of it".

Easy Entry Into New Markets

The ICT is a great leveller. It allows easy entry into new markets, especially geographically remote markets, as the playing field becomes more level between companies of different sizes and budgets, thereby giving SMEs the opportunity to compete with larger companies on an equal footing. BIL reports:"... all sites on the Internet are equal irrespective of company size. We regard the Internet as a great equaliser, where a smaller company like us can be a larger company in a global market". FP reports:"... eliminating time zones, natural barriers, and country borders not only aids a company with internal communications, it also levels the playing field for businesses".

Promotional and Advertising

The case evidence shows that the promotional and advertising benefits of the ICT are very important in the decision to adopt. All the SMEs view ICT as a medium for advertising to supplement the traditional media of television, radio, and print. AL reports: "ICT offers us an opportunity for promoting our products and its use has made us aware of our competitors and markets in general". The evidence demonstrates that most of the SMEs view their web sites as an important part of their advertising effort and consider its use as a major part of their publicity and a means to establish their companies in the global world. It offers them a real opportunity to do business round the clock and Web is an effective way to reach and test new international markets. It is regarded as one of the benefits that being online can offer SMEs particularly smaller companies that cannot afford to develop their business abroad through traditional channels.

Global Market Reach

SMEs market is bounded by the customers it can reach effectively. Two SMEs (AL and BPC) have used ICT to expand markets and contact customers previously out of reach. ICT removes geographic boundaries, allowing even the smallest business to easily and cheaply reach potential customers around the globe for a fraction of what it costs to do direct mail or run advertisements in a magazines or newspapers. Customers can make purchases from anywhere in the world as easily as they can from a shop down the street. Expanding customers and markets and reachability are the driving force in the adoption and use of ICT in business. AL reports: "We have generated sales outside our area that would not have occurred otherwise". SAH reports: We use it to provide information to the public regarding the activities of the hospice". BPC reports: "Long distance demonstrations can be made through video conferencing, which can achieve what a face-to-face meeting can but without any of the associated travel costs or time away from the office".

Easy Access to Global Information

All the SMEs use ICT to access information previously unavailable or unknown to them, this includes the ability to search databases worldwide. Three of the SMEs (AL, FP and MGL) report using the ICT to search for customer information and obtain specific information for marketing purposes. The result suggests that reducing operational costs of traditional communication and information access are some of the benefits of using ICT in business. This is evident in terms of speed of access to information and in terms of overcoming time zone restrictions. In general, the enhanced speed of communication is viewed as advantageously as is the speed of access to information. AL reports:"... ICT provides us with instant access to a myriad of information relevant to our business". FP reports: "We use ICT to easily access a repository of databases of information useful to the running of our business". MGL reports: "The use of ICT enables us to maintain communication with our overseas customers and business associates".

Perceived Usefulness of ICT

The perceived usefulness of ICT is defined as the prospective SMEs' subjective probability that using ICT will increase job performance and improve efficiency (Davis 1989). The use of ICT for communication is especially useful in that it provides an efficient, informal and inexpensive method of communicating with customers and business associates. ICT is also regarded as a useful tool for market research to find out about the movement and trends in marketplace, the actions of business competitors and partners. Across all SMEs, ICT is perceived as an extremely useful business tool for information dissemination to customers, to search and gather information, to communicate and to provide better customer service. FP reports: "The use of ICT has facilitated the collaboration of work with colleagues based in our overseas offices". CLR reports: "It has made us work more efficiently and helps us to interact with our customers and get feedback from them". MGL reports: "... ICT allows us to cast a wider net, which meant that retrieving information became much easier". BPC reports: "ICT provides the easiest, most efficient, and most cost-effective means of gathering information". The case result supports what other empirical studies have suggested that SMEs are more likely to adopt ICT if they perceive it as a useful tool to perform tasks (Davis et al., 1992). These findings support Adams et al. (1992) and Davis et al. (1989) that found SMEs' adoption of ICT is driven to a significant extent by perceived usefulness of the technology.

Perceived Ease of Use of ICT

Perceived ease of use of ICT refers to the degree to which ICT technology is perceived by SMEs as relatively easy to use (Davis, 1989). The perceived ease of use of ICT emerged in the case study as one of the categories directly influencing SMEs decision to adopt ICT in business. This finding supports Adams et al. (1992) which found both perceived usefulness and perceived ease of use as important determinants of system usage. Davis, Bagozzi and Warshaw (1989) identify perceived ease of use as an important determinant of system usage through perceived usefulness. The case evidence shows that across all SMEs, ICT was perceived as easy to use particularly email and searching for information. MGL reports that ICT is a quick and easy means to communicate to customers. In general, innovative ideas that are simpler to understand will be adopted more rapidly than innovations that require the adopter to develop new skills and understandings (Rogers, 2003). All else being equal, Davis claims, an application perceived to be easier to use than another is more likely to be adopted (Davis, 1989).

Organizational Factors

Organisational factors are those categories affecting the organisational structure that the organisation could adjust or change to suit its changing environment. Three categories that emerged from the analysis include management support, organisational resources and organisational size.

Management Support

Management support refers to the perceived level of widespread support offered by management. Management is not only expected to carry on the crusade for adoption within the organisation. They need to take responsibility for overcoming the apprehension and resistance to ICT, organising needed resources and being closely involved in various phases of adoption and implementation (Ramamurthy & Premkumar, 1995) and convince staff of the benefits that will accrue from adopting and using ICT in business. It is argued that SMEs with full management support would most likely consider adopting ICT in response to the current technological trends and market demands, where as a lack of it has often been cited as a barrier to effective use of technology (Lawrence, 2013). The case results show that across all SMEs, there is evidence of managerial enthusiasm towards ICT adoption and use in business. AL reports: "The managers at AL frequently use ICT in their work. The amount of information that we can get about things useful to our business is endless". BPC reports: "The owner of BPC, although not a hands-on user, encouraged all his employees to use the ICT". McMaster et al. (1997) report that active involvement and management support can provide the appropriate strategic vision and direction. Management support and commitment are crucial factors in the adoption and use of ICT in SMEs. The more support given by management, the more likely organisational resources would be allocated to the implementation of innovation decisions, which will in turn facilitates the adoption and success of an innovation. The case result is consistent with previous organisational and IS research (Wolfe 1994; Cragg & King, 1993), which found management support to be important in the adoption of innovation. This suggest that management support is much more important in small firms where the owner or CEO is commonly involved in most key operational decisions due to lack of managerial staff (Lawrence, 2008).

Organizational Resources

Organisational resources refer to the level of financial and technological resources of SMEs. The result shows that SMEs tend to lack the organisational resources (i.e., capital, people, and technology) that are necessary for ICT and other IT investments and this usually limits their ability to receive the full strategic benefits of the technology (Cragg & King, 1993). SMEs with adequate financial and technological resources are better equipped to undertake a complex innovation such as ICT and consequently are more likely to enjoy higher benefits from its use. This is consistent with the case study findings, which shows that if SMEs do not have the necessary resources, they are less likely to adopt ICT in business. Therefore, organisational resources are necessary key elements to the adoption of ICT. This is consistent with past research (Iacovou et al., 1995; MacGregor et al., 1998) that found organisational resources are influential in the adoption of IT. Clarke (1996) identifies lack of organisational resources as a specific impediment to the widespread adoption and usage of the Internet in organisation.

Organizational Size

The case evidence shows that size of SMEs is a key factor in the adoption of ICT in business. For large organisation, there may be a greater necessity to adopt some innovations than for smaller ones. This is not surprising because size, especially in financial measures indicate the resources available to larger SMEs than smaller ones. The medium businesses in the case study were more enthusiastic about ICT adoption and usage than the smaller businesses. The case study findings support others (DTI, 1998) which found that size of business is a key factor in the general adoption of computer technology. The DTI survey found that large companies have higher levels of ownership of hardware and infrastructure than SMEs. Although firm size was not included in Iacovou et al.'s (1995) model, they found size to be closely related to adoption of EDI.

Environmental Factors

Environmental factors are those changes in the business environment that create threats as well as opportunities for an organisation and are usually beyond the control of management of individual SME. The two categories that emerged as being influential in the adoption of ICT are competitive pressure and external pressure from trading partners.

Competitive Pressure

Competitive pressure refers to the level of ICT usage of the SMEs' industry and, most importantly, to that of its competitors. The case result shows that few of the SMEs adopted ICT in their business because of the perception of increased competition within and from other industries. These SMEs interpreted the pressures as threats to their competitive position and their profitability ratio. This is the view expressed by four of the SMEs (AL, FP, BPC and CLR), the nature of their business also means that ICT can help them to be more effective in their operations. Information is clearly a tool of key strategic value for SMEs, ICT can significantly alter the way business is conducted by improving business functions such as communication, marketing and customer service (Lawrence, 2002). SMEs can use ICT to differentiate their products or services they provide to their customers. ICT offers several opportunities that can turn into organisational advantages if they are combined with an appropriate business strategy (Lawrence, 2013). Chatterjee and Sambamurthy (1999) point out that the interactive capability of the technology enables SMEs to provide better customer service and to tap their existing and prospective customers for ideas to differentiate their individual products and services through quality features, brand name and packaging.

However, Reynolds (1997) argues that having an online presence is not a source of sustainable competitive advantage as the technology can easily be copied. Reynolds suggests that there are two strategic uses. First, ICT can be an information medium for new products and services. Second, it can be used to provide value-added services that cannot be easily provided otherwise. Porter (1984) identifies five competitive forces: new entrants, threat of substitute, bargaining power of customer, bargaining power of suppliers, and rivalry among current competitors. Porter suggests that, by adopting ICT, businesses will be able to change their competitive environment in three ways: by changing the industry structure, altering rules of competition, and giving businesses innovative ways to outperform their rivals.

The case evidence suggests that some SMEs are jumping on the ICT bandwagon to maintain their competitive positions. MGL reports: "As you know to compete in today's competitive market, organisations have to follow the trend and join the ICT revolution". AL explains:"... one of the main reasons that encouraged us to use ICT is because almost every other company in the world is using it". SAH reports: "We started to use ICT just to keep in line with the way information technology is going, we do not want to be left behind". A high level of competition among firms in a certain industry may enlarge the pressure on an individual SME to adopt certain technological innovation. As more competitors and trading partners adopt and use ICT, SMEs are more inclined to adopt the technology to maintain their own competitive position. The case result is consistent with previous research on IT (Porter, 1984; Cragg and King, 1993) that found competitive pressure as influential in the innovation adoption decision. In cases where firms do not do so, they may find that the adoption of that specific innovation by other firms may create a competitive disadvantage for it (Frambach, 1993).

External Pressure

External pressure refers to influences from the organisational environment, for example an imposition from trading partners. A few SMEs report external pressure as a very influential factor in adopting and using ICT in business. In three cases (BIL, MGL and BPC) external influences affected adoption, including ICT's increasing popularity and the rising number of online users. Two of these SMEs (BIL and BPC) indicated being pressured to adopt and use ICT technology in business. BIL reports: "We started using ICT, because we were asked to use it by our trading partner (Peugeot manufactures), and as a dealer with them, we have no choice but to start using it or risk losing our dealership". MGL reports: "We started using ICT, because we think conducting business online is getting popular and there are more and more people using Internet for every day transactions". BPC reports: "... unless you appear to be installing the latest technology and keeping it or you will be in danger of losing your clients".

The case result shows that the adoption of ICT seems to be prompted by external pressure rather than by a serious business decision. This is in line with other studies (Iacovou et al., 1995), which found external pressure as the strongest explanatory variable influencing small businesses to adopt EDI. Iacovou et al. (1995) reveal that a firm's decision to adopt EDI "is primarily based on what its business partners are doing and not on the characteristics of EDI". The pressure from large trading partners is especially significant and influential in the case of EDI because of the need for networking between them (Iacovou et al., 1995).

Small businesses have used EDI in a way that was originally established by their principal customers and they have not used the technology because of the opportunities it offers them or as part of business strategy (Lawrence, 2008). The imposition from trading partners is one of the most critical factors for ICT adoption by SMEs, they are the weaker partners in inter-organisational relationships and they are extremely susceptible to impositions by their larger partners (Iacovou et al., 1995).

FUTURE RESEARCH DIRECTIONS

The research has drawn conclusions about the adoption of ICT in SMEs' business and has laid a foundation on which further longitudinal studies could be undertaken. The study has identified SME characteristic, technological, organisational and environmental factors as influential in the adoption of ICT in SMEs' business. Additional research could be conducted to determine if other kinds of technological innovations are affected by these factors. Further empirical study is needed to assess the validity of the theoretical model proposed in this study to develop an appreciation of the relative contributions of the model's constructs. As with any other simple model, there is a danger that additional significant factors have not been included in the model. Longitudinal investigations would allow researchers to measure the explanatory factors that emerged from the study before the adoption of ICT and more objectively assess the impact of ICT on the organisations. Further research should also examine the impact of ICT adoption on the performance of SMEs.

CONCLUSION

The central concern of this study has been in gaining deep insight into the factors that influence SMEs' decision to adopt ICT in business. The study has identified and discussed the factors that positively influenced SMEs' ICT adoption in business. The study has developed an adoption model that considered the SME characteristics, technological, organisational and environmental factors, which explained the adoption of ICT in SMEs. The author has argued both theoretically and where possible using empirical evidence, why these categories helped to better understand and explain ICT adoption in SMEs. The study's results provided significant support to past findings in innovation and information systems literature. The study was presented in a descriptive form and chronicles the perceptions and experiences of SMEs' adoption of ICT in business. Zeller (1991) cited in Miles and Huberman (1994) suggests that studies with an interpretive perspective don't report out "data", they report "scenes" i.e. accounts of researchers' engagement over time with participants in their surroundings. Hammersley (1992) adds that "an account is valid or true if it represents accurately those features of the phenomenon that it is intended to describe, explain or theorise". The study has presented the current picture of the factors that influenced SMEs' decision to adopt ICT in business. It has told story of ICT adoption from the perspective of the SME cases examined in the study.

The conclusions of the study were based on the analysis of the SMEs studied and not on a population. It is not the goal of an interpretive study to make generalisations from the examined SMEs, but rather to offer understanding or insights about the adoption of ICT in SMEs business. A rich, thick description of the cases allows readers to make decisions regarding transferability of the research (Merriam, 1988). This study has presented considerable progress in explaining the factors influencing the adoption of ICT in SMEs. The findings provided theoretical and practical insights into the adoption and use of ICT in SMEs. The study has contributed to the existing body of research on technology usage in organisation in general and particularly ICT adoption in SMEs. Finally, the research reported here contributes to what is hoped will be a continually expanding body of empirical evidence that can increase knowledge of ICT adoption and usage in business.

DISCUSSION QUESTIONS

1.   What are the key driving forces of ICT adoption and usage in Small to Medium-sized Enterprises?
2.   What are the distinctive characteristics that differentiate SMEs from large companies
3.   How does SMEs benefit from using ICT as a competitive tool?
4.   What are the challenges for SMEs in using ICT as a competitive tool?
5.   How does using ICT gives SMEs competitive advantage?
6.   Discuss how SMEs could use ICT to become competitive
7.   Discuss the factors limiting ICT adoption and usage in SMEs
8.   What are the perceived benefits of adopting and using ICT in SMEs' business operations?
9.   How does using ICT impact on SMEs performance?
10.   Identify the major barriers hindering ICT adoption and usage in SMEs' business?

REFERENCES

Adams, D. A., Nelson, R. R., & Todd, P. A. (1992). Perceived usefulness, ease of use and usage of information technology: Replication. *Management Information Systems Quarterly*, *16*(June), 227–247. doi:10.2307/249577

Agarwal, R., & Prasad, J. A. (1998). Conceptual and Operational Definition of Personal Innovativeness in the Domain of Information Technology. *Information System Research*, *19*(2), 204-215.

Ajzen, I., & Fishbein, M. (1980). *Understanding attitudes and predicting social behavior*. Englewood Cliffs, NJ: Prentice-Hall.

Ashrafi, R., & Murtaza, M. (2008). Use and impact of ICT on SMEs in Oman. *The Electronic Information Systems Evaluations*, *11*(3), 125–138.

Auger, P., & Gallaugher, J. (1997). Factors affecting the adoption of an Internet-based sales presence for small businesses. *The Information Society*, *13*(1), 55–74. doi:10.1080/019722497129287

Barnes, D., Dyerson, R., & Harindranath, G. (2008). *If it isn't broken, don't fix it*. Retrieved from http://www.rhul.ac.uk/Management/Research/PRISM/index.html

Benbasat, I., Goldstein, D. K., & Mead, M. (1987). The Case Research Strategy in Studies of Information Systems. *Management Information Systems Quarterly*, *11*(3), 369–385. doi:10.2307/248684

BERR. (2008). Retrieved from July 15, 2015 http://stats.berr.gov.uk/ed/sme

Blili, S., & Raymond, L. (1993). Information technology: Threats and Opportunities for Small and Medium Enterprises. *International Journal of Information Management*, *13*(6), 439–448. doi:10.1016/0268-4012(93)90060-H

Bogdan, R. C., & Biklen, S. K. (1982). *Qualitative research for education: An introduction to theory and methods*. Boston: Allyn and Bacon.

Burgess, L., & Cooper, J. (1999). A Model for Classification of Business Adoption of Internet Commerce Solution. *Twelfth Bled Electronic Commerce Conference, Global Networked Organizations*.

Cameron, J., & Clarke, R. (1996). Towards a Theoretical Framework for Collaborative Electronic Commerce Projects Involving Small and Medium-Size Enterprises. *Proc. Of the 9th International Conference EDI-IOS*.

CFIB. (2000). *Internet Use among Small and Medium-sized Firms*. Retrieved from August 10, 2015 www.bcstats.gov.bc.ca/pubs/sbq/sbq01q1.pdf

Chatterjee, D., & Ramamurthy, V. (1999). Business Implications of Web Technology: An Insight into Usage of the World Wide Web by US Companies. *The International Journal of Electronic Commerce and Media*, *9*(1/2), 9–13.

Clarke, R. (1996). *Issues in Technology-Based Consumer Transactions*. Retrieved from http://www.anu.edu.au//Roger.Clarke/SOS/SCOCAP96.html

Cragg, P., & King, M. (1993). Small-Firm Computing: Motivators and Inhibitors. *Management Information Systems Quarterly*, *17*(1), 47–59. doi:10.2307/249509

Davis, F. D. (1989). Perceived Usefulness, Perceived Ease of Use, and User Acceptance of Information Technology. *Management Information Systems Quarterly*, *13*(3), 319–340. doi:10.2307/249008

Davis, F. D., Bagozzi, R. P., & Warshaw, P. R. (1989). User Acceptance of Computer Technology: A Comparison of Two Theoretical Models. *Management Science*, *35*(8), 982-1003

Department of Trade and Industry (DTI). (1997, 1998). *Moving into the Information Age: An International Benchmarking Study*. Retrieved July 25, 2010 http://www.dti.gov.uk

Department of Trade and Industry. (1999). *How the Internet can work for you*. Retrieved July 25, 2010 http://www.dti.gov.uk

Dey, I. (1993). *Qualitative Data Analysis: A user-friendly guide for social scientists*. London: Routledge. doi:10.4324/9780203412497

Dixon, T., McAllister, P., & Thompson, B. (2002). *The value of ICT for SMEs in the UK: A critical Literature Review*. Retrieved from http://www.cem.ac.uk/itribe.htm

Eisenhardt, K. M. (1989). Building theories from Case Study Research. *Academy of Management Review*, *14*(4), 532–550.

European Commission. (1998). *Awareness creation activities in electronic commerce for SMEs* (2nd ed.). Retrieved July 2, 2010 http://ispo.cec.be/ecommerce/books/awarenessbook.html

Fichman, R. G. (1992). Information technology diffusion: A review of empirical research. *Proceedings of the Thirteenth International Conference on Information Systems*, 195-206.

Finger, G., Jamieson-Proctor, R., & Grimbeek, P. (2013). *Teaching teachers for the future project: building TPACK confidence and capabilities for eLearning*. Paper presented at the 5th International Conference on Educational Technologies, Malé, Maldives.

Frambach, R. T. (1993). An integrated model of organizational adoption and diffusion of innovation. *European Journal of Marketing*, *27*(5), 22–41. doi:10.1108/03090569310039705

Galliers, B., & Swan, J. (1999). Information systems and strategic change: A critical review of business process reengineering. In W. Currie & B. Galliers (Eds.), *Rethinking Management Information Systems*. Oxford, UK: University Press.

Gefen, D., Karahanna, E., & Straub, D. (2003). Trust and Tam in Online Shopping: An Integrated Model. *MIS Quarterly*, *27*(1), 51-90.

Gefen, D., & Straub, D. (2000). The Relative Importance of Perceived Ease of Use in IS Adoption: A Study of E-Commerce Adoption. *Journal of Association for Information Systems*, *1*(8), 1-22.

Glaser, E. G., & Strauss, A. L. (1967). *The Discovery of Grounded Theory: Strategies for Qualitative Research*. London: Weidenfeld and Nicolson.

Golden, W., & Griffin, M. (2000). The World Wide Web: Savior of small firms. *13th International Bled Electronic conference*, Bled, Slovenia.

Hammersley, M. (1992). *What's wrong with ethnography? Methodological explorations*. London: Routledge.

Iacovou, C., Benbasat, I., & Dexter, A. (1995). Electronic Data Interchange and Small Organizations: Adoption and Impact of technology. *Management Information Systems Quarterly*, *19*(4), 465–485. doi:10.2307/249629

Kaplan, B., & Maxwell, J. A. (1994). Qualitative Research Methods for Evaluating Computer Information Systems. In J. G. Anderson, C. E. Aydin, & S. J. Jay (Eds.), *Evaluating Health Care Information Systems: Methods and Applications* (pp. 45–68). Thousand Oaks, CA: Sage publications.

Karatas, I., Tunc, M. P., Yilmaz, N., & Karaci, G. (2017). An Investigation of Technological Pedagogical Content Knowledge, Self-Confidence, and Perception of Pre-Service Middle School Mathematics Teachers towards Instructional Technologies. *Journal of Educational Technology & Society*, *20*(3), 122–132. Retrieved from http://www.ifets.info/journals/20_3/10.pdf

Kimbrough, S.O., & Lee, R.M. (1997). Special Issue: Systems for Computer-Mediated Digital Commerce. *IJEC, 1*(4), 3-10.

Koehler, M., & Mishra, P. (2009). What is Technological Pedagogical Content Knowledge (TPACK)? *Contemporary Issues in Technology and Teacher Education, 9*(1), 60-70. Retrieved January 9, 2018 from https://www.learntechlib.org/p/29544/

Kotey, B., & Folker, C. (2007). Employee training in SMEs: Effects of size and firm type. *Journal of Small Business Management, 45*(2), 214–234. doi:10.1111/j.1540-627X.2007.00210.x

Lawrence, J. E. (2002). *The Use of Internet in Small to Medium-Sized Enterprises* (Unpublished PhD thesis). University of Salford, UK.

Lawrence, J. E. (2008). The Challenges and Utilization of e-Commerce: The Use of Internet by Small to Medium-sized Enterprises in the United Kingdom. *Information. Social Justice (San Francisco, Calif.), 1*(2).

Lawrence, J. E. (2009). The Utilization of E-Commerce by Small to Medium-sized Enterprises: A U K Perspective. *Proceedings of the IADIS International Conference Information Systems*. Barcelona, Spain.

Lawrence, J. E. (2013). *Adoption and Usage of Internet in Small to Medium-sized Enterprises*. Lap Lambert Academic Publishing.

Lawrence, J. E. (2015). Examining the Factors that Influence ICT Adoption in SMEs: A Research Preliminary Findings. *International Journal of Technology Diffusion, 6*(4), 40–57. doi:10.4018/IJTD.2015100103

Lincoln, Y. S., & Guba, E. G. (1985). *Naturalistic Inquiry*. Newbury Park, CA: Sage.

MacGregor, R. C., Bunker, D. J., & Waugh, P. (1998). Electronic Commerce and Small / Medium Enterprises (SMEs) in Australia: An Electronic Data Interchange (EDI) Pilot Study. *Eleventh International Bled Electronic Commerce Conference*, Bled, Slovenia.

Mason, R. M. (1997). SME adoption of electronic commerce technologies: Implication for emerging national information infrastructure. *Proceedings of the Thirtieth Hawaii International Conference on Information Systems*, 495-504.

McMaster, T., Vidgen, R. T., & Wastell, D. G. (1997). Towards an understanding of technology in transition: Two conflicting theories. In T. McMaster, E. Mumford, E. B. Swanson, B. Warboys, & D. G. Wastell (Eds.), Facilitating technology transfer through partnership: Learning from practice and research. IFIP TC8 WG 8.6, international working conference on diffusion, adoption and implementation of information technology (pp. 64–75). Ambleside, UK: Academic Press. doi:10.1007/978-0-387-35092-9_4

Merriam, S. B. (1988). *Case study research in education: A qualitative approach*. San Francisco: Jossey-Bass.

Miles, M. B., & Huberman, A. M. (1984). *Qualitative Data Analysis: A sourcebook of new methods*. Thousand Oaks, CA: Sage Publications Inc.

Miles, M. B., & Huberman, A. M. (1994). *An Expanded Sourcebook: Qualitative Data Analysis*. Thousand Oaks, CA: Sage Publications Inc.

Ndubisi, N., & Sinti, Q. (2006). Consumer Attitudes, System's Characteristics and Internet Banking Adoption in Malaysia. *Management Research News*, *29*(1/2), 16-27.

Observatory of European SMEs. (2007). *Competence Development in SMEs*. Brussels: European Commission.

OECD. (2000). *OECD Small and Medium Enterprise Outlook*. OECD Publication Services.

OECD. (2004). *ICTs, e-business and SMEs*. Paper prepared for the 2nd OECD Conference of Ministers responsible for SMEs, Istanbul, Turkey.

Oftel SME Survey. (2000). *Internet use among SMEs*. Retrieved May 25, 2010 http://www.oftel.gov.uk/cmu/research/brint1000.htm

Orlikowski, W. J. (1991). Integrated information environment or matrix of control? The contradictory implications of information technology. *Accounting Management and Information Technologies*, *1*(1), 9–42. doi:10.1016/0959-8022(91)90011-3

Orlikowski, W. J. (1993). CASE tools as organizational change: Investigating incremental and radical changes in systems development. *Management Information Systems Quarterly*, *17*(3), 309–340. doi:10.2307/249774

Patel, H., & Connolly, R. (2007). *Factors Influencing Technology Adoption: A Review*. 8th International Business Information Management Conference, Dublin, Ireland. Retrieved February 15, 2018 https://www.researchgate.net/publication/273140050

Pool, P. W., Parnell, J. A., Spillan, J. E., Carraher, S., & Lester, D. L. (2006). Are SMEs meeting the challenge of integrating e-commerce into their businesses? A review of the development, challenges and opportunities. *International Journal of Information Technology and Management*, *5*(2/3), 97–113. doi:10.1504/IJITM.2006.010112

Poon, S., & Swatman, P. (1998). Small Business Internet commerce Experience: A Longitudinal Study. *Eleventh International Bled Electronic Commerce Conference*, Bled, Slovenia

Porter, M. E. (1984). *Competitive Strategy: Creating and Sustaining Superior Performance*. New York: Free Press.

Ramamurthy, K., & Premkumar, G. (1995). Determinants and outcomes of electronic data interchange diffusion. *IEEE Transactions on Engineering Management*, *42*(4), 325–347. doi:10.1109/17.482083

Reynolds, J. (1997). The Internet as a strategic resource. In L. Willcocks, D. Feeny, & G. Islei (Eds.), *Managing IT as a strategic resource*. McGraw Hill.

Rogers, E. M. (1995, 2003). Diffusion of innovations. New York: Free Press.

Schiller, J. (2003). Working with ICT Perceptions of Australian Principals. *Journal of Educational Administration*, *41*(2), 171–185. doi:10.1108/09578230310464675

Strauss, A. L., & Corbin, J. (1990, 1998). Basics of Qualitative Research: Techniques and Procedures for developing Grounded Theory. London: Sage Publications.

Tornatzky, L., & Klein, K. (1982). Innovation Characteristics and innovation adoption-implementation: A Meta-Analysis of findings. *IEEE Transactions on Engineering Management, EM-29*(1), 28–45. doi:10.1109/TEM.1982.6447463

UNESCO. (2004). *Integrating ICTs into Education: lessons learned.* Asia and Pacific Regional Bureau for Education. Retrieved from http://unesdoc.unesco.org/images/0013/001355/135562e.pdf

Walsham, G. (1993). *Interpreting Information Systems in Organization.* Chichester, UK: John Wiley & Sons Ltd.

Walsham, G. (1995). Interpretive case studies in IS research: Nature and Method. *European Journal of Information Systems, 4*(2), 74–81. doi:10.1057/ejis.1995.9

Wolfe, R. A. (1994). Organizational innovation: Review, critique and suggested research directions. *Journal of Management Studies, 31*(3), 405–431. doi:10.1111/j.1467-6486.1994.tb00624.x

Wymer, S. A., & Regan, E. A. (2005). Factors influencing e-commerce adoption and use by small and medium businesses. *Electronic Markets, 15*(4), 438–453. doi:10.1080/10196780500303151

Yap, C.S., Soh, C.P.P., & Raman, K.S. (1992). Information systems success factors. *Small Business International Journal of Management Science, 20*, 597.

Yin, R. K. (1994). Case Study Research, Design and Methods. Newbury Park, CA: Sage Publications.

Chapter 14
Web-Based PHR (Personal Health Records) Systems Adoption:
Patients' Perspectives

Changsoo Sohn
St. Cloud State University, USA

Younsook Yeo
St. Cloud State University, USA

ABSTRACT

The purpose of this study is to find factors which explain patients' intention to use web-based personal health records (PHR). It is hypothesized that patients' perceived value of information, perceived worthwhileness of searching, concerns about privacy issues, trust in information, and perceived security on web-based PHR systems are related to patients' intention to use PHRs. Using data from health information national trends survey (HINTS), direct and indirect effects of these factors on patients' intention to use PHRs were analyzed. The results show that perceived value of information, privacy, information trust, and security have significant and direct associations to intention to use PHRs. Meanwhile, perceived value of information is a strong antecedent of perceived worthwhileness of searching; however, it has no direct association to intention to use PHRs. The findings suggest that the efforts should be targeted to increase perceived value of the information and trust in privacy and security as well as the information to increase patients' intention to use PHRs.

INTRODUCTION

Previous studies have shown that new IT systems in the healthcare industry, such as electronic medical records (EMRs) for physicians and web-based personal health records (PHRs) for patients, may reduce costs and improve efficiency, quality (Thompson & Brailer, 2004; Menachemi et al., 2007; Li et al., 2014; Menachemi, 2006; Simon et al., 2008; Simon et al., 2007), and the safe delivery of health care (Li et al., 2014). The American Telemedicine Association (2010) has found that patients believe that new

DOI: 10.4018/978-1-5225-6367-9.ch014

e-health care systems will improve access to, and the quality of, healthcare. For example, web-based PHRs that are connected to EMRs are patient-focused IT applications (for details see Goldzweig et al., 2009) that can empower patients to be responsible for their own health by allowing them to check and manage their personal health information, while also facilitate communications with their health care practitioners (Institute of Medicine, 1997).

However, even though the e-health care systems have potential benefits, either health care providers or patients were not willing to adopt the e-health care systems (Bhattacherjee & Hikmet, 2007; LaPointe & Rivard, 2005). According to Ilie et al. (2009), four reasons have been identified that explains why new IT adoptions among health care providers are slow from a provider's perspectives: complexity, dual organizational structure, different characteristics of physicians and general IT users, and concerns about changes in the power structure between patients and physicians. Ilie et al. (2009) also found that both physical accessibility (i.e., the availability of computers to access EMRs) and logical accessibility (i.e., the ease or difficulty of logging into the system) were significant indicators of a physician's decision to use EMRs. However, relatively few studies have examined why patients are hesitating to adopt PHRs or what makes patients adopt PHRs. Therefore, this study focuses on the patients' viewpoints related to the adoption of web-based PHR systems. Specifically, the purpose of this study is to explain patients' intentions to use web-based PHR systems by examining patients' perceptions of the issues around PHRs, such as information quality, value of the information, and privacy and security concerns.

This study will contribute academic and practical areas. Currently, relatively few studies have been conducted from patients' viewpoints, compared to studies from providers' viewpoints. This study will fill the gap by focusing on patients' adoption factors. Practically, the results of this study will provide guidelines for both program developers and health care providers in regard to how to develop and implement web-based PHR to reduce costs and improve service quality.

Using an interpretive review analysis of qualitative research studies, a study (Hare, Law, & Brennan, 2013) identified that patients' experiences with health care services can be classified into seven themes: patients' life experiences; service design to address patients' complex needs; point of service delivery; accessibility to service and decision-making processes; availability of choices; education and training of service providers for users, and consumer typology of not being empowered. According to these classifications, the present study belongs to the categories of accessibility and point of delivery because it focuses on how patients make decisions to use web-based PHR systems (i.e., accessibility) and how PHR systems could be improved to be more patient-friendly (i.e., the point of delivery).

The following section reviews existing literature on this topic and proposes hypotheses derived from this literature review. The data analysis section explains the procedures used to collect and analyze the data. The discussion will follow the analysis of the results. This study concludes with some implications and limitations.

LITERATURE REVIEW

Electronic PHRs refer to "a universally accessible, layperson comprehensible, lifelong tool for managing relevant health information, promoting health maintenance, and assisting with chronic disease management via an interactive, common data set of electronic health information and e-health tools" (Institute of Medicine [IOM], 2009, p. 95). This definition implies that PHRs are one type of IT used in the healthcare industry. In regard to considering the adoption of new IT, many studies have discussed and used the Technology Acceptance Model (TAM) that Davis et al. (1989) developed. The TAM has been widely used in health care (Hu et al., 1999; Chau & Hu, 2001; Pare et al., 2006; Bhattacherjee & Hikmet, 2007) and information systems (IS) research (Lee et al., 2003).

In IS research, the TAM has been used to explain the adoption of technology (Klein, 2007), such as e-mail systems (Gefen & Straub, 1997), health information systems (Wilson & Lankton, 2004), microcomputers (Igbaria, 1993), operating systems (Karahanna et al., 1999), spreadsheets (Chau, 1996), and the World Wide Web (Agarwal & Prasad, 1997). The main idea of TAM is that people's intentions determine their personal behaviors as to whether they adopt new technology. The intention to use is indirectly affected by a person's belief via the person's attitudes toward the use of the technology. In the TAM, the perceived ease of use (PEOU) and perceived usefulness (PU) are factors used to explain technology adoption. Davis et al. (1989) defined perceived usefulness as "the degree to which a person believes that using a particular system would enhance his or her job performance (p. 320)," while perceived ease of use is defined as "the degree to which a person believes that using a particular system would be free of effort (p. 320)."

Many studies have used two dimensions (i.e., PEOU and PU) in various settings, showing that perceived ease of use is significantly related to perceived usefulness (Escobar-Rodriguez et al., 2012; Ilie et al., 2009; Klein, 2007; Wirtz et al., 2012). Some studies have considered only two dimensions, while other studies have added more dimensions. Liu et al. (2013) used the TAM for research in health care area by analyzing intentions to use PHRs, focusing on the physician-patient relationship. The study identified how perceived ease of use indirectly affects patients' intentions to use PHRs through 'perceived usefulness.' Meanwhile, some studies have targeted different technology, such as the adoption of the eHealth Card (Wirtz et al., 2012) or EMRs from physicians' perspectives (Ilie et al., 2009). However, these findings are not applicable to the e-health care area when attempting to analyze patients' web-based PHRs adoption decision because the purposes of these studies are not identical.

The TAM is based on the Theory of Reasoned Action (TRA), which is one of the most popular models of persuasion. According to the TRA, 'belief' affects personal 'attitude' (Ajzen & Fishbein, 1980; Fishbein & Ajzen, 1975). In other words, belief about a new technology influences one's personal attitude to decide to adopt the new technology. Thus, the TAM is used to explain that users will adopt the technology if they perceive that the technology is useful and easy to use. The technology was traditionally defined as "a well-understood physical artifact with known attributes and uses," but, currently, the meaning of technology has expanded to include "social context to the interpretation, trial, and ongoing use of any technology" (Tornatzky et al., 1983). The traditional definition implies that technology is a tool, while the expanded definition includes a diffusion of the tool and method to individuals and organizations. Thus, if we follow the definition used by Tornatzky et al. (1983), 'technology adoption' includes two steps: the adoption of the technology itself as a tool and usage of the adopted technology for certain purposes. From this viewpoint, the TAM might be useful in regard to explaining technology adoption as a tool. The two dimensions (i.e., PEO and PU) in the TAM are well-developed in regard to explaining technology adoption as a tool.

However, the TAM may not be enough to explain web-based PHR adoption behaviors because the two dimensions may explain the use of World Wide Web, the Internet. That is, when users make decisions to adopt a technology as a tool, it is critical to consider how it is useful or easy it is to use. Once users adopt a technology, the issue is how to use the technology for certain purposes. In the case of the Internet as a new technology during the late 1990s and early 2000s, the adoption of the Internet as a tool was an issue. However, today, adopting the Internet may not be an issue. Instead, the issue may be how much users are willing to obtain and use contents from Internet websites, such as PHRs websites. That is, the concern to program developers and healthcare providers would be whether they would visit the website frequently and use the contents within the website. Therefore, this study focuses on 'contents or usage' such as information obtained through searching activities from the technology, rather than focusing on the technology itself.

When patients visit and use PHRs websites, they expect to have valuable information from PHR systems. Moreover, when they think information from the web-based PHR is valuable, they perceive that searching information from the web-based PHR is worthwhile. Then, the patients adopt and use the web-based PHR regularly.

This study identifies the dimensions necessary that will help determine the patients' use of web-based PHR systems. Several factors explain intention to use web-based PHR systems. This study argues that the key reason to use web-based PHR systems is the contents that patients derive from the website. In other words, patients may use web-based PHR systems based on how much information from the PHR is valuable and how much searching the information from PHR is worthwhile.

Sweeney and Soutar (2001) classified perceived value into four dimensions: quality value, emotional value, monetary value, and social value. Quality value relates to a person's performance as a consumer who has used a product based on the perceived quality and the expected performance of the product. Emotional value refers to the feelings or affective states that consumers feel from the product when they are using. Monetary value reflects monetary benefits versus the perceived short-term and long-term costs from using the product. Social value implies public recognition for using the service. Considering these four dimensions, the 'value of the information' used for this study refers to the 'quality' and 'emotional' values of the information that web-based PHR systems can generate for patients. As shown in the study presented by Kim and Han (2009), patients believe that information has a high value if they perceive the information to be useful and helpful for their health. Thus, the first hypothesis is related to the perceived value of the information and the second hypothesis is related to the perceived worthwhileness of searching the information. That is, we hypothesize that the patients are willing to search for information within web-based PHR systems if they perceive that the information is valuable. We also hypothesize that the perceived value of the information is the antecedent of the perceived worthwhileness of searching.

Along with the perceived value of the information and perceived worthwhileness of searching, privacy concerns related to using web-based PHR systems influence patients' intentions to use the systems. Information privacy means the ability of individuals to control how and when their personal information is exchanged with others (Culnan & Bies, 2003; Stone et al., 1983). As healthcare providers manage patients' personal data and provide the data to users, privacy concerns exist (Angst & Agarwal, 2009). Many studies have also reported that PHR systems raise concerns about privacy, confidentiality, standardization, and accuracy (Endsley et al., 2006; Kim & Johnson, 2002). For example, Bishop et al. (2005) found that 67% of the study participants worried about the privacy of their personal medical records. Bernhardt et al. (2002) also claim that privacy is a major concern for patients, suggesting that privacy may be a major dimension by which to determine intention to use as it is related to web-based PHR systems (Li et al., 2014). Angst and Agarwal (2009) also found that privacy negatively affected patients' use e-health care systems, while Li et al. (2014) discovered that privacy cannot explain intention to use significantly. According to Whetstone and Goldsmith (2008), health care innovativeness, privacy concerns, and perceived usefulness are significantly related to intention to use. As such, we hypothesize that privacy is negatively related to intention to use web-based PHR systems.

Trust is also related to intention to use web-based PHR systems (Li et al., 2014; Notberg et al., 2003) because it is critical in creating healthy relationships with healthcare practitioners and compliance with medical care (Hesse et al., 2005). Mayer et al. (1995) defined trust as "the willingness of a party to be vulnerable to the actions of another party based on the expectation that the other will perform a particular action important to the trustor, irrespective of the ability to monitor or control that other party" (p. 712). Xiao et al. (2014) explained trust as users' beliefs in the accuracy of the contents about medical information online. Thus, once users have trust in the online health information, they are more likely to perceive the information to be useful and invest more time and effort in searching. Trust is a type of trade-off relationship with privacy because consumers who trust a vendor that provides web-based PHR systems have a tendency to have low privacy-related risks (Li et al., 2014), suggesting a hypothesis that trust has a positive relationship with intention to use web-based PHR systems.

Along with privacy and confidentiality, security has been identified as a factor by which to determine adoption decisions related to using web-based PHRs (Sabnis & Charles, 2012). Therefore, perceived security is positively related to the intention to use web-based PHRs.

In summary, the review of the literature related to technology adoption enables us to develop the following hypotheses:

H1: The patient who perceives that information from web-based PHR systems is valuable is more likely to have an intention to use that information.

H2: The patient who perceives that searching information within web-based PHR systems is worthwhile is more likely to have the intention to use that information.

H3: The patient who perceives that information from web-based PHR systems is valuable is more likely to search information within web-based PHR systems.

H4: The patient who is concerned with privacy is less likely to have an intention to use web-based PHR systems.

H5: The patient who trusts health information is more likely to have an intention to use web-based PHR systems.

H6: The patient who is concerned with data security is less likely to have an intention to use web-based PHR systems.

METHODOLOGY

Sampling and Data Collection

In order to answer the research question and verify the hypotheses, this study used publicly-released data from the National Cancer Institute (NCS). The NCS conducts the Health Information National Trends Survey (HINTS), for which the data are collected from a nationally representative U.S. adult population biannually in order to assess the impact of the health information environment on the public. This data have been collected since 2003 (National Cancer Institute, n.d. a). For the HINTS Cycle 1 survey, a two-stage design was used. The first stage consisted of a stratified sample of addresses from a file of residential addresses, while the second stage consisted of sampling adults within the sampled households

(Westat, 2012). This study used the HINTS 4 and Cycle 1 (2011) data. This data was collected between October 2011 and February 2012.

Two methods were used to determine which adult in the household would fill out the survey. For the first method (i.e., All Adults Method), two questionnaires were sent with each mailing and each adult residing in a sampled household was asked to complete the questionnaire. In the second method (i.e., Next Birthday Method), one questionnaire was sent with each mailing and the adult with the next upcoming birthday was asked to complete the questionnaire (National Cancer Institute, n.d., b). In order to encourage responses, follow-up questionnaires were sent to non-responding households (Westat, 2012). The materials were also provided in Spanish in order to increase participation by Hispanic respondents. The data contains 3,959 respondents, which were used for the present study.

Measures

This study's outcome variable is one's intention to adopt PHR systems. It was measured by asking the respondents to indicate how important the following statement is to them: "You should be able to get to your own medical information electronically." The explanatory dimensions used to explain the patients' intentions to adopt PHR systems were: (1) perceived value of information, (2) perceived worthwhileness of searching, (3) privacy, (4) information trust, and (5) security. Each of the five dimensions consisted of two items.

- *Perceived value of information.* This study used the items operationalized as follows: "Based on the results of your most recent search for information about health or medical topics, how much do you agree or disagree with each of the following statements?" (a) "It took a lot of effort to get the information you needed" and (b) "You were concerned about the quality of the information."
- *Perceived worthwhileness of search.* This dimension was measured by asking: "Based on the results of your most recent search for information about health or medical topics, how much do you agree or disagree with each of the following statements?" (a) "You felt frustrated during your search for the information" and (b) "The information you found was hard to understand."
- *Privacy:* The following questions were used: (a) "If your medical information is sent by fax from one health care provider to another, how concerned are you that an unauthorized person would see it?" and (b) "If your medical information is sent electronically from one health care provider to another, how concerned are you that an unauthorized person would see it?"
- *Trust of information.* The measures asked: (1) "In general, how much would you trust information about health or medical topics from the Internet?" and (2) "How much attention do you pay to information about health or medical topics on the Internet?"
- *Security.* The questions used for this study were as follows: (1) "How confident are you that safeguards (including the use of technology) are in place to protect your medical records from being seen by people who aren't permitted to see them? Having safeguards (including the use of technology) in place has to do with the security of your medical records" and (2) "How confident are you that you have some say in who is allowed to collect, use, and share your medical information? Having a say in who can collect, use, and share your medical information has to do with the privacy of your records."

DATA MANAGEMENT AND PRELIMINARY ANALYSIS

To clean up the data, we removed any respondents with missing data and reversed the scales for some of the variables to make them consistent with the other data. Based on the scales used for the question responses, negative response, such as "not important" were coded as 1, while positive response, such as "very important" were coded as either 3 or 5, depending on the scale used. After cleaning the data, the exploratory factor analysis (EFA) confirmed the five dimensions as the relevant constructs developed for the present study. The EFA used the principal component analysis and VARIMAX rotation method. The outcome values of EFA are summarized in Table 1.

In order to check the scale reliability (i.e., internal consistency), Cronbach's alpha was used. Cronbach's alpha measures how closely each item is related in each dimension as a group. The last column in Table 1 shows that the measures are reliable, even though Information Trust (0.630) was relatively low. To check dimensionality, the EFA was performed. The results of the EFA proved that the items were correctly grouped into each dimension. This fact confirms that the measures for this study have construct validity. Since the data for this study are reliable and valid, at least statistically, further analyses were conducted to test the hypotheses.

RESULTS

The Structural Equation Modeling technique was used to test the hypotheses. As shown in Table 2, most of the values for the path analyses were statistically acceptable (Chi-square = 7.706 (p = 0.564), GFI=0.998, AGFI=0.994, RMR=0.005, NFI=0.989, RMSEA=0.000, CFI=1.000). Thus, we continued to test the six hypotheses.

According to the structural equation modeling methods, most of the dimensions significantly explained the intention of the individual to adopt the web-based PHRs. The results of the path analysis can be found in Figure 1. The solid line in Figure 1 indicates a significant coefficient, while the dotted line displays an insignificant coefficient.

Table 1. Exploratory factor analysis

Dimensions	Items	Loadings					Cronbach's Alpha
		1	2	3	4	5	
1.Perceived Worthwhileness of Searching	a	*.884*	.032	-.023	.269	.023	.847
	b	*.862*	.009	.016	.349	.021	
2. Privacy	a	.002	*.941*	.014	-.016	.016	.872
	b	.029	*.941*	.028	.004	.005	
3. Security	a	-.024	.026	*.914*	.019	.009	.805
	b	.020	.015	*.914*	-.014	-.016	
4. Information Trust	a	.239	-.009	-.004	*.911*	.107	.630
	b	.511	-.008	.013	*.707*	-.099	
5. Perceived Value of Information	a	-.007	.020	-.014	.003	*.856*	.755
	b	.023	.000	.008	.037	*.850*	

Table 2. Results and recommended criteria

	Results	Recommended
Chi-square	7.706 (p = .564)	P ≥ 0.05
RMR	.005	≤ 0.08
GFI	.998	≥ 0.90
AGFI	.994	≥ 0.80
NFI	.989	≥ 0.90
RMSEA	.000	≤ 0.10
CFI	1.000	≥ 0.90

Figure 1. Results of path analysis

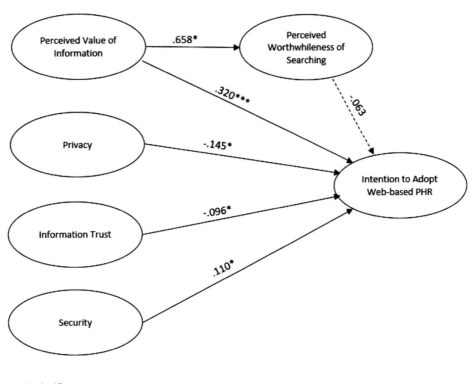

*: significant at 1 %
**: significant at 5 %

The results of SEM analysis show that all of the hypotheses were significant, except for H2 (i.e., the patient who perceives that searching information from web-based PHR systems is worthwhile is more likely to have the intention to use). 'Perceived value of information' (H1), 'privacy' (H4), 'information trust' (H5), and 'security' (H6) significantly explained the patients' intention to adopt web-based PHR systems. However, 'perceived worthwhileness of searching' (H2) did not have the statistical significance necessary to explain the individual's intention to adopt web-based PHRs. The 'perceived value of information' was a statistically significant precedent of 'perceived worthwhileness of searching' (H3).

DISCUSSION

The main purpose of this study was to explain what dimensions are important in regard to patients' intentions to use web-based PHR systems. The 'perceived value of information' and 'perceived worthwhileness of searching' were used to account for the patients' intention to use PHRs along with privacy, information trust, and security. The results of this study show that patients are more likely to intend to adopt web-based PHR systems when they perceive that the information is valuable, that information is trustworthy, and that the systems are secured so as to protect their privacy. The followings are the discussion of these findings, followed by several implications of this study.

Considering the coefficients of the structural equation modeling, the perceived value of information (0.320) was the most influential dimension related to an individual's intention to use web-based PHR systems. The other important dimensions were privacy (0.145) and security (0.110). Information trust was statistically significant (0.096), but the coefficient size was minimal. However, perceived worthwhileness of searching (-0.063) did not show any significance. Meanwhile, the results in Figure 1 also shows the statistical significance (0.658) of the perceived value of information as it is related to the perceived worthwhileness of searching. This result means that the 'perceived value of information' is the antecedent of the perceived worthwhileness of searching, which can be interpreted as searching itself may not stimulate patients to intention to adopt web-based PHR systems although patients who think that the information from the searching is valuable will be more likely to search for the information. Thus, if health care providers want patients to use web-based PHR systems more frequently, then they should provide information that the patients perceive as valuable. Such valuable information would entice the patients to search the information using web-based PHR systems. However, this result leads to the question of what information is valuable to patients. Valuable information may include medical test results, upcoming appointments, and communications with doctors and nurses. However, this study did not intend to identify what information is valuable to patients. As such, future studies may consider what types of information are valuable to patients.

Another significant indicator of patients' intention to use PHRs was privacy. As expected, the patients were concerned about their privacy when using web-based PHR systems, even though a study by Li et al. (2014) showed an insignificant connection between privacy and intention to adopt. The negative coefficient (-0.145) of privacy in this study indicates that the higher the concerns of the patient related to privacy, the less likely that patient is to use web-based PHR systems. Thus, health care providers need to create policies and strategies to emphasize privacy protection for patients, so as to entice them to be more likely to use the web-based PHR systems.

Security was also a significant indicator of intention to adopt web-based PHR systems. While privacy is related to protecting personal information, security is related to protecting web-based PHR systems from unauthorized users, such as hackers. In other words, privacy is related to information, while security is related to the system itself. According to the coefficients, security (0.110) was less of a concern than privacy (-0.145) for the patients. While little difference existed between the sizes of the coefficients, the direction of the coefficients was important. Security was positively-related, while privacy was negatively-related, to patients' intention to use PHRs, which implies that patients are more likely to adopt systems if the systems are highly secured and thus clear of patients' privacy issues.

The result also shows that 'information trust' had a negative and significant coefficient (-0.096) related to the intention to adopt web-based PHR systems, which suggests that patients who trust the information available in the web-based PHR systems are more likely to intend to adopt web-based PHR.

As patients who trust information are more likely to adopt web-based PHR systems, this result is opposite of what we would expect. However, considering the value of the coefficient, the impact of this variable on a patient's intention to adopt is small. Another interpretation may be that patients may take the information trust for granted. Thus, they do not care that much about the quality of the information.

This study provides ideas for future studies. First, as this study is based on published data from HINTS, the survey instruments may not be designed for and matched perfectly to the purpose of our study although the survey data provides valuable insights regarding patients' intentions to adopt the web-based PHRs. Hence, future research may be necessary to verify these results. This study was based on data from HINTS that was conducted between 2011 and 2012. More recent survey results may have changed the results of this study as the respondents may now be more familiar with web-based PHRs. It may be useful to compare the results of this study to the results of future studies using more recent data. In addition, a longitudinal study may provide useful insights into the trends related to patients' intention to adopt web-based PHR systems. This study focused on patient-level information. As such, a study focused on physician-level information that analyzed the variables that entice providers to adopt electronic medical systems would be useful so that researchers can understand the full adoption picture.

CONCLUSION

In order to reduce costs and improve the effectiveness of healthcare delivery, patients' use of PHR systems is critical. However, the rates of patients' adoption of the web-based rates are low. Hence, the goal of this study was to examine the variables important to patients in regard to their intentions to adopt web-based PHR systems. The findings suggest that patients prefer to have systems that provide valuable information. Once the information is proven to be valuable, they perceive it as worthwhile to search the information provided within web-based PHR systems. Privacy, information trust, and security were also factors that helped determine the patients' intentions to use web-based PHR systems.

DISCUSION QUESTIONS

1. If you have not used the PHR systems linked to your physicians' EMRs, then list some of the reasons why you have not.
2. If you have ever used the PHR systems linked to your physicians' EMRs, then list some of the positive and negative experiences that you have had related to these systems?
3. Based on your personal experience, what do you think is the most important factor for patients (1) to adopt web-based PHR systems and (2) to not adopt web-based PHR systems?
4. This study shows that the perceived value of the information, privacy, information trust, and security can explain the intention to adopt web-based PHR systems. List some other factors that may explain patients' intention to adopt web-based PHR systems.
5. If you were a medical service provider and wanted to follow the suggestions made by this study, which suggestion would you implement first in order to help patients adopt the web-based PHR systems? Why?

REFERENCES

Agarwal, R., & Prasad, J. (1997). The Role of Innovation Characteristics and Perceived Voluntariness in the Acceptance of Information Technologies. *Decision Sciences*, *28*(3), 557–582. doi:10.1111/j.1540-5915.1997.tb01322.x

Ajzen, I., & Fishbein, M. (1980). *Understanding Attitudes and Predicting Social Behavior*. Englewood Cliffs, NJ: Prentice-Hall.

American Telemedicine Association (AHA). (2013). *What is Telemedicine?* Retrieved from http://www.americantelemed.org/learn/what-is-telemedicine

Angst, C. M., & Agarwal, R. (2009). Adoption of Electronic Health Records in the Presence of Privacy Concerns: The Elaboration Likelihood Model and Individual Persuasion. *Management Information Systems Quarterly*, *33*(2), 339–370. doi:10.2307/20650295

Bernhardt, J. M., Lariscy, R. A. W., Parrott, R. L., Silk, K. J., & Felter, E. M. (2002). Perceived Barriers to Internet-based Health Communication on Human Genetics. *Journal of Health Communication*, *7*(4), 325–340. doi:10.1080/10810730290088166 PMID:12356290

Bhattacherjee, A., & Hikmet, N. (2007). Physicians' Resistance Toward Healthcare Information Technology: A Theoretical Model and Empirical Test. *European Journal of Information Systems*, *16*(6), 725–737. doi:10.1057/palgrave.ejis.3000717

Bishop, L. S., Holmes, B. J., & Kelley, C. M. (2005). *National Consumer Health Privacy Survey*. Oakland, CA: California HealthCare Foundation.

Chau, P. Y. K. (1996). An Empirical Assessment of a Modified Technology Acceptance Model. *Journal of Management Information Systems*, *13*(2), 185–204. doi:10.1080/07421222.1996.11518128

Chau, P. Y. K., & Hu, P. J. (2002). Examining a Model of Information Technology Acceptance by Individual Professionals – An Exploratory Study. *Journal of Management Information Systems*, *18*(4), 191–229. doi:10.1080/07421222.2002.11045699

Culnan, M. J., & Bies, R. J. (2003). Consumer Privacy: Balancing Economic and Justice Consideration. *The Journal of Social Issues*, *59*(2), 323–342. doi:10.1111/1540-4560.00067

Davis, F. D., Bagozzi, R. P., & Warshaw, P. R. (1989). User Acceptance of Computer Technology: A Comparison of Two Theoretical Models. *Management Science*, *7*(3), 982–1003. doi:10.1287/mnsc.35.8.982

Endsley, S., Kibbe, D. C., Linares, A., & Colorafi, K. (2006). An Introduction to Personal Health Records: Here's What You Need to Know About This Growing Trend To Give Patients Access To A Portable Health record. *Family Practice Management*, *13*(5), 57. PMID:16736906

Escobar-Rodriguez, T., Monge-Lozano, P., & Romero-Alonso, M. M. (2012). Acceptance of E-Prescriptions and Automated Medication-Management Systems in Hospitals: An Extension of the Technology Acceptance Model. *Journal of Information Systems*, *26*(1), 77–96. doi:10.2308/isys-10254

Fishbein, M., & Ajzen, I. (1975). *Belief, Attitude, Intention, and Behavior*. Reading, MA: Addison-Wesley.

Gefen, D., & Straub, D. W. (1997). Gender Differences in the Perception and Use of E-mail: An Extension to the Technology Acceptance Model. *Management Information Systems Quarterly, 21*(4), 389–401. doi:10.2307/249720

Goldzweig, C. L., Towfigh, A., Maglione, M., & Shekelle, P. G. (2009). Costs and Benefits of Health Information Technology: New Trends from the Literature. *Health Affairs, 28*(2), 376–386. doi:10.1377/hlthaff.28.2.w282 PMID:19174390

Hare, C., Law, J., & Brennan, C. (2013). The Vulnerable Healthcare Consumer: An Interpretive Synthesis of The Patient Experience Literature. *International Journal of Consumer Studies, 37*(3), 299–311. doi:10.1111/ijcs.12006

Hesse, B. W., Nelson, D. E., Kreps, G. L., Croyle, R. T., Arora, N. K., Rimer, B. K., & Viswanath, K. (2005). Trust and Sources of Health Information. The Impact of the Internet and its Implications for Health Care Providers: Findings from the First Health Information National Trends Survey. *Archives of Internal Medicine, 165*(22), 1–7. doi:10.1001/archinte.165.22.2618 PMID:16344419

Hu, P. J., Chau, P. Y. K., Sheng, O. R. L., & Tam, K. Y. (1999). Examining the technology Acceptance Model Using Physician Acceptance of Telemedicine Technology. *Journal of Management Information Systems, 16*(2), 91–112. doi:10.1080/07421222.1999.11518247

Igbaria, M. (1993). User Acceptance of Microcomputer Technology: An Empirical Test. *Omega, 21*(1), 73–90. doi:10.1016/0305-0483(93)90040-R

Ilie, V., Slyke, C. V., Parikh, M. A., & Courtney, J. F. (2009). Paper Versus Electronic Medical records: The Effects of Access on Physicians' Decisions to Use Complex Information Technologies. *Decision Sciences, 40*(2), 213–241. doi:10.1111/j.1540-5915.2009.00227.x

Institute of Medicine. (2009). *Health Literacy, eHealth, and Communication: Putting the Consumer First: Workshop Summary*. Washington, DC: The National Academies Press.

Institute of Medicine (IOM). (1991). *The Computer-Based Patient Record: An Essential Technology For Healthcare*. National Academy Press.

Institute of Medicine (IOM). (1997). *The Computer-based Patient Record: An Essential Technology for Health Care*. National Academy Press.

Karahanna, E., Straub, D. W., & Chervany, N. L. (1999). Information Technology Adoption Across Time: A Cross-sectional Comparison of Pre-adoption and Post-adoption Beliefs. *Management Information Systems Quarterly, 23*(2), 183–213. doi:10.2307/249751

Kim, B., & Han, I. (2009). What Drives the Adoption of Mobile Data Services? An Approach from a Value Perspective. *Journal of Information Technology, 24*(1), 35–45. doi:10.1057/jit.2008.28

Kim, M. I., & Johnson, K. B. (2002). Personal Health Records: Evaluation of Functionality and Utility. *Journal of the American Medical Informatics Association, 9*(2), 171–180. doi:10.1197/jamia.M0978 PMID:11861632

Klein, R. (2006). Internet-based Patient Physician Electronic Communication Applications: Patient Acceptance and Trust. *e-Service Journal, 5*(2), 27–51. doi:10.2979/esj.2007.5.2.27

Lapointe, L., & Rivard, S. (2005). A Multilevel Model of Resistance to Information Technology Implementation. *Management Information Systems Quarterly*, *29*(3), 461–491. doi:10.2307/25148692

Lee, Y., Kozar, K., & Larsen, K. (2003). The Technology Acceptance Model: Past, Present, and Future. *Communications of the Association for Information Systems*, *12*, 752–780.

Li, H., Gupta, A., Zhang, J., & Sarathy, R. (2014). Examining the Decision to Use Standalone Personal health Record Systems as a Trust-Enabled fair Social Contract. *Decision Support Systems*, *57*, 376–386. doi:10.1016/j.dss.2012.10.043

Liu, C. F., Tsai, Y. C., & Jang, F. L. (2013). Patients' Acceptance Towards a Web-based Personal Health Record System: An Empirical Study in Taiwan. *International Journal of Environmental Research and Public Health*, *10*(10), 5191–5208. doi:10.3390/ijerph10105191 PMID:24142185

Mayer, R. C., Davis, J. H., & Schoorman, F. D. (1995). An Integration Model of Organizational Trust. *Academy of Management Review*, *20*(3), 709–734.

Menachemi, N. (2006). Barriers to Ambulatory EHR: Who Are 'Imminent Adopters' And How Do They Differ From Other Physicians? *Informatics in Primary Care*, *14*(2), 101–108. PMID:17059699

Menachemi, N., Saunders, C., Chukmaitov, A., Matthews, M. C., & Brooks, R. G. (2007). Hospital adoption of information technologies and improved patient safety: A study of 98 hospitals in Florida. *Journal of Healthcare Management*, *52*(6), 398–409. doi:10.1097/00115514-200711000-00008 PMID:18087980

National Cancer Institute. (n.d.a). *Frequently Asked Questions About HINTS*. Retrieved from http://hints.cancer.gov/faq.aspx

National Cancer Institute. (n.d.b). *Survey Instrumens*. Retrieved from https://hints.cancer.gov/data/survey-instruments.aspx

Noteberg, A., Christiaanse, E., & Wallage, P. (2003). Consumer Trust in Electronic Channels: The Impact of Electronic Commerce Assurance on Consumers' Purchasing Likelihood and Risk Perceptions. *e-Service Journal*, *2*(2), 46–67. doi:10.2979/esj.2003.2.2.46

Pare, G., Sicotte, C., & Jacques, H. (2006). The Effects of Creating Psychological Ownership on Physicians' Acceptance of Clinical Information Systems. *Journal of the American Medical Informatics Association*, *13*(2), 197–205. doi:10.1197/jamia.M1930 PMID:16357351

Prady, S. L., Norris, D., Lester, J. E., & Hoch, D. B. (2001). Expanding the Guidelines for Electronic Communication with Patients Application to a Specific Tool. *Journal of the American Medical Informatics Association*, *8*(4), 344–348. doi:10.1136/jamia.2001.0080344 PMID:11418540

Sabnis, S., & Charles, D. (2012). Opportunities and Challenges: Security in eHealth. *Bell Labs Technical Journal*, *17*(3), 105–112. doi:10.1002/bltj.21561

Simon, S. R., Kaushal, R., Cleary, P. D., Jenter, C. A., Volk, L. A., Poon, E. G., ... Bates, D. W. (2007). Correlates Of Electronic Health Record Adoption In Office Practices: A Statewide Survey. *Journal of the American Medical Informatics Association*, *14*(1), 110–117. doi:10.1197/jamia.M2187 PMID:17068351

Simon, S. R., McCarthy, M. L., Kaushal, R., Jenter, C. A., Volk, L. A., Poon, E. G., ... Bates, D. W. (2008). Electronic Health Records: Which Practices Have Them, and How Are Clinicians Using Them? *Journal of Evaluation in Clinical Practice, 14*(1), 43–47. doi:10.1111/j.1365-2753.2007.00787.x PMID:18211642

Stone, E. F., Gueutal, H. G., Gardner, D. G., & McClure, S. (1983). A Field Experiment Comparing Information-Privacy Values, Beliefs, And Attitudes Across Several Types Of Organizations. *The Journal of Applied Psychology, 68*(3), 459–468. doi:10.1037/0021-9010.68.3.459

Sweeney, J. C., & Soutar, G. N. (2001). Consumer Perceived Value: The Development of A Multiple Item Scale. *Journal of Retailing, 77*(2), 203–220. doi:10.1016/S0022-4359(01)00041-0

Thompson, T. G., & Brailer, D. J. (2004). *The decade of health information technology: Delivering consumer-centric and information-rich health care: Framework for strategic action.* Washington, DC: Department of Health and Human Services, National Coordinator for Health Information Technology. Retrieved from http://www.hhs.gov/onchit/framework/hitframework.pdf

Tornatzky, L. G., Eveland, J. D., Boylan, M. G., Hetzner, W. A., Johnson, E. C., Roitman, D., & Schneider, J. (1983). The Process of technological innovation: reviewing the literature. Productivity Improvement Research Section, Division of Industrial Science and Technological Innovation, National Science Foundation, Washington, DC.

Westat. (2012). *Health Information National Trends Survey 4 (HINTS 4): Cycle 1 Methodology Report.* Bethesda, MD: National Cancer Institute. Retrieved from https://hints.cancer.gov/docs/HINTS4_Cycle1_Methods_Report_revised_Jun2012.pdf

Whetstone, M., & Goldsmith, R. E. (2008). Some factors Associated with Adoption of Personal Health Records. In W. J. Kehoe & L. K. Whitten (Eds.), *Advances in Marketing: Issues, Strategies, and Theories* (pp. 258–259). Tuscaloosa, AL: Society for Marketing Advances.

Wilson, E. V., & Lankton, N. K. (2004). Modeling Patients' Acceptance of Provider-delivered E-health. *Journal of the American Medical Informatics Association, 11*(4), 241–248. doi:10.1197/jamia.M1475 PMID:15064290

Wirtz, B. W., Mory, L., & Ullrich, S. (2012). eHealth in the Public Sector: An Empirical Analysis of the Acceptance of Germany's Electronic Health Card. *Public Administration, 90*(3), 642–663. doi:10.1111/j.1467-9299.2011.02004.x

Xiao, N., Sharman, R., Rao, H. R., & Upadhyaya, S. (2014). Factors Influencing Online Health Information Search: An Empirical Analysis of a national Cancer-Related Survey. *Decision Support Systems, 57*, 417–427. doi:10.1016/j.dss.2012.10.047

Chapter 15
Conceptualizing the Domain and an Empirical Analysis of Operations Security Management

Winfred Yaokumah
Pentecost University College, Ghana

ABSTRACT

Operations security management integrates the activities of all the information systems security controls. It ensures that the entire computing environment is adequately secured. This chapter conducts an in-depth review of scholarly and practitioner works to conceptualize the domain of operations security management. Drawing upon the existing information systems security literature, the chapter classifies operations security management into 10 domains. Following, the chapter performs an empirical analysis to investigate the state-of-practice of operations security management in organizations. The findings show that the maturity level of operations security management is at the Level 3 (well-defined). The maturity levels range from Level 0 (not performed) to Level 5 (continuously improving). The results indicate that operations security processes are documented, approved, and implemented organization-wide. Backup and malware management are the most applied operations security controls, while logging, auditing, monitoring, and reviewing are the least implemented controls.

INTRODUCTION

Operations security management is the day-to-day activities involved in ensuring that people, applications, computer systems, computer networks, processes, and the entire computing environment are properly and adequately secured (Gregory, 2010). It pertains to the activities that take place while keeping computing environment up and running in a secured and protected manner (Harris, 2013; Shaqrah, 2010). Operations security management integrates the activities of all the information systems security controls (Henrya, 2011). To attain a high level of operations security organizations need to put in place

DOI: 10.4018/978-1-5225-6367-9.ch015

appropriate measures that will ensure that the routine security activities are carried out in a controlled manner (Prabhu, 2013). These activities may include documenting operating procedures; ensuring that changes to information assets are carried out efficiently; protecting information resources from malware and other threats; performing backups and ensuring timely availability of information; and carrying out logging, auditing, monitoring, and reviewing user activities (Prabhu, 2013). In order to keep up with these tasks, operations security personnel (network administrators, system administrators, and database administrators) need in-depth understanding of the domain of operations security. This knowledge will help them to fully implement and adequately handle the day-to-day operations security challenges.

However, there seems to be varying views as to what constitutes the domain of operations security. According to Gregory (2010), operations security includes security monitoring, vulnerability management, change management, configuration management, and information handling procedures. Harris (2013) considers operations security as the activities involved in ensuring that physical and environmental security (such as temperature and humidity control, media reuse and disposal, and destruction of media containing sensitive information) concerns are addressed. Moreover, the International Information System Security Certification Consortium's (ISC²) Body of Knowledge (CBK, 2017) extends operations security to cover operational support of highly available systems, fault tolerance, and mitigation of security-related cyber attacks. Also, ISO/IEC 27002 (2013) defines the scope of operations security as consisting of security procedures, roles and responsibilities; management of security in the third-party products and services; securing systems and data from malware activities; backup of data to safeguard against data lost and system corruption; and logging, monitoring, auditing, and reviewing of system activities.

Considering these different perspectives, there is the need to identify, classify, and clarify the domain of operations security for better implementation and management of operations security controls in organizations. Therefore, the objectives of this chapter are: (a) to conduct a review of scholarly and practitioner works to conceptualize the domain of operations security management, and (b) to perform an empirical analysis to ascertain the level of operations security management in organizations based on ISO/IEC 27002:2013 framework. Information security programs will be successful when measured with IT security maturity models (McFadzean, Ezingeard, & Birchall, 2011). These models are based on international standards and best practices. Information security maturity models consist of structured set of elements that describe levels of security improvement (maturity). They are often used as tools for measuring the performance of security programs in organizations (Stevanović, 2011).

Therefore, this chapter's empirical analysis of operations security management is based on the information security control objectives defined by the International Organization for Standardization/International Electrotechnical Commission - security techniques - code of practice for information security management (ISO/IEC 27002:2013 framework). This framework is a widely accepted information technology security techniques and contains 14 security control clauses with a total of 35 main security categories and 114 controls (ISO/IEC 27002:2013, 2013). In particular, the objectives of this chapter will be achieved by answering the following three research questions:

1. What is the domain of operations security management?
2. What is the maturity level of operations security management in Ghanaian organizations?
3. Are there any significant differences among the organizations with regard to the levels of operations security management?

BACKGROUND

Context

Legal and regulatory compliance required organizations to protect critical and sensitive data of their customers. Computer Security Institute (2011) reported that organizational information security has improved by 64% owing to regulatory compliance efforts. Compliance with legal requirements, such as Sarbanes-Oxley (SOX) for financial reporting and governance, impacted the management of information systems security (Brown & Nasuti, 2005). The Health Insurance Portability and Accountability Act (HIPPA) required healthcare organizations to "safeguard the confidentiality, integrity, and availability of electronic protected health information" (Hoffman & Podgurski, 2007, p. 7). Also, the Federal Information Security Management Act (FISMA) required all U.S. federal agencies and international banking industry to develop, document, and implement a program that would provide information security for the systems that support their operations and assets (Pabrai, 2006).

Developing countries enacted laws and regulations to protect information resources. A recent Data Protection Act 843 of Ghana was aimed at protecting the privacy and personal data of individuals (Data Protection Act, 2012). Moreover, the Electronic Transaction Act 772 of Ghana (Electronic Transactions Act 772, 2008) focused on developing "a safe, secure and effective environment for the consumer, business and the government to conduct and use electronic transactions" (p. 6). Despite these regulatory compliance efforts, a recent study found a decline in fundamental security practices (PWC, 2015). For example, a recent report ranked Ghana second in Africa and seventh in the world with respect to Internet related crimes (Joy Online, 2013). The report also indicated that about 82 cyber crimes occurred in Ghana every month - on average about 1000 crimes occurred in a year (Joy Online, 2013).

Empirical Work

According to Harris (2013), operations security can be achieved through configuration settings, performance monitoring, fault tolerance, and accounting and verification management. Operations security management practices are based on the fundamental security concepts of need-to-know (users have only the information required to perform specific duties), least privilege (users have the fewest or lowest number of privileges required to accomplish their duties), separation of duties (high-value or high-risk tasks required two or more different individuals to complete), and job rotation (moving users through a range of job assignments) (Gregory, 2010). According to ISO/IEC27002 (2013), operations security tasks could be achieved through performing operational procedures and responsibilities; managing security in third-party systems; malware protection; backup and restoration; and logging, monitoring, auditing, and reviewing.

Operational Procedures and Responsibilities

Operational procedures and responsibilities ensure protected operations of information processing facilities (ISO/IEC27002, 2013). It includes documentation of operating procedures, change management, capacity management, and separation of development and testing from operational environments. Change management involves changes to the organization, business processes, information processing facilities, and systems that can affect information security. Capacity management is the monitoring, tuning, and projections made of future capacity requirements to ensure that required system performance is sustained. To reduce the risks of unauthorized access or changes made to the operational environment, system development, testing, and operational environments should be segregated (ISO/IEC27002, 2013).

Concerning security roles and responsibilities, senior executives of the organization have legal obligations, compliance and regulatory requirements to ensure that resources are protected, safety measures are in place, and security mechanisms are tested to guarantee that required level of protection is maintained (Harris, 2013). In order to achieve this, organizations have to consider threats, including disclosure of confidential data, theft of assets, corruption of data, interruption of services, and destruction of the physical or logical environment (Harris, 2013). Moreover, it is important that organizations maintain security configuration standards for information systems and segregation of security duties to ensure that unintentional or unauthorized modifications of information systems can be detected.

Information security is an important concern for not only the senior executives. The users have critical role and responsibility to play by following security policies and procedures to safeguard information. Human aspects of information security should be taken into consideration as ignorance, negligence, mischief, resistance, and lack of information security awareness on the part of users can have adverse effect on the security of the organizational data (Safa, von Solms, & Furnell, 2016). In a study that assessed major information security risks within the health care sector, Deursen, Buchanan, and Duff (2013) enumerated the main risks to patients' health records: staff leaving data unattended to in their offices, staff sharing passwords with others, and staff sending emails containing personal patient data to wrong addressees.

Security in Third-party Systems

In today's interconnected business world, more data is generated and shared with business partners and suppliers. Internet security (Zolait, Ibrahim, & Farooq, 2010) and database outsourcing become threats nowadays because they pose substantial security and privacy risks (Evdokimov, Fischmann, & Günther, 2010). It is important that the third-party and other stakeholders protect organizational data. Recent study reported that organizations do not pay much attention to third-party security (PWC, 2015). The study investigated whether organizations perform appropriate protections of vendors to ensure their ability to safeguard information. It further assessed whether organizations conduct ongoing monitoring to ensure that the third-party is protecting organizational sensitive data (PWC, 2015). From the results, only 50% of the organizations performed risk assessments on third-party vendors; 50% conducted an inventory of all third parties that handle personal data of employees and customers; and only 54% have a formal policy requiring third parties to comply with their privacy policies (PWC, 2015).

The third party systems, particularly the cloud computing, though have the benefits of scalability, cost reduction, portability, flexibility, and availability, are also faced with serious security issues (Bachlechner et al., 2014; Karadsheh, 2012). Concerns were raised over unauthorised access to third party cloud based systems - which can cause large scale exposure of organizational private data (Scanlon, Farina, & Kechadi, 2015). Thus, the need for due diligence in the selection of a trusted cloud service provider (Tang & Liu, 2015) and the establishment of appropriate security policies, service level agreement and compliance for enhancing cloud security (Karadsheh, 2012). Accordingly, it is crucial organizations put processes in place to assess and monitor third-party compliance with security requirements.

Malware Protection

Malware protection is important to ensure that information resources are protected (ISO/IEC27002:2013) from destruction and damage. Malware is "a program that is covertly inserted into another program with the intent to destroy data, run destructive or intrusive programs, or otherwise compromise the confidentiality, integrity, or availability of the victim's data, applications, or operating system" (Souppaya & Scarfone, 2013, p. 2). Malware can gather the user's sensitive information, gain read or write access to the user's files, activate the device's microphone or camera to secretly record information, or even upload files to specific locations (US GAO, 2012). On the contrary, in the area of computer forensics, Ramalho (2014) noted that malware can be used as a means of obtaining digital evidence.

The frequency of malware incursions has heightened the need for security awareness and education, law enforcement, and installation of current security software (Martin & Rice, 2011). Fake anti-virus attacks are the current trend for malware distribution by which the attackers disguise malware as legitimate anti-virus software and convince users to install it (Kim, Yan, & Zhang, 2015). But, Nissim et al., (2015) developed a method that can detect malicious non-executable files (such .pdf, .docx) containing malware which users may mistakenly consider less suspicious or malicious. Therefore, users' ability to exhibit malware avoidance behaviours require repeated trainings (Dang-Pham & Pittayachawan, 2015). Also, organizations should implement mechanisms to detect, quarantine, and eradicate known malicious codes on all its computing systems, including workstations, servers, and mobile computing devices.

Backup and Restoration

Data loss as a result of malware activities and system crashes represents a significant threat to individuals and organizations. Therefore, taking regular backups ensures protection against loss of data (ISO/IEC27002:2013). According to Mbowe et al. (2014), security breaches of sensitive information remained a difficult problem to solve owing to the increasing number of malware programs. In a study, Computer Security Institute (2011) found that 97% of the 234 respondents had installed anti-virus software to protect organizational data. Conversely, the study reported that malware infection accounted for 67.1 percent of all security attacks (Computer Security Institute, 2011). Accordingly, Menard et al. (2014) recommended a cloud-based backup solution as a sufficient backup alternative. Jarraya and Laurent (2010) proposed a novel Peer-to-Peer (P2P) reliable and secure backup system that utilizes the hard disk space attached to the Internet to implement a distributed backup service.

Additionally, the frequency of data backup process should be consistent with the availability requirements and the restore procedures should be routinely tested to ensure the integrity of the backup. Similarly, a study found that a very large proportion of discarded computer disks were potentially exposed to the possibility of a compromise of sensitive information (Jones, Dardick, Davies, Sutherland, & Valli, 2009). Moreover, Kljun, Mariani, and Dix (2016) found that a fifth of all computers are not backed up, and a quarter of most important files and a third of most important folders could not be (fully) restored in the event of computer failure.

Logging, Monitoring, Auditing, and Reviewing

A log is a record of events that occur within an organization's computing systems arising from network activities, application software, and operating systems (Kent & Souppaya, 2006). The purpose is to record events and generate evidence (ISO/IEC27002:2013, 2013). The evident can help in troubleshooting, optimizing system and network performance, identifying security incidents and policy violations, and recording of user actions (Kent & Souppaya, 2006). Logs can provide data useful for investigating attacks, fraud, and inappropriate system usage (Kent & Souppaya, 2006). Data logging on networks helps in detecting and troubleshooting faults (Connolly, 2010). In particular, website log data can be used to reconstruction the website (Shieh, 2012). It can reveal user's behaviour (Arshad & Ameen, 2015) and provide trends in the use of information systems (Park & Lee, 2013).

Organizations can monitor the workforce as their activities are logged when interacting with organizational computing facilities (Alampay & Hechanova, 2010). Transaction logs can provide evidence of usage patterns of resources (Avery & Tracy, 2014). Besides, data logging over an extended period can help diagnose intermittent faults (Connolly, 2010), provide evidence for accountability (Vance, Lowry, & Eggett, 2013), and enhance intrusion detection and problem identification (United States Patent and Trademark Office [USPTO], 2009). Therefore, processes should be put in place to automatically log the utilization of information system resources and routinely monitor logs to detect unauthorized and anomalous activities. Accordingly, logging facilities and log information should be protected against tampering and unauthorized access (ISO/IEC27002:2013, 2013).

IT Maturity Models

Various IT maturity models exist for measuring the performance of IT security and related processes. Notable among them are ISO/IEC 21827, the Control Objectives for Information and Related Technology (COBIT), and the Capability Maturity Model Integration (CMMI). ISO/IEC 21827 is an international standard based on the Systems Security Engineering Capability Maturity Model (SSE-CMM) developed by the International Systems Security Engineering Association (ISO/IEC 21827:2008, 2008). It is a standard metrics that captures security engineering practices generally observed in the industry. The metrics measures the development, operation, maintenance and decommissioning activities; management, organizational and engineering activities; system, software, hardware, and human factors; system management, operation and maintenance; and acquisition, system management, certification, accreditation and evaluation (ISO/IEC 21827:2008, 2008).

The COBIT maturity model, developed by IT Governance Institute, consists of set of best practices for IT governance and management. It ensures that IT sustains business goals, optimizes IT investment, and manages IT-related risks and opportunities (ITGI, 2010). Similarly, the CMMI is aimed at providing guidance for improving organization's processes and ability to manage the development, acquisition, and maintenance of products or services, focussing on systems engineering, software engineering, integrated product and process development, and supplier sourcing (Software Engineering Institute, 2002). Table 1 shows the maturity levels contained in ISO/IEC 21827:2008 model, which can be mapped to both COBIT maturity model and that of CMMI. However, the models differ with respect with their area of focus. Essentially, COBIT focuses on assessing the maturity of IT governance processes; CMMI model measures the maturity of software processes, and ISO/IEC 21827:2008 focuses on IT security management. Hence, ISO/IEC 21827:2008 maturity model is suitable for this study.

Table 1. Scales for measuring IT maturity levels

Maturity Scale		International Standards for Measuring IT Maturity			
Level	(%)	ISO 21827	COBIT	CMMI	Definition/Meaning
0	0	Not Performed (NP)	Non-Existent (NE)	Non-Existent (NE)	• No security controls or plans in place. • The controls are non-existent.
1	20	Performed Informally (PI)	Ad-hoc and Initial (AI)	Ad-hoc (AD)	• Base practices of the control areas are generally performed on an ad hoc basis. • There is general agreement within the organization that identified actions that should be performed, and they are performed when required. • But the practices are not formally adopted, tracked, and reported on.
2	40	Planned (PL)	Repeatable but Intuitive (RI)	Repeatable (RE)	• The base requirements for the control areas are planned, implemented, and repeatable.
3	60	Well Defined (WD)	Defined Process (DP)	Defined and Implemented (DI)	• In addition to Level 2, the processes used are documented, approved, and implemented organization-wide.
4	80	Quantitatively Controlled (QC)	Managed and Measurable (MM)	Managed (MA)	• In addition to Level 3, the processes are measured and verified (e.g., auditable).
5	100	Continuously Improving (CI)	Optimized (OP)	Optimized (OP)	• In addition to Level 4, standard processes are regularly reviewed and updated. • Improvements reflect an understanding of and response to vulnerability's impact.

METHOD

Research Methodology, Population and Samples

This chapter conducted a review of scholarly and practitioner literature to conceptualize the domain of operations security management. Following, the chapter utilized quantitative research methodology with a cross-sectional survey research approach (Malhotra & Grover, 1998) to assess the level of maturity of operations security management among industry sectors. Four hundred and eighty questionnaires were sent to information security officers, chief information officers, IT managers, IT specialists, and Internal Auditors who were familiar with their organizations' security environment by post, by email and by self delivery in 56 organizations drawn from five major industry sectors in three large regional capitals of Ghana. The industry sectors include (a) government public service institutions, (b) public utility companies (water, electricity, and telecommunication), (c) financial institutions, (d) educational institutions, (e) healthcare institutions, and others (manufacturing, oil and gas, IT, etc). The survey instrument was adopted from Higher Education Information Security Council (HEISC, 2013). It was modified to focus on operations security controls of the widely-accepted ISO/IEC 27002:2013 framework.

Instrument Reliability

The questionnaire consisted of operations security management (with five controls of 20 items) (see Table 2) and a section for demographic data. Apart from the demographic data, all the items on the

Table 2. Instrument reliability

Variables	No. of Items	Reliability Coefficient (Cronbach's Alpha)
Administrative Management	4	.785
Security in Third-Party Products and Services	4	.739
Malware Management	2	.747
Backup and Restoration	2	.765
Logging, Monitoring, Auditing and Reviewing	8	.891

$N = 223$

questionnaire used a 6-point Likert scale (*Not performed = 0, Performed informally = 1, Planned = 2, Well defined = 3, Quantitatively controlled = 4, and Continuously improving = 5*). The scale generated continuous data on all the items. The demographic data consisted of industry sector, job title, and the number of years of experience on the current job. The inter-organizational security program maturity was measured using ISO/IEC 21827 maturity model. The collected data were coded and analyzed using Statistically Package for Social Scientists (SPSS).

Firstly, the Cronbach's alpha reliability coefficient which measures the internal consistency of the items on the questionnaire was computed. Table 2 shows that the coefficients were within the acceptable range of 0.7 and above as according to Nunnuly (1978). Secondly, descriptive statistics using the mean and percentages was conducted to ascertain the information security maturity levels of the operations security controls and the individual security measures of the controls. Moreover, the Cross-tab was used to compare the organizations. Thirdly, with the intent of comparing and benchmarking the inter-organizational information security maturity levels, analysis of variance (ANOVA) was employed to analyze the significance differences among the organizations by their type.

MAIN FOCUS OF THE CHAPTER

This section conceptualizes the domain of operations security management based of the previous works. It follows with empirical analysis to assess the state-of-practice (maturity levels) of operations security management.

Proposed Domain of Operations Security Management

Figure 1 identifies and classifies operations security into ten domains as follows:

- Resource Protection
- Access Management
- Malware Management
- System Availability Management
- Administrative Management

Figure 1. Conceptualizing the domain of operations security management

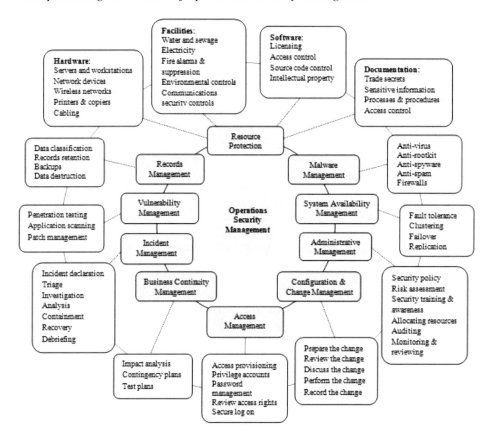

- Configuration and Change Management
- Business Continuity Management
- Incident Management
- Vulnerability Management
- Records Management

Resource Protection

Resource protection is the set of activities to protect the organization's resources. These resources include facilities (such as electricity, fire alarms, communications lines, and temperature controls), hardware (such as computers and network devices), software (such as source code and intellectual property), and documentations (processes, procedures, and instruction manuals).

Access Management

Access management consists of security policies, procedures, and controls that determine how and who should access information (Gregory, 2010). It includes user account provisioning, managing privilege accounts, password management, and review of access rights.

Malware Management

Malware management is the use of software (referred to as anti-malware) to block, detect, and clean malicious and unwanted software on a computer system. Malware is often classified as viruses, worms, and Trojan Houses. Viruses self-replicate and insert copies of themselves into other programs or data files. Viruses can be activated by user interaction with infested files through activities such as opening a file or running a program. Unlike viruses, worms are self-contained programs that normally execute themselves without user interaction (Souppaya & Scarfone, 2013). Trojan Horses are the type of malware that disguise themselves and hide within the user's legitimate file (US GAO, 2012). Data loss as a result of malware activities represents a significant threat to individuals and organizations. Therefore, installing anti-virus, anti-rootkit, anti-spyware, anti-spam, and firewalls can ensure protection against data loss.

System Availability Management

This is the process of ensuring that critical systems are continuously available (Negi & Pandey, 2012) to authorized users. Several measures are available to make systems resilient to failures. These include fault tolerance (duplication of components such that failure of one component will not result in the failure of the entire system), clustering (a group of two or more systems operate functionally as a single logical unit such that the system continues to operate if one of the systems fail), failover (switching over to a passive system when the active system fails), and replication (data transmission from one storage system to a counterpart storage system).

Administrative Management

This involves management oversight and control over all activities related to the protection of organizational information assets. Management control and oversight responsibilities include establishing and enforcing security policies, risk assessment, security training and awareness, allocating resources, auditing, monitoring, and reviewing.

Configuration and Change Management

Configuration management is the process of recording configuration changes that take place in a computing environment (Gregory, 2010). It aims at systematically controlling and monitoring the changes that have incurred in the configuration of systems during the entire lifetime (Gasparotti, 2013). Change management is a management process whereby each proposed change in an environment is formally planned and reviewed by peers and stakeholders prior to making the change (Gregory, 2010). It aims at improving stability and reducing unscheduled downtime in an environment (Gregory, 2010). Change management is carried out together with configuration management to record approved changes to systems (Gregory, 2010).

Business Continuity Management

The increasing levels of business disruptions and disaster events have created the need for business continuity management (Asgary, 2016). A potential threat to business continuity management is globalization

(Ee, 2014). Business continuity is a management activity where analysis is performed to better understand the risks associated with potential disasters and the steps that can be taken to reduce the impact of a disaster should one occur. Organizations will implement high-resilience systems that will permit critical business functions to continue operating even when a disaster strikes (Gregory, 2010). Business continuity management involves continuity planning (set of activities required to ensure continuation of critical business processes when a disaster occurs) and disaster recovery planning (set of activities concerned with assessment, salvaging, repairing, and restoration of damaged facilities and assets that support critical business processes) (Gregory, 2010). It also includes business impact analysis (catalog of all organization's important business processes and the criticality of each), contingency planning, and test plans (Gregory, 2010).

Incident Management

The objective of information security incident management is to provide a quick, efficient and organized response in case a security incident occurs. An incident is an unexpected event that results in an interruption of normal operations (Gregory, 2010). It aims at providing sufficient information regarding the event and ensures that such an incident do not occur (Finat, 2014). An incident can be managed systematically as follows: a) incident declaration (declaration of security incident when a policy violation has occurred), b) triage (search for clues that will hopefully lead to a root cause of the incident and the ability to apply corrective measures), c) investigation (closer study of information that may lead to the cause of the incident), d) analysis (deeper study of the information that is directly related to the incident), e) containment (measures to halt the incident and to prevent its spread), f) recovery (restoring the system to its pre-incident condition), and g) debriefing (reflecting on the incident and the organization's response to it in order to learn from the incident activities) (Gregory, 2010).

Vulnerability Management

Vulnerability management is the process of identifying weaknesses in systems and then acting to mitigate those weaknesses (Harris, 2013). Vulnerability is an inherent characteristic of any system (hardware or software). Its identification and management are essential for improving the system's resilience (Agarwal, 2015). Vulnerabilities in systems can be discovered through penetration testing, application scanning, and patch management. Penetration testing is a technique that mimics the actions of a hacker who scans a system or network for opened ports and services. Application scanning is the process of performing security tests on an application in order to find vulnerabilities in the application code itself. Patch management is a process that manages the installation of patches on systems (Gregory, 2010).

Records Management

Activities under records management involve data classification (establishing data sensitivity levels and handling procedures) and records retention (how long information must be kept). It also includes backups (making sure information is not lost due to system failure or malfunction) and data destruction (how information should be safely discarded when no longer needed) (Gregory, 2010).

RESULTS OF EMPIRICAL DATA ANALYSIS

This section begins by presenting the characteristics of the respondents. It is followed by the assessment of operations security maturity levels using ISO/IEC 21827 maturity scale. Following, the significant differences in the levels of operations security management among Ghanaian organizations were verified.

Characteristics of the Respondents

Out of the 480 survey questionnaires sent to the participants, 223 were returned, yielding a 46.5 percent response rate. Of this total, 17.6% of the respondents (corresponding to 40 participants) were from Educational Institutions (University colleges, polytechnics, universities), 10.8% of the respondents (corresponding to 24 participants) were from Public Utility Companies (Water, Electricity, Telecom), 24.3% (corresponding to 54 participants) were from Financial Institutions, 16.2% (corresponding to 36 participants) were from Government Public Service, 13.5% (corresponding to 30 participants) were from Health Care Institutions, and 17.6% were from other organizations (IT Companies, Oil and Gas, Manufacturing, etc).

The vast majority of the respondents (120 in total or 53.1%) who participated in the study were IT managers (specialists), who had the responsibility of managing and performing IT security functions in their various organizations. Thirty-three respondents (representing 14.9%) were chief information officers. Thirty information security officers (representing 13.5%), fifteen internal auditors (also representing 6.7%) also took part in the study. Twenty five (representing 11.2%) were other IT personnel (i.e., IT consultants) also participated in the study. For the number of years respondents had worked on the current job position, over 22.9% had 1-5 years of experience, 35.4% had 6 to 10 years experience, 37.7% had 11 to 15 years experience, and 4% had 16 to 20 years experience.

Assessing Operations Security Maturity Levels

Operations security controls that were measured composed of operational procedures and responsibilities, security in third-party products and services, malware protection, data backups, and logging and monitoring activities. Frequency distributions of the operations security controls and the individual security measures were measured using percentages, the mean and the standard deviation. Following, a crosstab was used to assess the levels of maturity of operations security management within the organizations:

- **Operational Procedures and Responsibilities:** To measure the level of operational procedures and responsibilities, participants responded to the extent to which their organizations maintained security configuration standards for information systems (IS) and applications; tested, authorized, and reported changes to information systems; segregated duties to ensure unintentional or unauthorized modification of information was detected; and how production systems were separated from other stages of the development life cycle. The results show that the level of operational procedures and responsibilities is at maturity Level 3 (mean = 3.04 or 60.8%) (see Table 4). This is an indication that the organizations' security operational procedures and responsibilities are well-defined. This suggests that security operational procedures and responsibilities processes used in the organizations are documented, approved, and implemented organization-wide;

Table 3. Sample characteristics

Respondents	No. of Participants Responded	Percent (%)
Industry Sector		
Education Institution	40	17.6
Public Utility Company	24	10.8
Financial Institution	54	24.3
Government	36	16.2
Health Care	30	13.5
Others (IT Companies, Oil and Gas, Manufacturing, etc.)	39	17.6
Job Function		
Information Security Officers	30	13.5
Chief Information Officers	33	14.9
IT Manager /IT Specialists	120	53.1
Internal Auditors	15	6.7
Others	25	11.2
Experience (Years)		
1-5	51	22.9
6-10	79	35.4
11-15	84	37.7
16-20	9	4.0

$N = 233$

- **Security in Third-party Products and Services:** With regard to management of security in third-party products and services, the participants responded to the degree to which their organizations had agreements with external IS services that met the organization's specific security requirements; put processes in place for assessing that external information system providers complied with security requirements; monitored the external information system services providers' compliance with security controls; and that the external information system service agreements were executed and routinely reviewed. From Table 4, the majority of the respondents (33.8%) reported that security in third-party products and services are generally at the stage of *well-defined*. Overall, the level of maturity is a little above Level 3 (mean = 3.14 or 62.4%). This level portrays that processes used in managing security in third-party products and services are documented, approved, and implemented organization-wide;

- **Malware Protection:** Moreover, regarding *malware protection*, the respondents assessed the degree to which their organizations put in place mechanisms to detect, quarantine, and eradicate known malicious code on information systems (including workstations, servers, and mobile computing devices) and eradicated known malicious code transported by electronic mail, the web, or removable media. From Table 4, malware protection recorded a mean of 3.08 (61.6), depicting maturity Level 3. Among the five security controls of operations security management, the vast majority of the respondents reported that their organizations malware protection is quantitatively controlled (37.8%). Information security processes are quantitatively controlled when the organizational security processes are being measured and verified (e.g., auditable);

- **Data Backup:** Likewise, the respondent assessed the extent to which data backup processes were consistent with the availability requirements and that system restore procedures were routinely tested. The results show that the maturity level is above Level 3, which has the mean of 3.32 (66.4%). Apparently, backup processes recorded the highest maturity among all the five controls of operations security management;

- **Logging, Monitoring and Reviewing:** Moreover, regarding logging and monitoring, the respondent assessed the extent to which their organizations: Put in place processes to monitor the utilization of key system resources and to mitigate the risk of system downtime; performed security-related activities that automatically logged system events; and implemented processes to routinely monitor logs to detect unauthorized and anomalous activities. Logging, monitoring and reviewing processes also included records log reviews; securing log data to prevent unauthorized access and tampering; regularly reviewing administrative and operative access to audit logs; use of file-integrity monitoring tools to alert personnel of unauthorized modification; and processes to ensure synchronization of system clocks with an authoritative source. Logging and monitoring security measures recorded the lowest maturity level among all the five controls of operations security management. It had a mean of 2.93 (58.6%), indicating the maturity level below Level 3.

- **Overall Operations Security Management:** Overall, the organizations' maturity level of operations security management was approximately at Level 3 (*well-defined*) with a mean score of 3.06 (*SD* = .808). As can be observed from Table 4, 4.1% of the organizations operations security management are *performed informally*, 17.6% are *planned*, 51.4% are *well defined*, 25.7% are *quantitatively controlled*, and only 1.4 are *continuously improving*.

Observably, the majority of the organizations have their operations security management maturity at the *planned* and *well defined* stages (see Table 5). It is interesting to note that apart from Education Institutions (15%) and Public Utility Companies (12.5%), no other organization's operations security

Table 4. Levels of operations security management

Information Security Controls	Levels in Percentages (%)						Mean	ML (%)	SD
	NP	PI	PL	WD	QC	CI			
Security Procedures and Responsibilities	1.4	4.1	18.9	44.6	27.0	4.1	3.04	60.8	.954
Security in third-party Products and Services	1.4	4.1	21.6	32.4	33.8	6.8	3.14	62.4	1.048
Malware Management	-	8.1	21.6	28.4	37.8	4.1	3.08	61.6	1.040
Backup and Restoration	-	4.1	10.8	43.2	32.4	9.5	3.32	66.4	.935
Logging, Monitoring and Review	1.4	6.8	21.6	37.8	32.4	-	2.93	58.6	.967
Maturity of Operations Security Management	-	4.1	17.6	51.4	25.7	1.4	3.06	61.2% (WD)	.808

Not Performed (NP – 0%); Performed Informally (PI – 20%); Planned (PL – 40%); Well Defined (WD – 60%); Quantitatively Controlled (QC – 80%); Continuously Improving (CI – 100%); ML - Maturity Level, N=223

Table 5. Maturity levels of operations security controls

Level	Maturity Scale	Industry Sectors (Frequency and Percentages)					
		Education Institution	Public Utility Company	Financial Institution	Government	Health Care	Others
0	Not Performed (NP)	-	-	-	-	-	-
1	Performed Informally (PI)	6	3	0	0	0	0
		15.0%	12.5%	.0%	.0%	.0%	.0%
2	Planned (PL)	10	6	6	9	0	9
		25.0%	25.0%	11.1%	25.0%	.0%	23.1%
3	Well Defined (WD)	15	6	27	24	15	27
		37.5%	25.0%	50.0%	66.7%	50.0%	69.2%
4	Quantitatively Controlled (QC)	9	9	18	3	15	3
		22.5%	37.5%	33.3%	8.3%	50.0%	7.7%
5	Continuously Improving (CI)	0	0	3	0	0	0
		.0%	.0%	5.6%	.0%	.0%	.0%
	No. of Respondents	40	24	54	36	30	39

management is at the *low level* maturity (*not performed* and *performed informally*). Also, the Government Public Services had 91.7% (PL and WD) and Financial Institutions had 61.1%, which are the *moderate level of maturity*. Comparing the organizations, the results show that only 22.5% (QC and CI) of Education Institutions are at the *high level* maturity, 37% for Public Utility Company, 38.9% for Financial Institutions, 8.3% for Government public service, 50% for Health Care, and 7.7% of other organizations. Thus, the maturity of operations security management is higher within Financial and Healthcare institutions than all other organizations, with Government Public Services recorded the lowest maturity levels.

- **Individual Operations Security Measures:** Further analysis of the individual operations security measures reveals interesting findings. The majority of the security measures fall below the stage of *well defined* (mean of 3.0 or 60%). In particular, only seven (7) operations security measures attain maturity Level 3 and above, falling within 61.6% and 64.0% (mean values of 3.08 and 3.20) (see Table 6). The highest operations security measures put in place is that the organizations ensure that external information systems services providers' compliance with security controls is monitored (64.0%). Moreover, many of the organizations ensure that data backup process is frequency consistent with the availability data security requirements (63.0%). However, it can be seen that as large as 6.8% of the organizations studied do not have external service providers' compliance with security measures. In addition, routine review of external information systems service agreements (54.8%) and file-integrity monitoring tools to alert security personnel of unauthorized modifications (54.6%) occupied the lowest levels of operations security measures.

Inter-Organizational Operations Security Management

The previous section assessed the maturity levels of operations security management. This section verifies whether there are significant differences in the levels of operations security management among

Table 6. Operations security control measures

No		Operations Security Controls/Measures	NP (%)	PI (%)	PL (%)	WD (%)	QC (%)	CI (%)	Mean	ML (%))	SD
	Operational Procedures and Responsibilities
	1	Maintains security configuration standards for information systems (IS) and applications.	2.7	9.5	24.3	32.4	21.6	9.5	2.89	59.8	1.207
	2	Changes to IS are tested, authorized, and reported.	1.4	9.5	23.0	35.1	25.7	5.4	2.91	58.2	1.096
	3	Segregation of duties to ensure unintentional or unauthorized modification of information is detected.	1.4	10.8	18.9	33.8	28.4	6.8	2.97	59.4	1.143
	4	Production systems are separated from other stages of the development life cycle.	2.7	12.2	21.6	27.0	27.0	9.5	2.92	58.4	1.264
	Security in Third-Party Products and Services
	5	Agreements for external IS services specify appropriate security requirements.	2.7	13.5	17.6	33.8	20.3	12.2	2.92	58.4	1.286
	6	Processes are in place for assessing that external IS providers comply with security requirements.	1.4	9.5	21.6	28.4	25.7	13.5	3.08	61.6	1.232
	7	External IS services providers' compliance with security controls is monitored.	6.8	6.8	17.6	24.3	23.0	23.0	3.20	64.0	1.457
	8	External IS service agreements are executed and routinely reviewed.	2.7	5.4	35.1	35.1	35.1	5.4	2.74	54.8	1.070
	Protection Against Malware
	9	Methods are used to detect, quarantine, and eradicate known malicious codes on IS including workstations, servers, and mobile computing devices.	2.7	5.4	31.1	24.3	32.4	4.1	2.91	58.2	1.121
	10	Methods are used to detect and eradicate known malicious code transported by electronic mail, the web, or removable media.	-	17.6	21.6	32.4	24.3	4.1	2.76	55.2	1.129
	Backup and Restoration
	11	Data backup process is frequency consistent with the availability requirements.	-	6.8	14.9	44.6	24.3	9.5	3.15	63.0	1.013
	12	Routinely tests the restore procedures.	1.4	10.8	23.0	33.8	24.3	6.8	2.89	57.8	1.138
	Logging, Monitoring, and Auditing
	13	Processes are in place to monitor the utilization of key system resources and to mitigate the risk of system downtime.	2.7	4.1	17.6	41.9	23.0	10.8	3.11	62.2	1.114
	14	Security-related activities are automatically logged.	-	12.2	23.0	28.4	24.3	12.2	3.01	60.2	1.206
	15	Processes are in place to routinely monitor logs to detect unauthorized and anomalous activities.	1.4	5.4	23.0	35.1	27.0	8.1	3.05	62.0	1.206
	16	Records log reviews.	1.4	8.1	24.3	33.8	24.3	8.1	2.96	59.2	1.124
	17	Steps are taken to secure log data to prevent unauthorized access and tampering.	2.7	9.5	17.6	29.7	39.2	1.4	2.97	59.4	1.118
	18	Regularly reviews administrative and operative access to audit logs.	-	9.5	20.3	35.1	20.3	14.9	3.11	62.2	1.173
	19	File-integrity monitoring tools are used to alert personnel to unauthorized modification.	5.4	8.1	23.0	23.0	20.3	4.1	2.73	54.6	1.158
	20	Processes in place to ensure synchronization of system clocks with an authoritative source.	4.1	9.5	21.6	33.8	27.0	4.1	2.82	56.4	1.171

N=223, NP- Not Performed, PI- Performed Informally, PL - Planned, WD - Well Defined, QC - Quantitatively Controlled, CI - Continuously Improving, ML - Maturity Level the organizations. Analysis of variance (ANOVA) was employed to test six null hypotheses in turn. For each hypothesis, descriptive statistics is conducted to ascertain the mean, standard deviation and 95% confidence intervals for the independent variables and the organization type: Education Institutions, Public Utility Company, Financial Institutions, Government, Health Care, and Others (IT, Oil and Gas, Manufacturing, etc.).

The following hypotheses were tested:

H$_1$: *There are no significant differences among organizations regarding the level of managing security procedures and responsibilities.*

H$_2$: *There are no significant differences among organizations regarding the level of managing security in the third-party products and services.*

H$_3$: *There are no significant differences among organizations regarding the level of malware management.*

H$_4$: *There are no significant differences among organizations regarding the level of backup management*

H$_5$: *There are no significant differences among organizations regarding the level of logging and monitoring management*

H$_6$: *There are no significant differences among organizations regarding the level of operations security management*

One of the assumptions of a one-way ANOVA is that the variances of the groups being compared should be similar. As such, the Levene's test of homogeneity of variance was tested for similar variances. Levene's *F* Statistic has a significance value of $p < .05$, indicating that the assumption of homogeneity of variances was not met. Therefore, the variances in the levels of information security management among the organizations were statistically significantly different. A post hoc test (Games-Howell *post-hoc*) of multiple comparisons was conducted to determine which organizations are significantly and statistically different. The results of the ANOVA analyses are presented in Table 7.

Hypothesis H$_1$ proposed that the level of operations *security procedures and responsibilities* is the same among the organizations. A one-way ANOVA was conducted to test significant differences among the organizations. Table 7 shows the mean and standard deviation of the organization types: Education Institutions was 2.30 ($N = 40$; $SD = .92$); Public Utility Companies was 3.22 ($N = 24$; $SD = .84$); Financial Institutions was 3.26 ($N = 54$; $SD = .51$); Government Public Service was 2.73 ($N = 36$; $SD = .44$); Health Care was 3.73 ($N = 30$; $SD = .51$), and other organizations (IT, Oil and Gas, Manufacturing) was 2.42 ($N = 39$; $SD = .75$). A one-way ANOVA shows (see Table 8) that there was at least one significant difference between the organizations ($N = 233$; $F (5, 217) = 17.567$; $p < .05$). The results indicated statistical significant differences in the level of operations *security procedures and responsibilities* among the organization types. As a result, the null hypothesis was not supported and therefore rejected. Table 8 shows a significant difference between the Education Institutions (46.0%) and Public Utility (64.4%), Financial Institutions (65.2%), Health Care Institutions (74.6%). Moreover, significant differences can be observed between Government Public Services (54.6%) and Financial Institutions (65.2%), Health Care Institutions (74.6%). Observably, the Public Utility, Financial Institutions, and Health Care Institutions outperform Education Institutions. Also, Financial Institutions and Health Care outperform Government Public Service.

Hypothesis H$_2$ proposed that the level of *managing security in third-party products and services* is the same among the organizations. Table 7 shows the mean and standard deviation of the organization types: Education Institutions was 2.39 ($N = 40$; $SD = 1.19$); Public Utility Companies was 2.78 ($N = 24$;

Table 7. Differences in inter-organizational operations security management

Security Controls	Organizations/ Institutions	N	Mean	SD	ML(%)/ (Ranking)	Maturity Level *	Organizational Differences (Post Hoc – Games Howell)
Security Roles, Responsibilities, Procedures & Security	Education Institution	40	2.30	.92	46.0 (6)	PL (2)	Educational -> Public Utility, Financial, Health Care. Government -> Financial, Health Care.
	Public Utility Company	24	3.22	.84	64.4 (3)	WD (3)	
	Financial Institution	54	3.26	.94	65.2 (2)	WD (3)	
	Government	36	2.73	.51	54.6 (4)	WD (3)	
	Health Care	30	3.73	.51	74.6 (1)	QC (3)	
	Others	39	2.42	.75	48.4 (5)	PL (3)	
Third-Party Security	Education Institution	40	2.39	1.19	47.8 (6)	PL (2)	Educational -> Financial, Health Care. Public Utility -> Health Care. Financial -> Public Utility.
	Public Utility Company	24	2.78	.96	55.6 (3)	WD (3)	
	Financial Institution	54	3.50	.84	70.0 (2)	WD (3)	
	Government	36	2.77	.52	55.4 (4)	WD (3)	
	Health Care	30	3.63	.55	72.6 (2)	WD (3)	
	Others	39	2.65	.77	53.0 (5)	WD (3)	
Malware Protection	Education Institution	40	2.14	1.07	42.8 (6)	PL (2)	Educational -> Financial, Government -> Health Care.
	Public Utility Company	24	2.88	1.11	57.6 (3)	WD (3)	
	Financial Institution	54	3.03	.88	60.6 (2)	WD (4)	
	Government	36	2.79	.78	55.8 (5)	WD (3)	
	Health Care	30	3.40	.93	68.0 (1)	WD (3)	
	Others	39	2.81	.92	56.3 (4)	WD (3)	
Backup & Restoration	Education Institution	40	2.74	.99	54.8 (5)	WD (3)	Educational -> Financial. Financial -> Government. Government -> Health Care.
	Public Utility Company	24	3.06	.97	60.2 (3)	WD (3)	
	Financial Institution	54	3.39	.82	67.8 (1)	WD (4)	
	Government	36	2.67	.52	53.4 (6)	WD (3)	
	Health Care	30	3.30	.65	66.0 (2)	WD (4)	
	Others	39	2.85	1.08	57.0 (4)	WD (3)	
Logging, Monitoring, & Auditing	Education Institution	40	2.46	1.04	49.2 (6)	PL (2)	Educational -> Financial, Health Care. Financial -> Government.
	Public Utility Company	24	2.88	.91	57.6 (4)	WD (3)	
	Financial Institution	54	3.45	.73	69.0 (1)	WD (4)	
	Government	36	2.65	.62	53.0 (5)	WD (3)	
	Health Care	30	3.25	.83	65.0 (2)	WD (3)	
	Others	39	2.95	.58	59.0 (3)	WD (3)	
Overall: Operations Security	Education Institution	40	2.41	.90	48.2 (6)	PL (2)	Educational -> Financial, Health Care. Health Care -> Government.
	Public Utility Company	24	2.94	.86	59.8 (3)	WD (3)	
	Financial Institution	54	3.38	.67	67.6 (2)	WD (3)	
	Government	36	2.70	.44	54.0 (5)	WD (3)	
	Health Care	30	3.44	.59	68.8 (1)	WD (3)	
	Others	39	2.76	.77	55.2 (4)	WD (3)	

Not Performed (NP – 0%); Performed Informally (PI – 20%); Planned (PL – 40%); Well Defined (WD – 60%); Quantitatively Controlled (QC – 80%); Continuously Improving (CI – 100%); N=233. * Nearest to maturity scale point, *N*=223

SD = .96); Financial Institutions was 3.50 (*N* = 54; *SD* = .84); Government Public Service was 2.77 (*N* = 36; *SD* = .52); Health Care was 3.63 (*N* = 30; *SD* = .55), and other organizations (IT, Oil and Gas, Manufacturing) was 2.65 (*N* = 39; *SD* = .77). A one-way ANOVA shows (see Table 8) that there was at least one significant difference between the organizations (*N* = 233; F (5, 217) = 13.289; $p < .05$). This indicated statistical significant differences in the level of *managing security in third-party products and services* among the organization types. Consequently, the null hypothesis was not supported and therefore rejected. Table 8 shows that Educational Institutions (47.8%) differ significantly from Financial Institutions (70.0%) and Health Care Institutions (72.6%); Public Utility (55.6%) differs significantly from Health Care Institutions (74.6%); and Financial Institutions (70.0%) differ significantly from Public Utility (55.6%). Therefore, Financial Institutions and Health Care Institutions perform better than Educational Institutions and Public Utility organizations.

Hypothesis H₃ also proposed that the level of *malware protection* is the same among the organizations. A one-way ANOVA was conducted to test the hypothesis that *malware protection* do no differ significantly among the organizations. The mean and standard deviation of the organization types were: Education Institutions was 2.14 (*N* = 40; *SD* = 1.07); Public Utility Companies was 2.88 (*N* = 24; *SD* = 1.11); Financial Institutions was 3.03 (*N* = 54; *SD* = .88); Government Public Service was 2.79 (*N* = 36; *SD* = .78); Health Care was 3.40 (*N* = 30; *SD* = .93), and other organizations (IT, Oil and Gas, Manufacturing) was 2.81 (*N* = 39; *SD* = .92) (see Table 7). A one-way ANOVA shows that there was at least one significant difference between the organizations (*N* = 233; F (5, 217) = 7.006; $p < .05$) (see Table 8). Accordingly, the null hypothesis was not supported and therefore rejected. Table 8 shows the mean and significant differences in the levels of *malware protection:* Educational Institutions (42.8%) differ significantly from Financial Institutions (67.8%) and Government Public Service (54.8%) also differs significantly from Health Care Institutions (68.0%). As can be observed from the table, Financial Institutions outperform Educational Institutions and Health Care Institutions outperform Government Public Service.

Hypothesis H₄ proposed that the level of *backup management* is not different among the organizations. Table 7 shows the mean and standard deviation of the organization types: Education Institutions was 2.74 (*N* = 40; *SD* = .99); Public Utility Companies was 3.06 (*N* = 24; *SD* = .97); Financial Institutions was 3.39 (*N* = 54; *SD* = .82); Government Public Service was 2.67 (*N* = 36; *SD* = .52); Health Care was 3.30 (*N* = 30; *SD* = .65), and Other organizations (IT, Oil and Gas, Manufacturing) was 2.85 (*N* = 39; *SD* = 1.08). A one-way ANOVA shows (see Table 8) that there was at least one significant difference between the organizations (*N* = 233; F (5, 217) = 5.003; $p < .05$). Hence, the null hypothesis was not supported and therefore rejected. Observably, Educational Institutions (54.8%) differ significantly from Financial Institutions (67.8%), Financial Institutions (67.8%) differ significantly from Government *Public Service* (53.4%), and Government Institutions (53.4) differ significantly from Health Care Institutions (66.0%). Evidently, Financial Institutions outperform Educational Institutions and Government Institutions. Also, Health Care Institutions outperform Government Public Service.

Hypothesis H₅ proposed that the level of security logging and monitoring is different among the organizations. Table 7 shows the mean and standard deviation of the organization types: Education Institutions was 2.46 (*N* = 40; *SD* = 1.04); Public Utility Companies was 2.88 (*N* = 24; *SD* = .91); Financial Institutions was 3.45 (*N* = 54; *SD* = .73); Government Public Service was 2.65 (*N* = 36; *SD* = .62); Health Care was 3.25 (*N* = 30; *SD* = .83), and Other organizations (IT, Oil and Gas, Manufacturing) was 2.95 (*N* = 39; *SD* = .58). A one-way ANOVA shows (see Table 8) that there was at least one significant difference between the organizations (*N* = 233; F (5, 217) = 9.381; $p < .05$). As a result, the null hypothesis was not supported and therefore rejected. Noticeably, Educational Institutions (49.2%) differ significantly from Financial Institutions (69.0%) and Health Care Institutions (65.0%). Again, Financial Institutions (69.0%) differ significantly from Government Public Service (53.0%). Obviously, Financial Institutions outperform Educational Institutions and Government Public Service. Likewise, Health Care Institutions outperform Educational Institutions.

Hypothesis H_6 proposed that the overall level of *operations security* is the same among the organizations. Table 7 shows the mean and standard deviation of the organization types: Education Institutions was 2.41 ($N = 40$; $SD = .90$); Public Utility Companies was 2.94 ($N = 24$; $SD = .86$); Financial Institutions was 3.38 ($N = 54$; $SD = .67$); Government Public Service was 2.70 ($N = 36$; $SD = .44$); Health Care was 3.44 ($N = 30$; $SD = .59$), and Other organizations (IT, Oil and Gas, Manufacturing) was 2.76 ($N = 39$; $SD = .77$). A one-way ANOVA shows that there was at least one significant difference between the organizations ($N = 233$; $F (5, 217) = 14.181$; $p < .05$). This indicated statistical significant differ-

Table 8. Significant differences between and within organizations using ANOVA

Hypotheses	Variables		Sum of Squares	df	Mean Square	F	Sig.	Result
H_1	Security Roles, Responsibilities, Procedures & Security	Between Groups	54.280	5	10.856	17.567	.000	Not supported
		Within Groups	134.101	217	.618			
		Total	188.381	222				
H_2	Third-Party Security	Between Groups	47.497	5	9.499	13.289	.000	Not supported
		Within Groups	155.118	217	.715			
		Total	202.614	222				
H_3	Malware Protection	Between Groups	31.157	5	6.231	7.006	.000	Not supported
		Within Groups	193.022	217	.890			
		Total	224.179	222				
H_4	Backup & Restoration	Between Groups	18.599	5	3.720	5.003	.000	Not supported
		Within Groups	161.360	217	.744			
		Total	179.960	222				
H_5	Logging, Monitoring, & Auditing	Between Groups	29.179	5	5.836	9.381	.000	Not supported
		Within Groups	134.992	217	.622			
		Total	164.171	222				
H_6	Overall: Operations Security	Between Groups	32.128	5	6.426	14.181	.000	Not supported
		Within Groups	98.329	217	.453			
		Total	130.457	222				

$N = 233$

ences in the level of *operations security* among the organization types. As a result, the null hypothesis was not supported and therefore rejected. The results show that Educational Institutions (48.2%) differ significantly from Financial Institutions (67.6%) and Health Care Institutions (68.8%). Also, Health Care Institutions (68.8%) differ significantly from Government Public Service (54.0%). Overall, Financial Institutions and Health Care Institutions outperform Educational Institutions. Moreover, Health Care Institutions outperform Government Public Service.

SOLUTIONS AND RECOMMENDATIONS

Operations security management integrates the activities of all the other information systems security controls (Henrya, 2011). Previous studies noted the multifaceted nature of operations security management (Gregory, 2010; Harris, 2013; ISC2 CBK, 2017; ISO/IEC 27002:2013, 2013). However, few studies attempted to specify its domain for better understanding and effective management of the entire computing environment. In this chapter, ten domains of operations security management were identified. Each control of the domain was presented and discussed along with its sub-themes and countermeasures.

Following, an assessment was conducted to ascertain the maturity levels of some key domain controls of operations security management and their sub-themes (managing operational procedures, roles and responsibilities; security in third-party products and services; malware protection; data backup; and logging and monitoring activities). The study found that operations security maturity was 61.2%, which represented the maturity Level 3 (*Well-Defined*). This level suggested that operations security processes and controls were documented, approved, and implemented organization-wide. Though this level provided reasonable level of protection, ISO/IEC 27002 (2013) noted that for sustained information security, higher levels of security would be required. For example, Level 4 suggested that information security processes were measured and verified (e.g., auditable), while Level 5 (the highest level of maturity) ensured that standard processes were regularly reviewed and updated in response to vulnerability's impact. Ideally, organizations should improve operations security processes to Level 5 in order to sustain improved information security.

Among the operations security controls, backup was the most implemented security measures. Conversely, logging, monitoring, auditing, and reviewing were the least implemented measures of operations security management. The majority of the respondents reported that in their organizations malware protection was quantitatively controlled (Level 5). Logging and monitoring recorded the lowest maturity level of the mean of 2.93 (below Level 3). In terms of individual operations security measures, the highest security measures put in place were: (a) ensuring that external information systems services providers' compliance with security controls and (b) data backup processes were consistent with the organizations' data security requirements. In terms of organizational performance, the maturity of operations security management was higher within Financial and Healthcare institutions than all other organizations. The Government Public Services recorded the lowest maturity levels. A further analysis was conducted to determine the significant differences among the organizations. Consistently, among the hypotheses tested for significant differences, Financial and Health Care Institutions significantly differed from Educational Institutions and Government Public Service.

FUTURE RESEARCH DIRECTIONS

This chapter is a preliminary study toward series of in-depth studies on information security management in organizations. The current study is limited to operations security management, although there are other security controls. However, the choice is because operations security is the centre of all information security activities (Henrya, 2011). Another limitation is that, even within the domain of operations security management identified in the chapter, only some of the measures (managing operational procedures, roles and responsibilities; security in third-party products and services; malware protection; data backup; and logging and monitoring activities) were used in the empirical analysis. Therefore, future works will include assessing other controls within the operations security domain, including incident management, vulnerability management, and business continuity management.

CONCLUSION

For the need of integrating and better understanding of the domain of operations security, this chapter classified operations security into ten domains based on the analysis of existing scholarly and practitioner literature. Each domain has been presented and discussed with its sub-themes and appropriate security measures. This categorization would assist operations security personnel in their day-to-day activities of protecting the organization's information assets. Moreover, the chapter assessed the maturity of operations security controls and the inter-organizational information security levels. The evaluation provided information about how well operations security controls were applied in organizations. This could serve as a benchmark for making security investments decisions. The study further provided the basis for comparing inter-organizational security measures, the results of which might be useful for benchmarking performance. This might lead to competitiveness and general improvement in information security management. Finally, the findings of this chapter could be used by organizations as the basis for improving operations security in particular and information security in general.

DISCUSSION QUESTIONS

1. Why should organizations apply the following information security concepts when implementing operations security
    a. Need-to-know
    b. Least privilege
    c. Separation of duties
    d. Job rotation.
2. Identify the threats to operations security and discuss the countermeasures.
3. What measures should an organization take to in order improve the maturity of its operations security?

4. Given the proposed domain of operations security management as in Figure 1, explain two major activities/tasks (under the following list) operations security personnel should perform to keep their computing environment continuously secured.

    a. Resource protection
    b. Access management
    c. Malware management
    d. System availability management
    e. Administrative management
    f. Configuration and change management
    g. Business continuity management
    h. Incident management
    i. Vulnerability management
    j. Records management

REFERENCES

Agarwal, J. (2015). Improving resilience through vulnerability assessment and management. *Civil Engineering and Environmental Systems*, *32*(1/2), 5–17. doi:10.1080/10286608.2015.1025065

Alampay, E. A., & Hechanova, R. M. (2010). Monitoring employee use of the Internet in Philippine organizations. *The Electronic Journal on Information Systems in Developing Countries*, *40*(5), 1–20. doi:10.1002/j.1681-4835.2010.tb00287.x

Arshad, A., & Ameen, K. (2015). Usage patterns of Punjab University Library website: A transactional log analysis study. *The Electronic Library*, *33*(1), 65–74. doi:10.1108/EL-12-2012-0161

Asgary, A. (2016). Business continuity and disaster risk management in business education: Case of York University. *AD-Minister*, (28): 49–72. doi:10.17230/ad-minister.28.3

Avery, S., & Tracy, D. G. (2014). Using transaction log analysis to assess student search behavior in the library instruction classroom. *RSR. Reference Services Review*, *42*(2), 320–335. doi:10.1108/RSR-08-2013-0044

Bachlechner, D., Thalmann, S., & Maier, R. (2014). Security and compliance challenges in complex IT outsourcing arrangements: A multi-stakeholder perspective. *Computers & Security*, *40*, 38–59. doi:10.1016/j.cose.2013.11.002

Brown, W. C., & Nasuti, F. (2005). Sarbanes-Oxley and enterprise security: IT governance - what it takes to get the job done. *Information Systems Security*, *14*(5), 15–28. doi:10.1201/1086.106589 8X/45654.14.5.20051101/91010.4

Bulgurcu, B., Cavusoglu, H., & Benbasat, I. (2010). Information security policy compliance: An empirical study of rationality-based beliefs and information security awareness. *Management Information Systems Quarterly*, *34*(3), 523–548. doi:10.2307/25750690

Computer Security Institute. (2011). *The 2010 / 2011 CSI Computer Crime and Security Survey*. Retrieved from www.GoCSI.com

Connolly, C. (2010). A review of data logging systems, software and applications. *Sensor Review*, *30*(3), 192–196. doi:10.1108/02602281011051362

Data Protection Act. (2012). *Protecting the privacy of the individual and personal data*. Retrieved from http://www.dataprotection.org.gh/data-protection-act

DBIR. (2013). *The 2013 Data Breach Investigations Report*. Retrieved from http://www.verizonenterprise.com/DBIR/

Deursen, N. V., Buchanan, W. J., & Duff, A. (2013). Monitoring information security risks within health care. *Computers & Security*, *37*, 31–45. doi:10.1016/j.cose.2013.04.005

Ee, H. (2014). Business continuity 2014: From traditional to integrated business continuity management. *Journal of Business Continuity & Emergency Planning*, *8*(2), 102–105. PMID:25416371

Electronic Transactions Act 772. (2008). *Ghana's Electronic Transaction Act 772*. Retrieved from www.unesco.org

Evdokimov, S., Fischmann, M., & Günther, O. (2010). Provable security for outsourcing database operations. *International Journal of Information Security and Privacy*, *4*(1), 1–17. doi:10.4018/jisp.2010010101

Finat, C. (2014). Information security management incidents in research - development. *Romanian Review Precision Mechanics, Optics & Mecatronics*, (45), 137-141.

Gasparotti, C. (2013). Importanţa managementului configuraţiei, cu Exemplificare în domeniul instalaţiilor navale. *Review of Management & Economic Engineering*, *12*(4), 41–52.

Gregory, P. (2010). *CISSP Guide to Security Essentials*. Cengage Learning. Course Technology. Retrieved from https://www.cengage.com/c/cissp-guide-to-security-essentials-2e.../9781285060422

Harris, S. (2013). *All-In-One CISSP Exam Guide* (6th ed.). McGraw Hill.

HEISC. (2013). *Information Security Program Assessment Tool*. Retrieved from http://www.educause.edu/library/resources/information-security-program-assessment-tool

Hoffman, S., & Podgurski, A. (2007). Securing the HIPPA security rule. *Journal of Internet Law*, *10*(8), 1–11.

ISC2 CBK. (2017). *The (ISC)2 Body of Knowledge*. Retrieved from https://www.isc2.org/Certifications/CBK

ISO/IEC 21827:2008. (2008). *Information technology - Security techniques - Systems Security Engineering - Capability Maturity Model (SSE-CMM)*. Retrieved from http://www.iso.org/iso/catalogue_detail.htm?csnumber=44716

ISO/IEC 27002:2013. (2013). *Information technology Security techniques - Code of practice for information security controls*. Retrieved from http://www.iso.org/iso/catalogue_detail?csnumber=54533 ISO/IEC

ITIL. (2010). *Benefits of standard IT governance frameworks*. Retrieved from http://www.itil-officialsite. com

Jarraya, H., & Laurent, M. (2010). A secure peer-to-peer backup service keeping great autonomy while under the supervision of a provider. *Computers & Security*, *29*(2), 180–195. doi:10.1016/j.cose.2009.10.003

Jones, A., Dardick, G. S., Davies, G., Sutherland, I., & Valli, C. (2009). The 2008 analysis of information remaining on disks offered for sale on the second hand market. *Journal of International Commercial Law & Technology*, *4*(3), 162–175.

Joy Online. (2013). *Cyber crime: Ghana 2nd in Africa, 7th in the world*. Retrieved from http://edition. myjoyonline.com/pages/news/201307/110530.php

Karadsheh, L. (2012). Applying security policies and service level agreement to IaaS service model to enhance security and transition. *Computers & Security*, *31*(3), 315–326. doi:10.1016/j.cose.2012.01.003

Kent, K., & Souppaya, M. (2006). *NIST Special Publication 800-92: Guide to Computer Security Log Management - Recommendations of the National Institute of Standards and Technology*. Retrieved from csrc.nist.gov/publications/nistpubs/800-92/SP800-92.pdf

Kim, D. W., Yan, P., & Junjie Zhang, J. (2015). Detecting fake anti-virus software distribution webpages. *Computers & Security*, *49*, 95–106. doi:10.1016/j.cose.2014.11.008

Kljun, M., Mariani, J., & Dix, A. (2016). Toward understanding short-term personal information preservation: A study of backup strategies of end users. *Journal of the Association for Information Science and Technology*, *67*(12), 2947–2963. doi:10.1002/asi.23526

Kolkowska, E., & Dhillon, G. (2013). Organizational power and information security rule compliance. *Computers & Security*, *33*, 3–11. doi:10.1016/j.cose.2012.07.001

Malhotra, M. K., & Grover, V. (1998). An assessment of survey research in POM: Form constructs to theory. *Journal of Operations Management*, *16*(4), 407–425. doi:10.1016/S0272-6963(98)00021-7

Martin, N., & Rice, J. (2011). Cybercrime: Understanding and addressing the concerns of stakeholders. *Computers & Security*, *30*(8), 803–814. doi:10.1016/j.cose.2011.07.003

Morrow, B. (2012). BYOD security challenges: *Control and protect your most sensitive data. Network Security*, *5-8*. doi:10.1016/S1353-4858(12)70111-3

Negi, M., & Pandey, D. K. (2012). High availability using virtualization. *International Transactions in Applied Sciences*, *4*(2), 195–200.

Nissim, N., Cohen, A., Glezer, C., & Elovici, Y. (2015). Detection of malicious PDF files and directions for enhancements: A state-of-the art survey. *Computers & Security*, *48*, 246–266. doi:10.1016/j. cose.2014.10.014

Nunnally, J. C. (1978). *Psychometric theory* (2nd ed.). New York, NY: McGraw-Hill.

Pabrai, U. A. (2006). Rules and regulations: The impact of compliance on IT. *Certification Magazine*, *8*(3), 38–40.

Park, M., & Lee, T. (2013). Understanding science and technology information users through transaction log analysis. *Library Hi Tech, 31*(1), 123–140. doi:10.1108/07378831311303976

Prabhu, P. R. (2013). *ISO/IEC 27001:2013: Insight on Operations Security & Communications Security Domain*. Retrieved from https://wings2i.wordpress.com/2013/10/31/isoiec-270012013-insight-on-operations-security-communications-security-domain/

Ramalho, D. S. (2014). The use of malware as a means of obtaining evidence in Portuguese criminal proceedings. *Digital Evidence and Electronic Signature Law Review, 11*.

Report, P. W. C. (2015). *The Global State of Information Security Survey 2015*. Retrieved from http://www.pwc.com

Safa, N. S., Von Solms, R., & Furnell, S. (2016). Information security policy compliance model in organizations. *Computers & Security, 56*, 70–82. doi:10.1016/j.cose.2015.10.006

Scanlon, M., Farina, J., & Kechadi, M. (2015). Network investigation methodology for BitTorrent Sync: A Peer-to-Peer based file synchronisation service. *Computers & Security, 54*, 27–43. doi:10.1016/j.cose.2015.05.003

Shaqrah, A. A. (2010). The influence of internet security on e-business competence in Jordan: An Empirical Analysis. *International Journal of Technology Diffusion, 1*(4), 13–28. doi:10.4018/jtd.2010100102

Shieh, J. (2012). From website log to findability. *The Electronic Library, 30*(5), 707–720. doi:10.1108/02640471211275747

Software Engineering Institute. (2002). *Capability maturity model integration for software engineering*. Retrieved from ftp://192.58.107.24/pub/documents/02.reports/pdf/02tr028.pdf

Souppaya, M., & Scarfone, K. (2013). *NIST Special Publication 800-83 Revision 1 (2013). Guide to Malware Incident Prevention and Handling for Desktops and Laptops*. Retrieved from http://nvlpubs.nist.gov/nistpubs/SpecialPublications/NIST.SP.800-83r1.pdf

Stevanović, B. (2011). Maturity models in information security. *International Journal of Information and Communication Technology Research, 1*(2), 44–47.

Tang, C., & Liu, J. (2015). Selecting a trusted cloud service provider for your SaaS program. *Computers & Security, 50*, 60–73. doi:10.1016/j.cose.2015.02.001

Thielens, J. (2013). Why API are central to a BYOD security strategy. *Network Security*, 5-6. doi:10.1016/S1353-4858(13)70091-6

United States Patent and Trademark Office (USPTO). (2009). *Network and AIS audit, logging, and monitoring policy*. Retrieved from www.uspto.gov/about/vendor_info/current_acquisitions/sdi_ng/ocio_6011_09.pdf

US GAO. (2012). *Information Security: Better implementation of controls for mobile devices should be encouraged*. Retrieved from http://www.gao.gov/products/GAO-12-757

Vance, A., Lowry, P. B., & Eggett, D. (2013). Using accountability to reduce access policy violations in information systems. *Journal of Management Information Systems*, *29*(4), 263–289. doi:10.2753/MIS0742-1222290410

Willison, R., & Warkentin, M. (2013). Beyond deterrence: An expanded view of employee computer abuse. *Management Information Systems Quarterly*, *37*(1), 1–20. doi:10.25300/MISQ/2013/37.1.01

Wu, M., & Yu, M. (2013). Enterprise information security management based on context-aware RBAC and communication monitoring technology. *Mathematical Problems in Engineering*, *2013*, 1–11. doi:10.1155/2013/569562

Zolait, A. H., Ibrahim, A. R., & Farooq, A. (2010). A study on the Internet security and its implication for e-commerce in Yemen. *International Journal of Technology Diffusion*, *1*(3), 34–47. doi:10.4018/jtd.2010070102

KEY TERMS AND DEFINITIONS

Access Management: Activities organizations carry out to control users' access to computer systems, networks, and facilities (buildings, rooms, workspaces). It also includes the tasks users are permitted to perform when access is granted.

Backup: The process of making a copy of important information from a computer system to another device for recovery or archival purposes.

Business Continuity Management: When an unexpected event occurs, organizations must recover and restore work to normal operations. This involves measures that are taken to reduce or prevent the effect of a disaster.

Change Management: The processes involved when changes to computing environment are formally planned and reviewed before the changes are implemented.

Configuration Management: Activities to monitor and set up the configuration of computer systems and software applications so that they can perform the needed functionality.

Malware Management: The use of software (known as antimalware) to block, detect, and clean malicious and unwanted software on a computer system.

Operation Security: The day-to-day activities that ensure that computer systems, networks, applications, and the entire computing environment are secured and protected.

Resource Protection: Security measures and processes that are put in place to protect information assets and resources, including facilities, hardware, software, networks, documentation, and records.

Vulnerability Management: The process of identifying weaknesses in systems and putting in place measures to mitigate the threats that may exploit the weaknesses.

Chapter 16
Executing a Real–Time Response in an Agile Information System

Pankaj Chaudhary
Indiana University of Pennsylvania, USA

James A. Rodger
Indiana University of Pennsylvania, USA

Micki Hyde
Indiana University of Pennsylvania, USA

ABSTRACT

Agile information systems (AIS) is a current topic of interest in the IS industry. An AIS is defined as one that has ability to sense a change in real time, diagnose it in real time, and select and execute an action in real time. This study focuses on the properties or attributes of an AIS to execute an action in real time. The properties outlined in this research enable an AIS to select a response in real time and then execute a response in real time. The attributes are derived using industry literature, refined using interviews with industry practitioners and then verified for importance using a survey. From the exercise it is concluded that most properties or attributes are important for real-time execution in an AIS. Dimensions underlying these attributes are identified using EFA. Some recent frameworks and paradigms related to IS configurations that can respond to changes in real time are discussed. These frameworks incorporate many of the properties that were arrived for executing a change in real time in an agile IS and hence provide additional validation for the research.

INTRODUCTION

The current business environment and environment in general is characterized by change, uncertainty, and turbulence. The rate of change is fast and unpredictable. There are many sources of change. Changing and evolving technology, change in consumer demographics (e.g. aging in certain societies), change in customer demand, new competitors (in the same product category and serving as substitute products),

DOI: 10.4018/978-1-5225-6367-9.ch016

etc., are all sources of change that an organization in today's environment has to deal with on a regular basis. The seamless flow of information on a global scale and global competition means that the impact of a change can occur fast and come from any corner of the world, not just locally or even from within the country. Organizations need to be proactive in anticipating change and responding to it in real-time, to stay competitive in the marketplace. Organizations also need to be able to react in real-time to a change that has occurred, again not just to stay competitive but also for survival. Organizations then need to develop the capability to respond to a change in real-time (refer to Pankaj et al., (2009) for a more detailed treatment). This capability may be defined as agility. As per a Computer Associates survey, 84% of the executives believe that the capability to respond more quickly to new opportunities will give them a distinct advantage, 65% believe that improved agility will result in higher customer satisfaction, and 58% believe that it will result in a higher employee productivity and retention (Orton-Jones, 2017).

Agility is a multi-faceted concept which pervades all aspects of an organization (Pankaj, 2009). Information is an integral part of any organization's operations, functions, and processes (Tushman & Nadler, 1978), and Information Systems (IS) are a necessity for any modern organization where information processing is concerned (Pankaj & Hyde, 2003). Additionally, IS are needed for organizational agility on account of their ability to provide shared, distributed and integrated, current, and fast-flowing information (Bajgoric, 2000; Bal, Wilding, & Gundry, 1999; Christopher, 2000; Hoek, 2000; Mason-Jones & Towill, 1999; Sharifi & Zhang, 1999; Yusuf, Sarahadi, & Gunasekaran, 1999). Hence information and the information processing mechanisms (IS) in a modern organization are an integral consideration in agility of an organization.

Modern business processes in organizations use IS as a core resource or component (Pankaj & Hyde, 2003). In many and most cases, IS may completely or significantly embed a business process (e.g., Internet banking). The pivotal role of IS in modern organizational business processes means that an organization (agile or striving to be) cannot change its business processes unless the IS changes as well. Thus, an agile organization would need an agile IS. As per the ORACLE cloud agility survey (ORACLE, 2015) the ability of the competitor to launch innovative services more rapidly was identified as a top threat by 27% of the respondents. Also, as per the survey, a majority of businesses believe they are agile but cannot flexibly manage workloads or rapidly develop, test, and launch new applications, leaving them poorly prepared to deal with competitive threats. What Boynton indicated in 1993 still holds true: current IS are not easy to change though several are getting closer in some aspects. Markets change but IS do not. Though more organizations are experimenting with Agile Development methods, most IS have been developed and are still being built, to cover a closed/defined set of requirements using the waterfall development methodology, especially in contracting and outsourcing arrangements. The performance of an IS is also optimized for these requirements. The result of this optimization is that IS changes are often arduous and complicated, especially in cases where the requirements were not explicitly foreseen by the designers. But such requirements are frequent in today's environment. The problems in changing an IS are further aggravated by other factors such as outsourcing, where the knowledge about the architectural and technical aspects of IS may primarily reside outside the organization. The inability of IS to change quickly impedes organizational agility. The challenge for an organization is to structure its IS to meet a variety of changing requirements, many of which are not even known when the IS are built. In summary, an agile organization needs an agile IS.

So, what is an agile IS? We arrive at the definition or construct of an agile IS based on prior work done in this area by the authors. Agility in general is defined (Pankaj, 2005; Pankaj, Hyde, Ramaprasad,

& Tadisina, 2009) as a formative construct comprised of the ability to sense a change, diagnose a change, select a response, and execute the response in real-time:

1. **Sense:** Ability to sense the stimuli for change (as they occur) in real-time;
2. **Diagnose:** Ability to interpret or analyze stimuli in real-time to determine the nature, cause, and impact of change:
   a. **Respond:** Ability to respond to a change in real-time, further disaggregated into *select* and *execute*;
   b. **Select:** Ability to s*elect* a response in real-time (very short planning time) needed to capitalize on the opportunity or counter the threat;
   c. **Execute:** Ability to *execute* the response in real-time.

Real-time is defined as the span of time in which the correctness of the task performed not only depends upon the logical correctness of the task performed but also upon the time at which the result is produced. If the timing constraints of the system are not met, system failure is said to have occurred (Unknown, 2002).

Thus, an Agile IS may be defined as one that has the ability to sense a change in real-time, diagnose the change in real-time, select a response in real-time, and execute the response in real-time. Due to the formative nature of the construct, several, or some, of these abilities might exist in the absence of others.

This chapter is organized as follows. It starts with a definition of the formative construct of an "Agile IS" and the construct's components: Sense, Diagnose, and Select and Execute. The Introduction is followed by a Literature Review and general discussions of Information Systems and Sources of Change in Information Systems to provide context for the analysis and results that follow. The Research Approach and Objectives of the paper are discussed followed by a conceptualized set of attributes for Selecting and Executing a Response to a Change in an Agile IS. These attributes are verified and refined and then validated through the empirical analysis of a survey. The Survey Administration, Analysis, and Results are detailed followed by the Summary, Comments, and Limitations.

LITERATURE REVIEW

Based on the review of the current peer-reviewed academic work there appears to be few studies addressing the topic of IS agility and/or agile IS directly. Many studies have explored the concept of flexible IS, and agility in other aspects of the organizations. It should be noted that flexibility is a related, though different and distinct, concept (Pankaj et al., 2009). Flexibility does not imply agility but can aid in agility (Pankaj et al., 2009). This section summarizes some studies in the area of flexibility and agility in relation to IS.

A flexible IS infrastructure allows sharing of data and applications through communication networks. It pertains to the arrangement of hardware, software, and networks so that data and applications can be accessed and shared within and between suppliers, customers, and vendors (Broadbent, Weil, & St. Clair, 1999). A flexible IS infrastructure helps in integrating disparate and geographically distributed systems and makes IS applications cost effective in their operations and supports. Therefore, a flexible infrastructure becomes a critical source of advantage to the firm. In both academics and industry, "companies increasingly adopt process-aware information systems (PAISs), which offer promising perspectives for more flexible enterprise computing" (Weber, Reichert, & Rinderle-Ma, 2008). Gottfried and Herwig (2014) believe that recent economic developments indicate that greater flexibility in manufacturing is more important than ever and they present an applicable approach that shows exactly how to evaluate the manufacturing flexibility and how to measure an improvement of flexibility in business practice. A flexible IS infrastructure is an integrated shared system that is built piece by piece over time (Bharadwaj, 2000). That means, as a firm learns to work with a system and gradually becomes proficient in using the system, it continually works to add other pieces in the infrastructure that can set it apart from other firms.

Based on the Resource-Based View (RBV) of the firm, we consider IS as a key resource of a firm. Even though many systems can be purchased from the marketplace, the use and customization of these systems is recognized as anchoring the IS competencies of the firm. For example, Bharadwaj (2000) and Rockart et al. (1996) view IS infrastructure as an IS competence, because not all the firms can equally capitalize on information technology (IT) without using a flexible IS infrastructure. Firm competencies inherit the following properties: they are valuable, rare, inimitable, and non-substitutable. These attributes cannot be easily imitated by competitors in the short-run because capabilities are deeply rooted in the history of the firm, and some capabilities could arise just by being in the right place at the right time (Barney, 1991).

It can be argued that Business Process Management (BPM) practices continue to gain interest among managers who seek to improve their organization's efficiency, effectiveness, agility, and competitive position (Goeke & Antonucci, 2013). The knowledge-based organization must be agile and apply substantial knowledge, when and where it's needed, to affect organizational goals (Nissen, 2005). A model proposed by Hefu et al. (2013) proposes to examine how IT capabilities (i.e., flexible IT infrastructure and IT assimilation) affect firm performance through absorptive capacity and supply chain agility in the supply chain context (Hefu, Weiling, Kwok, & Zhongsheng, 2013). Their research shows that absorptive capacity and supply chain agility fully mediate the influences of IT capabilities on firm performance.

A conceptual framework developed and empirically tested by Yang (2014) investigates the antecedents of manufacturers supply chain agility and posits that cost efficiency mediates the relationship between agility and performance (Yang, 2014).

Given the nature of collaboration and the high degree of interoperability between partner IS, processes need to be agile in order to respond to changes in context; to apply agility mechanisms; and to detect the significant events that will lead to a subsequent evolution of the situation; and to design the structure of the part of the system that is in charge of IS agility (Barthe-Delanoë, Truptil, Bénaben, & Pingaud, 2014).

Organizational workers improve their perceived job performance through the use of Mobile Enterprise Systems (MES), while also investigating the impact of perceived organizational agility and location independence on technology acceptance of MES (Sunghun, Kyung, & Kimin, 2014). Organizational agility is positively associated with both perceived ease of use and perceived usefulness (Sunghun et al., 2014).

The link between dimensions of agile supply chains, competitive objectives, and business performance was assessed by Yusuf et al. (2014). They identify the most important dimensions and attributes of supply chain agility and provide a deeper insight into those characteristics of agility that are most relevant.

A cross-sectional field study was employed to analyze how key defining features of enterprise systems environment, including integration, process optimization, and best practices affect agility (Seethamraju & Sundar, 2013).

In summary, there are studies addressing different aspects of flexibility and agility in an organization. This study addresses IS agility as a distinct concept in an explicit and direct fashion.

Information Systems

IS in this study are restricted to computer-based information systems and we categorize IS components into human and IT components (Byrd & Turner, 2000) operating within an organizational context (please refer to Figure 1). This is a simplistic conceptualization of an IS by the authors and is used in this research to put a boundary around the domain of interest, since IS in their holistic view can be all encompassing. Several alternative ways of classifying components, such as having a database component and/or including storage in hardware, is possible. Each has its own merits and advantages.

The organizational context for an IS may be described in different ways depending upon the purpose of the research question. Conceptualization of the organizational context is based on the work of Ein-Dor and Segev (1978). Organizational context may be viewed as a combination of uncontrollable, partially controllable, and controllable factors. Uncontrollable factors are those whose status is given with respect to IS and include organizational size, organizational structure, organizational time-frames, and extra-organizational situations. The partially controllable factors are those whose change can be affected by the IS in many situations like organizational resources, organizational maturity, and the psychological climate in the organization. Controllable factors are those for which changes can be affected by the IS like rank and location of the top IS executives, and existence of a steering committee. Organizational policies and rules also play an important part as they control and guide all organizational actions and imperatives.

The human component of IS consists of the IS staff responsible for planning, development, operation, and maintenance of the IS. The human IS component should have four types of knowledge and skills. These are technology management knowledge and skills; business and functional knowledge and skills; interpersonal and management skills; and technical knowledge and skills (Lee, Trauth, & Farwell, 1995).

Figure 1. A model of information systems

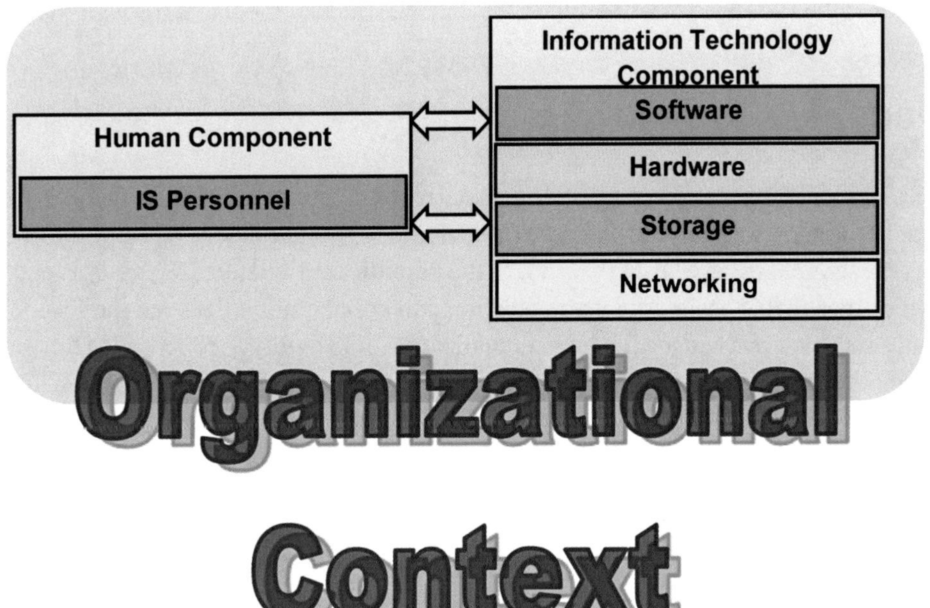

The IT component consists of the computing, storage (including databases with the data model and other data), and networking equipment, and software that runs on this equipment. The absence of data as an explicit component may be seen as an issue. The rationale for not providing data as an explicit component is that data is a contextual component rather than an independent component and can be subsumed in software and storage. The logic of the business processes is embedded into the configuration of IT components. The human component of the IS is responsible for embedding or programming this logic and associated data into the IT components.

SOURCES OF CHANGE IN INFORMATION SYSTEMS

IS need to change continuously. There are several motivators/causes for an IS change. IS may change because of internal changes, organizational changes, and/or environmental changes. IS form the core of information processing in all modern organizations. An IS has to continuously improve its performance to improve organizational performance, thus requiring continuous changes. Such changes to the IS that emanate from considerations within the IS itself, are termed as *internal changes* in this study. In modern organizations, IS and business processes are tightly coupled (Edwards, Millea, Mcleod, & Coults, 1998). Business processes have to change in response to changes in the organization's strategy and its short-term and medium-term choices. A change in the business process will require a change in the IS. Conversely, an IS's ability to change may permit, or prohibit, changes in business processes. An IS has to change to enable changes in business processes. Such changes in IS that are driven by the organization, are termed as *organizational changes*. Environmental changes may impact an IS directly and warrant change. Issues such as technical compatibility with suppliers, customers, and other partners; termination of support for obsolete technologies; upgrade of the hardware and software products; increase in viruses and cyber-attacks; changes in licensing terms; etc. pose a requirement for changes in IS. Such changes are termed as *environmental changes*. These are primarily driven by the changes in the environment that directly and exclusively affect the IS. These would exclude the changes that are mediated through the organization.

RESEARCH APPROACH AND OBJECTIVES

Though there is a lot of discussion of agility in the current practitioner literature, theories in the area of IS agility are in the early formative stages (see (Eisenhardt, 1989) for theory building). IS agility is also an area where practitioners have taken the lead. In the practitioner literature, IS agility is equated to a set of technologies that enable seamless interconnection and collaboration between the IT components to achieve rapid configuration changes. The conceptualization of IS agility as proposed in this study is much broader and more comprehensive in scope. This study therefore aims to fulfill the following objectives:

1. Arrive at a conceptualized set of attributes for selecting and executing a response to a change in an agile IS. (Work on sensing attributes (Pankaj, Hyde, & Rodger, 2013b) and diagnosis attributes (Pankaj, Hyde, & Rodger, 2013a) has been presented separately due to length considerations);
2. Verify and refine the conceptualized set of attributes for selecting and executing a response to change in an agile IS based on the feedback from practitioners and to arrive at a comprehensive set of attributes selecting and executing a response for IS agility;

3. Validate the attributes for selecting and executing a response in an agile IS as conceptualized in this study provided through a survey.

Response Selection and Execution in an Agile Information System

Sensing means that relevant signals are received and the information on the level/measure of parameter(s) with which the signal is concerned, is recorded. Signals come from everywhere (Quinn, 1980). IS employs a wide variety of sensors that include machines, living entities, and social entities to sense the stimuli. An agile IS has several attributes (Pankaj et al., 2013b) for sensing a change in real-time. Sensing a change is an important ability. After a change is sensed it has to be diagnosed.

Given that the stimuli have been sensed accurately and in a timely fashion, an accurate and timely diagnosis is needed. The diagnosis provides answers to questions like what the change is, where is it occurring, when has it occurred or will occur, who is affected by the change, and what is the cause of the change. Former Intel chairman Andy Grove (1999) argued that this is perhaps one of the most difficult tasks that an organization faces. Recognizing whether a change has happened or is going to happen is a non-trivial task. An important objective of the diagnosis is to distinguish signal from noise. Stimuli need to be interpreted to determine the nature and cause of change. Diagnosis of the change in an agile IS takes additional importance since most modern IS are fairly complex. This complexity often makes it difficult to infer the linkages between cause and effect. Inference of cause is necessary to arrive at a response to the change. For a modern IS, what the change is and why it is happening are the minimal answers needed from diagnosis. There are several attributes that enable an agile IS to diagnose in real-time (Pankaj et al., 2013a).

Once a change has been diagnosed, a response is selected. This response may range from doing nothing, to a complete reengineering, or replacement of the existing IS. The primary criterion for arriving at a response in agility is execution within the time constraints (real-time). For this reason, a quick patch job that meets the time constraints may be preferred when compared to an exceptionally effective and sound rational response that is late. Additional criteria for a response are cost of change, scope of change, and robustness of change (Dove, 1994). These additional constraints may be used if several responses satisfy the time constraints. Together these four constraints constitute the core criteria for selection of a response and may subsume other constraints. For instance, constraints on time and cost will help in choosing between the alternatives of outsourcing vs. in-house development; constraint on robustness will help in choosing between use of new technologies (with higher probability of instability and bugs) vs. trusted old technologies; etc. An agile IS chooses a response that can be executed within the given time constraint, with minimum cost, maximum scope, and maximum robustness. Time, in an agile IS, is the primary constraint.

Execution of the response within the given constraints is contingent upon the resources available for execution which in turn depends upon the accuracy of the estimation of resource requirements and constraints (sometimes still an art) during the response selection. The selection process itself may be short at most times to meet the real-time constraints and may not involve exhaustive attention to details, thus cutting down the planning time during selection. This, coupled with complexity associated with IS changes, may result in unforeseen contingencies during execution. An agile IS should be able to resolve these contingencies within the given time constraints. This may pose the need for having viable alternatives when selecting and executing a response. For example, if an application cannot be developed in-house then it may be outsourced. In the worst-case scenario, it may be necessary to start the cycle of sense, diagnose, select, and execute again by seeking additional stimuli while still staying within the original time constraints. An agile IS has alternatives for the execution of a chosen response, and also has alternative responses for a given change. An agile IS has properties like loose coupling of components with standard interfaces; flexibility in the technical components to be reconfigured, scaled, and reused; multi-skilled human resources, etc.; that allow for alternative executions of a response and/or execution of a different response within the given constraints.

Attributes for Response Selection and Execution in an Agile IS

The human and IT components of an agile IS have several attributes which allows the IS to select and respond to internal, organizational, and environmental changes in real-time. These changes may affect the human or IT components or both.

Due to paucity of the peer-reviewed academic literature, most attributes have been derived from a survey of practitioner literature (about 250 in number) and the consulting experiences of the authors. Some academic articles in the area of IS flexibility were also referenced (e.g., Allen & Boynton, 1991; Weil, Subramani, & Broadbent, 2002).

Attributes for Response Selection in an Agile IS

One of the attributes needed in an agile IS for the selection of a response is good estimation skills for the evaluation of responses for satisfaction of the given constraints. The IS staff should be able to rate the available responses on the four constraints of time, cost, robustness, and scope with confidence so that a few responses may be selected. A prerequisite to estimation is an accurate assessment of the capabilities of the IS organization in terms of controllable, partially controllable, and uncontrollable factors so that only feasible/viable responses are selected. IS staff leading projects and tasks should have an accurate knowledge of these factors for accurate estimation. Formal methods of estimation (e.g., COCOMO, COCOMO II, Function Point Analysis) may be used within the IS function for estimation (Pendharkar, Subramanian, & Rodger, 2005). Human experience may be used exclusively or complement formal methods. Many times, access to the knowledge-bases external to the organizations like those of the IT vendors and others (Kris & Jan, 2010) may be needed during estimation for the purpose of effort-estimation and sizing of the IS components (number of processors in the server, number of people needed in the implementation, etc.).

Often it may not be possible to select a response that fulfills all the constraints (including those posed by IS) by only altering the IS. In many such cases a small change in the business processes, rules, and/or policies, can yield a response that fulfills all the given constraints. This attribute is necessary since the traditional wisdom in the MIS area is for an IS to conform to business process requirements. IS-driven changes in business processes are often seen as problematic by most executives since there is a perception that such changes are devoid of any good business logic and seek to fulfill only technical goals. Thus, IS should possess the capability to influence the organizational context by driving limited changes in business processes, rules, and policies to the extent where justification for such change can be provided. We focus on these three factors for the sake of parsimony. But the capability as to what factors in the organizational context can be changed, and the extent to which they can be changed, would depend upon the perceived necessity of the IS change. The attributes of agile IS relevant to the selection of a response are described in Table 1.

Table 1. Attributes for selecting a response in an agile Information System

1. IS staff that lead tasks and projects with an accurate knowledge of controllable, partially controllable, and uncontrollable factors for the IS department/function.
2. Estimation methods
a. Scientific and formal estimation methods that can estimate the time, cost, robustness, and scope of a response.
b. Experienced and knowledgeable IS staff for estimating the time, cost, robustness, and scope of a response.
c. Access to knowledge-bases (e.g., sizing guidelines) of vendors of IT components to aid in estimation.
3. Capability of IS to drive changes in the business processes to a limited extent.
4. Capability of IS to drive changes in organizational rules and policies to a limited extent.

Attributes for Executing a Response in an Agile IS

Execution in this study is defined as the creation of a new configuration in IS using the IT components and the IS staff such that the selected response is incorporated as a functionality of this IS configuration. The IS configuration may be created by altering the existing IT components and staff, adding on new IT components and staff, or both. These new configurations include alternatives like application services providers, outsourcing, co-location in third-party data centers, and "computing on demand" (*all of these collectively subsume cloud computing*) being offered by various vendors like IBM, Google, Amazon, RackSpace, etc. These alternatives may also be used in conjunction with the reconfiguration of the in-house IS functionality within the organization. Execution in an agile IS should meet the constraints by creating the IS configuration within the time and cost with the requisite robustness and scope. The resulting configuration should be stable. This is an important point to stress since the distributed nature of the current IS, coupled with the number of components and their complexity increases the number of failure points significantly. Execution should also allow for alternative methods of execution of the same response and ability to switch to an alternative response during a contingency.

IT components in general should have properties that allow for rapid execution. Reusable, scalable, and rapidly reconfigurable modular components may allow for rapid execution (Dove, 1995). Several attributes of the IS components facilitate reconfiguration. The IT components should scale, implying that it should be possible to add a similar IT component to an existing component to obtain an increase in capacity. There have been some significant recent developments in modular software artifacts that facilitate scaling. With the improvement in clustering and virtualization including containers (Lederman, 2016), it is now possible to achieve rapid horizontal appliction scaling including auto-scaling (Yu & Huang, 2015). Docker container technology has emerged as a popular mechanism to scale applications horizontally (Ellingwood, 2015a) and even be deployed on irregular architecture.

Most IT components scale at a rate that is below linear and hence, the closer the scaling is to being linear, the more agile the IS would be in some contexts. Similar to IT components, IS staff strength and skills may need to be augmented. This can be achieved through a network of vendors and/or contractors who are able to provide on-site and off-site person-power. Reconfiguration of IS may need in-depth technical skills in the IT components. An agile IS should have access to staff within the organization or external parties who have these skills. When technical skills exist in-house, a multi-skilled IS staff provides more flexibility in allocation of resources during the execution of tasks, especially those that are on the critical path. Therefore, IS staff with a wider range of skills would be desired in an agile IS.

In scaling, similar components are added to the IS. The IS should also allow for the addition of components and the replacement of existing components with components that may be different from the existing component. When such components are added, the IS should be able to integrate these components fast. For example, if new components are bought off the shelf then these new components should easily interoperate with the existing components. This integration and interoperability can be done rapidly if the IS architecture uses modular IT components that are integrated through some common framework/standard. Hence an agile IS should use modular IT components.

Modularity is pervasive in an agile IS. A module is a collection of functionality that can be treated as logically separate from all other functionality under consideration. Each module has a well-defined functionality that is offered to other modules through well-defined and often standardized interfaces. The use of modules allows for plug-and-play operation where one module can be replaced by another similar module to result in fast recovery in case of an error, added functionality, and/or superior performance. Modules also allow reusability when they are loosely coupled. For example, in software, an existing module can be reused in new software programs. For IT components, modules can exist at various levels of abstraction. At the lowest level, these may be monolithic components like a single mainframe or one big program without functions/subroutines. The second level comprises of components that are configured through an intermediary like middleware or enterprise application integration software (EAI). At the third level, components are able to interact without the use of any intermediary. The final and the last level is one where each IS (not just IT) component is seen as service and can be called when needed through some defined mechanisms. Existing IS should move towards higher levels of modularity for agility. The final level of modularity, where the IS components are seen as services, is the desired level for an agile IS though it is also the most difficult to attain. An IS architecture based on the philosophy that each IS component presents itself as a service has been termed as the "Service Oriented Architecture" (SOA). An IS would seek to move to an SOA for agility.

The concept of Service Orientation has taken roots in the current era as various cloud computing services. Services like Infrastructure as a Service (IaaS) and Platform as a Service (PaaS) provide IT infrastructure as service. Such services are becoming more and popular and to the extent that is it estimated that 83% of the enterprise workload will be in the cloud by 2020 as per a cloud study by LogicMonitor (Columbus, 2018). As per a survey by Unisys of 400 IT executives across eight countries, improving agility is the overall top driver of cloud adoption with 78% of the respondents saying that it is critical or very important (Young, 2017). Sawas and Wafta (2015) found that there was an association between IaaS and improvement of infrastructure agility (Sawas & Wafta, 2015). In the realm of software with the popularization of containers there has been an increased emphasis on micro-services (Ellingwood, 2015b). Hasselbring and Steinacker (2017) describe properties of microservice architectures that facilitate scalability, agility and reliability at otto.de, which is one of the biggest European e-commerce platforms. Service-oriented architecture for software through the use of technologies like Web services has been existence for several years and is also postulated to increase the ability to change software. Moammadi and Mukhtar (2018) point to the fact that supply chain processes have shifted toward IT-based business processes using service-oriented architecture (SOA) to augment the agility, integration, and flexibility of IT-based applications in enterprise networks.

In the execution of a response in an IS, the major challenges often come from the issues in reconfiguration of the software components. Software components implement the business logic and are invariably, and directly, impacted by changes and responses to these changes. The complex interdependencies between the various software components and the adverse and often indeterminate impact of a change in one component on another component (on account of complexity) has promoted higher and higher levels of abstraction. Higher levels of abstractions also allow for reuse of code and functionality in software and thus save development time. In this area, SOA again presents the highest levels of abstraction. Each component of the IS can evolve and change independently of other components, and in the process, minimize any adverse impacts of change. Micro-services running in containers is the latest development in the area of SOA for applications. Jahromi et al. (2018) propose a network function virtualization and micro-services based architecture for on-the-fly content delivery network component provisioning to handle flash crowds.

Modularity with respect to the human IS staff can be viewed as considerations regarding the internal structure of the IS department/function and its position and role within the organization. The position and role of the IS department/function may be partially uncontrollable, but the internal structure can be organized for agility. The parameters to be considered for internal structure would include issues like the number of teams, areas of expertise of teams, their interfacing mechanisms, etc. Successful organization of the IS department may range from a two-person team in the case of extreme programming (XP) to specialized cross-functional teams for system integration projects. The preference for an agile IS would be a team of well-qualified and multi-skilled IS staff though they are difficult to procure and retain. Requirements for depth of technical knowledge also makes it a challenge. Such staff will allow for dynamic configuration of project teams as per the requirement of the response to be executed. For an agile IS, all IS staff should have technology management knowledge and skills; business and functional knowledge and skills; and interpersonal and management skills (Lee et al., 1995); along with technical knowledge and specialized skills. Another skill required in an agile IS, and especially relevant in today's outsourcing scenario, is for the IS staff designated to lead IS projects/tasks, to have the requisite IS project management skills to integrate external and internal staff into the current tasks. This would include the ability to formalize requirements to be passed on to external parties, establishing lines of communication and workflows, tracking and monitoring progress, etc.

Relevant to the ability of the modules for plug-and-play and fast reconfiguration is the role of standards. These standards may be de facto and/or open standards. For IT components, standards operate at both functional and technical levels. Standards at the functional level may be a base set of best business practices, interpretation of government rules and regulation, technical requirements formulated by professional bodies like IEEE and W3C, etc. Standardization of the functionality allows development of IS that can be deployed quickly. Further standardization may be achieved when the standard functionality at the top level is decomposed into a standard set of modules. Existence of standard modules further aids in rapid reconfiguration. For example, an address book based on the 'vcard' standard incorporates a base set of standard functionality and, therefore, it may be integrated into any email client. Standards for the interface between modules allow modules from different vendors to interoperate. Such standards include definition of the interface (functionality offered, inputs needed, outputs returned, etc.) and definition of information exchange mechanisms like specification of the message format or packet format used to exchange the data. This implies that the IS has access to a wider resource base when considering a set of functionality, and this decreases the time to respond by reducing dependency on a narrow set of resources. Interface standards are needed both at the functional and technical levels. Existence of technical standards for building the modules and/or components like standard ways of naming variables, PCI express interface specification for peripheral cards, etc., also aid in faster reconfiguration of the IT components.

As far as standards for IS staff are concerned, they relate to standards for skill assessment. The IS organization may have a set of skill assessment standards that may be based on industry certifications or other professional body standards, to assess the skills of IS staff (including those of vendors and contractors). This set of standards would be based on considerations such as the dominant technology used in the IS, structure of the IS organization, etc. These standards ensure that IS staff can be assumed to have certain skills with a certain level of depth for execution purposes.

With respect to standards, an SOA benefits immensely from the use of open or de facto standards. An SOA based on standards allows for collaboration between IS components belonging to different vendors, organizations, and/or partners hence broadening the base of available services that can be used to create the requisite functionality in an IS. The collaboration between IS components from different organizations demands existence of mechanisms for advertising of the services provided by the components that the IS wants to share; mechanisms to access these services; and appropriate security mechanisms to control the access to these components. An agile IS should have these facilities to enable collaboration and delivering functionality by collaboration. Many of these mechanisms, facilities, and technologies exist currently and are continuously evolving.

If a new functionality cannot be implemented through available IT components, modules, or services then new functionality has to be developed and implemented. For software components, development of this functionality needs to be managed properly. This can be done using existing and emerging software engineering tools and methods. An agile IS may use automated software engineering methods for faster and reliable development of new functionality. This includes maintaining comprehensive business process/logic specification in a technically independent format, mechanisms to translate these business specifications into code using code-generation tools, automated testing in a test environment to ensure robustness, and automated rollout with versioning, and change management.

In case of machine diagnosis of the change, automatic reconfiguration of IT components may be possible to a limited extent. This is currently possible for many recovery responses. The initiatives in this area include self-healing servers, self-reorganizing databases, storage virtualization, and others. IS now have the limited capability for automatic diagnosis of simple changes and execution of scripted responses to these changes. It is also possible to generate scripted responses based on some artificial intelligence, algorithms, and/or rules pre-built into the IT components. An agile IS may incorporate these capabilities to speed up the response time.

The top-level properties/attributes of an agile IS relevant to the execution of a response are summarized in Table 2.

Refining Attributes for Selecting and Executing Response in an Agile IS

Attribute refinement was done through interviews with ten IS executives. Interviews were conducted to obtain their opinion on, and validation of, various aspects of IS agility, including response selection and execution. The IS executives targeted were involved with both business and technological aspects of IS and could give a balanced perspective on different aspects of an agile IS ranging from organizational rules and policies to IT components. As per Bonoma's verification guidelines (Bonoma, 1985), multiple interviews were proposed for purposes of literal replication. The selection of the interviewees was done from a list of organizations that were enlisted in a discussion round table of a research center in the business school of a major university. The only criterion for selection of the organizations was to select those organizations that were expected to have a need for IS agility based on an informal assessment of the antecedents of IS agility for those organizations (Pankaj, 2005).

The interviewees demonstrated diversity in organizations in terms of industry and size; diversity in role and responsibilities; and diversity in organizations in terms of their approach to developing and managing IS. For example, while one interviewee's company tried to be on the forefront of new and

Table 2. Attributes for executing the response in an agile Information System

---

1. IT components:
   a. Scalable IT components.
   b. Modular IT components.
   c. Existence of a common underlying framework like middleware, EAI, etc., to integrate existing and legacy IT components.
   d. Loosely coupled IT components.
2. Standards:
   a. Standards for processes, practices, functions, and activities that can be incorporated into IS.
   b. Standards for decomposition of functionality into lower levels modules or components (IT components and/or modules with a base set of standard functionality).
   c. Standards (message formats, protocols, etc.) for information exchange between modules/components.
   d. Technical interface (e.g., PCI and other bus standards) standards for IT components.
   e. Technical standards (like the naming of variables) for building of the modules and/or components.
   f. Standards for assessing and certifying the skills of the IS staff (including those of contractors).
3. Service oriented architecture for IS:
   a. Availability of IS components that may be viewed as services.
   b. Ability to collaborate with external parties to use services provided by their IS components through advertising of services and specification of the access mechanisms.
   c. Existence of security mechanisms to control access to service provided by IS components inside and outside the organization.
4. Speeding up software development:
   a. Maintenance of comprehensive business process/logic documentation.
   b. Generation tools for generating code from business specifications.
   c. Existence of a testing environment and automated testing tools.
   d. Automated roll out tools with change management/versioning facilities.
   e. Reusable software components like objects and libraries.
5. IS personnel attributes:
   a. IS staff with in depth technical knowledge of IT components in chosen areas.
   b. Multi-skilled IS staff with ability to work in different areas.
   c. Access to external consultants with in-depth knowledge of IT components.
   d. Lead IS staff with project management skills that allow for adding staff to the task though outsourcing or through contracting temporary workers.
   e. Continuous training and learning of IS staff in new and evolving technologies and other skills.
6. Automated execution and reconfiguration:
   a. Automated and scripted responses within IS for commonly occurring problems, tasks, and changes.
   b. Generation of responses using artificial intelligence and rules-base built into the IT components.

---

developing technologies, another interviewee's company still used a large number of legacy systems and was cautious in its use of cutting-edge technologies. The interviewees held roles that spanned from strategic, to a mix of strategic and technical, to more specialized technical roles.

Content analysis was done on the interviews and attributes for selection and execution of response were refined as a result of content analysis (Pankaj, 2005). Interviewees mentioned 43 attributes/items related to selection and execution. For selection many participants stressed automated selection of response or having a set of defined responses that are selected for routine and/or simple situations and time as the primary criterion for selection of a response. Some attributes additional to those in Table 2, were mentioned for execution of a response. Attitude of the IS staff was mentioned as an important attribute for execution. The IS staff needs to have the 'get it done' attitude to navigate around the constraints of bureaucratic policies, resources, lack of time, and the like. Another attribute of the IS staff stressed in the interviews was the ability of the IS staff to learn constantly. This would be needed to fully utilize the emerging technologies. An IS infrastructure that is stable, robust, resilient, flexible, standards-based, and forms the framework on which all enterprise applications are developed is needed.

An enterprise-level data model with enterprise-wide metadata is also needed for quick execution. Flexible and universal user interfaces using the web-browser and portals were mentioned as an important attribute as they allow one interface to be customized and presented for different applications and cuts down on user training. The last attribute mentioned to support execution was the use of rules-based, process-driven, and workflow-based applications that can be easily modified in case of process changes. An example of a recent development in the area of automated execution and configuration is the use of configuration stores with container technologies like Docker (Ellingwood, 2015c) which allows an application or component to discover information about its environment and neighbors. It also allows one to separate the run-time configuration from the actual container allowing the use of the same image in a number of environments. There is also provision for dynamic configuration which allows for configuration changes in the containers on the fly depending upon the new and updated information in the configuration store. An example might a load balancer that automatically adjust the scheduling to exclude a server in the backend that has failed as indicated by a health-check.

A refined set of attributes for sensing is presented in Table 3 and Table 4. New attributes have been italicized.

SURVEY DEVELOPMENT AND ADMINISTRATION

Survey development and administration was performed using the well-documented steps for survey development, administration and analysis (Bailey & Pearson, 1983; Goodhue, 1988; Ives, Olson, & Baroudi, 1983; Ricketts & Jenkins, 1985). The development and validation of the survey was performed as per the guidelines by Churchill (1979): generate sample items, pilot test, and develop final measures.

The items for the questionnaire were generated from the list of post-interview refined attributes. There were 8 items for attributes needed for "selecting a response in real time" in an agile IS, and 34 items for attributes needed for "executing the response in real time" in an agile IS (the original questionnaire included items related to sensing, diagnosis, and selection and execution). Demographic information about the organization and respondent was also collected using 6 items. These were standard items compiled from analyses of ten surveys designed by peer researchers. The demographic information collected included the title and department, industry, the number of IS personnel, annual IS budget, and annual revenue. The draft survey was pilot-tested with practitioners (paper version) and students (web version) for assessing the understandability of the questions, clarity of the instructions, unambiguity in the wording of the items, and the overall format of the questionnaire. The pilot test used the paper questionnaire as the primary mechanism to test for quality of content. Participants in the pilot test of

Table 3. Refined attributes for selecting a response in an agile Information System

1. IS staff that leads tasks and projects with an accurate knowledge of controllable, partially controllable, and uncontrollable factors for the IS department/function.
2. Estimation methods
a. *Time with the highest priority as criterion.*
b. Scientific and formal estimation methods that can estimate the time, cost, robustness, and scope of a response.
c. Experienced and knowledgeable IS staff for estimating the time, cost, robustness, and scope of a response.
d. Access to knowledge bases (e.g., sizing guidelines) of vendors of IT components to aid in estimation.
3. Automated selection of response or having a set of defined responses for routine and/or simple situations based on defined rules and algorithms.
4. Capability of IS to drive changes in the business-processes to a limited extent.
5. Capability of IS to drive changes in organizational rules and policies to a limited extent.

Table 4. Refined attributes for executing a response in an agile Information System

1. IT components
    a. Scalable IT components.
    b. Modular IT components.
    c. Existence of a common underlying framework like middleware, EAI, etc., to integrate existing and legacy IT components.
    d. Loosely coupled IT components.
2. Standards
    a. Standards for processes, practices, functions, and activities that can be incorporated into IS.
    b. Standards for decomposition of functionality into lower levels modules or components (IT components and/or modules with a base set of standard functionality).
    c. Standards (message formats, protocols, etc.) for information exchange between modules/components.
    d. Technical interface (e.g., PCI and other bus standards) standards for IT components.
    e. Technical standards (e.g., naming of variables) for building the modules and/or components.
    f. Standards for assessing and certifying the skills of the IS staff (including those of contractors).
3. Service-oriented architecture for IS
    a. Availability of IS components that may be viewed as services.
    b. Ability to collaborate with external parties to use services provided by their IS components through advertising of services and specification of the access mechanisms.
    c. Existence of security mechanisms to control access to service provided by IS components inside and outside the organization.
4. Speeding up software development
    a. Maintenance of comprehensive business process/logic documentation.
    b. Generation tools for generating code from business specifications.
    c. Existence of a testing environment and automated testing tools.
    d. Automated roll-out tools with change management/versioning facilities.
    e. Reusable software components like objects and libraries.
    f. Flexible and universal user interfaces using the web-browser and portals.
5. IS personnel attributes
    a. IS staff with in-depth technical knowledge of IT components in chosen areas.
    b. Multi-skilled IS staff with ability to work in different areas.
    c. Access to external consultants with in-depth knowledge of IT components.
    d. Lead IS staff with project management skills that allow for adding staff to the task through outsourcing or through contracting temporary workers.
    e. Continuous training and learning of IS staff in new and evolving technologies and other skills.
    f. IS staff needs to have the 'get it done' attitude (overcome constraints of bureaucratic policies, resources constraints, lack of time, etc.).
6. IS infrastructure
    a. Stable, robust, resilient, flexible, and standards based infrastructure.
    b. Architectural framework on which all enterprise applications are developed.
    c. An enterprise-level data model with enterprise-wide metadata.
    d. Use of rules-based, process-driven, and workflow-based applications (can be easily modified in case of process changes).
7. Automated execution and reconfiguration
    a. Automated and scripted responses within IS for commonly occurring problems, tasks, and changes.
    b. Generation of responses using artificial intelligence and rules-base built into the IT components.

the paper survey included four practitioners and three MIS researchers. The primary concern was the length of the survey which was stated to be slightly long but participants commented that the questionnaire could be completed within a reasonable time and without extensive effort. It was suggested that items be grouped together. For example, items relating to personnel may be grouped together and items relating to the IT components may be grouped together. The idea of contacting people through a paper letter was supported since emails run the danger of being dropped by the SPAM filters. The changes suggested by the researchers included the phrasing of five items and the layout of the balloon graphic providing the definition of agility on the second page.

The pilot test for the web questionnaire was oriented towards visual appeal, layout and design, and not content. These were done with the help of university students. The first task was testing on different browsers to verify that all the buttons and scripts worked and there were no run-time errors. The pause-

and-resume functionality; clarity of the images and fonts; visual appeal of colors; amount of scrolling at standard resolution of 800 X 600; and download times were tested. Some changes in fonts and layout were done as a result of the tests.

Survey Administration

The survey was mailed to the potential respondents for self-administration. A list of IS executives was purchased from a market-research company. The purchased list contained 5000 names and addresses. Of these, 2718 executives were from companies with between 100-1500 employees and 2282 were from companies with 1-100 employees. Due to budgetary constraints, it was decided to mail the survey to 2718 executives (IS staff strength of between 100-1500). The survey included a cover letter, a paper copy of the questionnaire and a prepaid return envelope. The only incentive for responding to the survey was to share the results of the survey. The cover letter specified that the survey could also be completed online if desired by the respondent. A reminder for the survey was mailed approximately three weeks after the original mailing. After mailing the questionnaires, emails were sent to about 30 potential respondents using referrals from IS executives known to the researchers. The emails contained an executive summary of the research concepts, a copy of the questionnaire, and a link to the web-based questionnaire. A second mailing of the survey was done. The survey was mailed to 2,448 addresses and a reminder postcard was mailed approximately three weeks after the mailing.

Survey Analysis and Results

A total of 154 responses were received (it is estimated that 11 responses were from referrals). Of these, 105 were paper responses and 49 were web responses. There were a total of 2,539 solicitations (accounting for incorrect addresses). This gives a 5.7% response rate. This response rate was considered acceptable considering the questionnaire had 112 items (pertaining to sensing, diagnosis, selection, execution, and self-assessment), budgetary constraints on the survey, and the fact that executives in organizations receive many surveys to complete that contain some financial incentive (gift card).

All the data was entered into SPSS for analysis. The demographic data items (except for the title and department) representing various demographic categories were assigned numerical codes. The rating for all items for benefits and attributes were entered as marked on the questionnaire except for "Not Applicable" which was assigned a code of 0 (zero). To verify the correctness of data entry from the paper survey, a random sample of 20 questionnaires was selected and checked by a fellow researcher. No data entry errors were found. There were few missing values in the entire data set. Missing values were treated as pair-wise exclusive for correlational analyses like factor analysis. They were treated as list-wise exclusive otherwise, e.g., for purposes like calculating descriptive statistics.

Respondent Demographics

The demographics of the respondents are shown in Tables 5 to 8. Education, government, finance, healthcare, and information technology companies are prominently represented in the survey. For IS personnel, 62% of the respondents had fewer than 250 IS personnel. 61% of the organizations had an

Table 5. Industry distribution of survey respondents

Industry	Frequency	Percent
Retail	3	2.0%
Finance & Insurance	23	15.0%
Government	24	15.7%
Information Technology	18	11.8%
Mining & Oil	1	0.7%
Manufacturing	9	5.9%
Education	32	20.9%
Recreation & Leisure	1	0.7%
Utilities	3	2.0%
Trading (Wholesale)	4	2.6%
Media/Publishing/Broadcasting	5	3.3%
Professional Services	3	2.0%
Healthcare	20	13.1%
Other	7	4.6%
Total Valid	**153**	**100.0%**
Missing	1	
Total	154	

Table 6. IS personnel distribution of survey respondents

IS Personnel	Frequency	Percent	Cumulative Percent
1-100	39	25.3%	25.3%
101-250	56	36.4%	61.7%
251-500	29	18.8%	80.5%
501-750	12	7.8%	88.3%
751-1000	3	1.9%	90.3%
1001-1500	3	1.9%	92.2%
1501-2000	1	0.6%	92.9%
2001-5000	3	1.9%	94.8%
>5000	8	5.2%	100.0%
Total	**154**	**100.0**	

annual IS budget between $1 million and $50 million. 40% of the respondents had revenues between $1 billion and $25 billion. In summary, the survey had respondents from various segments of the population and it captured opinions from a variety of organizations in different industries both small and large in terms of annual revenue, IS budget, and number of IS personnel.

Table 7. Distribution of annual IS budget of survey respondents

Annual IS Budget ($millions)	Frequency	Percent	Cumulative Percent
< 0.5	11	7.2%	7.2%
0.5 – 1	10	6.5%	13.7%
1 - 50	93	60.8%	74.5%
50 -100	20	13.1%	87.6%
100 - 500 Million	15	9.8%	97.4%
500 -1000	3	2.0%	99.3%
> 1000	1	0.7%	100.0%
Total Valid	**153**	**100.0%**	
Missing	1		
Total	154		

Table 8. Distribution of annual revenue of survey respondents

Annual Revenue	Frequency	Percent	Cumulative Percent
< $1 Million	8	5.5%	5.5%
$1 Million-$50 Million	18	12.4%	17.9%
$50 Million-$100 Million	9	6.2%	24.1%
$100 Million-$500 Million	25	17.2%	41.4%
$500 Million-$1 Billion	21	14.5%	55.9%
$1 Billion-$25 Billion	58	40.0%	95.9%
> $25 Billion	6	4.1%	100.0%
Total Valid	**145**	**100.0%**	
Missing	9		
Total	154		

Respondent Bias

Since the survey was anonymous, it prevented testing for demographical differences between respondents and non-respondents. The respondents from the two mailings were, however, compared for differences. The number of responses for each medium and for each mailing is detailed in Table 9. The number of responses in the second mailing was about half of those in the first mailing.

To ensure that there were no significant unexplainable factors operating between the first and second mailing, cross-tabulations were computed to examine the differences on the demographic variables of industry, IS personnel, IS budget, and annual revenue. Chi-square tests were not conducted since many of the cells had an expected count of less than 5 and combining various categories led to mitigation of the differences with respect to the categories for the two mailings of the survey. There was a noticeable difference in the profile of the respondents between the first and second mailing. In addition, mean

Table 9. Paper and web responses for first and second survey mailing

		Mailing		Total
		First	Second	
Type of Medium for Survey	Paper	67	38	105
	Web	36	13	49
Total		**103**	**51**	**154**

ratings of benefits of an agile IS (not covered in this manuscript) and the attributes of an agile IS were compared using independent sample t-tests. The means of the ratings were not found to be different between the two mailings at a significance level of 0.01.

Attribute Importance for Selection of Response and Execution of Response

Respondents were asked to rate the importance of 8 items for selecting a response in real time. The mean rating for each of the items is significantly different (greater) from the mid-point of the scale (rating of 4 indicating neutral) at 0.01 level of significance, on a two-tailed test. Table 10 shows the frequency, mean, and standard deviation of the rating of the attributes for diagnosing a change in real time.

Respondents also rated the attributes for execution of response in real-time. These ratings are shown in Table 11. The mean rating for each of the items is significantly different (greater) from the mid-point of the scale (rating of 4 indicating neutral) at 0.01 level.

Table 10. Survey ratings of the attributes for selecting a response in an agile Information System

Attribute for Selecting a Response in Real Time	Frequency of Rating[1]								N	Mean[2]	Std. Dev
	1	2	3	4	5	6	7	N/A			
Familiarity of IS personnel with the controllable and uncontrollable organizational factors	1	1	3	15	48	62	21	1	152	5.50**	1.03
IS personnel expertise in estimation	1	0	8	17	51	55	21	1	154	5.39**	1.09
Capability of the IS to alter business processes (albeit to a limited extent)	1	2	6	22	47	51	24	1	154	5.36**	1.17
Predefined set of responses for common changes	1	4	7	23	51	48	19	1	154	5.22**	1.20
Formal methods of estimating time and cost of a response	2	1	8	20	55	48	18	2	154	5.24**	1.16
Timely completion of response as the primary criterion for selecting a response	4	4	7	24	47	44	19	4	153	5.11**	1.35
Capability of the IS to alter organizational rules and policies	2	6	9	24	50	44	18	1	154	5.08**	1.31
Access to vendor knowledge bases on sizing/ estimation	2	4	16	24	59	34	12	3	154	4.88**	1.26

Notes:

1. The shaded boxes show the rating with the highest frequencies.

2. Items are arranged in ascending order of mean rating.

** Mean is significantly greater than 4 at 0.00 level of significance in a two-tailed test.

Table 11. Survey ratings of the attributes for executing the response in an agile Information System

Attribute for Executing the Response in Real Time	Frequency of Rating[1]								N	Mean[2]	Std. Dev
	1	2	3	4	5	6	7	N/A			
IS personnel with a "get it done" attitude	0	0	0	4	7	41	101	0	153	6.56**	0.71
Existence of a test environment	0	0	2	8	14	47	82	1	154	6.30**	0.93
IS personnel with in-depth technical knowledge in selected technologies	0	0	1	6	26	56	64	1	154	6.15**	0.89
Interface standards for IT components	0	2	1	5	20	62	63	1	154	6.14**	0.96
Standards for information exchange between software applications	0	0	4	6	20	60	63	1	154	6.12**	0.96
Scalable IT components	0	1	1	6	27	59	60	0	154	6.09**	0.94
Multi-skilled IS personnel with skills in more than one area	0	0	3	9	21	75	46	0	154	5.99**	0.92
Stable and flexible standards-based infrastructure	0	1	3	9	29	70	42	0	154	5.88**	0.98
Standards for business activities, functions, processes, and practices	0	0	3	9	24	69	47	2	154	5.97**	0.94
Collaboration between services offered by IS from different organizations and vendors	0	2	6	16	39	69	22	0	154	5.51**	1.07
Change/version management tools for automated software rollout	0	0	3	5	18	65	60	3	154	6.15**	0.90
Use of rules-based, process-driven, and/or workflow based software applications	0	1	4	19	31	65	33	1	154	5.66**	1.07
Framework (middleware, EAI, etc.) for integrating new and existing applications	0	0	4	18	33	64	34	1	154	5.69**	1.03
Architectural framework/standards for all enterprise application development	1	2	1	7	35	63	44	1	154	5.86**	1.06
Use of service-oriented architecture for IS	2	2	5	14	42	63	25	1	154	5.49**	1.18
Continuous training of IS personnel in new and evolving technologies	0	3	2	17	35	61	36	0	154	5.67**	1.11
Access to external consultants to supplement/complement the skills of IS personnel	3	3	10	15	38	58	25	2	154	5.34**	1.34
Security mechanisms for collaboration of IS services	0	1	4	9	29	57	54	0	154	5.94**	1.06
Technical standards for building IS components	1	1	0	10	31	56	54	1	154	5.96**	1.04
Modular IT components	0	1	3	10	35	56	49	0	154	5.88**	1.04
Standard functionality for lowest level modules/ components	0	1	2	18	50	54	27	2	154	5.55**	1.00
Scripted responses for commonly occurring situations	0	4	9	20	43	53	24	0	153	5.33**	1.21
Reusable software components	0	1	3	13	38	52	46	1	154	5.80**	1.07
Universal web browser-based user interfaces like those offered by portals	0	4	6	16	37	51	40	0	154	5.59**	1.24
Project leaders with project management skills needed for outsourcing	1	5	9	16	28	51	38	5	153	5.50**	1.38
Automated test tools	1	1	4	15	44	51	36	2	154	5.61**	1.13
Comprehensive documentation for application software	1	3	7	16	43	51	33	0	154	5.48**	1.24

continued on following page

Table 11. Continued

Attribute for Executing the Response in Real Time	Frequency of Rating[1]								N	Mean[2]	Std. Dev
	1	**2**	**3**	**4**	**5**	**6**	**7**	**N/A**			
Intelligent software/tools to generate responses for routine/simple situations	1	6	15	22	42	48	19	0	153	5.08**	1.35
Standards for assessing and certifying skills of IS personnel	2	5	13	25	43	46	17	0	151	5.04**	1.34
Enterprise level metadata	1	4	2	20	40	45	35	6	153	5.51**	1.25
Intelligent software/tools to automatically execute scripted or generated responses	1	5	16	22	43	43	21	2	153	5.08**	1.35
Loosely coupled IT components	2	9	9	22	52	30	27	2	153	5.06**	1.43
Code generation tools	3	10	17	32	46	33	10	3	154	4.64**	1.39
Enterprise-level data model	1	3	4	17	44	43	38	4	154	5.54**	1.24

Notes:

1. The shaded boxes show the rating with the highest frequencies.

2. Items are arranged in ascending order of mean rating.

** Mean is significantly greater than 4 at 0.00 level of significance in a two-tailed test.

Exploratory Factor Analysis for Identification of Dimensions Underlying Selection and Execution of Response Attributes

An exploratory factor analysis (EFA) was conducted to identify possible dimensions underlying the attributes for selection and execution of response in real-time. Though broad categories were defined, when arriving at attributes and so it would be possible to do a confirmatory factor analysis, it was felt that an EFA is appropriate given the exploratory nature of the study. For selection there were 8 attributes for a sample of 154 and for execution there were 34 attributes for sample size of 154. While the rule of thumb of 5:1 for observations-item ratio was satisfied for selection attributes, it was close (4.5:1) for the execution attributes.

To test the appropriateness of the correlation matrix for factor analysis the Kaiser-Meyer-Olkin's Measure of Sampling Adequacy (KMO MSA) was examined. The KMO MSA for selection was 0.80 or at a meritorious level. The KMO MSA for execution was 0.89 or at a meritorious level.

An EFA was conducted using principal axis factoring since the objective was to identify underlying dimensions based on the common variance shared by the attributes. Varimax rotation was used to arrive at a simple structure for the factors. Other rotations oblimin, quatrimax, and promax were also tested. Varimax rotation provided the simplest and most interpretable factor structure. The number of factors to be extracted was based on a combination of the scree-test, eigen-value criterion, and simple structure. Simplicity of structure was given preference over parsimony. Initial factor extraction was based on the criteria of the eigen-value greater than 1. Then, the scree plot was examined for a visible elbow such that all factors with an eigen-value of greater than 1 were included in the solution. The factor analysis was run again with the number of factors indicated by the elbow. Both solutions were examined and the factor structure that was simple and interpretable was chosen. The cut-off for factor loading was taken as 0.4. Guidelines suggest (Hair, Anderson, Tatham, & Black, 1995) loadings of greater than $\pm$ 0.3 to meet the minimal level while loadings of $\pm$ 0.40 are considered more important.

Exploratory Factor Analysis Results for Response-Selection

For selecting a response, three factors were extracted based on the scree-plot and interpretability of the factors. The three factors explain approximately 69% of the variance. Table 12 provides the details of the factors and the items loading for each factor. The factors have been provided with some indicative names.

The first factor was labeled as "*IS Induced Organizational Change*". The two items that loaded onto this factor related to the ability of the IS to drive some changes in the organization. Often this makes the choice of responses easier since IS have inherent constraints and cannot fully adapt to the organizational requirement many times. Selection in real time may happen if an IS is allowed to alter organizational processes and policies.

The second factor was labeled as "*Selection Aids*". The three items that load onto this factor relate to things that will aid in selection. This appeared to be a factor with a general theme and items that do not fall in with other factors loaded on this factor. The three items covered different themes. Addition of more items that fit into the themes of these three items may eliminate this general factor and can be explored in future studies.

The third factor was labeled as "*Estimation Skills*". Items that loaded on this factor relate to estimation of the time and effort for various available responses.

The item "familiarity of IS personnel with the controllable and uncontrollable organizational factors" did not load on any of the factors though it did have a small loading on the second factor (Selection Aids). The item relates to the knowledge of IS personnel in what they can change and control in the organization and what they cannot. This is related to the first factor but may be more informal in nature in terms of "what the IS function can get away with" as compared to the items in the first factor which would need to be more formal. As such, this item may be subsumed in the other two items. It is possible that a better factor structure may be obtained with more items and different wording of the existing items. For instance, "access to vendor knowledge-bases on sizing/estimation" may load on the third factor instead

Table 12. Factors for selecting a response in an agile Information System

Attribute for Selecting a Response in Real Time	Factors		
	1 (IS Induced Organizational Change)	2 (Selection Aids)	3 (Estimation Skills)
Capability of the IS to alter business processes (albeit to a limited extent)	.788		
Capability of the IS to alter organizational rules and policies	.780		
Predefined set of responses for common changes		.719	
Access to vendor knowledge bases on sizing/estimation		.521	
Timely completion of response as the primary criterion for selecting a response		.508	
Familiarity of IS personnel with the controllable and uncontrollable organizational factors			
IS personnel expertise in estimation			.843
Formal methods of estimating time and cost of a response		.404	.538

of the second factor if it was worded differently and it did have a small 0.35 loading on the third factor. Overall, the factor structure appears to be acceptable. It may be explored more in future studies in view of the results in this study.

Exploratory Factor Analysis Results for Response-Execution

Executing a response in real time had 34 attributes and it was the largest category. Focus in the practitioner world and the IS industry has been on execution and there are several new technologies and concepts evolving in this area at any time. Based on the scree-plot and the eigen-value criterion, 9 factors were extracted. The factors explained approximately 70% of the variance in the data. Table 13 provides the details of the factors and the items loading for each factor. The factors have been provided with some indicative names.

The first factor extracted was "*Automated Execution*". The first three items that loaded on this factor relate to automatic execution. The item "*standards for assessing and certifying skills of IS personnel*" cross-loaded on this factor. This item appears to be a completely different item as compared to others in the factor. If the item is dropped from the factor analysis, the factor structure remains the same though the loadings change. In our original discussion, this item was needed so that the number of personnel could be easily increased through subcontracting and other means when such a need arose. Standard assessment enables, to some extent, automatic selection of personnel in times of need without an elaborate selection process. The selection process may be considered automatic to an extent. Based on this reasoning, the loading of the item may be considered appropriate. However, in future research, further investigation may be needed, and the item may need to be reworded to reflect its context.

The second factor was labeled as "*Standards*". The item "*reusable software components*" loaded on this item since reusable software components are based on standard interfaces and functionality. The item "*architectural framework/standards for all enterprise application development*" cross-loaded on this factor. Since this item deals with standards, its cross-loading onto this factor was considered appropriate. To avoid the cross-loading, this item could be split into two items, one dealing with standards and framework at the micro level and other dealing with standards and framework at the enterprise level. The word enterprise may be removed to avoid its loading with enterprise related items.

The third factor was labeled as "*IS Development*". All items that loaded onto this factor relate to the building of IS components (both IT and human). The item "*standards for assessing and certifying skills of IS personnel*" cross-loaded on this factor and the "*Automated Execution*" factor. This item appears to be, on face value, relevant to standards; however, it may be more pertinent to development. It may need to be reworded or split to pertinent items that are relevant to each of the first three factors.

The fourth factor was labeled as "*Enterprise Application Infrastructure*". All the items that loaded onto this factor relate to the enterprise-level infrastructure specific to application development and deployment. The item "Architectural framework/standards for all enterprise application development" cross-loaded on this factor and "Standards" factor since it relates to both concepts. It may need to be modified as discussed before or may need to split up.

The fifth factor was labeled as "*Modular IS*" since all items that loaded onto this factor relate to modularity in IS. Scalability is related to modularity since, at most times, components cannot be added for scalability (to increase the capacity or capability of the IS component) unless the design of the component and the system is modular.

The sixth factor was labeled as *"Capability Supplementation"*. The items that loaded onto this factor related to supplementing the skills of the IS personnel in the development and deployment of IS. The use of Service Oriented Architecture (SOA) for IS is towards this goal, where services from various sources (including services like application service providers) can be combined in real time to execute a response.

The seventh factor was labeled as *"Personnel Versatility"* as items related to orientation of the IS personnel to execute a response in real time.

The eighth factor was labeled as *"Testing"* since the loaded items relate to testing and the roll out of IT components.

The ninth factor was labeled as *"Service Collaboration"*. These items capture the mechanisms that need to be put in place for secure and robust collaboration between services that would be offered by different vendors as part of the SOA paradigm. These items may be considered to relate to the theme of the sixth factor – "Skill Supplementation", since they cover collaboration between services that allows an execution within the given time constraints using resources not available within the organization. Still these two factors may be considered as different since the sixth factor is somewhat general in nature; the ninth factor relates more to specific technologies, standards, mechanisms, etc. to enable collaboration.

Some of the items did not load onto any factor. The item labeled *"use of rules-based, process-driven, and/or workflow-based software applications"* did not load on any factor. The item deals with a higher layer of abstraction for better integration of applications and business processes. It deals with modularity, service-oriented architecture, and other related aspects. This may be the reason that it did not load onto any of the factors and it would need to be investigated further. In future research, it may be useful to add a set of items relating to logical abstraction. The item *"universal web browser-based user interfaces like those offered by portals"* also did not load onto any factor. This item specifically deals with quick deployment and rolling out of changes through a standard web-based user-interface. Since it is related to standards, it may load onto the *"Standards"* factor if worded differently. This may be tested and studied in future research. The item *"IS personnel with in-depth technical knowledge in selected technologies"*, did not load onto any factor. It loaded with a 0.38 loading on the *"IS Development"* factor (factor # 3), which appears appropriate. All of the three non-loading items need further research. They may need to be split into more specific items and/or reworded based on the factors on which they are expected to load.

SURVEY COMMENTS

The survey data supports the importance of attributes pertaining to selection of a response in real time and execution of a response in real time in an Agile IS. These may serve as indicative guidelines for practitioners to improve the ability of their IS to select and execute a response in real time. The EFA identifies dimensions that make logical sense at this stage of exploration.

As it was concluded with respect to the attributes for sensing a change in real-time (Pankaj et al., 2013b) and diagnosing a change in real-time (Pankaj et al., 2013a), people do matter, though automated execution has an important role when it comes to selecting and executing a response in real-time. "Familiarity of IS personnel with the controllable and uncontrollable organizational factors", and "IS personnel expertise in estimation" were the highest rated attributes for selecting a response in real-time. "IS personnel with a get it done attitude", "IS personnel with in-depth technical knowledge in selected technologies", and "Multi-skilled IS personnel with skills in more than one area" were amongst the high-

Table 13. Factors for executing a response in an agile Information System

Attribute for Executing the Response in Real Time	Factors								
	1 (Automated Execution)	2 (Standards)	3 (IS Development)	4 (Enterprise Application Infrastructure)	5 (Modular IS)	6 (Capability Complementation)	7 (Personnel Versatility)	8 (Testing)	9 (Service Collaboration)
Intelligent software/tools to automatically execute scripted or generated responses	.911								
Intelligent software/tools to generate responses for routine/simple situations	.850								
Scripted responses for commonly occurring situations	.629								
Standards for assessing and certifying skills of IS personnel	.482		.405						
Standards for information exchange between software applications		.729							
Standards for business activities, functions, processes, and practices		.646							
Interface standards for IT components		.623							
Standard functionality for lowest level modules/ components		.479							
Reusable software components		.400							
Comprehensive documentation for application software			.640						
Continuous training of IS personnel in new and evolving technologies			.542						
Technical standards for building IS components			.536						
Stable and flexible standards-based infrastructure			.479						
Enterprise level metadata				.806					
Enterprise level data model				.805					
Architectural framework/ standards for all enterprise application development		.442		.466					

continued on following page

Table 13. Continued

Attribute for Executing the Response in Real Time	Factors								
	1 (Automated Execution)	2 (Standards)	3 (IS Development)	4 (Enterprise Application Infrastructure)	5 (Modular IS)	6 (Capability Complementation)	7 (Personnel Versatility)	8 (Testing)	9 (Service Collaboration)
Modular IT components					.786				
Scalable IT components					.594				
Loosely coupled IT components					.526				
Use of service-oriented architecture for IS						.588			
Access to external consultants to supplement/ complement the skills of IS personnel						.512			
Framework (middleware, EAI, etc.) for integrating new and existing applications						.484			
Code generation tools						.477			
Project leaders with project management skills needed for outsourcing						.414			
Multi-skilled IS personnel with skills in more than one area							.750		
IS personnel with "get it done" attitude							.726		
Automated test tools								.502	
Existence of a test environment								.479	
Change/version management tools for automated software rollout								.462	
Collaboration between services offered by IS from different organizations and vendors									.641
Security mechanisms for collaboration of IS services									.410
IS personnel with in-depth technical knowledge in selected technologies									

continued on following page

356

Table 13. Continued

Attribute for Executing the Response in Real Time	Factors								
	1 (Automated Execution)	2 (Standards)	3 (IS Development)	4 (Enterprise Application Infrastructure)	5 (Modular IS)	6 (Capability Complementation)	7 (Personnel Versatility)	8 (Testing)	9 (Service Collaboration)
Use of rules-based, process-driven, and/or workflow based software applications									
Universal web browser-based user interfaces like those offered by portals									

est rated attributes for execution in real-time. In the comments that accompanied the survey, respondents stressed the importance of people. The stress on personnel implies that organizations need to focus on issues like training and retention of good IS personnel.

Another important conclusion is that a more well-rounded and holistic approach may be needed (in the true spirit of IS). Here IT and organization interact more closely with the realization that organizational change may be driven to some extent by IT.

In recent times there has been a great movement towards a services-based model in the IS. These include: Infrastructure as a Service (IaaS), Platform as a Service (PaaS), Software as a Service (SaaS), Storage as a Service, etc. These new frameworks along with increased modes of collaboration, are enabling some faster execution and rapid reconfiguration, increasing the IS agility. At the same time the increasing complexity and evolution of algorithms and technology will lead to more automatic sensing, automatic diagnosis, and automatic selection and execution. On the whole, the integral role of IS in organizations and the increasing rate of change will mean that IS agility will be an area of increasing concern to most organizations in coming times.

AGILE INFORMATION SYSTEMS DEVELOPMENTS

As mentioned before, today there are several technologies and new frameworks/paradigms that are available for making an IS agile and developing an AIS. This section describes in some detail some of these emerging paradigms/frameworks.

These paradigms and frameworks are based on the attributes/properties as outlined earlier in the paper. However, they have been implemented or, to say more appropriately, operationalized in a given fashion. This does not take away from the generic nature of the attributes or properties previously outlined. For instance, Service Oriented Architecture or SOA was mostly implemented as web services when it debuted in the industry. Today the emphasis appears to be on micro-services running in containers in data centers which may be abstracted as a public or private cloud. Web services and containers are not exclusive since a container may be running a web service. The user of containers enables DevOps which accelerates the development to deployment cycle. The DevOps is further facilitated or complemented by Agile software development methodologies like Scrum and XP where software is developed in small portions and its functionality is continuously delivered. Though there is still some learning curve involved, the technologies involved are more main stream than at any other time in the history of IS due to the realization that IS significantly impacts organizational performance. IS are a part of every major organization today. They are the indispensable means by which we manage and communicate in today's world. As ubiquitous as they may be, more can be done and done better.

According to Martinez-Simarro et al (2015), the strategic use of information technology (IT) is a matter of concern for researchers and managers. Firms need to make decisions regarding IT use in response to technological evolution and changes in business activity. Previous studies indicate that, without a solid information systems (IS) strategy, IT contribution to organizational performance may fall short of expectations. In a similar approach, Bach et al. (2016), wrote that modern organizations generate huge amounts of information, which has become a major competitive factor in today's business world. Transformation of useful information into knowledge leads to higher competitive advantage. Providing the right persons with the information which is complete, correct, relevant and in-time is important to support strategic decision making.

Cloud Computing

Cloud computing has been discussed previously in relation to scaling. Cloud computing is however a totally new way of thinking about computing resources.

The race for the next innovative idea is causing the business process environment to be more competitive than ever. Companies that incorporate the finest modes of information access will have the inside track to computing successful outcomes. The most popular method of monitoring one's information network is in Cloud Computing. Cloud computing is a model for enabling ubiquitous, convenient, on-demand network access to a shared pool of configurable computing resources (e.g., networks, servers, storage, applications, and services) that can be rapidly provisioned and released with minimal management effort or service provider interaction (Mell et al., 2010). With Cloud Computing, vast swaths of data can be stored and accessed in real time, on demand from any means of network linkage. Cloud systems automatically control and optimize resource use by leveraging a metering capability at some level of abstraction appropriate to the type of service (e.g., storage, processing, bandwidth, and active user accounts) (Mell et al., 2010). Resource usage can be monitored, controlled, and reported, providing transparency for both the provider and consumer of the utilized service (Mell et al., 2010). It becomes easy to benchmark progress and outcomes or research competitive advantages in your target market. Cloud computing assembles large networks of virtual services, including hardware (CPU, storage, and network) and software resources (databases, message queuing systems, monitoring systems, and load-balancers) (Wang et al., 2017). As the Cloud continues to revolutionize applications in academia, industry, government, and many other fields, the transition to this efficient and flexible platform presents serious challenges at both theoretical and practical levels—ones that will often require new approaches and practices in all areas (Wang et al., 2017). Cloud Computing can help small and medium business enterprises—and governments—in optimizing expenditures on application-host (Wang et al., 2017).

Virtualization

Technology has become advanced enough to allow users to multitask on levels on par with the speed of human thought. Through the process of Virtualization people can process information and communicate on a level equal to one's own personal capabilities. Virtualization is a process in computing that allows one computer or server to use more than one operating system or application simultaneously (Dziak, 2016). It has made technology more efficient, allowing one computer to take on the strength of many. This in turn has increased profits and productivity as well as reduced costs and waste for many companies and individuals. Three sub-sets in virtualization are server, desktop, and storage virtualization. Server virtualization allows one server to use multiple operating systems and applications, thus reducing the need for numerous machines and all the necessary upkeep (Dziak, 2016). Desktop virtualization allows single computers or other devices to access information and abilities from other sources, allowing, for instance, a company to provide virtual desktops to mobile and outsource workers to keep everyone working on the same project with the same tools and data (Dziak, 2016). Storage virtualization gathers data from many sources and stores it in a safe place that is accessible to any number of registered users (Dziak, 2016). Network virtualization allows multiple heterogeneous network architectures to cohabit on a shared physical substrate (Chowdhury & Boutaba, 2009). Network virtualization provides flexibility, promotes diversity, and promises security and increased manageability (Chowdhury & Boutaba, 2009).

This idea is most like that of cloud computing, one of the most popular uses of virtualization (Dziak, 2016). In cloud computing, computer users connect their devices to a virtual cloud, or a storage area containing software and data that is accessible to users at any time or place through any Internet-capable device (Dziak, 2016). Cloud computing allows companies greater flexibility and saves money on hardware, software, and maintenance (Dziak, 2016). Companies choose virtualization for many reasons. Likely, the primary reason is its efficiency, since fewer machines can do the task formerly done by many (Dziak, 2016). Machines that previously used only 15 percent of their capabilities can use 80 percent with proper virtualization (Dziak, 2016). This reduces the needs for costly extra machines, upkeep, and energy, and therefore helps a business reduce expenditures (Dziak, 2016). At the same time, the reduced number of machines means less waste and energy requirements that, in turn, cuts down on environmental wear and damage (Dziak, 2016). Virtualization, once correctly set up, may also make software installation and system administration much simpler (Dziak, 2016). When deploying applications in complex environments, complex scenarios can be defined by many things in the environment—adjusting communication ports for application delivery, handling particular applications, adapting company policies to the implementation, securing the environment, and so on (Alvarez, 2012). Virtualized solution design is complex; by taking a measured approach that involves both hard data (metric collection) as well as organizational input (questionnaire), the chances of a suitable design increases drastically (Langone & Leibovici, 2012). It is important for an organization to be able to adapt its IT systems and quickly respond to changing business conditions.

Related to virtualization, a concept that is gaining traction and has been discussed previously is the concept of containers. Docker has emerged as one of the leaders in the container world and along with micro-services (part of service-oriented architecture) it has emerged as another significant framework to manage and deploy applications.

Service Oriented Architecture (SOA) and Service Oriented Enterprise (SOE)

The System Design Life Cycle is further advanced by new operational ideologies that seize the opportunities of high performance computing platforms, such as Service Oriented Architecture and Service Oriented Enterprise. Service Oriented Architecture is a new computing paradigm for building IT systems (Li & Madnick, 2015). Service-oriented architecture refers to an architecture style that supports loosely coupled interoperable services to enable business flexibility and agility (Li & Madnick, 2015). SOA has several potential benefits and advantages, including enhanced IS agility and improved IT-business alignment, and many organizations invested in service- oriented architecture are expecting to reap those potential benefits (Li & Madnick, 2015). An enterprise system often has applications in a stack of infrastructure including databases, operating systems, and networks (Tsai, 2005). As pointed out in Table 4, agile organizations require a stable, robust, resilient, flexible, and standards-based infrastructure. Service-Oriented Computing (SOC) is applicable to these layers. SOC is a new paradigm that evolves from component-based computing paradigms by splitting the developers into three independent but collaborative entities: the application builders (also called service requestors), the service brokers (or publishers), and the service developers (or providers) (Tsai, 2005). The responsibility of the service developers is to develop software services that are loosely coupled. The service brokers publish or market the available services. The application builders find the available services through service brokers and use the services to develop new applications. The application development is done via discovery and composition rather than traditional design and coding (Tsai, 2005). In other words, the application development is a collaborative effort from three parties: application builders, service developers, and service brokers (Tsai, 2005). Furthermore, services are platform-independent and loosely coupled so that services developed by different providers can be used in a composite service (Tsai, 2005). The service-oriented enterprise (SOE) is often considered as the future model of organization (Janssen, 2008). SOE emerges and evolves from the implementation of new projects. New banking products and services can be created by deploying service centers (Janssen, 2008). Some of the key benefits are functionality, cost effectiveness, responsiveness, transformation, and optimization. Service oriented structure has advantages concerning the time to-market of products, reduction of duplicate activities and systems, and clarity of the governance structure (Janssen, 2008). This idea of the Service-Oriented Enterprise originates from the introduction of service-oriented architectures (SOAs), in which an application is constructed from well-defined and readily available components (Janssen, 2008). Figure 2 provided a hierarchy of how the services evolve and mature.

Figure 2. Service evolution and maturity

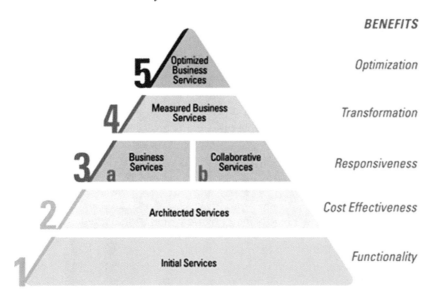

As pointed out earlier in Table 4, these components may include Scalable IT components, Modular IT components, Existence of a common underlying framework like middleware, EAI, etc., to integrate existing and legacy IT components; loosely coupled IT components; standards for decomposition of functionality into lower levels modules or components (IT components and/or modules with a base set of standard functionality); standards (message formats, protocols, etc.) for information exchange between modules/components; technical interface (e.g., PCI and other bus standards) standards for IT components; technical standards (e.g., naming of variables) for building the modules and/or components; availability of IS components that may be viewed as services; ability to collaborate with external parties to use services provided by their IS components through advertising of services and specification of the access mechanisms; and the existence of security mechanisms to control access to service provided by IS components inside and outside the organization.

Service-oriented architectures are becoming the prominent paradigm for building enterprise information systems. To date, most the focus on SOA and web service has been on technical details of defining interfaces (Janssen, 2008). The service-oriented architecture (SOA) enables the introduction of the SOE and the parallel evolutions of business and IT raise the new challenge of establishing a tighter linkage between business strategy and IT (Janssen, 2008). A SOA is essentially an architecture that describes the interactions between services communicating with each other, with functions and with their operations (Janssen, 2008). The complexities of the SDLC demand monumental information storage requirements that can only be facilitated by groups of specially routed server farms.

As mentioned previously, the latest development in the area of SOA is the advent of micro-services which are supposed to be used in containers. Using software like Docker if the application functionality can be decomposed into a set of microservices then these services can be deployed in containers (Ellingwood, 2015a) and can be easily scaled. At the same time, the services can be dynamically reconfigured using service discovery (Ellingwood, 2015c) through distributed configuration stores.

Server Farms and Data Centers

Huge data centers containing thousands of servers has transformed IS over the last few years. The discipline has matured tremendously over a period of the last ten years leading to server consolidation on account of increasing network quality and bandwidth and economies of scale. The evolution of data centers has led to cloud computing which in turn has led to an increased use of virtualization leading to enablement of dynamic capacity allocation and better resource utilization.

The amount of data accumulated over years of business cycles is nothing if it cannot be stored and retrieved for future analysis. Server Farms in data centers provide the function of compiling logs of operational memory for clients around the globe—giving easy access to important files. Current server farms have simple resource allocation models (Agrawal et al., 2001). One such model used is to dedicate a server or a group of servers for each client. Another model partitions physical servers into logical servers and assigns one to each client (Agrawal et al., 2001). However, both of these approaches prevent resource sharing and reduce the ability to handle peak loads except at the cost of having to reserve resources that will lie idle most of the time (Agrawal et al., 2001). The goal is to assign each client to a server to minimize the total number of servers needed to host all the clients (Agrawal et al., 2001). Server farms, also known as data centers and web server clusters, offer managed clusters of servers to host the IT infrastructure and web applications of various businesses (Agrawal et al., 2001). It allows businesses to focus on their core competencies, while availing of up-to-date technical skills, fast scalability, and high availability of servers at such farms (Agrawal et al., 2001). Each farm hosts multiple clients, achieving economies of scale. Resources on servers include CPU, memory, network bandwidth, and disk I/O, etc. (Agrawal et al., 2001). The simplest approach adopted by server farms for hosting clients is to dedicate resources to each client. Access rates of web sites are typically observed to have periodicity that exists on multiple time scales (Agrawal et al., 2001). Time scales of interest are daily, weekly, and seasonal. Different web sites experience their peak loads at different times (Agrawal et al., 2001). For example, a weather forecast application may be accessed mainly in the morning, while stock quotes may be heavily accessed in the evening. This will also be true for two sites accessed from opposite time zones. It is reasonable to assume that these observations also hold for the resource utilization of various web sites or web applications, due to close correlation with access rates (Agrawal et al., 2001).

Data centers have revolutionized the IS landscape and have led to several new developments that form the foundations of AIS.

DevOps

DevOps is oriented towards reducing the barriers between software development discipline and the operations discipline (responsible for deployment new and changed applications into the production environment). DevOps is about continuous delivery: reliable software releases through build, test, and deployment automation (Bass et al., 2005). It is formally defined as set of practices intended to reduce the time between committing a change to a system and change being placed in normal production, while ensuring high quality (Bass et al, 2005).

Bass et al. (2005) state that the quality of the deployed change to the system is important. This has been discussed before by stating that when a system is changed the resulting configuration has to be stable. Quality means suitability for use by various stakeholders including end-users, developers or system administrators. It also includes availability, security, reliabilies and other "ilities". One way of ensuring quality is to have a variety of automated test cases that must be passed prior to placing changed code into production, another method is to change in production with a limited set of users prior to opening it to the whole world. Still another method is to closely monitor newly deployed code for a period of time.

Containers (discussed previously) and DevOps are a good marriage. Kang et al. (2016), provide a proof of efficiency of container-based microservices-style DevOps compared to a VN-based approach. They also show that OpenStack DevOps using containers benefit greatly from fast deployment time, ease of rolling upgrade, and simplification of failure recovery and high availability.

DevOps is important for AIS since it can lead to faster deployment of the application from the test environment to the production environment. DevOps are considered an important component of an AIS. Cloud computing and the DevOps movement are two pillars that facilitate software delivery with extreme agility (Oliveira et al., 2016). "Born on the cloud" companies, such as Netflix, have demonstrated rapid growth to their business and continuous improvement to the service they provide, by reportedly applying DevOps principles (Oliveira et al., 2016). Perera et. al. (2016), show that software professionals in Sri Lanka are of the perception that the implementation of DevOps has a positive impact on Quality, Responsiveness to Business Needs, and Agility.

As many of the recent developments in the AIS, DevOps may involve some amount of learning curve for organizations. Achieving DevOps goals can involve fundamental changes in the architecture of the systems and in the roles and responsibilities required to get systems into production and support them once they are there (Bass et al., 2015). It represents a fascinating interplay between design, process, tooling, and organizational structure (Bass et al, 2015).

Software Defined Networks (SDN) and Network Function Virtualization (NFV)

Networking today is an important component of all IS. With the advent of cloud computing and the popularity of distributed systems especially, those that may be comprised of business processes made by stitching a variety of software services running on different systems, networks are central to IS. Software-defined networking is a new paradigm to manage networks. Open Network Foundation defines SDN as "the physical separation of the network control plane from the forwarding plane, and where a control plane controls several devices." Furthermore, it's "an emerging architecture that is dynamic, manageable, cost-effective and adaptable, making it ideal for the high-bandwidth, dynamic nature of today's applications. SDN is more about separating the network control logic from network hardware. Over time SDN can come to describe an open networking environment where elements such as switches, servers, and storage may be configured and managed centrally while running on standard hardware components (Tittel, 2014). In essence that means SDN control software sitting atop a physical infrastructure layer composed of networked devices with which it communicates via a control plane interface such as Open-Flow (Tittel, 2014). By minimizing hands-on work on physical devices, the network can change faster according to the needs of the applications and enterprises.

NFV aims to facilitate the deployment of new network services by virtualizing network devices and appliances, though not through the proliferation of physical devices to fill specialized roles such as routing, switching, content filter, spam filter, load balancer, WAN acceleration and optimization, unified threat management, and so forth (Tittel, 2014). Ultimately NFV is concerned with virtualizing hardware resources in software so that virtual implementations may be used to provide important network functions rather than requiring the presence of one or more specialized physical devices (Tittel, 2014).

Both SDN and NFV enhance agility of the IT infrastructure through rapid configuration and provisioning of resources. There are several recent examples of organizations using these to enhance agility by responding to changes in real-time fashion. When used in conjunction, SDN and NFV can result in both agility and economic benefits for organizations. In a case study involving LTE-based mobile networks Zhang and Hämmäinen (2015), found that SDN increases network agility while less redundancy is needed in network and equipment investments. At the same time, SDN may ease network management and deployment, which further reduces mobile network operator's (MNO's) costs (Zhang & Hämmäinen, 2015). On the other hand, it does make data centers more complex due to virtualization and increased control intelligence (Zhang & Hämmäinen, 2015). Overall the quantitative results show that SDN reduces the network related annual CAPEX by 7.72% and OPEX by 0.31% compared to non-SDN LTE in the case of a Finnish MNO (Zhang & Hämmäinen, 2015).

Agile Software Development

As mentioned before, software development has been traditionally done using the Waterfall Methodology which is not very conducive to changing requirements. Iterative methodologies like prototyping., Rapid Application Development, and the Unified Process have existed for a long time. However, the focus on iterative software development methodologies was thrust into the forefront with the publication of the Agile Manifesto (2001). There was an increasing realization that traditional development using the Waterfall Methodology was no longer sufficient. Since then a variety of methodologies (Scrum, Kanban, XP, etc.) based on the concept of iterative development have been proposed. "Agile software development describes an approach to software development under which requirements and solutions evolve through collaborative effort of self-organizing cross-functional teams and their customers and end users" (Wikipedia, 2018a):

Agile methods generally promote a disciplined project management process that encourages frequent inspection and adaptation, a leadership philosophy that encourages teamwork, self-organization and accountability, a set of engineering best practices that allow for rapid delivery of high-quality software, and a business approach that aligns development with customer needs and company goals. Conceptual foundations of this framework are found in modern approaches to operations management and analysis, such as lean manufacturing, soft systems methodology, speech act theory (network of conversations approach), and Six Sigma. (Wiztech Inc., 2011)

Artificial Intelligence

"Artificial Intelligence (AI) is the study of "intelligent agents" or any device that perceives it environment and takes actions that maximize its chance of successfully achieving its goals" (Wikipedia, 2018b; Russel & Norwig, 2009). "It is applied when a machine mimics cognitive functions that humans associate with other human minds such as learning and problem solving" (Gandhi, 2017; Russel & Norwig, 2009). AI has made significant progress in the last few years and is being employed in various domains to make better decisions while cutting the down the time to make these decisions significantly. The progress in AI is being driven primarily by significant increase in processing power coupled with enhanced ability to process both structured and unstructured data.

One of the hallmarks of an agile information system is that sensing, diagnosis, and execution happens in real time. Diagnosis (though not discussed here) can be significantly enhanced using AI and once the change has been diagnosed an action can be selected and executed again using AI. AI can significantly automate the cycle without need for human intervention and thereby speeding the process. Burre (2018), states that AI technologies have evolved from simple isolated automation systems to integrated enterprise-class digital automation solutions. These systems have diverse abilities like Runbook automation (a sequence of steps leading to the implementation of automated tasks started by system or a user), AI Ops (AI Ops platforms (leveraging big data and AI or machine learning functionality to improve and partially replace a myriad of IT operations processes and tasks), and AI-led Intelligent Automation (context-aware robots that cement a strong foundation for applications and services) (Burre, 2018). Burre (2018), goes on to further emphasize that AI-based systems are the next game changers in the IT operations area. These systems can detect and analyze vast quantities of data and automate complete IT processes or workflows while learning and adapting in the process (Burre, 2018). This key feature allows them to facilitate autonomous and seamless decision making even when there are aberrations in the process implementation. Some of the practical applications of AIS that incorporate AI would include predictive maintenance, interdependency analytics, self-healing and autonomous remediation.

Incorporation of AI into the AIS will usher a new era of responsiveness where the real-time may further shrink to the level of processing the bottlenecks of processing algorithms. One can possibly conceive a scenario where an increase in incoming traffic will automatically spin up a cluster in a public cloud service like Amazon with parameters derived from machine learning. The AIS can then automatically deploy new instances of applications by spinning up relevant containers again configuring them dynamically based on the given conditions. The WAN (Wide Area Network) may be reconfigured using NFV and SDN to provide better response times to the end users.

Summary

These current paradigms/frameworks which are both a combination of technologies that are old and new, as well as a new way of thinking borne out of the necessity of IS to become agile, are paving a new era in the development of an AIS. The reason we mention old and new is really on account of the fact that some of these technologies are not really new. Containers have been in existence for a long time through artifacts like BSD jails. Docker kind of brought this mainstream and combined it with DevOps and micro-services to make it an integral part of the AIS landscape. If one were to summarize how to summarize an agile IS with these paradigms, then one could say that the IS would involve applications that are structured as a set of loosely coupled micro-services that are developed using agile software development methodologies like Scrum and XP. The developed micro-services are tested and deployed using DevOps principles on an infrastructure that is composed of a combination of public and private cloud and being maintained and provisioned using the principles of clusters, virtualization, containers, SDN, and NFV. Once the applications have been deployed, the data collection and processing using big data and AI principles can lead to automated management and automatic reconfiguration of the technology components of the IS.

CONCLUSION AND DISCUSSION

There are some limitations in this study. This research represents the state at a particular point in time. In the IS area where technologies, practices, and concepts are continuously evolving, the research may need to be continually refreshed to be more meaningful with the times. It has been explained previously that there are several new frameworks and paradigms that are popular in the current IT industry and they do incorporate the properties outlined in the research that are specified in more generic and conceptual terms. Sometimes it is more appropriate to solicit opinions using specific terms rather than generic terms, which can be done if the research is replicated or repeated. Items may need to be further refined to avoid cross-loadings and non-loading items in EFA. The response rate for the survey was 5.7% and though this response rate was considered acceptable for the purpose of this survey there is still room to improve the response rate. This could be done, for example, through collaboration with some special interest groups and research groups with an interest in the area of IS agility.

The subject of big data and big data analytics is not addressed in this research and the reason for that is that this research is focused on the execution aspect of an agile IS. Big Data Analytics and big data can lead to building knowledge bases which can form the basis of automated response selection and execution. However, the building of knowledge bases may be viewed as a resource provision exercise.

The attributes for selection of an action in real-time, and execution of an action in real-time, in an agile IS as identified in this study, are based on a continuous and rigorous monitoring of IS industry developments. The shifting ideas and thoughts have been consolidated into the attribute list for selection and execution in an agile IS in this chapter (similar to the manner as it was done for sensing and diagnosis). This list could serve as a starting point for further research.

The instrument and the items may be examined and revised based on the data collection and analyses in this research, and the study may then be replicated. The replicated results may be used to come up with a scale for measuring selection and execution abilities of an agile IS.

CLASS DISCUSSION QUESTIONS

1. Discuss and critique the definition of agility as proposed in this chapter. Discuss the importance of "Real-time" in the definition. (for a detailed treatment of the construct of "Agility" reader may refer to (Pankaj et al.2009).
2. It may be argued (as also expressed by some industry practitioners) that if "Real-time" is an essence of an Agile IS then this may be achieved using total automation. Comment on this statement. Also think of this statement considering AI and the ability of machines to respond to changes in environmental conditions. Can AI result in a truly Agile IS?
3. One of the most important attributes of an Agile IS for execution was "IS personnel with get-it-done-attitude". Do you agree with this assessment? Are there any other attributes of IS personnel that you consider important for an Agile IS?
4. There is an increasing emphasis in the IS industry to abstract all components of an IS as services. For example, IaaS abstracts all hardware to be provisioned as a service. Can you think of some advantages and disadvantages of such an approach with respect to an Agile IS?
5. One factor that is not focused on in this chapter is "Organization Size". We treat IS as a necessity for all organizations. Given the complexity of IS, small- to medium-size organizations often procure IS from external sources (think of buying packaged software as opposed to custom software). Do you think that a small- to medium-size organization can have a truly Agile IS or is this something only large organizations with significant resources can attain?
6. What do agile software development and an agile organization have in common? How do the differ? Compare and contrast.

REFERENCES

Agarwal, V., Chafie, G., Karnik, N., Kumar, A., Kundu, A., Shahabuddin, J., & Varma, P. (2001). *An architecture for virtual server farms. Research Report*. IBM India Research Lab.

Allen, B. R., & Boynton, A. C. (1991). Information Architecture: In Search of Efficient Flexibility. MIS Quarterly, 435-445.

Alliance, A. (2001). *Agile manifesto.* Retrieved from http://www.agilemanifesto.org

Alvarez, A. (2012). Microsoft Application Virtualization Advanced Guide: Master Microsoft App-V by Taking a Deep Dive into Advanced Topics and Acquire All the Necessary Skills to Optimize Your Application Virtualization Platform. Birmingham, UK: Packt Publishing.

Bach, M. P., Čeljo, A., & Zoroja, J. (2016). Technology Acceptance Model for Business Intelligence Systems: Preliminary Research. *Procedia Computer Science, 100,* 995–1001. doi:10.1016/j.procs.2016.09.270

Bailey, J. E., & Pearson, S. W. (1983). Development of a Tool for Measuring and Analyzing Computer User Satisfaction. *Management Science*, *29*(5), 530–545. doi:10.1287/mnsc.29.5.530

Bajgoric, N. (2000). Web-based Information Access for Agile Management. *International Journal of Agile Management Systems*, *2*(2), 121–129. doi:10.1108/14654650010337131

Bal, J., Wilding, R., & Gundry, J. (1999). Virtual Teaming in the Agile Supply Chain. *International Journal of Logistics Management*, *10*(2), 71–82. doi:10.1108/09574099910806003

Barney, J. B. (1991). Firm Resources and Sustained Competitive Advantage. *Journal of Management*, *17*(1), 24. doi:10.1177/014920639101700108

Barthe-Delanoë, A. M., Truptil, S., Bénaben, F., & Pingaud, H. (2014). Event-driven agility of interoperability during the Run-time of collaborative processes. *Decision Support Systems*, *59*, 171–179. doi:10.1016/j.dss.2013.11.005

Bass, L., Weber, I., & Zhu, L. (2015). *DevOps: A Software Architect's Perspective*. Addison-Wesley Professional.

Bharadwaj, A. S. (2000). A Resource-Based Perspective on Information Technology Competences and Firm Performance: An Empirical Investigation. *Management Information Systems Quarterly*, *24*(1), 28. doi:10.2307/3250983

Bonoma, T. V. (1985). Case Research in Marketing: Opportunities, Problems, and a Process. *JMR, Journal of Marketing Research*, *22*(2), 199–208. doi:10.2307/3151365

Boynton, A. C. (1993). Achieving Dynamic Stability Through Information Technology. *California Management Review*, *35*(Winter), 58–77. doi:10.2307/41166722

Broadbent, M., & Weil, P. (1999). The Implications of Information Technology Infrastructure for Business Process Redesign. *Management Information Systems Quarterly*, *23*(2), 159–182. doi:10.2307/249750

Burre, P. (2018). AI-Driven Cognitive Operations Driving Enterprise Agility. *BWDisrupt*. Retrieved from http://bwdisrupt.businessworld.in/article/AI-Driven-Cognitive-Operations-Driving-Enterprise-Agility/21-02-2018-141356/

Byrd, T. A., & Turner, D. E. (2000). Measuring the Flexibility of Information Technology Infrastructure. *Journal of Management Information Systems*, *17*(1), 167–208. doi:10.1080/07421222.2000.11045632

Chowdhury, N. M. K., & Boutaba, R. (2009). Network virtualization: State of the art and research challenges. *IEEE Communications Magazine*, *47*(7), 20–26. doi:10.1109/MCOM.2009.5183468

Christopher, M. (2000). The Agile Supply Chain: Competing in Volatile Markets. *Industrial Marketing Management*, *29*(1), 37–44. doi:10.1016/S0019-8501(99)00110-8

Churchill, G. A. (1979). A Paradigm for Developing Better Measures of Marketing Constructs. *JMR, Journal of Marketing Research*, *16*(1), 64–73. doi:10.2307/3150876

Columbus, L. (2018). *83% Of Enterprise Workloads will be in The Cloud by 2020*. Retrieved from http://www.forbes.com/sites/louiscolumbus/2018/01/07/83-of-enterprise-workloads-will-be-in-the-cloud-by-2020/#521a089e6261

Dove, R. (1994). The Meaning of Life & The Meaning of Agile. *Production, 106*(11), 14–15.

Dove, R. (1995). Agility Engineering: Lego Lessons. *Production, 107*(3), 12–15.

Dziak, M. (2016). Virtualization (Computing). In *Salem Press Encyclopedia: Research Starters*. Academic Press.

Edwards, J., Millea, T., Mcleod, S., & Coults, I. (1998, 11 Jun 1998). *Agile System Design and Build*. Paper presented at the IEEE Colloquium on Managing Requirements Change: A Business Process Re-Engineering Perspective, London, UK.

Ein-Dor, P., & Segev, E. (1978). Organizational Context and the Success of Management Information Systems. *Management Science, 24*(10), 1064–1078. doi:10.1287/mnsc.24.10.1064

Eisenhardt, K. M. (1989). Building Theories from Case Study Research. *Academy of Management Review, 14*(4), 532–550.

Ellingwood, J. (2015a). The Docker Ecosystem: An introduction to Common Components. *The Docker Ecosystem*. Retrieved from https://www.digitalocean.com/community/tutorials/the-docker-ecosystem-an-introduction-to-common-components

Ellingwood, J. (2015b). The Docker Ecosystem: An Overview of Containerization. *The Docker Ecosystem*. Retrieved from https://www.digitalocean.com/community/tutorials/the-docker-ecosystem-an-overview-of-containerization

Ellingwood, J. (2015c). The Docker Ecosystem: Service Discovery and Distributed Configuration Stores, An Overview of Containerization. *The Docker Ecosystem*. Retrieved from https://www.digitalocean.com/community/tutorials/the-docker-ecosystem-service-discovery-and-distributed-configuration-stores

Gandhi, S. (2017). *Artificial Intelligence-Demystified*. Retrieved from https://towardsdatascience.com/artificial-intelligence-demystified-a456328e193f

Goeke, R. J., & Antonucci, Y. L. (2013). Differences in Business Process Management Leadership and Deployment: Is There a Connection to Industry Affiliation? *Information Resources Management Journal, 26*(2), 43–64. doi:10.4018/irmj.2013040103

Goodhue, D. L. (1988). *Supporting Users of Corporate Data (Ph.D. Doctoral)*. Boston: Massachusetts Institute of Technology.

Gottfried, S., & Herwig, W. (2014). Evaluating Flexibility in Discrete Manufacturing based on Performance and Efficiency. *International Journal of Production Economics, 153*, 340–352. doi:10.1016/j.ijpe.2014.03.018

Grove, A. S. (1999). *Only the Paranoid Survive*. New York: Doubleday.

Hair, J. H. Jr, Anderson, R. E., Tatham, R. L., & Black, W. C. (1995). *Multivariate Data Analysis*. Prentice Hall.

Hasselbring, W., & Steinacker, G. (2017). *Microservice Architectures for Scalability, Agility and Reliability in E-Commerce. In 2017 IEEE International Conference on Software Architecture Workshops* (pp. 243–246). Gothenburg: ICSAW; http://ieeexplore.ieee.org/stamp/stamp.jsp?tp=&arnumber=7958 496&isnumber=7958419, doi:10.1109/ICSAW.2017.11

Hefu, L., Weiling, K., Kwok, K. W., & Zhongsheng, H. (2013). The Impact of IT Capabilities on Firm Performance: The Mediating Roles of Absorptive Capacity and Supply Chain Agility. *Decision Support Systems, 54*(3), 1452–1463. doi:10.1016/j.dss.2012.12.016

Hoek, R. I. Van. (2000). The Thesis of Leagility Revisited. *International Journal of Agile Manufacturing Management Systems, 2*(3), 196-201.

Ives, B., Olson, M. H., & Baroudi, J. J. (1983). The Measurement of User Information Satisfaction. *Communications of the ACM, 26*(10), 785–793. doi:10.1145/358413.358430

Jahromi, N. T., Glitho, R. H., Larabi, A., & Brunner, R. (2017). An NFV and Microservice Based Architecture for On-the-fly Component Provisioning in Content Delivery Networks. *The 15th IEEE Consumer Communications and Networking Conference (CCNC).*

Janssen, M. (2008, January). Exploring the service-oriented enterprise: Drawing lessons from a case study. In *Hawaii International Conference on System Sciences, Proceedings of the 41st Annual* (pp. 101-101). IEEE. 10.1109/HICSS.2008.166

Kang, H., Le, M., & Tao, S. (2016, April). Container and microservice driven design for cloud infrastructure devops. In *Cloud Engineering (IC2E), 2016 IEEE International Conference on* (pp. 202-211). IEEE. 10.1109/IC2E.2016.26

Kris, V., & Jan, V. (2010). Determinants of the Use of Knowledge Sources in the Adoption of Open Source Server Software. *International Journal of Technology Diffusion, 1*(4), 53–70. doi:10.4018/jtd.2010100105

Langone, J., & Leibovici, A. (2012). *VMware View 5 Desktop Virtualization Solutions.* Packt Publishing Ltd.

Lederman, S. (2016). *Geek Guide - Containers 101.* Retrieved from www.puppet.com

Lee, D. M. S., Trauth, E., & Farwell, D. (1995). Critical Skills and Knowledge Requirements of IS Professionals: A Joint Academic/Industry Investigation. *Management Information Systems Quarterly, 19*(3), 313–340. doi:10.2307/249598

Li, X., & Madnick, S. E. (2015). Understanding the Dynamics of Service-Oriented Architecture Implementation. *Journal of Management Information Systems, 32*(2), 104–133. doi:10.1080/07421222.201 5.1063284

Martinez-Simarro, D., Devece, C., & Llopis-Albert, C. (2015). How information systems strategy moderates the relationship between business strategy and performance. *Journal of Business Research, 68*(7), 1592–1594. doi:10.1016/j.jbusres.2015.01.057

Mason-Jones, R., & Towill, D. R. (1999). Total Cycle Time Compression and the Agile Supply Chain. *International Journal of Production Economics, 62*(1-2), 61-73.

Mell, P., & Grance, T. (2010). The NIST definition of cloud computing. *Communications of the ACM*, *53*(6), 50.

Mohammadi, M., Mukhtar, M., & Malaysia, M. M. U. K. (2018). Comparison of Supply Chain Process Models based on Service-oriented Architecture. *Industrial Engineering (American Institute of Industrial Engineers)*, *9*(1).

Nissen, M. E. (2005). Delineating Knowledge Flows for Enterprise Agility. In Encyclopedia of Information Science and Technology (II) (pp. 779-785). Academic Press.

Oliveira, F., Eilam, T., Nagpurkar, P., Isci, C., Kalantar, M., Segmuller, W., & Snible, E. (2016). Delivering software with agility and quality in a cloud environment. *IBM Journal of Research and Development*, *60*(2-3), 10–11. doi:10.1147/JRD.2016.2517498

ORACLE. (2015). *New Oracle Research Reveals that Businesses are Unaware of Competitive Advantages of Cloud Agility.* Retrieved from https://www.oracle.com/corporate/pressrelease/oracle-cloud-agility-survey-na-082715.html

Orton-Jones, C. (2017). Identify threats and strike before they flourish. *Enterprise Agility.* Retrieved from https://www.raconteur.net/enterprise-agility-2017

Pankaj, H., Micki, R. A., & Rodger, J. A. (2013a). Attributes for Change Diagnosis in an Agile Information System. *International Journal of Computers and Technology*, *10*(10), 2095–2109.

Pankaj, H., Hyde, M., & Ramaprasad, A. (2013b). Sensing Attributes of an Agile Information System. *Intelligent Information Management*, *5*(5), 150–161. doi:10.4236/iim.2013.55016

Pankaj, H., & Micki, R. A., & Tadisina, S. (2009). Revisiting Agility to Conceptualize Information Systems Agility. In M. Lytras & P. O. D. Pablos (Eds.), Emerging Topics and Technologies in Information Systems (pp. 19-54). Hershey, PA: IGI Global.

Pankaj, & Hyde, M. (2003). *Organizations and the Necessity of Computer Based Information Systems.* Paper presented at the 9th Americas Conference on Information Systems, Tampa, FL.

Pankaj. (2005). *An Analysis and Exploration of Information Systems Agility* (Ph.D.). Southern Illinois University, Carbondale, IL.

Pendharkar, P. C., Subramanian, G. H., & Rodger, J. A. (2005). A Probabilistic Model for Predicting Software Development Effort. *IEEE Transactions on Software Engineering*, *31*(7), 615–624. doi:10.1109/TSE.2005.75

Perera, P., Bandara, M., & Perera, I. (2016, September). Evaluating the impact of DevOps practice in Sri Lankan software development organizations. In *Advances in ICT for Emerging Regions (ICTer), 2016 Sixteenth International Conference on* (pp. 281-287). IEEE. 10.1109/ICTER.2016.7829932

Quinn, J. B. (1980). Managing Strategic Change. *Sloan Management Review*, *21*(4), 3–20. PMID:10249849

Ricketts, J. A., & Jenkins, A. M. (1985). *The Development of an MIS Satisfaction Questionnaire: An Instrument for Evaluating User Satisfaction with Turnkey Decision Support Systems* Discussion Paper no. 296. Bloomington, IN: Indiana University School of Business.

Rockart, J. F., Earl, M. J., & Ross, J. W. (1996). Eight Imperatives for the New IT Organization. *Sloan Management Review, 38*(1), 13.

Sawas, M., & Watfa, M. (2015). The Impact of Cloud Computing on Information Systems Agility. *AJIS. Australasian Journal of Information Systems, 19*. doi:10.3127/ajis.v19i0.930

Seethamraju, R., & Sundar, D. K. (2013). Influence of ERP Systems on Business Process Agility. *IIMB Management Review, 25*(3), 137–150. doi:10.1016/j.iimb.2013.05.001

Sharifi, H., & Zhang, Z. (1999). A Methodology for Achieving Agility in Manufacturing Organizations: An Introduction. *International Journal of Production Economics, 62*(1), 7–22. doi:10.1016/S0925-5273(98)00217-5

Sunghun, C., Kyung, L. Y., & Kimin, K. (2014). Job Performance through Mobile Enterprise Systems: The Role of Organizational Agility, Location Independence, and Task Characteristics. *Information & Management, 15*, 605–618.

Tittel, E. (2014). *Understanding How SDN and NFV van Work Together*. Retrieved from https://www.cio.com/article/2379216/business-analytics/understanding-how-sdn-and-nfv-can-work-together.html

Tsai, W. T. (2005, October). Service-oriented system engineering: a new paradigm. In *Service-oriented system engineering, 2005. sose 2005. IEEE International Workshop* (pp. 3-6). IEEE.

Tushman, M. L., & Nadler, D. A. (1978). Information Processing as an Integrating Concept in Organizational Design. *Academy of Management Review, 3*(3), 613–624.

Unknown. (2002). *Comp.realtime: Frequently Asked Questions (FAQs) 3.6*. Retrieved 1/1/03, 2002, from http://www.faqs.org/faqs/realtime-computing/faq/

Wang, L., Ranjan, R., Chen, J., & Benatallah, B. (Eds.). (2017). *Cloud computing: methodology, systems, and applications*. CRC Press.

Weber, B., Reichert, M., & Rinderle-Ma, S. (2008). Change Patterns and Change Support Features – Enhancing Flexibility in Process-Aware Information Systems. *Data & Knowledge Engineering, 66*(3), 438–467. doi:10.1016/j.datak.2008.05.001

Weil, P., Subramani, M., & Broadbent, M. (2002, Fall). Building IT Infrastructure for Strategic Agility. *MIT Sloan Management Review*, 57–65.

Wikipedia. (2018a). *Agile Software Development*. Retrieved from https://en.wikipedia.org/wiki/Agile_software_development

Wikipedia. (2018b). *Artificial Intelligence*. Retrieved from https://en.wikipedia.org/wiki/Artificial_intelligence

Wiztech Inc. (2011). *AGILE Methodology*. Retrieved from http://www.wiztechinc.com/AGILE-methodology.html

Yang, J. (2014). Supply Chain Agility: Securing Performance for Chinese Manufacturers. *International Journal of Production Economics, 150*, 104–114. doi:10.1016/j.ijpe.2013.12.018

Young, A. (2017). *Global Survey Reveals Cost, Benefit, & Challenges of Cloud Migration.* Retrieved from http://itbrief.com.au/story/global-survey-reveals-costs-benefits-challenges-cloud-migration

Yu, H. E., & Huang, W. (2015). *Building a Virtual HPC Cluster with Auto Scaling by the Docker.* Retrieved 02-03, 2018, from https://sshelco-primo.hosted.exlibrisgroup.com/primo-explore/fulldisplay?docid=TN_ar xiv1509.08231&context=PC&vid=IUP&search_scope=default_scope&tab=default_tab&lang=en_US

Yusuf, Y. Y., Gunasekaran, A., Musa, A., Dauda, M., El-Berishy, N. M., & Cang, S. (2014). A Relational Study of Supply Chain Agility, Competitiveness, and Business Performance in the Oil and Gas Industry. *International Journal of Production Economics, 147,* 531–544. doi:10.1016/j.ijpe.2012.10.009

Yusuf, Y. Y., Sarahadi, M., & Gunasekaran, A. (1999). Agile Manufacturing: The Drivers, Concepts, and Attributes. *International Journal of Production Economics, 62*(1-2), 33-43.

Zhang, N., & Hämmäinen, H. (2015, March). Cost efficiency of SDN in LTE-based mobile networks: Case Finland. In *Networked Systems (NetSys), 2015 International Conference and Workshops on* (pp. 1-5). IEEE.

Chapter 17
The Rate of Adoption in Households and Organizations:
A Comparative Study

Henrik Vejlgaard
Copenhagen Business Academy, Denmark

ABSTRACT

The aim of this study is to investigate if households or organizations are faster in their adoption of an innovation. There does not appear to be existing research on this area of diffusion of innovations research. In this comparative study, the study object is digital terrestrial television (DTT), specifically the implementation of DTT in Denmark. By taking a service theory approach, DTT can be categorized as a service innovation. The rate of adoption is a concept in diffusion of innovations theory, which is used as the study's theoretical framework. For both units of analysis, three surveys were carried out. Based on the data, the rate of adoption for households and for organizations was established. It is clear that organizations adopt an innovation faster than households during the entire adoption process. Based on this research, a predictive model is constructed conceptually.

INTRODUCTION

Diffusion of innovations research has shown that organizations adopt innovations in a process that is different from individuals (Rogers, 2003, Chapter 10). However, we do not know if organizations are slow or fast in their adoption of innovations.

If we want to know if organizations as a whole are slow or fast in their adoption of innovations, we have to have another type of unit of analysis to which we can compare them. The only option we have if we want to find out if organizations are fast or slow with respect to adoption of innovations is to compare them to individuals or, as this study will do, to households. What has to be investigated is the rate of adoption, that is, the outcome of an adoptive process for both households and organizations for the exact same innovation in the exact same geographical area, at the same time, in the same culture. These requirements can be fulfilled by investigating the rate of adoption of digital terrestrial television (DTT) in Denmark.

DOI: 10.4018/978-1-5225-6367-9.ch017

The adoptive process is part of the diffusion of innovations discipline, which is a cross between sociology and communication research, or rather integrates both these disciplines in research. Diffusion of innovations (DOI) has been studied for more than a hundred years (Rogers, 2003, Chapter 2), resulting in a mainly empirically-driven science (Greenhalgh et al., 2004), based on quantitative research (Rogers, 2003, p. 196), and this study will also follow this empirical, quantitative tradition. Much of the research that took place in the 20th century has been summed up by Everett M. Rogers in his book *Diffusion of Innovations* (2003).

At first glance, DTT is likely to be categorized as a technological innovation. However, technology is not just technology: Technology is typically also part of something else: a product or a service. A clear analysis of the category that an innovation belongs to may give us more nuanced insights. This study will exemplify that—when studying technological innovations—a multidisciplinary approach to understanding the innovation may be meaningful. In this study, a service theory approach is introduced to correctly categorize DTT in an industry.

A SERVICE THEORY APPROACH

Research has made it clear that DTT is not, as some might think, about technology, or rather, not just about technology (Vejlgaard, 2018). At first glance, because of the word digital, DTT could be assumed to be about a technological innovation. This will quite naturally lead to the understanding that the adoptive process of DTT is about technology diffusion. However, this may be a premature conclusion. While there is no doubt that, in technical terms, DTT is transmission of television signals as digital units (bits) through the air (Benoit 2008), this cannot lead to the conclusion that DTT in a diffusion context "automatically" is a technological innovation. Vejlgaard (2018) established that DTT is a service innovation, not a technological innovation.

With fluid and blurred boundaries between technology and service offerings, the perception of an innovation may also be open to interpretation legally. In the beginning of the 2010s many digital innovations were introduced, for instance, as apps. The Uber taxi company and the company's drivers and customers may have viewed Uber as an app-based tech company but the European Court of Justice has determined that it is a transportation company, that is, a service company (BBC News, 2017). Therefore, it is important to analyze an innovation and put it into the correct industry and product category, and not just assume that an innovation is one or the other. This approach has been applied to research on cloud computing, which was viewed as "a technology and service innovation." (Hwang, Huang & Yang, 2016). Service innovation is a subject in itself, a subject that is closely related to service theory, for instance, services marketing theory.

Services marketing is one of the disciplines that studies the service sectors and the service industries. Services marketing theory was established in the 1980s (John & Lee-Ross, 1998, p. 21) and in the 21st century has become a fully established field (cf. Grönroos, 2015). In services marketing, a service offering is typically thought of as a service package (see, for instance, Normann, 2007, p. 75; Grönroos, 2015, p. 206). There are several ways to describe service packages (for instance, Grönroos, 2015; Fitzsimmons, Fitzsimmons & Bordoloi, 2014; Lovelock & Wirtz, 2004). The Grönroos basic service package model has five elements: the core service; enabling services and enabling physical goods; enhancing services and enhancing physical goods. Enabling services and/or enabling goods are often required for the core service to be used by customers. Enhancing services and enhancing goods do not facilitate the consumption of a service and are not obligatory for the core service to work. Enhancing services and enhancing goods are used to increase the value of or differentiate the service. The point is that a service may have physical elements and/or technology in them (Grönroos, 2015, pp. 207-209).

If we look at DTT in a service perspective, it becomes apparent that DTT fits with an established service sector. Service management categorizes services into service sectors and service industries. Guile and Quinn (1988) have made an overview of service sectors and service industries. One sector, the infrastructure services sector, consists of the communications, transportation, utilities, and banking industries. Television is part of a communications industry subcategory, the broadcasting industry, which offers different types of services: TV content production companies, TV-channels (broadcasters), and TV-signal distribution companies (distribution can take place via different platforms: cable, satellite, terrestrial, online). From a purely industry point of view, terrestrial television, whether analogue or digital, is a distribution service. The core service of television distribution companies is distribution of TV-signals. With this perspective, DTT is an innovation in a service industry, making DTT a service innovation, not a technological innovation. It is a physical (technological) element in the core service that is innovated. In a physical product. this element would be considered a technological innovation but when part of a service offering, it becomes a service innovation.

According to Johnson, Menor, Roth, and Chase (2000), a service innovation involves the creation of new and/or improved service offerings, service processes, and service business models. As the service itself, distribution of analogue TV-signals, already exists, DTT must be considered an improvement. In other words, in this analysis, DTT is an improved service innovation.

This insight leads to two points: 1. In the 21st century it makes sense to have multidisciplinary approaches to technology diffusion. 2. The adopters, whether they are individuals in households or in organizations, may have a different perception of DTT depending on perceiving DTT as a technological innovation or as a service innovation. If perceived as a technological innovation, this may stir technology anxiety (TA), which is well-known even with every day technology use (see, for instance, Lee, 2010). A professional facility manager in an organization may understand DTT as a service. If an innovation is viewed as a service innovation, there may be less of an issue of TA being a barrier to the adoptive process.

ADOPTIVE PROCESSES

The rate of adoption is one of the key concepts in diffusions of innovations research, as it is the outcome of the adoptive process. Diffusion research findings have concluded that the rate of adoption of an innovation typically follows a curve shaped like an italicized S. Rogers points out that the slope of the S curve can vary. Some innovations diffuse rapidly, and the S curve is then quite steep. Some innovations have a slower rate of adoption, which makes the S curve more gradual. The rate of adoption is typically measured by the length of time required for a certain percentage of the members of a social system to adopt an innovation. "Therefore, we see that the rate of adoption is measured for innovation in a system, rather than for an individual as the unit of analysis. [...] This system may be a community, an organization, or some other structure." (Rogers, 2003, p. 23). This other structure can, for instance, also be a segment of users/customers sharing the same trait(s).

The rate of adoption concept is the same for individuals and for organizations. But what determines the rate of adoption and the actual decision-making processes are different for individuals and organizations. The determinants and the innovation-decision process are not investigated in this study, and in principle they could be rendered a black box. However, key aspects of the two different processes that may be relevant to understand and possibly predict the relative speed of the adoptive process of individuals and of organizations are summarily summarized here.

Individuals

The rate of adoption is the confirmation of a decision making process that consists of (1) knowledge, (2) persuasion, (3) decision, (4) implementation, and (5) confirmation (Rogers, 2003, p. 20). This process is also termed the innovation-decision period (Rogers, 2003, p. 21). The length of the innovation-period is well documented for individuals (Rogers, 2003).

The S curve illustrates that people have different approaches to innovations: Some people adopt innovations right away, others need longer time, and some people need a very long time. This led Rogers to categorize people by adopter categories, the classifications of members of a social system on the basis of innovativeness (Rogers, 2003, p. 22). He identified five adopter categories: innovators, early adopters, early majority, late majority, and laggards. The first three categories are bundled together as early adopters; the remaining two categories are bundled together as late adopters.

The adopter categories have different personalities, interests, financial circumstances, and educational levels. Individuals who are innovators are different from the late adopters. Innovators are more open and curious than late adopters, and they want an innovation as soon as they hear about it. Laggards are the opposite and take the longest time to adopt.

The innovativeness dimension is used to understand and define the five adopter categories in quantitative terms. This dimension is measured by the time at which an individual adopter category adopts an innovation. Rogers partitioned the adopter categories into the five categories by calculating the standard deviation from the average time of adoption. This gave the following result: Innovators: The first 2,5% to adopt. Early adopters: The following 13,5% to adopt. Early majority: The following 34% to adopt. Late majority: The following 34% to adopt. Laggards: The remaining 16% to adopt (Rogers, 2003, p. 281).

In this study, the above is considered the adoption process representative of households, or rather an individual in a household.

Organizations

Rogers also summed up the innovation-decision process in organizations, and it is different from that of individuals (Rogers, 2003, pp. 402-435). However, the individual leader(s) in the organization are also likely to have an attitude towards change and innovations, and this attitude will also have an influence on the organization's adoptive process. It seems that the adopter category profiles of individuals can be reflected also in organizations (Rogers, 2003, p. 410).

Rogers also describes six internal characteristics of organizational structure that influence the organizations' innovativeness. 1. Centralization. 2. Complexity. 3. Formalization. 4. Interconnectedness. 5. Organizational slack. 6. Size (Rogers, 2003, p. 411). The more centralized an organization is, the less innovative the organization is. Complexity is about the employees' level of knowledge and expertise; complexity increases with higher levels of knowledge and expertise, based on, for instance, the employees' formal training and professionalism. "Complexity encourages organizational members to grasp the value of innovations [...]." (Rogers, 2003, p. 412). Formalization is about following rules and procedures. Formalization may inhibit innovativeness but encourage the implementation of innovations. Interconnectedness is about how networked the employees are. The more networked they are, the more innovative the organization. Organizational slack is about having uncommitted resources in an organization; having such resources are positively linked to innovativeness in organizations (Rogers, 2003, p. 412). Research has shown that larger organizations are more innovative (Rogers, 2003, p. 409). Beside these six internal factors, one external factor plays a role: The more open to the world an organization is, the more innovative it is (Rogers, 2003, p. 411).

An organization's actual innovation-decision process consists of two phases: Initiation and Implementation. The initiation phase consists of two sub phases: i. Agenda-setting and ii. Matching a problem from the organization's agenda with an innovation. The implementation phase consists of three sub phases: iii. Refining, iv. Clarifying, and v. Routinizing (Rogers, 2003, p. 421). Thus, it is notable that there is an implementation phase for both individuals and organizations.

Decisions in an organization may be made by one or more individuals, at different levels of the organization. Based on the number of people involved in the decision-making process inside the organization, three types of innovation-decisions can be identified: 1. Optional innovation-decisions. 2. Collective innovation-decisions. 3. Authority innovation-decisions (Rogers, 2003, p. 403).

Optional innovation-decisions refer to situations when an individual in an organization can choose to adopt an innovation independently of others in the organization. Collective innovation-decisions refer to situations when there is a consensus to adopt an innovation among a group of people in an organization. Authority innovation-decisions refer to situations when relatively few people in an organization decide to adopt an innovation (Rogers, 2003, pp. 407-408).

Both households and organizations go through a decision-making process. However, the process appears to be more complex in organizations than it is for individuals. Rogers has also noted that 'Compared to the innovation-decision process by individuals, the innovation-decision process in organizations is much more complex. Implementation typically involves a number of individuals, each of whom plays a different role in the innovation-decision process.' (Rogers, 2003, pp. 402-403). Furthermore, as Rogers also has pointed out, 'Once a decision to adopt has been made in an organization, implementation does not always follow directly.' (Rogers, 2003, p. 402). This could lead to the assumption that organizations are slower than households to adopt an innovation.

LITERATURE REVIEW

In literature, there is little research to support this assumption. It appears that no research on the topic of this study has been carried out. Literature that compares the rate of adoption of the same innovation for households and organizations in the same geographical area, at the same time, in the same culture, appears to be non-existent. Research has been carried out that makes other comparisons of the adoptive process, for instance, adoption in SMEs (small and medium-sized enterprises) and large companies (for instance, Buoanno et al. (2004), adoptions of product innovations and of process innovations inside the same company (for instance, Damanpour & Gopalakrishnan, 2001), and adoptive processes across cultures (for instance, Im, Hong & Kang, 2011). It appears that we do not know if organizations are slow or fast in their adoption of an innovation. There is a lack in this very specific area of diffusion of innovations research.

Research on the rate of adoption among individuals, among households, and among organizations has been carried out but not comparatively. But some existing research can help in further informing us on what makes a household slow or fast and on what makes an organization slow or fast.

Vejlgaard (2018) has noted that the adoptive process of DTT in Denmark was not voluntary, as it was mandated by the Danish government. Thus, with respect to organizations, it was an authority innovation-decision process. When the process is not a question of *if* innovation is to take place, only *when* it is to be implemented, this is in all likelihood a much simpler process within an organization. This could speed up the rate of adoption in organizations. While the mandatory policy can affect organizations, especially government organizations, it may not necessarily affect households in the same way.

Literature says that organization size is an important predictor of organizational innovation, as is complexity (Blau & McKinley, 1979; Camison-Zornoza, Boronat-Navarro & Segarra, 2004; Damanpour, 1996). It appears that size has an influence on the implementation stage whereas the influence of complexity on the implementation phase is mixed (Damanpour & Schneider, 2006). DOI research suggests that manager characteristics influence the adoption of innovations, for instance, that organizational managers may have a pro-innovation bias, which can speed up the adoptive process in an organization (Rogers, 2003, p. 412). One could speculate that managers working in public institutions (which represent organizations in this study) do not have a pro-innovation attitude. But research has shown that (also) among managers working in public institutions there may be a pro-innovation attitude (Damanpour & Schneider, 2008; Damanpour, 1991). However, it does not appear that sociodemographic characteristics of managers play a role in the adoptive process (Damanpour & Schneider, 2006). It is more about the employees' level of knowledge and expertise, as is well-established in DOI research.

In classic DOI research, the most referenced unit of analysis is an individual, which is a uniform size, namely one person. However, households are a different unit of analysis than individuals and can have different sizes. A household may consist of only one person (single-person households) or two-persons (households without children), or more persons (multi-person households). In a study of household technology (including television sets), it was found that multi-person households (with children) had the highest rate of adoption of a number of household electronic products. The research found that, "In general, one-adult households were slower to adopt new household technology when compared to other types of households." (Ironmonger, Lloyd-Smith, & Soupourmas, 2000). The study pointed out that demographically, single-person households tend to be older and female.

RESEARCH QUESTION

The research question is as follows:

- **RQ:** Which of the two, households or organizations, adopt an innovation the fastest?

As pointed out in the Introduction, the RQ can only be answered with data from the exact same innovation in the exact same geographical area, at the same time, in the same culture. Such data are available from when analogue terrestrial television (ATT) was terminated and digital terrestrial television (DTT) was implemented and made the only option for watching terrestrial television in Denmark. Thus, in this study, the rate of adoption of DTT is the study object. Both households and organizations are presented as single units of analysis, that is, the study is not about the adoptive process inside organizations and inside households, solely about the outcome of the adoptive process.

The RQ aims to investigate the units of analysis as general categories. However, because it has been established that unit size can influence the innovative nature of both households and organizations, unit size will also be part of this research.

From DOI research, it has been documented that larger organizations are more innovative. However, organizational unit size is relative, therefore, organizational unit size has to be put in a relevant geographical context, which in this study, is Denmark. In many countries, private enterprises are often categorized into three categories: small ('50 employees), medium-sized (50-249), and large (250+). The categorization can also be applied to government and non-government organizations. The categories will vary from country to country, sometimes also from industry to industry. Sometimes a fourth category is added: micro enterprises with less than 10 employees. This categorization often serves a policy purpose, for instance, with respect to eligibility for government grants. Therefore, the categories are not necessarily meaningful for other purposes, and one can add to that that the two words, enterprise and organization, have different meanings: Organization includes all types of organizations, private, non-government, and government organizations, whereas enterprise refers to private companies as businesses.

The average small private enterprise in Denmark has 3,6 employees; however, few stand-alone public institutions have fewer than 10 employees. The average large enterprise has 900 employees (*DSTanalyse*, 2016). In other countries, the number may be many times higher. What should factor in, in a meaningful categorization, is also the relative distribution of organization sizes. In Denmark, a majority of companies are micro enterprises, and there are no extremely large organizations (Erhvervsudvalget, 2005). However, with respect to public or government-funded organizations, the majority is a mix of small, medium-sized, and large organizations. A point here is to make a distinction between the typical small organization and larger organizations. Therefore, the following categories will be utilized: Small organization = ' 10 employees. Medium-sized organization = 10–249 employees. Large organization = 250+ employees. Medium-sized and large organizations are grouped together, representing "larger" organizations.

With respect to households, the following categories will be utilized in this study: Single-person household = 1 adult. Two-person household = 2 adults. Multi-person household = family in the broadest sense of the word.

Based on DOI research, the Literature Review, the RQ, and the definitions of the size of the units of analysis, this study will also include the following proposition: medium-sized and large organizations will be faster than single-person and two-person households with late adopter category profiles in adopting an innovation.

The RQ involves two affective variables, the rate of adoption of DTT for households and the rate of adoption of DTT for organizations. The proposition involves one variable (unit size), with one unit characteristic for households (adopter category profiles). The research populations have to live up to these criteria in order to either validate or invalidate the proposition.

METHOD

There are two separate (that is, unconnected) variables in this study: the rate of adoption of DTT in households and the rate of adoption of DTT in organizations. With quantitative data on these two variables, it will be possible to compare the two variables and establish whether households or organizations are the fastest in the adoption of DTT.

Making a comparative study between two units of analysis requires that a meaningful comparison can be made. Some clear criteria must be met, some of which has already been mentioned: They must involve the same object and subject matter for both units. They must be in the same geographical area, in the same culture. They must be compared during the same period; with preferably the same number of measuring points. It must be possible to gather data that are equally valid and reliable for both units of analysis. Neither unit must be manipulated in any biased way, that is, for instance, if they are influenced by a change agent, both units must be influenced by the change agent in an equal or at least balanced way.

This study lives up to these criteria. Therefore, the basis for a quantitative study comparing the rate of adoption for households and institutions, based on the case of implementing DTT in Denmark, is present. In order to measure the two affective variables, the research design is based on conducting a series of surveys over a period of time. Rogers indicated that three points at which data are gathered can form an S curve if you also have a zero (Rogers, 2003, p. 113).

In order to investigate the proposition, the research population must live up to the size definitions and the household characteristic stated in the RQ section. In this study, the two research populations have the following sizes:

- **Households:** Households with analogue terrestrial television; 601.000 households. Approx. 65% of the households were single-person households; approx. 30% were two-person households. The remaining 5% were a mix of household profiles. The profiles of the first two groups are typical of late adopters and laggards (middle-aged and older, little education, low income, outside of urban areas). The third group had an educated and urban profile;
- **Institutions:** Institutions with 24-hour living facilities with analogue terrestrial television; 2,215 institutions; Medium-sized and large organizations.

Institutions with 24-hour living facilities were the following types of institutions: asylum seekers' temporary housing facilities, boarding schools, college dormitories, halfway houses, hospitals, hospices, institutions for criminal youths, institutions for disadvantaged children and youths, institutions for drug addicts, institutions for the mentally handicapped, institutions for the physically handicapped, military barracks, nursing homes, and prisons. In this European context they are typically called 'public institutions', and in Denmark these are typically 100 percent government-funded institutions (the exceptions in this case are boarding schools, college dormitories, and halfway houses that may mainly have private funding). In this study, all the aforementioned organizations will be referred to as 'institutions'.

DATA GATHERING

It appears to be rare to have nationwide data on the adoption process of an innovation from an in-process adoption process for both households and organizations. However, such data were gathered when DTT was implemented in Denmark. The data were gathered in the following way: Three surveys were carried out for both households and institutions. With respect to households, the surveys were carried out in January 2009, September 2009, and November 2009. The institution surveys were carried out in May 2009, August 2009, and November 2009. It would have been ideal to have measuring points for the exact same months but measuring points at slightly different months were not expected to affect the findings of this study. However, it does require a need for an extra critical view of the results if they are in any way ambiguous.

Surveying television reception can be carried out in many ways. It is important to be aware of the technological issues involved and of the fact that some people have little or no knowledge of their own television reception. Therefore, to get valid and reliable data, survey methods have to be extraordinarily thorough and be based on insight into the technical part of television reception:

- **Households:** The three household surveys were all carried out using the same method: Approximately 1,000 persons, representative of the Danish population, aged 18+, with their own household, was selected randomly. After selection, the potential respondents received a letter informing them that they had been selected to participate in a survey of television habits. Each person in the 1,000-person sample was then contacted in one of two ways: 80 percent were contacted by telephone; 20 percent were visited in their own home by an interviewer. Irrespective of contact method the respondent selected for interviewing was the household member responsible for the TV equipment in the household. If a potential respondent could not be reached or refused to participate a new potential respondent with the same socio-demographic characteristics was selected and included in the sample. Thus, it was secured that there would be approximately 1,000 respondents in the sample population. Consequently, the survey in principle had a 100 percent response rate. The selection and interviewing process lasted four weeks.

A structured interview guide consisting of 72 questions was used for all respondents. The questions were of a socio-demographic nature and about TV habits and TV reception. For this study, the following survey question was asked:

- **Survey Question:** Has your household converted to the digital terrestrial television signal?

It was possible to crosscheck and to verify responses to this survey question by asking multiple behavioral and technical questions. For instance, if someone answered 'I don't know' to the survey question after the ATT switch-off it would, in fact, be possible to change this to a 'yes' or a 'no' in a simple way: Ask the respondent to turn on the television set and see if there is a signal. If the answer to that question was a 'yes', the answer to survey question would also be a 'yes'. It has been pointed out that the unit of analysis that organizations are compared to is households. Households are a type of unit that, as has already been pointed out, can vary in size and complexity, from single person units to large-size, maybe multi-generational, family units. However, in this study it is not the entire household that will be surveyed. It is an individual who is selected to be the respondent, not the entire household. The individual was also asked to respond as an individual, not after conferring with the entire household. (In general, presumably, most consumers who take part in surveys are supposedly members of a household. In other words, decision-making processes may be blurred with respect to the individual/household issue.) There is, therefore, no modification with respect to the innovation-decision process for individuals as described in the section on the Adoption Processes. It would be different if the entire household had been asked. Then it would probably be a different decision-making process because individual household members can have different adopter category profiles:

- **Institutions:** Three surveys were carried out, using two different methods. First, a questionnaire was emailed to the 4.043 institutions with 24-hour living facilities that had been established as the target group. For the remaining two surveys, the CATI (Computer-Assisted-Telephone-Interview) survey method was used.

In spring 2009, a written questionnaire with nine questions was mailed to 4,043 institutions, that is, to all individual addresses of all institutions in Denmark. The 2-page questionnaire only had multiple choice questions plus space to write contact person data. In the letter it was asked that the questionnaire was filled out by the person responsible for television reception at the institution. The questionnaire could be filled out on paper and returned in an enclosed envelope or could be filled out online. Twice reminders were sent to institutions. Based on the returned questionnaires, it was established that 2,215 institutions had analogue terrestrial television and would be affected by the ATT switch-off. They would be the population for the two remaining institution surveys. Based on the questionnaire, it could be established how many institutions that had converted to DTT at that time.

The 2,215 affected institutions would be the population for the two CATI surveys. Samples for the remaining CATI surveys would be randomly drawn from this population. Each sample would comprise a minimum of 200 institutions. The CATI surveys were carried out in August 2009 and November 2009. Because television reception and contact data for a relevant contact person had been established through the questionnaire different questions could be asked in the CATI surveys. Eight questions were asked in the CATI surveys, with different grammatical tense before and after the ATT switch-off. Based on these questions, it could be calculated if an institution had converted to DTT.

With respect to both households and institutions, adoption of DTT could not begin to take place until the DTT signal was in the air on March 31, 2006. Therefore, March 2006 is set as zero with respect to the rate of adoption.

SURVEY RESULTS

The results of the three household surveys are shown in Table 1. The statistical variance for the household surveys is shown in Table 2. The results of the three institution surveys are shown in Table 3. The response rates for the institution surveys are shown in Table 4. As a rule, numbers are rounded up or down.

The numbers from Table 1 and Table 3 have been turned into curves in Figure 1. The curve to the left represents the rate of adoption for institutions; the curve to the right represents the rate of adoption for households.

Table 1. Survey results for households survey questions

	March 2006	**January 2009**	**September 2009**	**November 2009**
Number of Respondents	-	1024	989	976
Has your household converted to the digital terrestrial television signal?	0	13%	26%	99,7%

Table 2. Statistical variance for household survey question

Household Survey Question	Result	Result With Statistical Variance	Response Rate
January 2009	13%	0-32%	100%
September 2009	26%	0-43%	100%
November 2009	99,7%	---	100%

Table 3. Survey results for institutions survey questions

	March 2006	May 2009	August 2009	November 2009
Number of Respondents	-	4,043	247	184
Has the institution converted to the digital terrestrial television signal?	0	39%	64%	99,6%

Table 4. Statistical variance for institutions survey question

Institution Survey Question	Result	Response Rate
May 2009	39%	55%
August 2009	64%	94%
November 2009	99,6%	91%

It does not appear to have an influence on the findings of this study that there was a difference in the months the two first surveys were carried out: There is a clear difference between the two rates of adoption, and they do not cross each other. In other words, no matter at what months the surveys were carried out within innovation-decision period, the overall findings would be the same.

CONCLUSION

The answer to the research question is that organizations are faster than households in adopting an innovation. In the entire process, organizations were faster than households at adopting the innovation. The latter finding is especially worth noting because if there were variations during the innovation-decision period, the conclusion could be said to be ambiguous. In the early part of the period, the difference is minor but as the deadline for the ATT switch-off gets nearer the difference widens until a couple of months before the ATT switch-off deadline when the differences again narrows, ending (when rounded up) in 100 percent adoption for both organizations and households.

The households in this study had different sizes, as did the organizations. The households were single-person and two-person households with late adopter category profiles. The organizations were medium-sized and large organizations.

Therefore, the proposition that medium-sized and large organizations will be faster than single-person and two-person households with late adopter category profiles in adopting an innovation can be validated.

Figure 1. The rate of adoption for institutions to the left (black line); the rate of adoption for households to the right (the grey line)

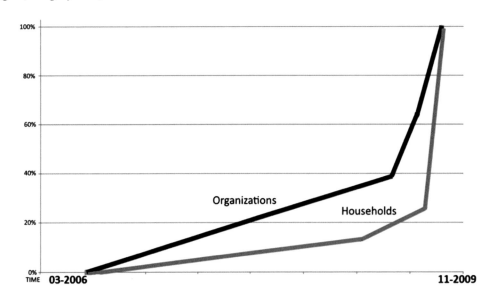

DISCUSSION

Due to the simpler decision-making process in a household, compared to the decision-making process in an institution, one could easily assume that households would be faster than organizations in adopting an innovation. The findings, however, are contrary to what may be a popular belief, namely that organizations are slow compared to households, due to bureaucratic structures, processes, and work cultures. The findings may not only have an effect on the image of organizations but also add to our general understanding of organizations.

The reason that institutions had the speediest rate of adoption could have to do with other aspects of the adoptive process than unit size: The institutions are staffed with employees who have knowledge and expertise, not necessarily with respect to the precise technology but with respect to be working in a service organization. It is also important to be aware that that the type of organizations studied here were institutions with 24-hour living facilities and in most instances these institutions have a 'built-in' responsibility for the people living in the facility. The staff may have an awareness of this responsibly towards other people that may be part of the organizational thinking of many of the institutions in this study. When employees are aware that they are acting on behalf of an organization and that there is a responsibility towards other people who cannot act themselves, they are probably not likely to delay the required decisions unduly. If the staff (for instance, a facility manager) has perceived DTT as a new service that needs to be implemented, staff has handled this in a professional way, for instance, by contacting a television repair person.

As pointed out, organizations are presented as a single unit of analysis in this study. Organizations may be anonymous entities but they are peopled with employees. These individuals do not act on their own behalf and as private persons. They act on behalf of an organization and thus represent organizational behavior, and they take part in decision processes that are different from individuals' decision processes.

However, with respect to innovation-decisions, it is open for discussion if employees will act according to their "private" adopter category profile at their work.

As most organizations are not just represented by one person, in many organizations employees and executives with different adopter category profiles, are likely to be involved. This could mean that change-oriented adopter category profiles within the organization will be setting the agenda no matter what their position in the organization is. If they are represented among the management, the management will make the decision relatively early on. If they are represented by an employee, this employee can push the management to decide faster. So, as long as these adopter categories are represented by some individuals involved in the innovation-decision process, at any level, this could speed up the process.

This leads to this observation: Employees are maybe more likely to act irrespective of their personal adopter category profile when acting on behalf of an organization. While it cannot be expected that employees who are laggards by nature will become innovators in their work life, they could act as majority adopters.

The organizations in this study were not representative of all types of organizations, as there were no private organizations in the study. Therefore, one can ask, would private organizations also be speedier than households investigated in this study? This study cannot say anything definitive in this respect. It will probably not matter if organizations are private or not with respect to hospitals, prisons, nursing homes etc. Whether privately or publicly owned they will be likely to act as the institutions in this study. But if the organizations are more broadly private enterprises, the answer is not obvious. But a point to be made here (and below) is that the households in this study were late adopters and laggards, that is, the two slowest adopter categories. In other words, only if the private organizations overwhelmingly also had these profiles, it would be difficult to predict which would be fastest. But, as it would be exceptional that all private organizations are late adopters, it is likely that private organizations also would be faster compared to the households investigated here.

One important question is, if the findings of this study are generalizable to other countries. One should always be careful to conclude any general validity based on just one study. Culture can have played a part: It has been documented that culture can affect organizations and organizational life (Hofstede et al., 2010). Before answering any questions with respect to generalization, the study must be put in a cultural context. The cultural context is Denmark, a country with specific cultural dimensions, as understood by, for instance (Hofstede et al., 2010). If one were to put 'efficient organizations' and 'bureaucratic organizations' at different ends of a continuum, it is likely that Denmark would be categorized as more efficient than bureaucratic. One can add to this that Denmark in 2010 had the no. 1 position on the Corruption Perceptions Index (Transparency International, 2014). In other words, Danish culture can have had an influence on the findings, and if that is the case, the findings may be generalizable only to cultures that are similar to Danish culture, that is, mainly countries in Northern Europe.

A PREDICTIVE MODEL

The present study has introduced new insight on an aspect of DOI theory that was lacking. We have not had knowledge about the comparative speed of the adoptive processes of households and organizations. With this study, new insights into the diffusion of innovations seem to emerge. Therefore, based on this insight, it is now possible to create a construct that can guide future research.

By just focusing on one variable for both units of analysis and adding adopter category characteristic to the household unit of analysis, this study can conceptually generate a deeper insight with respect to predicting the comparative speed of the rate of adoption of the two units. In this study, medium-sized and large organizations were faster than single-person and two-person households, consisting of late adopters. One can wonder what effect dissimilar households and dissimilar organizations will have on the speed. Here, a theoretical answer, based on a conceptual construct, is introduced.

Table 5 presents a conceptual construct of the relative speed of the rate of adoption of households and of organizations, each divided into two unit size categories. The household size variable also has a characteristic based on adopter category profiling. The predicted speed of the units of analysis is shown in the column to the left. The unit sizes (and the household characteristic) are presented in square A and in square D: D is faster than A, as per this study. According to another study, only 50 per cent of households had adopted DTT in Denmark one month before the deadline. The remaining 50 per cent of households adopted in the course of the last month out of a 3 year and 7 months period (Vejlgaard, 2016). This means that adoptive process was slow, indeed, very slow. An adoptive process can be slower but one can argue that an even slower diffusion process would be extreme. With this insight square B will be faster than square A. As mentioned in the Literature Review section, larger organizations will have a faster rate of adoption than small organizations. Therefore, square D represents the faster process with respect to organizations; square C will be slower.

As a forecasting model, Figure 1 has some limits: If the units of analysis are not uniform, it is likely to be more difficult to make a prediction based on this construct. In addition to that, the construct cannot predict if A or C is slowest or if B or D is fastest. However, the perspective is that if the unit sizes of the two units of analysis and the household unit characteristic can be established early in an adoptive process, one may be able to predict the relative speed of the rate of adoption. Here the conceptual construct is analytical theory. However, with empirical research on this construct, across different types of types of innovations, it may be possible to establish the model as scientific theory. Then the construct can be a de facto predictive model.

DISCUSSION QUESTIONS

1. What was most surprising to you when you read this chapter?
2. Search 5 innovations that can be either a new technology or a new service, and categorize them in an industry, and, if meaningful, in a product category. Discuss the challenges in categorizing innovations in an industry or as a product category.

Table 5. Conceptual construct of the relative speed of the rate of adoption with respect to two different units of analysis

Unit Type Predicted Speed	Households Unit Size	Organizations Unit Size
Slow	A. Single-person and two-person Late adopters	C. Small
Fast	B. Multi-person Early adopters	D. Medium-sized and large

3. Would you act differently with respect to adopting an innovation whether you perceive it as new technology or as a service innovation?
4. How likely is it that the findings of this study would be different if the study object (the innovation) had been different, for instance, in a completely different category?
5. How can the predictive model introduced in this chapter be of value to businesses or government institutions?

REFERENCES

BBC News. (2017). *Uber is officially a cab firm, says European Court*. Retrieved February 1, 2018 from http://www.bbc.com/news/business-42423627

Benoit, H. (2008). *Digital Television: Satellite, Cable, Terrestrial, IPTV, Mobile TV in the DVB Framework*. Oxford, UK: Focal Press.

Blau, J. R., & McKinley, W. (1979). Idea, Complexity, and Innovation. *Administrative Science Quarterly*, *24*(2), 200–219. doi:10.2307/2392494

Buoanno, G., Faverio, P., Pigni, F., Ravarini, A., Sciuto, D., & Tagliavini, M. (2004). Factors affecting ERP system adoption: A comparative analysis between SMEs and large companies. *Journal of Enterprise Information Management*, *18*(4), 384–426. doi:10.1108/17410390510609572

Camison-Zornoza, C., Lapiedra-Alcami, R., Segarra-Cipres, M., & Boronat-Navarro, M. (2004). A Meta-Analysis of Innovation and Organizational Size. *Organization Studies*, *25*(3), 331–361. doi:10.1177/0170840604040039

Damanpour, F. (1996). Organizational Complexity and Innovation: Developing and Testing Multiple Contingency Models. *Management Science*, *42*(5), 693–716. doi:10.1287/mnsc.42.5.693

Damanpour, F., & Gopalakrishnan, S. (2001). The Dynamics of the adoption of product and process innovations in organizations. *Journal of Management Studies*, *38*(1), 45–65. doi:10.1111/1467-6486.00227

Damanpour, F., & Schneider, M. (2006). Phases of the Adoption of Innovation in Organizations: Effects of Environment, Organization and Top Managers. *British Journal of Management*, *17*(3), 215–236. doi:10.1111/j.1467-8551.2006.00498.x

Damanpour, F., & Schneider, M. (2009). Characteristics of Innovation and Innovation Adoption in Public Organizations: Assessing the Role of Managers. *Journal of Public Administration: Research and Theory*, *19*(3), 495–522. doi:10.1093/jopart/mun021

DSTanalyse. (2016). *Hvornår er små virksomheder små?* Retrieved on February 1, 2018 from https://www.dst.dk/da/Statistik/Analyser/visanalyse?cid=27867

Erhvervsudvalget, F. (2005). *Bilag 230*. Retrieved on February 1. 2018 from http://www.ft.dk/samling/20101/almdel/eru/bilag/125/944066.pdf

Fitzsimmons, J. A., Fitzsimmons, M. J., & Bordoloi, S. K. (2014). *Service Management: Operation, Strategy, Information Technology*. New York: McGraw-Hill International.

Greenhalgh, T., Robert, G., Macfarlane, F., Bate, P., & Kyryiakidou, O. (2004). Diffusion of Innovations in Service Organizations: Systematic Review and Recommendations. *The Milbank Quarterly*, *82*(4), 581–629. doi:10.1111/j.0887-378X.2004.00325.x PMID:15595944

Grönroos, C. (2015). *Service Management and Marketing*. New York: Wiley.

Guile, B. R., & Quinn, J. B. (1988). *Technology of Services: Politics for Growth, Trade, and Employment*. Washington, DC: National Academy Press.

Hofstede, G., Hofstede, G. J., & Minkov, M. (2010). *Cultures and Organizations: Software of the Mind*. New York, NY: McGraw-Hill.

Hwang, B.-N., Huang, C.-Y., & Yang, C.-L. (2016). Determinants and their causal relationships affecting the adoption of cloud computing in science and technology institutions. *Innovation*, *18*(2), 164–190. doi:10.1080/14479338.2016.1203729

Im, I., Hong, S., & Kang, M. S. (2011). An international comparison of technology adoption: Testing the UTAUT model. *Information & Management*, *48*(1), 1–8. doi:10.1016/j.im.2010.09.001

Ironmonger, D. S., Lloyd-Smith, C. W., & Soupourmas, F. (2000). New Products of the 1980s and 1990s: The Diffusion of Household Technology in the Decade 1985-1995. *Prometheus*, *18*(4), 403–415. doi:10.1080/08109020020008514

Johns, N., & Lee-Ross, D. (1998). *Research Methods in Service Industry Management*. London: Cassell.

Johnson, S., Menor, L., Roth, A., & Chase, R. (2000). A Critical Evaluation of the New Service Development Process: Integrating Service Innovation and Service Design. In New Service Development: Creating Memorable Experiences. Thousand Oaks, CA: Sage Publications.

Lee, C.-P. (2010). The Impact of Technology Anxiety on the Use of Mobile Financial Applications. *International Journal of Technology Diffusion*, *1*(4), 1–12. doi:10.4018/jtd.2010100101

Lovelock, C., & Wirtz, J. (2004). *Services Marketing: People, Technology, Strategy*. Singapore: Pearson.

Normann, R. (2000). *Service Management: Strategy and leadership in service management*. New York: Wiley.

Rogers, E. M. (2003). *Diffusion of Innovations*. New York: Free Press.

Transparency International. (2014). Retrieved on February 1, 2018 from https://www.transparency.org/cpi2014

Vejlgaard, H. (2016). Late adopters can be fast: The case of digital television. *Communications*, *41*(1), 87–98. doi:10.1515/commun-2015-0029

Vejlgaard, H. (2018). Rate of adoption determinants of innovations: A case study of digital terrestrial television. *International Journal of Digital Television*, *9*(1), 7–26. doi:10.1386/jdtv.9.1.7_1

Chapter 18

Learning From Abroad on SIM Card Registration Policy:
The Case of Malawi

Frank Makoza
Cape Peninsula University of Technology, South Africa

ABSTRACT

This chapter presents an analysis of policy transfer in the context of a developing country. The case of Malawi was analyzed as an African country attempting to implement a mandatory subscriber identity module (SIM) card registration policy. The study used a qualitative research approach and secondary data including government reports and media reports. The findings showed that the SIM card registration policy was transferred through coercive transfer to meet security standards and international conventions, and voluntary transfer to address local social challenges related to the use of mobile technologies. Despite initiating the SIM card registration process on several occasions, the implementation process was met with constraints related to social, economic, and political factors that affected the policy transfer process.

INTRODUCTION

Mobile technologies have become more accessible and affordable across the continent of Africa. It is estimated that there are about 759 million users of mobile phones in Africa (ITU, 2017). Mobile phones are improving communication for individuals and organisations, access to information and services such as financial services (for instance banking, money transfer and insurance) and public services (health, education, agriculture and managing the environment). Further mobile phones have been heralded in creating employment opportunities and redressing social ills in communities, such as social exclusion. It is, therefore, not surprising that mobile phones are in a way influencing the social and economic conditions of many people in African countries (Ojo, Janowski & Awotwi, 2013; Shaik & Karjaluoto, 2015).

While there are potential benefits to be derived from the use mobile phones, some critics have argued that mobile phones are also being used in criminal activities that pose a threat to the well-being of the citizens (Ahmed, Hague, Guha et al., 2017; Ajayi, 2014; Donovan & Martin, 2012). For example, mo-

DOI: 10.4018/978-1-5225-6367-9.ch018

bile phones are being used in crimes such as kidnapping, terrorism, drug and human trafficking (Ajayi, 2014). Further, mobile phones are used in activities related to hate speech, glorification of violence, cyber laundering and SMS phishing and spamming (Aririguzo, & Agbaraji, 2016; Donovan & Martin, 2012). To remedy some of the challenges, African governments have adopted mandatory SIM card registration policies where all prepaid mobile phones users are required to register their personal identifiable data for their active SIM cards (Hemeson, 2012; Donovan & Martin, 2012; Jentzsch, 2012).

SIM card registration policy, like other public technology, is *"a set of actions that affect the generation, acquisition, adaptation, diffusion and use of technological knowledge in a way that government deems useful for society rather than the individual"* (Ghazinoory, Divsalar & Soofi, 2008:836). The SIM card registration policies may be transferred through lesson drawing, voluntary and coercive approaches (Dolowitz & Marsh, 2000). The majority of African countries (48 out of the 54 countries) have adopted the mandatory SIM card registration policies in response to the ratification of international and regional conventions for security (Jentzsch, 2012). There are consequently few countries without the mandatory SIM card registration policy (Donovan & Martin, 2014).

This study focuses on the context of Malawi, which is an example of a low-income economy in Africa. The country has not yet implemented the mandatory SIM card registration policy. It was interesting to note how the country will learn about SIM card registration policy from other countries and develop an understanding of technology policy transfer, and the challenges and opportunities of the SIM card registration policy. The study was guided by the research question: How are mandatory SIM card policies adopted in the countries without SIM card registration? The study was important in addressing the paucity of studies on technology policy transfer in the context of African countries (Donovan & Martin, 2012). The study may serve to inform policymakers and practitioners on issues that can inhibit the success of the SIM card registration in the countries without the policy.

POLICY TRANSFER

Policy transfer may be viewed from many perspectives depending on the context of the study. The different perspectives may include policy diffusion, policy convergence and policy transfer (Marsh & Sharman, 2009). To appreciate the differences the description of each term are summarised as follows:

- **Policy diffusion:** The process in which policy choices in one country affect those made in another country (Braud & Gilardi, 2006). Policy diffusion emphasises the roles of the structures of the policy process rather than the agents involved in the policy transfer (Marsh & Sharman, 2009);
- **Policy convergence:** The process in which policies in two or more countries become more alike over a period of time (Knill, 2005);
- **Policy transfer:** The process in which *"knowledge about policies, administrative arrangements, institutions and ideas in one political setting (past and present) is used in development of policies, administrative arrangements, institutions and ideas in another political setting"* (Dolowitz & Marsh, 2000:5).

The study used the term 'policy transfer' (Dolowitz & Marsh, 2000) to clarify the process of policy transfer for mandatory SIM card registration. The perspective of policy transfer is considered appropriate because it is more encompassing and addresses both agency and structure that are interactive and iterative in the sequence of activities where decisions are made and resources are used in activities that address specific social challenges (Marsh & Sharman, 2009), thus addressing the questions related to what, who, how and why in the policy transfer process.

Policy transfer can include policy goals, contents, programs, institutions, ideologies, ideas, attitudes and negative lessons. The transfer of these items may vary depending on the situation or policy issue being addressed (Dolowitz & Marsh, 2000). The process of policy transfer can happen at different levels of society involving diverse groups of policy actors, for example policy transfers at international, national or local levels. At international level, policy actors may include Intergovernmental Organisations (IGOs) for example World Bank, IMF, OECD, United Nations and governments. Politicians and government officials are involved in policy transfer at the national level. Non-governmental and private sector organisations (for example in partnerships) may also be engaged in policy transfer activities.

Policies can be transferred in three modes: lesson drawing (perfect and bounded rational evaluation of alternative policies to address challenges), voluntary transfer (driven by perceived necessity such as international acceptance) and coercive transfer (direct imposition by an aid agency or intergovernmental organisations) (Dolowitz & Marsh, 2000). Voluntary policy transfer is ideal in situations where the government is faced with problems which are complex or not is not clear in terms of how they can be addressed. Policy-makers may consider lesson-drawing from elsewhere to understand the problems and come up with solutions. In coercion, governments can be compelled to adopt policies against their will. This could also be a result of the governments' obligation to international regimes and structures (Marsh & Sharman, 2009).

There are barriers in policy transfer process that may lead to unsuccessful policy outcomes. The three causes of policy transfer failure are uninformed transfer (due to lack of sufficient information on how the policy operates), incomplete transfer (due to lack of transfer for crucial elements for the policy), and inappropriate transfer (due to differences in context such as social, political and economic structures) (Marsh & Sharman, 2009). The factors that inhibit successful policy transfer can be categorised into environmental, political opinion and cognitive obstacles (Evans, 2012). Cognitive obstacles for policy transfer may occur during the pre-decision phase may include the limited search for activities related to the policy, cultural assimilation challenges and complexity of the policy transfer process (Evans, 2012). Therefore, policy transfer should take into account the potential barriers in the process.

MANDATORY SIM CARD REGISTRATION

Mandatory SIM card registration is the process of recording prepaid mobile phones with their personal details for the active SIM cards (Jentzsch, 2012). The process involves agencies recording personal information details including name, national identification number, physical address and contact details of a SIM card holder. In some cases, biometric data is recorded, such as fingerprints and facial image of the SIM card holder (Donovan & Martin, 2012). Identification of the SIM card holder is crucial in the registration process.

One of the aims for the introduction of SIM card registration policies is to combat and prevent crimes and fraud where mobile devices are used in these activities, for example fraud, money laundering and terrorism. Hence, governments across the globe have ratified international conventions on Anti-Money Laundering and Combating the Financing of Terrorism (AML/CFT) (Chatain, Zerzan, Noor, Dannaoui & de Koker, 2011). The standards of AML/CFT require consumers to take reasonable steps when making a single payment for cash transactions. This relates to Know Your Customer (KYC) procedures that support the identification of any financial transaction. Part of the implementation of KYC involves enacting national laws and regulations which require verification of the identity of customers and their physical addresses (Johnson, 2008; Makulilo, 2011). The increase in mobile phone adoption and use of mobile payments has led to consideration for mandatory SIM registration in African countries (Chatain et al., 2011).

In Africa, regional economic groups have influenced the transfer of SIM card registration policies. For example, the East African Communication Organisation (EACO) promoted and supported SIM card registration policy transfer for countries in East Africa including Tanzania, Kenya, Uganda and Burundi (Jentzsch, 2012). The mandatory SIM card registration in the member states of EACO include enacting legislation, regulations and procedures for recording personal data of active mobile phone users. The SIM card registration policy implementation was achieved through the collaboration of governments, regulators and Mobile Network Operators (MNOs). The main role of government was enacting laws to support the regulation and enforcement of the mandatory SIM card registration process. The MNOs where engaged in the implementation of the policy in registering the mobile phone users (Jentzsch, 2012). Other regional economic groups also supported and promoted the mandatory SIM card registration for example the Economic Community of West African States (ECOWAS), East African Community (EAC) and Southern Africa Development communities (SADC) (Sumbwanyambe & Nel, 2013). Other African countries have implemented the mandatory policy without support from regional economic groups. However, there are a number of African countries that remain without the mandatory SIM card policies in place, for example Lesotho, Malawi, Mauritania, Namibia, Somalia and Swaziland (Annan & Sahoy, 2017; Jentzch, 2012).

It is interesting to note that while the majority of the African governments have willingly adopted the mandatory SIM card registration, other developed countries world-wide have rejected such mandatory SIM card registration policies (for example the Czech Republic, Romania and the United Kingdom). Part of the reasons highlighted in literature is skepticism about the relation between reduction in crimes related to mobile phones and the mandatory SIM card registration policies. Another point concerns privacy issues, where there are perceptions that privacy of individuals will be compromised when SIM card registration policies are implemented (Gow & Parisi, 2008). Hence, it is necessary to look at benefits and challenges of mandatory SIM card.

Benefits of SIM Card Registration

African governments have adopted SIM card registration mainly for security to protect citizens, assist law enforcement agencies to address crimes and knowing customers for financial services. The benefits of mandatory SIM card registration are the ability to track lost or stolen mobile phones, law enforcement agencies may track crimes conducted using mobile phones for example cyber laundering, stalking, SMS phishing and spamming. MNOs may generate revenue from switching costs and the data collected may be used for marketing purposes (Jentzsch, 2012; Donovan & Martin, 2014). SIM card registration has been considered as an incentive towards mobile commerce (m-commerce). The registered mobile phone users can access m-commerce services such as mobile money transfer, mobile ATM, mobile ticketing, mobile banking, location-based services, mobile marketing and advertising (Abu Tair & Abu-Shanab, 2014). M-commerce services can also support delivery of other service providers such as retailers, banks and governments, which may improve the economic status of mobile phone users. In addition, MNOs may develop value-added services and products using the information on the profiles of the registered mobile phone users (Abu-Shanab, 2012; Moqbel, Yani-De-Soriano & Yousafzai, 2010).

Challenges of SIM Card Registration

While there are benefits of implementing a mandatory SIM card policy, there are also challenges in implementing such policies. A number of studies have highlighted the challenges including resistance from the MNOs, lack of identification for the customers, limited awareness of the process, time frames for the registration, location of where the registration takes place, the cost of conducting the registration exercise and trust in the authorities keeping the data and lack of standards and best practices for managing the data (Ahmed et al., 2017; Ajayi, 2015; Annan et al., 2017; Aririguzo et al., 2016; Lesitaokana, 2014; Makulilo, 2011; Mteru-Behitsa et al., 2010; Sumbwanyambe et al., 2013).

Hemeson (2012) noted issues of consumer privacy and protection in relation to SIM card registration. There are perceptions that the implementation of the policy would violate the rights of consumers where data could be passed on to third parties and used for other purposes. This may be attributed to lack of laws to support registration in most African countries and the fact that data protection laws were not yet in place (Hemeson, 2012; Makulilo, 2011).

Jentzsch (2012) elucidated that SIM card registration can reduce customer subscriptions for MNOs due to disconnections. Similarly, Donovan and Martin (2014) highlighted that there was resistance from the MNOs to conduct the SIM card registration due to potential loss of revenue because of disconnections when SIM card registration was completed. Further, the cost of the SIM card registration activities was high because the resources for the registration were mainly mobilised by the MNOs (Annan et al., 2017; Jentzsch, 2012).

Another challenge was the geographical location to conduct the SIM card registration of customers residing in rural and remote areas. The MNOs operate in urban centres and have to make special arrangements to register customers in remote areas which may require additional financial resources (Mteru-Behitsa et al., 2010). Sumbwanyambe and Nel (2013) highlighted that some citizens do not possess identification documents such as national ID, passport or driver's licences. This is the main challenge for the SIM card registration process and has been a persistent issue in a number of studies (for example Annan et al., 2017; Donovan et al., 2014; Hemeson, 2012; Jentzsch, 2012).

The challenges highlighted in literature can be categorised into technical, political, economic, social and legal challenges (See Table 1). Technical issues are conceptualised as the capacity of institutions and individuals in having resources, special knowledge and understanding of the operations to achieve the objectives of the SIM card registration. Some of the technical challenges are lack of standards in data management, limited resources to conduct the SIM card registration in remote areas, inability to verify the captured data of customers and lack of mechanisms to check data where customers have multiple SIM cards (Ahmed et al., 2017; Aririguzo et al., 2016; Donovan et al., 2014; Mteru-Behitsa et al., 2010; Terrant, 2009).

Economic challenges are conceptualised as the issues related to value in use of resources that may support production and consumption of services related to use of mobile technologies. The economic challenges may include the cost of the SIM card registration for both services providers conducting the registration and the customers participating in the registration process and the perceived value that can be obtained from the SIM card registration process (Ahmed et al., 2017; Annan et al., 2017; Hemeson, 2012).

Table 1. Summary of categories for SIM Card registration challenges

	Economic		Legal			Political		Social						Technical								
	Cost of registration	Value of registration	Laws	Policies	Regulations	Trust	Political victimization	Awareness	Engagement	Exclusion	Religious beliefs	Respect	Public support	Capacity	Data storage	Identification documents	Multiple cards	Location	Resources	Standards	Time	Verification of data
Ahmed et al., 2017	x	x	x			x	x							x		x		x	x		x	x
Ajayi, 2015			x	x	x																	
Annan et al., 2017	x															x						
Aririguzo et al., 2016			x					x							x					x		
Donovan et al., 2014	x		x			x		x		x	x					x	x	x	x			
Hemeson, 2012	x		x						x							x				x		
Jentzsch, 2012	x		x		x					x						x	x				x	
Lesitaokana, 2014						x				x			x									
Makulilo, 2011			x			x	x													x		
Mteru-Behitsa et al., 2010																x		x	x			
Sumbwanyambe et al., 2013	x		x			x		x		x						x		x			x	x
Terrant, 2009								x		x						x	x		x	x	x	

Political challenges are related to the use of power and status to impose their will on others. The political issues related to SIM card registration may include the use of the records of individuals to track those who are vocal against government leading to victimization and abuse of power for the institutions that can have access to the customer data once the SIM card registration is completed. Consequently, some stakeholders may not trust the agencies that are responsible for the SIM card registration (Ahmed et al., 2017; Ajayi, 2015).

Social challenges are related to issues about how the members of communities understood the purposes of SIM card registration and how it may affect the way their community is organized. Some of the social challenges include lack of awareness of the SIM card registration, limited engagement of some of the stakeholders of SIM card registration, lack of public support in the registration process and religious beliefs that SIM card registration is related to the apocryphal warning in the Bible (for the mark of the beast) (Aririguzo et al., 2016; Donovan et al., 2014; Hemeson, 2012; Lesitaokana, 2014).

Legal challenges are issues related to the absence of laws, regulations and policies that can support SIM card registration to promote fairness and social justice. The absence of data protection laws can affect the registration of customers where there were concerns over the disclosure and use of the collected data. Another issue is lack of policies to guide the SIM card registration in terms of allocation of resources and promoting best practices for data management once the SIM card registration commences (Ajayi, 2015; Aririguzo et al., 2016; Sumbwanyambe et al., 2013).

CONTEXT OF MALAWI

Malawi is located in the South East of Africa with a population of about 16.7 million people (NSO, 2016). The teledensity indicators for Malawi are very low despite the country having a national ICT policy to improve ICT access and support social economic development (See Table 2). The current ICT policy concentrates on infrastructure and creating an enabling environment for ICT investment among others (GoM, 2013). However, the policy does not address the issues of SIM card registration. The country has been attempting to conduct mandatory SIM card registration since 2012. In June 2014, the regulator announced the registration of SIM card, but the process was not successful due to lack of laws to support the process and absence of customer identification systems for the majority of the population. The SIM card registration process has not yet been fully conducted.

The telecommunication sector was liberalised in 2001 which led to split of the main telecommunications operator (Malawi Post and Telecommunications) into two: Malawi Postal Cooperation (MPC) and Malawi Telecommunications Limited (MTL). MPC focuses on postal services while MTL concentrates on telecommunication service for fixed landlines. Telecom Networks Limited (TNM) was formed to provide mobile services. Other mobile network operators have entered the telecommunication market in Malawi due to the liberalisation of the sector (Clarke, Gabreab & Mgombelo, 2003). These include Airtel and Access Limited. Table 3 summarises the telecommunication operators in Malawi.

The mobile services are available across the country. Almost all parts of the country have access to mobile phone reception (Mtingwi & van Belle, 2012). The MNOs have offices mainly in the urban areas and in some cases use agents for services such as selling of airtime, SIM cards and mobile money transfer services. This may mean that when developing strategies for SIM card registration, there is need to consider the consumers that may be located in remote areas. It should be noted that not all consumers will have access to the MNOs offices and branches.

The Communications Act 2016 is used as a legal framework for the Telecommunication sector. The Act addresses issues related to licensing, network interconnection, regulations and radio spectrum management, among others. In 2016, the Malawi Parliament enacted the Communications Act of 2016 which

Table 2. Summary of teledensity of Malawi

Index	Population	Fixed Line Teledensity	Mobile Phone Teledensity	Internet Teledensity	Fixed Broadband Teledensity
Value	16.7 million	0.06%	40.32%	9.61%	0.05%

(NSO, 2016; ITU, 2017)

Table 3. Telecommunications operators in Malawi

Operator	Type of Services	No. Subscribers
Access Ltd	Fixed landlines services	16 615
MTL	Fixed landlines services	29 063
Airtel	Mobile phone services	3 103 719
TNM	Mobile phone services	3 012 551

(NSO, 2016)

gives the mandate the Malawi Communications Regulatory Authority (MACRA) to enforce mandatory SIM card registration. The Act makes it the obligation of consumers and services providers to register SIM cards. In addition, the Parliament has enacted the Access to Information Act of 2016 and Electronic Transactions and Management Act of 2017 which can complement the Communication Act of 2016 to address some of the issues related to acceptable access and use of information gathered during the SIM card registration. However, there are still gaps in the existing legal frameworks to regulate issues related to use of ICT, including data protection and management, and privacy (Bande, 2011).

Malawi is a member of regional bodies such as the Southern Africa Development Community (SADC), Common Market for Southern and Eastern Africa (COMESA) and Communications Regulatory Association of Southern Africa (CRASA). These organisations influence the member states on the issues relating to ICTs. For example, in 2001 Malawi signed the SADC ICT declaration which promotes the commitment of member states to focus on ICT infrastructure development (Makoza & Chigona, 2012). COMESA promotes trade and investment, which includes the development of ICT infrastructures such as fibre connectivity projects and IT systems linking financial institutions in the COMESA region. CRASA promotes harmonisation of regulations in Southern Africa and concentrates on ICTs, postal and telecommunications. However, COMESA and CRASA do not have a formal binding agreement for all member states to implement mandatory SIM card registration (Sumbwanyambe & Nel, 2013).

RESEARCH METHODOLOGY

The study used a qualitative research approach to analyse SIM card registration policy transfer in the context of Malawi (Myers, 2009). The study was exploratory, where the purpose was to find out what was happening and clarify the problems related to policy transfer for mandatory SIM card registration (Saunders, Lewis & Thornhill, 2009). Secondary data comprising policy and legal documents were used in the study. Reports from regional organisations and media reports were also used to enrich the data and compare the facts presented in the data. The documents were obtained from Government departments and regulatory organisations. Other documents were obtained from the websites of the regional collaboration organisations. Table 4 summarises the documents used in the study.

The study employed context analysis to analyse the data (Zhang & Wildemuth, 2009). The content analysis technique was considered ideal because it supported deductive approach. The policy transfer concepts were used to guide the data analysis (Marsh & Sharman, 2009). The analysis followed the eight iterative steps, data preparation where documents were prepared in electronic format and were read several times; the unit of analysis was identified which was the SIM card registration policy. The coding units used in the study were themes in the documents; categories and a coding structure were developed from the constructs of policy transfer theory (Marsh & Sharman, 2009); the coding scheme was tested through an iterative process for assigning the sample data to codes and checking consistency of the codes. The categories were redefined where necessary until consistency was achieved; the data was coded where text was assigned to the codes and categories. This was repeated to check for new themes or concepts, if any, and to add them to the coding manual; the codes were assessed for consistency where text was re-read within the categories and ensure that there was consistency in the codes. Conclusions from the coded data were noted and the report was prepared to present the key findings answering the research question (Zhang & Wildemuth, 2009).

Table 4. Summary of documents analysed in the study

ID	Document Title	Type	Source
DC1	Access to Information Act 2016	Legislation	Government of Malawi
DC2	CRASA Roaming Project Report 2012	Report	CRASA
DC3	CRASA Harmonisation for typical standards and approval 2006	Report	CRASA
DC4	Media reports on SIM card registration	News articles	Daily times
DC5	Media reports on proposal for SIM card registration	News articles	The Nation
DC6	Anti-Money Laundering Act 2006	Legislation	Government of Malawi
DC7	Customer due diligence for banks and financial institutions (2005)	Policy document	Reserve Bank of Malawi
DC8	Communications Act 2016	Legislation	Government of Malawi
DC9	Electronic Transactions & Management Act 2017	Legislation	Government of Malawi

SUMMARY OF RESULTS

This section presents the results of data analysis. The first part focuses on lesson drawing on the mandatory SIM card registration. This is followed by the summary of results on voluntary policy transfer and coercive policy transfer.

Lesson Drawing on SIM Card Registration

From the analysis of media reports, it was clear that Malawi was drawing lessons from other countries which had implemented the mandatory SIM card registration policies. There was recognition that SIM card registration was being implemented in other countries:

Most countries in the Southern African Development Community (SADC) already have their SIM cards registered including Zambia, Tanzania and South Africa among others. (DC4)

Those who have travelled either to the Western World; the United Kingdom, United States of America, so on and so forth or in Africa; South Africa, Ethiopia, Botswana and in the larger SADC community, know that all these countries register SIM cards. Therefore, our registration of SIM cards is within our own legal requirement but most importantly, we are keeping up with the global trends in the communications sector. (DC5)

This may mean the officials from government and other ICT sector organisations were aware of the SIM card registration in other countries. Key area noted in lesson drawing was the attempt to commence the SIM card registration process in Malawi. However, there was no clarity of specific areas of the lessons learnt on the SIM registration from other countries to indicate perfectrationality (making the decision for actions that are logical, consistent and systematic using resources such as information) and bounded-rationality (making decisions for action under constraints such as information and time).

Thus, lesson drawing was mainly on ideas for SIM card registration in general rather than the specific use of information to support the plans, strategies and activities for the implementation of the SIM card registration.

One of the areas of lesson drawing is that countries may learn from another context when they experience social challenges with severe consequences and challenges in a particular area of the policy. In the case of Malawi, key social challenges for not having a SIM card registration was security threats:

Our Internet or ICT systems are porous and this puts the country at a higher risk of being attacked by cybercriminals. Another problem is that SIM cards are cheap and easily accessible even to people with evil intentions. (DC5)

… the mandatory registration of SIM cards and generic numbers will help prevent crime and fraudulent cases encountered in the absence of the provision. (DC5)

Apart from the security challenges, another problem was related to economic value from the use of the SIM cards. There were reports of misuse of the SIM cards which the MNOs imported from overseas and had implication on the use of foreign currency reserves for the country:

There has been an abuse of SIM cards since people have been taking advantage of buying from the streets. People buy SIM cards and destroy them as they wish since they know they will buy another one. (DC4)

A particular challenge related to policy was lack of legal frameworks to support the SIM card registration in terms of statutory mandate for the regulator and the stakeholders engaged in the process, for example MNOs and financial institutions: "People don't register when buying SIM cards because at the moment, there is no law or regulation that requires registration of the prepaid SIM cards in Malawi" (DC4). In addition, identification of customers was a key challenge where most people did not have any formal identification document: "Registration requires identification and Malawi currently does not have a national identification system … would, therefore, prefer to do the registration of SIM cards when the national identity system is in place" (DC4). This meant that the SIM card registration could only be done for those customers who had some form of identification such passport and drivers licence. However, it was noted that alternative identification systems such as a letter from the employer and village headmen could be used in the process for mandatory SIM card registration.

Despite the challenges of inadequate legal frameworks and lack of identification document to identify customers during the registration process, there was no indication that the challenges led the policymakers to learn from elsewhere. There were attempts to implement SIM card registration in 2014 without legal frameworks and identification of customers. However, the process was discontinued in 2015 to take advantage of the National Identity registration process:

It is a long process to embark on the project since we needed to plan and go through the necessary legal documentation process. We slowed down a bit waiting for the National Registration Exercise since everyone, even the people in rural areas will have a national ID unlike Driver's license or passport. (DC1)

Although absence of identification documents was one of the key challenges for the SIM card registration, this was an opportunity for the government to draw lessons from another context on how the issues of identification were addressed. However, the local stakeholders, including MNOs, were cooperating with the government and the regulator to address some of the challenges: "The project will be implemented in a phased approach involving all the licensed mobile operators in the country". (DC5). There was limited evidence to suggest that the process involved the exchange of information from other countries or contexts to support lesson drawing on SIM card registration process.

Voluntary Policy Transfer on SIM Card Registration

Malawi was facing challenges as a result of not having SIM card registration, such as misuse of SIM cards and security threats (See Table 5). However, there was no substantive evidence that the country was under crisis as a result of the absence of mandatory SIM card registration. The challenges did not compel the government to immediately implement the mandatory SIM card registration policy. The situation may partly explain why the country was among the few countries in Africa that did not have the mandatory SIM card registration policy. This meant that issues related to misuse of SIM cards and security threats were being addressed using the existing legal frameworks. However, the existing legal frameworks were outdated and could not address the complex issues that had emerged as a result of the use of mobile phones in criminal activities.

While there were no immediate crises to address issues that mandatory SIM card could address, the institutional practices in the country also contributed to the delays in developing legal and regulations for the policy. For example, the reforms for the Communications Act of 1998 and the enacting of the Electronic Transaction Management bill of 2012 took long following the legal procedures in Parliament and Government:

SIM card registration will also have to wait for the review of the Communications Act which she said is expected to be done this year. (DC5)

Table 5. Examples of challenges for SIM card registration

Theme	Description	Examples of Statements
Legal framework	Absence of laws to support the mandatory SIM card registration	"There is need for legal framework to regulate the process" (DC4) "Government is also reviewing the Electronic Transactions and Management Bill which will outline legal obligations to be placed on any person processing personal information" (DC5)
Effects on sector growth	The process of SIM card registration affecting the operations of the sector	"SIM card registration and new regulations introduced could have a negative impact on growth of the sector" (DC4)
Identification	Lack of identification documents for most of the mobile phone users	"Delay in implementing the project could come from lack of formal national identities for Malawi which is also compounded by the lack of post coding and physical address" (DC5)
Awareness	Lack of awareness for the user on the need and advantages of the SIM card registration	"I don't understand why we have to register our SIM cards" (DC4) "MPs expressed concern that there is need for further sensitisation and consideration on the period on how people will manage to register" (DC5)
Political issues	Fear for those who are vocal against government and government agencies violating privacy of individuals	"Some of the concerns from the public have been on suspicion that the on-going SIM card registration is a ploy by government to listen into people's private telephone conversations, check SMS and monitor internet activity in real time ..." (DC4)

Consultations on the regulations are still on-going with all key stakeholders, it is expected that the process will be finalized during the first half of 2016 to allow effective registration of the SIM cards in use by all subscribers. (DC5)

Parliament passed the Communications Act in 2016 and the Electronic Transactions Management Act in 2017 which supported the mandate of the telecommunications regulator to enforce the mandatory SIM card registration. There was no evidence to indicate external pressure to enact the legislations but that perceptions on addressing the perceived security threats and voluntarily follow the global trend: "SIM card registration which has been described as a global phenomenon is believed to reduce the misuse of mobile phone service which leads to increased acts of crime through unregistered usage." (DC5).

Coercive Policy Transfer on SIM Card Registration

Malawi adopted policies related to AML/CFT in response to the need to meet international standards. The Financial Action Task Force (FATF) proposed the standards for AML/CFT. In 1999, Malawi joined the Eastern and Southern Africa Anti-Money Laundering Group (ESAAMLG). The main role of ES-AAMLG is to support member countries in the implementation of legal frameworks, regulatory and procedures for combating AML/CFT. The country is also a member of the Southern Africa Development Community (SADC). The country, as a member state, strives to meet the SADC Protocol against corruption. Consequently, the Anti-Money Laundering Act was enacted in 2006. The Central Bank of Malawi, as a financial regulator, has also promoted regulations related AML/CFT policies. The policies have been adopted through coercive means as the country was striving to meet the standards set by the global and regional financial organisations:

To ensure that the financial sector (and the nation) complies with international conventions and initiatives by international bodies (for example the United Nations, Basle Committee on Banking Supervision and the Financial Action Task Force) in the prevention of the criminal use of the financial system. (DC6)

Despite implementing policies that address challenges AML/CFT, policies specific to mobile technologies are partly adopted. For example, policies related to mobile phone services have been implemented in commercial banks which are offering mobile banking services:

Some might recall a similar know-your-customer exercise by commercial banks in which they submitted similar information to what MACRA is demanding. (DC4)

Commercial banks have KYC policy which extends to mobile banking services. This means that customers for mobile banking are required to register their SIM cards. Similarly, MNOs (Airtel and MTN) were also offering mobile payment services where customers were required to register their SIM cards. This was part of the requirements of regulations for mobile payments set by the central bank noted in the following policy declaration:

Registration of users shall be subject to Data Protection (Privacy) policy; Enrolment of consumers should satisfy Know Your Customer (KYC) requirements as laid out in the Money Laundering, Proceeds of Serious Crime and Terrorist Financing Act (2006) and regulations thereto. (DC7)

We actively started registering most of our customers with the advent of our mobile financial service, Airtel Money, as far back as 2012 based on the central bank's prerequisite for customers to be registered to access and utilise the service. (DC5)

Compliance with standards such as AML/CFT was the major drive for coercive policy transfer related to SIM card registration which many countries have implemented in other countries in Africa. Malawi adopted the SIM card policy indirectly to comply with AML/CFT partly to meet the international standards and conventions for the financial sector and avoid exclusion. Therefore, there were no immediate crises that SIM card registration policies would address.

DISCUSSION OF RESULTS

The study set out to explore how a low-income status country in Africa without SIM card registration policy from learning from other countries. Using the case of Malawi, the findings from the study demonstrated that the need to address security issues and use of mobile phones in committing crimes led to the motivation to implement the mandatory SIM card registration policy. Further, the country attempted to have the exact number of active SIM card holders: "the exercise is likely to enable the government to monitor and verify the actual teledensity figures and active lines to ensure that tax revenues from mobile service providers correlate with the data they present" (DC4). In addition, compliance with international standards and conventions to combat fraud and criminal activities indirectly influence the need for mandatory SIM card registration. The SIM card registration policy was mainly being transferred through coercive and voluntary means (Marsh & Sharma, 2009). The country adopted the SIM card registration voluntarily to address their specific needs for combating crimes related to mobile technologies. The officials in the government departments perceived the need to comply with standards such as the AML/CFT propagated by the international organisations to avoid being sidelined. Hence, mandatory SIM card registration policy was perceived to be a global trend which many countries had implemented.

The findings from this study indicated some of the reasons why the mandatory SIM card registration policy has not been fully implemented in Malawi. Lack of legal frameworks and lack of identification documentation were the main constraints for transfer of SIM card registration policy. The results to some extent were consistent with the findings in other studies (Ahmed et al., 2017; Donovan & Martin, 2012; Lesitaokana, 2014). There were more issues highlighted in literature related to technical, economic, social, legal and political issues (Hemeson, 2012; Jentzsch, 2012; Sumbwanyambe & Nel, 2013). These presented opportunities for areas from which the officials engaged in the mandatory SIM card registration policy could learn.

A contribution of the study is the insights on the way the lessons could be drawn from other countries that have implemented SIM card policies. For instance, the lesson drawing in Malawi on SIM card registration was limited to experiences of the Government officials without proper formal transfer of information from other contexts. This presented an opportunity, but with limitations. It would be ideal for the Government officials to formally visit the countries that had implemented the policy and learn in detail how SIM cards registration was conducted in the countries and appreciate the challenges and how they were addressed. In addition, there was the need to consider the challenges for SIM card registration beyond identification documents and legal frameworks. Consideration of social issues related to awareness of the registration policy, political issues related to rights to privacy, economic issues related to cost of the registration process and technical issues such as data management after the registration process is completed (Ahmed et al., 2017; Lesitaokana, 2014; Sumbwanyambe et al., 2013). It was necessary for the country to consider these issues if it was to successfully implement the mandatory SIM card registration policy. Another interesting insight was the collaboration of local stakeholders in supporting the SIM card registration where there was limited lesson drawing from another context. This may imply that when there is no formal lesson from another context, policy stakeholders may use their own wisdom to address their challenges through collaborations.

While the results from the study highlighted coercive and voluntary transfer of policy, it is also important to acknowledge the challenges of policy learning in SIM card registration policies. Policymakers may face limitations in access to vital information for decision making, time constraints in making policy decisions, insufficient knowledge of the implications of policy and balancing the needs of policy stakeholders and beneficiaries (Benson & Jordan, 2011; Ettelt, Mays & Nolte, 2012). The study makes the following recommendations, especially to the few countries in Africa which are yet to implement SIM card registration policies:

- **Issues of identification of consumers:** Absence of identification documents may affect the registration process. Identification systems should be in place to support the SIM card registration process;
- **Awareness of the SIM card registration to the stakeholders:** Policymakers and policy implementation agencies should promote awareness of the SIM card registration policy to stakeholders who may be affected by the SIM card registration policy;
- **The cost of the registration process:** The cost of SIM registration process should be established and the resources made available to the policy implementation agencies. Regulators and MNOs should consider contingency plans to ensure that consumers are not affected during the SIM card registration process;
- **Legal and regulatory frameworks:** Enactment of laws and regulations is necessary before implementing SIM card registration policy to promote the rights of consumers such as privacy and address issues of surveillance;
- **Data management:** Developing data management strategies for accessing, updating, storage and security of the customer's data once the SIM card registration processes commences; and
- **Location of the customers:** Government agencies and MNOs should develop a plan for conducting SIM card registration of users located in rural and remote areas where the majority of the population live.

A limitation of this study is the inability to gather views from the stakeholders for the SIM card registration from the policy custodians. As an exploratory study, different sources of secondary data were used to confirm and relate the results of data analysis (Bowen, 2009). The focus was on highlighting how the SIM card registration policy can be transferred and learning on policy from another context. Further, the study attempted to develop an understanding of the challenges for policy transfer for countries without SIM card registration policies. Future research may systematically investigate policy transfer and gather primary data from the stakeholders promoting the policy as well as those adopting the policy.

CONCLUSION

The purpose of this study was to analyse how SIM card registration is transferred in the countries without the mandatory SIM card policy. Using the case of Malawi as an example of an African country that is yet to fully implement a mandatory SIM card policy, the study showed that such a policy can be transferred through (a) lesson drawing policy transfer, (b) voluntary policy transfer, (c) coercive policy transfer. The main reason for the country to adopt the SIM card registration was to address problems of security and meeting part of the international standards for international organisations. The study showed that lack of legal frameworks and identification documentation delayed the transfer and implementation of the SIM card policy. The study contributes towards the understanding of technology policy transfer in the context of African countries.

DISCUSSION QUESTIONS

1. Discuss how technology policies such as mandatory SIM card registration policies can be transferred within African counties.
2. Many African countries do not have Data protection laws to protect collected data during SIM card registration. What are the key challenges of absence of Data protection laws and how can these challenges be addressed?
3. How can advanced countries support developing countries in Africa in policy transfer of mandatory SIM card registration policies?
4. What are the key areas that developing countries can learn from advanced countries on mandatory SIM card registration policies?
5. Some developed countries in Europe have rejected implementation of mandatory SIM card registration on the basis of violation of the individual's rights to privacy. What can African countries learn from these countries related to the mandatory SIM card registration policies?

REFERENCES

Abu-Shanab, E., & Ghaleb, O. (2012). Adoption of Mobile Commerce Technology: An Involvement of Trust and Risk Concerns. *International Journal of Technology Diffusion*, *3*(2), 36–49. doi:10.4018/jtd.2012040104

Abu Tair, H. Y., & Abu-Shanab, E. A. (2014). Mobile Government Services: Challenges and Opportunities. *International Journal of Technology Diffusion*, *5*(1), 17–25. doi:10.4018/ijtd.2014010102

Ahmed, S. I., Haque, M. R., Guha, S., Rifat, M. R., & Dell, N. (2017). Privacy, security, and surveillance in the Global South: A study of biometric mobile SIM registration in Bangladesh. In *ACM Proceedings of the 2017 CHI Conference on Human Factors in Computing Systems* (pp. 906-918). ACM.

Ajayi, B. (2015). Telecommunications Law and Policy to Protect Subscribers' of Mobile Phones in Africa. *Journal Open Access Library*, *3*, 121–148.

Annan, F., & Sanoh, A. (2017). *Mobile infrastructure and rural business enterprises: Evidence from SIM registration mandate in Niger*. Research Policy Working Paper 8778. Poverty and Equity Global Practice Group, World Bank Group.

Aririguzo, M., & Agbaraji, E. (2016). Mobile phone registration for developing countries: Gains and constraints. *European Journal of Basic and Applied Science*, *3*(3), 44–52.

Bande, L. (2011). A case for cybercrime legislation in Malawi. *Malawi Law Journal*, *5*(2), 93–113.

Benson, D., & Jordan, A. (2011). What have we learned from policy transfer research? Dolowitz and Marsh revisited. *Political Studies Review*, *9*(3), 366–378. doi:10.1111/j.1478-9302.2011.00240.x

Bowen, G. (2009). Document Analysis as a Qualitative research method. *Qualitative Research Journal*, *9*(2), 28–40. doi:10.3316/QRJ0902027

Braun, D., & Gilardi, F. (2006). Taking 'Galton's problem' seriously: Towards a theory of policy diffusion. *Journal of Theoretical Politics*, *18*(3), 298–322. doi:10.1177/0951629806064351

Chatain, P., Zerzan, A., Noor, W., Dannaoui, N., & de Koker, L. (2011). *Protecting mobile money against financial crimes: Global policy challenges and solutions*. Washington, DC: The World Bank. doi:10.1596/978-0-8213-8669-9

Clarke, G., Gebreab, F., & Mgombelo, H. (2003). *Telecommunications reforms in Malawi*. Policy Research Working Paper 3036, The World Bank, Washington, DC.

Dolowitz, D., & Marsh, D. (2000). Learning from abroad: The role of policy transfer in contemporary policy-making. *Governance: An International Journal of Policy, Administration and Institutions*, *13*(1), 5–24. doi:10.1111/0952-1895.00121

Donovan, K., & Martin, A. (2012). *The Rise of African SIM Registration: Mobility, Identity, Surveillance & Resistance*. Information Systems and Innovation Group Working Paper no. 186, London School of Economics and Political Science, London, UK.

Donovan, K., & Martin, A. (2014). The rise of African SIM card Registration: The emerging dynamics of regulatory change. *First Monday*, *19*(2), 1–12. doi:10.5210/fm.v19i2.4351

Ettelt, S., Mays, N., & Nolte, E. (2012). Policy learning from abroad: Why it is more difficult than it seems. *Policy and Politics*, *40*(4), 491–504. doi:10.1332/030557312X643786

Evans, M. (2009). Policy transfer in critical perspective. *Policy Studies*, *30*(3), 243–268. doi:10.1080/01442870902863828

Ghazinoory, S., Divsalar, A., & Soofi, A. S. (2009). A new definition and framework for the development of a national technology strategy: The case of nanotechnology for Iran. *Technological Forecasting and Social Change*, *76*(6), 835–848. doi:10.1016/j.techfore.2008.10.004

GoM. (2013). *National Information and Communication Technology Policy*. Ministry of Information and Civic Education. Government of Malawi.

Gow, G., & Parisi, J. (2008). Pursuing the anonymous user: Privacy rights and mandatory registration of prepaid mobile phones. *Bulletin of Science, Technology & Society, 28*(1), 60–68. doi:10.1177/0270467607311487

Hemeson, C. (2012). *Directive on Consumer data for SIM card registration in the telecommunication sector: An African perspective.* Available at SSRN 1982033.

ITU. (2017). *International Telecommunications Union (ITU) Statistics.* Access on 15 February, 2018 from: http://www.itu.int/en/ITU-D/Statistics/Pages/stat/default.aspx

Jentzsch, N. (2012). Implications of mandatory registration for mobile users in Africa. *Telecommunications Policy, 36*(8), 608–620. doi:10.1016/j.telpol.2012.04.002

Johnson, J. (2008). Is the global financial system AML/CFT prepared? *Journal of Financial Crime, 15*(1), 7–21. doi:10.1108/13590790810841662

Knill, C. (2005). Introduction: cross-national policy convergence: concepts, approaches and explanatory factors. *Journal of European Public Policy, 12*(3), 764–774. doi:10.1080/13501760500161332

Lesitaokana, W. (2014). Key issues in the development of mobile telephony in Botswana (1998-2011): An empirical investigation. *New Media & Society, 16*(5), 840–855. doi:10.1177/1461444813495161

Makulilo, A. (2011). Registration of SIM cards in Tanzania: A critical evaluation of the Electronic and Postal Communication Act 2010. *Computer and Telecommunication Law Review, 17*(2), 48–54.

Marsh, D., & Sharman, J. (2009). Policy diffusion and policy transfer. *Policy Studies, 30*(3), 269–288. doi:10.1080/01442870902863851

Moqbel, A., Yani-De-Soriano, M., & Yousafzai, S. (2010). Mobile Commerce Use among UK Mobile Users: An Experimental Approach Based on a Proposed Mobile Network Utilization Framework. *International Journal of Technology Diffusion, 1*(2), 1–35. doi:10.4018/jtd.2010040101

Mteru-Behitsa, M., & Diyamett, B. (2010). Tanzania ICT sector Performance review 2009/2010. In Towards evidence-based ICT policy and Regulation (vol. 2). ICT Research Africa, Cape Town, South Africa.

Mtingwi, J., & van Belle, J. (2012). The state of e-government and m-government readiness in Malawi. *International Journal of Information Technology & Computer Science, 6,* 58–68.

Myers, M. (2009). *Qualitative research in business and management.* London: Sage.

NSO. (2016). *Statistical Yearbook. National Statistics Office.* Accessed on 15 February 2018 from: http://www.nsomalawi.mw/images/stories/data_on_line/general/yearbook/2016%20Statistical%20Yearbook.pdf

Ojo, A., Janowski, T., & Awotwi, J. (2013). Enabling development through governance and mobile technology. *Government Information Quarterly, 30,* S32–S45. doi:10.1016/j.giq.2012.10.004

Saunders, M., Lewis, P., & Thornhill, A. (2009). *Research methods for business students.* London: Prentice Hall.

Shaik, A., & Karjaluoto, H. (2015). Mobile banking adoption: A literature review. *Telematics and Informatics*, *32*(1), 129–142. doi:10.1016/j.tele.2014.05.003

Sumbwanyambe, M., & Nel, A. (2013). Assessing the implications of SIM card registration policy in the SADC region. IEEE IST-Africa Conference and Exhibition (IST-Africa), 1-9.

Terrant, H. (2009). *Why Rica will fail*. Moneyweb's Personal Finance.

Zhang, Y., & Wildemuth, B. M. (2009). Qualitative analysis of content. In B. Wildemuth (Ed.), Applications of social research methods to questions in information and library science (pp. 308–319). Academic Press.

KEY TERMS AND DEFINITIONS

Data Protection: The process involving use of laws to protect data of individuals from unauthorized disclosure or access.

Know Your Customer (KYC): The process of identifying and confirming the identity of a user of financial services to ensure that all financial transactions can be traced and combat the financing of criminal activities.

Mobile Commerce: The process of buying or selling goods and services over the internet but using a mobile device such as mobile phone or tablet.

Mobile Phones: A portable electronic device that is used to for communication, including talking, texting, and used to access applications from any location.

Policy: Government activities that are aimed at addressing social challenges and are executed through programs, processes, and politics.

Policy Transfer: The process through which government learns on programs, processes, and politics from other context to address its priority areas for meeting the needs of the public or citizens. Policy transfer involves ideas, institutions, laws, and policy stakeholders and beneficiaries.

SIM Card: A subscriber identification module is an electronic chip that contains information that is used to provide connection to a mobile phone operator to access different services for telecommunications including voice, data, and payment services.

SIM Card Registration: The process of recording the details of a SIM card holder using identification documents to such as proof of physical address, national identity documents, passport and driver's license and storage of the data on a database.

SMS: Simple message systems is a method of sending text using a mobile device such as mobile phone.

SMS Spamming: A process of sending unsolicited messages for advertising to mobile phone users without their consent or knowledge which develops unnecessary traffic on mobile phone networks.

Chapter 19
Framework and Guidelines to Industry Web Portal Business

Duanning Zhou
Eastern Washington University, USA

Arsen Djatej
Eastern Washington University, USA

Robert Sarikas
Eastern Washington University, USA

David Senteney
California State University – San Bernardino, USA & Ohio University, USA

ABSTRACT

This chapter discusses a growth framework for industry web portals which present a new opportunity in the internet business. The framework contains five stages: business plan stage, website development stage, attraction stage, entrenchment stage, and defense stage. The actions to be taken and strategies to be applied in each stage are set out. Two industry web portals are investigated in detail. The two examples illustrate the applicability of the proposed growth framework to the real world. The combination of a conceptual growth framework and the application of this conceptual framework to two real-world examples yields a set of guidelines based in large part on lessons learned from the two examples. Thus, this chapter provides a concept-based growth framework and a set of real-world-based guidelines that will very possibly provide a practical benefit to industry web portal business practitioners.

INTRODUCTION

Up to 2018, Internet World Stats (Internet World Stats, 2018) stated that more than 4.15 billion people (54.4% of the total world population) pursue various activities through the internet. More than 320 million people (88.1% of the total population) in North America access the internet for email activity, for information and to purchase products online. Web Portals became an essential part in all internet-based activities. At early stages, web portals identity referred "to the category of firms that have evolved from

DOI: 10.4018/978-1-5225-6367-9.ch019

early roots as World Wide Web search engines, but may now include features such as calendar management, chat, free e-mail, games, and shopping, among others" (Gallaugher & Downing, 2000). According to Rao, web portals started as digital doorways, however eventually they became destinations or permanent parking spaces for users (Rao, 2001). In Internet, there is no limitation of physical places and spaces, and accessing time. These characteristics make the general Internet business to have "winner-takes-all" effect. It is extremely challenging for new entrants to penetrate the general web portals segment.

On the other hand, taking into consideration the evidence of the emergence of professional virtual communities (Arinze, 2012; Chen & Hung, 2010; Franchi et al., 2013; Yu et al. 2009), professionals in different industries or specialized areas seem willing to utilize virtual platforms for information exchange and social support. For example, it is reported that up to October 2017, an online academic community (Chen et al., 2016; Xu et al., 2012), *ResearchGate*, had over 14 million registered researchers. Online academic communities enable researchers to construct profiles which contain researchers' information, like their name, photos, educational background, research interests and publications. Via engaging in online academic communities, researchers can obtain the benefits of maintaining contacts with old scholar-friends and finding new scholar-friends they might be interested. In addition, researchers could showcase to other researchers with their research progress and disseminating research results including papers, presentations, patents, and projects, which may ultimately raise their academic influence. Via online academic communities, researchers can be aware of the works being conducted by other researchers in their professional area, which can help them to discover new information and develop research ideas. The online academic communities can foster social awareness of researchers and facilitating academic collaboration among researchers (Xu et al., 2012).

Thus, industry or specialized web portals present an excellent opportunity. We will use the term industry web portals to refer to industry web portals, specialized web portals, and professional-specific web portals (Zhou et al., 2014). The major differences between general web portals and industry web portals involve the content and the users. An industry web portal's content is about the specific industry, which may include news, knowledge, recruitment information, various virtual sub-communities, and domain-specific features. For example, with the big number of users registered on an online academic portal, the information overload problem presents a great challenge for researchers to find relevant and reliable scholar friends there; in order to reduce the information overload, a very useful domain-specific feature for an online academic portal is scholar-friends recommendation, which sending more targeted recommendation information to users. The visitors of an industry web portal are individuals working in the industry, people working in a related industries, and others seeking job opportunities in respective business segments. Visitors come to an industry web portal for diverse purposes which may include individuals looking for news and jobs, learning new knowledge, seeking friendship, support, playfulness, self-esteem enhancement, and satisfaction, sharing knowledge, experiences, opinions, and ideas, and looking for co-creation of new knowledge, new products, and new services.

How does an industry web portal grow and evolve? What approaches and strategies should an industry web portal use to succeed? Little research addresses these issues which are quite important to practitioners. This paper aims to benefit web business practitioners by narrowing this gap through the development of a web portal growth framework and set of practical guidelines that result from the thoughtful application of the growth framework to two real world cases.

LITERATURE REVIEW

Damsgaad (2002) presents a portal life cycle model for web portal management. The life cycle model contains four phases: attraction phase, contagion phase, entrenchment phase, and defense phase, in which practitioners at each phase face the necessity to overcome certain challenges to advance to the next phase. The attraction phase of a web portal begins from the launching of the web portal with some unique/ innovative features that existing web portals do not provide. The primary objectives of practitioners in the attraction stage of the process involve on attracting visitors and keeping them coming back to the portal, with eventually visitors becoming recurring users. Practitioners in the contagion phase seek to "infect" the recurring users so that they can help spread the portal. Practitioners find themselves in the entrenchment phase comes when the number of users of the portal reaches a "critical mass". The web portal at this phase can then "tax" users by providing upgraded/enhanced services and accepting advertisements. Once the portal is well established, practitioners then must defend the successful position they have achieved by carefully monitoring the challenges from new entrants. The primary goal of these practitioners in each of these four phases is to "lock-in" users, so that they do not switch to competitors (Damsgaad, 2002).

A relevant research area relating to industry web portals is virtual (online) communities which have been widely discussed in the information systems discipline (Johnson et al., 2010). The bulk of research concerning virtual communities focuses on the determinants of participation and knowledge sharing (Casalo et al., 2010; Chiu et al., 2015; Sun et al., 2010; Tilly et al., 2017; Wasko & Faraj, 2005; Zhang et al., 2010), such as playfulness, self-esteem enhancement, emotional ties, attachment, engagement, and satisfaction. Other researchers have studied virtual communities from the viewpoint of the success factors and management (Bock et al., 2015; Chiu et al., 2015; Iriberri & Leroy, 2009; Leimeister et al., 2006; Rosenkranz & Feddersen, 2008). The common success factors identified include: high stability of the website, offering up-to-date contents, offering high-quality contents, offering customized contents, encouraging and fostering interaction between users, building trust among users, limiting the size of a clique, handling user data sensitively, achieving a short website reaction time, and achieving a user-directed evolution of the website (Koh et al., 2007; Liu et al., 2009; Leimeister et al., 2006; Rosenkranz & Feddersen, 2008). Based on the socio-technical theory, Lin et al. (2009, 2013) present a comprehensive model which posits that system quality, information quality, community governance, and pro-sharing norms collectively influence user satisfaction, sense of belonging, and usage. Navigation, reliability, download delay, screen design, ease of search, and ease of communication are the factors of system quality. The information quality includes accuracy, completeness, currency, scope, and understandability. Community governance includes rules, policies, and moderation.

THE GROWTH FRAMEWORK OF INDUSTRY WEB PORTALS

Based on the portal management model (Damsgaad, 2002), and the success factors and the current research of virtual communities from literature, and the in-depth interview with the owners/managers of two industry web portals (www.3c3t.com, www.wushuw.com), we propose a growth framework for industry web portals. The proposed framework contains five stages: business plan stage, website development stage, attraction stage, entrenchment stage, and defense stage (see Figure 1). The actions and strategies to be taken and used in each stage will be discussed in detail.

Figure 1. Industry web portal growth framework

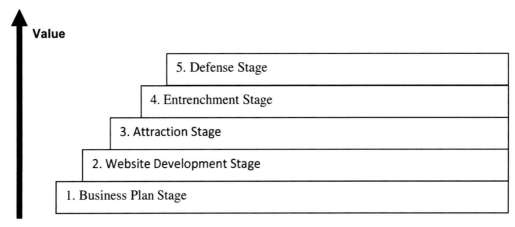

BUSINESS PLAN STAGE

Similar to starting a new economic entity elsewhere, the central tasks for an entity entering the industry web portal segment includes carefully assessing business context, analyzing customers, analyzing competitors and substitutes, and assessing the business network (Applegate et al., 2009; Leimeister & Krcmar, 2004; Porter, 1996). Therefore, the idea of creating an industry web portal usually comes from people working in the industry. Based on the expertise and experience of using the existing web portals or virtual communities, these industry participants identify certain shortcomings of the existing web portals in their industry, and then act on the opportunity to launch an e-commerce business. Because of the importance of domain knowledge and industry experience, the owners and the management team typically all possess deep industry experience, and it is the creative exploitation of this deep industry experience that powers the new web portal to success. A solid and complete business plan would include devising the ways and means to meet capital requirements, personnel requirements, market analysis needs, etc.

WEBSITE DEVELOPMENT STAGE

To start a new industry web portal, one important act is to analyze the successful web portals in other industries. The successful features and services available in the industry web portals of other industries display many features and they should be adopted and modified by other new industry portals. With regard to how to technically construct the website, as a result of the rapid development of the Internet technology, many mature software modules for constructing web sites are available for free (like open source products) or at low-cost. Customizing these software modules to construct the web portal not only greatly decreases the development time but also reduces costs. These software modules make it much easier for non-IT professionals to enter the industry web portal business.

Search engine optimization should be taken into consideration in the design of the web portal. Carefully designed keywords and internal structure can help the portal be listed in the front of the search results from search engines. It should be noted that no matter how good the analysis and the design are, a web portal's features and services need to be developed according to the web portal's real running situation.

System quality and information quality are the critical success factors of online communities (Lin et al., 2013; Tilly et al., 2017). System quality includes navigation, reliability, download delay, screen design, ease of search, and ease of communication. To maintain good system quality, the portal needs to carefully estimate the average page size, how many pages an average site visitor would visit during each visit, how many visitors will visit the site during the first month, how much the site traffic will grow each month during the first two years, and how many visitors would come at the same time (peak traffic). An appropriate server or servers can be purchased with server operating system, web server software, and database systems.

Usually an industry web portal has no resources with which to self-host the web server. Cloud-computing is a new trend for IT infrastructure. Hosting the server by a service provider, usually in a cloud, is a common practice. Choosing reliable service providers and managing strong vendor relationships are important (Applegate et al., 2009). If the portal owner/manager has no knowledge about server hardware and does not want to put large up-front investments, a dedicated hosting is also an option. In dedicated hosting, servers are owned and operated by the hosting provider. Functionality, reliability, scalability, security, backup and recovery, and cost are important considerations when choosing a service provider. An outsourcing deal (for example, website development, hosting) that is too one-sided and too favorable to one party usually ends up as a disappointment for all parties.

A portal should provide special features which fit the portal. For example, the scholar-friend recommendation feature for online academic communities. While online academic communities provide services to facilitate scientific collaboration in global context by transcending conventional organizational and geographical boundaries, the information overload problem occurring on these platforms presents a great challenge for researchers to find interesting and relevant information. The increasing number of registered researchers, together with the significant amount of relevant information in online academic communities, poses challenges for researchers to find scholar-friends they might be interested in. The information overload problem may subsequently lead to a degraded user experience which in turn could affect users' intention to continue their usage of online academic communities (Chen et al., 2016). Therefore, providing scholar-friends recommendation by an online academic portal is vital for the portal to succeed.

The portal should incorporate innovative multimedia tools and techniques to make the interaction between members more interesting and entertaining (Chiu et al., 2015). The portal should provide quality information which includes accuracy, completeness, currency, scope, and understandability (Tilly et al., 2017). Community governance is also a critical success factor of online communities (Lin et al., 2013). In sum, the main task of this stage is to have the website developed and have a good start regarding system quality, information quality, and community governance.

At this stage, it is important that potential clients and customers access and review the design and key features of the proposed layout as the primary appliance of presenting respective product, services, brand etc. Key customers can review and provide their feedback, specifically related to user friendliness, usage experience, process and procedures. For example, for the sports sector to gain collective benefits from web portals, customers and potential vendors must be more actively involved in the development of the portal. The Internet can provide improved efficiency and offer many new ways of doing business that can result in customer satisfaction and effective usage of Internet. But none of these benefits can be reached until sports fans directly participate in the portals' development effort (Hur et al., 2012).

Due to the increasing popularity of different mobile devices, the web portal needs to support mobile devices. Comparing to normal computers, mobile devices have a smaller screen, smaller disk storage, and slower speed. These characteristics of mobile devices need to be considered carefully when developing the web portal.

ATTRACTION STAGE

The launched web portal should have different features and services from other web portals to attract visitors. Also, because the web portal is new, promotion of the site is necessary. Advertising in an industry's magazines/newsletters is an effective way to reach professionals in the industry.

The main task of this stage is to attract visitors, and more importantly, keep visitors coming back and eventually becoming recurring visitors and members. Therefore, it is important to maintain good system quality, information quality, and community governance (Lin et al., 2013). In detail, keep the site running smoothly, and timely respond to the problems that occur (Leimeister et al., 2006). In addition, because there is not enough loyalty from visitors of the site, member-generated content alone is not enough to maintain the site's traffic. The website should provide high quality and up-to-date content to attract and retain users (Leimeister et al., 2006). Even within an industry, there are many special interest groups. The portal should create different virtual communities with different topics to meet the needs of visitors/members with different interests. These virtual communities can help attract and retain visitors/members (Bock et al., 2015; Armstrong & Hegal, 1996). Also, since the attachment and satisfaction are so important to the members, the portal should encourage their members to provide more interesting content and develop strategies to encourage interactions and the formation of relationships among members (Chiu et al., 2015).

The main objective for practitioners at this stage is to gain popularity and push the number of the visitors and members to reach a "critical mass" (Damsgaad, 2002). This "critical mass" is the indicator of the value of the portal, and different online communities have different measures for the "critical mass" of visitors and members (Raban et al., 2010). The strategy used at this stage aims at "infecting" the visitors and members to help spread the portal (Damsgaad, 2002). The way to "infect" the visitors and members is to give them a good experience with the portal so that they are willing to share this portal with their colleagues, classmates, and friends. As the portal accrues more visitors and members, protecting members' data becomes imperative. The portal should protect members' sensitive data to increase members' trust and loyalty to the portal. When the number of visitors/members of the portal has steadily increased, the portal can move to the next stage.

ENTRENCHMENT STAGE

When the number of visitors/members of the portal reaches the "critical mass", and the number is continuously increasing, it indicates that the portal has a certain amount of reputation and value. This is stage where it is desirable to "persuade" the visitors/members to use fee-based services provided by the portal (Damsgaad, 2002).

The visitors/members' willingness to use fee-based services is critical for the portal to entrench. Fee-based services not only generate the much-needed revenue, but also can better lock-in visitors/members who obviously, by now, value the portal. Fee-based services usually are upgraded/enhanced versions of the existing services. For example, fee-paying members can access more information and/or are given the priority to post promotional information.

At this stage, advertisements revenue will become an important part of revenue of the portal (Armstrong & Hagel, 1996). Because the visitors/members of the web portal are professionals in the industry, it is very valuable for targeted advertisements which can be charged in higher rates. At the same time, the portal should continuously maintain good system quality, information quality, including member-generated information quality (Tilly et al., 2017), and governance, which will positively affect members/ visitors satisfaction and then increase the "sense of belonging", and ultimately increase the members/ visitors' visit (Lin et al., 2013).

DEFENSE STAGE

When the portal has been well established, the next step is to maintain and secure the status of the portal. In essence, portals are constantly changing entities and require daily care and maintenance. Some of those essentials include live updates, changes and adjustments to the content and layout, new links etc. Furthemore, the visitors/members of the site are not static. Some visitors/members leave, and new visitors/members join. The factors that keep visitors/members coming back include the content, services, and communities of the portal, and the switching cost of the visitors/members. In this stage, the portal should always keep eyes on the new technology, new trends of web portals, and new features of web portals. The portal should be aware of the newly created competition portals and prevent the existing visitors/members from switching to the new competition portals (Damsgaad, 2002). If the portal finds new innovative features in the competitors, the portal should take timely actions to deal with this threat.

Another important point is that the revolutionary change of the portal may seriously affect the ability of the portal to run smoothly and the visitors and members' familiarity with the portal. Therefore, the portal should seek to have a continuously improving and evolving nature to avoid the need for revolutionary or emergency change (Damsgaad, 2002). When revising the portal, the portal should listen to visitors and members, allow visitors and members to participate, let visitors and members feel that the portal really serves and respects them, and let visitors and members feel that they also "own" the portal. In general, every portal is different and the primary features of a good portal include the following 1) intuitive, 2) easy to use, 3) reliable, 4) interfaced with other systems and 5) efficient (Roberts 2018).

REAL WORLD EXAMPLES

If examples of real life portals are investigated with the viewpoints developed in the growth framework presented previously, we believe that a set of guidelines for practitioners can emerge.

www.3c3t.com is an industry web portal for professionals of engineering supervision, testing, and inspection in China. The web portal not only provides a platform for professionals in the engineering supervision, testing, and inspection area to exchange and share information, but also provides professional services to the business and individuals in the engineering supervision and inspection area.

www.3c3t.com

www.3c3t.com was launched in January 2006. In December 2011, the number of the registered individual members was about 184,730, and the number of the institutional members was 437. The average daily traffic (page view) was more than 120,000. The web portal became the No. 1 website in the engineering supervision and inspection industry in China. The main features of the portal include news, recruitment, learning materials for downloading, technology forums, business directory, product supply and demand, exhibition, bidding information, and special business reports. The portal is still in the entrenchment stage.

Business Plan Stage (Before October 2005)

Before October 2005, there were some general industry web portals in China. However, these web portals were all-purpose oriented, and tried to include information from all industries. It is hard for professionals in a specific industry to have an "at home" feeling and experience when the visit those general industry web portals. Two professionals in the engineering supervision and inspection industry found the gap, and then the business opportunity. Because the number of China's infrastructure construction projects increases quickly, the demand of supervision and inspection engineers also increases rapidly. A web portal for the professionals in this area has the potential to succeed. The two professionals also decided to act as the managers of the web portal because they believe that only professionals in this industry can truly understand the needs, insights, and changes in the industry. A business plan was developed.

Website Development Stage (October 2005 to December 2005)

Web 2.0 platforms enable communication, cooperation, and collaboration of individuals and groups over the Internet. The two professionals chose forum based applications to start the web portal. Since the two professionals had no website development background, they were looking for software modules with the required features and at a low-cost. At the beginning, they adopted the Dvbbs -- a free forum software package. Later, they hired programmers to customize the system.

Due to the same reason of no information technology background, they use dedicated hosting service from a service provider to host the portal. This dedicated hosting can handle the issues of reliability, security, and scalability of the portal. The dedicated hosting can also have favorable cash flow profile, i.e., they do not need to put large up-front investments.

Because of the lack of knowledge of search engine optimization, at the beginning, the web portal had no effective keywords. Later in the attraction stage, the web portal re-designed the effective keywords, such as engineering supervision, engineering supervision consulting, engineering testing, engineering inspection, construction supervision, and construction inspection. The outcome shows that these well-designed keywords play an effective role in having the website listed in the front of the search results of search engines.

Attraction Stage (January 2006 –December 2009)

www.3c3t.com was launched in January 2006. A unique part of the portal is that it provides learning materials for the industry. There were several forums: consulting supervision, testing and inspection, and construction supervision. In the beginning, the web master uploaded news and learning materials, and encouraged visitors and members to share and exchange information. As member-generated learning materials increased, visitors found that this portal was quite useful, and more visitors started coming to the portal and registering as members.

The key features to attract visitors to the portal are the industry news, the learning materials, and the forums. The main objective of this stage is to gain popularity and reach "critical mass" of visitors and members. Different online communities have different measures of "critical mass" of visitors and members (Raban et al., 2010). Through the analysis of the engineering supervision, testing and inspection industry in China, we believe that 100,000 members can be considered as "critical mass" for this industry web portal.

As the content of the web portal became richer, visitors and members found this portal more useful. Through word of mouth, these visitors and members recommended the portal to their colleagues, classmates, and friends. Some visitors and members used QQ (the most popular instant messaging website in China) to "infect" others to come to www.3c3t.com. www.3c3t.com also used QQ to promote the web portal. However, the problem is that although at the beginning, the QQ promotion recruited a certain amount of visitors and members, later on, some visitors and members only used QQ to communicate and share; so they didn't come to www.3c3t.com, which caused an opposite outcome. This is an interesting phenomenon which is perhaps worthy of further research.

As the web portal built more and more virtual communities with different topics, more visitors and members can have specific platforms which they need. Also, the web portal started to provide the information and materials of certificate exams for the industry, as well as recruitment information and services. These new features and services played an important role in promoting the site's popularity. At the end of 2009, the number of the registered members of the web portal had reached 109,103.

Entrenchment Stage (January 2010 - Present)

The number of registered members and the site traffic kept increasing. At the end of 2010, the number of the registered members of www.3c3t.com had reached 138,730 (see Figure 2), of which there were 437 institutional and about 120 individual VIP members who pay membership fees. www.3c3t.com is ranked No. 1 in the engineering supervision, testing, and inspection industry in search engines Google and Baidu (a leading search engine in China), and is well ahead of other web portals in this area in China (see Table 1). The fee-based services and advertisements made the web portal had a positive cash flow in 2010 and 2011.

The next real world example examined illustrates some of the pitfalls possible.

www.wushuw.com

www.wushuw.com is an industry web portal for Chinese Kong Fu (Chinese martial art) in China. The web portal provides a platform for Kong Fu professionals and Kong Fu fans to exchange and share information. www.wushuw.com was launched in January 2010. Unfortunately, as of December 2013, the portal was still in the attraction stage. Nonetheless, there are lessons that can be learned from this portal.

Figure 2. The growth of the registered members of www.3c3t.com

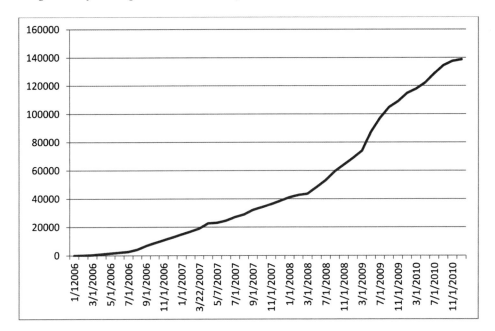

Table 1. The comparison of www.3c3t.com with other websites in engineering supervision, testing, and inspection area (query date 06/06/2010). China website rankings were from chinarank.org.cn, n.d.; World website rankings were from Alexa, n.d.

No.	Website Name	China Website Ranking	World Website Ranking
1	www.3c3t.com	11,487	112,348
2	www.163test.cn	1,997,188	13,603,128
3	www.ticc.cn	2,520,600	4,934,518
4	www.jianceshi.com	2,639,187	6,606,142
5	www.glsyjcw.com	2,267,608	12,979,035

Business Plan Stage (Before March 2007)

Chinese Kong Fu is quite popular in China. There are about 35,000 Chinese Kong Fu boarding schools as well as Chinese Kong Fu studios with more than 2 million students in the boarding schools and 20 million students in the studios (Chinese Martial Arts, 2002). In addition, there are 40 million Chinese Kong Fu practitioners who are not affiliated with any Chinese Kong Fu school or studio (Chinese Martial Arts, 2002). Before 2007, while there were some websites displaying Chinese Kong Fu school basic information, however at this point in time, a comprehensive and integrated Chinese Kong Fu portal did not exist.

One Chinese Kong Fu master, who was also the principal of a successful Chinese Kong Fu school, was inspired by the rapid development of Internet in China. He decided to create a comprehensive and general Chinese Kong Fu web portal. As there are so many Chinese Kong Fu schools and Chinese Kong Fu students and practitioners, a Chinese Kong Fu web portal has the potential for comprehensive success. The master also decided to act as the manager of the web portal because he believed that he truly understands the needs, insights, and changes in Chinese Kong Fu industry. A business plan was developed. However, the business plan was too optimistic and the available market share was overestimated.

Website Development Stage (March 2007 – December 2009)

Due to the lack of knowledge of website development, the Kong Fu master/owner contracted out the website development. However, since the master/owner thought the new website should have many new features, he insisted the website should be developed from scratch. An agreement was signed with an outside provider that was bold and aggressive in regard to website development. Unfortunately, after 12 months, the outside contractor had only provided a system with limited features and many bugs. After three months of testing and struggling, the Kong Fu master/owner and website owner had to abandon the system built from scratch and he bought a software module with which to construct the website. The website was online in January 2010 by using a collocating hosting service.

Attraction Stage (January 2010 –Present)

www.wushuw.com was launched in January 2010. The business plan starts from 2005, and the website was online in 2010. The web portal lost the momentum. The Internet use including the culture in China also changed rapidly. The web portal has had a hard time maintaining system quality and information quality. New competitors have appeared. The portal is struggling to get more members and visitors.

DISCUSSION

With the development of the Internet, professionals in different areas have increasing needs for information exchange and social support. Industry or specialized web portals have the opportunity to grow and meet the information exchange and social support needs of the professionals. How does an industry web portal grow and evolve? What approaches and strategies should an industry web portal use to succeed? We proposed a growth model of industry web portals. The growth model includes business plan stage, website development stage, attraction stage, entrenchment stage, and defense stage. Two industry web portals were discussed in detail as examples. Our study provides practical implications for industry web portal practitioners. The guidelines and lessons learned are summarized as below.

Business Plan Stage

Finding business opportunity and niche market and have a good business plan is the key. Because of the importance of the domain knowledge and industry experiences, it is important that the owners/co-owners and the management team come from the industry is vital for an industry web portal to be successful. One key lesson learned from the www.wushuw.com is that a business plan should be realistic and practical.

Website Development Stage

Internet technology develops rapidly. Industry web portals should take the advantage of existing software modules, adopt them, then later, develop their own technology if they can afford the cost and in require these capabilities. One key lesson learned from the www.wushuw.com is that there are too many uncertainties if a web portal starts developing the website from scratch. This would delay the launch of the website, waste the valuable time, and cause a loss of momentum.

Attraction Stage

The launched web portal should have unique different features and services from other web portals to attract visitors. Also, maintaining good system quality, information quality, and governance are so important to attract visitors. One key lesson learned from the www.wushuw.com is that if a web portal cannot maintain a good system quality and information quality then visitors will get frustrated and will not come again. In addition, the owner tried to promote the portal through a variety of methods and at different locations. However, lack of understanding that everyone should have a personal approach and no one-size-fits-all strategy significantly limited acquisition and retention of new and existing customers. While great promotion campaign generated strong push to sign up for the portal initially, the bottleneck came about when attempting to get customers to continue using it.

Entrenchment Stage

At this stage, a web portal can "persuade" the visitors/members to use fee-based services provided by the portal. The "pricing" strategy needs to be carefully crafted. At this stage, advertisements revenue will become an important part of revenue of the portal. Because the visitors/members of the web portal are professionals in the industry, it is very important for targeted advertisements which can be charged in higher rates. At the same time, the portal should continuously maintain good system quality, information quality, and governance, which will positively affect members/visitors' satisfaction and then increase the "sense of belonging", and ultimately increase the members/visitors' visit.

Defense Stage

When the portal has been well established, the next step is to maintain and secure the status of the portal. The factors that keep visitors/members coming back are the content, services, and communities of the portal, and the switching cost of the visitors/members. In this stage, the portal should be aware of the newly created competition portals and prevent the existing visitors/members from switching to the new competition portals. If the portal finds new innovative features in the competitors, the portal should take timely actions to deal with. At the same time, the portal should continuously maintain good system quality, information quality, and governance. The revolutionary change of the portal may seriously affect the ability of the portal to run smoothly and the visitors and members' familiarity with the portal. Therefore, the portal should keep up the evolutionary improvement to avoid revolutionary change. When revising the portal, the portal should listen to visitors and members, allow visitors and members to participate, let visitors and members feel that the portal really serves and respects them, and let visitors and members feel that they also "own" the portal.

CONCLUSION

This paper proposes a growth framework for industry web portals. The proposed framework contains five stages: business plan stage, website development stage, attraction stage, entrenchment stage, and defense stage. The actions to be taken and strategies to be applied in each stage are discussed. Two industry web portals are investigated in detail. The two examples illustrate the applicability of the proposed growth framework to the real world. The combination of a conceptual growth framework and the application of this conceptual framework to two real world examples yields a set of practical guidelines.

This research is in the preliminary status and more future studies are needed. Nevertheless, by providing a concept-based growth framework and a set of real world-based guidelines, this study will very possibly provide a practical benefit to industry web portal business practitioners.

DISCUSSION QUESTIONS

1. What are the success factors of a web portal business?
2. What is the best approach regarding technically constructing a website? What is the best approach regarding hosting a web portal?
3. There are five stages in the web portal growth framework. Which stage do you think is the most critical stage?
4. What are the challenges for a web portal to support mobile devices?
5. Please think about a possible new industry web portal business.

REFERENCES

Alexa. (n.d.). Retrieved from alexa.com

Applegate, L. M., Austin, R. D., & Soule, D. L. (2009). *Corporate Information Strategy and Management: Text and Cases*. Boston: McGraw-Hill.

Arinze, B. (2012). E-research collaboration in academia and industry. *International Journal of e-Collaboration*, *8*(2), 1–13. doi:10.4018/jec.2012040101

Armstrong, A., & Hagel, J. (1996, May). The real value of on-line communities. *Harvard Business Review*, 134–141.

Bock, G. W., Ahuja, M. K., Suh, A., & Yap, L. X. (2015). Sustainability of a virtual community: Integrating individual and structural dynamics. *Journal of the Association for Information Systems*, *16*(6), 3. doi:10.17705/1jais.00400

Casalo, L. V., Flavian, C., & Guinaliu, M. (2010). Relationship quality, community promotion and brand loyalty in virtual communities: Evidence from free software communities. *International Journal of Information Management*, *30*(4), 357–367. doi:10.1016/j.ijinfomgt.2010.01.004

Chen, C. C., Shih, S.-Y., & Lee, M. (2016). Who should you follow? Combining learning to rank with social influence for informative friend recommendation. *Decision Support Systems*, *90*, 33–45. doi:10.1016/j.dss.2016.06.017

Chen, C.-J., & Hung, S.-W. (2010). To give or to receive? Factors influencing members' knowledge sharing and community promotion in professional virtual communities. *Information & Management*, *47*(4), 226–236. doi:10.1016/j.im.2010.03.001

Chinarank.org. (n.d.). Retrieved from http://www.chinarank.org.cn

Chiu, C. M., Fang, Y. H., & Wang, T. G. (2015). Building community citizenship behaviors: The relative role of attachment and satisfaction. *Journal of the Association for Information Systems*, *16*(11), 1. doi:10.17705/1jais.00413

Damsgaard, J. (2002). Managing an Internet portal. *Communications of the Association for Information Systems*, *9*, 408–420.

Franchi, E., Poggi, A., & Tomaiuolo, M. (2012). Open social networking for online collaboration. *International Journal of e-Collaboration*, *9*(3), 50–68. doi:10.4018/jec.2013070104

Gallaugher, J., & Downing, C. (2000). Portal combat: An empirical study of competition in the Web portal industry. *Journal of Information Technology Management*, *11*(1–2), 13–24.

Hur, Y., Ko, Y. J., & Claussen, C. L. (2012). Determinants of using sports web portals: An empirical examination of the sport website acceptance model. *International Journal of Sports Marketing & Sponsorship*, *13*(3), 6–25. doi:10.1108/IJSMS-13-03-2012-B003

Internet World Stats. (2018). Retrieved on 02/26/2018 from https://www.internetworldstats.com/

Iriberri, A., & Leroy, G. (2009). A life-cycle perspective on online community success. *ACM Computing Surveys*, *41*(2), 11. doi:10.1145/1459352.1459356

Johnson, S. L., Butler, B., Faraj, S., Jarvenpaa, S., Kane, G., & Kudaravalli, S. (2010). New directions in online community research. *Proceedings of the Thirty First International Conference on Information Systems*.

Koh, J., Kim, Y. G., Butler, B., & Bock, G. W. (2007). Encouraging participation in virtual communities. *Communications of the ACM*, *50*(2), 69–73. doi:10.1145/1216016.1216023

Leimeister, J. M., & Krcmar, H. (2004). Revisiting the virtual community business model. *Proceedings of the Tenth Americas Conference on Information Systems*.

Leimeister, J. M., Sidiras, P., & Krcmar, H. (2006). Exploring success factors of virtual communities: The perspective of members and operators. *Journal of Organizational Computing and Electronic Commerce*, *16*(3&4), 277–298.

Lin, H., Fan, W., & Wallace, L. (2013). The effects of social and technical factors on user satisfaction, sense of belonging and knowledge community usage. *International Journal of e-Collaboration*, *9*(3), 13–30. doi:10.4018/jec.2013070102

Lin, H., Fan, W., & Zhang, Z. (2009). A qualitative study of web-based knowledge communities: Examining success factors. *International Journal of e-Collaboration, 5*(3), 39–57. doi:10.4018/jec.2009070103

Liu, C. T., Du, T. C., & Tsai, H. H. (2009). A study of the service quality of general portals. *Information & Management, 46*(1), 52–56. doi:10.1016/j.im.2008.11.003

Porter, M. (1996, May). What is strategy? *Harvard Business Review*, 134–141. PMID:10158475

Raban, D., Moldovan, M., & Jones, Q. (2010). An empirical study of critical mass and online community survival. *Proceedings of the 2010 ACM Conferences on Computer Supported Cooperative Work*, 71-80. 10.1145/1718918.1718932

Rao, S. S. (2001). Portal proliferation: An Indian scenario. *New Library World, 102*(9), 325–331. doi:10.1108/03074800110406204

Roberts, L. (2018). *5 Lessons from a Patient Portal Hiatus*. Retrieved from http://www.physicianspractice.com/ehr/5-lessons-patient-portal-hiatus

Rosenkranz, C., & Fessersen, C. (2008). A model for understanding success of virtual community management teams. *Proceedings of the Fourteenth Americas Conference on Information Systems*.

Sun, Y., Fang, Y., & Lim, K. H. (2010). Understanding sustained participation in transactional virtual communities. *Thirty First International Conference on Information Systems*.

Tilly, R., Posegga, O., Fischbach, K., & Schoder, D. (2017). Towards a conceptualization of data and information quality in social information systems. *Business & Information Systems Engineering, 59*(1), 1, 3–21. doi:10.100712599-016-0459-8

Wasko, M. M., & Faraj, S. (2005). Why should I share? Examining social capital and knowledge contribution in electronic networks of practice. *Management Information Systems Quarterly, 29*(1), 35–57. doi:10.2307/25148667

Xu, Y., Guo, X., Hao, J., Ma, J., Lau, R. Y. K., & Xu, W. (2012). Combining social network and semantic concept analysis for personalized academic researcher recommendation. *Decision Support Systems, 54*(1), 564–573.

Yu, M. Y., Lang, K. R., & Kumar, N. (2009). Internationalization of online professional communities: An empirical investigation of AIS-ISWorld. *International Journal of e-Collaboration, 5*(1), 13–31. doi:10.4018/jec.2009010102

Zhang, Y., Fang, Y., Wei, K. K., & Chen, H. (2010). Exploring the role of psychological safety in promoting the intention to continue sharing knowledge in virtual communities. *International Journal of Information Management, 30*(5), 425–436. doi:10.1016/j.ijinfomgt.2010.02.003

Zhou, D., Djatej, A., Sarıkas, R., & Senteney, D. (2014). The growth of industry web portals: Framework and guidelines. *International Journal of e-Collaboration, 10*(4), 17–31. doi:10.4018/ijec.2014100102

Chapter 20
Virtual Leadership:
How Millennials Perceive Leadership Attribution and Its Impact on Database System Development

Christian Graham
University of Maine, USA

Harold Daniel
University of Maine, USA

Brian Doore
University of Maine, USA

ABSTRACT

This chapter is an updated review of the results of a study completed in 2015 on leadership's impact on virtual team effectiveness and the quality of the completed virtual team project. Findings in 2015 suggested that leadership style and virtual team effectiveness did predict project quality, and specific leadership styles had a negative relationship with virtual team effectiveness. After summarizing the results of the studies purpose, methodology, and findings, the chapter concludes with a literature review of virtual team's leadership research between 2015 and present. It provides a discussion on the relationship between the previous studies' findings and what has been found since with recommendations on future research on shared leadership and relationship building in virtual teams.

INTRODUCTION

Virtual spaces continue to infiltrate themselves into various aspects of both our personal and professional lives. Millennials in particular know this having lived their whole lives immersed in the Internet. Some of the activities Millennials have done and continue to do include: social networking, synchronous real-time video gaming with friends who are geographically separated from them, and retrieving answers to every imaginable question they've ever had thanks to Internet search engines. Millennials have now reached

DOI: 10.4018/978-1-5225-6367-9.ch020

the age in which they are graduating from colleges and joining the workforce. Giving the ubiquitous nature of the Internet as a platform to communicate, coordinate, collaborate, and share information the research reviewed in this chapter sought to answer the question: "what is the effect of three leadership types on the quality of virtual team projects and what is the effect of these same leadership types on virtual team effectiveness?" This chapter is a review of the original research done by Graham, Daniel, and Doore (2015) titled: *Millennial Leadership: The Oppositional Relationship between Leadership Type and the Quality of Database System's Development in Virtual Environments*. The chapter also updates the literature review on the subject to better understand leadership types and its impact on database systems development and virtual team effectiveness in virtual environments.

The Millennial: The Net Generation

According to Williams and Chin (2009) Millennials, also referred to as "the Y generation" are those people who were born between 1977 and 2003. Another common term for Millennials is that they are the "net generation" (Tapscott 1998, 2008). Tapscott (2009) defined the net generation as:

- "People who grew up shaped fundamentally by technology and they are shaping it" (Tapscott, 2009);
- "People who use computer technology naturally and easily" (Tapscott, 2009);
- "People who prefer to learn and work collaboratively" (Tapscott, 2009);
- "People who anticipate fast and frequent communication" (Tapscott, 2009);
- People who judge corporations by their integrity, workplace practices, and concerns for the environment" (Tapscott, 2009);
- People who want to be evaluated on performance, not seniority or loyalty (Tapscott, 2009);
- People who don't make sharp distinctions between work and play, or their public and private spheres" (Tapscott, 2009).

Jones, Ramanau, Cross, and Healing (2010) reported that previous generations such as baby boomers (individuals born between 1946 and 1964) were "at least one step behind using new technologies than Millennials" and "unable to reach the kinds of natural fluency that comes with having grown up with new digital technologies".

Another interesting attribute of Millennials according to Bracey, Bevill, and Roach (2010) is that they have been discovered to be much more accepting of diversity and are more global-centric. All of this information demonstrates clear distinctions from previous generations. For example, Oblinger (2003) reported that while Millennials were more accepting diversity and global centric, baby boomers just beginning the civil rights movement and many were drafted into the Vietnam war. According to Billington and Billington (2010) in terms of working, baby boomers used experience and perspective to complete work or perform job tasks while Millennials who were more technically inclined preferred to use technology to complete tasks.

BACKGROUND

Failure in Information Systems Development

To begin, Hannola and Ovaska (2011) stated that a systems development project goal is to "develop and modify systems that satisfy customers and end users needs on schedule and within budget." (p. 66). Hannola and Ovaska added that "early activities involved in information systems development are critical and important steps. Poor execution of these activities will almost guarantee failure of the final information systems project. Dalcher and Drevin (2003) reported that "the greater part of database systems development projects end in failure. This is a problem not limited to database systems development, but most information systems development of any type. Warkentin, Moore, Bekkering, and Johnston (2009) added that "up to 80% of all systems development projects failed for a number of different reasons. Almost two decades ago Ewusi-Mensah (1997) found that these failures or cancellations of information systems projects can be attributed to any combination of the following factors:

- A lack of general agreement on a well-articulated set of project goals;
- A weak or problematic project team;
- Lack of clear project management;
- A deficiency in technical expertise, experience, or relevant application-domain knowledge;
- Current information technology infrastructure within the organization not able to support the system being developed;
- Senior management delegating decision-making at critical junctures in the development to the technical experts and not investing themselves into the project;
- The project costs and time going well beyond the original project plan.

Virtual Teams and Virtual Team Challenges

Today, many systems development projects are being done by teams that are physically separated by geographic space and time. That is, many members of systems development team projects work remote from one another. This remote team work is facilitated by telecommunication technologies that are no longer just limited to computers. Graham et al. (2015) stated it this way:

"People working together from remote locations can also use other electronic devices for communication such as tablets and the telephone. Today, the telephone would include smart phones with texting capabilities, email, and social networks. Kock (2005) added that Internet-enabled technologies such as smart phones have made collaboration significantly more mobile (p.35-36)."

Telecommunication technologies in its many forms, Internet connected computers, tablets, or smart phones to name just a few, have made possible the creation of virtual teams. In the original research, Graham et al. (2015) described virtual teams this way.

"According to Brandt, England, and Ward (2011), the ability to construct extremely adaptable and effective virtual teams is becoming essential to firms. Brandt et al. stated that virtual teams can be individuals working together who have never met in person and often will not meet face-to-face during the assigned project. There are variations of this definition. Virtual teams, according to Green and Roberts

(2010), are geographically separated teams that have little face-to-face contact and are dependent upon computers and telecommunication technologies to communicate with each other. (p.31). In research that followed the Graham et al. 2015 publication, Graham and Daniel (2016) further expanded the definition of virtual teams by citing the existing literature on the topic between 2004 and 2011.

"There are many variations of the definition of virtual teams. Virtual teams, according to Green and Roberts (2010), are geographically separated teams that have little face-to-face contact and are dependent upon computers and telecommunication technologies to communicate with each other. Martins, Gilson, and Maynard (2004) developed their own definition of virtual teams as "teams whose members use technology to varying degrees in working across locational, temporal, and relational boundaries to accomplish an interdependent task" (p. 808). Martins et al. (2004) added that virtual teams are teams first, and that the 'virtualness' is a team characteristic. Powell, Piccoli, and Ives, (2004) stated that virtual teams are "groups of geographically, organizationally, and or dispersed workers brought together by information and telecommunication technologies to accomplish one or more organizational tasks (2004; p. 7)."

It should be noted that these virtual teams bring with them certain value to the organization that use them. For example, Zivick (2012) stated that organizations are using virtual teams to accomplish business goals. Martins et al. (2004) reported that the use of virtual teams that use technology to interact with each other across geographic, organizational, and other boundaries are becoming very common in organizations (p. 805). Not only are virtual teams used more frequently in organizations, Brandt, England, and Ward (2011) stated that firms report these teams must have the ability to be constructed rapidly and be extremely adaptable to meet each individual project's goals. Kayworth and Leidner (2000) reported that many benefits are derived from these virtual teams: cost reductions, cycle-time reductions, integration of distant members, and improved decision-making and problem-solving skills. Arguably, the significance of virtual teams is best stated by Hargrove (1998) who stated: "in the future, the source of human achievement will not be extraordinary individuals, but extraordinary combinations of people."

That said, virtual teams, like information systems development, come with their own set of challenges that must be overcome or mitigated to achieve their goals. Some of the challenges associated with virtual teams include:

- Difficulty in establishing trust among team members that may have never met face to face (Brandt et al., 2011);
- Cultural and language differences become more pronounced and can result in increased distrust in virtual teams (Brandt et al., 2011);
- Lack of rules for communication, combined with cultural and language differences, can lead to a "break down" of communication amongst virtual team members. Like cultural and language differences, a lack of rules for communication can also result in increased distrust in virtual team members (Brandt et al., 2011);
- Inadequate social skills. Brandt et al. (2011) reported that expertise should not be the only reason for assembling a virtual team. Social skills are required for the effective exchange of "know how" among virtual team members;
- Like one of the reasons for any information systems development projects cancellation, a lack of clear well-articulated set of project goals keep virtual teams from performing effectively as well (Brandt et al., 2011);

- Ruggieri (2009) stated that another challenge virtual teams must overcome is the ability of team leaders or managers to "encourage, reward, and motivate" their employees through physical presence and comments. In virtual teams, the lack of physical presence makes rewarding employees more difficult. Differences in cultural norms can contribute to this as well as it makes it harder to create a common award system for all virtual team members;
- Decreased time. Sridhar, Nath, Paul, and Kapur (2007) reported that trust and relationships between virtual team members and team leaders improves over time and this more mature relationship among virtual team members and team leaders has been shown to impact the quality of outcomes both for virtual team projects and virtual team cohesiveness. Shorter term virtual projects do not get the opportunity to mature their relationships and resultant team cohesiveness;
- Blackburn, Furst, and Rosen (2003) report that in addition to what is listed above, that certain "knowledge, Skills, and Abilities (KSAs)" are also required in successful virtual teams. According to Blackburn et al. these KSAs include: comfort with technology and technology change.

Bhat, Pande, and Ahuja (2017) found that virtual teams face problems that face-to-face teams do not. Specifically, they found that virtual teams experience "decreased social interaction, communication and emotional expression (p. 35)". The findings presented by Bhat et al. (2017) state that virtual team may suffer a consequence for this. This is supported by research conducted by Brandt et al. (2011) and Hoegl and Muethel (2016) that have emphasized the importance of quality communication within virtual teams as requirement for successful virtual team project outcomes. Pozin, Nawi, and Romle (2016) report much of the same. Pozin et al. (2016) investigated he effect of communication on difference project stages and identified key factors to enhance virtual team communication. The findings primarily supported previous research that virtual teams are an effective way to have project teams communicate but add that the ability to rapidly develop communication technology that is flexible enough to support multi-national communication is necessary.

Virtual Leadership Impact on Virtual Teams Study

The original study conducted by Graham et al. (2015) was described this way:

This was a cross-sectional study that examined the impact of the type of leadership among Generation Y leaders and the effectiveness of leadership on virtual team project quality and virtual team effectiveness. The study was conducted with sophomore students at the Maine Business School. Millennial students worked in randomly assigned teams on the design and development of an MS Access database management system. The quality of the completed team project was defined as one that met the team project criteria which included:

- *Creating a list of three to five business requirements which state how the database management system should work;*
- *An entity-relationship (ER) model that graphically represents specific database management systems entities such as tables, relationship types, fields, and field data types;*
- *The completed database management system itself which would need to include physical tables, relationships, forms, queries, and reports.*

The Virtual Environment

According to Graham et al. (2015), the virtual environment was described this way:

The environment available for use in this study was Google Sites. Google Sites allowed students to work on the group / team project in a virtual environment. This virtual environment allowed students to communicate, asynchronously and synchronously; upload and download files such as word documents and database files; and collaborate on documents. Students were told at the beginning of the study that they must conduct all communication within the Google Sites. (Graham et al., 2015)

To determine leadership types impact on both virtual team project quality and virtual team effectiveness, Graham et al. (2015) developed three hypotheses for the study. They were:

H1: In comparison to Transactional and management by exception leadership types, Transformational leadership type will be most effective in leading a virtual team in developing a database management system.

H2: In comparison to Transformational and management by exception leadership types, Transactional leadership type will be most effective in leading a virtual team in developing a database management system.

H3: In comparison to both Transformational and Transactional leadership types, Management-by-Exception leadership type will be most effective in leading virtual team in developing a database management system. Figure 1 shows the structural model used in this study (Graham et al., 2015).

Figure 1. Structural model for determining the effect of leadership type impact on virtual team effectiveness and quality of completed team project

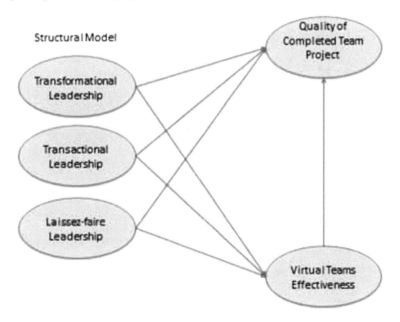

Instruments Used to Measure Leadership Type and Virtual Team Effectiveness

Graham et al. (2015) described the instruments used in the study to measure leadership type and virtual team effectiveness this way:

At the end of the study period, team members and leaders were required to complete the Multifactor Leadership Questionnaire (MLQ) survey and the Virtual Teams Survey (VTS) instruments through Qualtrics, a web-based survey tool. The MLQ measured leadership attributes and ascribed a leadership type to the team leaders based on leader attributes. Leadership types as measured by the MLQ are Transformational leadership, Transactional leadership, and Management-by-Exception (passive-avoidant) leadership. Virtual Team Effectiveness was measured by the global average of measurements of Team Formation, Team Member Relations, Team Leader Processes & Attributes and Overall Performance & Satisfaction with Team Members on the VTS. The resulting data were analyzed to understand which leadership type resulted in a successfully completed team project.

Study Findings in 2015

Graham et al. (2015) analyzed the data using a combination of descriptive statistics and Partial Least Squares – Structural Equation Modeling with WarpPLS. Figure 2 presents the findings of PLS-SEM analysis of the effect of leadership type on virtual team effectiveness and quality of completed team project.

Graham et al. (2015) in their original publication of this research reported the findings of the three hypotheses investigated in the study. The results for each hypothesis is below:

Figure 2. Findings of PLS-SEM analysis on the effect of leadership type impact on virtual team effectiveness and quality of completed team project

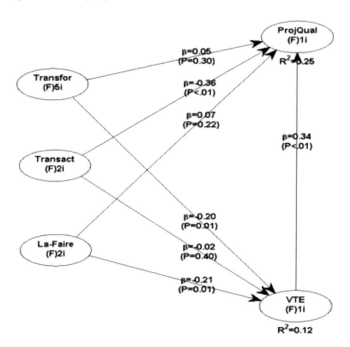

H1: In comparison to Transactional and Management by Exception leadership types, Transformational leadership type will be most effective in leading a virtual team in developing a database management system. Upon data analysis, the study found that H1 was not supported. Rather, Transformational leadership style achieves a statistically significant and negative relationship with Virtual Team Effectiveness (β=-.20).

Factors of Transformational leadership that were significant included idealized influence and intellectual stimulation, however, they showed an inverse relationship, meaning they negatively influenced database systems development in a virtual team environment. One interpretation of the negative correlation of idealized influence associated with Transformational leadership on the quality of completed virtual team projects is that in the virtual environment, leaders do not get the opportunity to arouse and inspire those they lead due to the lack of face to face interaction. According to Purvanova and Bono (2009) Transformational behaviors exhibited by leaders are "emotional in nature and may occur less frequently in virtual teams" (p. 344). Purvanova and Bono (2009) went on to state that idealized influence in particular employ nonverbal and para-verbal cues and as such it may be hard to display and perceive those Transformational behaviors in computer mediated communication settings. Thompson and Coovert (2003) stated that an additional problem for Transformational leadership in virtual teams is that communication is much more labor intensive and more cognitively taxing than face to face communication. Purvanova and Bono (2009) stated that, for example, it takes at least four times longer to type than to speak and as a result these Transformational leaders may engage in less intellectual stimulation because "challenging team members to re-think their assumptions and engage employees in the decision-making process may prove too difficult and time consuming in virtual environments" (p. 345). One explanation of the negative correlation of intellectual stimulation associated with Transformational leadership on virtual team effectiveness is that according to Hambley, O'Neill, and Kline (2007) in the virtual environment leaders tend to use a one-way, top-down approach to communication and these leaders tend to micromanage. This suggests, according to Hambley et al. (2007), that virtual followers will not find their leaders to be very intellectually stimulating. Additionally, Chidambaram (1996) suggested that managers think of computer-mediated communication as a tool to achieve goals rather than a tool for relationship building. As such, if socio-relational communication is displaced by a more task orientated communication, Transformational leadership behaviors may suffer as well. In virtual environments both idealized influence and intellectual stimulation proved to have a significant and negative influence on database systems development. The rationale for these outcomes was stated above and suggests that virtual team leaders cannot successfully convey much of the required communication, verbal, nonverbal, and para-verbal, in the virtual environment necessary to inspire and arouse team members to follow them, much less motivate team members to think on their own about problem-solving. This finding reinforces Purvanova's et al. (2009) findings that "technology-deterministic communication theories predict and preliminary data from qualitative studies reveals, that each of the Transformational leadership behaviors will be harder to display in virtual than in face to face teams" (p. 345). This study's research on leadership types agreed with Purvanova et al. (2009) Technology-facilitated communication has been shown to have an overall negative effect on leadership behavior, as well as on followers' perceptions of leadership behaviors."

Graham et al. (2015) Reported Findings on H2:

In comparison to Transformational and management by exception leadership types, Transactional leadership type will be most effective in leading a virtual team in developing a database management system. Upon data analysis, the study found that H2 was not supported. Transactional Leadership Style achieved a statistically significant and negative relationship with Project Quality (β=-.36).

Graham et al. (2015) Reported Findings on H3:

In comparison to both Transformational and Transactional leadership types, Management-by-Exception leadership type will be most effective in leading a virtual team in developing a database management system. This Laissez-Faire leadership style achieved a statistically significant and negative relationship with Virtual Team Effectiveness (β=-.21).

Additional Findings Reported in 2015

- Leadership style and Virtual Team Effectiveness predict Project Quality ($R2 = .25$);
- Virtual Team Effectiveness achieves a statistically significant positive relationship with Project Quality (β=.34);
- Leadership style predicts Virtual Team Effectiveness ($R2 = .12$).

All three leadership styles influence project quality. Transactional Leadership style influenced project quality directly, while Transformational and Management-by-Exception styles influenced project quality indirectly through their direct influence on virtual team effectiveness.

Summary of Graham et al. (2015) Findings

The 2015 findings proposed that leadership type and virtual team effectiveness did predict project quality and virtual team effectiveness. However, the relationship yielded some surprising outcomes such as:

- Transformational leadership had a negative relationship with virtual team effectiveness;
- Transactional leadership has a negative relationship with project quality;
- Management-by-Exception (Laissez-Faire) had a negative relationship with virtual team effectiveness.

Recent Findings on the Topic of Leadership and Virtual Teams

The findings of Graham et al. (2015) study provides a few interesting associations for those leading millennials in the development of database management systems and more generalizable, information systems as a whole, in virtual environments. The first finding that leaders should take away is that the more they assert specific leadership attributes, the quality of the completed system goes down. What does this suggest in terms of leadership in virtual teams? Gilson, Maynard, Jones-Young, and Hakonen (2015) reported that in terms of transformational leadership, leaders that focused on relationships instead of project tasks were "perceived as more intelligent, creative, and original (p.7)." While Graham et al. (2015) study focused on team effectiveness and project quality, the leadership attributes measured did not address relationship building. The research proposed by Gilson et al. may suggest that if transformational leaders focused more on relationship building among virtual team members they may create a more positive result on virtual team effectiveness. That research is supported by previous research by Sridhar et al. (2007) that found that virtual teams could be more effective if they had the time to develop better relationships among the virtual team members.

In another recent study, Carlson, Carlson, Hunter, Vaughn, and George (2017) investigated the moderating role of experience with instant messaging on team cohesion and openness had on virtual team effectiveness. Carlson et al. found that team cohesion had a major effect on virtual team effectiveness and that experience with instant messaging had a major effect on team openness; i.e., *this type of communication strengthened relationships among virtual team members*. This research by Carlson et al. (2017) reinforces finding presented here by both Gilson et al. (2015) and Hoegl et al. (2016) that relationship building in virtual teams seems paramount to improving virtual team effectiveness which should result in improved virtual team project quality.

Developing better relationships within virtual teams however will be more difficult for leaders than those leaders who benefit from co-location. For example, Liao (2017) stated that leadership in virtual teams is more challenging than face-to-face teams and building trust, forming shared mental models, and managing conflict will require more effort. Liao pointed out that "while relationship development in traditional teams can be organic and natural, virtual leaders might need to proactively guide the relationship building process, given the reduced richness of social information through computer mediated communication tools (p.649)".

In a more recent study, Hoegl et al. (2016) reported that many virtual teams perform better when leadership is shared. Their findings suggested that virtual team leaders who asserted more of their individual authority often tended to underestimate virtual team member's ability to lead themselves. Hoegl et al. (2016) goes on to state that this underestimation creates an environment in which virtual team members may feel that they do not have sufficient levels of autonomy to complete their specific tasks and that this lack of autonomy contributes to lower quality on the project. This research conducted by Hoegl et al. (2016) appears to reinforce the negative influence leadership styles had on both virtual team effectiveness and virtual team project quality as reported by Graham et al. (2015). Paradoxically, Hoegl et al. (2016) reported that "it is thus team leaders themselves hindering leadership effectiveness in virtual teams. (p.7)."

Hoch and Dulebohn (2017) define shared leadership as "a collective leadership process, whereby multiple team members step up to take the lead or to participate (p.681)." Hoch and Dulebohn (2017) go on to state that shared leadership is a mutual influence process carried out by team members where they lead each other toward the achievement of goals. According to Bell and Kozlowski (2002) and Hoch and Dulebohn (2013) this shared leadership in virtual teams makes sense since most virtual teams are made up of team members who possess skills and abilities that include: collaborative decision-making processes, foster motivation, take responsibility for project outcomes, and can influence and support other team members.

CONCLUSION

The Graham et al. (2015) original study on leaderships impact on the successful completion of database management systems and team effectiveness in virtual environments found that all three leadership styles influence outcomes (project quality). Transactional Leadership style influenced project quality directly, while Transformational and Laissez-Faire styles influenced project quality indirectly through their direct influence on Virtual Team Effectiveness. The research literature since 2015 suggests several reasons why this is but really appear to point to traditional styles of leadership as not being effective when leading virtual teams. Some of this is likely the result of the obvious differences between teams that work remotely from one another and teams that are co-located. The research literature in this area has plainly stated that the lack of physical presence in leaders diminishes traditional leadership attribution and that perhaps new approaches to leadership in virtual teams should be investigated more and developed. For example, research in the area of shared leadership approaches within virtual teams makes sense since each member of the team is likely a subject matter expert in their area and would not benefit from managers trying to assert themselves into how something should be done that they themselves are not experts in! Additionally, the research literature on relationship building among virtual team members appears to point towards better outcomes in virtual team projects as well. Intuitively this makes sense as well. We as human beings generally like to know that our leaders, managers, and teammates care about our well-being and have some emotional investment in us. Having a more stable relationship with us appears from the recent literature to lend themselves towards more successful project outcomes. Future research should investigate the relationship between shared leadership and improved relationships between team leaders and team members, improved relationships amongst virtual team members, and the links between them.

Another area of future research could investigate the linkages between improved collaboration technologies that create a greater sense of presence within virtual teams. The use of avatars for example in synchronous environments that allow for the acknowledgement and communication of non-verbal cues and its resultant impact of the quality of completed virtual team projects and or its impact of virtual team effectiveness.

QUESTIONS FOR PROFESSORS TO ASK

1. What are some challenges that virtual teams must overcome to successfully complete assigned tasks?
2. Why does the author of this chapter feel that shared leadership can benefit the performance of virtual teams?
3. Why does the author of this chapter feel that improved relationships among leaders and teammates can improve both the rate of successful virtual team projects and improve virtual team effectiveness?
4. Is the author of the chapter missing something? Beyond concepts related to shared leadership and improved relationships, what else could improve the success rate for successfully completed virtual team projects and improve virtual team effectiveness?

REFERENCES

Bell, B. S., & Kozlowski, S. W. J. (2002). A typology of virtual teams: Implications for effective leadership. *Group & Organization Management*, *27*(1), 14–49. doi:10.1177/1059601102027001003

Bhat, S. K., Pande, N., & Ahuja, V. (2017). Virtual Team Effectiveness: An Empirical Study Using SEM. *Procedia Computer Science*, *122*, 33–41. doi:10.1016/j.procs.2017.11.338

Billington, M., & Billington, P. (2010). Innovative business education methods for leaders and managers. *The Journal of Applied Business and Economics*, *11*(4), 44–55.

Blackburn, R., Furst, S., & Rosen, B. (2003). *Building a winning virtual team. Virtual teams that work: Creating conditions for virtual team effectiveness*. San Francisco, CA: Jossey-Bass.

Bracy, C., Bevill, S., & Roach, T. D. (2010). The millennial generation: Recommendations for overcoming teaching challenges. *Proceedings of the Academy of Educational Leadership*, *15*(2), 21–25.

Brandt, V., England, W., & Ward, S. (2011). Virtual teams. *Research Technology Management*, *54*(6), 62–63.

Carlson, J. R., Carlson, D. S., Hunter, E. M., Vaughn, R. L., & George, J. F. (2017). Virtual team effectiveness: Investigating the moderating role of experience with computer-mediated communication on the impact of team cohesion and openness. In Remote Work and Collaboration: Breakthroughs in Research and Practice (pp. 687-706). IGI Global.

Dalcher, D., & Drevin, L. (2003). Learning from information systems failures by using narrative and ante-narrative methods. In *Proceedings of the 2003 annual research conference of the South African Institute of Computer Scientists and Information Technologists on Enablement through technology* (pp. 137-142). South African Institute for Computer Scientists and Information Technologists.

Ewusi-Mensah, K. (1997). Critical issues in abandoned information systems development projects. *Communications of the ACM*, *40*(9), 74–80. doi:10.1145/260750.260775

Gilson, L. L., Maynard, M. T., Jones Young, N. C., Vartiainen, M., & Hakonen, M. (2015). Virtual teams research: 10 years, 10 themes, and 10 opportunities. *Journal of Management*, *41*(5), 1313–1337. doi:10.1177/0149206314559946

Graham, C. M., Daniel, H., & Doore, B. (2015). Millennial Leadership: The Oppositional Relationship between Leadership Type and the Quality of Database System's Development in Virtual Environments. *International Journal of e-Collaboration*, *11*(3), 29–48. doi:10.4018/ijec.2015070103

Graham, C. M., Daniel, H., & Doore, B. (2016). Millennial Teamwork and Technical Proficiency's Impact on Virtual Team Effectiveness: Implications for Business Educators and Leaders. [IJeC]. *International Journal of e-Collaboration*, *12*(3), 34–50. doi:10.4018/IJeC.2016070103

Green, D., & Roberts, G. (2010). Personnel implications of public sector virtual organizations. *Public Personnel Management*, *39*(1), 47–57. doi:10.1177/009102601003900103

Hambley, L. A., O'Neill, T. A., & Kline, T. J. (2007). Virtual team leadership: The effects of leadership style and communication medium on team interaction styles and outcomes. *Organizational Behavior and Human Decision Processes*, *103*(1), 1–20. doi:10.1016/j.obhdp.2006.09.004

Hannola, L., & Ovaska, P. (2011). Challenging frontend-of-innovation in information systems. *Journal of Computer Information Systems*, *52*(1), 66–75.

Hargrove, R. A. (1998). *Mastering the art of creative collaboration*. New York, NY: McGraw-Hill.

Hoch, J. E., & Dulebohn, J. H. (2013). Shared leadership in enterprise resource planning and human resource management systems implementation. *Human Resource Management Review, 23*(1), 114–125. doi:10.1016/j.hrmr.2012.06.007

Hoch, J. E., & Dulebohn, J. H. (2017). Team personality composition, emergent leadership and shared leadership in virtual teams: A theoretical framework. *Human Resource Management Review, 27*(4), 678–693. doi:10.1016/j.hrmr.2016.12.012

Hoegl, M., & Muethel, M. (2016). Enabling shared leadership in virtual project teams: A practitioners' guide. *Project Management Journal, 47*(1), 7–12. doi:10.1002/pmj.21564

Jones, C., Ramanau, R., Cross, S., & Healing, G. (2010). Net generation or Digital Natives: Is there a distinct new generation entering university? *Computers & Education, 54*(3), 722–732. doi:10.1016/j.compedu.2009.09.022

Kayworth, T., & Leidner, D. (2000). The global virtual manager: A prescription for success. *European Management Journal, 18*(2), 183–194. doi:10.1016/S0263-2373(99)00090-0

Kock, N. (2005). What is e-collaboration. *International Journal of e-Collaboration, 1*(1), 1–7.

Lenhart, A., Purcell, K., Smith, A., & Zickuhr, K. (2010). *Social Media & Mobile Internet Use among Teens and Young Adults. Millennials.* Pew internet & American Life Project.

Liao, C. (2017). Leadership in virtual teams: A multilevel perspective. *Human Resource Management Review, 27*(4), 648–659. doi:10.1016/j.hrmr.2016.12.010

Oblinger, D. (2003). Boomers gen-xers millennials. *EDUCAUSE Review, 500*(4), 37–47.

Powell, A., Piccoli, G., & Ives, B. (2004). Virtual teams: A review of current literature and directions for future research. *ACM Sigmis Database, 35*(1), 6–36. doi:10.1145/968464.968467

Pozin, A. M. A., Nawi, M. M. N., & Romle, A. R. (2016). Effectiveness of virtual team for improving communication breakdown in IBS project delivery process. *International Journal of Supply Chain Management, 5*(4), 121–130.

Purvanova, R. K., & Bono, J. E. (2009). Transformational leadership in context: Face-to-face and virtual teams. *The Leadership Quarterly, 20*(3), 343–357. doi:10.1016/j.leaqua.2009.03.004

Ruggieri, S. (2009). Leadership in virtual teams: A comparison of transformational and transactional leaders. *Social Behavior and Personality, 37*(8), 1017–1021. doi:10.2224bp.2009.37.8.1017

Sridhar, V., Nath, D., Paul, R., & Kapur, K. (2007). Analyzing Factors that Affect Performance of Global Virtual Teams. *Proceedings of the Second International Conference on Management of Globally Distributed Work,* 159-169.

Tapscott, D. (2009). *Grown up digital* (Vol. 361). New York: McGraw Hill.

Thompson, L. F., & Coovert, M. D. (2003). Teamwork online: The effects of computer conferencing on perceived confusion, satisfaction and post-discussion accuracy. *Group Dynamics, 7*(2), 135–151. doi:10.1037/1089-2699.7.2.135

Warkentin, M., Moore, R. S., Bekkering, E., & Johnston, A. C. (2009). Analysis of systems development project risks: An integrative framework. *SIGMIS Database*, *40*(2), 8–27. doi:10.1145/1531817.1531821

Williams, J., & Chinn, S. (2009). Using Web 2.0 to support the active learning experience. *Journal of Information Systems Education*, *20*(2), 165–174.

Zivick, J. (2012). Mapping global virtual team leadership actions to organizational roles. *The Business Review, Cambridge*, *19*(2), 18–25.

Chapter 21

What Motivates Immigrants for ICT Adoption and Use?
A Systematic Review of the 21ˢᵗ Century Literature (2001–2017)

Bhanu Bhakta Acharya
University of Ottawa, Canada

ABSTRACT

Several studies demonstrate that most immigrants feel positively about technology adoption and use, and they use information and communication technologies (ICTs) more than non-immigrants or earlier immigrants. What motivates immigrants to use ICTs? Is their motivation to use ICTs for back home connection with their families and friends, or to adjust to their new environment? What are the factors that influence immigrants' ICT behaviors most often? For this study, the author chose 24 peer-reviewed journal articles published in English between 2001-2017 to assess immigrants' motivations for ICT adoption and use. The chapter, based on the systematic review of the existing literature for a longitudinal assessment, will discuss primary motives for immigrants' ICT adoption and use, as well as identify factors that influence immigrants' behavior with respect to ICT adoption and use. Based on these influencing factors, the chapter proposes a framework of technology adoption and use by immigrants.

INTRODUCTION

Immigration refers to the movement of people, usually from their country of birth to another country for the purpose of permanent residence (Perry, 2017). There are several socio-economic and socio-political reasons to migrate from a home country to a host country. These include poverty, unemployment, conflicts, threats, and political captivity. During the 1950s and 1960s, the influx of people in foreign countries was at the highest point as consequences of World War II, the fall of colonial regimes in Asia and Africa, and natural calamities (Perry, 2017). Nowadays, people's movement towards foreign countries, often more developed ones, has become a global phenomenon. Searching for better opportunities (such

DOI: 10.4018/978-1-5225-6367-9.ch021

as, employment and education), joining with family members (spouses, children, parents), and escaping from humanitarian crises (war, conflicts, and natural calamities) are the primary reasons for today's immigration (Perry, 2017; Wellman, 2015).

However, leaving a community known since birth and adjusting to a new environment can be challenging for immigrants mainly because of the socio-cultural differences. For instance, a lack of proficiency in the host-country's language, lack of familiarity with government services and legal systems, attitudes towards work traditions, cultural perceptions on gender, race, and other issues may create difficult a situation for immigrants in integrating into the life of a host-country. On one hand, immigrants feel disconnected and isolated from their friends and family that they have left behind. On the other hand, there is a lack of strong networks with people in their new community. Restricted communication due to a limited knowledge of the host country's language may also cause feelings of loss.

Several studies assessing immigrants' struggles in adjusting to the host country's environment have identified that ICTs—mobile devices, computers, and the Internet—play pivotal roles in the successful resettlement of immigrants. By using ICTs, immigrants can:

- Reconnect and maintain sociocultural networks back home (Bacigalupe & Càmara, 2012; Benitez, 2006; Chen, 2010; Gonzalez, & Katz, 2016; Peile & Híjar, 2016; Williams, Gavino & Jacobson, 2017);
- Familiarize themselves with and adjust to a new environment (Benitez, 2006; Kabbar & Crump, 2006; Khvorostianov, Elias & Nimrod, 2011; Peile & Híjar, 2016; Williams et al., 2017; Yoon, 2016);
- Explore information and provide various support services (Alam & Imran, 2015; Barth & Veit, 2011; Peeters & d'Haenens, 2005; Peile & Híjar, 2016);
- Retrieve health information (Bacigalupe & Cámara, 2012; Mikal & Woodfield, 2015; Selsky, Luta, Noone, Huerta, & Mandelblatt, 2013);
- Enhance children's education (Gonzalez & Katz, 2016; Kabbar & Crump, 2006, 2007; Tripp, 2010);
- Entertain people in their leisure time (Khvorostianov et al., 2011; Peile & Híjar, 2016).

Studies have noticed different purposes of ICT adoption and use by immigrants in different parts of the world.

Several studies indicate that limited income, low-level education, lack of skills, and language barriers cause recent immigrants to have lower rates of access to computers and the Internet than the locals (Barth & Veit, 2011; Chen, 2010; Haight, Quan-Haase, & Corbett, 2014; Kabbar & Crump, 2006; Mossberger, Tolbert, Bowen, & Jimenez, 2012; Tsai, 2006; Williams et al., 2017). Ahmed and Veronis (2016), Gonzalez and Katz (2016), and Haight et al. (2014) noted that recent immigrants are more likely to be affected by the digital divide—"The gap between individuals, households, businesses, and geographic areas at different socio-economic levels with regard to both their opportunities to access information and communication technologies and their use of the Internet for a wide variety of activities" (OECD, 2001, p. 5).

When recent immigrants do have access to the Internet, they have higher levels of online activities and social media interactions (Haight et al., 2014; Williams et al., 2017). Similarly, Kabbar and Crump (2006, 2007), Peile and Híjar (2016), and Yoon (2016) observed that immigrants view ICTs, particularly the mobile device, computer, and the Internet, positively and want to use them as soon as they have the opportunity. Other scholars, such as Mossberger et al. (2012) and van Dijk (2012) argue that some immigrants consciously choose not to adopt and use ICT devices because they fear technological risks or have negative feelings about technology. Different findings lead to important questions, such as: What motivates immigrants to use (or not use) ICTs? What factors influence immigrants' decisions to adopt ICTs?

Immigrants have unique socio-economic and socio-cultural backgrounds. Therefore, they may have different perceptions in regard to ICT adoption and use because of the costs, requirement of skills, and usefulness of ICT devices. Identifying immigrants' motivations to adopt ICTs, as well as the factors that influence immigrants' decisions with respect to ICT adoption, is important for a smooth transition and successful integration of immigrants into a host country. Countries including Australia, Canada, Germany, the United Kingdom, and the United States welcome millions of immigrants each year. It is important to understand global trends influencing immigrants' use or non-use of ICTs so that both the host countries and the immigrants can develop better strategies to facilitate transition process. The following section will review literature on diaspora communication, technology adoption patterns of immigrants, and challenges created by the digital divide.

LITERATURE REVIEW

A number of studies have revealed that ICT adoption and use by immigrants is influenced by their communication patterns and states of the digital divide. This section, therefore, briefly reviews literature in three specific areas: (a) Diaspora communication, which refers to the communication behavior of immigrants within their communities, with their family members in their country of origin, and with other communities in the host country or beyond (Benitez, 2006); (b) The digital divide, which refers to a disparity between people in terms of computer and Internet access, skills and knowledge, affordability of ICT devices and services, language, and other factors (van Dijk, 2012); and (c) Technology adoption, which refers to the acceptance and appropriation of any technological device by users based on the device's usefulness and simplicity in use (Davis, Bagozzi, & Warshaw, 1989).

Diaspora Communication

The flow of international migration forms a multicultural society in the host country, establishes a network of communication across national spaces, and enriches a distinct diaspora (Benitez, 2006). Frequent communication, which is crucial for diasporas, is made possible by using various ICT devices. In addition to computers and the Internet, social media applications—including Facebook, Viber, and Skype—make international communication accessible and affordable. They also transform traditional communication into lively virtual meetings between transnational families using text, symbols, and audio-visual apparatus for regular contact and day-to-day information sharing.

Virtual relationships between transnational members have fostered a new sense of community called the "digital diaspora" (Brinkerhoff, 2009). The digital diaspora is an electronic community of immigrants living in different locations who interact through ICTs (Brinkerhoff, 2009; Everett, 2009). Suitable for connecting diaspora around the world, ICT devices provide a forum for sharing information, exchanging ideas, and building virtual communities through social media platforms (Brinkerhoff, 2009; Everett, 2009).

Some research scholars worry about the mental health effects of long-term separation from family and community members in an immigrant's country of origin. Bacigalupe and Cámara (2012, p. 1426) noted "Grief and loss resulting in stress, trauma, depression, and other symptoms are often the themes associated with a clinical view of immigration." There are two prevalent aspects of the psychological construct. The first is a grief over the separation from the community and family members in the country of origin. The second is a loss of identity in the host country and stress created by acculturation in a new society. With the emergence of ICTs into the lives of immigrant families, mental health effects have become more favorable (Bacigalupe & Cámara, 2012). ICTs reconnect loved ones despite geographic distance and play a catalytic role in alleviating mental stress and psychological trauma in immigrants.

Immigrants may not be able to return home to meet family and community members for reasons including: cost, legal status, and security. The Internet and social media can unite immigrants who are living in different countries. Scholars have noted that the opportunities created by the Internet and social media have created and shaped the identity of virtual diaspora (Brinkerhoff, 2009; Everett, 2009). Hence, the virtual world has played a significant role in creating and reforming diaspora communications. Yet, immigrants face two major difficulties with respect to communicating virtually with people from their country of origin: (1) a digital divide (in the form of access, affordability, skills, or perception) among immigrants and/or their loved ones in the country of origin; and (2) immigrants' reluctance to adopt technology.

Digital Divide

The concept of the digital divide denotes the gap between people with respect to their access to, skills in, usage of, and motivation to use computers and the Internet (van Dijk, 2012). The digital divide occurs when there is a disparity between people for their (in)ability to use ICT devices (such as, mobile phones, laptops, and desktop computers, and the Internet) because of several indicators, such as age, education, employment, and income (Harambam et al., 2013; Niehaves & Plattfaut, 2014; Sparks, 2013; van Dijk, 2012).

The understanding of factors contributing to various facets of the digital divide has been evolving and expanding since it was first popularized in the mid-1990s. Early studies on the digital divide focused on access and interpreted the concept as an unequal access of people to ICTs and the Internet (Compaine, 2001; Katz & Aspden, 1997; Norris, 2001). Katz and Aspden (1997) conducted a telephone survey to assess the barriers to the access to computers and the Internet, and found that low-income, low education, and ethnicity were the major causes of the digital access divide. The U.S. Department of Commerce published a series of reports, entitled *Falling Through the Net* (see, NTIA, 1995, 1998, 1999) highlighting the importance of access to computer and the Internet to the American public. When ICT devices and Internet services became more affordable and widely accessible, the digital divide continued in another form: disparity of skills among people with respect to using these devices (Dewan & Riggins, 2005). Studies from the early 21st century extended the concept of the digital divide to a second level and included gaps in skills and knowledge of handling ICT devices (Hargittai, 2002; Selwyn et al., 2005; Warschauer, 2003). For instance, Hargittai's (2002) study identified that age, gender, education, and past experience with technology were the key factors that affect users' skills and abilities to navigate web content. Her study concluded that providing access to ICTs to everyone could not solve the digital divide, unless their ICT handling skills were developed.

A few years later, scholars, such as Hargittai and Hinnant (2008) and Hohlfeld et al. (2008) argued that the digital divide should be assessed based on usage of ICTs and the Internet, to see whether these devices brought positive change to users' livelihoods. Their studies were focused on usage disparity of ICTs and the Internet (i.e. how frequently specific ICT devices are used, what types of applications were used, and what kinds of changes, such use of ICTs, brought to users' lives) that was responsible for fostering changes in users' livelihoods. Hence, a third layer of the digital divide was identified: the digital usage/outcome divide. This level focuses on the inequality of users' capacities to exploit ICT devices for productive purposes.

During the second decade of the 21ˢᵗ century, the concept of the digital divide extended to a new connection between socio-cultural and psychological spheres. Scholars assumed that ICT infrastructure is one of several factors affecting the extent of the digital divide (Haight et al., 2014; Harambam et al., 2013; Nguyen, 2012; Sparks, 2013; van Dijk, 2012). For instance, Harambam et al. (2013) identified that cultural attitude influences users' decision-making with regard to ICT adoption and use. For them, the digital divide is a "reproduction [...] of already existing [socio-economic] disparities, favoring the rich and aggrieving the poor" (p. 1094). Furthermore, van Dijk (2012), Sparks (2013), and Nguyen (2013) argued that socio-cultural and psychological aspects (i.e., attitude toward technology, anxiety, or techno-phobia) were important to motivate people to use or not use ICT devices. Access to ICTs, according to van Dijk (2012), is more of a culturally informed decision than the outcome of socio-economic disparities. Sparks (2013) argued that, "The digital divide remains a reality even in the most developed online economies. It is neither an artifact of the pattern of diffusion, nor of the relative scarcity of technical resources. Rather, it is a function of deep-seated and enduring social inequalities" (p. 38). According to Haight et al. (2014), the digital divide may never be bridged without addressing socio-cultural factors pivotal to technology adoption in many societies.

To sum up, over the last 20 years, the digital divide has been manifested in different forms, caused by various demographic, socio-economic, and socio-cultural factors. In order to address these divides, a number of strategies, such as providing universal access to ICTs, developing ICT handling skills, and focusing on proper use of ICTs, were discussed. However, recent studies have signaled towards addressing the long-rooted socio-economic and socio-cultural disparities to mitigate and gradually end the digital gaps.

Technology Adoption

Modern societies increasingly rely on information and communication technologies (ICT), and advances in ICT devices have substantial effects in society with respect to facilitating everyday activities of individual users and organizations. When users are offered an opportunity to use a new technology, a number of factors influence their decision-making process. Niehaves and Plattfaut's (2014) study identified various socio-demographic factors (i.e., age, culture, ICT skills, language, income, ethnicity, privacy and trust, psychology and attitude, and awareness) that can play important roles in ICT adoption. Similarly, in a study on the nature of the digital divide with respect to the use of the e-government portal in Nigeria, scholars Okunola et al. (2017) found that access to computing facilities, past experience with Internet use, and various socio-demographic factors, including age, gender, education, income, and geographic location were affecting potential users in accessing and using ICTs and online services.

Baum and Mahizhnan's (2015) study on Singapore's e-government practices, and Conteh and Smith's (2015) study on Ghana and Kenya's e-government service delivery identified that a lack of or limited ICT skills created considerable barriers to adopting and using ICTs and government online programs. Comparing government service delivery channels in Canada, Reddick, and Turner (2012) concluded that owing to limited ICT handling skills, a large proportion of the Canadian public preferred traditional channels, such as telephone calls and in-person visits to public offices for tasks that could be done online at home. Middleton and Byus's (2011) study examined Hispanic immigrants in the U.S. with respect to their adoption and use of ICTs in their small and medium-sized business enterprises. The study found that Hispanic immigrants "not only failed to adopt a full range of ICTs, but they were also less likely to use ICTs long-term" because of factors such as income, language, and non-practice by community members (p. 98).

Several scholars (e.g., Ebbers, Jansen & van Deursen 2016; Reddick & Turner, 2012; Roy, 2006) argue that people are hesitant to accept any new form of technology due to uncertainty, and privacy and trust-related concerns. A study by Ebbers et al. (2016) found that ICT skills were not highly relevant factors in influencing Dutch citizens' motivation towards the adoption and use of online services. Rather, users' trust and satisfaction with the services could motivate them to use online services in the long run, regardless of the users' expertise in handling ICT devices. Reddick and Turner (2012) revealed that a large number of Canadians were hesitant to use online services due to privacy concerns, among others. Highlighting public concerns over transparency, trust, and security of service delivery, Roy (2006) argued that creation of a secure, reliable, and transparent channel of service delivery and citizen participation through online platforms can enhance trust among e-government users.

Furthermore, scholars, such as Persaud and Persaud (2015) and Shareef et al. (2011) have pointed out that awareness is one of the key factors to motivate people in decision-making with respect to technology adoption and use. In order to increase awareness on technological innovations (e.g., ICTs and e-government programs), as discussed and emphasized by scholars such as Shareef et al. (2011), digital literacy entails gaining the requisite knowledge and technical skills to engage meaningfully with ICTs in a confident manner. Digital competencies can help users to explore, evaluate, and utilize digital information to increase the benefits of using digital media, and eventually enable users to make informed decisions.

Different studies reviewed in this section have demonstrated two significant challenges for effective diaspora communications: (1) the digital divide (affordability and capability to adopt ICTs); and (2) immigrants' attitudes toward technology adoption. Moreover, researchers (Barth & Veit, 2011; Haight et al., 2014) identified that immigrants have limited opportunities to access ICT devices compared to their local counterparts. Yet, they have positive attitudes with respect to technology adoption and, with access to ICTs, are more interactive online. Due to the lack of longitudinal assessment of past research, there is limited understanding about what motivates immigrants to use ICT devices and what factors influence their motivation. This study, therefore, is designed to assess past studies on immigrants' motivations with respect to ICT adoption and factors influencing immigrants' motivations to use ICT devices.

RESEARCH METHODOLOGY

By employing Okoli and Schabram's (2010) systematic literature review (SLR) method, this study aims to assess the most relevant literature with regard to the following research question: What motivates immigrants to use or not use ICT devices? SLR is a "systematic, explicit, and reproducible method for identifying, evaluating, and synthesizing the existing body of completed and recorded work produced by researchers, scholars, and practitioners" (Okoli & Schabram, 2010, p. 4). In other words, SLR helps to identify the most appropriate scholarly literature related to specific research questions, assess the quality of the literature, synthesize the findings in a systematic way, and identify the gaps that may require further research. Okoli and Schabram's (2010) model, one of the most comprehensive research methods, proposes eight steps to conducting an SLR: (1) determine the purpose of the review; (2) adhere to protocol and undergo training; (3) search for the literature; (4) screen for practicality; (5) perform quality appraisal; (6) extract data; (7) synthesize studies; and (8) write the review.

Using various research methods over the past 17 years, several global studies were conducted on the use of the Internet and/or ICTs by immigrants. This included refugee immigrants. However, there are no scholarly articles to substantially and systematically assess the trends in immigrants' motivation or demotivation to use ICTs. The current study, therefore, will be relevant in assessing the trends in immigrants' motivations to use or not use the Internet and/or ICT devices. Often referred to as a "stand-alone literature review," a SLR can stand on its own as a complete research project and can be a paradigm shifter because of its scope and rigor (Okoli & Schabram, 2010).

Data Collection and Analysis

In consultation with two librarians at the University of Ottawa specializing in communication and information technology, seven databases were identified and searched. These databases were ABI/INFORM Global, ACM Digital, Communication Source, ProQuest, Scholars' Portal, Scopus, and Web of Science. The keywords or phrases used to search an online database at the University of Ottawa (https://biblio. uottawa.ca/en/databases) were immigrant* OR newcomer* AND motiv* OR "motivation factor*" OR adopt* AND Internet OR ICT* OR "communication technolog*." The articles search was conducted in two phases. In the first phase, articles were searched between 2001 and 2015. Due to the 15-year publication period, thousands of articles were identified, making this research project very intractable and complex. Several limiters (such as English language, peer-reviewed, scholarly journals, articles, and full text) were used to make the SLR practical, manageable, and relevant to the research topic (see Table 1). Despite these limiters, 8,301 articles were retrieved through the ProQuest database. With a high number of articles found in ProQuest, a keyword search was limited to the abstracts. Sixty-nine results were generated. Altogether, 134 articles were retrieved. Twenty-five of the articles were deleted due to repetition. Hence, 109 articles were selected from the first phase of article collection for the review.

The second phase of articles selection was conducted mainly for updating this article and developing it as a book chapter. So, articles published in 2016 and 2017 were searched in the above-mentioned seven databases in which the same key terms were used, and the same limiters were applied (see Table 1). Because of a high number of results, the key terms were searched in abstracts only. As a result, 61 articles were identified, among them, 16 articles were deleted due to repetition, and 45 articles were selected for the review.

Table 1. Criteria for article selection

Database (Number of Articles)	Boolean/ Phrase Used	Published Date Range	Journal Type	Article Type	Language
ABI/INFORM Global (4+3) ACM Digital (7+6) Communication Source (7+5) ProQuest (ab*69+30) Scholars Portal (15+6) Scopus (18+4) Web of Science (14+7)	immigrant* OR newcomer* AND motiv* and "motivation factor*" OR adopt* AND Internet OR ICT* OR "communication technolog*"	2001 to 2015 2016 to 2017	Scholarly article	Peer-reviewed Full text	English

Among the total 154 (109 in the first phase and 45 in the second phase) selected articles, abstracts and keywords were carefully reviewed and rated on a Likert Scale (1 = least relevant to the research topic, 5 = most relevant to the research topic). Forty-four articles rated 4 or 5 were selected for quality appraisal, which is the fifth stage of a systematic literature review (Okoli & Schabram, 2010). In this stage, the main parts of the articles (for example, introduction, research questions, and discussion/conclusion sections) were read to make sure that the articles were highly relevant to the research topic. Finally, a total of 24 articles were selected for the review. (See Figure 1 for the article selection process).

Before starting data extraction, contacting thematic experts "to receive an assessment of the completeness of the search" was recommended to ensure whether relevant articles were missed during the selection process (Okoli & Schabram, 2010, p. 20). For this purpose, the author contacted Professor Daniel J. Paré of the University of Ottawa with a description of the research project and a list of the selected articles. Professor Paré suggested that the author look at two specific books and various articles to gain background. He also noted that these publications would be relevant for the literature review and data analysis.

As seen in Figure 1, data that answers the research question would be extracted systematically from each article. The data would be coded into small thematic units; meaningful connections between these units would be explored by developing a thematic layout. In other words, collected data would be organized into themes and links between the themes would be explored to make comprehensive sense of the themes. Finally, the SLR would conclude with a description of novel findings.

Figure 1. SLR flow diagram

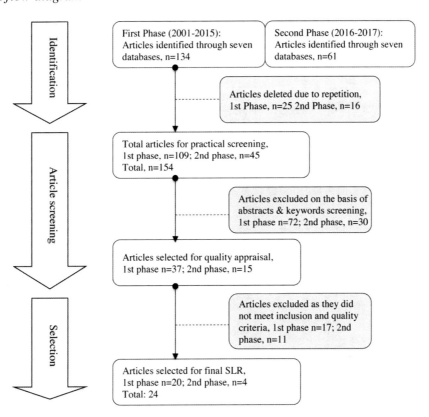

FINDINGS

General Overview

To assess immigrants' ICT adoption and use, the selected articles for this study covered a range of geography, diverse ethnicity, multiple languages, and various methodologies (Table 2). Eight studies discussed the issues of immigrants in the U.S, and three articles were about the immigrants to Canada. Eight studies (two from each country) focused on immigrants in New Zealand, Israel, Germany, and The Netherlands. Three studies (one from each country) examined immigrants' ICT adoption in the U.K., Australia, and Singapore. The two remaining articles were based on the literature review. These articles demonstrated a trend that immigrants mostly from developing countries (i.e., South America, Africa, and Asia) resided in developed countries in North America (U.S. and Canada), West Europe (U.K., Germany and the Netherlands), and Australia (Australia and New Zealand). Interestingly, two small, but developed, Asian nations (Israel and Singapore) were also among the countries that received immigrants.

Table 2. Articles selected for the systematic literature review

Articles	Coverage	Study Subjects	Research Method	Key Findings/Arguments
Alam & Imran (2015)	Queensland, Australia	Refugee migrants	Focus groups, (n=28)	Examines factors influencing refugee migrants' adoption of ICT and its relevance to their social inclusion
Bacigalupe & Cámara (2012)	Global	Psychological patients of immigration background	Literature review	Argues that ICTs may influence and mainstream transnational experiences
Bacigalupe & Lambe (2011)	Global	Immigrant/ transnational families	Literature review	Investigates the potential impact of ICTs on the lives of transnational families and how these families utilize them
Barth & Veit (2011)	Germany	Immigrants	Case study [semi-structured interview (n=28)]	Analyzes the influence of migration background on the capability to use public e-services
Baycan, Sahin, & Nijkamp (2012)	Amsterdam, The Netherlands	Turkish entrepreneurs in The Netherlands	Multivariate qualitative classification method (in-depth interviews)	Addresses motivations of second generation Turkish immigrants for socio-economic emancipation
Benitez (2006)	Washington D.C., U.S.	Salvadoran immigrants	Ethnography [in-depth interviews, (n=67), participant observation]	Identifies how transmigrants and immigrant communities appropriate and make use of the ICTs based on various influence factors
Chen (2010)	Singapore	Chinese immigrants	Telephone survey (n=710)	Argues that immigrants who frequently communicate with locals via the Internet are more adaptive in terms of overall sociocultural adaptation
Gonzalez & Katz (2016)	U.S. California, Arizona, & Colorado	Latino and Hispanic immigrants and their children	45-60 minutes long interview (n=166 children, n=170 parent)	Examines how inter-country family communication need influences immigrants' technology adoption and use.
Haight et al. (2014)	Canada	Canadian residents including immigrants	Meta-analysis based on the Canadian Internet Use Survey-2010	Finds that recent immigrants who are online have significantly higher levels of online activity than Canadian-born residents and earlier immigrants
Kabbar & Crump (2006)	Wellington, New Zealand	Refugee immigrants from Asia and Africa	Semi-structured interviews (n=32)	Identifies factors influencing ICT adoption/non-adoption by immigrants (such as literacy, language skill, and cultural background)
Kabbar & Crump (2007)	New Zealand, Wellington	Refugee immigrants from Asia and Africa	In-depth interview (n=32)	Finds that the most common factor in ICT adoption for immigrants who were new to computing was via friends and family

continued on following page

Table 2. Continued

Articles	Coverage	Study Subjects	Research Method	Key Findings/Arguments
Khvorostianov et al., (2011)	Israel	Older Jewish immigrants from the Former Soviet Union in Israel	In-depth interviews (n=32)	finds that old immigrants in Israel use ICTs for managing health, nurturing professional interests, extending social networks, and enjoying leisure.
Mesch (2012)	Israel	Internet users (minorities and immigrants)	Online survey	Finds that disadvantaged groups show greater motivation to use ICTs to expand business and occupational contacts
Mikal & Woodfield (2015)	U.S.	Iraqi and Sudanese Refugee immigrants	Five focus groups (n=25)	Observes four trends of refugee immigrants' ICT use: (1) Internet use was related to culture of origin; (2) refugees were reluctant to explore online; (3) children served as brokers of online knowledge; and (4) limited Internet access
Mossberger et al. (2012)	Chicago, U.S.	Latino immigrants	Telephone survey (n=3,453)	Interprets neighborhood and individual factors influencing ICT adoption and use
Peeters & d'Haenens (2005)	The Netherlands	Ethnic minorities (Turkish, Moroccan, Surinamese, & Antillean)	Face-to-face interview (n=1913)	Analyzes immigrants' ICT adoption and use in two terms: (1) bonding and (2) bridging, and argues that ICT communication slants toward country of origin.
Peile & Hijar (2016)	London, U.K.	Spanish youth immigrants	Semi-structured interviews (n=25) and participant observation	Analyzes the prospects and challenges of mobile communication need of 25 Spanish youth migrated to London in search of better opportunities.
Selsky et al. (2013)	Washington D.C., U.S.	Latino immigrants (*attending safety-net clinics in the U.S.*)	Survey questionnaire (n=1,273)	Investigates access to and intended use of the Internet for cancer information among low income, immigrant Latinos
Spaiser (2013)	Germany	Turkish and East European immigrants in Germany	Survey (n=2,082)	Explores young immigrants' online political activities based on the sociological rational-choice theory and theoretical resource models
Tripp (2010)	Los Angeles, U.S.	First generation Latino immigrants in the U.S.	Participant observations and in-depth interviews	Analyzes how Latino immigrants in the U.S. negotiated and debated home access to the internet, as well as how they regulated children's use of the internet
Tsai (2006)	U.S.	Taiwanese immigrants in the U.S.	Ethnography (semi-structured interview and set of questionnaire)	Assesses how new computer technology promotes immigrant families' adaptation and alleviates stress associated with resettlement
Williams, Gavino, & Jacobson (2017)	U.S.	Latino entrepreneurs in the U.S.	Surveys and workshops (n=116)	Finds that Latino entrepreneurs in the U.S. use less business-technology than their non-Latino counterparts, but they tend to use more social media tools and linguistic communication software than the non-Latinos.
Yoon (2016)	Canada	South Korean immigrants to Canada	Semi-structured interviews with young immigrants (n=57) between 19 & 29 years	Assesses how Korean immigrants compare their home country experiences of ICTs use with their host-country environment in Canada, during their post-migration adjustment.
Zaidi, Fernando, & Ammar (2015)	Canada	Women, who are victims of IPV	Semi-structured interview (n=49)	Argues that ICTs can be both a tool of empowerment, and liberation or can involve harassment, threats, and victimization

Of the 24 articles, 21 were empirical studies. The three remaining performed meta-analysis on immigrants' adjustment to their new environment, as well as their use of ICTs to facilitate their transition. Among the empirical studies: seven used semi-structured interviews; six used survey methods; three used ethnographic studies; two used focus groups; and three used in-depth interviews. Of the three meta-analyses, two studies were based on the literature review and one study used data from the Canadian Internet Use Survey-2010. Four articles were published in 2012; three articles were published each year in 2016, 2015, 2011, and 2006. Two articles were published each year in 2013 and 2010. One article was published each year in 2017, 2014, 2007, and 2005. These articles covered various subjects with respect to immigrants' motivation, adoption, and use of ICTs. Seventeen studies looked at first generation immigrants, two studies looked at second generation immigrants, three studies looked at parent-child relationships, one study looked at elderly immigrants, and one study looked at refugee women (Table 2).

Immigrants' Motivations for ICT Use

Scholars found that immigrants show greater motivation to adopt and use ICTs for the following reasons: familiarizing themselves with their new environment; connecting with family and friends in their country of origin; getting information updates; performing job searches; enhancing children's education; spending leisure time in old age; and establishing ethnic and cultural identity in host societies (Haight et al., 2014; Mesch, 2012; Yoon, 2016). Most of the articles focused on two points often referred to as "bonding" and "bridging" (Peeters & d'Haenens, 2005). Bonding refers to immigrants' frequent contact with family and friends in their country of origin. Bridging refers to immigrants' desires to integrate into and familiarize themselves with the host country. Fourteen of the 24 studies discussed the use of ICTs by immigrants for both home connection and adjustment in the host country. Seven studies focused on immigrants' endeavors to familiarize themselves with and adjust to the host country. Three studies prioritized immigrants' connection with family and friends back home as the major purpose of ICT adoption and use (Figure 2).

ICTs for Home Connection

Immigrants may face a series of pre- and post-migration stresses related to family separation and settlement in a new environment (Mikal & Woodfield, 2015; Peile & Híjar, 2016; Tsai, 2006; Yoon, 2016). They worry about careers, job opportunities, financial status, social connections, and reputation. Fifteen of the studies identified and discussed the importance of ICTs in coping with and overcoming these

Figure 2. Focus of articles on immigrants' motivation of ICT adoption

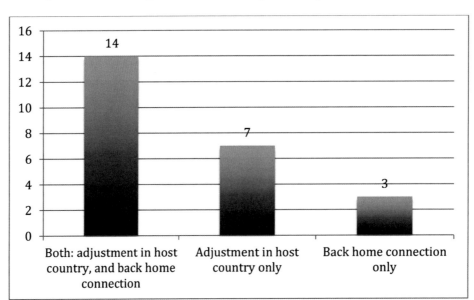

challenges by making a connection with people back home. A key theme of these studies was that the mainstreaming of ICTs increasingly allowed immigrant families to maintain social ties across national borders despite vast geographic distances (Bacigalupe & Càmara, 2012; Bacigalupe & Lambe, 2011; Benitez, 2006; Chen, 2010; Gonzalez & Katz, 2016; Mesch, 2012; Yoon, 2016).

Immigrants encounter various challenges related to their adjustment in their new environment. These include language problems, lack of jobs and income sources, and disconnection from society. Consequently, they may feel socially isolated and residentially segregated from their new community (Peile & Hijar, 2016; Tsai, 2006; Yoon, 2016). ICTs provide platforms for immigrants to maintain existing relationships with people back home in order "to compensate for their lack of social capital" in their host country (Mesch, 2012, p. 317). Bacigalupe and Lambe (2011, p. 14) noted that ICTs may "fill a relational, emotional, and social void for [immigrant] families who have more than one country as their home." Similarly, ICTs can provide a source of "emotional sustenance," create "a feeling of collective family-hood," and maintain relationships despite geographic distances (Bacigalupe & Càmara, 2012, p. 1431).

According to Gonzalez and Katz (2016), ICTs are useful tools to "provide opportunities to develop and maintain virtual intimacy with faraway relatives, to secure emotional support that can mitigate effects of isolation in the host country, and to provide opportunities to engage in transnational caregiving, in both directions (p. 2697)." A study by Peile and Hijar (2016) observed that Spanish youth migrating to London for better opportunities used mobile phones to maintain "family bonds across distance, as well as to keep in touch with relatives" (p. 414). Since ICTs provide a way of strengthening the connection between immigrants and people in the home country, their utilization among immigrants is increasing (Benitez, 2006; Chen, 2010; Gonzalez & Katz, 2016; Peile & Híjar, 2016; Yoon, 2016).

Scholars have identified several patterns used by immigrants when communicating via ICTs (Chen, 2010; Haight et al., 2014; Mesch, 2012; Peeters & d'Haenens, 2005). Mesch (2012) pointed out that non-immigrants and earlier immigrants (who are financially settled) used ICTs to maintain existing social ties in the host countries. Recent immigrants used ICTs to connect with their social circle back home and overcome existing physical and psychological barriers (Mesch, 2012; Peile & Hijar, 2016; Yoon, 2016). Similarly, Haight et al. (2014) found that recent immigrants to Canada were less likely to have Internet access. However, if they did have access, they had a higher level of online interactions with family and friends back home than they did with people in Canada. Gonzalez and Katz's (2016) study on parents and children of Mexican heritage, low-income families, in the U.S. found that children's pressure was the main reason of purchasing ICTs and accessing the Internet, but parents encouraged children to use ICTs to connect with transnational family members, understand their cultures, and keep virtual intimacy with them. Similarly, a study by Williams et al. (2017) found that Latino entrepreneurs in the U. S. were found using social media (such as *Facebook* and *Twitter* that were easy to communicate in their mother tongue) more than other ICTs and websites because of English language problems. Yoon's (2016) study found that online connection provided South Korean young immigrants to Canada "a sense of continuity and belonging" (Yoon, 2016, p. 373). But these youths observed that Canadian Internet service is very slow and costly in comparison to their back home Internet service. Therefore, many of these Korean youths abandoned their habits of online gaming and started engaging in outdoor activities.

Several articles selected for this review noted that recent immigrants' communication via the Internet usually slanted toward the country of origin. For instance, a study by Peeters and d'Haenens (2005) identified that Turkish immigrants in the Netherlands were more interested in accessing home country media through the Internet. Chen's (2010) study on Chinese immigrants in Singapore revealed two findings as immigrants lived for longer periods of time in the host country: (1) they were more likely to surf the host country's websites; and (2) they were less likely to surf websites of their country of origin. Similarly, these immigrants were more likely to use the official language of the host country and less likely to use their mother language during online interactions (Chen, 2010). Furthermore, Benitez (2006) and Haight et al. (2014) identified that the migratory status of immigrants shaped their appropriation, adoption, and usage of ICTs. In the U.S., Salvadoran immigrants who had temporary legal status and could not go back to Salvador because of a lack of legal documents were found frequently communicating via ICTs with their family and friends who were still in Salvador (Benitez, 2006). Similar legal obstruction was observed by Gonzalez and Katz (2016) in their study on Latino and Hispanic immigrants of Mexican heritage in the U. S., compelling them to use ICTs as the only means to keep a virtual intimacy with back home families and friends. Spanish youth immigrants to the U.K. downloaded Whatsapp, Skype, and Facebook Messenger on their smart phones mainly for the purpose of transnational communication with their parents in Spain in order to avoid costly international telephone calls. Hence, the above-mentioned study evidences demonstrate that back home connection is one of immigrants' key motives for ICT adoption. This connection reduces stress, mitigates their sense of loss, and relieves homesickness.

ICTs for Adjustment and Integration

Twenty-one of the articles identified adjustment and integration in the host country as the most important motivations for immigrants' use of ICTs. For instance, refugee immigrants in Australia (Alam & Imran, 2015) and Taiwanese immigrants in Washington, D.C. (Tsai, 2006) used computers and the Internet to participate in and to integrate into their new environment. Arab immigrants in Israel used ICTs to expand their social circle and overcome social isolation in the host country (Mesch, 2012). Refugees from Iraq and Sudan who immigrated to the U.S. used ICTs to overcome post-migration stress and re-establish "their lives, relationships, and identities in a new and unfamiliar context" (Mikal & Woodfield, 2015, p. 1319). A group of Latino immigrants in Chicago used the Internet in their homes to adjust to the neighborhood in which most of the residents were digitally connected (Mossberger et al., 2012). Another group of Latino immigrants in Washington, D.C. adopted ICTs to retrieve health information because they trusted the Internet more than other information sources (Selsky et al., 2013). Salvadoran immigrants in the U.S. (Benitez, 2006), and South Korean youth immigrants in Canada (Yoon, 2016) used ICTs to establish and sustain ethnic and sociocultural networks that provided them with sociability, support, new opportunities, and a sense of belonging. Turkish and East European immigrants in Germany used computers and the Internet for empowerment purposes (such as political participation) in their new home country (Spaiser, 2013). Moroccan immigrants in the Netherlands used the Internet to integrate with the local community through online discussion groups (Peeters & d'Haenens, 2005). In addition, some immigrants adopted and used ICTs to help their children adjust and integrate themselves into the new country. For instance, Asian and African immigrants in New Zealand (Kabbar & Crump, 2007) and a group of Latino immigrants in Los Angeles (Tripp, 2010) used computers and the Internet to enhance their children's education and allow them to fit into the host country's competitive environment. As discussed, most of the selected studies demonstrated that the key motivation for ICT adoption and use was to adjust to and integrate within the host country's environment.

Immigrants' psychological factors (such as attitude, stress, isolation, and confidence) were equally important with respect to ICT adoption and use (Chen, 2010; Khvorostianov et al., 2011). Tsai (2006) contended that ICT devices provided immigrants with new opportunities and strategies to overcome psychological consequences, including stress created by resettlement and social isolation. Khvorostianov et al. (2011) found that older immigrants from the former Soviet Union who resided in Israel used ICTs to cope with cultural isolation, depression, the host country's language, poverty, and ageing. These immigrants believed that ICTs enhanced their sense of independence, built positive attitudes toward ageing, and initiated "a process of empowerment" (Khvorostianov et al., 2011, p. 3). Chen (2010, p. 388) observed that "immigrants who are more active in interpersonal communication are better adjusted psychologically and physically" to the host country. These immigrants were more likely to communicate with local people via the Internet while using the host country's language (Chen, 2010). A group of young Spanish immigrants, according to Peile and Hijar (2016), searched information online to find out the best immigration destination in terms of cost, opportunities, and living standards. Later, they migrated to the U.K., purchased brand new smart phones, and downloaded various mobile apps to adjust to the mobile-friendly ICT environment in London.

However, the adoption and use of ICTs is not free of challenges. Williams et al. (2017) observed that a lack of self-efficacy—ability to perform assigned/desired talk through the technology—made a majority of the Latino immigrant entrepreneurs in the U.S. very unlikely to adopt, access, and use ICTs for business purpose. Similarly, Peile and Hijar (2016) noted that immigrants' technological adjustments, such as purchase of ICTs and subscription of services, depend on their economic conditions. Their study found that Spanish youths who migrated to London lacked a regular income source, and had limited or no Internet connection to their mobile devices. Mesch (2012) warned that the increased use of ICTs might foster social alienation and residential segregation of immigrants in specific contexts. Several immigrants in the selected studies were found to be alienated in the host country: former Soviet Union immigrants in Israel (Khvorostianov et al., 2011); Chinese immigrants in Singapore (Chen, 2010); Mexican heritage families in the U.S. (Gonzalez & Katz, 2016); and young Turkish immigrants in the Netherlands (Peeters & d'Haenens, 2005). Alienation of immigrants to the host country may cause a long and complex integration process. In addition, some immigrants worried that ICT usage would allow their children to come across inappropriate content and have contact with strangers (Kabbar & Crump, 2006; Trip, 2010). These immigrants believed that "not everything is useful on the Internet" (Kabbar & Crump, 2006, p. 116) and that the Internet is "a gateway to harm" (Tripp, 2010, p. 558). These immigrants felt that it was important to monitor their children's online activities in accordance with their cultural, religious, and social norms that may be challenged by adopting ICTs (Kabbar & Crump, 2006; Tripp, 2010). On one hand, various opportunities motivated immigrants to use ICTs. On the other hand, challenges demotivated immigrants to use ICTs due to various influential factors.

Influence Factors of Immigrants' Motivation

Authors of the selected articles identified several factors influencing immigrants' motivation to adopt and use ICT devices and services. The most common factors included age, culture, education, income, language, ICT skills, and attitude. These factors are described below[1]:

- **Age:** Based on the results of original articles that are reviewed for this study, fifteen of them found an association between age of immigrants and their individual decision-making in regards to ICT adoption (see, Bacigalupe & Lambe, 2011; Barth & Veit, 2011; Baycan et al., 2012; Benitez, 2006; Chen, 2010; Haight et al., 2014; Kabbar & Crump, 2006, 2007; Peeters & d'Haenens, 2005; Peile & Hijar, 2016; Spaiser, 2013; Tripp, 2010; Tsai, 2006; Yoon, 2016; Zaidi et al., 2015). For instance, a young person was highly likely to adopt and use ICTs in comparison with his/her older counterparts. In Tripp's (2010) study, all teen participants expressed confidence and familiarity in using computers and the Internet. However, their parents had limited knowledge about handling ICTs. When it became difficult for parents to monitor their children's online activities, parents were less likely to adopt ICTs (Tripp, 2010). Therefore, older individuals cannot take advantage of the potential for bonding offered by the Internet (Barth & Veit, 2011; Peeters & d'Haenens, 2005);

- **Culture:** Eleven of the selected studies noted that immigrants' cultural backgrounds in the country of origin and the contemporary culture in the host country influenced their decisions about ICT adoption (see, Alam & Imran, 2015; Barth & Veit, 2011; Chen, 2010; Haight et al., 2014; Kabbar & Crump, 2006, Khvorostianov et al., 2011; Mikal & Woodfield, 2015; Peeters & d'Haenens, 2005; Tsai, 2006; Yoon, 2016; Zaidi et al., 2015). Some immigrants used ICTs to bridge cultural gaps (Mikal & Woodfield, 2015; Peeters & d'Haenens, 2005) and engage in the contemporary culture of the host country (Khvorostianov et al., 2011; Tsai, 2006). Other immigrants refrained from ICT use because they felt that "Internet content conflicted with their cultural and social norms" (Kabbar & Crump, 2006, p. 116). In some cultures, female members were not allowed to or did not feel comfortable using computers and the Internet outside of the home and/or in public places (Kabbar & Crump, 2006);

- **Education:** Eleven of the articles selected for this study highlighted that highly educated immigrants who want to receive an education in the host country are more likely to adopt ICTs compared to their counterparts with medium or low education (Alam & Imran, 2015; Bacigalupe & Lambe, 2011; Baycan et al., 2012; Benitez, 2006; Chen, 2010; Kabbar & Crump, 2007; Khvorostianov et al., 2011; Mesch, 2012; Selsky et al., 2013; Tripp, 2010; Williams et al., 2017). Baycan et al. (2012, p. 985) maintained, "Educational attainment ... appears as decisive factor toward orientation to the ICT sector." Some Latin American parents purchased computers to assist children with school assignments. However, they were hesitant to adopt these ICTs because of the risks associated with the devices (Benitez, 2006; Tripp, 2010). In New Zealand, Asian immigrants who had relatively higher educational backgrounds were found to be more likely to adopt and frequently use ICTs (Kabbar & Crump, 2007);

- **Income:** Twelve of the selected studies (Barth & Veit, 2011; Benitez, 2006; Kabbar & Crump, 2006; Gonzalez & Katz, 2016; Haight et al., 2014; Mesch, 2012; Mossberger et al., 2012; Peile & Hijar, 2016; Selsky et al., 2013; Tripp, 2010; Tsai, 2006; Zaidi et al., 2015) found that income positively influenced immigrants in ICT adoption and use. According to these studies, immigrants with more economic capital, professional jobs, or satisfactory employment used the Internet to maintain sociocultural networks. Limited or inconsistent income, however, caused immigrants to refrain from adopting ICTs. Barth and Veit (2011), for instance, identified low income as one of three characteristics of immigrants. The other two characteristics were cultural differences and lack of language ability of the host country. Income status directly affected ICT use because of costs associated with hardware, software, service, maintenance, and training (Mossberger et al., 2012);

- **Language:** Fourteen of the selected articles considered language as a significant factor influencing immigrants' decisions to adopt and use ICTs (Barth & Veit, 2011; Benitez, 2006; Chen, 2010; Kabbar & Crump, 2006, 2007; Mikal & Woodfield, 2015; Mossberger et al., 2012; Peeters & d'Haenens, 2005; Peile & Hijar, 2016; Selsky et al., 2013; Tripp, 2010; Tsai, 2006; Williams et al., 2017; Yoon, 2016). Learning the language and norms of the host country is a part of resettlement; it is a way to rebuild immigrants' social images of themselves (Barth & Veit, 2011; Tsai,

2006). Without proficient knowledge of the host country's language, immigrants face difficulties in carrying out tasks, exploring job opportunities, and building social ties with local community members (Benitez, 2006; Chen, 2010; Kabbar & Crump, 2006; Peile & Hijar, 2016). Recent immigrants often used language translating software or mobile apps to convert host-country information into their mother tongues (Peile & Hijar, 2016; Williams et al., 2017; Yoon, 2016). Due to limited knowledge of English language, Spanish youths avoided British government websites, and rather visited social media community portals in Spanish for easier understanding (Peile & Hijar, 2016). A limited proficiency in the host country's language negatively influenced immigrants' decisions with respect to ICT adoption (Mikal & Woodfield, 2015; Tripp, 2010; Tsai, 2006);

- **ICT Skills:** Fourteen of the selected articles recognized ICT handling skills as an important factor influencing immigrants' motivation to adopt ICTs (Alam & Imran, 2015; Bacigalupe & Cámara, 2012; Bacigalupe & Lambe, 2011; Barth & Veit, 2011; Baycan et al., 2012; Benitez, 2006; Chen, 2010; Haight et al., 2014; Kabbar & Crump, 2006, 2007; Khvorostianov et al., 2011; Mossberger et al., 2012; Peeters & d'Haenens, 2005; Williams et al., 2017; Yoon, 2016). According to these articles, immigrants perceived ICTs as innovative tools that provided them with advantages for successful post-migration settlement. Skills and usage related to the digital divide, however, appeared as major barriers to immigrants in adopting ICTs. Some scholars (such as Barth & Veit, 2011; Tsai, 2006; Williams et al., 2017) found that immigrants were consequently motivated to use ICTs for simple activities; they avoided partaking in professional activities because of their lack of or limited knowledge and skills with respect to handling ICTs. Immigrant parents felt uncomfortable about adopting ICTs because of potential risks to their children (Tripp, 2010);
- **Attitude:** A positive attitude toward technology is found an important factor in influencing ICT adoption. Eight of the selected articles demonstrated that individuals' perceptions and attitudes influenced their motivation with respect to ICT adoption (Chen, 2010; Kabbar & Crump, 2006, 2007; Mossberger et al., 2012; Peile & Hijar, 2016; Peeters & d'Haenens, 2005; Tripp, 2010; Yoon, 2016). Lack of confidence, technological anxiety, privacy concerns, and fear of unintended consequences of ICT use may negatively influence people with respect to ICT adoption and use (Mossberger et al., 2012). Similarly, some cultures do not permit female immigrants to use computers and the Internet outside of the home and/or in public places, including the host country (Kabbar & Crump, 2006, 2007). As detailed above, some immigrants consciously choose not to adopt ICTs for cultural or psychological reasons.

To conclude this section, ICT adoption is important for two fundamental reasons: (a) connecting with family and friends in the country of origin, and (b) successfully adapting and socializing in the host country (Alam & Imran, 2015; Benitez, 2006; Peeters & d'Haenens, 2005; Selsky et al., 2013; Spaiser, 2013; Tsai, 2006, Williams et al., 2017; Yoon, 2016). Moreover, the selected articles identified seven factors influencing immigrants' motivation to adopt and use ICTs. These included age, culture, education, income, language, ICT skills, and attitude. The following section will discuss and analyze the findings.

DISCUSSION AND CONCLUSION

Migration is a global phenomenon. Every year, millions of people migrate as immigrants from their countries of origin to other countries in search of better opportunities and higher levels of livelihood

(Bacigalupe & Lambe, 2011; Barth & Veit, 2011). Due to specific socio-cultural and socio-economic backgrounds, immigrants possess unique characteristics that play an important role in their adjustment to and integration into a new country environment. Adjusting to a new environment is not easy for many immigrants because of several factors, including linguistic and cultural differences, limited or no education, low income, high competition for job opportunities, and others. Moreover, several studies show that ICTs, including mobile devices, personal computers and the Internet, can help immigrants with a successful transition (Alam & Imran, 2015; Barth & Veit, 2011; Benitez, 2006; Chen, 2010).

What Motivated Immigrants to Use ICTs?

This study identified two key motivations for ICT adoption and use by immigrants. First, adjustment to and integration within the new host country environment through ICTs was the most discussed theme among the selected articles. The second most important theme was the transnational connection of immigrants with their family and friends back home through various ICTs, web applications, and mobile apps. Specifically, 14 of the 24 articles emphasized both motivations of immigrants with respect to ICT adoption and use. Seven articles focused on the first motivation and three articles highlighted the second motivation.

Twenty-one (14+7) of the 24 articles discussed various reasons for immigrants to use ICTs: expanding their social circle; adjusting to their neighborhood; establishing and sustaining ethnic and sociocultural networks in their host countries; retrieving information required for everyday activities (such as banking and shopping); familiarizing children with the new country and back home family members; establishing ethnic identity, and enhancing education (Alam & Imran, 2015; Mesch, 2012; Mikal & Wodfield, 2015; Tripp, 2010; Tsai, 2006; Yoon, 2016).

Seventeen (14+3) of the studies emphasized that back home connections through ICTs are important for motivating immigrants during the difficult transition. It provided them with a sense of collective familyhood as it helped them to overcome social isolation and post-migration stress (Gonzalez & Katz, 2016; Mikal & Woodfield, 2015; Selsky et al., 2013; Spaiser, 2013). Accordingly, Mikal and Woodfield (2015, p. 1330) described ICTs as "tools for stress reduction." For Gonzalez and Katz (2016), ICTs adoptions and usages by immigrants are primarily motivated for virtual intimacy between families separated in different countries, emotional support, and transnational caregiving to mitigate social isolation from one another.

The aforementioned two major motivations of immigrants with respect to adopting and using ICTs are a part of diaspora communication. There are four categories of diaspora communication: (1) intra-diaspora (immigrants' communications with other local immigrants of the same ethnicity); (2) inter-diaspora (immigrants' communications with immigrants of different ethnicities in the host country or beyond); (3) diaspora-host (immigrants' communications with people from different communities and ethnicities within the host country); and (4) diaspora-homeland communication (immigrants' communications with family and friends living in the home country) (Benitez, 2006). Since immigrants, particularly more recent ones, generally have poor intra-diaspora and inter-diaspora communication skills because of their limited abilities in using the host country language, limited ICT skills, and cultural differences, the articles selected for this study focused mainly on diaspora-host and diaspora-homeland communication (Benitez, 2006; Chen, 2010).

Drawing from the selected articles, it was found that immigrants' motivation for ICT adoption and use was unique among various immigrant communities, and did not remain intact for a long time. Rather, immigrants' communication with people back home slowly faded. In turn, interaction with local people in the host country gradually increased. In comparison to recent immigrants, more settled immigrants were less likely to interact with people back home and less likely to visit websites from the country of origin (Benitez, 2006; Chen, 2010; Mesch, 2012). They were more likely to use the host country language in communication, interact with local people in the community, visit and use host country websites, and read or watch local news media (Chen, 2010). Likewise, immigrants' legal status in the host country influenced their use of ICTs. Immigrants with temporary residence status were more likely to interact with their family and friends back home than were other permanent residents because of a lack of proper documentation for international visits from the host country (Gonzalez & Katz, 2016; Mikal & Woodfield, 2015). Similarly, second-generation immigrants were generally completely engaged in the host country environment and seldom connected with anyone living in the country of origin (Baycan et al., 2012). Older immigrants, however, used ICTs to look at information from their past and disengage from the unfamiliarity of the host community (Khvorostianov et al., 2011).

A couple of recent studies (Peile & Hijar, 2016; Yoon, 2016) identified some unique characteristics of ICT adoption and use by recent immigrants from developed countries such as Spain and South Korea. Spanish youth immigrants to the U.K. were more familiar with personal computers and laptops in their home country, but they shifted to smart phones because of London's mobile-friendly digital environment. In the case of South Korean immigrants to Canada (Yoon, 2016), they abandoned online gaming habits because of slow Internet experience in Canada compared to their home country, and, consequently, they started to engage in outdoor activities. Some immigrants, who were already familiar with various ICTs, mobile apps, and online applications, found past experience of ICT handling was very important for them to adjust and integrate into a new host society smoothly because ICTs are the primary gateways to search for information in the host country (Peile & Hijar, 2016; Williams et al., 2017; Yoon, 2016).

Interestingly, immigrants tended to use the same ICTs, online platforms, and mobile apps that they were familiar with in home country in the host-country environment, but that did not work properly. For example, Korean immigrants used KakaoTalks for chats in South Korea, but they shifted to Facebook Messenger in Canada in order to communicate with host-country peers. So, immigrants not only change their countries of living, but they may also change their ICT appropriation habits based on the technology-friendly environment of the host country.

Which Factors Influenced Immigrants' Adoption of ICTs?

There were several factors influencing immigrants' decisions to adopt and use ICTs. The following were commonly referred to in the selected articles; (1) age; (2) education; (3) income; (4) culture; (5) ICT skills; (6) language; and (7) attitude. Age, referred to in 15 of the articles, significantly influenced immigrants' decisions to adopt or not to adopt ICTs. A young immigrant, for instance, was more likely to use ICTs because of his or her physical ability and passion to learn. An older immigrant tended to avoid complex technological devices. Immigrants with high incomes (referred to in 12 articles), education (referred to in 11 articles), proficiency in the host country language (referred to in 14 articles), skillful handling of ICT devices (referred to in 14 articles), and positive attitudes (referred to in 8 articles) toward new technology were very likely to adopt and use ICT devices during their settlement process in the host country. When their socio-cultural values (referred to in 11 articles) were not directly challenged by ICTs or the host country environment, immigrants were more likely to use ICTs and interact with locals (Chen, 2010; Tripp, 2010; Tsai, 2006). Based on these influencing factors, there was a low probability that an elderly immigrant with a limited education, low income, unfamiliarity with the local language, and limited ICT skills would adopt and use a computer or the Internet.

Some cultures are restrictive and do not permit children and women to use computers and the Internet because they are considered to be a gateway to inappropriate content (Kabbar & Crump, 2006; Tripp, 2010). They are also afraid that children and women would come into contact with strangers. Finally, some cultures fear the risk of privacy infringement through ICT devices. Technology adoption (or non-adoption) is also related to the attitude, willingness, and motivation of individual users (Davis et al., 1989). It has been shown that some immigrants are hesitant and/or demotivated with respect to ICT adoption and use because of the stress and anxiety that they feel toward complex technology.

Based on the influence factors discussed in the selected articles, a framework is developed (see, Figure 3) to help explain immigrants' dynamics of motivation with respect to ICTs adoption and use. In this framework, the seven factors (age, education, income, culture, ICT skills, language and attitude) are placed as neutral variables. When all or most of the factors point upward, an immigrant is more likely to adopt and use ICTs. For instance, an immigrant with young age, high education, high income, technology-accepting culture, high ICT skills, a positive attitude, and knowledge of the host country language (or the language of the web content) is highly likely to adopt and use ICTs, which in turn, facilitate his/her adjustment to and integration within the host country. On the other hand, when all or most of the seven factors point downward, an immigrant is less likely to adopt and use ICTs, making the adjustment and integration process in the host country difficult. These factors cannot, however, be generalized within all contexts because just one single factor could motivate or demotivate immigrants with respect to their ICTs adoption and usage. For instance, if a person has a negative attitude towards ICTs, he or she might avoid ICTs adoption and use despite scoring positively with respect to the other influence factors, such as high education, ICT skills, young age, high income, and so on.

Figure 3. Framework of ICT motivation

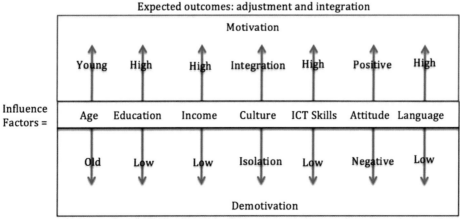

These influence factors are also causes of various digital divides ranging from the digital access divide to the digital outcome divide. Low income, for example, directly restricts access to ICTs, a lack of ICT skills, and knowledge of the language of the web content may create digital skills/knowledge gap and isolation from the host country's culture, and a negative attitude can foster a usage and outcome divide (Van Dijk, 2012). Most of the studies demonstrate that immigrants are affected from a digital divide with respect to access to, skills in, and usage of ICTs, and the Internet (Barth & Veit, 2014). Since most immigrants tend to migrate from developing countries to developed countries, they face a unique situation with respect to digital divide. Similarly, immigrants' family and friends back in the immigrants' country of origin may be affected from a digital access divide because of a lack of Internet infrastructure and availability of digital information in said country. The reverse of this situation can also be seen where immigrants in the host country experience a skills and usage level divide. In Germany, immigrants who lack sufficient skills and knowledge of computers and the Internet are unlikely to use the government's e-services available to the general public (Barth & Veit, 2011). In some of the selected studies (see Bacigalupe & Càmara, 2012; Chen, 2010; Gonzalez & Katz, 2016; Kabbar & Crump, 2006, 2007; Selsky et al., 2013; Williams et al., 2017), for instance, immigrants were found to be hesitant and confused with respect to ICT adoption in that they wanted to experience the benefits of ICT use but they feared the risks (for example, privacy infringement).

To conclude, the articles selected for this study emphasized two key motivations with respect to immigrants' ICT adoption and use: (1) adjustment to and integration within the host country environment and (2) connections to individuals back home. Not surprisingly, immigrants adopt and use ICTs for a smooth transition into and adjustment to a new setting. ICTs facilitate their learning of the host country language, their understanding of its socio-cultural values, and their exploration of opportunities (for example, education, employment, and socialization). Likewise, a connection through ICTs is important as it allows immigrants to keep in touch with family and friends in the country of origin, avoid negative psychological effects of isolation in the host country, connect with ethnic people in host countries, and build and sustain transnational identities. However, this study demonstrates that immigrants can change their habits of technology appropriation depending on the host-country environment. For instance, mobile-friendly environment in London, and slow Internet in Canada influenced Spanish and South Korean immigrants respectively to change their habits of ICT adoption and use. As discussed, there are seven identified factors (i.e., age, culture, education, income, language, ICT skills, attitude) that influence immigrants' motivation positively or negatively with respect to ICT adoption and use. Furthermore, these influencing factors are indicators of digital divides, which are not "singular or static, but multiple, changing over time, and affecting diverse regions and social groups" (Peile & Hijar, 2016, p. 419). Without bridging these divides, immigrants may not adopt and use ICTs for a smooth transition within a new country environment.

DISCUSSION QUESTIONS

1. Do motivation factors change over time when other variables remain the same?
2. To what extent does the culture influence immigrants of different ethnic backgrounds?
3. Do immigrants of the same country but migrated in different countries have similar patterns of ICT adoption and use?

REFERENCES

Ahmed, R., & Veronis, L. (2016). Multicultural media use and immigrant settlement: A comparative study of four communities in Ottawa, Canada. *Journal of International Migration and Integration*, 1–26. doi:10.100712134-016-0488-7

Alam, K., & Imran, S. (2015). The digital divide and social inclusion among refugee migrants: A case in regional Australia. *Information Technology & People*, *28*(2), 344–365. doi:10.1108/ITP-04-2014-0083

Bacigalupe, G., & Cámara, M. (2012). Transnational families and social technologies: Reassessing immigration psychology. *Journal of Ethnic and Migration Studies*, *38*(9), 1425–1438. doi:10.1080/1369 183X.2012.698211

Bacigalupe, G., & Lambe, S. (2011). Virtualizing intimacy: Information communication technologies and transnational families in therapy. *Family Process*, *50*(1), 12–26. doi:10.1111/j.1545-5300.2010.01343.x PMID:21361921

Barth, M., & Veit, D. J. (2011, February). *How digital divide affects public e-services: The role of migration background*. Paper presented at the meeting of Wirtschaftinformatik, Zurich. Retrieved from http://aisel.aisnet.org/wi2011/118

Baum, S., & Mahizhnan, A. (2015). Government-with-you: E-government in Singapore. In A. DeMarco (Ed.), *Public Affairs and Administration: Concepts, Methodologies, Tools, and Applications* (pp. 711–725). Hershey, PA: Information Resources Management Association. doi:10.4018/978-1-4666-8358-7.ch033

Baycan, T., Sahin, M., & Nijkamp, P. (2012). The urban growth potential of second-generation migrant entrepreneurs: A sectoral study on Amsterdam. *International Business Review*, *21*(6), 971–986. doi:10.1016/j.ibusrev.2011.11.005

Benitez, J. L. (2006). Transnational dimensions of the digital divide among Salvadoran immigrants in the Washington DC metropolitan area. *Global Networks*, *6*(2), 181–199. doi:10.1111/j.1471-0374.2006.00140.x

Brinkerhoff, J. M. (2009). *Digital diasporas: Identity and transnational engagement*. Cambridge, UK: Cambridge University Press. doi:10.1017/CBO9780511805158

Chen, W. (2010). Internet-usage patterns of immigrants in the process of intercultural adaptation. *Cyberpsychology, Behavior, and Social Networking*, *13*(4), 387–399. doi:10.1089/cyber.2009.0249 PMID:20712497

Compaine, B. M. (2001). *The digital divide: Facing a crisis or creating a myth?* Cambridge, MA: The MIT Press.

Conteh, C., & Smith, G. (2015). Towards an interactive e-government system in sub-Saharan Africa: Prospects and challenges. *Public affairs and administration: Concepts, methodologies, tools, and applications*, 213.

Davis, F. D., Bagozzi, R. P., & Warshaw, P. R. (1989). User acceptance of computer technology: A comparison of two theoretical models. *Management Science*, *35*(8), 982–1002. doi:10.1287/mnsc.35.8.982

Dewan, S., & Riggins, F. J. (2005). The digital divide: Current and future research directions. *Journal of the Association for Information Systems, 6*(12), 298–337. doi:10.17705/1jais.00074

Ebbers, W. E., Jansen, M. G., & van Deursen, A. J. (2016). Impact of the digital divide on e-government: Expanding from channel choice to channel usage. *Government Information Quarterly, 33*(4), 685–692. doi:10.1016/j.giq.2016.08.007

Everett, A. (2009). *Digital diaspora: A race for cyberspace.* Albany, NY: SUNY Press.

Gonzalez, C., & Katz, V. S. (2016). Transnational family communication as a driver of technology adoption. *International Journal of Communication, 10,* 21.

Gordano Peile, C. G., & Ros Híjar, A. R. (2016). Immigrants and mobile phone uses: Spanish-speaking young adults recently arrived in London. *Mobile Media & Communication, 4*(3), 405–423. doi:10.1177/2050157916655375

Haight, M., Quan-Haase, A., & Corbett, B. A. (2014). Revisiting the digital divide in Canada: The impact of demographic factors on access to the Internet, level of online activity, and social networking site usage. *Information Communication and Society, 17*(4), 503–519. doi:10.1080/1369118X.2014.891633

Harambam, J., Aupers, S., & Houtman, D. (2013). The contentious gap: From digital divide to cultural beliefs about online interactions. *Information Communication and Society, 16*(7), 1093–1114. doi:10.1080/1369118X.2012.687006

Hargittai, E. (2002). Second-level digital divide: Differences in people's online Skills. *First Monday, 7*(4). Retrieved from http://firstmonday.org/ article/view/942/864

Hargittai, E., & Hinnant, A. (2008). Digital inequality: Differences in young adults' use of the Internet. *Communication Research, 35*(5), 602–621. doi:10.1177/0093650208321782

Hohlfeld, T. N., Ritzhaupt, A. D., Barron, A. E., & Kemker, K. (2008). Examining the digital divide in K-12 public schools: Four-year trends for supporting ICT literacy in Florida. *Computers & Education, 51*(4), 1648–1663. doi:10.1016/j.compedu.2008.04.002

Kabbar, E. F., & Crump, B. J. (2006). The factors that influence adoption of ICTs by recent refugee immigrants to New Zealand. *Informing Science: International Journal of an Emerging Transdiscipline, 9,* 111–121. doi:10.28945/475

Kabbar, E. F., & Crump, B. J. (2007). Promoting ICTs Uptake Among the Refugee Immigrant Community in New Zealand. In P. Kommers (Ed.), *Proceedings of the IADIS International Conference e-Society* (pp. 55-62). Lisbon: IADIS Press.

Katz, J., & Aspden, P. (1997). Motivations for and barriers to Internet usage: Results of a national public opinion survey. *Internet Research, 7*(3), 170–188. doi:10.1108/10662249710171814

Khvorostianov, N., Elias, N., & Nimrod, G. (2011). 'Without it I am nothing': The Internet in the lives of older immigrants. *New Media & Society, 14*(4), 583–599. doi:10.1177/1461444811421599

Mesch, G. S. (2012). Minority status and the use of computer-mediated communication: A test of the social diversification hypothesis. *Communication Research, 39*(3), 317–337. doi:10.1177/0093650211398865

Middleton, K. L., & Byus, K. (2011). Information and communications technology adoption and use in small and medium businesses: The influence of Hispanic ethnicity. *Management Research Review*, *34*(1), 98–110. doi:10.1108/01409171111096496

Mikal, J. P., & Woodfield, B. (2015). Refugees, post-migration stress, and Internet use: A qualitative analysis of intercultural adjustment and Internet use among Iraqi and Sudanese refugees to the United States. *Qualitative Health Research*, *25*(10), 1319–1333. doi:10.1177/1049732315601089 PMID:26290542

Mossberger, K., Tolbert, C. J., Bowen, D., & Jimenez, B. (2012). Unraveling different barriers to Internet use: Urban residents and neighborhood effects. *Urban Affairs Review*, *48*(6), 771–810. doi:10.1177/1078087412453713

Nguyen, A. (2012). The digital divide versus the 'digital delay': Implications from a forecasting model of online news adoption and use. *International Journal of Media & Cultural Politics*, *8*(2-3), 251–268. doi:10.1386/macp.8.2-3.251_1

Niehaves, B., & Plattfaut, R. (2014). Internet adoption by the elderly: Employing IS technology acceptance theories for understanding the age-related digital divide. *European Journal of Information Systems*, *23*(6), 708–726. doi:10.1057/ejis.2013.19

Norris, P. (2001). *Digital divide: Civic engagement, information poverty, and the Internet worldwide.* Cambridge, UK: Cambridge University Press. doi:10.1017/CBO9781139164887

NTIA. (1995). *Falling through the Net: A survey of the "have nots" in rural and urban America.* Retrieved from, https://www.ntia.doc.gov/ntiahome/fallingthru.html

NTIA. (1998). *Falling through the Net: New data on the digital divide.* Retrieved from https://www.ntia.doc.gov/ ntiahome/net2

NTIA. (1999). *Falling through the Net: Defining the digital divide.* Retrieved from https://www.ntia.doc.gov/ report/1999/falling-through-net-defining-digital-divide

Okoli, C., & Schabram, K. (2010). A guide to conducting a systematic literature review of information systems research. *Sprouts: Working Papers on Information Systems, 10*(26).

Okunola, O. M., Rowley, J., & Johnson, F. (2017). The multi-dimensional digital divide: Perspectives from an e-government portal in Nigeria. *Government Information Quarterly*, *34*(2), 329–339. doi:10.1016/j.giq.2017.02.002

Organization for Economic Co-operation and Development (OECD). (2001). *The wellbeing of nations: The role of social and human capital.* Paris: Organization for Economic Co-operation and Development.

Peeters, A. L., & d'Haenens, L. (2005). Bridging or bonding? Relationships between integration and media use among ethnic minorities in the Netherlands. *Communications*, *30*(2), 201–231. doi:10.1515/comm.2005.30.2.201

Perry, S. (2017, September 20). Immigration. *Encyclopedia Britannica*. Retrieved from, https://www.britannica.com/topic/immigration

Persaud, A., & Persaud, P. (2015). Rethinking E-government adoption: a user-centered model. In A. DeMarco (Ed.), *Public Affairs and Administration: Concepts, Methodologies, Tools, and Applications* (pp. 657–676). Hershey, PA: Information Resources Management Association. doi:10.4018/978-1-4666-8358-7.ch030

Reddick, C. G., & Turner, M. (2012). Channel choice and public service delivery in Canada: Comparing e-government to traditional service delivery. *Government Information Quarterly*, *29*(1), 1–11. doi:10.1016/j.giq.2011.03.005

Roy, J. (2006). Government of Canada. In *E-government in Canada: Transformation for the digital age* (pp. 111–137). Ottawa: University of Ottawa Press.

Selsky, C., Luta, G., Noone, A. M., Huerta, E. E., & Mandelblatt, J. S. (2013). Internet access and online cancer information seeking among Latino immigrants from safety net clinics. *Journal of Health Communication*, *18*(1), 58–70. doi:10.1080/10810730.2012.688248 PMID:23066874

Selwyn, N., Gorard, S., & Furlong, J. (2005). Whose Internet is it anyway? Exploring adults' (non) use of the Internet in everyday life. *European Journal of Communication*, *20*(1), 5–26. doi:10.1177/0267323105049631

Shareef, M. A., Kumar, V., Kumar, U., & Dwivedi, Y. K. (2011). e-government adoption model (GAM): Differing service maturity levels. *Government Information Quarterly*, *28*(1), 17–35. doi:10.1016/j.giq.2010.05.006

Spaiser, V. (2013). Young immigrants' Internet political participation in Germany: Comparing German east Europeans and German Turks. *International Journal of E-Politics*, *4*(1), 1–17. doi:10.4018/jep.2013010101

Sparks, C. (2013). What is the "digital divide" and why is it important? *Javnost-The Public*, *20*(2), 27–46. doi:10.1080/13183222.2013.11009113

Tripp, L. M. (2010). 'The computer is not for you to be looking around, it is for schoolwork': Challenges for digital inclusion as Latino immigrant families negotiate children's access to the Internet. *New Media & Society*, *13*(4), 552–567. doi:10.1177/1461444810375293

Tsai, J. H. C. (2006). Use of computer technology to enhance immigrant families' adaptation. *Journal of Nursing Scholarship*, *38*(1), 87–93. doi:10.1111/j.1547-5069.2006.00082.x PMID:16579329

van Dijk, J. A. G. M. (2012). The evolution of the digital divide: The digital divide turns to inequality of skills and usage. In J. Bus, M. Crompton, M. Hildebrandt, & G. Metakides (Eds.), Digital Enlightenment Yearbook 2012 (pp. 57-75). Amsterdam, The Netherlands: IOS Press.

Warschauer, M. (2003). Dissecting the "digital divide": A case study in Egypt. *The Information Society*, *19*(4), 297–304. doi:10.1080/01972240309490

Wellman, C. H. (2015). Immigration. *The Stanford encyclopaedia of philosophy* (Summer 2015 Edition). Retrieved from, https://plato.stanford.edu/archives/sum2015/entries/immigration/

Williams, D. E., Gavino, M. C., & Jacobson, D. W. (2017). Latino Entrepreneurs and Technology Usage: Ethnic Identity, Resistance, Self-Efficacy. *Journal of Business Diversity*, *17*(1).

Yoon, K. (2016). The migrant lives of the digital generation. *Continuum, 30*(4), 369–380. doi:10.1080/10304312.2016.1141867

Zaidi, A. U., Fernando, S., & Ammar, N. (2015). An exploratory study of the impact of information communication technology (ICT) or computer mediated communication (CMC) on the level of violence and access to service among intimate partner violence (IPV) survivors in Canada. *Technology in Society, 41*, 91–97. doi:10.1016/j.techsoc.2014.12.003

ENDNOTE

[1]   Scholars use various terms to denote influence factors with respect to immigrants' ICT adoption and use, such as employment, cost, affordability, peer-pressure, neighborhood factor, and gender. For the purpose of this article, the terms employment, cost, and affordability are incorporated within income, peer-pressure, and neighborhood factor are incorporated within attitudes, and self-efficacy is incorporated within ICT skills. Similarly, gender is incorporated within culture because different treatment based on gender in a particular ethnicity is a cultural issue.

Compilation of References

Abdelghaffar, H. (2009). Citizens' Readiness for E-government in Developing Countries (CREG). In *Proceedings of the 8th European Conference on Information Warfare and Security, Military Academy, Lisbon and the University of Minho, Braga, Portugal, 6-7 July 2009* (p. 11). Academic Conferences Limited.

Abdelghaffar, H., & Magdy, Y. (2012). The Adoption Of Mobile Government Services In Developing Countries: The case of Egypt. *International Journal of Information*, 2(4), 333–341.

ABET. (2017). Retrieved from ABOUT ABET.: Http://www.abet.org/about-abet/

Abu Tair, H. Y., & Abu-Shanab, E. A. (2014). Mobile Government Services: Challenges and Opportunities. *International Journal of Technology Diffusion*, 5(1), 17–25. doi:10.4018/ijtd.2014010102

Abu-Shanab, E., & Ghaleb, O. (2012). Adoption of Mobile Commerce Technology: An Involvement of Trust and Risk Concerns. *International Journal of Technology Diffusion*, 3(2), 36–49. doi:10.4018/jtd.2012040104

Abu-Taieh, E. (2016). Social Network Service for Scientists Difficulties Facing E-Publishing over Cloud Computing. International Journal of Technology Diffusion, 7(3), 10-20. doi:10.4018/IJTD.2016070102

Abu-Taieh, E. (2017). *Cyber Security Body of Knowledge. SC2 IEEE Conference*. IEEE. Retrieved from https://grid.chu.edu.tw/sc2-2017/AcceptedPaperList.php

Academia.edu. (2016). About academia.edu. Retrieved from http://www.academia.edu

ACM & IEEE. (2013). *Curriculum Guidelines for Undergraduate Degree Programs in Computer Science*. New York: ACM IEEE; doi:10.1145/2534860

ACM & IEEE. (2016). *Curriculum Guidelines for Undergraduate Degree Programs in Computer Engineering*. New York: ACM IEEE; doi:10.1145/3025098

ACM & IEEE. (2017). Information Technology Curricula 2017. ACM IEEE. doi:10.1145/3173161

ACM. (2017). *About*. Retrieved from The ACM Orgnization: www.acm.org

Adams, D. A., Nelson, R. R., & Todd, P. A. (1992). Perceived usefulness, ease of use and usage of information technology: Replication. *Management Information Systems Quarterly*, 16(June), 227–247. doi:10.2307/249577

Adcock, R., Hutchison, N., & Nielsen, C. (2016). Defining an architecture for the Systems Engineering Body of Knowledge. *2016 Annual IEEE Systems Conference (SysCon)* (pp. 1-7). Orlando, FL: IEEE. 10.1109/SYSCON.2016.7490640

Ademola, F. S. (2007). Theories of social conflict in best, 5.An Edited Introduction to Peace and Conflict Studies in. Ibadan: Spectrum Books limited.

Adida, B., & Birbeck, M. (2008). RDFa primer - bridging the human and data webs. *W3C Recommendation*. Retrieved from http://www.w3.org/TR/xhtml-rdfa-primer/

Agarwal, R., & Prasad, J. A. (1998). Conceptual and Operational Definition of Personal Innovativeness in the Domain of Information Technology. *Information System Research, 19*(2), 204-215.

Agarwal, J. (2015). Improving resilience through vulnerability assessment and management. *Civil Engineering and Environmental Systems, 32*(1/2), 5–17. doi:10.1080/10286608.2015.1025065

Agarwal, R., & Prasad, J. (1997). The Role of Innovation Characteristics and Perceived Voluntariness in the Acceptance of Information Technologies. *Decision Sciences, 28*(3), 557–582. doi:10.1111/j.1540-5915.1997.tb01322.x

Agarwal, V., Chafie, G., Karnik, N., Kumar, A., Kundu, A., Shahabuddin, J., & Varma, P. (2001). *An architecture for virtual server farms. Research Report*. IBM India Research Lab.

Agnes, M. (2017). *3 Important Crisis Management Trend Projections For 2017*. Retrieved on January, 2018, from https://www.forbes.com/sites/melissaagnes/2017/01/11/3-important-crisis-management-trend-projections-for-2017/#39d5a22663e0

Ahmad, N., Omar, A., & Ramayah, T. (2010). Consumer Lifestyles and Online shopping continuance intention. *Business Strategy Series, 11*(4), 227–243. doi:10.1108/17515631011063767

Ahmed, S. I., Haque, M. R., Guha, S., Rifat, M. R., & Dell, N. (2017). Privacy, security, and surveillance in the Global South: A study of biometric mobile SIM registration in Bangladesh. In *ACM Proceedings of the 2017 CHI Conference on Human Factors in Computing Systems* (pp. 906-918). ACM.

Ahmed, R., & Veronis, L. (2016). Multicultural media use and immigrant settlement: A comparative study of four communities in Ottawa, Canada. *Journal of International Migration and Integration*, 1–26. doi:10.100712134-016-0488-7

Aiken, L., & West, S. (1991). *Multiple regression: Testing and Interpreting Interactions*. Newbury Park, CA: Sage Publications.

Ainin, S., Naqshbandi, M. M., & Dezdar, S. (2016). Impact of adoption of Green IT practices on organizational performance. *Quality & Quantity, 50*(5), 1929–1948. doi:10.100711135-015-0244-7

Ajayi, B. (2015). Telecommunications Law and Policy to Protect Subscribers' of Mobile Phones in Africa. *Journal Open Access Library, 3*, 121–148.

Ajjan, H., Kumar, R. L., & Subramaniam, C. (2013). Understanding differences between adopters and non-adopters of information technology. Project portfolio management. *International Journal of Information Technology & Decision Making, 12*(6), 1151–1174. doi:10.1142/S0219622013400129

Ajzen, I. (1985). From intentions to actions: A theory of planned behavior. In J. Kuhl & J. Beckman (Eds.), *Action-control: From cognition to behavior* (pp. 11–39). Heidelberg, Germany: Springer. doi:10.1007/978-3-642-69746-3_2

Ajzen, I. (1988). *Attitudes, personality and behaviour*. Milton Keynes, UK: Open University Press.

Ajzen, I. (1991). The theory of planned behavior. *Organizational Behavior and Human Decision Processes, 50*(2), 179–211. doi:10.1016/0749-5978(91)90020-T

Ajzen, I., & Fishbein, M. (1980). *Understanding attitudes and predicting social behavior*. Englewood Cliffs, NJ: Prentice-Hall.

Ajzen, I., & Fishbein, M. (1980). *Understanding Attitudes and Predicting Social Behavior*. Englewood Cliffs, NJ: Prentice-Hall.

Akhter, S., & Rahman, N. (2015). Building a customer inquiry database system. *International Journal of Technology Diffusion, 6*(2), 59–76. doi:10.4018/IJTD.2015040104

Akhter, S., Rahman, N., & Rahman, M. N. (2014). Competitive strategies in the computer industry. *International Journal of Technology Diffusion, 5*(1), 73–88. doi:10.4018/ijtd.2014010106

Alam, K., & Imran, S. (2015). The digital divide and social inclusion among refugee migrants: A case in regional Australia. *Information Technology & People, 28*(2), 344–365. doi:10.1108/ITP-04-2014-0083

Alampay, E. A., & Hechanova, R. M. (2010). Monitoring employee use of the Internet in Philippine organizations. *The Electronic Journal on Information Systems in Developing Countries, 40*(5), 1–20. doi:10.1002/j.1681-4835.2010.tb00287.x

Alario-Hoyos, C., Bote-Lorenzo, M. L., Gómez-Sánchez, E., Asensio-Pérez, J. I., Vega-Gorgojo, G., & Ruiz-Calleja, A. (2013). GLUE! An architecture for the integration of external tools in Virtual Learning Environments. *Computers & Education, 60*(1), 122–137. doi:10.1016/j.compedu.2012.08.010

Alba, A., Coden, A., Gentile, A. L., Gruhl, D., Ristoski, P., & Welch, S. (2017, December). Multi-lingual Concept Extraction with Linked Data and Human-in-the-Loop. In *Proceedings of the Knowledge Capture Conference*. ACM. 10.1145/3148011.3148021

Alberts, C., & Dorofee, A. (2012). *Mission Risk Diagnostic (MRD) Method Description(CMU/SEI-2012-TN-005)*. Carnegie Mellon University. Retrieved 12 12, 2017, from https://resources.sei.cmu.edu/asset_files/Technical-Note/2012_004_001_15431.pdf

Alberts, C., & Woody, C. (2017). *Prototype Software Assurance Framework (SAF):Introduction and Overview (CMU/SEI-2017-TN-001)*. Carnegie Mellon University. Retrieved 12 12, 2017, from https://resources.sei.cmu.edu/asset_files/TechnicalNote/2010_004_001_15191.pdf

Alberts, C., Allen, J., & Stoddard, R. (2010). *Integrated Measurement and Analysis Framework for Software Security(CMU/SEI-2010-TN-025)*. Carnegie Mellon University. Retrieved 9 5, 2017, from http://resources.sei.cmu.edu/library/asset-view.cfm?AssetID=9369

Al-Debei, M. M., Mamoun, N., Akroush, N. M., & Ashouri, I. M. (2015). Consumer attitudes towards online shopping: The effects of trust, perceived benefits, and perceived web quality. *Internet Research, 25*(5), 707–733. doi:10.1108/IntR-05-2014-0146

Alexa. (n.d.). Retrieved from alexa.com

Alexander, K., Cyganiak, R., Hausenblas, M., & Zhao, J. (2009). Describing linked datasets. *Proceedings of the WWW Workshop on Linked Data on the Web*.

Allemang, D., & Hendler, J. (2011). *Semantic Web for the Working Ontologist, Effective Modeling in RDFS and OWL* (2nd ed.). Morgan Kaufmann publishers.

Allen, B. R., & Boynton, A. C. (1991). Information Architecture: In Search of Efficient Flexibility. MIS Quarterly, 435-445.

Alliance, A. (2001). *Agile manifesto*. Retrieved from http://www.agilemanifesto.org

Alvarez, A. (2012). Microsoft Application Virtualization Advanced Guide: Master Microsoft App-V by Taking a Deep Dive into Advanced Topics and Acquire All the Necessary Skills to Optimize Your Application Virtualization Platform. Birmingham, UK: Packt Publishing.

Amara, S., Macedo, J., Bendella, F., & Santos, A. (2016). Group Formation in Mobile Computer Supported Collaborative Learning Contexts: A Systematic Literature Review. *Journal of Educational Technology & Society, 19*(2), 258–273.

American Telemedicine Association (AHA). (2013). *What is Telemedicine?* Retrieved from http://www.americantelemed. org/learn/what-is-telemedicine

Anderson, A., Dossick, C. S., Iorio, J., & Taylor, J. E. (2017). The impact of avatars, social norms and copresence on the collaboration effectiveness of AEC virtual teams. *Journal of Information Technology in Construction, 22*(15), 287–304.

Anderson, T. (2008). *The Theory and Practice of Online Learning.* Athabasca University Press.

ANECA. (2017). Retrieved from National Agency for Quality Assessment and Accreditation of Spain ANECA: www. aneca.es/

Angst, C. M., & Agarwal, R. (2009). Adoption of Electronic Health Records in the Presence of Privacy Concerns: The Elaboration Likelihood Model and Individual Persuasion. *Management Information Systems Quarterly, 33*(2), 339–370. doi:10.2307/20650295

Annan, F., & Sanoh, A. (2017). *Mobile infrastructure and rural business enterprises: Evidence from SIM registration mandate in Niger.* Research Policy Working Paper 8778. Poverty and Equity Global Practice Group, World Bank Group.

Antoniadis, I., Saprikis, V., & Politis, K. (2014). Investigating internet users' perceptions towards online shoping: An empirical study on Greek university students. *2nd International Conference on Contemporary Marketing Issues*, 66-71.

Applegate, L. M., Austin, R. D., & Soule, D. L. (2009). *Corporate Information Strategy and Management: Text and Cases.* Boston: McGraw-Hill.

ARC. (2018, Feb 18). Retrieved from The Australian Research Council: http://www.arc.gov.au/news-media/media-releases/arc-seeks-sectors-views-journal-rankings-era-initiative

Arias-Báez, M. P., Pavlich-Mariscal, J. A., & Ramos, A. C. (2013). Forming adapted teams oriented to collaboration: Detailed design and case study. *journal. Dyna (Bilbao), 10*(1), 87–94.

Arinze, B. (2012). E-Research Collaboration in Academia and Industry. *International Journal of e-Collaboration, 8*(2), 1–13. doi:10.4018/jec.2012040101

Aririguzo, M., & Agbaraji, E. (2016). Mobile phone registration for developing countries: Gains and constraints. *European Journal of Basic and Applied Science, 3*(3), 44–52.

Armstrong, A., & Hagel, J. (1996, May). The real value of on-line communities. *Harvard Business Review*, 134–141.

Arpaci, I. (2013). *Organizational adoption of mobile communication technologies* (Doctoral dissertation). Department of Information Systems, Middle East Technical University.

Arpaci, I. (2015). A qualitative study on the adoption of bring your own device (BYOD) Practice. *International Journal of E-Adoption, 7*(2), 1–14. doi:10.4018/IJEA.2015070101

Arpaci, I. (2016). Understanding and predicting students' intention to use mobile cloud storage services. *Computers in Human Behavior, 58*, 150–157. doi:10.1016/j.chb.2015.12.067

Arpaci, I. (2017). Antecedents and consequences of cloud computing adoption in education to achieve knowledge management. *Computers in Human Behavior, 70*, 382–390. doi:10.1016/j.chb.2017.01.024

Arpaci, I., Yardimci Cetin, Y., & Turetken, O. (2015). A cross-cultural analysis of smartphone adoption by Canadian and Turkish organizations. *Journal of Global Information Technology Management, 18*(3), 214–238. doi:10.1080/109 7198X.2015.1080052

Arpaci, I., Yardimci Cetin, Y., & Turetken, O. (2015). Impact of Perceived Security on Organizational Adoption of Smartphones. *Cyberpsychology, Behavior, and Social Networking*, *18*(10), 602–608. doi:10.1089/cyber.2015.0243 PMID:26383763

Arshad, A., & Ameen, K. (2015). Usage patterns of Punjab University Library website: A transactional log analysis study. *The Electronic Library*, *33*(1), 65–74. doi:10.1108/EL-12-2012-0161

Arthur, C. (2011). Egypt blocks social media websites in attempted clampdown on unrest. *The Guardian*. Retrieved from http://www.guardian.co.uk/world/2011/jan/26/egypt-blocks-social-media-websites

Asgary, A. (2016). Business continuity and disaster risk management in business education: Case of York University. *AD-Minister*, (28): 49–72. doi:10.17230/ad-minister.28.3

Ashcroft, L. S. (1997). Crisis Management - Public Relations. *Journal of Managerial Psychology*, *12*(5), 325–332. doi:10.1108/02683949710183522

Ashrafi, R., & Murtaza, M. (2008). Use and impact of ICT on SMEs in Oman. *The Electronic Information Systems Evaluations*, *11*(3), 125–138.

Auer, S., Buhmann, L., & Dirschl, C. (2012). Managing the life-cycle of linked data with the lod2 stack. *Proceedings of the International Semantic Web Conference, ISWC*. 10.1007/978-3-642-35173-0_1

Auer, S., & Lehmann, J. (2010). Creating knowledge out of interlinked data. *Semantic Web Journal*, *1*(1), 97–104.

Auger, P., & Gallaugher, J. (1997). Factors affecting the adoption of an Internet-based sales presence for small businesses. *The Information Society*, *13*(1), 55–74. doi:10.1080/019722497129287

Avery, S., & Tracy, D. G. (2014). Using transaction log analysis to assess student search behavior in the library instruction classroom. *RSR. Reference Services Review*, *42*(2), 320–335. doi:10.1108/RSR-08-2013-0044

Ax, C., & Greve, J. (2017). Adoption of management accounting innovations: Organizational culture compatibility and perceived outcomes. *Management Accounting Research*, *34*, 59–74. doi:10.1016/j.mar.2016.07.007

Bachlechner, D., Thalmann, S., & Maier, R. (2014). Security and compliance challenges in complex IT outsourcing arrangements: A multi-stakeholder perspective. *Computers & Security*, *40*, 38–59. doi:10.1016/j.cose.2013.11.002

Bach, M. P., Čeljo, A., & Zoroja, J. (2016). Technology Acceptance Model for Business Intelligence Systems: Preliminary Research. *Procedia Computer Science*, *100*, 995–1001. doi:10.1016/j.procs.2016.09.270

Bachour, K., Kaplan, F., & Dillenbourg, P. (2010). An interactive table for supporting participation balance in face-to-face collaborative learning. *IEEE Transactions on Learning Technologies*, *3*(3), 203–213. doi:10.1109/TLT.2010.18

Bacigalupe, G., & Cámara, M. (2012). Transnational families and social technologies: Reassessing immigration psychology. *Journal of Ethnic and Migration Studies*, *38*(9), 1425–1438. doi:10.1080/1369183X.2012.698211

Bacigalupe, G., & Lambe, S. (2011). Virtualizing intimacy: Information communication technologies and transnational families in therapy. *Family Process*, *50*(1), 12–26. doi:10.1111/j.1545-5300.2010.01343.x PMID:21361921

Bailey, J. E., & Pearson, S. W. (1983). Development of a Tool for Measuring and Analyzing Computer User Satisfaction. *Management Science*, *29*(5), 530–545. doi:10.1287/mnsc.29.5.530

Bajgoric, N. (2000). Web-based Information Access for Agile Management. *International Journal of Agile Management Systems*, *2*(2), 121–129. doi:10.1108/14654650010337131

Balcı, A., Medeni, T. D., & Nohutçu, A. (2013). Turkish Case of E-Government Strategy Development and Policy-Formulation Process: Recent Developments on Evaluations of E-Government Rankings. *International Journal of Technology Diffusion*, *4*(4), 27–44. doi:10.4018/ijtd.2013100102

Bal, J., Wilding, R., & Gundry, J. (1999). Virtual Teaming in the Agile Supply Chain. *International Journal of Logistics Management*, *10*(2), 71–82. doi:10.1108/09574099910806003

Bande, L. (2011). A case for cybercrime legislation in Malawi. *Malawi Law Journal*, *5*(2), 93–113.

Banerjee, S. (2017). *Top 10 Best Selling Computer Servers & Accessories. RS-WebSols.* Retrieved on 2/19/2018 from: https://www.rswebsols.com/reviews/product-reviews/top-10-best-selling-computer-servers-accessories

Bankole, F., Osei-Bryson, K.-M., & Brown, I. (2013). The Impact of ICT Investments on Human Development: A Regression Splines Analysis. *Journal of Global Information Technology Management*, *16*(2), 59–85. doi:10.1080/1097198X.2013.10845636

Banks, K. F. (2001). *Crisis Communications: A case Book Approach 2nd Edi.* Mahwah, NJ: Lawrence Erlbaum.

Bardhan, I., Krishnan, V., & Lin, S. (2013). Research note—business value of information technology: Testing the interaction effect of IT and R&D on Tobin's Q. *Information Systems Research*, *24*(4), 1147–1161. doi:10.1287/isre.2013.0481

Barnes, A., & Indie Bound, N. (2017). *How to Communicate Effectively During a Crisis.* Retrieved on January, 2018, from https://www.entrepreneur.com/article/290446

Barnes, D., Dyerson, R., & Harindranath, G. (2008). *If it isn't broken, don't fix it.* Retrieved from http:// www.rhul.ac.uk/Management/Research/PRISM/index.html

Barney, J. B. (1991). Firm Resources and Sustained Competitive Advantage. *Journal of Management*, *17*(1), 24. doi:10.1177/014920639101700108

Barth, M., & Veit, D. J. (2011, February). *How digital divide affects public e-services: The role of migration background.* Paper presented at the meeting of Wirtschaftinformatik, Zurich. Retrieved from http://aisel.aisnet.org/wi2011/118

Barthe-Delanoë, A. M., Truptil, S., Bénaben, F., & Pingaud, H. (2014). Event-driven agility of interoperability during the Run-time of collaborative processes. *Decision Support Systems*, *59*, 171–179. doi:10.1016/j.dss.2013.11.005

Barton, L. (2011). *Crisis in Organizations II* (2nd ed.). Cincinnati, OH: College Divisions South-Western.

Bass, L., Weber, I., & Zhu, L. (2015). *DevOps: A Software Architect's Perspective.* Addison-Wesley Professional.

Baum, S., & Mahizhnan, A. (2015). Government-with-you: E-government in Singapore. In A. DeMarco (Ed.), *Public Affairs and Administration: Concepts, Methodologies, Tools, and Applications* (pp. 711–725). Hershey, PA: Information Resources Management Association. doi:10.4018/978-1-4666-8358-7.ch033

Baycan, T., Sahin, M., & Nijkamp, P. (2012). The urban growth potential of second-generation migrant entrepreneurs: A sectoral study on Amsterdam. *International Business Review*, *21*(6), 971–986. doi:10.1016/j.ibusrev.2011.11.005

BBC News. (2017). *Uber is officially a cab firm, says European Court.* Retrieved February 1, 2018 from http://www.bbc.com/news/business-42423627

Beall, J. (2014). *Google Scholar is Filled with Junk Science.* Retrieved 3 30, 2016, from Scholarly Open Access: https://scholarlyoa.com/2014/11/04/google-scholar-is-filled-with-junk-science/

Bechhofer, S., Buchan, I., de Roure, D., Missier, P., Ainsworth, J., Bhagat, J., & Goble, C. (2013). Why linked data is not enough for scientists. *Future Generation Computer Systems*, *29*(2), 599–611. doi:10.1016/j.future.2011.08.004

Beckett, D. (2004). Rdf/XML syntax specification (revised). *W3C Recommendation*. Retrieved from HTTP:// www. w3.org/TR/rdf-syntax-grammar/

Beile, P. M. (2005). *Development and Validation of the Beile Test of Information Literacy for Education (B-TILED)* (PhD thesis). College of Education, Central Florida Univ., Orlando, FL.

Beil, R., Ford, G., & Jackson, J. (2005). On the relationship between telecommunications investment and economic growth in the United States. *International Economic Journal*, *19*(1), 3–9. doi:10.1080/1351161042000320399

Bellaaj, M., Bernard, P., Pecquet, P., & Plaisent, M. (2008). Organizational, environmental, and technological factors relating to benefits of web site adoption. *International Journal of Global Business*, *1*(1), 44–64.

Bell, B. S., & Kozlowski, S. W. J. (2002). A typology of virtual teams: Implications for effective leadership. *Group & Organization Management*, *27*(1), 14–49. doi:10.1177/1059601102027001003

Benbasat, I., Goldstein, D. K., & Mead, M. (1987). The Case Research Strategy in Studies of Information Systems. *Management Information Systems Quarterly*, *11*(3), 369–385. doi:10.2307/248684

Benitez, J. L. (2006). Transnational dimensions of the digital divide among Salvadoran immigrants in the Washington DC metropolitan area. *Global Networks*, *6*(2), 181–199. doi:10.1111/j.1471-0374.2006.00140.x

Benoit, H. (2008). *Digital Television: Satellite, Cable, Terrestrial, IPTV, Mobile TV in the DVB Framework*. Oxford, UK: Focal Press.

Benslimane, Y., Yang, Z., & Bahli, B. (2016). Information Security between Standards, Certifications and Technologies: An Empirical Study. *Information Science and Security (ICISS), 2016 International Conference on* (pp. 1-5). Pattaya, Thailand: IEEE. doi:10.1109/ICISSEC.2016.7885859

Benson, D., & Jordan, A. (2011). What have we learned from policy transfer research? Dolowitz and Marsh revisited. *Political Studies Review*, *9*(3), 366–378. doi:10.1111/j.1478-9302.2011.00240.x

Bergman, M. K., & Giasson, F. (2008). *Umbel ontology*. Technical report, Structured Dynamics LLC. Retrieved from https://github.com/structureddynamics/UMBEL/blob/master/Doc/UMBEL_TR-11-2-10.pdf

Berners Lee, T. (2009). *Linked data design issues*. Retrieved from http://www.w3.org/DesignIssues/LinkedData.htmls

Bernhardt, J. M., Lariscy, R. A. W., Parrott, R. L., Silk, K. J., & Felter, E. M. (2002). Perceived Barriers to Internet-based Health Communication on Human Genetics. *Journal of Health Communication*, *7*(4), 325–340. doi:10.1080/10810730290088166 PMID:12356290

Bernroider, E. W. N., & Schmöllerl, P. (2013). A technological, organisational, and environmental analysis of decision making methodologies and satisfaction in the context of IT induced business transformations. *European Journal of Operational Research*, *224*(1), 141–153. doi:10.1016/j.ejor.2012.07.025

Bernstein, J. (2016). *The 10 Steps of Crisis Communications*. Retrieved on January 31, 2018, from https://www.bernsteincrisismanagement.com/the-10-steps-of-crisis-communications/

BERR. (2008). Retrieved from July 15, 2015 http://stats.berr.gov.uk/ed/sme

Bertot, J., Paul, J., & Justin, G. (2012). Promoting Transparency and Accountability through ICTs, Social Media, and Collaborative E-Government. Transforming Government: People, Process, and Policy, 6(1), 78–91.

Best Reviews. (2018). Best Chromebooks - Updated February 2018. *Best Reviews*. Retrieved on 2/19/2018 from: http:// bestreviews.com/best-chromebooks

Betts, K. (2017). *Crisis management for entrepreneurs: how to deal with PR disasters*. Retrieved on January, 2018, from https://www.theguardian.com

Beyer, L. M., & Browning, L. D. (1999). Transforming an industry in crisis: Charisma, routinization, and supportive cultural leadership. *The Leadership Quarterly*, *10*(3), 483–520. doi:10.1016/S1048-9843(99)00026-0

Bharadwaj, A. S. (2000). A Resource-Based Perspective on Information Technology Competences and Firm Performance: An Empirical Investigation. *Management Information Systems Quarterly*, *24*(1), 28. doi:10.2307/3250983

Bhat, S. K., Pande, N., & Ahuja, V. (2017). Virtual Team Effectiveness: An Empirical Study Using SEM. *Procedia Computer Science*, *122*, 33–41. doi:10.1016/j.procs.2017.11.338

Bhattacherjee, A., & Hikmet, N. (2007). Physicians' Resistance Toward Healthcare Information Technology: A Theoretical Model and Empirical Test. *European Journal of Information Systems*, *16*(6), 725–737. doi:10.1057/palgrave.ejis.3000717

Biddle, B., White, A., & Woods, S. (2010). How many standards in a laptop? (And other empirical questions). *Proceedings of the ITU-T, Beyond the Internet? – Innovations for Future Networks and Services, Kaleidoscope Conference.* Available at SSRN: http://ssrn.com/abstract=1619440

Biessmann, F., & Harth, A. (2010). Analysing dependency dynamics in Web data. *Proceedings of the Linked AI: AAAI Spring Symposium.*

Bijwe, A., & Mead, N. (2010). *Adapting the SQUARE Process for Privacy Requirements Engineering (CMU/SEI-2010-TN-022). Carnegie Mellon University.* Retrieved from https://resources.sei.cmu.edu/library/asset-view.cfm?AssetID=9357

Bilgihan, A. (2016). Gen Y customer loyalty in online shopping: An integrated model of trust, user experience and branding. *Computers in Human Behavior*, *61*, 103–113. doi:10.1016/j.chb.2016.03.014

Billington, M., & Billington, P. (2010). Innovative business education methods for leaders and managers. *The Journal of Applied Business and Economics*, *11*(4), 44–55.

Birdsall, W. F. (2007). Web 2.0 as a Social Movement. *Webology*, *4*(2), 5–11.

Bishop, L. S., Holmes, B. J., & Kelley, C. M. (2005). *National Consumer Health Privacy Survey*. Oakland, CA: California HealthCare Foundation.

Bizer, C., & Heath, T. (2011). *Evolving the Web into a Global Data Space*. Morgan and Claypool Publishers. doi:10.1007/978-3-642-24577-0_1

Bizer, C., Heath, T., & Berners Lee, T. (2009). Linked data – the story so far. *International Journal on Semantic Web and Information Systems*, *5*(3), 1–22. doi:10.4018/jswis.2009081901

Bizer, C., & Schultz, A. (2009). The Berlin SPARQL benchmark. *International Journal on Semantic Web and Information Systems*, *5*(2), 1–24. doi:10.4018/jswis.2009040101

Blackburn, R., Furst, S., & Rosen, B. (2003). *Building a winning virtual team. Virtual teams that work: Creating conditions for virtual team effectiveness*. San Francisco, CA: Jossey-Bass.

Black, S. (1989). *Introduction to Public Relations*. West African Book Publishers Ltd.

Blau, J. R., & McKinley, W. (1979). Idea, Complexity, and Innovation. *Administrative Science Quarterly*, *24*(2), 200–219. doi:10.2307/2392494

Blili, S., & Raymond, L. (1993). Information technology: Threats and Opportunities for Small and Medium Enterprises. *International Journal of Information Management*, *13*(6), 439–448. doi:10.1016/0268-4012(93)90060-H

Blocker, C. P., Flint, D. J., Myers, M. B., & Slater, S. F. (2011). Proactive customer orientation and its role for creating customer value in global markets. *Journal of the Academy of Marketing Science, 39*(2), 216–233. doi:10.100711747-010-0202-9

Bobrowski, M., Marrie, M., & Yankelevich, D. (1999). A homogeneous framework to measure data quality. *Proceeding of Information Quality workshop.*

Bock, G. W., Ahuja, M. K., Suh, A., & Yap, L. X. (2015). Sustainability of a virtual community: Integrating individual and structural dynamics. *Journal of the Association for Information Systems, 16*(6), 3. doi:10.17705/1jais.00400

Bogdan, R. C., & Biklen, S. K. (1982). *Qualitative research for education: An introduction to theory and methods.* Boston: Allyn and Bacon.

Bojars, U., Passant, A., Breslin, J., & Decker, S. (2008). Social Network and Data Portability using Semantic Web Technologies. *Proceedings of the Workshop on Social Aspects of the Web.*

Bonoma, T. V. (1985). Case Research in Marketing: Opportunities, Problems, and a Process. *JMR, Journal of Marketing Research, 22*(2), 199–208. doi:10.2307/3151365

Bouras, C., Giannaka, E., & Tsiatsos, T. (2009). E-Collaboration Concepts, Systems, and Applications. In N. Kock (Ed.), *E-Collaboration: Concepts, Methodologies, Tools, and Applications* (pp. 8–16). Hershey, PA: Information Science Reference. doi:10.4018/978-1-60566-652-5.ch002

Bourque, P., & Fairley, R. (2014). Guide to the Software Engineering Body of Knowledge (Swebok(R)): Version 3.0 (3rd ed.). Los Alamitos, CA: IEEE Computer Society Press.

Bowen, G. (2009). Document Analysis as a Qualitative research method. *Qualitative Research Journal, 9*(2), 28–40. doi:10.3316/QRJ0902027

Boyce, C., & Neale, B. (2006). *Conducting In-depth Interviews: A Guide for Designing and Conducting In-Depth Interviews for Evaluation Input.* Pathfinder International.

Boynton, A. C. (1993). Achieving Dynamic Stability Through Information Technology. *California Management Review, 35*(Winter), 58–77. doi:10.2307/41166722

Bracher, S., & Krishnan, P. (2012). Supporting Secure Information Flow: An Engineering Approach. *International Journal of e-Collaboration, 8*(1), 17–35. doi:10.4018/jec.2012010102

Bracy, C., Bevill, S., & Roach, T. D. (2010). The millennial generation: Recommendations for overcoming teaching challenges. *Proceedings of the Academy of Educational Leadership, 15*(2), 21–25.

Brandt, V., England, W., & Ward, S. (2011). Virtual teams. *Research Technology Management, 54*(6), 62–63.

Bratitsis, T., & Demetriadis, S. (2012). Perspectives on Tools for Computer-Supported Collaborative Learning. *International Journal of e-Collaboration, 8*(4), 1–7. doi:10.4018/jec.2012100101

Bratitsis, T., & Demetriadis, S. (2013). Research approaches in computer-supported collaborative learning. *International Journal of e-Collaboration, 9*(1), 1–8. doi:10.4018/jec.2013010101

Braumoeller, B. (2004). Hypothesis Testing and Multiplicative Interaction Terms. *International Organization, 58*(4), 807–820. doi:10.1017/S0020818304040251

Braun, D., & Gilardi, F. (2006). Taking 'Galton's problem' seriously: Towards a theory of policy diffusion. *Journal of Theoretical Politics, 18*(3), 298–322. doi:10.1177/0951629806064351

Breazeal, C., Kidd, C. D., Thomaz, A. L., Hoffman, G., & Berlin, M. (2005). Effects of nonverbal communication on efficiency and robustness in human-robot teamwork. *IEEE/RSJ International Conference on Intelligent Robots and Systems*, 383-388. 10.1109/IROS.2005.1545011

Breindl, Y., & Francq, P. (2008). Can Web2.0 Applications Save E-Democracy? A Study Of How New Internet Applications May Enhance Citizen Participation In Political Process Online. *International Journal of E-Democracy, 1*(1), 14-31.

Brentani, U. D., & Droge, C. (1988). Determinants of the new product screening decision: A structural model analysis. *International Journal of Research in Marketing, 5*(2), 91–106. doi:10.1016/0167-8116(88)90062-6

Bresnahan, T. F., Brynjolfsson, E., & Hitt, L. M. (2002). Information technology, workplace organization, and the demand for skilled labor: Firm level evidence. *The Quarterly Journal of Economics, 117*(1), 339–376. doi:10.1162/003355302753399526

Bridges, T. (2014). Retrieved 3 30, 2016, from MyScienceWork raises $1.1 million to fuel its international growth and roll-out new services: http://www.rudebaguette.com/2014/04/10/mysciencework-raises-1-1-million-fuel-international-growth/

Briguglio, P. (2004). *Crisis Management: A White Paper.* Retrieved on August, 2013, from MMI Public Relations: http://www.mmipublicrelations.com/white/paper/crisis-management-a-white-paper/

Brinkerhoff, J. M. (2009). *Digital diasporas: Identity and transnational engagement.* Cambridge, UK: Cambridge University Press. doi:10.1017/CBO9780511805158

Britton, C. (2017). *Crisis Management Planning in 2017: 3 Emerging Threats.* Retrieved on January 31, 2018, from https://www.rockdovesolutions.com/blog/crisis-management-planning-in-2017-3-emerging-threats

Broadbent, M., & Weil, P. (1999). The Implications of Information Technology Infrastructure for Business Process Redesign. *Management Information Systems Quarterly, 23*(2), 159–182. doi:10.2307/249750

Brohman, M. K., Parent, M., Pearce, M. R., & Wade, M. (2000). The business intelligence value chain: Data-driven decision support in a data warehouse environment: An exploratory study. In *Proceedings of the 33rd Hawaii International Conference on System Sciences (HICSS-33).* IEEE. 10.1109/HICSS.2000.926905

Brown, W. C., & Nasuti, F. (2005). Sarbanes-Oxley and enterprise security: IT governance - what it takes to get the job done. *Information Systems Security, 14*(5), 15–28. doi:10.1201/1086.1065898X/45654.14.5.20051101/91010.4

Brusilovsky, P., & Peylo, C. (2003). Adaptive and Intelligent Web-Based Educational Systems. *International Journal of Artificial Intelligence in Education, 13*, 156–169.

Brynjolfsson, E., & Hitt, L. M. (1996). Paradox lost: Firm level evidence on returns to information systems spending. *Management Science, 42*(4), 541–558. doi:10.1287/mnsc.42.4.541

Buettner, R. (2016). Getting a Job via Career-oriented Social Networking Sites: The Weakness of Ties. In *49th Hawaii International Conference on System Sciences (HICSS-49).* Kauai, Hawaii: IEEE. 10.1109/HICSS.2016.272

Bulgurcu, B., Cavusoglu, H., & Benbasat, I. (2010). Information security policy compliance: An empirical study of rationality-based beliefs and information security awareness. *Management Information Systems Quarterly, 34*(3), 523–548. doi:10.2307/25750690

Buonanno, G., Faverio, P., Pigni, F., Ravarini, A., Sciuto, D., & Tagliavini, M. (2004). Factors affecting ERP system adoption: A comparative analysis between SMEs and large companies. *Journal of Enterprise Information Management, 18*(4), 384–426. doi:10.1108/17410390510609572

Burden, P. (2010). *A subject guide to quality Web sites.* Scarecrow Press, Inc. Retrieved from https://dl.acm.org/citation.cfm?id=1942832

Burgess, L., & Cooper, J. (1999). A Model for Classification of Business Adoption of Internet Commerce Solution. *Twelfth Bled Electronic Commerce Conference, Global Networked Organizations.*

Burgos, D., Tattersall, C., & Koper, R. (2007). Representing Adaptive and Adaptable Units of Learning. In B. Fernández Manjon, J. M. Sanchez Perez, J. A. Gómez Pulido, M. A. Vega Rodriguez, & J. Bravo (Eds.), *Computers and Education: E-learning – From Theory to Practice* (pp. 41–56). Springer. doi:10.1007/978-1-4020-4914-9_4

Burnham, J. F. (2006, March 8). Scopus database: A review. *Biomedical Digital Libraries, 3*(1), 1. doi:10.1186/1742-5581-3-1 PMID:16522216

Burre, P. (2018). AI-Driven Cognitive Operations Driving Enterprise Agility. *BWDisrupt.* Retrieved from http://bwdisrupt.businessworld.in/article/AI-Driven-Cognitive-Operations-Driving-Enterprise-Agility/21-02-2018-141356/

Bush, T. (2012). Developing an organization's competitive strategies: Staying ahead of the competition. In *Proceedings of the 2nd International Conference on Management and Artificial Intelligence (IPEDR)* (*Vol. 35,* pp. 88-92). Academic Press.

Byrd, T. A., & Turner, D. E. (2000). Measuring the Flexibility of Information Technology Infrastructure. *Journal of Management Information Systems, 17*(1), 167–208. doi:10.1080/07421222.2000.11045632

Caballé, S., Daradoumis, T., & Xhafa, F. (2007). Efficient embedding of information and knowledge into CSCL applications. In *International Conference on Technologies for E-Learning and Digital Entertainment* (pp. 548-559). Springer. 10.1007/978-3-540-73011-8_53

Cameron, J., & Clarke, R. (1996). Towards a Theoretical Framework for Collaborative Electronic Commerce Projects Involving Small and Medium-Size Enterprises. *Proc. Of the 9th International Conference EDI-IOS.*

Camison-Zornoza, C., Lapiedra-Alcami, R., Segarra-Cipres, M., & Boronat-Navarro, M. (2004). A Meta-Analysis of Innovation and Organizational Size. *Organization Studies, 25*(3), 331–361. doi:10.1177/0170840604040039

Cappiello, C., Di Noia, T., Marcu, B. A., & Matera, M. (2016, June). A quality model for linked data exploration. In *International Conference on Web Engineering* (pp. 397-404). Springer. 10.1007/978-3-319-38791-8_25

Carlson, J. R., Carlson, D. S., Hunter, E. M., Vaughn, R. L., & George, J. F. (2017). Virtual team effectiveness: Investigating the moderating role of experience with computer-mediated communication on the impact of team cohesion and openness. In Remote Work and Collaboration: Breakthroughs in Research and Practice (pp. 687-706). IGI Global.

Carro, R. M., Ortigosa, A., Martin, E., & Schlichter, J. (2003). Dynamic Generation of Adaptive Web-based Collaborative Courses. *Journal of Lecture Notes on Computer Science, 2806,* 191–198. doi:10.1007/978-3-540-39850-9_17

Casalo, L. V., Flavian, C., & Guinaliu, M. (2010). Relationship quality, community promotion and brand loyalty in virtual communities: Evidence from free software communities. *International Journal of Information Management, 30*(4), 357–367. doi:10.1016/j.ijinfomgt.2010.01.004

Casillas, L., & Daradoumis, T. (2012). An Ontological Structure for Gathering and Sharing Knowledge among Scientists through Experiment Modeling. *Collaborative and Distributed E-Research: Innovations in Technologies, Strategies and Applications: Innovations in Technologies, Strategies and Applications,* 165.

Casillas, L., & Jara, I. (2018). Learning Avatar's Locomotion Patterns Through Spatial Analysis in FPS Video Games. *International Journal of Organizational and Collective Intelligence, 8*(1), 28–45. doi:10.4018/IJOCI.2018010103

Casillas, L., Peña, A., & Gutierrez, A. (2016). Towards an Automated Model to Evaluate Collaboration through Non-Verbal Interaction in Collaborative Virtual Environments. *International Journal of e-Collaboration, 12*(4), 7–23. doi:10.4018/IJeC.2016100102

Cavanaugh, R., Ellis, M., Layton, R., & Ardis, M. (2004). *Automating the Process of Assigning Students to Cooperative-Learning Teams.* Paper presented at the American Society for Engineering Education Annual Conference and Exposition, Salt Lake City, UT.

Caves, D., Christensen, L., & Diewert, W. (1982). Multilateral comparisons of output, input and productivity using superlative index numbers. *Economic Journal (London)*, *92*(365), 73–86. doi:10.2307/2232257

CFIB. (2000). *Internet Use among Small and Medium-sized Firms.* Retrieved from August 10, 2015 www.bcstats.gov.bc.ca/pubs/sbq/sbq01q1.pdf

Chabrow, E. (2016). *IST Unveils a Cybersecurity Self-Assessment Tool:Gauging the Effectiveness of Risk Management Initiatives.* Princeton, NJ: Information Security Media Group, Corp. Retrieved from https://www.bankinfosecurity.com/aligning-cyber-framework-organizations-strategy-goals-a-9401

Chadwick, A. (2003). Bringing E-Democracy Back. *Social Science Computer Review*, *21*(4), 443–455. doi:10.1177/0894439303256372

Chadwick, A. (2008). Web 2.0: New challenges for the study of e-democracy in an era of informational exuberance. *ISJLP*, *5*, 9.

Chahal, P. (2015). A study on the role of consumers gender and age on online shopping. *International Journal in Comerce, IT &. Social Sciences*, *2*(7), 33–41.

Chakraborty, R., Lee, J., Bagchi-Sen, S., Upadhyaya, S., & Rao, R. (2016). Online shopping intention in the context of data breach in online retail stores: An examination of older and younger adults. *Decision Support Systems*, *83*, 47–56. doi:10.1016/j.dss.2015.12.007

Chakravarty, A., Grewal, R., & Sambamurthy, V. (2013). Information technology competencies, organizational agility, and firm performance: Enabling and facilitating roles. *Information Systems Research*, *24*(4), 976–997. doi:10.1287/isre.2013.0500

Chang, C.-T., & Cheng, Z.-H. (2015). Tugging on heartstrings: Shopping orientation, mindset, and consumer responses to cause-related marketing. *Journal of Business Ethics*, *127*(2), 337–350. doi:10.100710551-014-2048-4

Chang, I. C., Hwang, H. G., Hung, M. C., Lin, M. H., & Yen, D. C. (2007). Factors affecting the adoption of electronic signature: Executives' perspective of hospital information department. *Decision Support Systems*, *44*(1), 350–359. doi:10.1016/j.dss.2007.04.006

Chang, Y. B., & Gurbaxani, V. (2013). An empirical analysis of technical efficiency: The role of IT intensity and competition. *Information Systems Research*, *24*(3), 561–578. doi:10.1287/isre.1120.0438

Chatain, P., Zerzan, A., Noor, W., Dannaoui, N., & de Koker, L. (2011). *Protecting mobile money against financial crimes: Global policy challenges and solutions.* Washington, DC: The World Bank. doi:10.1596/978-0-8213-8669-9

Chatterjee, D., & Ramamurthy, V. (1999). Business Implications of Web Technology: An Insight into Usage of the World Wide Web by US Companies. *The International Journal of Electronic Commerce and Media*, *9*(1/2), 9–13.

Chaudhuri, S., Dayal, U., & Narasayya, V. (2011). An overview of business intelligence technology. *Communications of the ACM*, *54*(8), 88–98. doi:10.1145/1978542.1978562

Chau, P. Y. K. (1996). An Empirical Assessment of a Modified Technology Acceptance Model. *Journal of Management Information Systems*, *13*(2), 185–204. doi:10.1080/07421222.1996.11518128

Chau, P. Y. K., & Hu, P. J. (2002). Examining a Model of Information Technology Acceptance by Individual Professionals – An Exploratory Study. *Journal of Management Information Systems, 18*(4), 191–229. doi:10.1080/07421222.2002.11045699

Chavula, H. (2013). Telecommunications development and economic growth in Africa. *Information Technology for Development, 19*(1), 5–23. doi:10.1080/02681102.2012.694794

CHEA. (2017). Retrieved from Council for Higher Education Accreditation: http://www.chea.org/

Chen, P., Dean, M., Ojoko-Adams, D., Osman, H., Lopez, L., & Xie, N. (2004). *Systems Quality Requirements Engineering (SQUARE) Methodology: Case Study on Asset Management System* (CMU/SEI-2004-SR-015). Carnegie Mellon University. Retrieved 07 12, 2017, from https://resources.sei.cmu.edu/library/asset-view.cfm?assetid=6841

Chen, C. A. (2009). Information-oriented Online Shopping Behavior in Electronic Commerce Environment. *Journal of Software, 4*(4), 307–314. doi:10.4304/jsw.4.4.307-314

Chen, C. C., Shih, S.-Y., & Lee, M. (2016). Who should you follow? Combining learning to rank with social influence for informative friend recommendation. *Decision Support Systems, 90*, 33–45. doi:10.1016/j.dss.2016.06.017

Chen, C.-J., & Hung, S.-W. (2010). To give or to receive? Factors influencing members' knowledge sharing and community promotion in professional virtual communities. *Information & Management, 47*(4), 226–236. doi:10.1016/j.im.2010.03.001

Chen, P., & Hitt, L. (2002). Measuring switching costs and the determinants of customer retention in internet enabled businesses: A study of online brokerage industry. *Information Systems Research, 13*(3), 255–274. doi:10.1287/isre.13.3.255.78

Chen, W. (2010). Internet-usage patterns of immigrants in the process of intercultural adaptation. *Cyberpsychology, Behavior, and Social Networking, 13*(4), 387–399. doi:10.1089/cyber.2009.0249 PMID:20712497

Chester, V. (2009). *The relationship between cooperative learning and physics achievement in minority students (Doctoral dissertation)*. Walden University.

Chieu, V. M. (2007). COFALE: An Authoring System for Creating Web-based Adaptive Learning Environments Supporting Cognitive Flexibility. *Journal of Computers, 2*(5), 27–37. doi:10.4304/jcp.2.5.27-37

Chinarank.org. (n.d.). Retrieved from http://www.chinarank.org.cn

Chiu, C. M., Fang, Y. H., & Wang, T. G. (2015). Building community citizenship behaviors: The relative role of attachment and satisfaction. *Journal of the Association for Information Systems, 16*(11), 1. doi:10.17705/1jais.00413

Chong, A. Y. L., Ooi, K. B., Lin, B. S., & Raman, M. (2009). Factors affecting the adoption level of c-commerce: An empirical study. *Journal of Computer Information Systems, 50*(2), 13–22.

Chowdhury, N. M. K., & Boutaba, R. (2009). Network virtualization: State of the art and research challenges. *IEEE Communications Magazine, 47*(7), 20–26. doi:10.1109/MCOM.2009.5183468

Cho, Y. C., & Sagynov, E. (2015). Exploring factors that affect usefulness, ease of use, trust, and purchase intention in the online environment. *International Journal of Management & Information Systems, 19*(1), 21–36.

Christodoulopoulos, C. E., & Papanikolaou, K. A. (2007). *A Group Formation Tool in an E-Learning Context.* Paper presented at the 19th IEEE International Conference on Tools with Artificial Intelligence (ICTAI 2007), Patras, Greece. 10.1109/ICTAI.2007.155

Christopher, M. (2000). The Agile Supply Chain: Competing in Volatile Markets. *Industrial Marketing Management, 29*(1), 37–44. doi:10.1016/S0019-8501(99)00110-8

Chudnov, D. (2006). 6). COinS for the Link Trail. *Library Journal, 131*(12), 8–10.

Churchill, G. A. (1979). A Paradigm for Developing Better Measures of Marketing Constructs. *JMR, Journal of Marketing Research, 16*(1), 64–73. doi:10.2307/3150876

Cieślika, A., & Kaniewska, M. (2004). Telecommunications Infrastructure and Regional Economic Development: The Case of Poland. *Regional Studies, 38*(6), 713–725. doi:10.1080/003434042000240996

Ciganek, A. P., Haseman, W. D., & Ramamurthy, K. (2014). Time to decision: The drivers of innovation adoption decisions. *Enterprise Information Systems, 8*(2), 279–308. doi:10.1080/17517575.2012.690453

CIPS. (2017). *Accredited Programs.* Retrieved from Canada's Association of I.T. Professionals: http://www.cips.ca/

CiteSeer. (2016). *History.* Retrieved 11 11, 2016, from CiteSeer: http://csxstatic.ist.psu.edu/about/history

Clarivate. (2018). *Databases.* Retrieved from clarivate: https://clarivate.com/products/web-of-science/databases/

Clarke, G., Gebreab, F., & Mgombelo, H. (2003). *Telecommunications reforms in Malawi.* Policy Research Working Paper 3036, The World Bank, Washington, DC.

Clarke, R. (1996). *Issues in Technology-Based Consumer Transactions.* Retrieved from http://www.anu.edu.au//Roger.Clarke/SOS/SCOCAP96.html

Clemes, D.-M., Gan, C., & Zhang, J. (2014). An empirical analysis of online shopping adoption in Beijing, China. *Journal of Retailing and Consumer Services, 21*(3), 364–375. doi:10.1016/j.jretconser.2013.08.003

Cogan, A., & Valabjee, J. (2004). *How to migrate access forms to. NET windows forms.* Retrieved on 02/15/2018 from: http://www.ssw.com.au/ssw/Standards/DeveloperDotNet/MSUS_02_How_To_Migrate_Access_Forms_To_Dot_Net_Whitepaper_ver15.doc

Cohen, J. R. (1999). Advising Clients to Apologize. California Law Review, 129-131.

Cohen, S. G., Ledford, G. E. Jr, & Spreitzer, G. M. (1996). A predictive model of self-managing work team effectiveness. *Journal of Human Relations, 49*(5), 643–676. doi:10.1177/001872679604900506

Coldow, J. (2004). *E-Democracy: Putting Down Global Roots.* Institution of Electric Government.

Colecchia, A., & Schreyer, P. (2002). ICT Investment and Economic Growth in the 1990s: Is the United States a Unique Case? A Comparative Study of Nine OECD Countries. *Review of Economic Dynamics, 5*(2), 408–442. doi:10.1006/redy.2002.0170

Columbus, L. (2018). *83% Of Enterprise Workloads will be in The Cloud by 2020.* Retrieved from http://www.forbes.com/sites/louiscolumbus/2018/01/07/83-of-enterprise-workloads-will-be-in-the-cloud-by-2020/#521a089e6261

Compaine, B. M. (2001). *The digital divide: Facing a crisis or creating a myth?* Cambridge, MA: The MIT Press.

Complinet. (2010). *DFSA Takes Action Over Damas Failures.* Thomson Reuters.

Computer Security Institute. (2011). *The 2010 / 2011 CSI Computer Crime and Security Survey.* Retrieved from www.GoCSI.com

Connolly, C. (2010). A review of data logging systems, software and applications. *Sensor Review, 30*(3), 192–196. doi:10.1108/02602281011051362

Conteh, C., & Smith, G. (2015). Towards an interactive e-government system in sub-Saharan Africa: Prospects and challenges. *Public affairs and administration: Concepts, methodologies, tools, and applications,* 213.

Coombs, W. T. (2007). Ongoing Crisis Communication: Planning, Managing, and Responding. Academic Press.

Coombs, W. T. (2004). Structuring Crisis Discourse Knowledge: The West Pharmaceutics Case. *Public Relations Review*, 467–474. doi:10.1016/j.pubrev.2004.08.007

Coombs, W. T. (2007). *Crisis Management and Communications.* Institute of PR.

Coombs, W. T. (2007). Protecting Organization Reputations During a Crisis: The Development and Application of Situational Crisis Communication Theory. *Corporate Reputation Review*, 1–14.

Cooper, W. W., & Tone, K. (1997). Measures of inefficiency in data envelopment analysis and frontier estimation. *European Journal of Operational Research*, 99(1), 72–88. doi:10.1016/S0377-2217(96)00384-0

Corbin, J., Strauss, A., & Strauss, A. L. (2014). *Basics of qualitative research.* Newbury Park, CA: Sage.

Cormode, G., & Krishnamurthy, B. (2008). Key Differences between Web 1.0 and Web 2.0. *First Monday, 13*(6). Retrieved December, 2012, from http://www.uic.edu/htbin/cgiwrap/bin/ojs/index.php/

Coronel, C., & Morris, S. (2014). Database systems: Design, implementation, & management (11th ed.). Cengage Learning.

Cragg, P., & King, M. (1993). Small-Firm Computing: Motivators and Inhibitors. *Management Information Systems Quarterly, 17*(1), 47–59. doi:10.2307/249509

Craigen, D., Diakun-Thibault, N., & Purse, R. (2014). Defining Cybersecurity. *Technology Innovation Management Review, 4*(10), 13-21. Retrieved from http://timreview.ca/article/835

Creswell, J. W. (2013). *Research design: Qualitative, quantitative, and mixed methods approaches.* Thousand Oaks, CA: Sage Publications.

Cristea, A. I., & Ghali, F. (2011). Towards adaptation in e-learning 2.0. *Journal of New Review of Hypermedia and Multimedia, 17*(2), 199–238. doi:10.1080/13614568.2010.541289

Crossman, A. (2017). *An Overview of Qualitative Research Methods.* Retrieved on January 31, 2018 from https://www.thoughtco.com/qualitative-research-methods-3026555

Cui, X. (2009). In-depth analysis of PC industry in China. *International Journal of Business and Management, 4*(11), 150–157. doi:10.5539/ijbm.v4n11p150

Culnan, M. J., & Bies, R. J. (2003). Consumer Privacy: Balancing Economic and Justice Consideration. *The Journal of Social Issues, 59*(2), 323–342. doi:10.1111/1540-4560.00067

Cyganiak, R., Stenzhorn, H., Delbru, R., Decker, S., & Tummarello, G. (2008). Semantic sitemaps: Efficient and flexible access to datasets on the semantic web. *Proceedings of the 5th European Semantic Web Conference.* 10.1007/978-3-540-68234-9_50

D'Aquin, M., Motta, E., Sabou, M., Angeletou, S., Gridinoc, L., Lopez, V., & Guidi, D. (2008). Toward a new generation of semantic web applications. *IEEE Intelligent Systems, 23*(3), 20–28. doi:10.1109/MIS.2008.54

Dahlberg, L. (2001). The Internet and Democratic Discourse: Exploring the Prospects of Online Deliberative Forums Extending the Public Sphere. *Information Communication and Society, 4*(4), 615–633. doi:10.1080/13691180110097030

Dalcher, D., & Drevin, L. (2003). Learning from information systems failures by using narrative and ante-narrative methods. In *Proceedings of the 2003 annual research conference of the South African Institute of Computer Scientists and Information Technologists on Enablement through technology* (pp. 137-142). South African Institute for Computer Scientists and Information Technologists.

Damanpour, F. (1996). Organizational Complexity and Innovation: Developing and Testing Multiple Contingency Models. *Management Science*, *42*(5), 693–716. doi:10.1287/mnsc.42.5.693

Damanpour, F., & Gopalakrishnan, S. (2001). The Dynamics of the adoption of product and process innovations in organizations. *Journal of Management Studies*, *38*(1), 45–65. doi:10.1111/1467-6486.00227

Damanpour, F., & Schneider, M. (2006). Phases of the Adoption of Innovation in Organizations: Effects of Environment, Organization and Top Managers. *British Journal of Management*, *17*(3), 215–236. doi:10.1111/j.1467-8551.2006.00498.x

Damanpour, F., & Schneider, M. (2009). Characteristics of Innovation and Innovation Adoption in Public Organizations: Assessing the Role of Managers. *Journal of Public Administration: Research and Theory*, *19*(3), 495–522. doi:10.1093/jopart/mun021

Damas. (2013). *About Damas*. Retrieved on August 31, 2013, from Damas: http://www.damasjewel.com/articledisplay.aspx?mid=33&id=25

Damsgaard, J. (2002). Managing an Internet portal. *Communications of the Association for Information Systems*, *9*, 408–420.

Data Protection Act. (2012). *Protecting the privacy of the individual and personal data*. Retrieved from http://www.dataprotection.org.gh/data-protection-act

Datta, A., & Agarwal, S. (2004). Telecommunications and economic growth: A panel data approach. *Applied Economics*, *36*(15), 1649–1654. doi:10.1080/0003684042000218552

Daveri, F. (2002). The New Economy in Europe, 1992-2001. *Oxford Review of Economic Policy*, *18*(3), 345–362. doi:10.1093/oxrep/18.3.345

Davis, F. D., Bagozzi, R. P., & Warshaw, P. R. (1989). User Acceptance of Computer Technology: A Comparison of Two Theoretical Models. *Management Science*, *35*(8), 982-1003

Davis, Z. (2017). Definition of computer security. *PCMag*. Retrieved 11 3, 2017, from http://www.pcmag.com/encyclopedia/term/40169/computer-security

Davis, F. D. (1989). Perceived usefulness, perceived ease of use, and user acceptance of information technology. *Management Information Systems Quarterly*, *13*(3), 319–339. doi:10.2307/249008

Davis, F. D. (1993). User acceptance of information technology: System characteristics, user perceptions and behavioral impacts. *International Journal of Man-Machine Studies*, *38*(3), 475–487. doi:10.1006/imms.1993.1022

Davis, F. D., Bagozzi, R. P., & Warshaw, P. R. (1989). User acceptance of computer technology: A comparison of two theoretical models. *Management Science*, *35*(8), 982–1003. doi:10.1287/mnsc.35.8.982

Davis, L., & Metcalf, G. (2016). Does Better Information Lead to Better Choices? Evidence from Energy-Efficiency Labels. *Journal of the Association of Environmental and Resource Economists*, *3*(3), 589–625. doi:10.1086/686252

DBIR. (2013). *The 2013 Data Breach Investigations Report*. Retrieved from http://www.verizonenterprise.com/DBIR/

De Bra, P., & Calvi, L. (1998). AHA! An open adaptive hypermedia architecture. *Journal of New Review of Hypermedia and Multimedia*, *4*, 15–139.

Dean, J., & Tam, P. (2005, June 9). The laptop trail - The modern PC is a model of hyper-efficient production and geopolitical sensitivities. *The Wall Street Journal*.

Dean, D. H. (2004). Consumer Reaction to Negative Publicity: Effects of Corporate Reputation, Response, And Responsibility For a Crisis Event. *Journal of Business Communication*, *41*(2), 192–211. doi:10.1177/0021943603261748

Debattista, J., Lange, C., Auer, S., & Cortis, D. (2017). Evaluating the Quality of the LOD Cloud: An Empirical Investigation. *Semantic Web Journal.*

Dedrick, J., & Kraemer, K. L. (2002). *Globalization of the personal computer industry: Trends and implications. Globalization of I.T. CA.* Center for Research on Information Technology and Organizations, UC Irvine.

Dedrick, J., Venkatesh, M., Stanton, J. M., Zheng, Y., & Ramnarine-Rieks, A. (2015). Adoption of smart grid technologies by electric utilities: Factors influencing organizational innovation in a regulated environment. *Electronic Markets*, *25*(1), 17–29. doi:10.100712525-014-0166-6

Dehler, J., Bodemer, D., Buder, J., & Hesse, F. W. (2011). Guiding knowledge communication in CSCL via group knowledge awareness. *Computers in Human Behavior*, *27*(3), 1068–1078. doi:10.1016/j.chb.2010.05.018

Deirdre, L. (2012). *Linked open data.* Retrieved from http://fr.slideshare.net/deirdrelee/linked-opendata-15303345

De-la-Fuente-Vanentin, L., Pardo, A., & Kloos, C. D. (2011). Generic service integration in adaptive learning experiences using IMS learning design. *Computers & Education*, *57*(1), 1160–1170. doi:10.1016/j.compedu.2010.12.007

Demetriadis, S., & Karakostas, A. (2009). Introduction to Adaptive Collaboration Scripting: Pedagogical and Technical Issues. *Journal of Intelligent Collaborative e-Learning Systems and Applications Studies in Computational Intelligence*, *246*, 1-18.

Dennis, C., Fenech, T., & Merrilees, B. (2004). *E-retailing.* Abingdon, UK: Routledge.

Dennis, C., Merrilees, B., Jayawardhena, C., & Wright, L. T. (2009). E-consumer behaviour. *European Journal of Marketing*, *43*(9), 1121–1139. doi:10.1108/03090560910976393

Department of Trade and Industry (DTI). (1997, 1998). *Moving into the Information Age: An International Benchmarking Study.* Retrieved July 25, 2010 http://www.dti.gov.uk

Department of Trade and Industry. (1999). *How the Internet can work for you.* Retrieved July 25, 2010 http://www.dti.gov.uk

Deursen, N. V., Buchanan, W. J., & Duff, A. (2013). Monitoring information security risks within health care. *Computers & Security*, *37*, 31–45. doi:10.1016/j.cose.2013.04.005

Dewan, S., & Kraemer, K. (2000). Information Technology and Productivity: Evidence from Country Level Data. *Management Science*, *46*(4), 548–562. doi:10.1287/mnsc.46.4.548.12057

Dewan, S., & Riggins, F. J. (2005). The digital divide: Current and future research directions. *Journal of the Association for Information Systems*, *6*(12), 298–337. doi:10.17705/1jais.00074

Dey, I. (1993). *Qualitative Data Analysis: A user-friendly guide for social scientists.* London: Routledge. doi:10.4324/9780203412497

Dilenschneider, R. L. (2000). *The Corporate Communications Bible: Everything you Need to Know to Become a Public Relations Expert.* Beverly Hills, CA: New Millennium.

Dillenbourg, P. (2002). Over-scripting CSCL: The risks of blending collaborative learning with instructional design. In Three worlds of CSCL. Can we support CSCL? Heerlen, Open Universiteit Nederland.

Dillenbourg, P., Baker, M., Blaye, A., & O'Malley, C. (1996). The evolution of research on collaborative learning. In E. Spada & P. Reiman (Eds.), *Learning in Humans and Machine: Towards an interdisciplinary learning science* (pp. 189–211). Oxford, UK: Elsevier.

Dillenbourg, P., Zufferey, G., Alavi, H., Jeremann, P., Do-Lenh, S., Bonnard, Q., & Kaplan, F. (2011). Classroom Orchestration: The third circle of usability. In *Proceedings of the 9th International Conference on Computer Supported Collaborative Learning* (pp. 510-517). Hong Kong: International Society of the Learning Sciences.

DiMaggio, P. J., & Powell, W. (1983). The iron cage revisited: Institutional isomorphism and collective rationalizing in organizational fields. *American Sociological Review, 48*(2), 147–160. doi:10.2307/2095101

Dimitracopoulou, A., & Petrou, A. (2005). Advanced collaborative distance learning systems for young students: Design issues and current trends on new cognitive and metacognitive tools. *THEMES in Education, International Journal.*

Ding, L., Lebo, T., Erickson, J. S., DiFranzo, D., Williams, G. T., Li, X., & Hendler, J. A. (2011). Twc logd: A portal for linked open government data ecosystems. *Journal of Web Semantics, 9*(3), 325–333. doi:10.1016/j.websem.2011.06.002

Ding, L., Pan, R., Finin, T., Joshi, A., Peng, Y., & Kolari, P. (2005). Finding and ranking knowledge on the semantic web. *Proceedings of the 4th International Semantic Web Conference.* 10.1007/11574620_14

Dividino, R. Q. (2017). *Managing and using provenance in the semantic web* (Doctoral dissertation). Universität Koblenz-Landau.

Dixon, T., McAllister, P., & Thompson, B. (2002). *The value of ICT for SMEs in the UK: A critical Literature Review.* Retrieved from http://www.cem.ac.uk/itribe.htm

Dlab, M. H., Boticki, I., Hoic-Bozic, N., & Looi, C.-K. (2017). Adaptivity in Synchronous Mobile Collaborative Learning. *Proceedings 9th International Conference on Education and New Learning Technologies.* 10.21125/edulearn.2017.1097

Dolkart, V. M., & Pronina, L. V. (2007). Change in computer hardware and software paradigms. *Russian Electrical Engineering, 78*(10), 548–553. doi:10.3103/S1068371207100082

Dolowitz, D., & Marsh, D. (2000). Learning from abroad: The role of policy transfer in contemporary policy-making. *Governance: An International Journal of Policy, Administration and Institutions, 13*(1), 5–24. doi:10.1111/0952-1895.00121

Domingo, J. S. (2018). The Best Laptops of 2018. *PC Magazine.* Retrieved on 2/18/2018 from: https://www.pcmag.com/article2/0,2817,2369981,00.asp

Domingo, J. S., & Brant, T. (2017). The Best Desktop Computers of 2018. *PC Magazine.* Retrieved on 2/19/2018 from: https://www.pcmag.com/article2/0,2817,2372609,00.asp

Domingue, J., Fensel, D., & Hendler, J. (2011). *Handbook of semantic web technologies.* Springer. doi:10.1007/978-3-540-92913-0

Donovan, K., & Martin, A. (2012). *The Rise of African SIM Registration: Mobility, Identity, Surveillance & Resistance.* Information Systems and Innovation Group Working Paper no. 186, London School of Economics and Political Science, London, UK.

Donovan, K., & Martin, A. (2014). The rise of African SIM card Registration: The emerging dynamics of regulatory change. *First Monday, 19*(2), 1–12. doi:10.5210/fm.v19i2.4351

Dorogovtsev, S., & Mendes, J. (2015). Ranking Scientists. *Nature Physics, 11*(11), 882–884. doi:10.1038/nphys3533

Dove, R. (1994). The Meaning of Life & The Meaning of Agile. *Production, 106*(11), 14–15.

Dove, R. (1995). Agility Engineering: Lego Lessons. *Production, 107*(3), 12–15.

Downes, L., & Nunes, P. F. (2013). The big idea: Big-bang disruption. *Harvard Business Review,* 1–12.

Downing, J. R. (2003). American Airlines' Use of Mediated Employee Channels After the 9/11 Attacks. *Public Relations Review*, 37–48.

Doyle, T., & Tagg, J. (2008). *Helping Students Learn in a Learner-Centered Environment: A Guide to Facilitating Learning in Higher Education*. Stylus Publishing.

Drnevich, P. L., & Croson, D. C. (2013, June). Information technology and business-level strategy: Toward an integrated theoretical perspective. *Management Information Systems Quarterly*, *37*(2), 483–509. doi:10.25300/MISQ/2013/37.2.08

DSTanalyse. (2016). *Hvornår er små virksomheder små?* Retrieved on February 1, 2018 from https://www.dst.dk/da/Statistik/Analyser/visanalyse?cid=27867

Duarte, A., Duarte, D., & Thiry, M. (2016). aceBoK: Toward a Software Requirements Traceability Body of Knowledge. In *2016 IEEE 24th International Requirements Engineering Conference (RE)* (pp. 236-245). Beijing: IEEEXPLORE. doi:10.1109/RE.2016.32

DuBois, S. (2013). *How IKEA Can Get Back On The Horse After a Meat Scandal.* Retrieved on September 01, 2013, from CNN Money: http://management.fortune.cnn.com/2013/02/26/ikea-horsemeat/

DuBois, F. L., Toyne, B., & Oliff, M. D. (1993). International manufacturing strategies of U.S. multinationals: A conceptual framework based on a four-industry study. *Journal of International Business Studies*, *24*(2), 307–333. doi:10.1057/palgrave.jibs.8490234

Dziak, M. (2016). Virtualization (Computing). In *Salem Press Encyclopedia*: *Research Starters*. Academic Press.

Ebbers, W. E., Jansen, M. G., & van Deursen, A. J. (2016). Impact of the digital divide on e-government: Expanding from channel choice to channel usage. *Government Information Quarterly*, *33*(4), 685–692. doi:10.1016/j.giq.2016.08.007

Ebersole, G. (2013). *The Importance of Public Relations and Crisis Management Planning To Your Business.* Retrieved on September 1, 2013, from Crisis Management: http://www.crisistraining.net/crisis-media-training_workshops_The-Importance-of-Public-Relations-and-Crisis-Management-Planning-To-Your-Business.htm

E-Commerce Europe. (2013). *Europe B2C E-Commerce Report 2013.* Retrieved February 1, 2014, from http://www.paymentscardsandmobile.com/wp-content/uploads/2013/08/Europe-B2C-Ecommerce-Report-2013.pdf

E-Commerce Europe. (2015). *Europe B2C E-Commerce Report 2015.* Retrieved January 15, 2016, from http://www.ecommerce-europe.eu/press/2015/european-e-commerce-turnover-grew-by-14.3-to-reach-423.8bn-in-2014

E-Commerce Foundation. (2017). *European E-Commerce Report.* Retrieved January 18, 2018, from https://ecommercenews.eu/ecommerce-europe-e602-billion-2017/

Edwards, J., Millea, T., Mcleod, S., & Coults, I. (1998, 11 Jun 1998). *Agile System Design and Build.* Paper presented at the IEEE Colloquium on Managing Requirements Change: A Business Process Re-Engineering Perspective, London, UK.

EEC. (2018). *About EEC.* Retrieved from Education Evaluation Commission (EEC): https://www.eec.gov.sa/

Ee, H. (2014). Business continuity 2014: From traditional to integrated business continuity management. *Journal of Business Continuity & Emergency Planning*, *8*(2), 102–105. PMID:25416371

Eilu, E., & Auma, T. O. (2017). Mobile Money Services as a Panacea to Financial Inclusion in Sub-Saharan Africa: The Case of Uganda. *International Journal of Technology Diffusion*, *8*(4), 77–88. doi:10.4018/IJTD.2017100106

Ein-Dor, P., & Segev, E. (1978). Organizational Context and the Success of Management Information Systems. *Management Science*, *24*(10), 1064–1078. doi:10.1287/mnsc.24.10.1064

Eisenhardt, K. M. (1989). Building theories from Case Study Research. *Academy of Management Review, 14*(4), 532–550.

Eisenhardt, K. M. (1989). Building Theories from Case Study Research. *Academy of Management Review, 14*(4), 532–550.

Electronic Transactions Act 772. (2008). *Ghana's Electronic Transaction Act 772*. Retrieved from www.unesco.org

Ellingwood, J. (2015a). The Docker Ecosystem: An introduction to Common Components. *The Docker Ecosystem.* Retrieved from https://www.digitalocean.com/community/tutorials/the-docker-ecosystem-an-introduction-to-common-components

Ellingwood, J. (2015b). The Docker Ecosystem: An Overview of Containerization. *The Docker Ecosystem.* Retrieved from https://www.digitalocean.com/community/tutorials/the-docker-ecosystem-an-overview-of-containerization

Ellingwood, J. (2015c). The Docker Ecosystem: Service Discovery and Distributed Configuration Stores, An Overview of Containerization. *The Docker Ecosystem.* Retrieved from https://www.digitalocean.com/community/tutorials/the-docker-ecosystem-service-discovery-and-distributed-configuration-stores

Ellison, N. B. (2007). Social network sites: Definition, history, and scholarship. *Journal of Computer-Mediated Communication, 13*(1), 210–230. doi:10.1111/j.1083-6101.2007.00393.x

El-Mahied, M. T., & Abu-Taieh, E. (2006). Information Systems in Developing Countries: Reasons for Failure –Jordan, Case Study. In M. Khosrow-Pour (Ed.), *IRMA-2006. 1* (p. 868). Idea Group Inc. Retrieved from http://www.irma-international.org/viewtitle/32934/

El-Mahied, M. T., Alkhaldi, F., & Abu-Taieh, E. M. (2009). Discovering Knowledge Channels in Learning Organization: Case Study of Jordan. In E. Abu-Taieh, A. El-Sheikh, & J. Abu-Tayeh (Eds.), *Utilizing Information Technology Systems Across Disciplines: Advancements in the Application of Computer Science* (pp. 190–209). Hershey, PA: IGI Global; doi:10.4018/978-1-60566-616-7.ch013

Elstub, S., & McLaverty, P. (2014). Conclusion: The future of deliberative democracy. In *Deliberative democracy: Issues and cases*. Edinburgh, UK: Edinburgh University Press.

Eltrun. (2014). *Anuual e-Commerce survey in Greece*. Retrieved February 1, 2014, from http://www.eltrun.gr/wp-content/uploads/2013/12/ELTRUN_ecommerce_survey_20131.pdf (in Greek).

Eltrun. (2015). *Anuual e-Commerce survey in Greece*. Retrieved January 15, 2016, from http://www.eltrun.gr/wp-content/uploads/2015/12/%CE%97%CE%BB%CE%95%CE%BC%CF%80%CE%BF%CF%81%CE%B9%CE%BF2015-1.pdf (in Greek).

Eltrun. (2017). *Anuual e-Commerce survey in Greece*. Retrieved January 15, 2018, from http://www.greekecommerce.gr/gr/resources/ereynes-gia-ellada/etisia-ereuna-ecommerce-b2c-2017-2018/

Emirates247. (2013). *Global-village Rides Closed After Visitors Death Arrested*. Retrieved on September 1, 2013, from Emirates 247: http://www.emirates247.com/news/emirates/global-village-rides-closed-after-visitor-s-death-3-arrested-2013-01-26-1.492484

Endsley, S., Kibbe, D. C., Linares, A., & Colorafi, K. (2006). An Introduction to Personal Health Records: Here's What You Need to Know About This Growing Trend To Give Patients Access To A Portable Health record. *Family Practice Management, 13*(5), 57. PMID:16736906

ENQA. (2017). Retrieved from ENQA:European Association for Quality Assurance in Higher Education: Enqa.eu

era-2018. (2018, Feb 21). Retrieved from Excellence in Research for Australia (ERA): http://www.arc.gov.au/era-2018

Erhvervsudvalget, F. (2005). *Bilag 230*. Retrieved on February 1. 2018 from http://www.ft.dk/samling/20101/almdel/eru/bilag/125/944066.pdf

Ernst and Young. (2000). *Global Online Retailing*. Retrieved January 27, 2003, from http://www.ey.com

Ernst, D. (2000). Inter-organizational knowledge outsourcing: What permits small Taiwanese firms to compete in the computer industry? *Asia Pacific Journal of Management*, *17*(2), 223–255. doi:10.1023/A:1015809609118

Escobar-Rodriguez, T., Monge-Lozano, P., & Romero-Alonso, M. M. (2012). Acceptance of E-Prescriptions and Automated Medication-Management Systems in Hospitals: An Extension of the Technology Acceptance Model. *Journal of Information Systems*, *26*(1), 77–96. doi:10.2308/isys-10254

Ettelt, S., Mays, N., & Nolte, E. (2012). Policy learning from abroad: Why it is more difficult than it seems. *Policy and Politics*, *40*(4), 491–504. doi:10.1332/030557312X643786

EU Crisis Management and Conflict Prevention. (2002). *Guidelines on Fact-Finding Missions Col 15461/02*. Author.

European Commission. (1998). *Awareness creation activities in electronic commerce for SMEs* (2nd ed.). Retrieved July 2, 2010 http://ispo.cec.be/ecommerce/books/awarenessbook.html

Eurostat. (2017). *E-commerce statistics for individuals*. Retrieved January 20, 2018, from http://ec.europa.eu/eurostat/statistics-explained/index.php/E-commerce_statistics_for_individuals

Evans, M. (2009). Policy transfer in critical perspective. *Policy Studies*, *30*(3), 243–268. doi:10.1080/01442870902863828

Evdokimov, S., Fischmann, M., & Günther, O. (2010). Provable security for outsourcing database operations. *International Journal of Information Security and Privacy*, *4*(1), 1–17. doi:10.4018/jisp.2010010101

Everett, A. (2009). *Digital diaspora: A race for cyberspace*. Albany, NY: SUNY Press.

Evermann, J. (2008). An exploratory study of database integration processes. *IEEE Transactions on Knowledge and Data Engineering*, *20*(1), 99–115. doi:10.1109/TKDE.2007.190675

Evertiq. (2017). *List: Top10 EMS-providers of 2016*. Manufacturing Market Insider (MMI). Retrieved on 2/19/2018 from: http://evertiq.com/news/41361

Ewusi-Mensah, K. (1997). Critical issues in abandoned information systems development projects. *Communications of the ACM*, *40*(9), 74–80. doi:10.1145/260750.260775

Ey-Ling, S. (2011). Practice Analysis: Professional Competencies and Work Categories in Public Relations Today. *Public Relations Review*, 187–196.

Fabri, M., Moore, D. J., & Hobbs, D. J. (2004). Mediating the expression of emotion in educational collaborative virtual environments: An experimental study. *International Journal of Virtual Reality*, *7*(2), 66–81. doi:10.100710055-003-0116-7

Falakmasir, M. H., Hsiao, I. H., Mazzola, L., Grant, N., & Brusilovsky, P. (2012). The Impact of Social Performance Visualization on Students. In *Proceedings of the 12th International Conference on Advanced Learning Technologies*, (pp. 565-569). Washington, DC: IEEE Computer Society Press. 10.1109/ICALT.2012.218

Fare, R., Grosskopf, S., Norris, M., & Zhang, Z. (1994). Productivity growth, technical progress, and efficiency change in industrialized countries. *The American Economic Review*, *84*(1), 66–83.

Farouk, A. (1987). *Retail marketing in Dhaka city, Research Report*. Dhaka, Bangladesh: Bureau of Business Research, University of Dhaka.

Feagin, J., Orum, A., & Sjoberg, G. (1991). *A Case for Case Study*. Chapel Hill, NC: University of North Carolina Press.

Fearn-Banks, K. (2007). *Crisis Communications: A Casebook Approach* (3rd ed.). Mahwah, NJ: Lawrence Erlbaum.

Federal Financial Institutions Examination Council. (2015). *FFIEC Cybersecurity Assessment Tool.* Federal Financial Institutions Examination Council. Retrieved 6 6, 2017, from https://www.ffiec.gov/pdf/cybersecurity/FFIEC_CAT_June_2015_PDF2.pdf

Fichman, R. G. (1992). Information technology diffusion: A review of empirical research. *Proceedings of the Thirteenth International Conference on Information Systems*, 195-206.

figshare. (2016). *About figshare.* Retrieved from figshare: figshare.com/

Fildes, N. (2017). PC market set to return to growth in 2018. *Financial Times.* Retrieved on February 19, 2018, from https://www.ft.com/content/1d525464-b282-11e7-aa26-bb002965bce8

Finat, C. (2014). Information security management incidents in research - development. *Romanian Review Precision Mechanics, Optics & Mecatronics,* (45), 137-141.

Finger, G., Jamieson-Proctor, R., & Grimbeek, P. (2013). *Teaching teachers for the future project: building TPACK confidence and capabilities for eLearning.* Paper presented at the 5th International Conference on Educational Technologies, Malé, Maldives.

Fink, S. (1986). *Crisis Management: Planning For The Inevitable.* New York: AMACOM.

Fishbein, M., & Ajzen, I. (1975). *Belief, attitude, intention and behavior: An introduction to theory and research.* Reading, MA: Addison-Wesley.

Fishbein, M., & Ajzen, I. (1975). *Belief, Attitude, Intention, and Behavior.* Reading, MA: Addison-Wesley.

Fitzsimmons, J. A., Fitzsimmons, M. J., & Bordoloi, S. K. (2014). *Service Management: Operation, Strategy, Information Technology.* New York: McGraw-Hill International.

Flak, L., Olsen, D., & Wolocott, P. (2005). Local E-Government in Norway: Local status and emerging issues. *Scandinavian Journal of Information Systems*, *17*(2), 41–84.

Fornell, C., & Larcker, D. F. (1981). Evaluating Structural Equation Models with Unobservable Variables and Measurement Error. *JMR, Journal of Marketing Research*, *18*(1), 39–50. doi:10.2307/3151312

Foutsitzis, C. G., & Demetriadis, S. (2013). Scripted collaboration to leverage the impact of algorithm visualization tools in online learning: Results from two small scale studies. *International Journal of e-Collaboration*, *9*(1), 42–56. doi:10.4018/jec.2013010104

Frambach, R. T. (1993). An integrated model of organizational adoption and diffusion of innovation. *European Journal of Marketing*, *27*(5), 22–41. doi:10.1108/03090569310039705

Franchi, E., Poggi, A., & Tomaiuolo, M. (2012). Open social networking for online collaboration. *International Journal of e-Collaboration*, *9*(3), 50–68. doi:10.4018/jec.2013070104

Gallaugher, J., & Downing, C. (2000). Portal combat: An empirical study of competition in the Web portal industry. *Journal of Information Technology Management*, *11*(1–2), 13–24.

Galliers, B., & Swan, J. (1999). Information systems and strategic change: A critical review of business process reengineering. In W. Currie & B. Galliers (Eds.), *Rethinking Management Information Systems.* Oxford, UK: University Press.

Gallivan, M. J., & Benbunan-Fich, R. (2005). A Framework for Analyzing Levels of Analysis Issues in Studies of E-Collaboration. *IEEE Transactions on Professional Communication*, *48*, 87–104.

Gandhi, S. (2017). *Artificial Intelligence-Demystified*. Retrieved from https://towardsdatascience.com/artificial-intelligence-demystified-a456328e193f

Garcia, M. (2017). *Avoiding Social Media Turbulence and PR Disasters: Airline CEOs Speak Out on Crisis Communications*. Retrieved January 30, 2018, from https://apex.aero/2017/06/09/avoiding-social-media-turbulence-pr-disasters-airline-ceos-crisis-communications

Gardner, B. S., & Korth, S. J. (1997). Classroom strategies that facilitate transfer of learning to the workplace. *Journal of Innovative Higher Education*, *22*(1), 45–60. doi:10.1023/A:1025151609364

Garfield, E. (1955). Citation Indexes for Science: A New Dimension in Documentation through Association of Ideas. *Science*, *122*(3159), 108–111. doi:10.1126cience.122.3159.108 PMID:14385826

Gartner, Inc. (2018). *Gartner Says Worldwide Device Shipments Will Increase 2.1 Percent in 2018*. Gartner, Inc. Retrieved on February 19, 2018 from https://www.gartner.com/newsroom/id/3849063

Garvin, D. A. (1987, November). Competing on the eight dimensions of quality. *Harvard Business Review*, 101–109.

Gasparotti, C. (2013). Importanţa managementului configuraţiei, cu Exemplificare în domeniul instalaţiilor navale. *Review of Management & Economic Engineering*, *12*(4), 41–52.

Gasser, M. (1988). *Building a Secure Computer System* (1st ed.). Van Nostrand Reinhold. Retrieved from https://ece.uwaterloo.ca/~vganesh/TEACHING/S2014/ECE458/building-secure-systems.pdf

Gatignon, H., & Robertson, T. S. (1989). Technology diffusion: An empirical test of competitive effects. *Journal of Marketing*, *53*(1), 35–49. doi:10.2307/1251523

Gefen, D., & Straub, D. (2000). The Relative Importance of Perceived Ease of Use in IS Adoption: A Study of E-Commerce Adoption. *Journal of Association for Information Systems*, *1*(8), 1-22.

Gefen, D., Karahanna, E., & Straub, D. (2003). Trust and Tam in Online Shopping: An Integrated Model. *MIS Quarterly*, *27*(1), 51-90.

Gefen, D., & Straub, D. W. (1997). Gender Differences in the Perception and Use of E-mail: An Extension to the Technology Acceptance Model. *Management Information Systems Quarterly*, *21*(4), 389–401. doi:10.2307/249720

George, S., & Venkatesan, N. (2012). Marketing strategies for laptop using conjoint analysis. *International Academic Research Journal of Business and Management*, *1*(1), 39–48.

Ghanam, Y., & Maurer, F. (2011). Using acceptance tests for incremental elicitation of variability in requirements: An observational study. *Proceedings of AGILE 2011 Conference (AGILE'11), IEEE 2011*. 10.1109/AGILE.2011.21

Ghazinoory, S., Divsalar, A., & Soofi, A. S. (2009). A new definition and framework for the development of a national technology strategy: The case of nanotechnology for Iran. *Technological Forecasting and Social Change*, *76*(6), 835–848. doi:10.1016/j.techfore.2008.10.004

Gibbs, J. L., & Kraemer, K. L. (2004). A cross-country investigation of the determinants of scope of e-commerce use: An institutional approach. *Electronic Markets*, *14*(2), 124–137. doi:10.1080/10196780410001675077

Gilson, L. L., Maynard, M. T., Jones Young, N. C., Vartiainen, M., & Hakonen, M. (2015). Virtual teams research: 10 years, 10 themes, and 10 opportunities. *Journal of Management*, *41*(5), 1313–1337. doi:10.1177/0149206314559946

Glaser, E. G., & Strauss, A. L. (1967). *The Discovery of Grounded Theory: Strategies for Qualitative Research*. London: Weidenfeld and Nicolson.

Goeke, R. J., & Antonucci, Y. L. (2013). Differences in Business Process Management Leadership and Deployment: Is There a Connection to Industry Affiliation? *Information Resources Management Journal, 26*(2), 43–64. doi:10.4018/irmj.2013040103

Golden, W., & Griffin, M. (2000). The World Wide Web: Savior of small firms. *13th International Bled Electronic conference*, Bled, Slovenia.

Goldzweig, C. L., Towfigh, A., Maglione, M., & Shekelle, P. G. (2009). Costs and Benefits of Health Information Technology: New Trends from the Literature. *Health Affairs, 28*(2), 376–386. doi:10.1377/hlthaff.28.2.w282 PMID:19174390

GoM. (2013). *National Information and Communication Technology Policy*. Ministry of Information and Civic Education. Government of Malawi.

Gomez, R., & Pather, S. (2012). ICT Evaluation: Are we asking the right questions? *The Electronic Journal on Information Systems in Developing Countries, 50*(1), 1–14. doi:10.1002/j.1681-4835.2012.tb00355.x

Gonzalez, C., & Katz, V. S. (2016). Transnational family communication as a driver of technology adoption. *International Journal of Communication, 10*, 21.

Goodhue, D. L. (1988). *Supporting Users of Corporate Data (Ph.D. Doctoral)*. Boston: Massachusetts Institute of Technology.

Google Scholar Blog. (2011). *Google Scholar Citations Open To All*. Retrieved 3 30, 2016, from Google Scholar Blog: googlescholar.blogspot.com/2011/11/google-scholar-citations-open-to-all.html

Goolsbee, A. (2001). Competition in the computer industry: Online versus retail. *The Journal of Industrial Economics, XLIX*(4).

Gordano Peile, C. G., & Ros Híjar, A. R. (2016). Immigrants and mobile phone uses: Spanish-speaking young adults recently arrived in London. *Mobile Media & Communication, 4*(3), 405–423. doi:10.1177/2050157916655375

Gottfried, S., & Herwig, W. (2014). Evaluating Flexibility in Discrete Manufacturing based on Performance and Efficiency. *International Journal of Production Economics, 153*, 340–352. doi:10.1016/j.ijpe.2014.03.018

Gouli, E., Gogoulou, A., & Grigoriadou, M. (2006). Supporting Self- Peer- and Collaborative-Assessment through a Web-based Environment. In E. Pearson, & P. Bohman (Eds.), *Proceedings of World Conference on Educational Multimedia, Hypermedia and Telecommunications* (pp. 2192-2199). Chesapeake, VA: AACE.

Gow, G., & Parisi, J. (2008). Pursuing the anonymous user: Privacy rights and mandatory registration of prepaid mobile phones. *Bulletin of Science, Technology & Society, 28*(1), 60–68. doi:10.1177/0270467607311487

Graf, S., & Bekele, R. (2006). Forming heterogeneous groups for intelligent collaborative learning systems with ant colony optimization. LNCS, 4053, 217–226. doi:10.1007/11774303_22

Graf, S., Ives, C., Rahman, N., & Ferri, A. (2011). AAT: a tool for accessing and analysing students' behaviour data in learning systems. In *Proceedings of the 1st International Conference on Learning Analytics and Knowledge* (pp. 174-179). New York, NY: ACM. 10.1145/2090116.2090145

Graham, C. M., Daniel, H., & Doore, B. (2016). Millennial Teamwork and Technical Proficiency's Impact on Virtual Team Effectiveness: Implications for Business Educators and Leaders. [IJeC]. *International Journal of e-Collaboration, 12*(3), 34–50. doi:10.4018/IJeC.2016070103

Graham, C. M., & Doore, B. (2015). Millennial leadership: The oppositional relationship between leadership type and the quality of database system's development in virtual environments. *International Journal of e-Collaboration, 11*(3), 29–48. doi:10.4018/ijec.2015070103

Green, D., & Roberts, G. (2010). Personnel implications of public sector virtual organizations. *Public Personnel Management, 39*(1), 47–57. doi:10.1177/009102601003900103

Greenhalgh, T., Robert, G., Macfarlane, F., Bate, P., & Kyryiakidou, O. (2004). Diffusion of Innovations in Service Organizations: Systematic Review and Recommendations. *The Milbank Quarterly, 82*(4), 581–629. doi:10.1111/j.0887-378X.2004.00325.x PMID:15595944

Greer, J., McCalla, G., Collins, J., Kumar, V., Meagher, P., & Vassileva, J. (1998). Supporting Peer Help and Collaboration in Distributed Workplace Environments. *International Journal of Artificial Intelligence in Education, 9*, 159–177.

Gregory, P. (2010). *CISSP Guide to Security Essentials*. Cengage Learning. Course Technology. Retrieved from https://www.cengage.com/c/cissp-guide-to-security-essentials-2e.../9781285060422

Grönroos, C. (2015). *Service Management and Marketing*. New York: Wiley.

Grove, A. S. (1999). *Only the Paranoid Survive*. New York: Doubleday.

Grublješič, T., & Jaklič, J. (2015). Business intelligence acceptance: The prominence of organizational factors. *Information Systems Management, 32*(4), 299–315. doi:10.1080/10580530.2015.1080000

Guile, B. R., & Quinn, J. B. (1988). *Technology of Services: Politics for Growth, Trade, and Employment*. Washington, DC: National Academy Press.

Guye-Vuillème, A., Capin, T. K., Pandzic, I. S., Thalmann, N. M., & Thalmann, D. (1998). *Nonverbal communication interface for collaborative virtual environments. Collaborative Virtual Environments*. University of Manchester.

Hagel, J., & Brown, J. S. (2017). Shaping Strategies for the IoT. *Computer, 50*(8), 64–68. doi:10.1109/MC.2017.3001254

Haider, A., & Tang, S. S. (2016). Maximising Value Through IT and Business Alignment: A Case of IT Governance Institutionalisation at a Thai Bank. *International Journal of Technology Diffusion, 7*(3), 33–58. doi:10.4018/IJTD.2016070104

Haight, M., Quan-Haase, A., & Corbett, B. A. (2014). Revisiting the digital divide in Canada: The impact of demographic factors on access to the Internet, level of online activity, and social networking site usage. *Information Communication and Society, 17*(4), 503–519. doi:10.1080/1369118X.2014.891633

Hair, J. H. Jr, Anderson, R. E., Tatham, R. L., & Black, W. C. (1995). *Multivariate Data Analysis*. Prentice Hall.

Hall, E. T., Birdwhistell, R. L., Bock, B., Bohannan, P., Diebold, A. R. Jr, Durbin, M., ... La Barre, W. (1968). Proxemics. *Current Anthropology, 9*(2/3), 83–108. doi:10.1086/200975

Halpin, H., Hayes, P., & Mccusker, J. (2010). When owl: same as is not the same: An analysis of identity in linked data. In *Proceedings of the International Semantic Web Conference, ISWC* (pp. 305-320). Springer Berlin Heidelberg.

Hambley, L. A., O'Neill, T. A., & Kline, T. J. (2007). Virtual team leadership. The effects of leadership style and communication medium on team interaction styles and outcomes. *Organizational Behavior and Human Decision Processes, 103*(1), 1–20. doi:10.1016/j.obhdp.2006.09.004

Hammersley, M. (1992). *What's wrong with ethnography? Methodological explorations*. London: Routledge.

Hane, P. (2013). *Sharing Research Data—New figshare For Institutions*. Retrieved 3 3, 2016, from Against The Grain Designed: www.against-the-grain.com/2013/09/sharing-research-data-new-figshare-for-institutions-2/

Hannola, L., & Ovaska, P. (2011). Challenging frontend-of-innovation in information systems. *Journal of Computer Information Systems, 52*(1), 66–75.

Haque, H., Tarofder, A. K., Mahmud, S. A., & Ismail, A. Z. (2007). Internet advertisement in Malaysia: A study on attitudinal differences. *The Electronic Journal on Information Systems in Developing Countries, 31*(9), 1–15. doi:10.1002/j.1681-4835.2007.tb00218.x

Harambam, J., Aupers, S., & Houtman, D. (2013). The contentious gap: From digital divide to cultural beliefs about online interactions. *Information Communication and Society, 16*(7), 1093–1114. doi:10.1080/1369118X.2012.687006

Hare, C., Law, J., & Brennan, C. (2013). The Vulnerable Healthcare Consumer: An Interpretive Synthesis of The Patient Experience Literature. *International Journal of Consumer Studies, 37*(3), 299–311. doi:10.1111/ijcs.12006

Hargittai, E. (2002). Second-level digital divide: Differences in people's online Skills. *First Monday, 7*(4). Retrieved from http://firstmonday.org/ article/view/942/864

Hargittai, E., & Hinnant, A. (2008). Digital inequality: Differences in young adults' use of the Internet. *Communication Research, 35*(5), 602–621. doi:10.1177/0093650208321782

Hargrove, R. A. (1998). *Mastering the art of creative collaboration.* New York, NY: McGraw-Hill.

Harindranath, G. (2008). ICT in a Transition Economy: The Case of Hungary. *Journal of Global Information Technology Management, 11*(4), 33–55. doi:10.1080/1097198X.2008.10856478

Harris, S. (2013). *All-In-One CISSP Exam Guide* (6th ed.). McGraw Hill.

Hartig, O., Bizer, C., & Freytag, J.-C. (2009). Executing SPARQL queries over the Web of Linked Data. *Proceedings of the International Semantic Web Conference.* 10.1007/978-3-642-04930-9_19

Hartig, O., & Zhao, J. (2009). Using web data provenance for quality assessment. *CEUR Workshop Proceedings.*

Hasan, B. (2016). Perceived irritation in online shopping: The impact of website designcharacteristics. *Computers in Human Behavior, 54*, 224–230. doi:10.1016/j.chb.2015.07.056

Hashim, A., Ghani, E. K., & Said, J. (2009). Does consumers' demographic profile influence online shopping? *Canadian Social Science, 5*(5), 19–31.

Hassan, L., & Abdelghaffar, H. (2016). Social Development of Rules: Can Social Networking Sites Benefit E-Rulemaking? *Transforming Government: People, Process and Policy. Emerald, 10*(2).

Hasselbring, W., & Steinacker, G. (2017). *Microservice Architectures for Scalability, Agility and Reliability in E-Commerce. In 2017 IEEE International Conference on Software Architecture Workshops* (pp. 243–246). Gothenburg: ICSAW; http://ieeexplore.ieee.org/stamp/stamp.jsp?tp=&arnumber=7958496&isnumber=7958419, doi:10.1109/ICSAW.2017.11

Hausenblas, M. (2009). *Linked data applications. First Community Draft.* DERI.

Hausmann, R. G. M., van de Sande, B., & VanLehn, K. (2008). Are Self-explaining and Coached Problem Solving More Effective When Done by Pairs of Students Than Alone? *Proceedings of the 30th Annual Cognitive Science Society* (p. 744). Washington, DC: Cognitive Science Society

Hayes-Roth, F. (1983). *Building knowledge based systems* (1st ed.). Addison-Wesley.

Hayne, S. C., & Smith, C. A. P. (2005). The relationship between e-collaboration and cognition. *International Journal of e-Collaboration, 1*(3), 17–34. doi:10.4018/jec.2005070102

Hazarika, B. (2016). *The Role of PR in Crisis Management.* Retrieved February 1st, 2018, from http://www.dsc.edu.in/the-role-of-pr-in-crisis-management/

HE_India. (2017). *HE_India.* Retrieved from Higher Education in India: www.education.nic.in/higedu.asp

HEAC. (2018). *about HEAC.* Retrieved from Accreditation and Quality Assurance Commission for Higher Education: http://heac.org.jo

Hearit, K. M. (2006). *Crisis Management By Apology: Corporate Response to Allegations of Wrongdoing.* Lawrence Erlbaum Associates.

Heeks, R., & Molla, A. (2009). *Impact Assessment of ICT-for-Development Projects: A Compendium of Approaches.* IDPM Development Informatics Working Paper no. 36. Retrieved from http://www.sed.manchester.ac.uk/idpm/research/publications/wp/di/index.htm

Heeks, R. (2010). Do information and communication technologies (ICTs) contribute to development? *Journal of International Development, 22*(5), 625–640. doi:10.1002/jid.1716

Heer, J., & Shneiderman, B. (2012). Interactive dynamics for visual analysis. *Communications of the ACM, 55*(4), 45–54. doi:10.1145/2133806.2133821

Hefu, L., Weiling, K., Kwok, K. W., & Zhongsheng, H. (2013). The Impact of IT Capabilities on Firm Performance: The Mediating Roles of Absorptive Capacity and Supply Chain Agility. *Decision Support Systems, 54*(3), 1452–1463. doi:10.1016/j.dss.2012.12.016

Heil, O. P., & Walters, R. G. (1993). Explaining competitive reactions to new products: An empirical signaling study. *Journal of Product Innovation Management, 10*(1), 53–65. doi:10.1016/0737-6782(93)90053-S

Heinrich, B., Hristova, D., Klier, M., Schiller, A., & Szubartowicz, M. (2018). Requirements for Data Quality Metrics. *Journal of Data and Information Quality, 9*(2), 12. doi:10.1145/3148238

HEISC. (2013). *Information Security Program Assessment Tool.* Retrieved from http://www.educause.edu/library/resources/information-security-program-assessment-tool

Heitmann, B., Kim, J. G., Passant, A., Hayes, C., & Kim, H. G. (2010). An architecture for privacy-enabled user profile portability on the Web of Data. In *Proceedings of the 1st International Workshop on Information Heterogeneity and Fusion in Recommender Systems* (pp. 16-23). ACM Publishers. 10.1145/1869446.1869449

Hemeson, C. (2012). *Directive on Consumer data for SIM card registration in the telecommunication sector: An African perspective.* Available at SSRN 1982033.

Hendriks, C. (2015). Coupling citizens and elites in deliberative systems: The role of institutional design. *Europena Joural of Politicial Research, 55*, 43–60.

Herman, I. (2010). Introduction to semantic web technologies. *Proceedings of the Semantic Web Activity Lead World Wide Web Consortium. Semantic Technology Conference.*

Hernandez, M. J. (2013). Database design for mere mortals: A hands-on guide to relational database design (3rd ed.). Addison-Wesley Professional.

Hersey, P., & Blanchard, K. H. (1988). *Management of organizational behavior: utilizing human resources.* Prentice-Hall.

Hesse, B. W., Nelson, D. E., Kreps, G. L., Croyle, R. T., Arora, N. K., Rimer, B. K., & Viswanath, K. (2005). Trust and Sources of Health Information. The Impact of the Internet and its Implications for Health Care Providers: Findings from the First Health Information National Trends Survey. *Archives of Internal Medicine, 165*(22), 1–7. doi:10.1001/archinte.165.22.2618 PMID:16344419

Hindmarsh, J., Fraser, M., Heath, C., & Benford, S. (2002). Virtually missing the point: Configuring CVEs for object-focused interaction. In E. F. Churchill, D. Snowdon, & A. Munro (Eds.), *Collaborative virtual environments: Digital places and spaces for interaction* (pp. 115–139). London: Springer.

Hirsch, J. E. (2005). An index to quantify an individual's scientific research output. *Proceedings of the National Academy of Sciences.* 102, pp. 16569–16572. 10.1073/pnas.0507655102

HKCAAVQ. (2017). Retrieved from Hong Kong Council For Accreditation Of Academic & Vocational Qualifications HKCAAVQ: https://www.hkcaavq.edu.hk/en/

Hoch, J. E., & Dulebohn, J. H. (2013). Shared leadership in enterprise resource planning and human resource management systems implementation. *Human Resource Management Review, 23*(1), 114–125. doi:10.1016/j.hrmr.2012.06.007

Hoch, J. E., & Dulebohn, J. H. (2017). Team personality composition, emergent leadership and shared leadership in virtual teams: A theoretical framework. *Human Resource Management Review, 27*(4), 678–693. doi:10.1016/j.hrmr.2016.12.012

Hoegl, M., & Muethel, M. (2016). Enabling shared leadership in virtual project teams: A practitioners' guide. *Project Management Journal, 47*(1), 7–12. doi:10.1002/pmj.21564

Hoek, R. I. Van. (2000). The Thesis of Leagility Revisited. *International Journal of Agile Manufacturing Management Systems, 2*(3), 196-201.

Hoffman, S., & Podgurski, A. (2007). Securing the HIPPA security rule. *Journal of Internet Law, 10*(8), 1–11.

Hofstede, G., Hofstede, G. J., & Minkov, M. (2010). *Cultures and Organizations: Software of the Mind.* New York, NY: McGraw-Hill.

Hogan, A. (2014). Linked Data and the Semantic Web Standards. In *Linked Data Management* (pp. 3–48). CRC Press. doi:10.1201/b16859-3

Hohlfeld, T. N., Ritzhaupt, A. D., Barron, A. E., & Kemker, K. (2008). Examining the digital divide in K-12 public schools: Four-year trends for supporting ICT literacy in Florida. *Computers & Education, 51*(4), 1648–1663. doi:10.1016/j.compedu.2008.04.002

Hong, W., & Zhu, K. (2006). Migrating to Internet-based e-commerce: Factors affecting e-commerce adoption and migration at the firm Level. *Information & Management, 43*(2), 204–221. doi:10.1016/j.im.2005.06.003

Hope, T. G. (2009). *Damas Says It Must Restructure, Delay Debt Payments to Survive.* Retrieved August 30, 2013, from The National: http://www.thenational.ae/business/banking/damas-says-it-must-restructure-delay-debt-payments-to-survive

Hórreo, V. S., & Carro, R. M. (2007). Studying the Impact of Personality and Group Formation on Learner Performance. *Journal of Lecture Notes in Computer Science, 4715*, 287–294. doi:10.1007/978-3-540-74812-0_22

Hoskisson, R., Eden, L., Lau, C., & Wright, M. (2000). Strategy in Emerging Economies. *Academy of Management Journal, 43*(3), 249–267. doi:10.2307/1556394

Howard, J. (2013). *Posting Your Latest Article? You Might Have to Take It Down.* Retrieved 3 3, 2016, from The Chronicle of Higher Education: https://www.chronicle.com/blogs/wiredcampus/posting-your-latest-article-you-might-have-to-take-it-down/48865

Howard, C., & Mathews, W. K. (2000). *On Deadline: Managing Media Relations* (3rd ed.). Lone Grove, IL: Waveland Press.

Huang, H. L. (2013). Performance effects of aligning service innovation and the strategic use of information technology. *Service Business*. doi:10.100711628-013-0192-z

Hull, D., West, H. G., & Cecez-Kecmanovi, D. (2011). Two Models of E-Democracy: A Case Study of Government Online Engagement with the Community. University of New South Wales, Australia.

Hu, P. J., Chau, P. Y. K., Sheng, O. R. L., & Tam, K. Y. (1999). Examining the technology Acceptance Model Using Physician Acceptance of Telemedicine Technology. *Journal of Management Information Systems*, 16(2), 91–112. doi: 10.1080/07421222.1999.11518247

Hur, Y., Ko, Y. J., & Claussen, C. L. (2012). Determinants of using sports web portals: An empirical examination of the sport website acceptance model. *International Journal of Sports Marketing & Sponsorship*, 13(3), 6–25. doi:10.1108/IJSMS-13-03-2012-B003

Hwang, B.-N., Huang, C.-Y., & Yang, C.-L. (2016). Determinants and their causal relationships affecting the adoption of cloud computing in science and technology institutions. *Innovation*, 18(2), 164–190. doi:10.1080/14479338.2016.1203729

Iacovou, C., Benbasat, I., & Dexter, A. (1995). Electronic data interchange and small organisations: Adoption and impact of technology. *Management Information Systems Quarterly*, 19(4), 465–485. doi:10.2307/249629

IBIS World. (2011). *IBIS world industry report 33411a: Computer manufacturing in the US*. Retrieved October 1, 2013 from www.ibisworld.com

IDC. (2017). *IDC: Worldwide Tablet Market Declines 5.4% in Q3 2017*. XDA Developers. Retrieved on 2/19/2018 from: https://www.xda-developers.com/idc-q3-2017-tablet-market-decline/

Idris, N., & Ahmad, K. (2011). Managing data source quality for data warehouse in manufacturing services. *Proceedings of the 2011 IEEE International Conference on Electrical Engineering and Informatics*. 10.1109/ICEEI.2011.6021598

Ifinedo, P. (2011). Internet/E-Business technologies acceptance in Canada's SMEs: An exploratory investigation. *Internet Research*, 21(3), 255–281. doi:10.1108/10662241111139309

Igbaria, M. (1993). User Acceptance of Microcomputer Technology: An Empirical Test. *Omega*, 21(1), 73–90. doi:10.1016/0305-0483(93)90040-R

Ikeda, M., Go, S., & Mizoguchi, R. (1997). *Opportunistic group formation*. Paper presented at the 8th World Conference on Artificial Intelligence in Education, Amsterdam, The Netherlands.

Ilie, V., Slyke, C. V., Parikh, M. A., & Courtney, J. F. (2009). Paper Versus Electronic Medical records: The Effects of Access on Physicians' Decisions to Use Complex Information Technologies. *Decision Sciences*, 40(2), 213–241. doi:10.1111/j.1540-5915.2009.00227.x

Imai, T., Qui, Z., Behara, S., Tachi, S., Aoyama, T., & Johnson, A. (2000). *Overcoming time-zone differences and time management problem with tele-immersion*. 10th Annual Internet Society Conference (INET), Yokohama, Japan.

IMF. (2000). *Transition Economies: An IMF Perspective on Progress and Prospects*. Retrieved May 20, 2009 from http://www.imf.org/external/np/exr/ib/2000/110300.htm#I

Im, I., Hong, S., & Kang, M. S. (2011). An international comparison of technology adoption: Testing the UTAUT model. *Information & Management*, 48(1), 1–8. doi:10.1016/j.im.2010.09.001

Im, K. S., Grover, V., & Teng, J. T. C. (2013). Research note - Do large firms become smaller by using information technology? *Information Systems Research*, *24*(2), 470–491. doi:10.1287/isre.1120.0439

IMS-LD. (2003). *IMS Global Learning Consortium: Learning Design Specification*. Retrieved February 2, 2015, from http://www.imsglobal.org/learningdesign/

IMS-LTI. (2014). *IMS Global Learning Consortium: Learning Tools Interoperability*. Retrieved February 2, 2015, from http://www.imsglobal.org/lti/

Indjikian, R., & Siegel, D. (2005). The Impact of Investments in IT on Economic Performance: Implications for Developing Countries. *World Development*, *33*(5), 681–700. doi:10.1016/j.worlddev.2005.01.004

Inmon, W. H. (2002). *Building the data warehouse* (3rd ed.). John Wiley.

INQAAHE. (2017). *INQAAHE*. Retrieved from The International Network for Quality Assurance Agencies in Higher Education: http://www.inqaahe.org/presentation

Institute of Medicine (IOM). (1991). *The Computer-Based Patient Record: An Essential Technology For Healthcare*. National Academy Press.

Institute of Medicine (IOM). (1997). *The Computer-based Patient Record: An Essential Technology for Health Care*. National Academy Press.

Institute of Medicine. (2009). *Health Literacy, eHealth, and Communication: Putting the Consumer First: Workshop Summary*. Washington, DC: The National Academies Press.

Internet World Stats. (2018). Retrieved on 02/26/2018 from https://www.internetworldstats.com/

Iriberri, A., & Leroy, G. (2009). A life-cycle perspective on online community success. *ACM Computing Surveys*, *41*(2), 11. doi:10.1145/1459352.1459356

Ironmonger, D. S., Lloyd-Smith, C. W., & Soupourmas, F. (2000). New Products of the 1980s and 1990s: The Diffusion of Household Technology in the Decade 1985-1995. *Prometheus*, *18*(4), 403–415. doi:10.1080/08109020020008514

Irvin, R. A., & Stansbury, J. (2004). Citizen Participation In Decision Making: Is It Worth The Effort? *Public Administration Review*, *64*(1), 55–65. doi:10.1111/j.1540-6210.2004.00346.x

ISC2 CBK. (2017). *The (ISC)2 Body of Knowledge*. Retrieved from https://www.isc2.org/Certifications/CBK

ISO/IEC 21827:2008. (2008). *Information technology - Security techniques - Systems Security Engineering - Capability Maturity Model (SSE-CMM)*. Retrieved from http://www.iso.org/iso/catalogue_detail.htm?csnumber=44716

ISO/IEC 27002:2013. (2013). *Information technology Security techniques - Code of practice for information security controls*. Retrieved from http://www.iso.org/iso/catalogue_detail?csnumber=54533 ISO/IEC

ITIL. (2010). *Benefits of standard IT governance frameworks*. Retrieved from http://www.itil-officialsite.com

ITU. (2017). *International Telecommunications Union (ITU) Statistics*. Access on 15 February, 2018 from: http://www.itu.int/en/ITU-D/Statistics/Pages/stat/default.aspx

Ives, B., & Learmonth, G. P. (1984). The information system as a competitive weapon. *Communications of the ACM*, *27*(12), 1193–1201. doi:10.1145/2135.2137

Ives, B., Olson, M. H., & Baroudi, J. J. (1983). The Measurement of User Information Satisfaction. *Communications of the ACM*, *26*(10), 785–793. doi:10.1145/358413.358430

Jabr, W., Mookerjee, R., Tan, Y., & Mookerjee, V.S. (2014). Leveraging philanthropic behavior for customer support: The case of user support firms. *MIS Quarterly, 38*(1), 187-208.

Jaccard, J., Turrisi, R., & Wan, C. (1990), Interaction effects in multiple regression. Thousand Oaks, CA: Sage Publications. Series: Quantitative Applications in the Social Sciences, No.72.

Jacsó, P. (2010). Metadata mega mess in Google Scholar. *Online Information Review, 31*(1), 175–191. doi:10.1108/14684521011024191

Jaffri, A. (2010). *Linked data for the enterprise - an easy route to the semantic web.* Retrieved from HTTP:// www.capgemini.com/blog/capping-it-off/2010/03/linked-data-for-the-enterprise-an-easy-route-to-thesemantic-web

Jahromi, N. T., Glitho, R. H., Larabi, A., & Brunner, R. (2017). An NFV and Microservice Based Architecture for On-the-fly Component Provisioning in Content Delivery Networks. *The 15th IEEE Consumer Communications and Networking Conference (CCNC).*

Jain, P., Hitzler, P., Yeh, P. Z., Verma, K., & Sheth, A. P. (2010). Linked Data Is Merely More Data. *Proceedings of the AAI Spring Symposium: linked data meets artificial intelligence.*

Jamal, A.-H., & Tilchin, O. (2016). Teachers' Accountability for Adaptive Project-Based Learning. *American Journal of Educational Research, 4*(5), 420–426.

Janssen, M. (2008, January). Exploring the service-oriented enterprise: Drawing lessons from a case study. In *Hawaii International Conference on System Sciences, Proceedings of the 41st Annual* (pp. 101-101). IEEE. 10.1109/HICSS.2008.166

Jarraya, H., & Laurent, M. (2010). A secure peer-to-peer backup service keeping great autonomy while under the supervision of a provider. *Computers & Security, 29*(2), 180–195. doi:10.1016/j.cose.2009.10.003

Jayawardhena, C., Wright, L. T., & Dennis, C. (2007). Consumers online: Intentions, orientations and segmentation. *International Journal of Retail & Distribution Management, 35*(6), 515–526. doi:10.1108/09590550710750377

Jennex, M. E. (2004). Emergency Response Systems: The Utility Y2K Experience. *Journal of Information Technology Theory and Application, 6*(3), 85–102.

Jentzsch, N. (2012). Implications of mandatory registration for mobile users in Africa. *Telecommunications Policy, 36*(8), 608–620. doi:10.1016/j.telpol.2012.04.002

Jimenez, J. M., & Polasek, W. (2003). E-democracy and Knowledge. A multi criteria Framework for The New Democratic Area. *Journal of Multi-Criteria Decision Analysis, 12*, 163-176.

Johns, N., & Lee-Ross, D. (1998). *Research Methods in Service Industry Management.* London: Cassell.

Johnson, S., Menor, L., Roth, A., & Chase, R. (2000). A Critical Evaluation of the New Service Development Process: Integrating Service Innovation and Service Design. In New Service Development: Creating Memorable Experiences. Thousand Oaks, CA: Sage Publications.

Johnson, E. J., Moe, W. W., Fader, P. S., Bellman, S., & Lohse, G. L. (2007). On the depth and dynamics of online search behaviour. *Management Science, 50*(3), 299–309. doi:10.128//mnsc.1040.0194

Johnson, J. (2008). Is the global financial system AML/CFT prepared? *Journal of Financial Crime, 15*(1), 7–21. doi:10.1108/13590790810841662

Johnson, S. L., Butler, B., Faraj, S., Jarvenpaa, S., Kane, G., & Kudaravalli, S. (2010). New directions in online community research. *Proceedings of the Thirty First International Conference on Information Systems.*

Jones, A., Dardick, G. S., Davies, G., Sutherland, I., & Valli, C. (2009). The 2008 analysis of information remaining on disks offered for sale on the second hand market. *Journal of International Commercial Law & Technology, 4*(3), 162–175.

Jones, C., Ramanau, R., Cross, S., & Healing, G. (2010). Net generation or Digital Natives: Is there a distinct new generation entering university? *Computers & Education, 54*(3), 722–732. doi:10.1016/j.compedu.2009.09.022

Jorden, C. (1993). Prepare for Business-Related Crises. *The Public Relations Journal,* 34–35.

Jorgenson, D. W. (2003). *Information Technology and the G7 Economies.* Conference on Digital Transformations: ICT's Impact on Productivity, London Business School, London, UK.

Joy Online. (2013). *Cyber crime: Ghana 2nd in Africa, 7th in the world.* Retrieved from http://edition.myjoyonline.com/pages/news/201307/110530.php

JU. (2018, Feb 20). *Deanship of Academic Research and Quality Assurance.* Retrieved from The University of Jordan: http://research.ju.edu.jo/ar/arabic/Pages/AccreditedJournals.aspx

Juslin, P. N., & Scherer, K. R. (2005). Vocal expression of affect. The new handbook of methods in nonverbal behavior research, 65-135.

Kabbar, E. F., & Crump, B. J. (2006). The factors that influence adoption of ICTs by recent refugee immigrants to New Zealand. *Informing Science: International Journal of an Emerging Transdiscipline, 9,* 111–121. doi:10.28945/475

Kabbar, E. F., & Crump, B. J. (2007). Promoting ICTs Uptake Among the Refugee Immigrant Community in New Zealand. In P. Kommers (Ed.), *Proceedings of the IADIS International Conference e-Society* (pp. 55-62). Lisbon: IADIS Press.

Kaiser, U. (2009). *A primer in entrepreneurship.* Retrieved February 19, 2018, from http://www.business.uzh.ch/professorships/entrepreneurship/teaching/past/hs08/primer/Kap1primerentrepreneuruka.pdf

Kajko-Mattsson, M., Sjögren, A., & Lindbäck, L. (2017). Everything Is Possible to Structure - Even the Software Engineering Body of Knowledge. In *2017 IEEE/ACM 1st International Workshop on Software Engineering Curricula for Millennials (SECM)* (pp. 61-67). Buenos Aires: IEEE. doi:10.1109/SECM.2017.5

Kang, H., Le, M., & Tao, S. (2016, April). Container and microservice driven design for cloud infrastructure devops. In *Cloud Engineering (IC2E), 2016 IEEE International Conference on* (pp. 202-211). IEEE. 10.1109/IC2E.2016.26

Kaplan, B., & Maxwell, J. A. (1994). Qualitative Research Methods for Evaluating Computer Information Systems. In J. G. Anderson, C. E. Aydin, & S. J. Jay (Eds.), *Evaluating Health Care Information Systems: Methods and Applications* (pp. 45–68). Thousand Oaks, CA: Sage publications.

Karadsheh, L. (2012). Applying security policies and service level agreement to IaaS service model to enhance security and transition. *Computers & Security, 31*(3), 315–326. doi:10.1016/j.cose.2012.01.003

Karahanna, E., Straub, D. W., & Chervany, N. L. (1999). Information Technology Adoption Across Time: A Cross-sectional Comparison of Pre-adoption and Post-adoption Beliefs. *Management Information Systems Quarterly, 23*(2), 183–213. doi:10.2307/249751

Karatas, I., Tunc, M. P., Yilmaz, N., & Karaci, G. (2017). An Investigation of Technological Pedagogical Content Knowledge, Self-Confidence, and Perception of Pre-Service Middle School Mathematics Teachers towards Instructional Technologies. *Journal of Educational Technology & Society, 20*(3), 122–132. Retrieved from http://www.ifets.info/journals/20_3/10.pdf

Karoui, M., Dudezert, A., & Leidner, D. E. (2015). Strategies and symbolism in the adoption of organizational social networking systems. *The Journal of Strategic Information Systems, 24*(1), 15–32. doi:10.1016/j.jsis.2014.11.003

Katz, J., & Aspden, P. (1997). Motivations for and barriers to Internet usage: Results of a national public opinion survey. *Internet Research*, *7*(3), 170–188. doi:10.1108/10662249710171814

Kavoussi, B. (2013). *Ikea Horse Meat Controversy Hurts Company's Reputation: Analysis*. The Huffington Post.

Kayworth, T., & Leidner, D. (2000). The global virtual manager: A prescription for success. *European Management Journal*, *18*(2), 183–194. doi:10.1016/S0263-2373(99)00090-0

Keil, M., & Carmel, E. (1995). Customer-developer links in software development. *Communications of the ACM*, *38*(5), 33–44. doi:10.1145/203356.203363

Kellerman, B. (2006). When Should a Leader Apologize and When Not? *Harvard Business Review*, 73–81. PMID:16579415

Kent, K., & Souppaya, M. (2006). *NIST Special Publication 800-92: Guide to Computer Security Log Management - Recommendations of the National Institute of Standards and Technology*. Retrieved from csrc.nist.gov/publications/nistpubs/800-92/SP800-92.pdf

Kent, M. T. (2007). Taxonomy of mediated crisis responses. *Public Relations Review*, 140–146.

Kersten, G. E. (2003). E-Democracy and Participatory Decision Processes: Lessons From-Negotiation Experiments. *Journal of Multi-Criteria Decision Analysis*, *12*(2-3), 127–143. doi:10.1002/mcda.352

Khabsa, M., & Giles, C. (2014). The Number of Scholarly Documents on the Public Web. *PLoS One*, *9*(5), e93949. doi:10.1371/journal.pone.0093949 PMID:24817403

Khan, S. M. (2017). Multimodal Behavioral Analytics in Intelligent Learning and Assessment Systems. In *Innovative Assessment of Collaboration* (pp. 173–184). Cham: Springer. doi:10.1007/978-3-319-33261-1_11

Kharuddin, S., Foong, S. Y., & Senik, R. (2015). Effects of decision rationality on ERP adoption extensiveness and organizational performance. *Journal of Enterprise Information Management*, *28*(5), 658–679. doi:10.1108/JEIM-02-2014-0018

Khramov, Y. (2006). The cost of code quality. In *Proceedings of the Agile 2006 Conference (AGILE'06)*. IEEE. 10.1109/AGILE.2006.52

Khvorostianov, N., Elias, N., & Nimrod, G. (2011). 'Without it I am nothing': The Internet in the lives of older immigrants. *New Media & Society*, *14*(4), 583–599. doi:10.1177/1461444811421599

Kim, B., & Han, I. (2009). What Drives the Adoption of Mobile Data Services? An Approach from a Value Perspective. *Journal of Information Technology*, *24*(1), 35–45. doi:10.1057/jit.2008.28

Kimbrough, S. O., & Lee, R. M. (1997). Special Issue: Systems for Computer-Mediated Digital Commerce. *IJEC*, *1*(4), 3-10.

Kim, D. W., Yan, P., & Junjie Zhang, J. (2015). Detecting fake anti-virus software distribution webpages. *Computers & Security*, *49*, 95–106. doi:10.1016/j.cose.2014.11.008

Kim, J. H., Kim, M., & Kandampully, J. (2009). Buying environment characteristics in the context of e-service. *European Journal of Marketing*, *43*(9/10), 1188–1204. doi:10.1108/03090560910976438

Kim, M. I., & Johnson, K. B. (2002). Personal Health Records: Evaluation of Functionality and Utility. *Journal of the American Medical Informatics Association*, *9*(2), 171–180. doi:10.1197/jamia.M0978 PMID:11861632

Kim, S. H., Jang, S. Y., & Yang, K. H. (2017). Analysis of the determinants of Software-as-a-Service adoption in small businesses: Risks, benefits, and organizational and environmental factors. *Journal of Small Business Management*, *55*(2), 303–325. doi:10.1111/jsbm.12304

Kim, Y. J., Kang, H. G., Sanders, L., & Lee, S.-Y. T. (2008). Differential effects of IT investments: Complementarity and effect of GDP level. *International Journal of Information Management, 28*(6), 508–516. doi:10.1016/j.ijinfomgt.2008.01.003

Kirat, M. (2005). Public relations practice in the Arab World: A critical assessment. *Public Relations Review, 31*(3), 323–332. doi:10.1016/j.pubrev.2005.05.016

Kirat, M. (2006). Public relations in the United Arab Emirates. *Public Relations Review, 32*(3), 254–260. doi:10.1016/j.pubrev.2006.05.006

Kissel, R. (2013). *Glossary of Key Information Security Terms*. doi: 10.6028/NIST.IR.7298R2

Klein, D., & Chiang, E. (2004). 4 1). The Social Science Citation Index: A Black Box—with an Ideological Bias? *Econ Journal Watch, 1*(1), 134–165.

Klein, R. (2006). Internet-based Patient Physician Electronic Communication Applications: Patient Acceptance and Trust. *e-Service Journal, 5*(2), 27–51. doi:10.2979/esj.2007.5.2.27

Kljun, M., Mariani, J., & Dix, A. (2016). Toward understanding short-term personal information preservation: A study of backup strategies of end users. *Journal of the Association for Information Science and Technology, 67*(12), 2947–2963. doi:10.1002/asi.23526

KMK. (2017). *KMK*. Retrieved from German Council of Science and Humanities: http://www.akkreditierungsrat.de/

Knill, C. (2005). Introduction: cross-national policy convergence: concepts, approaches and explanatory factors. *Journal of European Public Policy, 12*(3), 764–774. doi:10.1080/13501760500161332

Kock, N. (2004). The Psychobiological Model: Toward a New Theory of Computer-Mediated Communication Based on Darwinian Evolution. *Organization Science, 15*(3), 327–348. doi:10.1287/orsc.1040.0071

Kock, N. (2005). What is e-collaboration. *International Journal of e-Collaboration, 1*(1), 1–7.

Kock, N. (2005). What is E-collaboration? *International Journal of e-Collaboration, 1*(1), i–vii.

Kock, N. (2006). Car Racing and Instant Messaging: Task Constraints as Determinants of E-Collaboration Technology Usefulness. *International Journal of e-Collaboration, 2*(2), i–v.

Kock, N. (2008). E-Collaboration and E-Commerce in Virtual Worlds: The Potential of Second Life and World of Warcraft. *International Journal of e-Collaboration, 4*(3), 1–13. doi:10.4018/jec.2008070101

Kock, N. (2013). Using WarpPLS in e-collaboration studies: What if I have only one group and one condition? *International Journal of e-Collaboration, 9*(3), 1–12. doi:10.4018/jec.2013070101

Kock, N. (2016). Visualizing Moderating Effects in Path Models with Latent Variables. *International Journal of e-Collaboration, 12*(1), 1–7. doi:10.4018/IJeC.2016010101

Kock, N. (Ed.). (2008). *Encyclopedia of e-collaboration*. Hershey, PA: Information Science Reference. doi:10.4018/978-1-59904-000-4

Kock, N., & Antunes, P. (2007). Government Funding of E-Collaboration Research in the European Union: A Comparison with the United States Model. *International Journal of e-Collaboration, 3*(2), 36–47. doi:10.4018/jec.2007040103

Kock, N., & D'Arcy, J. (2002). Resolving the E-collaboration Paradox: The Competing Influences of Media Naturalness and Compensatory Adaptation. *Inform. Manage. Consulting, 17*(4), 72–78.

Kock, N., Davison, R., Ocker, R., & Wazlawick, R. (2001). E-collaboration: A look at Past Research and Future Challenges. *Journal of Systems and Information Technology, 5*(1), 1–9. doi:10.1108/13287260180001059

Kock, N., & DeLuca, D. (2007). Improving Business Processes Electronically: An action Research Study in New Zealand and the US. *Journal of Global Information Technology Management, 10*(3), 6–27. doi:10.1080/1097198X.2007.10856447

Kock, N., & Nosek, J. (2005). Expanding the Boundaries of E-Collaboration, IEEE *Transactions on Professional Communication. Special Issue on Expanding the Boundaries of E-Collaboration, 48*(1), 1–9.

Koehler, M., & Mishra, P. (2009). What is Technological Pedagogical Content Knowledge (TPACK)? *Contemporary Issues in Technology and Teacher Education, 9*(1), 60-70. Retrieved January 9, 2018 from https://www.learntechlib.org/p/29544/

Koh, J., Kim, Y. G., Butler, B., & Bock, G. W. (2007). Encouraging participation in virtual communities. *Communications of the ACM, 50*(2), 69–73. doi:10.1145/1216016.1216023

Kohli, R., Devaraj, S., & Ow, T. T. (2012). Does information technology investment influence a firm's market value? A case of non-publicly traded healthcare firms. *Management Information Systems Quarterly, 36*(4), 1145–1163.

Kolb, A. Y., & Kolb, D. A. (2005). *The Kolb Learning Style Inventory, version 3.1: 2005 technical specifications*. Boston: Hay Resources Direct.

Kolb, D. A. (1984). *Experiential Learning: Experience as the Source of Learning and Development*. Englewood Cliffs, NJ: Prentice-Hall Inc.

Kolkowska, E., & Dhillon, G. (2013). Organizational power and information security rule compliance. *Computers & Security, 33*, 3–11. doi:10.1016/j.cose.2012.07.001

Kompan, M., & Bieliková, M. (2016). Enhancing existing e-learning systems by single and group recommendations. *Int. J. Cont. Engineering Education and Life-Long Learning, 26*(4), 386–404. doi:10.1504/IJCEELL.2016.080980

Kontokostas, D., Westphal, P., Auer, S., Hellmann, S., Lehmann, J., Cornelissen, R., & Zaveri, A. (2014, April). Test-driven evaluation of linked data quality. In *Proceedings of the 23rd international conference on World Wide Web* (pp. 747-758). ACM.

Kosko, B., & Toms, M. (1993). *Fuzzy thinking: the new science of fuzzy logic*. New York: Hyperion.

Kotey, B., & Folker, C. (2007). Employee training in SMEs: Effects of size and firm type. *Journal of Small Business Management, 45*(2), 214–234. doi:10.1111/j.1540-627X.2007.00210.x

Kothari, R. (1979). *The North-South Issue*. Mazingria, No 10.

Kraemer, K. L., & Dedrick, J. (2002). Enter the dragon: China's computer industry. *Computer, 35*(2), 28–36. doi:10.1109/2.982913

Kristensen, K., & Kijl, B. (2010). Collaborative Performance: Addressing the ROI of Collaboration. *International Journal of e-Collaboration, 6*(1), 53–69. doi:10.4018/jec.2010091104

Kris, V., & Jan, V. (2010). Determinants of the Use of Knowledge Sources in the Adoption of Open Source Server Software. *International Journal of Technology Diffusion, 1*(4), 53–70. doi:10.4018/jtd.2010100105

Kroenke, D. M., & Auer, D. J. (2013). Database processing: fundamentals, design, and implementation (13th ed.). Prentice Hall.

Kulkarn, A., Aziz, B., Shams, I., & Busse, J. (2009, September 9). Comparisons of citations in Web of Science, Scopus, and Google Scholar for articles published in general medical journals. *Journal of the American Medical Association, 302*(10), 1092–1096. doi:10.1001/jama.2009.1307 PMID:19738094

Kumar, V., Jones, E., Venkatesan, R., & Leone, R. P. (2011). Is market orientation a source of sustainable competitive advantage or simply the cost of competing? *Journal of Marketing*, *75*, 1–31. doi:10.1509/jmkg.75.2.1

Kyprianidou, M., Demetriadis, S., Pombortsis, A., & Karatasios, G. (2009). PEGASUS: Designing a system for supporting group activity. *Journal of Multicultural Education and Technology*, *3*(1), 47–60. doi:10.1108/17504970910951147

Labbe, C. (2010). Ike Antkare one of the great stars in the scientific firmament. *ISSI Newsletter, 6*(2). Retrieved 6 6, 2016, from http://evaluation.hypotheses.org/files/2010/12/pdf_IkeAntkareISSI.pdf

Lambert, N. M., & McCombs, B. L. (1998). *How students learn: Reforming schools through learner-centered education.* Washington, DC: American Psychological Association. doi:10.1037/10258-000

Lam, W., Kong, E., & Chua, A. (2008). Managing Online Discussion Forums for Collaborative Learning. In N. Kock (Ed.), *Encyclopedia of E-Collaboration* (pp. 437–443). Hershey, PA: Information Science Reference. doi:10.4018/978-1-59904-000-4.ch067

Langone, J., & Leibovici, A. (2012). *VMware View 5 Desktop Virtualization Solutions.* Packt Publishing Ltd.

Lapointe, L., & Rivard, S. (2005). A Multilevel Model of Resistance to Information Technology Implementation. *Management Information Systems Quarterly*, *29*(3), 461–491. doi:10.2307/25148692

Latimore, D., Baskin, O., Heiman, S., Toth, E., & Van, J. (2004). *Public Relations: The Profession and the Practice.* New York: McGraw-Hill.

Latonero, M., & Shklovski, I. (2011). Emergency Management, Twitter, and Social Media Evangelism. *International Journal of Information Systems for Crisis Response and Management*, *3*(4), 1–16. doi:10.4018/jiscrm.2011100101

Lawless, M. W., & Fisher, R. J. (1990). Sources of durable competitive advantage in new products. *Journal of Product Innovation Management*, *7*(1), 35–44. doi:10.1016/0737-6782(90)90030-I

Lawrence, J. E. (2002). *The Use of Internet in Small to Medium-Sized Enterprises* (Unpublished PhD thesis). University of Salford, UK.

Lawrence, J. E. (2008). The Challenges and Utilization of e-Commerce: The Use of Internet by Small to Medium-sized Enterprises in the United Kingdom. *Information. Social Justice (San Francisco, Calif.)*, *1*(2).

Lawrence, J. E. (2009). The Utilization of E-Commerce by Small to Medium-sized Enterprises: A U K Perspective. *Proceedings of the IADIS International Conference Information Systems*. Barcelona, Spain.

Lawrence, J. E. (2013). *Adoption and Usage of Internet in Small to Medium-sized Enterprises.* Lap Lambert Academic Publishing.

Lawrence, J. E. (2015). Examining the Factors that Influence ICT Adoption in SMEs: A Research Preliminary Findings. *International Journal of Technology Diffusion*, *6*(4), 40–57. doi:10.4018/IJTD.2015100103

Lederman, S. (2016). *Geek Guide - Containers 101.* Retrieved from www.puppet.com

Lee, C. P., Chang, K., & Berry, F. S. (2011). Testing the Development and Diffusion of E-Government and E-Democracy: A Global Perspective. *Public Administration Review*, *71*(3), 444–454. doi:10.1111/j.1540-6210.2011.02228.x

Lee, C.-P. (2010). The Impact of Technology Anxiety on the Use of Mobile Financial Applications. *International Journal of Technology Diffusion*, *1*(4), 1–12. doi:10.4018/jtd.2010100101

Lee, D. M. S., Trauth, E., & Farwell, D. (1995). Critical Skills and Knowledge Requirements of IS Professionals: A Joint Academic/Industry Investigation. *Management Information Systems Quarterly*, *19*(3), 313–340. doi:10.2307/249598

Lee, S., Levendis, J., & Gutierrez, L. (2012). Telecommunications and economic growth: An empirical analysis of sub-Saharan Africa. *Applied Economics, 44*(4), 461–469. doi:10.1080/00036846.2010.508730

Lee, Y. W., Strong, D. M., Kahn, B. K., & Wang, R. Y. (2002). AIMQ: A methodology for information quality assessment. *Information & Management, 40*(2), 133–146. doi:10.1016/S0378-7206(02)00043-5

Lee, Y., Kozar, K., & Larsen, K. (2003). The Technology Acceptance Model: Past, Present, and Future. *Communications of the Association for Information Systems, 12*, 752–780.

Lehmann-Willenbrock, N., Hung, H., & Keyton, J. (2017). New frontiers in analyzing dynamic group interactions: Bridging social and computer science. *Small Group Research, 48*(5), 519–531. doi:10.1177/1046496417718941 PMID:29249891

Lehner, W., Hummer, W., & Schlesinger, L. (2002). In processing reporting function views in a data warehouse environment. In *Proceedings of the 18th International Conference on Data Engineering (ICDE'02)*. IEEE. 10.1109/ICDE.2002.994707

Leimeister, J. M., & Krcmar, H. (2004). Revisiting the virtual community business model. *Proceedings of the Tenth Americas Conference on Information Systems*.

Leimeister, J. M., Sidiras, P., & Krcmar, H. (2006). Exploring success factors of virtual communities: The perspective of members and operators. *Journal of Organizational Computing and Electronic Commerce, 16*(3&4), 277–298.

Lenhart, A., Purcell, K., Smith, A., & Zickuhr, K. (2010). *Social Media & Mobile Internet Use among Teens and Young Adults. Millennials.* Pew internet & American Life Project.

Lerbinger, O. (1997). *The Crisis Manager: Facing Risk and Responsibility.* Lawrence Erlbaum.

Lesitaokana, W. (2014). Key issues in the development of mobile telephony in Botswana (1998-2011): An empirical investigation. *New Media & Society, 16*(5), 840–855. doi:10.1177/1461444813495161

Levendis, J., & Lee, S. (2013). On the endogeneity of telecommunications and economic growth: Evidence from Asia. *Information Technology for Development, 19*(1), 62–85. doi:10.1080/02681102.2012.694793

Lian, J. W., Yen, D. C., & Wang, Y. T. (2014). An exploratory study to understand the critical factors affecting the decision to adopt cloud computing in Taiwan hospital. *International Journal of Information Management, 34*(1), 28–36. doi:10.1016/j.ijinfomgt.2013.09.004

Liao, C. (2017). Leadership in virtual teams: A multilevel perspective. *Human Resource Management Review, 27*(4), 648–659. doi:10.1016/j.hrmr.2016.12.010

Liao, Z., & Cheung, M. T. (2002). Internet-based e-banking and consumer attitudes: An empirical study. *Information & Management, 39*(4), 287–301. doi:10.1016/S0378-7206(01)00097-0

Li, H., Gupta, A., Zhang, J., & Sarathy, R. (2014). Examining the Decision to Use Standalone Personal health Record Systems as a Trust-Enabled fair Social Contract. *Decision Support Systems, 57*, 376–386. doi:10.1016/j.dss.2012.10.043

Lin, A., & Chen, N. C. (2012). Cloud computing as an innovation: Perception, attitude and adoption. *International Journal of Information Management, 32*(6), 533–540. doi:10.1016/j.ijinfomgt.2012.04.001

Lincoln, Y. S., & Guba, E. G. (1985). *Naturalistic Inquiry.* Newbury Park, CA: Sage.

Lin, H. F., & Lin, S. M. (2008). Determinants of e-business diffusion: A test of the technology diffusion perspective. *Technovation, 28*(3), 135–145. doi:10.1016/j.technovation.2007.10.003

Lin, H., Fan, W., & Wallace, L. (2013). The effects of social and technical factors on user satisfaction, sense of belonging and knowledge community usage. *International Journal of e-Collaboration, 9*(3), 13–30. doi:10.4018/jec.2013070102

Lin, H., Fan, W., & Zhang, Z. (2009). A qualitative study of web-based knowledge communities: Examining success factors. *International Journal of e-Collaboration*, *5*(3), 39–57. doi:10.4018/jec.2009070103

Lipner, S. (2015). Security Assurance. *Communications of the ACM*, *58*(11), 24–26. doi:10.1145/2822513

Liu, M. (2008). Determinants of e-commerce development: An empirical study by firms in Shaanxi, China. *4th International Conference on Wireless Communications, Networking and Mobile Computing*, 9177-9180. 10.1109/WiCom.2008.2143

Liu, C. F., Tsai, Y. C., & Jang, F. L. (2013). Patients' Acceptance Towards a Web-based Personal Health Record System: An Empirical Study in Taiwan. *International Journal of Environmental Research and Public Health*, *10*(10), 5191–5208. doi:10.3390/ijerph10105191 PMID:24142185

Liu, C. T., Du, T. C., & Tsai, H. H. (2009). A study of the service quality of general portals. *Information & Management*, *46*(1), 52–56. doi:10.1016/j.im.2008.11.003

Liu, S., Duffy, A. H. B., Whitfield, R. I., & Boyle, I. M. (2010). Integration of decision support systems to improve decision support performance. *Knowledge and Information Systems*, *22*(3), 261–286. doi:10.100710115-009-0192-4

Li, X., Hsieh, J. J. P., & Rai, A. (2013). Motivational differences across post-acceptance information system usage behaviors: An investigation in the business intelligence systems context. *Information Systems Research*, *24*(3), 659–682. doi:10.1287/isre.1120.0456

Li, X., & Madnick, S. E. (2015). Understanding the Dynamics of Service-Oriented Architecture Implementation. *Journal of Management Information Systems*, *32*(2), 104–133. doi:10.1080/07421222.2015.1063284

Li, Y. H. (2008). An empirical investigation on the determinants of e-procurement adoption in Chinese manufacturing enterprises. *15th International Conference on Management Science & Engineering*, 32-37. 10.1109/ICMSE.2008.4668890

Long, Y., & Aleven, V. (2011). Students' Understanding of Their Student Model. *International Journal of Artificial Intelligence in Education*, *67*(38), 179–186.

Lorenzo, C. M., Sicilia, M. A., & Sánchez, S. (2012). Studying the effectiveness of multi-user immersive environments for collaborative evaluation tasks. *Computers & Education*, *59*(4), 1361–1376. doi:10.1016/j.compedu.2012.06.002

Lotan, G., Graff, E., Amanny, M., Gaffney, D., Pearce, I., & Boyd, D. (2011). The Revolutions Were Tweeted: Information Flows During The 2011 Tunisian And Egyptian Revolutions. *International Journal of Communication*, *5*, 1375–1405.

Lovelock, C., & Wirtz, J. (2004). *Services Marketing: People, Technology, Strategy*. Singapore: Pearson.

Low, C., Chen, Y., & Wu, M. (2011). Understanding the determinants of cloud computing adoption. *Industrial Management & Data Systems*, *111*(7), 1006–1023. doi:10.1108/02635571111161262

Lunden, I. (2013). Confirmed: Elsevier Has Bought Mendeley For $69M-$100M To Expand Its Open, Social Education Data Efforts. *Techcrunch*. Retrieved 4 4, 2016, from https://techcrunch.com/2013/04/08/confirmed-elsevier-has-bought-mendeley-for-69m-100m-to-expand-open-social-education-data-efforts/

Lu, Y., & Ramamurthy, K. (2011). Understanding the link between information technology capability and organizational agility: An empirical examination. *Management Information Systems Quarterly*, *35*(4), 931–954. doi:10.2307/41409967

Maali, F., Cyganiak, R., & Peristeras, V. (2012). A publishing pipeline for linked government data. *The semantic web: Research and applications*, 778-792.

MacGregor, R. C., Bunker, D. J., & Waugh, P. (1998). Electronic Commerce and Small / Medium Enterprises (SMEs) in Australia: An Electronic Data Interchange (EDI) Pilot Study. *Eleventh International Bled Electronic Commerce Conference*, Bled, Slovenia.

Magnisalis, I., & Demetriadis, S. (2015). Tool Orchestration in e-Collaboration: A Case Study Analyzing the Developer and Student Perspectives. *International Journal of e-Collaboration, 11*(4), 40–63. doi:10.4018/ijec.2015100103

Magnisalis, I., Demetriadis, S., & Karakostas, A. (2011). Adaptive and intelligent systems for collaborative learning support: A review of the field. *IEEE Transactions on Learning Technologies, 4*(1), 5–20. doi:10.1109/TLT.2011.2

Magretta, J. (1998). The power of virtual integration: An interview with Dell computer's Michael Dell. *Harvard Business Review*, 73–84. PMID:10177868

Mahmood, M. A., Bagchi, K., & Ford, T. C. (2004). On-line shopping behavior: Cross-country empirical research. *International Journal of Electronic Commerce, 9*(1), 9–30.

Mahrer, H., & Krimmer, R. (2005). Towards The Enhancement of E-Democracy: Identifying The Notion Of The 'Middleman Paradox'. *Information Systems Journal, 15*(1), 27–42. doi:10.1111/j.1365-2575.2005.00184.x

Makulilo, A. (2011). Registration of SIM cards in Tanzania: A critical evaluation of the Electronic and Postal Communication Act 2010. *Computer and Telecommunication Law Review, 17*(2), 48–54.

Malhotra, M. K., & Grover, V. (1998). An assessment of survey research in POM: Form constructs to theory. *Journal of Operations Management, 16*(4), 407–425. doi:10.1016/S0272-6963(98)00021-7

Mallapragada, G., Chandukala, R. S., & Liu, G. (2016). Exploring the Effects of "What" (Product) and "Where" (Website) Characteristics on Online Shopping Behavior. *Journal of Marketing, 80*(2), 21–38. doi:10.1509/jm.15.0138

Malmquist, S. (1953). Index numbers and indifference curves. *Trabajos de Estatistica, 4*(1), 209–242. doi:10.1007/BF03006863

Manoharan, T., Taylor, H., & Gardiner, P. (2002). *A collaborative analysis tool for visualisation and interaction with spatial data.* 7th International Conference on 3D Web Technology, New York, NY.

Marsh, D., & Sharman, J. (2009). Policy diffusion and policy transfer. *Policy Studies, 30*(3), 269–288. doi:10.1080/01442870902863851

Martin, E., & Paredes, P. (2004). *Using learning styles for dynamic group formation in adaptive collaborative hypermedia systems.* Paper presented at the First International Workshop on Adaptive Hypermedia and Collaborative Web-based Systems (AHCW 2004). Retrieved from http://citeseerx.ist.psu.edu/viewdoc/download?doi=10.1.1.106.9315&rep=rep1&type=pdf

Martin, A. (2006). Successful IT application architecture design: An empirical study. *Information Systems and e-Business Management, 4*(2), 107–135. doi:10.100710257-005-0029-y

Martínez-Monés, A., Harrer, A., & Dimitriadis, Y. (2011). An interaction-aware design process for the integration of interaction analysis into mainstream CSCL practices. In *Analyzing interactions in CSCL* (pp. 269–291). Boston, MA: Springer. doi:10.1007/978-1-4419-7710-6_13

Martinez-Simarro, D., Devece, C., & Llopis-Albert, C. (2015). How information systems strategy moderates the relationship between business strategy and performance. *Journal of Business Research, 68*(7), 1592–1594. doi:10.1016/j.jbusres.2015.01.057

Martin, N., & Rice, J. (2011). Cybercrime: Understanding and addressing the concerns of stakeholders. *Computers & Security, 30*(8), 803–814. doi:10.1016/j.cose.2011.07.003

Martins, R., Oliveira, T., & Thomas, M. A. (2015). Assessing organizational adoption of information systems outsourcing. *Journal of Organizational Computing and Electronic Commerce, 25*(4), 360–378. doi:10.1080/10919392.2015.1087702

Mason, R. M. (1997). SME adoption of electronic commerce technologies: Implication for emerging national information infrastructure. *Proceedings of the Thirtieth Hawaii International Conference on Information Systems*, 495-504.

Mason-Jones, R., & Towill, D. R. (1999). Total Cycle Time Compression and the Agile Supply Chain. *International Journal of Production Economics, 62*(1-2), 61-73.

Masudi, F. (2013). *Meatballs on Menu Are Halal.* Retrieved on September 01, 2013, from Gulf News: http://gulfnews.com/news/gulf/uae/general/meatballs-on-menu-are-halal-ikea-says-1.1152651

Mathews, J. A. (2002). Competitive advantages of the latecomer firm: A resource-based account of industrial catch-up strategies. *Asia Pacific Journal of Management, 19*(4), 467–488. doi:10.1023/A:1020586223665

Mayer, R. C., Davis, J. H., & Schoorman, F. D. (1995). An Integration Model of Organizational Trust. *Academy of Management Review, 20*(3), 709–734.

McGettrick, A. (2013). *Toward Curricular Guidelines for Cybersecurity- Report of a Workshop on Cybersecurity Education and Training.* ACM. Retrieved 12 12, 2017, from https://www.acm.org/education/TowardCurricularGuidelinesCybersec.pdf

McGuckin, R. H., Streitwieser, M. L., & Doms, M. (1998). The effect of technology use on productivity growth. *Economics of Innovation and New Technology, 7*(1), 1–27. doi:10.1080/10438599800000026

McKinney, V., Yoon, K., & Zahedi, F. (2002). The measurement of web-customer satisfaction: An expectation and disconfirmation approach. *Information Systems Research, 13*(3), 296–315. doi:10.1287/isre.13.3.296.76

McMaster, T., Vidgen, R. T., & Wastell, D. G. (1997). Towards an understanding of technology in transition: Two conflicting theories. In T. McMaster, E. Mumford, E. B. Swanson, B. Warboys, & D. G. Wastell (Eds.), Facilitating technology transfer through partnership: Learning from practice and research. IFIP TC8 WG 8.6, international working conference on diffusion, adoption and implementation of information technology (pp. 64–75). Ambleside, UK: Academic Press. doi:10.1007/978-0-387-35092-9_4

Mead, N., Allen, J., Ardis, M., Hilburn, T., Kornecki, A., Linger, R., & McDonald, J. (2010). *Software Assurance Curriculum Project Volume I: Master of Software Assurance Reference Curriculum* (CMU/SEI-2010-TR-005). Software Engineering Institute. Carnegie Mellon University. Retrieved from http://resources.sei.cmu.edu/library/asset-view.cfm?AssetID=9415

Mead, N., Hilburn, T., & Linger, R. (2010). *Software Assurance Curriculum Project Volume II: Undergraduate Course Outlines* (CMU/SEI-2010-TR-019). Carnegie Mellon University. Retrieved 10 2017, 10, from http://resources.sei.cmu.edu/library/asset-view.cfm?AssetID=9543

Mell, P., & Grance, T. (2010). The NIST definition of cloud computing. *Communications of the ACM, 53*(6), 50.

Melnik, G., Maurer, F., & Chiasson, M. (2006). Executable acceptance tests for communicating business requirements: Customer perspective. *Proceedings of AGILE 2006 Conference (AGILE'06), IEEE 2006.* 10.1109/AGILE.2006.26

Menachemi, N. (2006). Barriers to Ambulatory EHR: Who Are 'Imminent Adopters' And How Do They Differ From Other Physicians? *Informatics in Primary Care, 14*(2), 101–108. PMID:17059699

Menachemi, N., Saunders, C., Chukmaitov, A., Matthews, M. C., & Brooks, R. G. (2007). Hospital adoption of information technologies and improved patient safety: A study of 98 hospitals in Florida. *Journal of Healthcare Management, 52*(6), 398–409. doi:10.1097/00115514-200711000-00008 PMID:18087980

Mendez, E., & Greenberg, J. (2012). Linked data for open vocabularies and hive's global framework. *El Profesional de la Información, 21*(3), 236–244. doi:10.3145/epi.2012.may.03

Mergel, I., & Bretschneider, S. (2013). A Three-Stage Adoption Process for Social Media Use in Government. *Public Administration Review, 73*(3), 390-400.

Merriam, S. B. (1988). *Case study research in education: A qualitative approach.* San Francisco: Jossey-Bass.

Mesch, G. S. (2012). Minority status and the use of computer-mediated communication: A test of the social diversification hypothesis. *Communication Research, 39*(3), 317–337. doi:10.1177/0093650211398865

Middleton, K. L., & Byus, K. (2011). Information and communications technology adoption and use in small and medium businesses: The influence of Hispanic ethnicity. *Management Research Review, 34*(1), 98–110. doi:10.1108/01409171111096496

Mikal, J. P., & Woodfield, B. (2015). Refugees, post-migration stress, and Internet use: A qualitative analysis of intercultural adjustment and Internet use among Iraqi and Sudanese refugees to the United States. *Qualitative Health Research, 25*(10), 1319–1333. doi:10.1177/1049732315601089 PMID:26290542

Miles, M. B., & Huberman, A. M. (1984). *Qualitative Data Analysis: A sourcebook of new methods.* Thousand Oaks, CA: Sage Publications Inc.

Miles, M. B., & Huberman, A. M. (1994). *An Expanded Sourcebook: Qualitative Data Analysis.* Thousand Oaks, CA: Sage Publications Inc.

Mislove, A., Marcon, M., Gummadi, K. P., Druschel, P., & Bhattacharjee, B. (2007). Measurement and analysis of online social networks. *Proceedings of the 7th ACM SIGCOMM conference on Internet measurement.* 10.1145/1298306.1298311

Mithas, S., Ramasubbu, N., & Sambamurthy, V. (2011). How information management capability influences firm performance. *Management Information Systems Quarterly, 35*(1), 237–256. doi:10.2307/23043496

Mohammadi, M., Mukhtar, M., & Malaysia, M. M. U. K. (2018). Comparison of Supply Chain Process Models based on Service-oriented Architecture. *Industrial Engineering (American Institute of Industrial Engineers), 9*(1).

Monsuwe, T. P., Dellaert, B., & Ruyter, K. (2004). What drives consumers to shop online A literature review. *International Journal of Service Industry Management, 15*(1), 102–121. doi:10.1108/09564230410523358

Moodle. (n.d.). Retrieved from https://moodle.org/

Moore, G. C., & Benbasat, I. (1991). Development of an instrument to measure the perceptions of adopting an information technology innovation. *Information Systems Research, 2*(3), 192–222. doi:10.1287/isre.2.3.192

Moqbel, A., Yani-De-Soriano, M., & Yousafzai, S. (2010). Mobile Commerce Use among UK Mobile Users: An Experimental Approach Based on a Proposed Mobile Network Utilization Framework. *International Journal of Technology Diffusion, 1*(2), 1–35. doi:10.4018/jtd.2010040101

Morgan, G. (1986). *Images of organization.* London: Sage.

Morris, T. (2012). *12 customer service quotes to inspire you this year.* Retrieved on 03/23/2014 from: http://www.parature.com/12-customer-service-quotes-to-inspire-you-this-year/

Morris, T. (2013). *12 customer service quotes to inspire you in 2013.* Retrieved on 02/15/2018 from: http://www.parature.com/12-customer-service-quotes-inspire-2013/

Morrow, B. (2012). BYOD security challenges: *Control and protect your most sensitive data. Network Security,* 5-8. doi:10.1016/S1353-4858(12)70111-3

Mossberger, K., Tolbert, C. J., Bowen, D., & Jimenez, B. (2012). Unraveling different barriers to Internet use: Urban residents and neighborhood effects. *Urban Affairs Review, 48*(6), 771–810. doi:10.1177/1078087412453713

Motro, A., & Rakov, I. (1998). Estimating the quality of databases. In *Flexible query answering systems* (pp. 298–307). Springer Berlin Heidelberg. doi:10.1007/BFb0056011

Mouratidis, H., & Giorgini, P. (2007). *Integrating Security and Software Engineering: Advances and Future Visions*. Hershey, PA: Idea Group Publishing. doi:10.4018/978-1-59904-147-6

Moy, R. L., & Terregrossa, R. (2009). Nerds: A case study of the PC industry. *Journal of Business Case Studies, 5*(6), 23–34. doi:10.19030/jbcs.v5i6.4729

Mteru-Behitsa, M., & Diyamett, B. (2010). Tanzania ICT sector Performance review 2009/2010. In Towards evidence-based ICT policy and Regulation (vol. 2). ICT Research Africa, Cape Town, South Africa.

Mtingwi, J., & van Belle, J. (2012). The state of e-government and m-government readiness in Malawi. *International Journal of Information Technology & Computer Science, 6*, 58–68.

Muehlenbrock, M. (2006). Learning Group Formation based on Learner Profile and Context. *International Journal on E-Learning, 5*(1), 19–24.

Mujkanovic, A., & Bollin, A. (2016). Improving learning outcomes through systematic group reformation: the role of skills and personality in software engineering education. *Proceedings of the 9th International Workshop on Cooperative and Human Aspects of Software Engineering*, 97-103. 10.1145/2897586.2897615

Munkvold, B. E., & Zigurs, I. (2005). Integration of e-collaboration technologies: Research opportunities and challenges. *International Journal of e-Collaboration, 1*(2), 1–24. doi:10.4018/jec.2005040101

Murphy, B., Jr. (2018). *Here Are the Best Inspirational Quotes for 2018*. Retrieved on 2/15/2018 from: https://www.inc.com/bill-murphy-jr/here-are-best-inspirational-quotes-for-2018.html

Murugesan, S. (2007). Understanding Web 2.0. *IT Professional, 9*(4), 34–41. doi:10.1109/MITP.2007.78

Myers, M. (2009). *Qualitative research in business and management*. London: Sage.

NACTE. (2017). Retrieved from National Accreditation Council for Teacher Education (NACTE): http://www.nacte.org.pk

NAEAC. (2017). Retrieved from About NAEAC: http://www.naeac.org.pk/

Nasir, V. A., Yoruker, S., Gunes, F., & Ozdemir, Y. (2006). Factor influencing consumers' laptop purchases. *Proceedings of the 6th Global Conference on Business & Economics*, 1-9.

National Cancer Institute. (n.d.a). *Frequently Asked Questions About HINTS*. Retrieved from http://hints.cancer.gov/faq.aspx

National Cancer Institute. (n.d.b). *Survey Instrumens*. Retrieved from https://hints.cancer.gov/data/survey-instruments.aspx

Naumann, F. (2002). *Quality-driven query answering for integrated information systems*. Springer Verlag. doi:10.1007/3-540-45921-9

NBEAC. (2017). Retrieved from National Business Education Accreditation Council (NBEAC): www.pbeac.org.pk/

Ncaaa. (2018, Feb 2). Retrieved from national center for acadmic accrediatation: https://www.ncaaa.org.sa/Pages/default.aspx

NCEAC. (2017). Retrieved from National Computing Education Accreditation Council: http://www.nceac.org

Ndubisi, N., & Sinti, Q. (2006). Consumer Attitudes, System's Characteristics and Internet Banking Adoption in Malaysia. *Management Research News*, *29*(1/2), 16-27.

Needleman, M. (2011). Linked data: What is it and what can it do? *Serials Review*, *37*(3), 234. doi:10.1080/00987913.2011.10765392

Negi, M., & Pandey, D. K. (2012). High availability using virtualization. *International Transactions in Applied Sciences*, *4*(2), 195–200.

Neumaier, S., Polleres, A., Steyskal, S., & Umbrich, J. (2017, July). Data Integration for Open Data on the Web. In Reasoning Web International Summer School. Springer.

News, C. (2013). *Horsemeat Found in Ikea Meatballs in Europe*. Retrieved on September 1, 2013, from CBC NEWS World: http://www.cbc.ca/news/world/story/2013/02/25/horse-meat-ikea-meat-balls.html

Ngomo, A. C. N., Auer, S., Lehmann, J., & Zaveri, A. (2014). Introduction to linked data and its lifecycle on the web. In *Reasoning Web. Reasoning on the Web in the Big Data Era* (pp. 1–99). Springer International Publishing. doi:10.1007/978-3-319-10587-1_1

Nguyen, A. (2012). The digital divide versus the 'digital delay': Implications from a forecasting model of online news adoption and use. *International Journal of Media & Cultural Politics*, *8*(2-3), 251–268. doi:10.1386/macp.8.2-3.251_1

Ngwenyama, O., & Morawczynski, O. (2009). Factors affecting ICT expansion in emerging economies: An analysis of ICT infrastructure expansion in five Latin American countries. *Information Technology for Development*, *15*(4), 237–258. doi:10.1002/itdj.20128

NICCS. (2017). Retrieved from National NSA/DHS Centers of Academic Excellence in Information Assurance/Cyber Defense Focus Areas: https://niccs.us-cert.gov/sites/default/files/documents/pdf/cae_ia-cd_focusareas.pdf?trackDocs=cae_ia-cd_focusareas.pdf

NICE. (2013). Retrieved from National Cybersecurity Workforce Framework: https://www.nist.gov/itl/applied-Cybersecurity/nice/resources/nice-Cybersecurity-workforce-framework

Niehaves, B., & Plattfaut, R. (2014). Internet adoption by the elderly: Employing IS technology acceptance theories for understanding the age-related digital divide. *European Journal of Information Systems*, *23*(6), 708–726. doi:10.1057/ejis.2013.19

Nissen, M. E. (2005). Delineating Knowledge Flows for Enterprise Agility. In Encyclopedia of Information Science and Technology (II) (pp. 779-785). Academic Press.

Nissim, N., Cohen, A., Glezer, C., & Elovici, Y. (2015). Detection of malicious PDF files and directions for enhancements: A state-of-the art survey. *Computers & Security*, *48*, 246–266. doi:10.1016/j.cose.2014.10.014

Normann, R. (2000). *Service Management: Strategy and leadership in service management*. New York: Wiley.

Norris, P. (2001). *Digital divide: Civic engagement, information poverty, and the Internet worldwide*. Cambridge, UK: Cambridge University Press. doi:10.1017/CBO9781139164887

Notcberg, A., Christiaanse, E., & Wallage, P. (2003). Consumer Trust in Electronic Channels: The Impact of Electronic Commerce Assurance on Consumers' Purchasing Likelihood and Risk Perceptions. *e-Service Journal*, *2*(2), 46–67. doi:10.2979/esj.2003.2.2.46

NSO. (2016). *Statistical Yearbook. National Statistics Office*. Accessed on 15 February 2018 from: http://www.nsomalawi.mw/images/stories/data_on_line/general/yearbook/2016%20Statistical%20Yearbook.pdf

NTIA. (1995). *Falling through the Net: A survey of the "have nots" in rural and urban America*. Retrieved from, https://www.ntia.doc.gov/ntiahome/fallingthru.html

NTIA. (1998). *Falling through the Net: New data on the digital divide*. Retrieved from https://www.ntia.doc.gov/ ntiahome/net2

NTIA. (1999). *Falling through the Net: Defining the digital divide*. Retrieved from https://www.ntia.doc.gov/ report/1999/falling-through-net-defining-digital-divide

Nunnally, J. C. (1978). *Psychometric theory* (2nd ed.). New York, NY: McGraw-Hill.

Nwosu, I. E. (1996). Mass Media and African War. Star Printing and Publishing Corporation Limited.

Oblinger, D. (2003). Boomers gen-xers millennials. *EDUCAUSE Review*, *500*(4), 37–47.

Observatory of European SMEs. (2007). *Competence Development in SMEs*. Brussels: European Commission.

OECD. (2000). *OECD Small and Medium Enterprise Outlook*. OECD Publication Services.

OECD. (2002). OECD Information technology outlook: ICTs and the information economy. Paris: OECD.

OECD. (2004). *ICTs, e-business and SMEs*. Paper prepared for the 2nd OECD Conference of Ministers responsible for SMEs, Istanbul, Turkey.

OECD. (2005c). The Contribution of ICTs to Pro-Poor Growth: No. 379. *OECD Papers*, *5*(1), 59–72.

Oftel SME Survey. (2000). *Internet use among SMEs*. Retrieved May 25, 2010 http://www.oftel.gov.uk/cmu/research/brint1000.htm

Ogata, H., & Yano, Y. (2004). Knowledge awareness map for computer-supported ubiquitous language-learning. In *Wireless and Mobile Technologies in Education, 2004. Proceedings. The 2nd IEEE International Workshop on* (pp. 19-26). IEEE.

Oguz, F. (2016). Organizational influences in technology adoption decisions: A case study of digital libraries. *College & Research Libraries*, *77*(3), 314–334. doi:10.5860/crl.77.3.314

Ojo, A., Janowski, T., & Awotwi, J. (2013). Enabling development through governance and mobile technology. *Government Information Quarterly*, *30*, S32–S45. doi:10.1016/j.giq.2012.10.004

Okafor, G., & Malizu, C. (2015). Effective Public Relations and Organizational Management: The Bond. *Journal of Social Sciences & Humanities Research*, *1*(1), 1–7.

Okoli, C., & Schabram, K. (2010). A guide to conducting a systematic literature review of information systems research. *Sprouts: Working Papers on Information Systems, 10*(26).

Okunola, O. M., Rowley, J., & Johnson, F. (2017). The multi-dimensional digital divide: Perspectives from an e-government portal in Nigeria. *Government Information Quarterly*, *34*(2), 329–339. doi:10.1016/j.giq.2017.02.002

Oliner, S. D., & Sichel, D. E. (2000). The Resurgence of Growth in the Late 1990's: Is Information Technology the Story? *The Journal of Economic Perspectives*, *4*(14), 3–22. doi:10.1257/jep.14.4.3

Oliveira, F., Eilam, T., Nagpurkar, P., Isci, C., Kalantar, M., Segmuller, W., & Snible, E. (2016). Delivering software with agility and quality in a cloud environment. *IBM Journal of Research and Development*, *60*(2-3), 10–11. doi:10.1147/JRD.2016.2517498

Olivera, F., & Straus, S. G. (2004). Group-to-individual transfer of learning: Cognitive and social factors. *Small Group Research*, *35*(4), 440–465. doi:10.1177/1046496404263765

ORACLE. (2015). *New Oracle Research Reveals that Businesses are Unaware of Competitive Advantages of Cloud Agility*. Retrieved from https://www.oracle.com/corporate/pressrelease/oracle-cloud-agility-survey-na-082715.html

Ordonez, C., & Garcia-Garcia, J. (2008). Referential integrity quality metrics. *Decision Support Systems*, *44*(2), 495–508. doi:10.1016/j.dss.2007.06.004

Orduña-Malea, E., Ayllón, J., Martín-Martín, A., & Delgado López-Cózar, E. (2014). About the size of Google Scholar: playing the numbers. *EC3 Working Papers*, 18. Retrieved from https://arxiv.org/abs/1407.6239

Oren, T. I. (2005). Toward the body of knowledge of modeling and simulation. In *Interservice/Industry Training, Simulation, and Education Conference (I/ITSEC) 2005*. Orlando, FL: Simulation Conference. Retrieved 7 13, 2017, from http://www.site.uottawa.ca/~oren/pubs-pres/2005/pub-0513-MSBOK-IITSEC.pdf

Oren, E., Delbru, R., Catasta, M., Cyganiak, R., Stenzhorn, H., & Tummarello, G. (2008). Sindice.com: A document-oriented lookup index for open linked data. *Journal of Metadata. Semantics and Ontologies*, *3*(1), 37–52. doi:10.1504/IJMSO.2008.021204

Organization for Economic Co-operation and Development (OECD). (2001). *The wellbeing of nations: The role of social and human capital*. Paris: Organization for Economic Co-operation and Development.

Orlikowski, W. J. (1991). Integrated information environment or matrix of control? The contradictory implications of information technology. *Accounting Management and Information Technologies*, *1*(1), 9–42. doi:10.1016/0959-8022(91)90011-3

Orlikowski, W. J. (1993). CASE tools as organizational change: Investigating incremental and radical changes in systems development. *Management Information Systems Quarterly*, *17*(3), 309–340. doi:10.2307/249774

Orton-Jones, C. (2017). Identify threats and strike before they flourish. *Enterprise Agility*. Retrieved from https://www.raconteur.net/enterprise-agility-2017

Osman, S., Yin-Fah, B. C., & Hooi-Choo, B. (2010). Undergraduates and Online Purchasing Behavior. *Asian Social Science*, *6*(10), 133–146. doi:10.5539/ass.v6n10p133

Oxford Internet Institute. (2005). *Oxford Internet Survey: Results of a Nationwide Survey of Britons aged 14 and Older*. Oxford, UK: Oxford Internet Institute.

Oyekola, O. (1995). *Foundations of Public Relations*. Ibadan Bombshell Publication.

Ozok, A. A., Benson, D., Chakraborty, J., & Norcio, A. F. (2008). A comparative study between tablet and laptop PCs: User satisfaction and preferences. *International Journal of Human-Computer Interaction*, *24*(3), 329–352. doi:10.1080/10447310801920524

Pabrai, U. A. (2006). Rules and regulations: The impact of compliance on IT. *Certification Magazine*, *8*(3), 38–40.

Paivarinta & Sæbo. (2006). Models Of E-Democracy. *Communications of the Association for Information Systems*, *17*, 818–840.

Palomino-Ramirez, L., Bote-Lorenzo, M. L., Asensio-Pérez, J. I., Vignollet, L., & Dimitriadis, Y. A. (2013). LeadFlow-4LD: A Method for the Computational Representation of the Learning Flow and Data Flow in Collaborative Learning. *Journal of Universal Computer Science*, *19*(6), 805–830.

Pankaj, & Hyde, M. (2003). *Organizations and the Necessity of Computer Based Information Systems*. Paper presented at the 9th Americas Conference on Information Systems, Tampa, FL.

Pankaj, H., & Micki, R. A., & Tadisina, S. (2009). Revisiting Agility to Conceptualize Information Systems Agility. In M. Lytras & P. O. D. Pablos (Eds.), Emerging Topics and Technologies in Information Systems (pp. 19-54). Hershey, PA: IGI Global.

Pankaj. (2005). *An Analysis and Exploration of Information Systems Agility* (Ph.D.). Southern Illinois University, Carbondale, IL.

Pankaj, H., Micki, R. A., & Rodger, J. A. (2013a). Attributes for Change Diagnosis in an Agile Information System. *International Journal of Computers and Technology, 10*(10), 2095–2109.

Pankaj, H., Hyde, M., & Ramaprasad, A. (2013b). Sensing Attributes of an Agile Information System. *Intelligent Information Management, 5*(5), 150–161. doi:10.4236/iim.2013.55016

Pan, M. J., & Jang, W. Y. (2008). Determinants of the adoption of enterprise resource planning within the technology-organization-environment framework: Taiwan's communications. *Journal of Computer Information Systems, 48*(3), 94–102.

Papadimitriou, A., & Gyftodimos, G. (2007). Use of Kolb's learning cycle through an adaptive educational hypermedia system for a constructivist approach of electromagnetism. *Proceedings of 4th WSEAS/IASME International Conference on Engineering Education*, 226-231.

Papadopoulos, Y. (2012). On the embeddedness of deliberative systems: Why elistist innovations matter more. In J. Parkinson & J. Mansbridge (Eds.), *Deliberative systems: Deliberative democracy at the large scale*. Cambridge, UK: Cambridge University Press. doi:10.1017/CBO9781139178914.007

Papanikolaou, K., & Gouli, E. (2013). Investigating influences among individuals and groups in a collaborative learning setting. *International Journal of e-Collaboration, 9*(1), 9–25. doi:10.4018/jec.2013010102

Pare, G., Sicotte, C., & Jacques, H. (2006). The Effects of Creating Psychological Ownership on Physicians' Acceptance of Clinical Information Systems. *Journal of the American Medical Informatics Association, 13*(2), 197–205. doi:10.1197/jamia.M1930 PMID:16357351

Park, E., & Kim, K. J. (2014). An integrated adoption model of mobile cloud services: Exploration of key determinants and extension of technology acceptance model. *Telematics and Informatics, 31*(3), 376–385. doi:10.1016/j.tele.2013.11.008

Park, M., & Lee, T. (2013). Understanding science and technology information users through transaction log analysis. *Library Hi Tech, 31*(1), 123–140. doi:10.1108/07378831311303976

Patel, H., & Connolly, R. (2007). *Factors Influencing Technology Adoption: A Review*. 8th International Business Information Management Conference, Dublin, Ireland. Retrieved February 15, 2018 https://www.researchgate.net/publication/273140050

Patterson, M. L. (1982). A sequential functional model of nonverbal exchange. *Psychological Review, 89*(3), 231–249. doi:10.1037/0033-295X.89.3.231

Patterson, M. L. (1983). *Nonverbal behavior. A functional perspective*. New York: Springer-Verlang. doi:10.1007/978-1-4612-5564-2

Patton, M. Q. (2002). *Qualitative Research & Evaluation Methods*. Thousand Oaks, CA: Sage Publications.

Peeters, A. L., & d'Haenens, L. (2005). Bridging or bonding? Relationships between integration and media use among ethnic minorities in the Netherlands. *Communications, 30*(2), 201–231. doi:10.1515/comm.2005.30.2.201

Pelikánová, Z. (2014). *Google Knowledge Graph*. Academic Press.

Peltz, C. (2003). Web services orchestration and choreography. *Computer, 36*(10), 46–52. doi:10.1109/MC.2003.1236471

Peña, A., & Jiménez, E. (2012). Virtual environments for effective training. *Revista Colombiana De Computación, 13*(1).

Peña, A., Rangel, N., & Lara, G. (2015). Nonverbal interaction contextualized in collaborative virtual environments. *Journal on Multimodal User Interfaces, 9*(3), 253–260. doi:10.100712193-015-0193-4

Pendharkar, P. C., Subramanian, G. H., & Rodger, J. A. (2005). A Probabilistic Model for Predicting Software Development Effort. *IEEE Transactions on Software Engineering, 31*(7), 615–624. doi:10.1109/TSE.2005.75

Penzenstadler, B., Fernandez, M., Richardson, D., Callele, D., & Wnuk, K. (2013). The requirements engineering body of knowledge (rebok). In *Requirements Engineering Conference (RE) 2013 21st IEEE International,* (pp. 377-379). Rio de Janeiro, Brazil: IEEE. 10.1109/RE.2013.6636758

Perera, P., Bandara, M., & Perera, I. (2016, September). Evaluating the impact of DevOps practice in Sri Lankan software development organizations. In *Advances in ICT for Emerging Regions (ICTer), 2016 Sixteenth International Conference on* (pp. 281-287). IEEE. 10.1109/ICTER.2016.7829932

Peristeras, V., Martínez-Carreras, M. A., Gómez-Skarmeta, A. F., Prinz, W., & Nasirifard, P. (2010). Towards a Reference Architecture for Collaborative Work Environments. *International Journal of e-Collaboration, 6*(1), 14–32. doi:10.4018/jec.2010091102

Perry, S. (2017, September 20). Immigration. *Encyclopedia Britannica.* Retrieved from, https://www. britannica.com/topic/immigration

Persaud, A., & Persaud, P. (2015). Rethinking E-government adoption: a user-centered model. In A. DeMarco (Ed.), *Public Affairs and Administration: Concepts, Methodologies, Tools, and Applications* (pp. 657–676). Hershey, PA: Information Resources Management Association. doi:10.4018/978-1-4666-8358-7.ch030

Pew Research Center. (2018). *Mobile Fact Sheet.* Retrieved on February 19, 2018 from: http://www.pewinternet.org/fact-sheet/mobile/

Piaget, J. (1983). Piaget's theory. In P. Mussen (Ed.), Handbook of Child Psychology (pp. 703–732). New York, NY: Wiley.

Piatkowski, M. (2003). *The Contribution of ICT Investment to Economic Growth and Labor Productivity in Poland 1995-2000.* TIGER Working Paper Series, No. 43.

Piatkowski, M. (2004). *Does ICT Investment Matter for Growth and Labor Productivity in Transition Economies?* Development and Comp Systems 0402008, EconWPA.

Pinkett, R. (2000). Bridging The Digital Divide: Sociocultural Constructionism and an Asset-Based Approach to Community Technology and Community Building. *Proceeding of the 81st annual meeting of the American educational research association (AERA).*

Pinsonneault, A., & Kraemer, K. L. (1993). Survey research methodology in management information systems: An assessment. *Journal of Management Information Systems, 10*(2), 75–105. doi:10.1080/07421222.1993.11518001

PNU. (2018, Feb 20). *Mechanism for Checking Journals Categorized under ISI or SCOPUS Databases.* Retrieved from Deanship of Scientific Research: http://www.pnu.edu.sa/arr/Deanships/Research/Documents/%D8%A2%D9%84%D9%8A%D8%A9%20%D8%A7%D9%84%D9%83%D8%B4%D9%81%20%D8%B9%D9%84%D9%89%20ISI%20or%20Scopus.pdf

Polleres, A., Hogan, A., Harth, A., & Decker, S. (2010). Can we ever catch up with the Web? *Semantic Web Journal, 1*(1), 45–52.

Pool, P. W., Parnell, J. A., Spillan, J. E., Carraher, S., & Lester, D. L. (2006). Are SMEs meeting the challenge of integrating e-commerce into their businesses? A review of the development, challenges and opportunities. *International Journal of Information Technology and Management, 5*(2/3), 97–113. doi:10.1504/IJITM.2006.010112

Poon, S., & Swatman, P. (1998). Small Business Internet commerce Experience: A Longitudinal Study. *Eleventh International Bled Electronic Commerce Conference*, Bled, Slovenia

Poon, W. C. (2008). Users' adoption of e-banking services: The Malaysian perspective. *Journal of Business and Industrial Marketing, 23*(1), 59–69. doi:10.1108/08858620810841498

Porter, M. (1996, May). What is strategy? *Harvard Business Review*, 134–141. PMID:10158475

Porter, M. E. (1984). *Competitive Strategy: Creating and Sustaining Superior Performance*. New York: Free Press.

Porter, M. E. (2008). The five competitive forces that shape strategy. *Harvard Business Review*, 1–18. PMID:18271320

Porter, M. E., & Millar, V. E. (1985, July). How information gives you competitive advantage. *Harvard Business Review*, 101–109.

Powell, A., Piccoli, G., & Ives, B. (2004). Virtual teams: A review of current literature and directions for future research. *ACM Sigmis Database, 35*(1), 6–36. doi:10.1145/968464.968467

Pozin, A. M. A., Nawi, M. M. N., & Romle, A. R. (2016). Effectiveness of virtual team for improving communication breakdown in IBS project delivery process. *International Journal of Supply Chain Management, 5*(4), 121–130.

Prabhu, P. R. (2013). *ISO/IEC 27001:2013: Insight on Operations Security & Communications Security Domain*. Retrieved from https://wings2i.wordpress.com/2013/10/31/isoiec-270012013-insight-on-operations-security-communications-security-domain/

Prady, S. L., Norris, D., Lester, J. E., & Hoch, D. B. (2001). Expanding the Guidelines for Electronic Communication with Patients Application to a Specific Tool. *Journal of the American Medical Informatics Association, 8*(4), 344–348. doi:10.1136/jamia.2001.0080344 PMID:11418540

Prahalad, C. K., & Hamel, G. (1990). The core competence of the corporation. *Harvard Business Review*, 1–15.

Preetam. (2017). 10 Best Netbooks – 2017. *Best World*. Retrieved on 2/19/2018 from: http://bestlaptopsworld.com/best-netbooks/

Price, R. (2012). The Future of Peer Review. *TechCrunch*. Retrieved 4 4, 2016, from https://techcrunch.com/2012/02/05/the-future-of-peer-review/

Prieto, L. P., Asensio-Pérez, J. I., Muñoz-Cristóbal, J. A., Jorrín-Abellán, I. M., Dimitriadis, Y., & Gómez-Sánchez, E. (2014). Supporting orchestration of CSCL scenarios in web-based Distributed Learning Environments. *Computers & Education, 73*, 9–25. doi:10.1016/j.compedu.2013.12.008

Prinz, W., Martínez-Carreras, M. A., & Pallot, M. (2010). From Collaborative Tools to Collaborative Working Environments. *International Journal of e-Collaboration, 6*(1), 1–13. doi:10.4018/jec.2010091101

PSRB. (2016). *Retrieved from Professional, Statutory and Regulatory Bodies (PSRBs) and professional accreditation of undergraduate programmes*. Higher Education Statistics Agency: www.hesa.ac.uk

Purvanova, R. K., & Bono, J. E. (2009). Transformational leadership in context: Face-to-face and virtual teams. *The Leadership Quarterly, 20*(3), 343–357. doi:10.1016/j.leaqua.2009.03.004

Qi, G., & Du, J. (2009). Model-based revision operators for terminologies in description logics. *Proceedings of the 21st International Joint Conference on Artificial Intelligence.*

Quezada-Sarmiento, P. A., Enciso-Quispe, L. E., Garbajosa, J., & Washizaki, H. (2016). Curricular design based in bodies of knowledge: Engineering education for the innovation and the industry. In *SAI Computing Conference (SAI), 2016* (pp. 843-849). London: IEEE. 10.1109/SAI.2016.7556077

Quinn, J. B. (1980). Managing Strategic Change. *Sloan Management Review, 21*(4), 3–20. PMID:10249849

Raban, D., Moldovan, M., & Jones, Q. (2010). An empirical study of critical mass and online community survival. *Proceedings of the 2010 ACM Conferences on Computer Supported Cooperative Work,* 71-80. 10.1145/1718918.1718932

Radulovic, F., Mihindukulasooriya, N., García-Castro, R., & Gómez-Pérez, A. (2017). A comprehensive quality model for linked data. *Semantic Web,* 1-22.

Rahman, N. (2018). Environmental Sustainability in the Computer Industry for Competitive Advantage. In Green Computing Strategies for Competitive Advantage and Business Sustainability (pp. 110-130). IGI Global. doi:10.4018/978-1-5225-5017-4.ch006

Rahman, N., Aldhaban, F., & Akhter, S. (2013). Emerging technologies in business intelligence. In *Proceedings of the IEEE Portland International Center for Management of Engineering and Technology (PICMET 2013) Conference.* San Jose, CA: IEEE.

Rahman, N. (2013). Measuring performance for data warehouses - A balanced scorecard approach. *International Journal of Computer and Information Technology, 4*(1), 1–7.

Rahman, N. (2016). Enterprise data warehouse governance best practices. *International Journal of Knowledge-Based Organizations, 6*(2), 21–37. doi:10.4018/IJKBO.2016040102

Rahman, N. (2017a). An empirical study of data warehouse implementation effectiveness. *International Journal of Management Science and Engineering Management, 12*(1), 55–63. doi:10.1080/17509653.2015.1113394

Rahman, N. (2017b, October-December). Lessons from a successful data warehousing project management. *International Journal of Information Technology Project Management, 8*(4), 30–45. doi:10.4018/IJITPM.2017100103

Rahman, N. (2018). A simulation model for application development in data warehouses. *International Journal of Operations Research and Information Systems, 9*(1), 66–80. doi:10.4018/IJORIS.2018010104

Rahman, N., & Akhter, S. (2010). Incorporating sustainability into information technology management. *International Journal of Technology Management & Sustainable Development, 9*(2), 95–111. doi:10.1386/tmsd.9.2.95_1

Rahman, N., Marz, J., & Akhter, S. (2012). An ETL metadata model for data warehousing. *CIT. Journal of Computing and Information Technology, 20*(2), 95–111. doi:10.2498/cit.1002046

Rahman, N., Rutz, D., Akhter, S., & Aldhaban, F. (2014, November). Emerging technologies in business intelligence and advanced analytics. *ULAB Journal of Science and Engineering, 5*(1), 7–17.

Rahman, N., & Sutton, L. (2016). Optimizing SQL performance in a parallel processing DBMS architecture. *ULAB Journal of Science and Engineering, 7*(1), 33–44.

Ramalho, D. S. (2014). The use of malware as a means of obtaining evidence in Portuguese criminal proceedings. *Digital Evidence and Electronic Signature Law Review, 11.*

Ramamurthy, K., & Premkumar, G. (1995). Determinants and outcomes of electronic data interchange diffusion. *IEEE Transactions on Engineering Management, 42*(4), 325–347. doi:10.1109/17.482083

Ramdani, B., Kawalek, P., & Lorenzo, O. (2009). Predicting SMEs' adoption of enterprise systems. *Journal of Enterprise Information Management*, 22(1/2), 10–24. doi:10.1108/17410390910922796

Rao, S. S. (2001). Portal proliferation: An Indian scenario. *New Library World*, 102(9), 325–331. doi:10.1108/03074800110406204

Raymond, L., Bergeron, F. O., & Blili, S. (2005). The assimilation of e-business in manufacturing SMEs: Determinants and effects on growth and internationalization. *Electronic Markets*, 15(2), 106–118. doi:10.1080/10196780500083761

Read, T., Barros, B., Barcna, E., & Pancorbo, J. (2006). Coalescing Individual and Collaborative Learning to Model User Linguistic Competences. *Journal of User Modeling and User-Adapted Interaction*, 16(3-4), 349–376. doi:10.100711257-006-9014-5

Reddick, C. G., & Turner, M. (2012). Channel choice and public service delivery in Canada: Comparing e-government to traditional service delivery. *Government Information Quarterly*, 29(1), 1–11. doi:10.1016/j.giq.2011.03.005

Reed, S., & Lenat, D. (2002). *Mapping ontologies into Cyc* (Technical report). Cycorp, Inc. Retrieved from http://www.cyc.com/doc/white papers/

Reinig, B. A., & Mejias, R. J. (2014). On the measurement of participation equality. *International Journal of e-Collaboration*, 10(4), 32–48. doi:10.4018/ijec.2014100103

Report, P. W. C. (2015). *The Global State of Information Security Survey 2015*. Retrieved from http://www.pwc.com

Rex, F. F. (1976). Building a Public Relations Definition. *Public Relations Review*, 2, 4.

Reynolds, J. (1997). The Internet as a strategic resource. In L. Willcocks, D. Feeny, & G. Islei (Eds.), *Managing IT as a strategic resource*. McGraw Hill.

RG facts. (2016). *Fact Sheet – ResearchGate*. Retrieved from ResearchGate: www.researchgate.net/aboutus.AboutUs-Press.downloadFile.html?

Ricketts, J. A., & Jenkins, A. M. (1985). *The Development of an MIS Satisfaction Questionnaire: An Instrument for Evaluating User Satisfaction with Turnkey Decision Support Systems* Discussion Paper no. 296. Bloomington, IN: Indiana University School of Business.

Riley, C. G., & Law, M. A. (2003). E-Governance & E-Democracy Equation. *Commonwealth Center for E-Governance*, 2-111.

Riley. C. G. (2003). The Changing Role of The Citizen In The E-Government And E-Democracy Equation. *Commonwealth Centre for E-Government*.

Roberts, L. (2018). *5 Lessons from a Patient Portal Hiatus*. Retrieved from http://www.physicianspractice.com/ehr/5-lessons-patient-portal-hiatus

Roberts, N., & Grover, V. (2012). Leveraging information technology infrastructure to facilitate a firm's customer agility and competitive activity: An empirical investigation. *Journal of Management Information Systems*, 28(4), 231–269. doi:10.2753/MIS0742-1222280409

Rockart, J. F., Earl, M. J., & Ross, J. W. (1996). Eight Imperatives for the New IT Organization. *Sloan Management Review*, 38(1), 13.

Rogers, E. M. (1995, 2003). Diffusion of innovations. New York: Free Press.

Rogers, E. M. (1986). *Communication technology: The new media in society*. New York: The Free Press.

Rogers, E. M. (2003). *Diffusion of innovations* (4th ed.). New York, NY: The Free Press.

Rogers, E. M. (2003). *Diffusion of Innovations*. New York: Free Press.

Romano, N. C. Jr, & Fjermestad, J. (2003). Electronic commerce customer relationship management: A research agenda. *Information Technology Management, 4*(2/3), 233–258. doi:10.1023/A:1022906513502

Rosenkranz, C., & Fessersen, C. (2008). A model for understanding success of virtual community management teams. *Proceedings of the Fourteenth Americas Conference on Information Systems*.

Roy, J. (2006). Government of Canada. In *E-government in Canada: Transformation for the digital age* (pp. 111–137). Ottawa: University of Ottawa Press.

Rubens, V., & Okamoto. (2009). Automatic group formation for informal collaborative learning. *Proceedings of the 2009 IEEE/WIC/ACM International Joint Conference on Web Intelligence and Intelligent Agent Technology, 3,* 231-234 10.1109/WI-IAT.2009.270

Ruggieri, S. (2009). Leadership in virtual teams: A comparison of transformational and transactional leaders. *Social Behavior and Personality, 37*(8), 1017–1021. doi:10.2224bp.2009.37.8.1017

Rutz, D., Nelakanti, T. K., & Rahman, N. (2012). Practical implications of real time business intelligence. *CIT. Journal of Computing and Information Technology, 20*(4), 257–264. doi:10.2498/cit.1002081

Sabnis, S., & Charles, D. (2012). Opportunities and Challenges: Security in eHealth. *Bell Labs Technical Journal, 17*(3), 105–112. doi:10.1002/bltj.21561

Safa, N. S., Von Solms, R., & Furnell, S. (2016). Information security policy compliance model in organizations. *Computers & Security, 56,* 70–82. doi:10.1016/j.cose.2015.10.006

Saldanha, T. J. V., & Krishnan, M. S. (2012). Organizational adoption of Web 2.0 technologies: An empirical analysis. *Journal of Organizational Computing and Electronic Commerce, 22*(4), 301–333. doi:10.1080/10919392.2012.723585

Sambamurthy, V., Bharadwaj, A., & Grover, V. (2003). Shaping agility through digital options: Reconceptualizing the role of information technology in contemporary firms. *Management Information Systems Quarterly, 27*(2), 237–263. doi:10.2307/30036530

Samoilenko, S. (2013). Investigating factors associated with the spillover effect of investments in telecoms: Do some transition economies pay too much for too little? *Information Technology for Development, 19*(1), 40–61. doi:10.1080/02681102.2012.677710

Samoilenko, S. (2014). Investigating the impact of investments in telecoms on microeconomic outcomes: Conceptual framework and empirical investigation in the context of transition economies. *Information Technology for Development, 20*(3), 251–273. doi:10.1080/02681102.2012.751572

Samoilenko, S. (2016). Where do Investments in Telecoms Come From? Developing and Testing a Framework of Sustained Economic Impact of Investments in ICT. *Journal of Information Technology for Development, 22*(4), 584–605. doi:10.1080/02681102.2014.927348

Samoilenko, S., & Ngwenyama, O. (2011). Understanding the human capital dimension of ICT and economic growth in transition economies. *Journal of Global Information Technology Management, 14*(1), 59–69. doi:10.1080/1097198X.2011.10856531

Samoilenko, S., & Osei-Bryson, K. M. (2008a). Strategies for Telecoms to Improve Efficiency in the Production of Revenues: An Empirical Investigation in the Context of Transition Economies. *Journal of Global Information Technology Management, 11*(4), 59–79. doi:10.1080/1097198X.2008.10856479

Samoilenko, S., & Osei-Bryson, K. M. (2008b). An Exploration of the Effects of the Interaction between ICT and Labor Force on Economic Growth in Transitional Economies. *International Journal of Production Economics, 115*(2), 471–481. doi:10.1016/j.ijpe.2008.07.002

Samoilenko, S., & Osei-Bryson, K.-M. (2017). Creating Theoretical Research Frameworks using Multiple Methods. *Insight (American Society of Ophthalmic Registered Nurses)*, ICT4D.

Samoilenko, S., & Weistroffer, H. R. (2010a). Improving the relative efficiency of revenue generation from ICT in transition economies: A product life cycle approach. *Information Technology for Development, 16*(4), 279–303. doi:10.1080/02681102.2010.510461

Samoilenko, S., & Weistroffer, H. R. (2010b). Spillover Effect of Telecom Investments on Technological Advancement and Efficiency Improvement in Transition Economies. *Proceedings of the SIG GlobDev 3rd Annual Workshop ICT in Global Development.*

Sandmire, D. A., Vroman, K. G., & Sanders, R. (2000). The Influence of Learning Styles on Collaborative Performances of Allied Health Students in a Clinical Exercise. *Journal of Allied Health, 29*(3), 143–149. PMID:11026115

Santamaria, P. G. (2006). *CA-OLE: a collaborative and adaptive online learning environment* (Master's thesis). Retrieved from: http://dspace.uta.edu/bitstream/handle/10106/229/umi-uta-1528.pdf?sequence=1

Saprikis, V., Chouliara, A., & Vlachopoulou, M. (2010). Perceptions Towards Online Shopping: Analyzing the Greek University Students' Attitude. *Communications of the IBIMA*, Article ID 854516.

Saprikis, V. (2013). Consumers' perceptions towards e-shopping advertisements and promotional actions in social networking sites. *International Journal of Electronic Adoption, 5*(4), 36–47. doi:10.4018/ijea.2013100103

Saunders, M., Lewis, P., & Thornhill, A. (2009). *Research methods for business students.* London: Prentice Hall.

Sawas, M., & Watfa, M. (2015). The Impact of Cloud Computing on Information Systems Agility. *AJIS. Australasian Journal of Information Systems, 19.* doi:10.3127/ajis.v19i0.930

Scanlon, M., Farina, J., & Kechadi, M. (2015). Network investigation methodology for BitTorrent Sync: A Peer-to-Peer based file synchronisation service. *Computers & Security, 54,* 27–43. doi:10.1016/j.cose.2015.05.003

Schaller, R. J. (1997). Moore's Law: Past, present and future. *IEEE Spectrum,* 53–59.

Schiller, J. (2003). Working with ICT Perceptions of Australian Principals. *Journal of Educational Administration, 41*(2), 171–185. doi:10.1108/09578230310464675

Schmachtenberg, M., Bizer, C., & Paulheim, H. (2014). Adoption of the linked data best practices in different topical domains. In *International Semantic Web Conference* (pp. 245-260). Springer. 10.1007/978-3-319-11964-9_16

Schroeder, R. (2011). *Being there together: Social interaction in shared virtual environments* (A. Kirlik, Ed.). New York: Oxford University Press.

Scopus. (2018, Feb 10). *About Scopus.* Retrieved from ELSEVIER: https://www.elsevier.com/solutions/scopus

Seethamraju, R., & Sundar, D. K. (2013). Influence of ERP Systems on Business Process Agility. *IIMB Management Review, 25*(3), 137–150. doi:10.1016/j.iimb.2013.05.001

Seitel, F. P. (2004). *The Practice of Public Relations*. Prentice Hall.

Selsky, C., Luta, G., Noone, A. M., Huerta, E. E., & Mandelblatt, J. S. (2013). Internet access and online cancer information seeking among Latino immigrants from safety net clinics. *Journal of Health Communication, 18*(1), 58–70. doi:10.1080/10810730.2012.688248 PMID:23066874

Selwyn, N., Gorard, S., & Furlong, J. (2005). Whose Internet is it anyway? Exploring adults'(non) use of the Internet in everyday life. *European Journal of Communication, 20*(1), 5–26. doi:10.1177/0267323105049631

Seter, J. (2017). *How PR Crises Impact Brand Reputation*. Retrieved on January 31, 2018, from http://www.instituteforpr. org/pr-crises-impact-brand-reputation/

Seybert, H. (2011). *Internet use in the households and by individuals in 2011*. Eurostat - Statistics in focus 66/2011. Retrieved 24 July 24, 2012, http://epp.eurostat.ec.europa.eu/cache/ITY_OFFPUB/KS-SF-11-066/EN/KS-SF-11-066-EN.PDF

Shadbolt, P. (2016). *How can a company repair a damaged reputation?* Retrieved on February 1st, 2018, from http://www.bbc.com/news/business-37630983

Shah, A., & Dalal, A. (2009). *The global laptop industry*. Retrieved October 1, 2013, from http://srl.gatech.edu/Members/ashah/laptop_industry_analysis_aditya_abhinav.pdf

Shaik, A., & Karjaluoto, H. (2015). Mobile banking adoption: A literature review. *Telematics and Informatics, 32*(1), 129–142. doi:10.1016/j.tele.2014.05.003

Shaqrah, A. A. (2010). The influence of internet security on e-business competence in Jordan: An Empirical Analysis. *International Journal of Technology Diffusion, 1*(4), 13–28. doi:10.4018/jtd.2010100102

Shareef, M. A., Kumar, V., Kumar, U., & Dwivedi, Y. K. (2011). e-government adoption model (GAM): Differing service maturity levels. *Government Information Quarterly, 28*(1), 17–35. doi:10.1016/j.giq.2010.05.006

Sharifi, H., & Zhang, Z. (1999). A Methodology for Achieving Agility in Manufacturing Organizations: An Introduction. *International Journal of Production Economics, 62*(1), 7–22. doi:10.1016/S0925-5273(98)00217-5

Shaw, G. L., & Harrald, J. (2006). The Core Competencies Required of Executive Level Business Crisis and Continuity Managers. Disaster Resource Guide. 11th Annual 2006/2007.

Shenker, J. (2011). Fury over advert claiming Egypt revolution as Vodafone's. *The Guardian*. Retrieved from http://www.guardian.co.uk/world/2011/jun/03/vodafone-egypt-advert-claims-revolution

Shi, L., Qudah, D., Qaffas, A., & Cristea, A. I. (2013). Topolor: A social personalized adaptive e-learning system. In User Modeling, Adaptation, and Personalization (pp. 338-340). Springer Berlin Heidelberg. doi:10.1007/978-3-642-38844-6_32

Shieh, J. (2012). From website log to findability. *The Electronic Library, 30*(5), 707–720. doi:10.1108/02640471211275747

Shiu, A., & Lam, P.-L. (2008). Causal Relationship between Telecommunications and Economic Growth in China and its Regions. *Regional Studies, 42*(5), 705–718. doi:10.1080/00343400701543314

Sila, I. (2013). Factors affecting the adoption of B2B e-commerce technologies *Electronic Commerce Research, 13*(2), 199–236. doi:10.100710660-013-9110-7

Simon, S. R., Kaushal, R., Cleary, P. D., Jenter, C. A., Volk, L. A., Poon, E. G., ... Bates, D. W. (2007). Correlates Of Electronic Health Record Adoption In Office Practices: A Statewide Survey. *Journal of the American Medical Informatics Association, 14*(1), 110–117. doi:10.1197/jamia.M2187 PMID:17068351

Simon, S. R., McCarthy, M. L., Kaushal, R., Jenter, C. A., Volk, L. A., Poon, E. G., ... Bates, D. W. (2008). Electronic Health Records: Which Practices Have Them, and How Are Clinicians Using Them? *Journal of Evaluation in Clinical Practice*, *14*(1), 43–47. doi:10.1111/j.1365-2753.2007.00787.x PMID:18211642

Simonson, M. R., Maurer, M., Montag-Torardi, M., & Whitaker, M. (1987). Development of a standardized test of computer literacy and a computer anxiety index. *Journal of Educational Computing Research*, *3*(2), 231–247. doi:10.2190/7CHY-5CM0-4D00-6JCG

Slater, S. F., & Narver, J. C. (2000). Intelligence generation and superior customer value. *Journal of the Academy of Marketing Science*, *28*(1), 120–127. doi:10.1177/0092070300281011

Slavin, R. E. (2010). Co-operative learning: what makes group-work? In D. Hanna, I. David, & B. Francisco (Eds.), *The nature of learning: Using research to inspire practice* (pp. 161–178). Chicago: OECD Publishing. doi:10.1787/9789264086487-9-en

Smith, A. W., Rahman, N., & Ullah, M. (2015). Intrapreneurship: Is more than just innovation. In *Proceedings of the 1st Biennial Conference of Bangladesh Academy of Business Administration (BABA'15)*, 19-20.

Soares-Aguiar, A., & Palma-Dos-Reis, A. (2008). Why do firms adopt e-procurement systems? Using logistic regression to empirically test a conceptual model. *IEEE Transactions on Engineering Management*, *55*(1), 120–133. doi:10.1109/TEM.2007.912806

Software Engineering Institute. (2002). *Capability maturity model integration for software engineering*. Retrieved from ftp://192.58.107.24/pub/documents/02.reports/pdf/02tr028.pdf

Soh, L. K., Khandaker, N., & Jiang, H. (2008). I-MINDS: A Multi-agent System for Intelligent Computer-Supported Collaborative Learning and Classroom Management. *International Journal of Artificial Intelligence in Education*, *18*(2), 119–151.

Soller, A., Martínez, A., Jermann, P., & Muehlenbrock, M. (2005). From mirroring to guiding: A review of state of the art technology for supporting collaborative learning. *International Journal of Artificial Intelligence in Education*, *15*(4), 261–290.

Sommerville, I. (2004). *Software engineering*. Pearson Education Limited.

Souppaya, M., & Scarfone, K. (2013). *NIST Special Publication 800-83 Revision 1 (2013). Guide to Malware Incident Prevention and Handling for Desktops and Laptops*. Retrieved from http://nvlpubs.nist.gov/nistpubs/SpecialPublications/NIST.SP.800-83r1.pdf

Spaiser, V. (2013). Young immigrants' Internet political participation in Germany: Comparing German east Europeans and German Turks. *International Journal of E-Politics*, *4*(1), 1–17. doi:10.4018/jep.2013010101

Sparks, C. (2013). What is the "digital divide" and why is it important? *Javnost-The Public*, *20*(2), 27–46. doi:10.108 0/13183222.2013.11009113

Spoelstra, H., van Rosmalen, P., Houtmans, T., & Sloep, P. (2015). Team formation instruments to enhance learner interactions in open learning environments. *Journal of Computers in Human Behavior*, *45*, 11–20. doi:10.1016/j.chb.2014.11.038

Srba, I., & Bieliková, M. (2015). Dynamic Group Formation as an Approach to Collaborative Learning Support. *IEEE Transactions on Learning Technologies*, *8*(2), 173–186. doi:10.1109/TLT.2014.2373374

Sridhar, V., Nath, D., Paul, R., & Kapur, K. (2007). Analyzing Factors that Affect Performance of Global Virtual Teams. *Proceedings of the Second International Conference on Management of Globally Distributed Work*, 159-169.

Staab, S., & Studer, R. (2010). *Handbook on ontologies*. Springer.

Stahl, B. C. (2005). The paradigm of e-commerce in e-government and e-democracy. *Electronic Government Strategies and Implementation, 9*(2) 1-19.

Stake, R. E. (2006). *Multiple Case Study Analysis*. New York: Guilford Press.

Statista. (2017). *Digital buyer penetration worldwide from 2016 to 2021*. Retrieved January 15, 2018, from https://www.statista.com/statistics/261676/digital-buyer-penetration-worldwide/

Stern, B. B., & Stafford, M. R. (2006). Individual and social determinants of winning bids in online auctions. *Journal of Consumer Behaviour, 5*(1), 43–55. doi:10.1002/cb.47

Stevanović, B. (2011). Maturity models in information security. *International Journal of Information and Communication Technology Research, 1*(2), 44–47.

Stone, E. F., Gueutal, H. G., Gardner, D. G., & McClure, S. (1983). A Field Experiment Comparing Information-Privacy Values, Beliefs, And Attitudes Across Several Types Of Organizations. *The Journal of Applied Psychology, 68*(3), 459–468. doi:10.1037/0021-9010.68.3.459

Storey, V. C., & Goldstein, R. C. (1993). Knowledge-based approaches to database design. *Management Information Systems Quarterly, 17*(1), 25–46. doi:10.2307/249508

Strauss, A. L., & Corbin, J. (1990, 1998). Basics of Qualitative Research: Techniques and Procedures for developing Grounded Theory. London: Sage Publications.

Subaihi, T. A. (2013). *Operator Warned Before Global Village Ferris Wheel Death*. Retrieved on September 01, 2013, from *The National*: http://www.thenational.ae/news/uae-news/operator-warned-before-global-village-ferris-wheel-death-says-family

Sucahyo, Y. G., Utari, D., Budi, N. F. A., Hidayanto, A. N., & Chahyati, D. (2016). Knowledge management adoption and its impact on organizational learning and non-financial performance. *Knowledge Management & E-Learning, 8*(2), 387–413.

Sumbwanyambe, M., & Nel, A. (2013). Assessing the implications of SIM card registration policy in the SADC region. IEEE IST-Africa Conference and Exhibition (IST-Africa), 1-9.

Sun, G., & Shen, J. (2014). Facilitating social collaboration in mobile cloud-based learning: A teamwork as a service (TaaS) approach. *IEEE Transactions on Learning Technologies, 7*(3), 207–220. doi:10.1109/TLT.2014.2340402

Sunghun, C., Kyung, L. Y., & Kimin, K. (2014). Job Performance through Mobile Enterprise Systems: The Role of Organizational Agility, Location Independence, and Task Characteristics. *Information & Management, 15*, 605–618.

Sun, Y., Fang, Y., & Lim, K. H. (2010). Understanding sustained participation in transactional virtual communities. *Thirty First International Conference on Information Systems*.

Suomalainen, P. (2010). A comparison of the usability of a laptop, communicator, and handheld computer. *Journal of Usability Studies, 5*(3), 111–123.

Suthers, D. D., Dwyer, N., Medina, R., & Vatrapu, R. (2010). A framework for conceptualizing, representing, and analyzing distributed interaction. *International Journal of Computer-Supported Collaborative Learning, 5*(1), 5–42. doi:10.100711412-009-9081-9

Swanson, E., & Ramiller, N. C. (2004). Innovating mindfully with information technology. *Management Information Systems Quarterly, 28*(4), 553–583. doi:10.2307/25148655

Sweeney, J. C., & Soutar, G. N. (2001). Consumer Perceived Value: The Development of A Multiple Item Scale. *Journal of Retailing*, *77*(2), 203–220. doi:10.1016/S0022-4359(01)00041-0

Swierczek, F., Shrestha, P., & Bechter, C. (2005). Information Technology, Productivity and Profitability in Asia-Pacific Banks. *Journal of Global Information Technology Management*, *8*(1), 6–26. doi:10.1080/1097198X.2005.10856388

Szymanski, D. M., & Henard, D. H. (2001). Customer satisfaction: A meta-analysis of the empirical evidence. *Journal of the Academy of Marketing Science*, *29*(1), 16–35. doi:10.1177/0092070301291002

Tambe, P., & Hitt, L. M. (2012). The productivity of information technology investments: New evidence from IT labor data. *Information Systems Research*, *23*(3), 599–617. doi:10.1287/isre.1110.0398

Tambini, D. (1999). New Media and Democracy: The Civic Networking Movement. *New Media & Society*, *1*(1), 305–329. doi:10.1177/14614449922225609

Tang, C., & Liu, J. (2015). Selecting a trusted cloud service provider for your SaaS program. *Computers & Security*, *50*, 60–73. doi:10.1016/j.cose.2015.02.001

Tao, P.-K. (1999). Peer collaboration in solving qualitative physics problems: The role of collaborative talk. *Research in Science Education*, *29*(3), 365–383. doi:10.1007/BF02461599

Tapscott, D. (2009). *Grown up digital* (Vol. 361). New York: McGraw Hill.

Teo, T. (2006). To buy or not to buy online: Adopters and non-adopters of online shopping in Singapore. *Behaviour & Information Technology*, *25*(6), 497–509. doi:10.1080/01449290500256155

Teo, T. S. H., & Ranganathan, C. (2009). Adopters and non-adopters of E-Procurement in Singapore. *Omega*, *37*(5), 972–987. doi:10.1016/j.omega.2008.11.001

Teo, T. S. H., Ranganathan, C., & Dhaliwal, J. (2006). Key dimensions of inhibitors for the deployment of web-based business-to-business electronic commerce. *IEEE Transactions on Engineering Management*, *53*(3), 395–411. doi:10.1109/TEM.2006.878106

Terrant, H. (2009). *Why Rica will fail*. Moneyweb's Personal Finance.

Thakur, R., & Srivastava, M. (2015). A study on the impact of consumer risk perception and innovativeness on online shopping in India. *International Journal of Retail & Distribution Management*, *43*(2), 148–166. doi:10.1108/IJRDM-06-2013-0128

The Learning Design Grid. (2017). *Tools*. Retrieved from http://www.ld-grid.org/resources/tools

TheTopTen. (2018). Best Computer Brands. *The Top Ten*. Retrieved on 2/18/2018 from: https://www.thetoptens.com/best-computer-brands/

Thielens, J. (2013). Why API are central to a BYOD security strategy. *Network Security*, *5-6*. doi:10.1016/S1353-4858(13)70091-6

Thomas, J. C., & Streib, G. (2005). E-Democracy, E-Commerce, and E-Research Examining the Electronic Ties between Citizens and Governments. *Administration & Society*, *37*(3), 259–280. doi:10.1177/0095399704273212

Thompson, L. F., & Coovert, M. D. (2003). Teamwork online: The effects of computer conferencing on perceived confusion, satisfaction and post-discussion accuracy. *Group Dynamics*, *7*(2), 135–151. doi:10.1037/1089-2699.7.2.135

Thompson, T. G., & Brailer, D. J. (2004). *The decade of health information technology: Delivering consumer-centric and information-rich health care: Framework for strategic action.* Washington, DC: Department of Health and Human Services, National Coordinator for Health Information Technology. Retrieved from http://www.hhs.gov/onchit/framework/hitframework.pdf

Thomson Reuters. (2016). *Fact Sheet.* Retrieved from Thomson Reuters.: thomsonreuters.com/content/dam/openweb/documents/pdf/scholarly-scientific-research/fact-sheet/wos-next-gen-brochure.pdf

Thore, S. (1996). Economies of scale in the US computer industry: An empirical investigation using data envelopment analysis. *Journal of Evolutionary Economics, 6*(2), 199–216. doi:10.1007/BF01202594

Tilly, R., Posegga, O., Fischbach, K., & Schoder, D. (2017). Towards a conceptualization of data and information quality in social information systems. *Business & Information Systems Engineering, 59*(1), 1, 3–21. doi:10.100712599-016-0459-8

Timeline: Egypt's revolution. (2011). *Aljazeera online.* Retrieved December, 2012, Accessed from http://www.aljazeera.com

Tittel, E. (2014). *Understanding How SDN and NFV van Work Together.* Retrieved from https://www.cio.com/article/2379216/business-analytics/understanding-how-sdn-and-nfv-can-work-together.html

Tornatzky, L. G., Eveland, J. D., Boylan, M. G., Hetzner, W. A., Johnson, E. C., Roitman, D., & Schneider, J. (1983). The Process of technological innovation: reviewing the literature. Productivity Improvement Research Section, Division of Industrial Science and Technological Innovation, National Science Foundation, Washington, DC.

Tornatzky, L., & Klein, K. (1982). Innovation Characteristics and innovation adoption-implementation: A Meta-Analysis of findings. *IEEE Transactions on Engineering Management, EM-29*(1), 28–45. doi:10.1109/TEM.1982.6447463

Toupikov, N., Umbrich, J., Delbru, R., Hausenblas, M., & Tummarello, G. (2009). DING! Dataset ranking using formal descriptions. *Proceedings of the WWW2009 Workshop on Linked Data on the Web.*

Transparency International. (2014). Retrieved on February 1, 2018 from https://www.transparency.org/cpi2014

Trending, R. G. (2016). *Discover the world's top research.* Retrieved from RG Trending: www.researchgate.net/trending/publications

Tripp, L. M. (2010). 'The computer is not for you to be looking around, it is for schoolwork': Challenges for digital inclusion as Latino immigrant families negotiate children's access to the Internet. *New Media & Society, 13*(4), 552–567. doi:10.1177/1461444810375293

Tsai, W. T. (2005, October). Service-oriented system engineering: a new paradigm. In *Service-oriented system engineering, 2005. sose 2005. IEEE International Workshop* (pp. 3-6). IEEE.

Tsai, J. H. C. (2006). Use of computer technology to enhance immigrant families' adaptation. *Journal of Nursing Scholarship, 38*(1), 87–93. doi:10.1111/j.1547-5069.2006.00082.x PMID:16579329

Turney, M. (2008). *Performing public relations during a crisis.* Retrieved on September 12, 2014, from The www.nku.edu/~turney/prclass/tips/crisis_response.pdf

Tushman, M. L., & Nadler, D. A. (1978). Information Processing as an Integrating Concept in Organizational Design. *Academy of Management Review, 3*(3), 613–624.

Tyler, L. (1997). Liability Means Never Being Able to Say You're Sorry: Corporate Guilt, Legal Constraints, and Defensiveness in Corporate Communication. *Management Communication Quarterly, 11*(1), 51–73. doi:10.1177/0893318997111003

U.S. Census Bureau. (2007). *NAICS 334: Computer and electronic product manufacturing.* Retrieved from http://www.census.gov/econ/industry/def/d334.htm

U.S. Department of Education. (2017, 8 9). Retrieved from Regional and National Institutional Accrediting Agencies: https://www2.ed.gov/admins/finaid/accred/accreditation_pg6.html

Ulmer, R. R. T. L. (2006). Effective Crisis Communication: Moving from Crisis to Opportunity. Thousand Oaks, CA: Sage.

Umar, A. (2005). IT infrastructure to enable next generation enterprises. *Information Systems Frontiers*, *7*(3), 217–256. doi:10.100710796-005-2768-1

UNESCO. (2004). *Integrating ICTs into Education: lessons learned*. Asia and Pacific Regional Bureau for Education. Retrieved from http://unesdoc.unesco.org/images/0013/001355/135562e.pdf

United States Patent and Trademark Office (USPTO). (2009). *Network and AIS audit, logging, and monitoring policy*. Retrieved from www.uspto.gov/about/vendor_info/current_acquisitions/sdi_ng/ocio_6011_09.pdf

Unknown. (2002). *Comp.realtime: Frequently Asked Questions (FAQs) 3.6*. Retrieved 1/1/03, 2002, from http://www.faqs.org/faqs/realtime-computing/faq/

US GAO. (2012). *Information Security: Better implementation of controls for mobile devices should be encouraged*. Retrieved from http://www.gao.gov/products/GAO-12-757

Van Ark, B., Inklaar, R., & McGuckin, R. (2002*). 'Changing Gear' - Productivity, ICT and Services Industries: Europe and the United States* (No. 02-02). Economics Program Working Papers, The Conference Board, Economics Program. Retrieved from http://econpapers.repec.org/RePEc:cnf:wpaper:0202

van Dijk, J. A. G. M. (2012). The evolution of the digital divide: The digital divide turns to inequality of skills and usage. In J. Bus, M. Crompton, M. Hildebrandt, & G. Metakides (Eds.), Digital Enlightenment Yearbook 2012 (pp. 57-75). Amsterdam, The Netherlands: IOS Press.

Van Ostrand, A., Wolfe, S., Arredondo, A., Skinner, A. M., Visaiz, R., Jones, M., & Jenkins, J. J. (2016). Creating Virtual Communities That Work: Best Practices for Users and Developers of E-Collaboration Software. *International Journal of e-Collaboration*, *12*(4), 41–60. doi:10.4018/IJeC.2016100104

Vance, A., Lowry, P. B., & Eggett, D. (2013). Using accountability to reduce access policy violations in information systems. *Journal of Management Information Systems*, *29*(4), 263–289. doi:10.2753/MIS0742-1222290410

Vatrapu, R., Teplovs, C., Fujita, N., & Bull, S. (2011). Toward visual analytics for teachers' dynamic diagnostic pedagogical decision-making. In *Proceedings of the 1st International Conference on Learning Analytics and Knowledge* (pp. 93-98). New York, NY: ACM. 10.1145/2090116.2090129

Vejlgaard, H. (2016). Late adopters can be fast: The case of digital television. *Communications*, *41*(1), 87–98. doi:10.1515/commun-2015-0029

Vejlgaard, H. (2018). Rate of adoption determinants of innovations: A case study of digital terrestrial television. *International Journal of Digital Television*, *9*(1), 7–26. doi:10.1386/jdtv.9.1.7_1

Venkataraman, S., & Haftka, R. T. (2004). Structural optimization complexity: What has Moore's law done for us? *Structural and Multidisciplinary Optimization*, *28*(6), 375–387. doi:10.100700158-004-0415-y

Venkatesh, V., & Davis, F. D. (2000). A theoretical extension of the technology acceptance model: Four longitudinal field studies. *Management Science*, *46*(2), 186–204. doi:10.1287/mnsc.46.2.186.11926

Venkatesh, V., Morris, M. G., Davis, G. B., & Davis, F. D. (2003). User acceptance of information technology: Toward a unified view. *Management Information Systems Quarterly*, *27*(3), 425–478. doi:10.2307/30036540

Vidal, V. M., Casanova, M. A., Arruda, N., Roberval, M., Leme, L. P., Lopes, G. R., & Renso, C. (2015, June). Specification and incremental maintenance of linked data mashup views. In *International Conference on Advanced Information Systems Engineering* (pp. 214-229). Springer. 10.1007/978-3-319-19069-3_14

Vosniadou, S. (2008). *International handbook of Research on Conceptual Change.* New York, NY: Taylor and Francis Group.

Vygotsky, L. S. (1978). *Mind in Society. The Development of Higher Psychological Processes.* Cambridge, MA: Harvard University Press.

Walker, E., Rummel, N., & Koedinger, K. R. (2014). Adaptive intelligent support to improve peer tutoring in algebra. *International Journal of Artificial Intelligence in Education, 24*(1), 33–61. doi:10.100740593-013-0001-9

Walrad, C. C. (2016). The IEEE Computer Society and ACM's Collaboration on Computing Education. *Computer, 49*(3), 88–91. doi:10.1109/MC.2016.67

Walsham, G. (1993). *Interpreting Information Systems in Organization.* Chichester, UK: John Wiley & Sons Ltd.

Walsham, G. (1995). Interpretive case studies in IS research: Nature and Method. *European Journal of Information Systems, 4*(2), 74–81. doi:10.1057/ejis.1995.9

Wang, L., Ranjan, R., Chen, J., & Benatallah, B. (Eds.). (2017). *Cloud computing: methodology, systems, and applications.* CRC Press.

Wang, Y. M., Wang, Y. S., & Yang, Y. F. (2010). Understanding the determinants of RFID adoption in the manufacturing industry. *Technological Forecasting and Social Change, 77*(5), 803–815. doi:10.1016/j.techfore.2010.03.006

Warkentin, M., Moore, R. S., Bekkering, E., & Johnston, A. C. (2009). Analysis of systems development project risks: An integrative framework. *SIGMIS Database, 40*(2), 8–27. doi:10.1145/1531817.1531821

Warschauer, M. (2003). Dissecting the "digital divide": A case study in Egypt. *The Information Society, 19*(4), 297–304. doi:10.1080/01972240309490

Wasko, M. M., & Faraj, S. (2005). Why should I share? Examining social capital and knowledge contribution in electronic networks of practice. *Management Information Systems Quarterly, 29*(1), 35–57. doi:10.2307/25148667

Weber, B., Reichert, M., & Rinderle-Ma, S. (2008). Change Patterns and Change Support Features – Enhancing Flexibility in Process-Aware Information Systems. *Data & Knowledge Engineering, 66*(3), 438–467. doi:10.1016/j.datak.2008.05.001

Weill, W., Subramani, M., & Broadbent, M. (2002). Building IT infrastructure for strategic agility. *MIT Sloan Management Review,* (Fall): 57–65.

Weil, P., Subramani, M., & Broadbent, M. (2002, Fall). Building IT Infrastructure for Strategic Agility. *MIT Sloan Management Review,* 57–65.

Wellman, C. H. (2015). Immigration. *The Stanford encyclopaedia of philosophy* (Summer 2015 Edition). Retrieved from, https://plato.stanford.edu/archives/sum2015/entries/immigration/

Westat. (2012). *Health Information National Trends Survey 4 (HINTS 4): Cycle 1 Methodology Report.* Bethesda, MD: National Cancer Institute. Retrieved from https://hints.cancer.gov/docs/HINTS4_Cycle1_Methods_Report_revised_Jun2012.pdf

Whetstone, M., & Goldsmith, R. E. (2008). Some factors Associated with Adoption of Personal Health Records. In W. J. Kehoe & L. K. Whitten (Eds.), *Advances in Marketing: Issues, Strategies, and Theories* (pp. 258–259). Tuscaloosa, AL: Society for Marketing Advances.

Wikipedia. (2018a). *Agile Software Development*. Retrieved from https://en.wikipedia.org/wiki/Agile_software_development

Wikipedia. (2018b). *Artificial Intelligence*. Retrieved from https://en.wikipedia.org/wiki/Artificial_intelligence

Williams Whyte, C. B., & Gulati, G. J. (2007). Social Networks in Political Campaigns. *Annual Meeting of The American Political Science Association*.

Williams, D. E., Gavino, M. C., & Jacobson, D. W. (2017). Latino Entrepreneurs and Technology Usage: Ethnic Identity, Resistance, Self-Efficacy. *Journal of Business Diversity, 17*(1).

Williams, J., & Chinn, S. (2009). Using Web 2.0 to support the active learning experience. *Journal of Information Systems Education, 20*(2), 165–174.

Williamson, A. (2007). Empowering Communities to Action: Reclaiming Local Democracy Through ICT. *Community Informatics Research Conference*.

Willison, R., & Warkentin, M. (2013). Beyond deterrence: An expanded view of employee computer abuse. *Management Information Systems Quarterly, 37*(1), 1–20. doi:10.25300/MISQ/2013/37.1.01

Wilson, E. V., & Lankton, N. K. (2004). Modeling Patients' Acceptance of Provider-delivered E-health. *Journal of the American Medical Informatics Association, 11*(4), 241–248. doi:10.1197/jamia.M1475 PMID:15064290

Wirtz, B. W., Mory, L., & Ullrich, S. (2012). eHealth in the Public Sector: An Empirical Analysis of the Acceptance of Germany's Electronic Health Card. *Public Administration, 90*(3), 642–663. doi:10.1111/j.1467-9299.2011.02004.x

Wiztech Inc. (2011). *AGILE Methodology*. Retrieved from http://www.wiztechinc.com/AGILE-methodology.html

Wolde-Rufael, Y. (2007). Another look at the Relationship between Telecommunications Investment and Economic Activity in the United States. *International Economic Journal, 21*(2), 199–205. doi:10.1080/10168730701345372

Wolfe, D. M., & Kolb, D. A. (1979). Career Development, Personal Growth, and Experiential Learning. In Organizational Psychology: A Book of Readings. Englewood Cliffs, NJ: Prentice-Hall Inc.

Wolfe, R. A. (1994). Organizational innovation: Review, critique and suggested research directions. *Journal of Management Studies, 31*(3), 405–431. doi:10.1111/j.1467-6486.1994.tb00624.x

Wolff, R., Roberts, D., Murgia, A., Murray, N., Rae, J., & Steptoe, W. (2008). *Communicating eye gaze across a distance without rooting participants to the spot*. Distributed Simulation and Real-Time Applications, 2008. DS-RT 2008. 12th IEEE International Symposium, Vancouver, British Columbia, Canada. 10.1109/DS-RT.2008.28

Wolfinbarger, M., & Gilly, M. C. (2002). *Q.com: dimensionalizing, measuring and predicting quality of the e-tail experience*. Working Paper No. 02-100, Marketing Science Institute, Cambridge, MA.

Wood, D., Zaidman, M., Ruth, L., & Hausenblas, M. (2014). *Linked Data, Structured Data on the Web*. Manning Publishers.

Wu, F., Mahajan, V., & Balasubramanian, S. (2003). An analysis of e-business adoption and its impact on business performance. *Journal of the Academy of Marketing Science, 31*(4), 425-447. DOI: 10.1177/0092070303255379

Wu, M., & Yu, M. (2013). Enterprise information security management based on context-aware RBAC and communication monitoring technology. *Mathematical Problems in Engineering, 2013*, 1–11. doi:10.1155/2013/569562

Wymer, S. A., & Regan, E. A. (2005). Factors influencing e-commerce adoption and use by small and medium businesses. *Electronic Markets, 15*(4), 438–453. doi:10.1080/10196780500303151

Xiaolan, Z., & Jun, J. (2010). A research on the selection and evaluation of supplier for laptop. *IEEE Xplore*, 674-676.

Xiao, N., Sharman, R., Rao, H. R., & Upadhyaya, S. (2014). Factors Influencing Online Health Information Search: An Empirical Analysis of a national Cancer-Related Survey. *Decision Support Systems*, *57*, 417–427. doi:10.1016/j.dss.2012.10.047

Xu, S., Zhu, K., & Gibbs, J. L. (2004). Global technology, local adoption: A cross-country investigation of Internet adoption by companies in the United States and China. *Electronic Markets*, *14*(1), 13–24. doi:10.1080/1019678042000175261

Xu, Y., Guo, X., Hao, J., Ma, J., Lau, R. Y. K., & Xu, W. (2012). Combining social network and semantic concept analysis for personalized academic researcher recommendation. *Decision Support Systems*, *54*(1), 564–573.

Yang, J. (2014). Supply Chain Agility: Securing Performance for Chinese Manufacturers. *International Journal of Production Economics*, *150*, 104–114. doi:10.1016/j.ijpe.2013.12.018

Yang, Q., Pang, C., Liu, L., Yen, C. D., & Tarn, M. (2015). Exploring consumer perceived risk and trust for online payments: An empirical study in China's younger generation. *Computers in Human Behavior*, *50*, 9–24. doi:10.1016/j.chb.2015.03.058

Yang, Z., Sun, J., Zhang, Y., & Wang, Y. (2015). Understanding SaaS adoption from the perspective of organizational users: A tripod readiness model. *Computers in Human Behavior*, *45*, 254–264. doi:10.1016/j.chb.2014.12.022

Yap, C.S., Soh, C.P.P., & Raman, K.S. (1992). Information systems success factors. *Small Business International Journal of Management Science*, *20*, 597.

Yin, R. K. (1994). Case Study Research, Design and Methods. Newbury Park, CA: Sage Publications.

Yin, R. K. (1993). *Applications of Case study Research*. Newbury Park, CA: Sage Publishing.

Yin, R. K. (2005). *Case Study Research: Design & Methods* (3rd ed.). Beverly Hills, CA: Sage.

Yong, A. (2014). Article *Notices of the American Mathematical Society*, *61*(9), 1040–1050. doi:10.1090/noti1164

Yoon, K. (2016). The migrant lives of the digital generation. *Continuum*, *30*(4), 369–380. doi:10.1080/10304312.2016.1141867

Yoon, T. E., & George, J. F. (2013). Why aren't organizations adopting virtual worlds? *Computers in Human Behavior*, *29*(3), 772–790. doi:10.1016/j.chb.2012.12.003

Young, A. (2017). *Global Survey Reveals Cost, Benefit, & Challenges of Cloud Migration*. Retrieved from http://itbrief.com.au/story/global-survey-reveals-costs-benefits-challenges-cloud-migration

Yu, H. E., & Huang, W. (2015). *Building a Virtual HPC Cluster with Auto Scaling by the Docker*. Retrieved 02-03, 2018, from https://sshelco-primo.hosted.exlibrisgroup.com/primo-explore/fulldisplay?docid=TN_arxiv1509.08231&context=PC&vid=IUP&search_scope=default_scope&tab=default_tab&lang=en_US

Yu, M. Y., Lang, K. R., & Kumar, N. (2009). Internationalization of online professional communities: An empirical investigation of AIS-ISWorld. *International Journal of e-Collaboration*, *5*(1), 13–31. doi:10.4018/jec.2009010102

Yusuf, Y. Y., Sarahadi, M., & Gunasekaran, A. (1999). Agile Manufacturing: The Drivers, Concepts, and Attributes. *International Journal of Production Economics*, *62*(1-2), 33-43.

Yusuf, Y. Y., Gunasekaran, A., Musa, A., Dauda, M., El-Berishy, N. M., & Cang, S. (2014). A Relational Study of Supply Chain Agility, Competitiveness, and Business Performance in the Oil and Gas Industry. *International Journal of Production Economics*, *147*, 531–544. doi:10.1016/j.ijpe.2012.10.009

Zadeh, L. A. (1983). The role of fuzzy logic in the management of uncertainty in knowledge based systems. *Fuzzy Sets and Systems*, *11*(1), 197–198.

Zaidi, A. U., Fernando, S., & Ammar, N. (2015). An exploratory study of the impact of information communication technology (ICT) or computer mediated communication (CMC) on the level of violence and access to service among intimate partner violence (IPV) survivors in Canada. *Technology in Society*, *41*, 91–97. doi:10.1016/j.techsoc.2014.12.003

Zakrzewska, D. (2009). Cluster Analysis in Personalized E-Learning. *Intelligent Systems for Knowledge Management*, *252*, 229–250. doi:10.1007/978-3-642-04170-9_10

Zaveri, A., Rula, A., Maurino, A., Pietrobon, R., Lehmann, J., & Auer, S. (2016). Quality assessment for linked data: A survey. *Semantic Web*, *7*(1), 63–93. doi:10.3233/SW-150175

Zeithaml, V. A., Parasuraman, A., & Malhotra, A. (2002). Service quality delivery through web sites: A critical review of extant knowledge. *Journal of the Academy of Marketing Science*, *30*(4), 362–375. doi:10.1177/009207002236911

Zemmouchi-Ghomari, L. (2015). Linked Data, Towards Realizing the Web of Data: An Overview. *International Journal of Technology Diffusion*, *6*(4), 20–39. doi:10.4018/IJTD.2015100102

Zemmouchi-Ghomari, L., & Ghomari, A. R. (2009). Reference Ontology. *Proceedings of the International IEEE Conference on Signal-Image Technologies and Internet-Based System*.

Zemmouchi-Ghomari, L., Sefsaf, R., & Azni, K. (2018). Using linked data resources to generate web pages based on a BBC case study. *Proceedings of the IEEE Computing Conference*.

Zhang, N., & Hämmäinen, H. (2015, March). Cost efficiency of SDN in LTE-based mobile networks: Case Finland. In *Networked Systems (NetSys), 2015 International Conference and Workshops on* (pp. 1-5). IEEE.

Zhang, Y., & Wildemuth, B. M. (2009). Qualitative analysis of content. In B. Wildemuth (Ed.), Applications of social research methods to questions in information and library science (pp. 308–319). Academic Press.

Zhang, P., & Von Dran, G. M. (2002). User expectations and rankings of quality factors in different web site domains. *International Journal of Electronic Commerce*, *6*(2), 9–33.

Zhang, Y., Fang, Y., Wei, K. K., & Chen, H. (2010). Exploring the role of psychological safety in promoting the intention to continue sharing knowledge in virtual communities. *International Journal of Information Management*, *30*(5), 425–436. doi:10.1016/j.ijinfomgt.2010.02.003

Zhou, D., Djatej, A., Sarikas, R., & Senteney, D. (2014). The growth of industry web portals: Framework and guidelines. *International Journal of e-Collaboration*, *10*(4), 17–31. doi:10.4018/ijec.2014100102

Zhou, K. Z., Yim, C. K., & Tse, D. K. (2005). The effects of strategic orientations on technology- and market-based breakthrough innovations. *Journal of Marketing*, *69*(2), 42–60. doi:10.1509/jmkg.69.2.42.60756

Zhu, K., Dong, S., Xu, S., & Kraemer, K. L. (2006). Innovation diffusion in global contexts: Determinants of post-adoption digital transformation of European companies. *European Journal of Information Systems*, *15*(6), 601–616. doi:10.1057/palgrave.ejis.3000650

Zhu, K., & Kraemer, K. L. (2005). Post-adoption variations in usage and value of e-business by organizations: Cross-country evidence from the retail industry. *Information Systems Research*, *16*(1), 61–84. doi:10.1287/isre.1050.0045

Ziemba, E., & Zelazny, R. (2013). Measuring the information society in Poland - dilemmas and a quantified image. FedCSIS, 1173-1180.

Zivick, J. (2012). Mapping global virtual team leadership actions to organizational roles. *The Business Review, Cambridge, 19*(2), 18–25.

Zolait, A. H., Ibrahim, A. R., & Farooq, A. (2010). A study on the Internet security and its implication for e-commerce in Yemen. *International Journal of Technology Diffusion, 1*(3), 34–47. doi:10.4018/jtd.2010070102

About the Contributors

Efosa C. Idemudia, an internationally known scholar, is an Associate Professor of Business Data Analytics at Arkansas Tech University. Also, Dr. Idemudia is the Director for the Interdisciplinary Research Center (IRC) at Arkansas Tech University. Dr. Idemudia holds degrees from universities located on three different continents: a PhD in Management Information Systems from Texas Tech University, a Master's in Computer Information Systems from the University of Texas at El Paso, and an MBA in International Business from the Helsinki School of Economics and Business Administration; he completed his Fulbright at the Lagos Business School and Carnegie Fellow at Covenant University. He participated as a member of the University System of Georgia's Academic Advisory Committee for Computer Disciplines for five years and is a member of Strathmore Who's Who of Professionals. Dr. Idemudia taught both graduate and undergraduate students as a visiting scholar in the Computer Information Systems (CIS) Department at Georgia State University, which the U.S. News & World Report ranked within the top ten CIS departments in the United States. Currently, Dr. Idemudia is a member of the editorial boards for the *International Journal of Technology Diffusion (IJTD)*; the *Journal of Information Technology Management (JITM)*; *Electronic Commerce Research and Applications*; *International Journal of Risk and Contingency Management (IJRCM)*; the *International Journal of Management Science of AASCIT*; the *Engineering and Technology of AASCIT*; *American Journal of Science and Technology of AASCIT*; the *Journal of the Southern Association for Information Systems*; the *International Journal of Economic and Business Management; Control and Systems Engineering.*

* * *

Hany Abdelghaffar is an associate professor of Information Systems at the German University in Cairo, Egypt. He holds MSc. and PhD from Middlesex University, London, UK in Information Systems. He has many publications in different fields including ERP, e-commence, e-government in different conferences and journals.

Evon M. O. Abu-Taieh (Associate Professor) is Past Dean of Information Systems & Technology Faculty in the University of Jordan – Aqaba. Prior she was chair of BIT and CIS Departments in the University of Jordan (Aqaba). Edited and authored many scholarly books on Simulation, IT, and Aviation. Published more than 40 papers on AI, KM, Simulation, Ciphering, Software engineering, OR, Multimedia, social media. Published more than 10 scholarly chapters in more than 7 scholarly books. Dr. Abu-Taieh has served as editorial board member and reviewer in a number of renowned Journals and conferences, furthermore, established the International Journal of Aviation Technology, Engineering and Management(IJATEM) with IGI as editor in chief. The work of Dr. Abu-Taieh is indexed in ACM digital Library, IEEE Xplore, Library of Congress, British Library, ISI Web of Knowledge, Scopus, Google scholar, Stanford University Libraries, University of Technology Sydney (UTS) Library and IGI.

Bhanu Bhakta Acharya is a researcher on media ethics and communication policy, affiliated to the Department of Communication at the University of Ottawa. He is currently researching on immigrants' motivation for Information and Communication Technology adoption and use in accessing and using government online services provided by the Federal, Provincial and Municipal Governments of Canada. Previously, Acharya worked as the communication officer of the National Human Rights Commission of Nepal for seven years. Author of five books on journalism and communication, Acharya has published several research articles in scholarly journals, attended international conferences, and advocated for capacity building of immigrants in accessing and using government services available online. His primary research interests include press freedom and media ethics, digital divide, immigrant's ICT use, diaspora communication, and e-government.

Shameem Akhter is an Information Technology (IT) Professional. She holds an M.S. in Management and Information Systems (MIS) from Western Oregon University, USA and a Master of Social Science (MSS) degree in Economics from the University of Dhaka, Bangladesh. She had been selected by Western Oregon University (WOU) faculty and staff committee for the Who's Who among Students in American Universities and Colleges recognition for 2011-2012. The committee selected her from a nominated pool of over 900 students to be recognized for her outstanding leadership, service, and scholarship at WOU. Her most recent publications appeared in the International Journal of Technology Diffusion (IJTD) and the ULAB Journal of Science and Engineering (JSE). Her research interest includes Database Systems, Data Warehousing, Decision Support System, and Information Systems Implementation.

Badreya Al-Jenaibi is a full Professor in Mass Communication at the UAEU. Her research interests include Pedagogy, international communication, public relations, as well as the uses and effects of mass media, and new media. Her research has appeared in the *Journal of Applied Journalism & Media Studies, International Journals of Information Systems & Social Change*, the *International Journal of E-adoption, Global Media Journal, Journal for Communication and Culture,* and the *Journal of Cross Cultural Communication.* She served in the editorial board in 18 peer-reviewed international journals, she published more than 43 peer-reviewed articles. Also, she received Khlifah Award for the best distinguished teacher and professor in the Arab world, Arab Youth and Academic Publishing Award, Arab Women Creative Award-best creative teacher, His Highness Hamdan Bin Mubarak Award for the best distinguished employee in specialized jobs – Academic, Quality Assurance and Community Service Award, UAEU Academic and Publishing Award, Volunteering Award. She is the director of Mubadrah student community engagement center, her activities were engaged with more than 116 local organizations.

Shaha Al-Otaibi is an assistant professor in the Department of Information Systems, College of Computer and Information Sciences, Princess Nourah Bint Abdulrahman University, Saudi Arabia. She got her MS in Computer Science and PhD in Artificial Intelligent from King Saud University. Her Research interests include Data Mining, Big Data, Social Media Analytics and bio-inspired computing.

Auhood Alfaries is as assistant professor in the IT department in King Saud University (KSU). Dr. Auhood received her PhD in semantic web and web services from the school of Computing and Information systems, Brunel University, UK. Held a number of IT related academic and Administrative positions both in KSU and Princes Noura bint Abdulrahman university (PNU). She has experience in Quality and program accreditation by serving in a number of Quality related roles since 2011. Auhood is Associated with a number of important bodies such as Associate of the UK Higher Education Academy, Member of the Institute of Electrical and Electronics Engineers (IEEE) and a member of the Saudi Computer Society. She is also an ABET program evaluator. She participated as conference and journal reviewer, a member of a number of national and international workshops and conference program committees. Served as vice Dean and Dean of E-learning and Distance Learning deanship in KSU and then in PNU for two years, also served as the assistant general director and then the director for the general directorate of information and communication technology (ITC) in PNU. Currently she is the Dean of the college of computer and information sciences. She is a member of a number of strategic committees in differing levels both university and Ministry of Education. Auhood's Research interest includes semantic web, ontology engineering, Natural Language Processing, Machine Learning and Cloud Computing. A member of IWAN research group.

Ibrahim Arpaci is Associate Professor and Chair of the Department of Computer Education and Instructional Technology at Gaziosmanpasa University, where he is also Director of Distance Education Application and Research Center. He was a visiting scholar at Ryerson University, Ted Rogers School of Information Technology Management, Toronto, ON, Canada (2012-2013). He holds a BSc in Computer Education and Instructional Technology (2005) from Anadolu University, an MSc in Information Systems (2009) and a PhD in Information Systems (2013) both from Middle East Technical University. His academic work focuses on how computational technology interact with psychological, educational and cultural dynamics. His research interests are in Computational Intelligence, Instructional Systems Design and Technology, Cyberpsychology and Behavior, Culture, Learning and Technology.

Luis Casillas holds a Ph.D. and a Master's Degree in Information and Knowledge Societies, as well as a Master's Degree in Information Systems and a B.Sc. in Informatics. He has been working as full-time professor for more than 23 years in the Computer Science Department from the University of Guadalajara (Mexico). He has published various papers and scientific chapters in diverse journals and books. He serves as member of the editorial board for a couple of journals, and reviewer for diverse journals and other scientific publications about: knowledge engineering, computer science and ICT in education. His research interests are: knowledge gathering and representation, bio-inspired systems, expert systems, complex networks analysis, soft-computing, data mining, and automated emotion-awareness.

Pankaj Chaudhary is currently a Professor of MIS in the ISDS department at Indiana University of Pennsylvania, USA. He holds a PhD in MIS from Southern Illinois University, USA, an MBA from Indian Institute of Management, Ahmedabad, India, and Bachelor of Technology in Computer Science & Engineering from Indian Institute of Technology, Delhi, India. His current research areas include Information Systems Agility, IS Infrastructure, IS-Centric organizational transformation, and Knowledge Management.

Harold Daniel is an Associate Professor of Marketing at the University of Maine's Business School. His research interests include: Development and Maintenance of Strategic Collaborations among Organizations, Development of Travel and Tourism Products, and Influence of Time and Timing on Buyer Behavior.

Stavros Demetriadis is currently faculty member at Computer Science Department, Aristotle University of Thessaloniki, Greece. He holds a BSc degree in Physics, MSc in Electronic Physics, and PhD in Multimedia educational technology from Aristotle University of Thessaloniki. He teaches courses and conducts research in the broader area of technology-enhanced learning with emphasis on Computer-supported collaborative learning (CSCL), Adaptive hypermedia systems for learning, Educational robotics and Tangible interfaces for programming, Conversational agents, Multimedia learning, Cognitive training technologies. He has published more than 150 research papers in international scientific journals (with IF) and international/national conference proceedings with more than 1200 third party citations. He is member of the scientific committee in several top ranking international Conferences each year (such as IEEE ICALT, ECTEL, CSEDU, etc.). His supervised PhD project "Cubes Coding" was presented with awards in two international competitions (Open Education Challenge 2014 and NUMA-2014). His conference articles have received three times "Best paper" awards and one article has been highlighted as "spotlight paper" at the IEEE Transactions of Learning Technologies journal. Since 1995 he has participated in many AUTH research projects and has been project leader in some of them (such as the "Kaleidoscope NoE" AUTH team).

Arsen Djatej is Professor, Eastern Washington University Spokane, Washington. College of Business and Public Administration. Teaching responsibilities, Accounting Information systems, Accounting Theory, Intermediate Accounting I, Intermediate Accounting II, International Accounting, Cost Accounting, Principles of Financial Accounting, Principles of Managerial Accounting, MBA Financial Accounting, MBA Managerial Accounting, and MBA Global Accounting Issues.

Brian Doore is the Director of Assessment at the University of Maine.

Christian Graham is an Assistant Professor of Management Information Systems at the University of Maine's Business School. He teaches several MIS courses that include database management, network design and applications, and enterprise architecture. His research interests are in the design of e-collaboration systems and the behavioral interactions between e-collaboration systems and virtual team members and leaders.

Alfredo Gutierrez holds a PhD in Engineering of Projects and Systems by Universitat Politécnica de Catalunya (BarcelonaTech). Professor at CUCEI Universidad de Guadalajara in México teaching to Computer Sciences students since 2001. Professor at Jalisco's Education Secretariat in México since 1994, where he has leaded the Virtual Education official at project and starting stage. From 2009 to 2011 member of TARIFA researching group in I2CAT in Barcelona, Spain. Granted by EMCW18 from European Community, and CONACYT from México, he developed his PhD thesis proposing a GDSS model and tools to generate web-based consensus based in Delphi Decision Making Process. His researching lines go on online evaluation and assessment, consensus opinion in collective workgroups, and Future Internet Socioeconomics.

Georgios Gyftodimos received a degree in mathematics and a PhD degree in informatics. He is currently an Associate Professor in the Department of Philosophy and History of Science, University of Athens, where he participates in the Interdisciplinary Postgraduate Program on Cognitive Science and teaches courses in AI, evolutionary programming, and simulation. His research interests lie in the domains of knowledge representation and modeling for cognitive purposes. He has published several publications in journals and has participated in various conferences. He has also served as a reviewer for several international journals. Retired Associate Professor Gyftodimos is an IEEE fellow.

Lobna Hassan is an information Systems researcher doing experimental work on motivational systems design and its influence on two-way government-citizens communications, and employee performance.

Micki Hyde is a Professor of MIS at Indiana University of Pennsylvania. She received her PhD in Management Information Systems from Southern Illinois University at Carbondale and her research interests include the development and success issues relating to information systems.

Magnisalis I. received the BSc degree in mathematics from Aristotle University of Thessaloniki, Greece, and the MSc degree in business systems analysis and design from the CITY University of London. He holds a PHD in the multi-disciplinary filed of Information Science and Educational technologies (2016, Aristotle University of Thessaloniki, Greece). His research interests include adaptive and intelligent systems for collaborative learning. He is a software engineer working since 1999 and has cooperated with various companies in Greece and Worldwide (e.g. INTRACOM, ERICSSON, SAP). He has experience in a variety of IT systems (CRM, Document Management, HR, Sales Operations, E-learning, Web-conference etc.). For the last 13 years, he has been working at the Greek Lottery Industry; he currently works as Head of Sales Support and Operations at OPAP S.A. (north Greece). His interests currently focus on deploying learning analytics solutions and collaborative games in diverse environments (in-class, at-work, web-based, gesture-based, on mobile devices, for people with special needs).

Japhet E. Lawrence received a doctoral degree in Computer Science from the University of Salford, UK, Master degree in Computer Science from London South Bank University, UK, Graduate Certificate in Higher Education from Deakin University, Australia, Bachelor degree in Applied Computing from University of Tasmania, Australia, BTEC HNC in Business and Finance from London Metropolitan University, UK and Diploma in French Language from Brussels, Belgium. He previously taught at the Department of Applied Computing and Information Technology, University of Kurdistan-Hawler, Erbil, Kurdistan Region of Iraq. Prior to joining Deakin University, Dr Lawrence worked as a Senior Lecturer at Nigerian Defence Academy.

Frank Makoza is a Lecturer in the Department of Entrepreneurship and Business Management at the Cape Peninsula University of Technology in South Africa. He holds a PhD in Information Systems and Masters degree in Information Systems from University of Cape Town, South Africa. His research interests are in assessing societal impact of ICT in the context of developing countries and ICT use in small businesses. His work has appeared in a number of Journals and international conferences.

Alexandros Papadimitriou received the diploma in Computer Science from the Department of Electrical and Computer Engineering, National Technical University of Athens (NTUA), Greece, in 1992 and the MSc degree in Automatic Control Systems and Robotics from the Department of Mechanical Engineering, NTUA, in 2004. He holds a PhD degree in Computer Science from the Department of Informatics and Telecommunications, University of Athens, since 2010. He taught for 21 years at the Technological Educational Institutions (TEI) and at the School of Pedagogical & Technological Education (ASPAITE), and for 21 years in Technical High Schools. He is now a School Advisor in the Greek Ministry of Education, and a visited Lecturer in the ASPAITE teaching courses of "Educational Applications with Computers" and "Educational Technology". His doctoral dissertation is on the "Web-based Adaptive Educational Hypermedia Systems in Science and Technology." His current research interests include the areas of educational technology, adaptive educational hypermedia systems, adaptive group formation and/or peer help, interactive problem-solving support, meta-adaptation techniques, and the didactics of science and technology. Dr. Papadimitriou has received several honors and distinctions including an Outstanding Paper Award from the ED-MEDIA 2008 conference, a Best Poster Paper Award from the ICALT 2009 conference and two invited papers from the IEEE TLT Journal and the Journal of Information Technology and Application in Education (JITAE). He has published several publications including journal articles and technical papers. He has also served as a reviewer for several international journals including the Journal of Knowledge-Based Systems, Elsevier.

Adriana Peña received her Ph.D. in Computer Science in 2009 from the Universidad Politécnica de Madrid, Spain. Her main research interest is on the user's avatar display of nonverbal communication in Collaborative Virtual Environments. She is a research professor at the Computer Science Department at the CUCEI of the Universidad de Guadalajara, Mexico

Mohammad Nirjhar Rahman is a Professor of Marketing at the Faculty of Business Studies, University of Rajshahi, Bangladesh. He served as the chair of the Department of Marketing, University of Rajshahi during 1996-1998. He teaches Marketing Management, Computer Applications in Business, Mathematics for Business, Quantitative Methods for Business, and Operations Research in BBA and MBA programs. He also supervises students' research projects. His principal research interests include e-commerce, customer relationship management, healthcare service quality, and green products.

Nayem Rahman is an Information Technology (IT) Professional. He has implemented several large projects using data warehousing and big data technology. He is currently working toward the Ph.D. degree in the Department of Engineering and Technology Management at Portland State University, USA. He holds an M.S. in Systems Science (Modeling & Simulation) from Portland State University, Oregon, USA and an MBA in Management Information Systems (MIS), Project Management, and Marketing from Wright State University, Ohio, USA. His most recent publications appeared in the International Journal of Business Analytics (IJBAN) and the International Journal of Operations Research and Information Systems (IJORIS). His principal research interests include Big Data Analytics, Big Data Technology Acceptance, Data Mining for Business Intelligence, and Simulation-based Decision Support System (DSS).

James A. Rodger is a Professor of Management Information Systems and Decision Sciences at Indiana University of Pennsylvania (IUP). He received his Doctorate in MIS from Southern Illinois University at Carbondale in 1997. Dr. Rodger has published several journal articles related to these subjects. His work has appeared in the following journals: Journal of Computer Information Systems, Issues in Information Systems, IEEE Transactions on Software Engineering, International Journal of Hybrid Intelligent Systems, Information and Software Technology, Information Technology and Management. Annals of Operations Research, Communications of ACM, Computers & Operations Research, Decision Support Systems, Expert Systems with Applications, Lecture Notes in Computer Science, International Journal of Human-Computer Studies, as well as several other journals.

Sergey Samoilenko is an Associate professor and the Chair of the Department of Computer Science & Computer Information Systems in Averett University, Danville, Virginia. A quick search on Google Scholar should provide an interested reader with Sergey's current scholarly pursuits and publications.

Vaggelis Saprikis is an Assistant Professor in e-Business at the Department of Business Administration, Western Macedonia University of Applied Sciences, Kozani, Greece. He received his undergraduate degree from the Department of Applied Informatics of the University of Macedonia, Thessaloniki, Greece in 2004. He also received his Master's degree in Information Systems and his PhD in B2B e-marketplaces from the same Department in 2007 and 2011 correspondingly. His research interests include e-business models, e-commerce, e-marketplaces, m-commerce and information systems. He has participated in international conferences and has published various papers in international journals.

Robert Sarikas is an Associate Professor of Accounting at Eastern Washington University in Spokane, Washington. He graduated with a PhD in Accountancy from the University of Illinois at Urbana-Champaign in 1992. Previous to joining Eastern Washington he held tenured faculty positions at Boise State University and Ohio University. He has taught overseas in Brazil, China, England, Germany, India, Russia, and Vietnam.

David Senteney holds Ph.D. degrees in Accountancy from University of Illinois at Urbana-Champaign and is a Licensed Certified Public Accountant. Professor Senteney has specialized in Financial Accounting and Reporting by business entities i.e., FASB and IASB Reporting Standards, SEC Regulation and Securities Markets for over 20 years as an academic accountant. He is a prolific scholarly author on financial statement analysis and equity valuation as well as economic aspects of FASB and IASB financial accounting standards, particularly relating to security market relevance of FASB and IASB financial accounting standards. Dr. Senteney is an active member of a number of professional and academic Accounting, Financial, and Statistical associations.

Changsoo Sohn is a professor at Department of Information Systems, St. Cloud State University, St. Cloud, Minnesota, USA. He received the Bachelor's degree from Seoul National University, Seoul, Korea, and MBA and Ph.D. degrees from Southern Illinois University, Carbondale, Illinois, USA. His major is Management Information Systems. His main research interests are business intelligence and healthcare information systems. His research has been published in many journals and proceedings such as Total Quality Management & Business Excellence, European Journal of Operational Research, and International Journal of Electronic Customer Relationship Management, and others.

Mahmud Ullah is an Associate Professor of Marketing at the Faculty of Business Studies, University of Dhaka, Bangladesh. He teaches Behavioral and Quantitative courses in Business, e.g. Psychology, Organizational Behavior, Consumer Behavior, Business Mathematics, Business Statistics, Quantitative Analyses in Business etc., in addition to the Basic and Specialized Marketing courses like Marketing Management, Non-Profit Marketing, E-Marketing etc. He also taught Basic & Advanced English, and IELTS in English language Schools in New Zealand during his stay over there between 2002 and 2006. He has conducted a number of research projects sponsored by different international and national organizations including the World Bank (RMB), UNICEF, UNFPA, and USAID. His research interests include ethical aspects of human behavior in all these relevant fields, specifically in the continuously evolving and changing field of Digital Business and Marketing.

Henrik Vejlgaard, M.Sc., MA, is a lecturer at Copenhagen Business Academy, Copenhagen, Denmark. He is the author of three books on lifestyle and trend sociology: *Anatomy of a Trend*, *The Lifestyle Puzzle,* and *Style Eruptions*.

Winfred Yaokumah is the Dean of the Faculty of Engineering, Science and Computing at the Pentecost University College, Accra, Ghana. He obtained his PhD in Information Technology with specialization in Information Assurance and Security. He has published extensively in several international journals, including the Information Management & Computer Security, Information Resources Management Journal, International Journal of E-Business Research, Journal of Information Technology Research, International Journal of Information Systems in the Service Sector, International Journal of Information Systems and Social Change, International Journal of IT/Business Alignment and Governance, and the International Journal of Technology Diffusion. His research interest includes information security, information security governance, IT governance, cyber security and ethics, e-services, and IT leadership.

Younsook Yeo is an assistant professor at Department of Social Work, St. Cloud State University, St. Cloud, Minnesota, USA. She received her Ph.D. in social work, Master of Applied Statistics (MAS), and Master of Social Work (MSW) from the University of South Carolina, Columbia, South Carolina, USA. Dr. Yeo's research has focused on health and health disparities. Using the empowerment perspective as a meta-theory, Dr. Yeo has examined individuals' behavioral factors in relation to contextual factors including welfare policy, cultural factors, and social determinant factors, which may promote or deter individuals' health and wellbeing.

Leila Zemmouchi-Ghomari received her Ph.D. in Computer Science from ESI, Algiers, in January 2014. Her research interests focus on ontology engineering, knowledge engineering, semantic web and linked data. She is currently a Lecturer at ENST: Ecole Nationale Supérieure de Technologie, Algiers, Algeria.

Duanning Zhou is a Professor of Management Information Systems, Chair of the department of Information Systems and Business Analytics, at the College of Business and Public Administration, Eastern Washington University, Spokane, Washington, USA. He received his Ph.D. in Information Systems from the City University of Hong Kong in 2000. His current research interests include electronic commerce, data mining, and health information systems. He has published in ACM Transaction on Internet Technology, Communication of Association for Information Systems, Global Perspective on Accounting Education, Group Decision and Negotiation, IEEE Transactions on Engineering Management, IEEE Transactions on Education, IEEE Transactions on Systems, Man, and Cybernetics, Information & Management, International Journal of Information Quality, Journal of Enterprise Information Management, and other journals.

Index

A

ability 3, 68, 131, 136-137, 141, 145-146, 151, 156, 160, 167, 191, 264, 266, 273, 277, 279, 281, 293-294, 307-309, 314, 331-333, 336-337, 339-341, 343, 352, 354, 361, 364, 392, 413, 418, 424-426, 431, 439, 449, 453

Access Management 312, 330

adoption 26, 41, 71, 114-117, 119-120, 123-124, 261-263, 265-270, 272-277, 279-284, 290-292, 294, 299, 340, 373, 375-384, 386, 392, 436-438, 440-441, 444, 446, 448-449, 451-455

AGILE INFORMATION SYSTEMS 331, 357

algorithm 130, 132, 134, 140-142, 146, 151

B

backup 304-306, 308, 322, 324-325, 330, 411

Business Continuity Management 313-314, 325, 330

BYOD 114-115, 120, 123-124

C

case study 42, 64, 71, 73, 76-77, 209, 214-222, 268-272, 274-277, 280-281, 363

change management 305-306, 313, 330, 342

Citation Index 235, 237, 240, 243, 247, 250, 252, 260

cloud computing 115, 194, 233-235, 237, 252, 260, 307, 339-340, 358-359, 361-363, 374

collaboration agreement 130, 132, 137, 144-146

collaboration analysis 2, 4-5, 10, 19

collaboration willingness 142

collaborative 1, 3-4, 10-11, 13, 19, 72, 131-136, 139, 141, 145, 152, 154, 156, 209-210, 212-213, 227, 360, 364, 431

communication strategies 64, 80

competitive strategy 191-192

computer industry 189-193, 196-198, 201, 203

configuration management 305, 313, 330

crises in the UAE 66, 81

cross-country 35, 42

Customer Information Database 166

D

Data Protection 306, 393-394, 396, 400, 406

database design 173

diaspora communication 438, 452

diffusion of innovations 265, 373-374, 377, 385

digital divide 154, 437-441, 455

Dyad 151

E

e-collaboration 64, 66, 71-72, 74-82, 147, 208-211, 213-220, 226-228

e-commerce 25-26, 34-35, 123, 340, 410

economic development 41-42, 55, 395

e-consumer behavior 25-27, 34

e-democracy 152-159, 161-162

Egypt 152, 158-159, 162

electronic commerce 262

email 73, 190, 262, 266, 275, 278, 280, 310, 341, 407, 424

entity-relationship 169, 172

e-publishing 233-235, 237, 252, 260

execution attributes 351

F

forecasting 386

fuzzy classification 1

G

grounded theory 261-262, 267-271, 273-274

group effectiveness 131-132, 137, 140-141, 145-146

H

Heterogeneous Group 151
HINTS 131, 290, 294-295, 299
Homogeneous Group 151

I

ICT 24, 40-43, 47, 55, 114-117, 119-120, 123, 156, 261-284, 395-398, 436-442, 444, 446, 448-449, 451-455
immigrants 436-439, 441-442, 444-449, 451-455
incident management 314, 325
industry web portal 407-408, 410-411, 413, 415, 417, 419
influence factors 449, 454-455
Informal Peer Help Network 145, 151
Information and Communication Technology 24, 114, 152
information trust 290, 295-299
institutions 71-72, 80, 237, 239, 243, 245-246, 310, 315, 317-318, 320, 322-324, 378-380, 382, 384-385, 391, 393-394, 396, 398, 406
Internet 24-28, 31, 33, 35, 66, 69, 71-72, 132, 154-157, 159, 162, 167, 190, 199, 201, 237, 243, 260, 262, 264, 275, 277-278, 281-282, 292-293, 306-308, 332, 398, 406-408, 410-411, 414, 416-418, 422-424, 437-440, 442, 445, 447-449, 452-455
investments in ICT 40-43, 47
IT consumerization 114, 120

K

Know Your Customer (KYC) 392, 400, 406

L

laptop 192-203
leadership types 423, 427-430
learning style 130, 132, 134, 136-137, 139-142, 145, 151
learning styles 132, 136-137, 139, 145-146
Linked Data 87-94, 97-99, 101-102, 104, 107

M

Malawi 389-390, 392, 395-401, 403
malware 304-306, 308, 313, 315, 322, 324-325, 330
Malware Management 304, 313, 330
Media Training 69
Millennials 422-423, 430

Mobile Commerce 392, 406
mobile phones 159, 389-392, 399, 401, 406, 439, 447
motivation 26, 131, 145, 151, 153, 210, 213, 401, 431, 436, 439, 441-442, 446, 448-449, 451-452, 454-455

N

negotiation protocol 130, 144, 151
nonverbal interaction 4-6

O

online shopping 24-26, 31-33, 190
Operation Security 330
operations security domain 325
organisation 262, 264-267, 269, 276, 280-281, 284, 392
organizational adoption 114, 116-117, 119, 123-124

P

peer help 130-135, 137, 139-140, 142-143, 145-146, 151
peer interaction 209-211, 213-215, 219, 221, 227
perceived value of information 290, 295, 297-298
perceived worthwhileness 290, 293, 295, 297-298
Perceptions Analysis 24
personal computer 190, 192-193, 195
Personal Health Records 290
policy 31, 124, 153, 195, 263, 307, 309, 314, 378-379, 389-393, 395-403, 406
policy transfer 389-392, 396-397, 399-403, 406
privacy 26, 28, 32-34, 114, 123-124, 290-291, 293-295, 297-299, 306-307, 392-393, 396, 400-401, 440-441, 454-455
problem-solving 131, 136, 139-141, 151, 425, 429

R

Reputation Management 64
Requirements Analysis 170
Resource Protection 312, 330
response selection 337-338, 342, 365

S

S curve 375-376, 380
search engines 93, 101, 190, 233-236, 239, 242, 246, 249, 252-253, 260, 408, 411, 414-415, 422
security 26, 28, 32-35, 114-117, 119, 123-124, 174, 192, 209, 265-266, 290-291, 294-295, 297-299,

304-315, 317-318, 320, 322-325, 330, 342, 359, 361-362, 389-390, 392, 398-401, 403, 411, 414, 439, 441
security monitoring 305
selection attributes 351
Semantic Web 87-88, 92, 97, 107
service innovation 373-375
service theory 373-374
shared leadership 422, 431-432
SIM card 389-403, 406
SIM card registration 389-403, 406
smartphone 115, 193, 195, 200-202
SME 262-263, 266-267, 269, 272-273, 275, 281-284
SMS 390, 392, 406
SMS Spamming 406
social media 69, 77, 80-81, 247, 250, 437-439, 447
Social network service for scientists 235-237, 252
social networks 24, 152-153, 155-159, 161-163, 235-236, 242, 424
software architecture 208, 213
SPARQL 87-88, 90, 94-96, 99, 107
systematic literature review 441, 443
systems development 423-425, 429

T

technology adoption 71, 114, 267, 292, 294, 436, 438, 440-441, 454

tool orchestration 208-212, 218-219, 224, 227
Total Factor Productivity 40-41, 44, 59
transition economies 40-42, 44, 59

V

Virtual relationships 438
virtual team effectiveness 422-423, 426-432
virtual teams 422, 424-426, 428-432
visualization 3, 107, 209-210, 214, 219-221
Vulnerability 237, 305, 314, 324-325, 330
Vulnerability Management 305, 314, 325, 330

W

web 44, 69, 79, 87-95, 97-99, 101-103, 107, 114, 124, 136, 152-155, 211-212, 214, 227-228, 237-238, 241-243, 267, 275-276, 278-279, 292, 340, 344-346, 354, 357, 361-362, 407-415, 417-419, 439, 442, 452, 454-455
Web of Data 87-89, 92, 102, 107
web portal management 409
Web services 211-212, 214, 228, 340, 357
willingness 131, 137, 141-142, 145, 151, 198, 269, 294, 412, 454

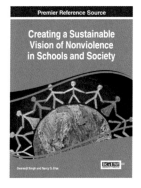

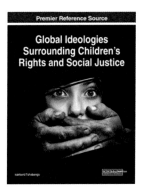
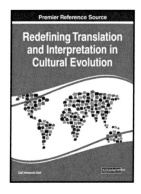

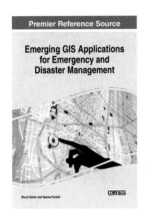
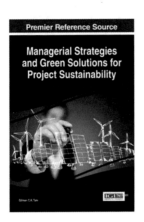

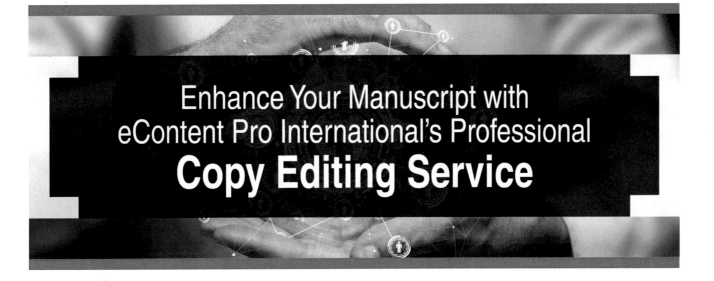

Printed in the United States
By Bookmasters